CW01501073

THE COUNCIL OF THE NAVY RECORDS SOCIETY 2009–10

PATRON

H.R.H. THE PRINCE PHILIP, DUKE OF EDINBURGH, K.G., O.M., F.R.S.

PRESIDENT

Admiral of the Fleet Sir Benjamin Bathurst, G.C.B., D.L.

VICE-PRESIDENTS

Professor D. Loades, M.A., D.Litt., F.S.A., F.R.Hist.S.
Professor N.A.M. Rodger, M.A., D.Phil., F.S.A., F.R.Hist.S.
B. Vale, B.A., C.B.E., M.Phil.
J.D. Davies, M.A., D.Phil.

COUNCILLORS

S.P. Rose, M.A., Ph.D.
Lt. Cdr. T.T.A. Lovering, M.B.E., B.Sc., M.St., R.N.
M.S. Seligmann, M.A., D.Phil., F.R.Hist.S.
S.B.A. Willis, M.A., Ph.D.
Professor E.J. Grove, M.A., Ph.D., F.R.Hist.S.
Dr H.L. Rubinstein, B.A., M.S., Ph.D., F.R.Hist.S.
C. Ware, M.A.
A.J. Webb, M.A., F.S.A., F.B.Cart.S.
Professor M. Duffy, M.A., D.Phil., F.R.Hist.S.
N.D. Black, M.A., Ph.D.
Professor A.D. Lambert, M.A., Ph.D., F.R.Hist.S.
Professor D. Law, M.A., F.C.L.I.P., F.I.Inf.Sc., F.K.C., F.L.A., F.R.S.E.
P. Nash, M.A., Ph.D., F.R.Hist.S.
M.J. Simpson, M.A., M.Litt., F.R.Hist.S.
Vice Admiral A. Massey, C.B.E., A.D.C.
V. Preston, M.A., Ph.D.
R.W.A. Suddaby, B.A.
Captain R. Woodman, M.N.I.
Lt. Cdr. F.L. Phillips, T.D., R.D., R.N.R.
Captain C.L.W. Page, M.A., R.N.
H. Doe, M.A., Ph.D.
M. Llewellyn-Jones, M.B.E., M.A., Ph.D., F.R.Hist.S.
O. Walton, M.A., Ph.D.

HON. SECRETARY

R.H.A. Brodhurst, B.A.

HON. TREASURER

P. Northcott, B.A., M.A.

GENERAL EDITOR

Dr R.A. Morriss, B.A., Ph.D.

MEMBERSHIP SECRETARY

Mrs A. Gould

NAVAL COURTS MARTIAL, 1793–1815

Edited by

JOHN D. BYRN

PUBLISHED BY ASHGATE
FOR THE NAVY RECORDS SOCIETY
2009

© The Navy Records Society, 2009

Crown copyright material is reproduced by permission of The Stationery Office.

All rights reserved. No part of this publication may be reproduced, stored in a retrieval system, or transmitted in any form or by any means, electronic, mechanical, photocopying, recorded, or otherwise without the prior permission of the publisher.

Published by
Ashgate Publishing Limited
Wey Court East
Union Road
Farnham
Surrey GU9 7PT
England

Ashgate Publishing Company
Suite 420
101 Cherry Street
Burlington, VT 05401–4405
USA

Ashgate website: http://www.ashgate.com

British Library Cataloguing in Publication Data

Byrn, John D., 1952–
Naval courts martial, 1793–1815. – (Navy Records Society publications)
1. Great Britain. Royal Navy – History – 18th century – Sources 2. Great Britain. Royal Navy – History – 19th century – Sources 3. Courts-martial and courts of inquiry – Great Britain – History – 18th century – Sources 4. Courts-martial and courts of inquiry – Great Britain – History – 19th century – Sources
I. Title II. Navy Records Society (Great Britain)
343.4'10143'0264

Library of Congress Cataloging-in-Publication Data

Byrn, John D., 1952–
Naval courts martial, 1793–1815 / John D. Byrn.
p. cm. – (Navy Records Society publications)
Includes index.
ISBN 978–0–7546–6781–0 (alk. paper)
1. Trials (Naval offenses) – Great Britain. 2. Courts-martial and courts of inquiry – Great Britain. I. Title.

KD6322.B97 2008
343.41'.0143–dc22 2008045714

ISBN 978–0–7546–6781–0

Printed on acid-free paper

Typeset in Times by Manton Typesetters, Louth, Lincolnshire, UK.

Mixed Sources
Product group from well-managed forests and other controlled sources
www.fsc.org Cert no. SA-COC-1565
© 1996 Forest Stewardship Council
FSC

Printed and bound in Great Britain by MPG Books Ltd, Bodmin, Cornwall.

This volume is dedicated to the memory of

The Honourable David Erskine

who was long a member of the Navy Records Society, served as its Honorary Secretary between 1963 and 1973, and was a benefactor to the Society.

CONTENTS

		Page
Preface		xi
Abbreviations		xiii
Glossary		xv
Introduction		xvii
1	Procedure	1
2	Social Crimes	147
3	Naval Crimes	347
4	Multiple Offences	559
Documents and Sources		753
Index		761

PREFACE

The present volume is a collection of British naval courts martial transcripts and related documents from the time of the French Revolutionary and Napoleonic Wars. In assembling and editing this collection, all of which are drawn from The National Archives, save for the first four, I have accumulated a number of personal debts. My friends and colleagues at the St Lucie County Library System in Fort Pierce, Florida, have been particularly helpful, most notably Mrs Carol Shroyer, Mrs Mary Wolf, Dr Edward Werner, Mrs Tammy Powley, Mrs Debie Hudson, Mrs Carla Niegelsen and Mr Robert Krause. With great kindness and skill, Dr Roger Morriss has guided the work to completion. Dr Nicholas Rodger graciously has given me counsel on several points of detail. As they have done for the last twenty years, the staff at The National Archives have treated me with the utmost courtesy and helpfulness. The Navy Records Society has extended me an extraordinary opportunity for which I am extremely grateful. And, as much as I am indebted to these people, I owe even more to my mother, Margaret D Byrn, who, despite a crippling stroke, has continued to offer encouragement and support. Needless to say, whatever errors there are to be found in what follows are mine and mine alone.

ABBREVIATIONS

ADM	Admiralty
CM	Court Martial

GLOSSARY

This list comprises terms mentioned in the text more than once.

Cheque During muster, this was a mark placed next to the names of men who were absent with leave.
Clerk of the cheque An official at a royal dockyard who mustered ships' companies when their vessel entered that port.
Cobbing A type of punishment in which the miscreant was hit upon the bottom with a board known as a cobbing board.
Crimp In a naval context, an individual whose job was to entice sailors to desert to merchantmen.
Cunning or **Conning** To direct the steering of a vessel. According to the 1815 revision of Falconer's *Universal Dictionary* by William Burney, this task fell to either the pilot or the quartermaster.
Gagging A punishment in which a noisy prisoner had a metal or wooden rod inserted in his mouth and affixed to his head. According to the 1815 revision of Falconer's *Universal Dictionary*, gagging was only administered 'under the most aggravating circumstances'.
Jolly boat A vessel, smaller than a yawl, that was kept on board ship and used either to go ashore or to perform other light duty.
Junk An old piece of cable that was cut into smaller portions and used to make such things as mats and points.
Lubber's hole The opening between the upper section of the lower mast and the top. According to the 1815 revision of Falconer, it acquired the name 'from a supposition that a lubber, not caring to trust himself up the futtock-shrouds, will prefer that way of getting into the top'.
Prick During the Middle Ages, this was a hole made with a pointed object, that was placed next to names on a muster; by the eighteenth century, it had become an ink dot placed against the names of men absent without leave.
Run To desert. An R was placed on a man's line in a muster book if he had missed three successive musters.
Starting An unsanctioned but customary punishment in which sailors were beaten with a rope's end or stick by a boatswain's mate on the

commanding officer's orders for want of alacrity. According to the 1815 revision of Falconer, by that time it was seldom inflicted.

INTRODUCTION

I

The study of British naval courts martial during the French Revolutionary and Napoleonic Wars is important for several reasons. Not only does it contribute to our understanding of military jurisprudence in the late eighteenth and early nineteenth centuries, but it furthers our knowledge of Georgian and Regency criminal law in general. Moreover, the transcripts of trials afloat, which form the core of the present volume, offer a unique window to the social conditions and behaviour aboard the King's ships at the time.

During the period under discussion, naval courts martial were the highest level of enforcement of the criminal code promulgated by *An Act for Amending, Explaining and Reducing into One Act of Parliament the Laws Relating to the Government of His Majesty's Ships Vessels, and Forces by Sea*, or, simply, the Consolidation Act of 1749 as revised by a statute passed in the nineteenth year of George III's reign. Known as the Articles of War, this code consisted of thirty-six clauses delineating virtually every naval offence and establishing their punishment.[1]

The Articles of War can be divided broadly into two general categories: social crimes and naval offences.[2] Social crimes include such phenomena as drunkenness, theft, buggery, profanity, murder, quarrelling and fighting – that is, the same types of infraction dealt with ashore by the Common Law. Naval offences consist of episodes like mutiny, desertion, insolence, loss of ship, cowardice, neglect of duty and unofficerlike behaviour – in other words, transgressions against the needs of the service.

[1]22 Geo. II c. 27; 19 Geo. III c. 27.

[2]In J. Byrn, *Crime and Punishment in the Royal Navy; Discipline on the Leeward Islands Station 1784–1812* (Aldershot: Scolar Press, 1989), pp. 12–15, I divided the Articles of War into four basic categories: first, 'contraventions against religion and morality' such as drunkenness, profanity and homosexuality; second, 'crimes against the king and his government' like treason, mutiny, destruction of naval property and disobedience of orders; third, 'infringements of the rights of individuals', including murder, theft, quarrelling and fighting; and fourth, 'strictly naval infractions', such as refusal to engage the enemy, cowardice and failure to provide convoy service. However, for the sake of simplicity, I have reduced that number to two groups here: social crimes and naval offences.

In addition to including the various clauses of the criminal code afloat, the Consolidation Act prescribed the authority of naval courts martial, their composition, several of the oaths to be taken at them and the penalties for prevarication, contempt of court and withholding evidence from a naval tribunal. These panels had a very limited jurisdiction. Only officers and men 'in actual service and in full pay' could be brought before them, and then only for offences enumerated by the Articles of War and perpetrated in areas where the Common Law did not have jurisdiction, that is 'upon the main seas, or in great rivers only, beneath the bridges of the said rivers nigh to the sea, or in any haven, river or creek within the jurisdiction of the Admiralty' and in all places which did not acknowledge the sovereignty of the British monarch.[1] Moreover, the alleged crime had to be committed within three years of the date of the formal letter of complaint containing the charges against the accused.[2]

As well as limiting the jurisdiction of courts martial, the Consolidation Act restricted their composition. Naval tribunals were to be composed of no more than thirteen, but no less than five, flag officers, captains or commanders. The first, second or third ranking officer present at the trial's location was to serve as president of the court, 'as shall be found most expedient, and for the good of his Majesty's service'. In cases in which there were more than thirteen flag officers and post captains able to attend a tribunal, the twelve next in seniority to that court's president were to serve. In instances where there were at least three, but not five, post captains able to sit as judges at a specific trial, then commanders of his Majesty's ships below that rank were eligible to do duty. No officer who met these criteria could be denied his seat on a court.[3]

Section 17 of the Consolidation Act established the penalties for witnesses prevaricating before, withholding from, or behaving contemptuously to a naval tribunal. Those found guilty of prevarication or withholding evidence could be imprisoned, at the court's discretion, for up to three months; those convicted of contempt could be incarcerated for a maximum of one month. This section further provided that individuals suspected of perjury, or subornation thereof, were to 'be prosecuted in his Majesty's Court of King's Bench by indictment or information', or by such county court as that panel directed.

Finally, the Consolidation Act of 1749 contained several of the oaths to be administered by the person executing the office of judge advocate at any given trial. The members of the quarter deck acting as judges were to take the following pledge:

[1]22 Geo. II c. 33.
[2]Ibid.
[3]Ibid.

> I, A. B., do swear that I will duly administer justice according to the articles and orders established by an Act passed in the twenty second year of the reign of his Majesty, King George the Second, for *Amending, Explaining and Reducing into One Act of Parliament the Laws Relating to the Government of his Majesty's Ships, Vessels and Forces by Sea*, without partiality, favour or affection; and if any case shall arise, which is not particularly mentioned in the said articles and orders, I will duly administer justice according to my conscience, the best of my understanding, and the custom of the navy in the like cases; and I do further swear that I will not upon any account, at any time whatsoever, disclose or discover the vote or opinion of any particular member of this court martial, unless thereunto required by Act of Parliament.
>
> So help me God.[1]

The Act further stipulated that, after the members of the court had taken this solemn oath, the judge advocate was to proclaim:

> I, A. B., do swear that I will not upon any account at any time whatsoever disclose or discover the vote or opinion of any particular member of this court martial, unless thereunto required by act of parliament.
>
> So help me God.[2]

The provisions regulating courts martial in the Consolidation Act were supplemented by those found in a volume entitled *Regulations & Instructions relating to his Majesty's Service at Sea*, which provided sea officers with a clear and concise reference manual 'describing the responsibilities of every member of the fleet and the proper methods and procedures to be followed for virtually the whole gamut of naval activities'.[3] During the age of sail, the Admiralty promulgated two editions of the *Regulations & Instructions*. The first, published in 1731, went through thirteen impressions before it was revised and expanded in 1806.

Both editions included chapters on courts martial, which contained many similar rules for the conduct of naval tribunals. For example, each stipulated that all charges intended as the basis for the convention of a court martial had to be made in writing, 'setting forth the particular facts, when and where and in what manner the same were committed'.[4]

[1]Ibid.

[2]Ibid.

[3]Byrn, *Crime and Punishment*, p. 18.

[4]*Regulations and Instructions Relating to His Majesty's Service at Sea*, 2nd edn (London, 1806), p. 405.

Similarly, both disqualified any captains involved in a specific case from sitting as a judge at the trial of that case. Moreover, each mandated that courts were to be held 'in the most public place of the ship' and that all persons wishing to attend were allowed to do so.[1] Furthermore, both stated that a majority of justices composing a tribunal determined the question of the guilt or innocence of a defendant, with the members voting in ascending order from most junior to most senior. Finally both established the procedure to be observed at execution, whereby the crews of all of his Majesty's ships at the location where the event was scheduled to occur were to be assembled upon deck as spectators and the crime or crimes for which the guilty party or parties were to be launched into eternity were read to them.

Despite these similarities, there were marked differences between the two editions. For instance, whereas the *Regulations & Instructions* of 1731 stated that commissions to hold courts martial were 'to be understood to be in force no longer than during the expedition', those of 1806 were silent on the duration of such commissions. Similarly, although the revised and expanded version mandated that 'a junior officer commanding a post ship' was to 'take precedence of his senior officer commanding a sloop' in being called to sit as a judge at a naval tribunal, the earlier edition was moot on this point. Correspondingly, whereas the 1806 volume established the oath to be administered to witnesses, the earlier book contained no such vow. Moreover, while the *Regulations* of 1731 prescribed only that the judge advocate at a court was 'to send timely before the trial' a copy of the charges against him to the defendant, the latter version specified that the presiding officer at the proceedings must 'take care that a copy of the charge or complaint be delivered to the person accused, as soon as may be after he shall have received the order to hold such court martial, and not less than twenty-four hours before the trial'.[2]

Beyond the Regulations and Instructions and the statutes governing justice at sea, the members of naval tribunals during the period under discussion had several manuals on courts martial at their disposal. The first of these to appear was John McArthur's *Principles and Practice of Naval and Military Courts Martial*, which was published originally in June 1792 and revised and expanded four times by 1813. McArthur intended his study as a compendium of information about the procedures and Common Law precedents of military trials ashore and afloat that would reduce the need to consult the appropriate legal authorities.[3] Thus,

[1]*Regulations and Instructions*, 1st edn (London, 1731), p. 4.

[2]*Regulations and Instructions*, 2nd edn, p. 405.

[3]J. McArthur, *Principles and Practices of Naval and Military Courts Martial, with an Appendix Illustrative of the Subject*, 2 vols, 4th edn (London, 1813).

it included discussions of such matters as courts of inquiry, parole evidence, determination of guilt and sentencing.[1] In 1805, a companion volume to *Principles and Practice* was published by John Delafons, entitled *Treatise on Naval Courts Martial*. Like McArthur, Delafons sought to provide his audience with a textbook for conducting judicial proceedings in the Royal Navy.[2] For this reason, he too discoursed on topics ranging from the jurisdiction of naval tribunals to the role of the judge advocate to 'the forms of drawing out the sentence'.[3]

II

In the Royal Navy, the judicial process began with a formal letter of complaint to the Lords Commissioners of the Admiralty in home waters or, on foreign stations, the commander in chief of that station, requesting a court martial. As noted above, both editions of the *Regulations and Instructions* required such letters to be precise in the charge or charges against the accused. They were to include a clear explanation of the alleged crime or crimes committed, the time and place each transgression had occurred, and how the alleged offences had been perpetrated. Failure to abide by any of these requirements often was grounds for dismissal of the case against the individual named in the complaint. According to McArthur, even charges properly drawn could be rejected at the discretion of the Lords Commissioners or commanders in chief acting in their stead.[4]

However, with the exception of cases in which the charges either were patently frivolous or likely to lead to a conviction, the Lords Commissioners or commanders of squadrons and foreign stations seldom acted summarily. Frequently, these authorities employed extra-constitutional devices, known as courts of inquiry, to determine the validity of letters of complaint. Such courts were analogous to grand juries ashore. As Delafons put it:

> It results, then, … that the intent of ordering courts of inquiry to be held is either to throw light on particular transactions and by the report made thereon to judge if there are sufficient grounds to bring the parties implicated to a trial for their conduct or to clear those who complain of aspersions cast on their character by persons in official capacity. Doubtless they frequently prevent an unnecessary assemblage of

[1] McArthur, *Principles and Practices*, *passim*.
[2] J. Delafons, *Treatise on Naval Courts Martial* (London, 1805).
[3] Delafons, *Treatise*, *passim*.
[4] McArthur, vol. 1, p. 225.

> officers to form a court martial, which is often attended with delays and considerable inconvenience to the public service. Courts of inquiry may be described as in some degree similar to grand juries, who are convened in order to decide on the truth of a bill of indictment.[1]

As extra-legal entities arising from the customs of the sea, courts of inquiry were much more informal than courts martial.[2] Composed of from three to five members depending on the seriousness of the matter under investigation, these bodies could not render legally binding decisions or inflict punishment based on their decisions.[3] Moreover, they were powerless to compel witnesses to testify before them. At the same time, although tradition dictated that they gather evidence through oral testimony, this testimony was not given under oath. Indeed, so relaxed were the procedures and safeguards at courts of inquiry that Delafons argued it was certainly within the authority of such inquests to deny defendants the fundamental right to confront those making the charges against them.[4]

When members of a court of inquiry had gathered enough evidence upon which to base a recommendation for or against a trial, they submitted their counsel to either the Lords Commissioners or the commander in chief of a foreign station. Depending on the collective inclination of the tribunal and the complexity of the case being investigated, the reports containing these opinions varied greatly in detail. Some were terse statements of advice; others included detailed accounts of the evidence upon which a decision was made. And, having issued its report, the court disbanded.

At this point, the Lords Commissioners or the commander in chief of a foreign station weighed and considered the court of inquiry's report and decided whether or not a case warranted adjudication by a court martial. In instances which the appropriate authority deemed worthy of a trial, that authority issued an order to convene a formal naval tribunal. These orders required and directed the second or third ranking officer of a station, as president of the court martial, to adjudicate the question at hand at the earliest convenience. Generally the earliest convenience translated into no more than two weeks, usually less than one. However, on occasion, it could mean considerably longer. Indeed the trial of John Bathie, in Hamoze on 1 October 1811, did not take place until more than six months after the order for his court martial had been issued by their Lordships [35].

[1]Delafons, pp. 57–8.
[2]Byrn, p. 36.
[3]Delafons, pp. 46–7.
[4]Ibid.

On the morning of the day chosen for trial by the president of the court, the members of the tribunal serving as justices assembled 'in the most convenient and public place of the ship'.[1] Once convened, naval courts martial followed a formal, structured procedure. The first order of business was to account for all officers who were qualified to sit as judges but not in attendance. There were two acceptable reasons for admirals, captains and ranking non-post commanders of ships not to attend a trial: either because of illness, as attested by a ship's surgeon, or Admiralty leave.[2]

After all qualified justices had been accounted for and those in attendance had been seated to the left and right of the president of the court martial according to seniority, the witnesses and audience were admitted; the prisoner was brought into court by the provost martial; and the order for the trial and warrant appointing the judge advocate were recited.[3] Then the members of the tribunal and the judge advocate swore their respective oaths. Next, the letter of complaint against the accused was read aloud before the assembly. At this point, all witnesses, except the first to testify, were ordered to withdraw; and, the proceedings entered the evidentiary phase.

During the evidentiary phase, all witnesses for the prosecution were called individually, followed by all those for the defence in like manner. Such evidences were examined first by the side that called them and then cross-examined by the other party. Witnesses could be called back and re-examined as often as the court thought necessary. According to McArthur, the general rule of thumb in the eighteenth and early nineteenth centuries was that, to obtain a conviction, the prosecution had to bring forward two evidences in support of the accusation, but in cases involving extremely private matters only one witness was sufficient to produce a

[1] *Regulations and Instructions*, 2nd edn, p. 405.

[2] Defendants also had a very limited right to challenge prospective justices at their trials. Both editions of the *Regulations and Instructions* contained virtually the same provision disqualifying ranking officers from sitting as judges in cases in which they had a vested interest. In the revised volume, the clause read: 'If any officer entitled by his rank to sit at a court martial be personally concerned in the matter to be tried, he is not to be permitted to be of the number of members by whom the court shall be composed'. Similarly, members of the quarterdeck serving on courts of inquiry could not adjudicate questions arising from that particular court's investigations. 'Those who have acted as members on a court of inquiry into the prisoner's conduct should not be permitted to sit on his court martial', observed Delafons, 'since they are held, in many respects in the light of a grand jury; and no indictor or grand juror can be put upon a petty jury for the trial of the same cause if challenged by the prisoner so indicted' (Delafons, p. 123). However, it appears that prisoners rarely exercised this type of challenge.

[3] According to the 1815 edition of William Falconer's classic maritime dictionary which was revised by William Burney, a provost martial had charge of a prisoner during his trial and subsequent punishment (*A New Universal Dictionary of the Marine* (London, 1815), p. 359).

guilty verdict.[1] While two was the usual minimum number of witnesses needed by the prosecutorial side, there was no limit on the maximum number. However, McArthur cautioned prosecutors that 'it would be to no good purpose to call too many to establish the same facts, as this could only tend unnecessarily to protract the trials, and perhaps ultimately so elude the justice of the case'.[2]

While depositions were allowed as evidence on infrequent occasions, *viva voce* testimony was the standard method used at courts martial for ascertaining the facts of a cause. As at criminal law ashore, oral declarations given publicly under oath held much greater weight than affidavits given privately and read at the trial. Not only did such testimony offer the defendant the opportunity to challenge his accuser, but it enabled the court to assess the veracity of witnesses. As McArthur put it:

> The court will be able to keep the witness from wandering from the point in issue and will have an opportunity of observing his quality, age, education, understanding, behaviour and inclination; all which necessary leading features cannot be collected from the depositions of witnesses when brought forward in writing and read to the court in the absence of those who made them; and, further, as much may be frequently collected from the manner in which the evidence is delivered, as from the matter of it.[3]

Indeed, parole evidence was so firmly embedded in naval jurisprudence that even testimony given at courts of inquiry had to be repeated *de novo* before the tribunal adjudicating charges arising from investigations by those courts.

At the conclusion of the examination of the last witness called by the prosecution, the prisoner entered his defence. Defences varied greatly, depending on the circumstances of the case rather than the rank or education of the accused.[4] As a rule, if the guilt of the prisoner was obvious, he threw himself upon the mercy of the court or introduced testimony regarding his character and service in the Royal Navy. Conversely, if the defendant believed that the charges against him could not be proved or if he was on trial for a crime carrying an almost certain death penalty, he mounted a vigorous rebuttal of the accusations against him.

Once the prisoner finished his defence, the court was cleared and 'proceeded to deliberate upon and form the sentence'.[5] During their

[1]McArthur, vol. 2, pp. 104–5.
[2]Ibid., p. 107.
[3]Ibid., p. 50.
[4]Byrn, p. 49.
[5]This was a standard phrase used in the courts martial transcripts.

deliberations, the members of a tribunal had to decide two basic questions. Was the defendant guilty of the crime or crimes with which he was accused? And if so, what was to be his punishment? The first of these issues was determined by a simple majority of justices, with the judge advocate asking each panellist in ascending order of rank one question: 'Are you of the opinion that the charge against the prisoner is proved or not proved?'[1]

Having reached a verdict, the tribunal took the appropriate steps. Needless to say, all defendants acquitted of the charge or charges against them were released as soon as the assembly was reconvened and its findings were announced. In cases involving officers (though not seamen) found innocent, it was customary for the court to exonerate them in the most emphatic way to preserve their honour and good name. 'The word unanimous is frequently inserted in sentences of acquittal,' Delafons observed 'in order to give greater energy and weight in restoring the officer in the good opinion of his country and efface the stain or tarnish his reputation might have suffered from the accusation brought against him; from which he is honourably acquitted'.[2] Moreover, if the allegations proved completely unfounded, it was not unknown for the justices to state their disapproval of the plaintiff's motives in the sentence.

If, on the other hand, the tribunal adjudged the defendant guilty either fully or in part, then it had to decide the type and degree of punishment to inflict. For a number of offences the penalty was predetermined by the Articles of War. Thus by Clause 28, the mandatory sentence for those convicted of murder was death. Correspondingly, all officers convicted of signing false musters were to 'be cashiered and rendered incapable of further employment in his Majesty's naval service'. In non-capital cases carrying prescribed penalties, all that the court could do was ameliorate the sentence by including any mitigating circumstances in its report, a practice frowned upon by the Admiralty.

Yet, not all crimes carried mandatory sentences. Indeed, most of the thirty-six clauses comprising the Articles of War gave courts martial considerable leeway in setting the penalties for the offences listed therein. Naval tribunals had a wide variety of punishments at their disposal; and the type of correction imposed varied greatly according to the rank of the miscreant. Warrant and commissioned officers adjudged guilty of violating the navy's code of criminal justice generally were dismissed their ships,

[1]Byrn, p. 51, n. 1. If the first poll of the panellists ended in a tie, a second was taken. Should the result still be a deadlock, the defendant was found innocent. As Delafons explained: 'Since it requires a majority of voices to condemn, an equality should of course acquit, as it neutralizes the opinion of the judges who can come to no decision' (p. 247).

[2]Delafons, p. 279.

disrated, reprimanded, admonished, reduced on the seniority list for their rank or received some combination thereof, depending on the circumstances of the crime.[1] Members of the lower deck routinely received death, 'flogging round the fleet', simple flogging, imprisonment or loss of pay, contingent on the severity of their transgression.[2]

The nature of the punishment inflicted upon those convicted by courts martial was settled by a majority vote of the justices hearing the case. However, due to the silence of the statutes regulating naval tribunals about which judges should be allowed a voice in determining penalties, some confusion on the matter arose. Delafons held that only those who had deemed the prisoner guilty should establish the punishment. McArthur, on the other hand, believed that all members of a tribunal, regardless of their opinion on the question of guilt or innocence, should determine the retribution. 'Unfortunately', as I argued in *Crime and Punishment in the Royal Navy*, 'it is impossible to estimate with any accuracy which of the two methods enjoyed a wider acceptance because the transcripts of naval trials uniformly and intentionally concealed the deliberations of every assembly from public knowledge'.[3]

No matter which method justices afloat used to determine a sentence, the Articles of War insisted they were to make sure that the punishment selected was appropriate for the crime committed. The sections not mandating a penalty routinely included the clause 'or such other

[1]Death sentences were not entirely unknown for members of the quarterdeck in the eighteenth century. Occasionally, naval tribunals condemned men like Lieutenants William Berry and Richard Stewart Gamage to suffer the ultimate penalty at the hands of a firing squad (Byrn, p. 59).

[2]Flogging round the fleet was a type of punishment involving a large number of lashes inflicted by the sentence of court martial. By this form of retribution, the commander in chief of a station or the commander of a squadron divided the total number of strokes imposed by the number of ships at the location where the punishment was to take place, with this figure to be administered at each of these vessels. On the day appointed to carry out the scourging, a yellow flag was flown from the foremast of the commander's ship; and, answering this signal, each vessel in the squadron sent a launch manned by seamen and marines under the command of a lieutenant to observe the proceedings. The prisoner, together with a surgeon and the provost martial, entered another launch and was stripped to the waist and bound to a grating constructed specially for the event. When this flotilla had assembled, it formed a line and set off to the first vessel to serve as a site of punishment. On its arrival, the sentence of the court was read aloud to the assembled ship's company and two boatswain's mates were sent on board to inflict the designated number of lashes. After all of these blows had been struck, the victim was examined by the surgeon to determine if he was capable of receiving further punishment and, if he was, a blanket was placed on his shoulders and the little flotilla proceeded to the next ship, where the entire ceremony was repeated. And so it continued until either the flogging was completed or the prisoner was unable to withstand further suffering. In the latter instance, the punishment was stopped and the miscreant was allowed to recuperate before it resumed. Each trip round the fleet could take several hours and multiple trips could take more than half a year to complete.

[3]Byrn, p. 52.

punishment as the nature and degree of the offence shall deserve'. That justices, as a rule, heeded this insistence is evinced paradoxically by a phrase frequently appearing in the reports of courts martial, which seems brutally callous to the twenty-first-century Western mind; often a sentence of several hundred lashes was prefaced by the words 'do only adjudge'. Yet, when it is considered that the maximum penalty for most offences was death, the passage was neither brutal or callous; rather it was a reminder that, even though an assembly possessed the authority to inflict the ultimate retribution upon the prisoner, it had chosen to exercise restraint and impose a penalty befitting the circumstances of the defendant's case.

A further indication that judicial bodies at sea sought to make the punishment fit the crime is the difference in penalties imposed upon warrant and commissioned officers:

> Considerable distinction should obtain in the mode of inflicting punishments of an inferior kind on officers and seamen: what may be regarded as a slight penalty inflicted on the one would be considered as of great magnitude to the other. Habits and education create essential differences in the minds and manners of men. To dismiss an officer from his Majesty's service would be esteemed a heavy punishment; whereas a common sailor would look upon it, in many cases, as a favour conferred upon him. Corporal punishment, which seldom operates on the feelings of common seaman or soldier, must affect a petty officer (such as a midshipman) so sensibly, if he has the sentiments of a gentleman, as to render his future life a burden to him.[1]

After the judges had reached a verdict and selected an appropriate sentence, their decisions were put in writing and signed by each member of the tribunal. Thereupon the court reconvened, the defendant was brought back in and the audience and witnesses readmitted to hear the judge advocate announce the justices' findings before the assembly. The proceedings then concluded and the judicial body was dissolved. Prisoners found innocent were freed immediately; those convicted were turned over to the provost martial to await their punishment.

The entire tribunal was conducted with great solemnity to impress upon both the defendant and the audience the gravity of the affair. On the morning of the day appointed for the trial, a cannon was fired and the union flag was flown from the top of the mainmast of the ship upon which the court was to assemble. Throughout the proceedings, the sober judges,

[1]Delafons, pp. 271–2.

in full dress uniform, sat at a long table on either side of the presiding officer in descending order of seniority. During the examination of witnesses, the provost marshal stood next to the prisoner with sword drawn.[1] And, it was ritual for the justices to cover their heads while the judge advocate publicly announced their findings.[2]

The judge advocate was the pivotal figure of the proceedings. Appointed by either the Lords Commissioners of the Admiralty or the commander in chief of a station, he read the warrant to convene the court and administered the oaths to both the judges and the witnesses alike. Moreover, he advised the magistrates at sea 'of the proper forms' and rendered opinions on problems as they arose during the trial. Furthermore, he questioned witnesses, directed the deliberations of the justices and drew up as well as announced the sentence. And, most important for the present purpose, he took the minutes of the proceedings, which he read to the members of the tribunal so that errors could be identified and revised.[3] As McArthur succinctly wrote, 'the judge advocate may be said to be the *primum mobile* of a court martial, as not only impelling it to action, but as being the person to whom, in great measure, depends that harmony of motion so necessary to constitute a regular court'.[4]

III

Both editions of the *Regulations and Instructions* required judge advocates to send their Lordships the 'original sentences', the minutes and accompanying documents of every court martial. The transcripts of these trials were collected and stored at the Admiralty.[5] They were arranged chronologically in bound volumes. Some time in the nineteenth century they were transferred to the Public Record Office, now The National Archives of the United Kingdom. For the period under consideration, there are now 122 volumes each covering from one month to over a year, bearing the references ADM 1/5330 to ADM 1/5452. While there is sufficient evidence to suggest that not all transcripts have survived, more than enough have to provide a clear picture of naval jurisprudence. Indeed, it is more likely than not that most of the records have been preserved. These documents vary greatly in detail. Some are meticulous records of

[1]R. R. S. Fisher, 'Courts Martial', *The Mariner's Mirror*, 56 (1970), p. 239.

[2]Dudley Pope, *Life in Nelson's Navy* (London: George Allen and Unwin, 1981), p. 243.

[3]*Regulations and Instructions*, 2nd edn, p. 406.

[4]McArthur, vol. 1, p. 279.

[5]See R. B. Pugh, 'The Early History of the Admiralty Record Office', in J Conway Davies (ed.), *Studies Presented to Sir Hilary Jenkinson* (London: Oxford University Press, 1957), pp. 326–36.

individual trials, offering a wealth of evidentiary and procedural data; others are mere drafts, consisting of nothing more than bare-boned notes.

Nevertheless, because of the abundance of the surviving records, several criteria for inclusion in the present compilation had to be imposed: First, the documents had to have been generated some time between 1793 and 1815. Second, the originals had to have been written in a legible hand that could be reproduced clearly by the copying service at The National Archives. Third, they could be no longer than ten handwritten pages (however, the remaining evidence dictates that this rule be set aside in some instances). Fourth, they had to contain cases representative of all types of crime adjudicated by naval tribunals, drawn from foreign as well as home stations. And fifth, they had to include examples of trials for these offences not only in which the defendant was found guilty, but also in which he was found innocent.

In presenting materials that meet these criteria, the following arrangement has been adopted. Chapter 1 deals with procedural matters. Chapter 2 covers trials arising from accusations of one kind of social crime – that is, transgressions of the laws of Georgian and Regency society such as drunkenness, theft, violence and homosexuality. Chapter 3 is devoted to proceedings against single types of naval offence, that is challenges to authority or maritime efficiency such as mutiny, insolence, desertion or loss of ship. Chapter 4 treats cases involving adjudications for multiple infractions.

The documents contained herein are complete transcriptions, with the exception of such extraneous passages as the salutations and conclusions of letters and the like in conformity with the Navy Records Society's editorial conventions. Thus archaic spelling has been modernized according to British orthographic practice as has punctuation and grammar, without – it is hoped – altering the intended meaning of the authors of the manuscripts. Moreover, all abbreviations used in the originals have been preserved. And the names of ships and officers mentioned in this volume have been rendered as they are found in such standard references as J. J. Colledge's *Ships of the Royal Navy: An Historical Index*, 2 vols (Newton Abbott: David and Charles, 1969–70); David Lyon's *The Sailing Navy List: All the Ships of the Royal Navy, Built, Purchased and Captured, 1688–1860* (London: Conway Maritime Press, 1983); and *The Commissioned Sea Officers of the Royal Navy, 1660–1815* edited by David Syrett and R. I. DiNardo (NRS Occasional Publications Vol. 1).

1

PROCEDURE

The documents in the present chapter have been selected to illustrate the precepts and practices of late eighteenth and early nineteenth century naval courts martial. The first four provide the legal and administrative framework within which his Majesty's tribunals at sea operated. Although several of the records that follow demonstrate that specific courts violated this or that axiom of law, these trials were the exception, not the rule. On the whole justice afloat abided by the rules established in *An Act for Amending, Explaining and Reducing into One Act of Parliament the Laws relating to the Government of His Majesty's Ships, Vessels and Forces by Sea* and the several editions of *Regulations and Instructions relating to His Majesty's Service at Sea* [1–4].

The various statutes and regulations governing justice afloat were very specific about how charges were to be drawn up and about the limited jurisdiction of naval courts martial. Once again, while a few courts violated these proscriptions [5, 43], most followed them closely. Thus, examples of compliance are much more common than violations. Indeed, inaccuracies in the charges or charges deemed beyond the purview of naval tribunals routinely led to the dismissal of cases [6, 15, 17, 19, 21, 28, 34, 38, 45].

Courts martial were not intended to deal with trivial offences. One device used to uphold this intention was the court of inquiry. Such courts commonly were ordered to determine if there were sufficient grounds to warrant the convention of a naval tribunal [30, 35, 41]. Moreover, courts martial were meant to instil a sense of their majesty in those who witnessed them by making examples of the individuals who were brought before them [16, 22]. Towards this end, justice afloat followed the same methods used by eighteenth-century common law courts. In *Crime and Punishment in the Royal Navy*, I argued that Douglas Hay's thesis that Georgian criminal trials ashore were based on an ideology of justice, terror and mercy was equally applicable to naval courts martial during the period under discussion [11, 23, 24].[1]

[1]Byrn, pp. 54–63.

Although such devices as courts of inquiry were safeguards against the terror and majesty of naval tribunals becoming too common (thus lessening their example), occasionally weak, frivolous or mute cases did reach trial. These cases usually resulted from the failure of either the prosecutor or defendant to appear [14, 36]. However, a few were the consequence of a lack of evidence.

Trials of this nature must have been particularly aggravating to commanders in chief of both foreign and home stations. Courts martial entailed, at times, much inconvenience. Because the Consolidation Act of 1749 specifically stated that courts martial must be composed of at least five captains and commanders, prisoners, particularly on foreign stations, could languish in confinement for months, if not years, until the minimum number of officers could be assembled [9, 10]. For this reason, when enough qualified officers were present on a station to hold a naval tribunal, that tribunal often disposed of a number of disparate cases at the same time [18, 29].

Whether a court martial tried one or more cases, its most important participant was the judge advocate. Judge advocates normally were well versed in the laws and regulations pertaining to naval tribunals. Often, they were men of much experience with justice afloat; in an extreme example, Moses Greetham was deputy judge advocate at Portsmouth for forty-five years, beginning as a substitute in 1785 and retiring in 1830. The documents presented below that pertain to judge advocates have not been selected to illustrate the important functions they performed (see the Introduction), as these are evident in all the transcripts in this volume; rather, materials have been chosen that shed light on their pay [12, 47], their appointment [20] and their requests to the Admiralty [46].

Part of the reason why judge advocates and officers composing judicial panels were able to follow the letter of the law as well as they did was that they could, and did, consult His Majesty's solicitor general for advice through the Lords Commissioners of the Admiralty. Questions to the solicitor ranged from petitions to carry out death sentences [37] to whether miscreants could be tried [44] to, on occasion, thorny points of law [27, 48, 49, 50].

Finally, a few of the documents in this chapter have been chosen to demonstrate various aspects of naval courts martial. For example, states evidence was known and used by the King's justice at sea [7]. At the same time, naval tribunals were, at least for officers, courts of honour [26]. Thus sentences of acquittal for members of the quarterdeck were often couched in terms that absolved the defendant of all dishonour [13]; conversely loss of rank, which was a common punishment for petty officers deemed guilty by courts martial, led not only to ill repute but also financial hardship [25].

In a similar vein, tribunals at sea enquiring into the loss of ships often 'honourably acquitted' the officers and crew, who usually were tried together. However, in rare cases where either a member or members of the group acted in a particularly opprobrious manner during the loss, he or they were tried either individually or as a group for their offences [31, 32]. Therefore, the materials contained herein are intended to give the reader a sense of the principles and procedures employed at courts martial in the Royal Navy during the period under consideration.

1. *An Act for Amending, Explaining and Reducing into One Act of Parliament the Laws relating to the Government of His Majesty's Ships, Vessels and Forces by Sea*

[22 Geo. II c. 33]

Whereas the several laws relating to the sea service made at different times and on different occasions have been found by experience not to be so full, so clear, so expedient or consistent with each other as they ought to be; for amending and explaining the said laws and for reducing them into one uniform Act of Parliament, be it enacted by the King's most excellent majesty, by and with the advice and consent of the lords spiritual and temporal and commons in this present Parliament assembled and by the authority of the same, that from and after the twenty fifth day of December one thousand seven hundred and forty nine, an Act passed in the thirteenth year of the reign of King Charles the Second, entitled *An Act for Establishing Articles and Orders for the Regulating and Better Government of His Majesty's Navies, Ships of War and Forces by Sea*; and also so much of an Act passed in the second year of the reign of King William and Queen Mary, entitled *An Act Concerning the Commissioners of the Admiralty*, as directs the form of an oath to be taken by every officer present upon all trials of offenders by courts martial to be held by virtue of any commission to be granted by the Lord High Admiral or the commissioners for executing the office of Lord High Admiral; and also so much of an Act passed in the sixth year of the reign of King George the First, entitled *An Act for Making Perpetual so much of an Act made in the Tenth Year of the Reign of Queen Anne for the Reviving and Continuing Several Acts of Parliament therein Mentioned as Relates to the Building and Repairing County Gaols*; and also an Act of the eleventh and twelfth years of the reign of King William the Third for the more effectual suppression of piracy and for making more effectual the Act of the thirteenth year of the reign of King Charles the Second, entitled *An Act for Establishing Articles and Orders for the Regulating and Better Government of His Majesty's Navies, Ships of War and Forces by Sea*, as relates to the trial and punishment of persons who shall commit any of the crimes or offences mentioned in the said articles upon the shore, in any foreign part or parts; and also so much of an Act passed in the eighth year of the reign of King George the First, entitled *An Act for the More Effectual Suppressing of Piracy*, as directs the punishment to be inflicted by a court martial upon any captain, commander or other officer of any His Majesty's ships or vessels of war, who shall receive on board or permit to be received on board any goods or merchandizes whatsoever in order to trade or merchandize with the same (except the goods and merchandizes therein excepted); and also an Act passed in the eighteenth year of the reign of His present Majesty, entitled *An Act for the Regulating and Better Government of His Majesty's Navies, Ships of War and Forces by Sea; and for Regulating the Proceedings upon Courts Martial in the Sea Service*; and also an Act passed in the twenty first year of the reign of His present Majesty, entitled *An Act for Further Regulating the proceedings upon Courts Martial in the Sea Service; and for Extending the Discipline of the Navy to the Crews of His Majesty's Ships Wrecked, Lost or Taken; and for Continuing to Them their Wages upon Certain Conditions*, shall be and the same are hereby repealed to all intents and purposes whatsoever.

II. And for the regulating and better government of His Majesty's navies, ships of war and forces by sea, whereon, under the good providence of God, the wealth, safety and strength of this kingdom chiefly depend, be it enacted by the King's most excellent majesty, by and with the advice and consent of the lords spiritual and temporal and commons in this present Parliament assembled and by the authority of the same that from and after the twenty fifth day of December one thousand seven hundred and forty nine, the articles and orders herein after following as well in time of peace as in time of war shall be duly observed and put in execution in manner herein after-mentioned.

1. All commanders, captains, and officers, in or belonging to any of His Majesty's ships or vessels of war, shall cause the public worship of Almighty God, according to the liturgy of the Church of England established by law, to be solemnly, orderly and reverently performed in their respective ships; and shall take care that prayers and preaching, by the chaplains in holy orders of the respective ships, be performed diligently; and that the Lord's day be observed according to law.
2. All flag officers, and all persons in or belonging to His Majesty's ships or vessels of war, being guilty of profane oaths, cursings, execrations, drunkenness, uncleanness, or other scandalous actions, in derogation of God's honour, and corruption of good manners, shall incur such punishment as a court martial shall think fit to impose, and as the nature and degree of their offence shall deserve.
3. If any officer, mariner, soldier, or other person of the fleet, shall give, hold, or entertain intelligence to or with any enemy or rebel, without leave from the King's majesty, or the Lord High Admiral, or the Commissioners for executing the office of Lord High Admiral,

commander in chief, or his commanding officer, every such person so offending, and being thereof convicted by the sentence of a court martial, shall be punished with death.

4. If any letter or message from any enemy or rebel, be conveyed to any officer, mariner, or soldier, or other in the fleet, and the said officer, mariner, soldier, or other as aforesaid, shall not, within twelve hours, having opportunity so to do, acquaint his superior officer or the officer commanding in chief with it or if any superior officer being acquainted therewith, shall not in convenient time reveal the same to the commander in chief of the squadron, every such person so offending and being convicted thereof by the sentence of the court martial, shall be punished with death or such other punishment as the nature and degree of the offence shall deserve and the court martial shall impose.
5. All spies, and all persons whatsoever, who shall come, or be found, in the nature of spies, to bring or deliver any seducing letters or messages from any enemy or rebel or endeavour to corrupt any captain, officer, mariner or other in the fleet, to betray his trust, being convicted of any such offence by the sentence of the court martial, shall be punished with death or such other punishment as the nature and degree of the offence shall deserve and the court martial shall impose.
6. No person in the fleet shall relieve an enemy or rebel with money, victuals, powder, shot, arms, ammunition or any other supplies whatsoever, directly or indirectly, upon pain of death or such other punishment as the court martial shall think fit to impose and as the nature and degree of the crime shall deserve.
7. All the papers, charter parties, bills of lading, passports, and other writings whatsoever, that shall be taken, seized or found aboard any ship or ships which shall be surprised or taken as prize, shall be duly preserved and the very originals shall by the commanding officer of the ship which shall take such prize, be sent entirely and without fraud to the Court of Admiralty or such other court of commissioners, as shall be authorized to determine whether such prize be lawful capture, there to be viewed, made use of, and proceeded upon according to law, upon pain that every person offending herein shall forfeit and lose his share of the capture and shall suffer such further punishment as the nature and degree of his offence shall be found to deserve, and the court martial shall impose.
8. No person in or belonging to the fleet shall take out of any prize, or ship seized for prize, any money, plate or goods, unless it shall be necessary for the better securing thereof, or for the necessary use

and service of any of His Majesty's ships or vessels of war, before the same be adjudged lawful prize in some Admiralty Court; but the full and entire account of the whole, without embezzlement, shall be brought in and judgement passed entirely upon the whole without fraud, upon pain that every person offending herein shall forfeit and lose his share of the capture and suffer such further punishment as shall be imposed by a court martial or such Court of Admiralty, according to the nature and degree of the offence.

9. If any ship or vessel shall be taken as prize, none of the officers, mariners or other persons on board her shall be stripped of their clothes or in any sort pillaged, beaten or evil-entreated upon pain that the person or persons so offending shall be liable to such punishment as a court martial shall think fit to inflict.

10. Every flag officer, captain and commander in the fleet, who upon signal or order of fight, or sight of any ship or ships which it may be his duty to engage or who, upon likelihood of engagement, shall not make the necessary preparations for fight and shall not in his own person and, according to his place, encourage the inferior officers and men to fight courageously shall suffer death or such other punishment, as from the nature and degree of the offence a court martial shall deem him to deserve and, if any person in the fleet shall treacherously or cowardly yield or cry for quarter, every person so offending and being convicted thereof by the sentence of a court martial shall suffer death.

11. Every person in the fleet, who shall not duly observe the orders of the admiral, flag officer, commander of any squadron or division, or other his superior officer, for assailing, joining battle with, or making defence against any fleet, squadron, or ship, or shall not obey the orders of his superior officer as aforesaid in time of action, to the best of his power, or shall not use all possible endeavours, to put the same effectually in execution, every such person so offending and being convicted thereof by the sentence of the court martial shall suffer death or such other punishment, as from the nature and degree of the offence a court martial shall deem his to deserve.

12. Every person in the fleet, who through cowardice, negligence, or disaffection, shall in time of action withdraw or keep back, or not come into the fight or engagement, or shall not do his utmost to take or destroy every ship which it shall be his duty to engage, and to assist and relieve all and every of His Majesty's ships, or those of his allies, which it shall be his duty to assist and relieve, every such person so offending and being convicted thereof by the sentence of a court martial shall suffer death.

13. Every person in the fleet, who through cowardice, negligence, or disaffection, shall forbear to pursue the chase of any enemy, pirate, or rebel, beaten or flying or shall not relieve or assist a known friend in view to the utmost of his power, being convicted of any such offence by the sentence of a court martial, shall suffer death.
14. If when action, or any service shall be commanded, any person in the fleet shall presume to delay or discourage the said action or service, upon pretence of arrears of wages, or upon any pretence whatsoever, every person so offending, being convicted thereof by the sentence of the court martial, shall suffer death or such other punishment as from the nature and degree of the offence a court martial shall deem him to deserve.
15. Every person in or belonging to the fleet, who shall desert to the enemy, pirate, or rebel, or run away with any of His Majesty's ships or vessels of war, or any ordnance, ammunition, stores, or provision belonging thereto, to the weakening of the service, or yield up the same cowardly or treacherously to the enemy, pirate, or rebel, being convicted of any such offence by the sentence of the court martial, shall suffer death.
16. Every person in or belonging to the fleet, who shall desert or entice others so to do, shall suffer death or such other punishment as the circumstances of the offence shall deserve and a court martial shall judge fit; and if any commanding officer of any of His Majesty's ships or vessels of war shall receive or entertain a deserter from any other of His Majesty's ships or vessels, after discovering him to be such deserter and shall not with all convenient speed give notice to the captain of the ship or vessel to which such deserter belongs or if the said ships or vessels are at any considerable distance from each other, to the secretary of the Admiralty or to the commander in chief, every person so offending, and, being convicted thereof by the sentence of the court martial, shall be cashiered.
17. The officers and seamen of all ships appointed for convoy and guard of merchant ships, or of any other, shall diligently attend upon that charge, without delay, according to their instructions in that behalf; and whosoever shall be faulty therein, and shall not faithfully perform their duty, and defend the ships and goods in their convoy, without either diverting to other parts or occasions, or refusing or neglecting to fight in their defence, if they be assailed, or running away cowardly, and submitting the ships in their convoy to peril and hazard; or shall demand or exact any money or other reward from any merchant or master for convoying of any ships or vessels entrusted to their care, or shall misuse the

masters or mariners thereof; shall be condemned to make reparation of the damage to the merchants, owners, and others, as the Court of Admiralty shall adjudge, and also be punished criminally according to the quality of their offences, be it by pains of death, or other punishment, according as shall be adjudged fit by the court martial.

18. If any captain, commander, or other officer of any of His Majesty's ships or vessels shall receive on board or permit to be received on board such ship or vessel any goods or merchandizes whatsoever, other than for the sole use of the ship or vessel, except gold, silver, or jewels, and except the goods and merchandizes belonging to any merchant, or other ship or vessel which may be shipwrecked, or in imminent danger of being shipwrecked, either on the high seas, or in any port, creek or harbour, in order to the preserving them for their proper owners, and except such goods or merchandizes as he shall at any time be ordered to take or receive on board by order of the Lord High Admiral of Great Britain, or the Commissioners for executing the officer of Lord High Admiral for the time being; every person so offending, being convicted thereof by the sentence of the court martial shall be cashiered and be for ever afterwards rendered incapable to serve in any place or office in the naval service of His Majesty, his heirs and successors.

19. If any person in or belonging to the fleet shall make or endeavour to make any mutinous assembly upon any pretence whatsoever, every person offending herein, and being convicted thereof by the sentence of the court martial, shall suffer death: and if any person in or belonging to the fleet shall utter any words of sedition or mutiny, he shall suffer death, or such other punishment as a court martial shall deem him to deserve and if any officer, mariner or soldier in or belonging to the fleet, shall behave himself with contempt to his superior officer, such superior officer being in the execution of his office, he shall be punished according to the nature of his offence by the judgement of a court martial.

20. If any person in the fleet shall conceal any traitorous or mutinous practice or design, being convicted thereof by the sentence of a court martial, he shall suffer death, or such other punishment as a court martial shall think fit; and if any person, in or belonging to the fleet, shall conceal any traitorous or mutinous words spoken by any, to the prejudice of His Majesty or government, or any words, practice, or design, tending to the hindrance of the service, and shall not forthwith reveal the same to the commanding officer, or being present at any mutiny or sedition, shall not use his utmost endeavours

to suppress the same, he shall be punished as a court martial shall think he deserves.

21. If any person in the fleet shall find cause of complaint of the unwholesomeness of the victual, or upon other just ground, he shall quietly make the same known to his superior, or captain, or commander in chief, as the occasion may deserve, that such present remedy may be had as the matter may require; and the said superior, captain, or commander in chief, shall, as far as he is able, cause the same to be presently remedied; and no person in the fleet, upon any disturbance, upon pain of such or other pretence, shall attempt to stir up any disturbance, upon pain of such punishment as a court martial shall think fit to inflict, according to the degree of the offence.
22. If any officer, mariner, soldier, or other person in the fleet shall strike any of his superior officers or draw or offer to draw or lift up any weapon against him, being in the execution of his office, on any pretence whatsoever, every such person being convicted of any such offence, by the sentence of a court martial, shall suffer death; and if any officer, mariner, soldier, or other person in the fleet, shall presume to quarrel with any of his superior officers, being in the execution of his office, or shall disobey any lawful command of any of his superior officers; every such person being convicted of any such offence, by the sentence of a court martial, shall suffer death, or such other punishment, as shall, according to the nature and degree of his offence, be inflicted upon him by the sentence of a court martial.
23. If any person in the fleet shall quarrel or fight with any other person in the fleet, or use reproachful or provoking speeches or gestures, tending to make any quarrel or disturbance, he shall, upon being convicted thereof, suffer such punishment as the offence shall deserve, and a court martial shall impose.
24. There shall be no wasteful expense of any powder, shot, ammunition, or other stores in the fleet, nor any embezzlement thereof, but the stores and provisions shall be carefully preserved, upon pain of such punishment to be inflicted upon the offenders, abettors, buyers, and receivers (being persons subject to naval discipline) as shall be by a court martial found just in that behalf.
25. Every person in the fleet, who shall unlawfully burn or set fire to any magazine or store of powder, or ship, boat, ketch, hoy or vessel, or tackle or furniture thereunto belonging, not then appertaining to an enemy, pirate, or rebel, being convicted of any such offence, by the sentence of a court martial, shall suffer death.

26. Care shall be taken in the conducting and steering of any of His Majesty's ships that through wilfulness, negligence, or other defaults, no ship be stranded or run upon any rocks or sands, or split or hazarded, upon pain, that such as shall be found guilty therein, be punished by death, or such other punishment, as the offence by a court martial shall be judged to deserve.
27. No person in or belonging to the fleet shall sleep upon his watch, or negligently perform the duty imposed on him or forsake his station upon pain of death or such other punishment as a court martial shall think fit to impose and as the circumstances of the case shall require.
28. All murders committed by any person in the fleet, shall be punished with death by the sentence of a court martial.
29. If any person in the fleet shall commit the unnatural and detestable sin of buggery or sodomy with man or beast, he shall be punished with death by the sentence of a court martial.
30. All robbery committed by any person in the fleet, shall be punished with death, or otherwise, as a court martial, upon consideration of circumstances, shall find meet.
31. Every officer or other person in the fleet, who shall knowingly make or sign a false muster or muster book, or who shall command, counsel, or procure the making or signing thereof, or who shall aid or abet any other person in the making or signing thereof, shall, upon proof of any such offence being made before a court martial, be cashiered, and rendered incapable of further employment in His Majesty's naval service.
32. No provost martial belonging to the fleet shall refuse to apprehend any criminal, whom he shall be authorized by legal warrant to apprehend, or to receive or keep any prisoner committed to his charge, or wilfully suffer him to escape, being once in his custody, or dismiss him without lawful order, upon pain of such punishment as a court martial shall deem him to deserve; and all captains, officers, and others in the fleet, shall do their endeavour to detect, apprehend, and bring to punishment all offenders, and shall assist the officers appointed for that purpose therein, upon pain of being proceeded against, and punished by a court martial, according to the nature and degree of the offence.
33. If any flag officer, captain, or commander, or lieutenant belonging to the fleet, shall be convicted before a court martial of behaving in a scandalous, infamous, cruel, oppressive, or fraudulent manner, unbecoming the character of an officer, he shall be dismissed from His Majesty's service.

34. Every person being in actual service and full pay, and part of the crew in or belonging to any of His Majesty's ships or vessels of war, who shall be guilty of mutiny, desertion, or disobedience to any lawful command, in any part of His Majesty's dominions on shore, when in actual service relative to the fleet, shall be liable to be tried by a court martial, and suffer the like punishment for every such offence as if the same had been committed at sea on board any of His Majesty's ships or vessel of war.
35. If any person, who shall be in the actual service and full pay of His Majesty's ships and vessels or war, shall commit upon the shore, in any place or places out of His Majesty's dominions, any of the crimes punishable by these articles and orders, the person so offending shall be liable to be tried and punished for the same, in like manner, to all intents and purposes, as if the said crimes had been committed at sea on board any of His Majesty's ships or vessels of war.
36. All other crimes not capital committed by any person or persons in the fleet, which are not mentioned in this Act, or for which no punishment is hereby directed to be inflicted, shall be punished according to the laws and customs in such cases used at sea.

III. Provided always that no person convicted of any offence shall, by the sentence of any court martial to be held by virtue of this Act, be adjudged to be imprisoned for a longer term than the space of two years.

IV. Provided also that nothing in this Act contained shall extend, or be construed to extend, to empower any court martial to be constituted by virtue of this Act to proceed to the punishment or trial of any of the offences specified in the several articles contained in this Act or of any offence whatsoever (other than the offences specified in the fifth, thirty fourth and thirty fifth of the foregoing articles and orders) which shall not be committed upon the main sea, or in great rivers only, beneath the bridges of the said rivers nigh to the sea, or in any haven, river or creek within the jurisdiction of the Admiralty and which shall not be committed by such persons as at the time of the offence committed shall be in actual service and full pay in the fleet or ships of war of His Majesty, his heirs or successors, such persons only excepted and for such offences only as are described in the fifth of the foregoing articles and orders.

V. Provided also that nothing in this Act contained shall extend, or be construed to extend, to empower any court martial to be constituted by virtue of this Act to proceed to the punishment or trial of any land officer or soldier on board any transport ship for any of the offences specified in the several articles contained in this Act.

VI. And it is hereby further enacted that from and after the twenty fifth day of December one thousand seven hundred and forty nine the Lord High Admiral of Great Britain or the Commissioners for executing the Office of Lord High Admiral of Great Britain for the time being shall have full power and authority to grant commissions to any officer commanding in chief any fleet or squadron of ships of war to call and assemble courts martial consisting of commanders and captains and that in case any officer commanding in chief any fleet or squadron of ships of war (who shall be authorized by the Lord High Admiral or the Commissioners for executing the office of Lord High Admiral for the time being to call and assemble courts martial in foreign parts) shall happen to die or be recalled or removed from his command, then the officer upon whom the command of the said fleet or squadron shall devolve, and so, from time to time, the officer who shall have the command of the fleet or squadron shall have the same power to call and assemble courts martial as the first commander in chief of the said fleet or squadron was invested with.

VII. Provided always, and it is hereby enacted and declared, that no commander in chief of any fleet or squadron of His Majesty's ships or detachment thereof consisting of more than five ships shall preside at any court martial in foreign parts, but that the officer next in command to such officer commanding in chief shall hold such court martial and preside thereat, any law, custom or usage to the contrary notwithstanding.

VIII. And it is hereby further enacted that from and after the twenty fifth day of December one thousand seven hundred and forty nine, in case any commander in chief in any fleet or squadron of His Majesty's ships or vessels of war in foreign parts shall detach any part of such fleet or squadron, every commander in chief shall and he is hereby authorized and required, by writing under his hand, to empower the chief commander of the squadron or detachment so ordered on such separate service (and in case of his death or removal, the officer to whom the command of such separate squadron or detachment shall belong) to hold courts martial during the time of such separate service or until the commander of the said detachment for the time being shall return to his commander in chief or shall come under the command of any other his superior officer or return to Great Britain or Ireland.

IX. Provided always, and it is hereby further enacted, that if any five or more of His Majesty's ships or vessels of war shall happen to meet together in foreign parts, then and in such case it shall be lawful for the senior officer of the said ships or vessels to hold courts martial and preside thereat from time to time as there shall be occasion during so long time as the said ships or vessels of war or any five or more of them shall continue together.

X. Provided nevertheless, and be it also enacted, that where any material objection occurs, which may render it improper for the person who is next in command to the senior officer or commander in chief of any fleet or squadron of His Majesty's ships of war in foreign parts to hold courts martial or preside thereat, in such cases it shall be lawful for the Lord High Admiral or Commissioners for executing the office of Lord High Admiral for the time being, as also the commander in chief of any such fleet or squadron of His Majesty's ships in foreign parts respectively to appoint the third officer in command to preside at or hold such court martial.

XI. And it is hereby further enacted that from and after the twenty fifth day of December one thousand seven hundred and forty nine, it shall be lawful for the Lord High Admiral of Great Britain or Commissioners for executing the office of Lord High Admiral for the time being, and they are hereby respectively authorized from time to time as there shall be occasion, to direct any flag officer or captain of any of His Majesty's ships of war who shall be in any port of Great Britain or Ireland to hold courts martial in any such port, provided such flag officer or captain be the first, second or third in command of such port as shall be found most expedient and for the good of His Majesty's service; and such flag officer or captain so directed to hold courts martial shall preside at such court martial, anything herein contained to the contrary notwithstanding.

XII. And it is hereby further enacted that from and after the twenty fifth day of December one thousand seven hundred and forty nine, no court martial, to be held or appointed by virtue of this present Act, shall consist of more than thirteen or less than five persons to be composed of such flag officers, captains or commanders then and there present as are next in seniority to the officer who presides at the court martial.

XIII. Provided always, and be it enacted by the authority aforesaid, that nothing herein contained shall extend, or be construed to extend, to authorize or empower the Lord High Admiral or the Commissioners for executing the office of Lord High Admiral or any officer empowered to order or hold courts martial to direct or ascertain the particular number of persons of which any court martial to be held or appointed by virtue of this present Act shall consist.

XIV. Provided always, and it is hereby enacted and declared, that in case any court martial shall, by virtue of this Act, be appointed to be held at any place where there are not less than three nor yet so many as five officers of the degree and denomination of a post captain or of a superior rank to be found, then it shall be lawful for the officer at the place appointed for holding such court martial who is to preside at the same to call to his assistance as many of the commanders of His Majesty's vessels under the rank and degree of a post captain as, together with the post captains then and there present, will make up the number of five to hold such court martial.

XV. And it is hereby further enacted that from and after the twenty fifth day of December one thousand seven hundred and forty nine, no member of any court martial after the trial is begun shall go on shore till sentence be given, but remain on board the ship in which the court shall first assemble, except in case of sickness, to be judged of by the court upon pain of being cashiered from His Majesty's service; nor shall the proceedings of the said court be delayed by the absence of any of its members, provided a sufficient number doth remain to compose the said court, which shall and is hereby required to sit from day to day (Sunday always excepted) until the sentence be given.

XVI. And it is hereby further enacted that from and after the twenty fifth day of December one thousand seven hundred and forty nine, upon all trials of offenders by any court martial, all the officers present who are to constitute the said court martial shall, before they proceed to such trial, take such oath as is herein after-mentioned upon the holy evangelists before the court, which oath the judge advocate, or his deputy or the person appointed to officiate as such, is hereby authorized and required to administer in the words following (that is to say):

> I, A. B., do swear that I will duly administer justice according to the articles and orders established by an Act passed in the twenty second year of the reign of His Majesty, King George the Second, for *Amending, Explaining and Reducing into One Act of Parliament the Laws Relating to the Government of His Majesty's Ships, Vessels and Forces by Sea*, without partiality, favour or affection; and if any case shall arise, which is not particularly mentioned in the said articles and orders, I will duly administer justice according to my conscience, the best of my understanding, and the custom of the navy in the like cases; and I do further swear that I will not upon any account, at any time whatsoever, disclose or discover the vote or opinion of any particular member of this court martial, unless thereunto required by Act of Parliament.
>
> So help me God.

And so soon as the said oath shall have been administered to the respective members, the president of the court is hereby authorized and required to administer to the judge advocate, or the person officiating as such, an oath in the following words:

> I, A. B., do swear that I will not upon any account at any time whatsoever disclose or discover the vote or opinion of any particular

member of this court martial, unless thereunto required by Act of Parliament.

So help me God.

XVII. And it is hereby further enacted that from and after the twenty fifth day of December one thousand seven hundred and forty nine, in case any person in the fleet, being called upon to give evidence at any court martial, shall refuse to give his evidence upon oath or shall prevaricate in his evidence or behave with contempt to the court, it shall and may be lawful for such court martial to punish every such offender by imprisonment at the discretion of the court, such imprisonment not to continue longer than three months, in case of such refusal or prevarication, nor longer than one month in the case of such contempt; and that all and every person and persons who shall commit any wilful perjury in any evidence or examination upon oath at any such court martial or who shall corruptly procure or suborn any person to commit such wilful perjury shall and may be prosecuted in His Majesty's Court of King's Bench by indictment or information; and every issue joined in any such indictment or information shall be tried by good and lawful men of the county of Middlesex, or such other county as the said Court of King's Bench shall direct; and all and every person and persons being lawfully convicted upon any such indictment or information shall be punished with such pains and penalties as are inflicted for the like offences respectively by two Acts of Parliament, the one made in the fifth year of the reign of Queen Elizabeth, entitled *An Act for Punishment of Such Persons as shall Procure or Commit any Wilful Perjury*, and the other made in the second year of the reign of His present Majesty entitled *An Act for the More Effectual Preventing and Further Punishment of Forgery, Perjury and Subornation of Perjury and to Make it Felony to Steal Bonds, Notes or other Securities for Payment of Money*.

XVIII. And be it further enacted by the authority aforesaid that in every information or indictment to be prosecuted by virtue of this Act for any such offence, it shall be sufficient to set forth the offence charged upon the defendant without setting forth the commission or authority for holding the court martial and without setting forth the particular matter tried or to be tried or directed or intended to be tried before such court.

XIX. And it is hereby further enacted that from and after the twenty fifth day of December one thousand seven hundred and forty nine, no sentence of death given by any court martial held within the narrow seas (except in cases of mutiny) shall be put in execution till after the report of the proceedings of the said court shall have been made to the Lord High Admiral or the Commissioners for executing the office of Lord High

Admiral and his or their directions shall have been given therein; and, if the said court shall have been held beyond the narrow seas, then such sentence of death shall not be carried into execution but by order of the commander of the fleet or squadron wherein sentence was passed; and in cases where sentence of death shall be passed in any squadron detached from any other fleet or squadron upon a separate service, then such sentence of death (except in cases of mutiny) shall not be put in execution, but by order of the commander of the fleet or squadron from which such detachment shall have been made or of the Lord High Admiral or Commissioners for executing the office of Lord High Admiral; and in cases where sentence of death shall be passed in any court martial held by the senior officer of five or more of His Majesty's ships, which shall happen to meet together in foreign parts pursuant to the power herein before given, then such sentence of death (except in cases of mutiny) shall not be carried into execution but by order of the Lord High Admiral or Commissioners for executing the office of Lord High Admiral.

XX. And it is hereby further enacted and declared that from and after the twenty fifth day of December one thousand seven hundred and forty nine, the judge advocate of any fleet for the time being or his deputy shall have full power and authority and is hereby required to administer an oath to any witness at any trial by court martial; and in the absence of the judge advocate and his deputy, the court martial shall have full power and authority to appoint any person to execute the office of judge advocate.

XXI. And be it further enacted by the authority aforesaid that from and after the twenty fifth day of December one thousand seven hundred and forty nine, all the powers given by the several articles and orders established by this Act shall remain and be in full force with respect to the crews of such of His Majesty's ships as shall be wrecked or be otherwise lost or destroyed; and all the command, power and authority given to the officers of the said ship or ships shall remain and be in full force as effectually as if such ship or ships to which they did belong were not so wrecked, lost or destroyed until they shall be regularly discharged from His Majesty's further service or removed into some other of His Majesty's ships of war or until a court martial shall be held pursuant to the custom of the navy in such cases to enquire into the causes of the loss of the said ship or ships; and if upon such enquiry it shall appear by the sentence of the court martial that all or any of the officers or seaman of the said ship or ships did their utmost to preserve, get off or recover the said ship or ships and since the loss thereof have behaved themselves obediently to their superior officers according to the discipline of the navy and the said articles and orders herein before established, then all the pay and wages of the said officers and seamen, or such of them as shall have done their duty as aforesaid, shall continue and go on and be paid to the time of their discharge or death; or if they shall be then alive, to the time of the holding of such court martial or removal into some other of His Majesty's ships of war and every such officer and seaman of any of His Majesty's ships of war, who after the wreck or loss of his ship shall act contrary to the discipline of the navy and the several articles and orders herein before established or any of them, shall be sentenced by the said court martial and punished as if the ship to which he did belong was not so wrecked, lost or destroyed.

XXII. And be it further enacted that from and after the twenty fifth day of December one thousand seven hundred and forty nine, all the pay and wages of such officers and seamen of any of His Majesty's ships as are taken by the enemy and upon enquiry at a court martial shall appear by the sentence of the said court to have done their utmost to defend the said ship or ships, and, since the taking thereof, to have behaved themselves obediently to their superior officers according to the discipline and the said articles and orders herein before established shall continue and go on and be paid from the time of their being so taken to the time of the holding of such court martial, or until they shall be regularly discharged from His Majesty's service or removed into some other of His Majesty's ships of war, or (if they shall die in captivity or not live to the time of the holding of such court martial) to the time of their death in such manner, and not otherwise, as if the said ship or ships to which they did belong respectively was not or were not so taken.

XXIII. Provided always, and be it further enacted, that no person or persons not flying from justice shall be tried or punished by any court martial for any offence to be committed against this Act, unless the complaint of such offence be made in writing to the Lord High Admiral or to the Commissioners for executing the Office of Lord High Admiral for the time being, or any commander in chief of His Majesty's squadrons or ships empowered to hold courts martial, or unless a court martial to try such offender shall be ordered by the said Lord High Admiral, or the said Commissioners, or the said commander in chief either within three years after such offence shall be committed or within one year after the return of the ship, or of the squadron, to which such offender shall belong into any of the ports of Great Britain or Ireland; or within one year after the return of such offender into Great Britain or Ireland.

XXIV. And whereas by the said Act, entitled *An Act for the More Effectual Suppressing of Piracy*, it is amongst other things enacted in the following words: 'that the said captain, commander or other officer of the said ship or vessel of war and all and every of the owners or proprietors of such goods and merchandizes put on board such ship or vessel of war as aforesaid shall lose, forfeit and pay the value of all and every such goods and merchandizes so put on board as aforesaid; one moiety of such full value to such person or persons as shall make the first discovery and give information of or concerning the said offence, the other moiety of such full value to and for the use of Greenwich Hospital; all which forfeitures shall and may be sued for and recovered in the High Court of Admiralty;' now for making the said in part recited Act more useful and effectual, be it enacted by the authority aforesaid that from and after the twenty fifth day of December one thousand seven hundred and forty nine, if any captain, commander or other officer of any of His Majesty's ships or vessels shall receive on board or permit or suffer to be received on board such ship or vessel any goods or merchandizes contrary to the true intent and meaning of the eighteenth article in this Act before mentioned and hereby enacted, every such captain, commander or other officer shall, for every such offence over and above any punishment inflicted by this Act, forfeit and pay the value of all and every such goods or merchandizes so received, or permitted or suffered to be received on board as aforesaid, or the sum of five hundred Pounds of lawful money of Great Britain at the election of the informer or person who shall sue for the same so that no more than one of these penalties or forfeitures shall be sued for and recovered by virtue of this and the said in part recited Act, or either of them, against the same person for one and the same offence, one moiety of which penalties or forfeitures shall be forfeited and paid to the person who shall inform or sue for the same and the other moiety thereof, to and for the use of the Royal Hospital at Greenwich, which forfeiture shall be sued for and recovered by action of debt, bill, plaint or information in any of His Majesty's courts of record at Westminster or in the High Court of Admiralty at the election of the informer or person who shall sue for the same; and the court shall award such costs to the parties as shall be just and in all cases where judgement or sentence shall be given against any such offender, the court, where such judgement or sentence shall be given, shall, with all convenient speed, certify the same to the Lord High Admiral or to the Commissioners for executing the said Office.

XXV. Provided always that nothing in this Act contained shall extend or be construed to extend to take away from the Lord High Admiral of Great Britain or the Commissioners for executing the office of Lord High Admiral of Great Britain, or any vice admiral, or any judge or judges of the Admiralty, or his or their deputy or deputies, or any other officers or ministers of the Admiralty, or any others having or claiming any admiral power, jurisdiction or authority within this realm or any other the King's dominions, or from any person or court whatsoever, any power, right, jurisdiction, pre-eminence or authority, which he or they, or any of them lawfully hath, have or had, or ought to have and enjoy before the making of this Act so as the same person shall not be punished twice for the same offence.

XXVI. Provided nevertheless and be it enacted that the repeal of the said before recited statutes, or any part thereof, or anything herein contained shall not extend or be deemed to extend to discharge or avoid, or prevent any prosecution or suit commenced or at any time hereafter to be commenced against any person or persons for any offence committed on or before the said twenty fifth day of December, one thousand seven hundred and forty nine or to be committed against the said statutes or any part or parts thereof, but that all persons who have been or shall, before said twenty fifth day of December, be guilty of any such offence shall and may be prosecuted, sued, condemned and punished for the same as well as before the said twenty fifth day of December as if the said statutes had not been repealed.

2. *An Act to Explain and Amend an Act Made in the Twenty Second Year of the Reign of His Late Majesty King George the Second, Entitled An Act for Amending, Explaining and Reducing into One Act of Parliament the Laws Relating to the Government of His Majesty's Ships, Vessels and Forces by Sea*

[19 Geo. III c. 17]

Whereas by an Act made in the twenty second year of the reign of His late Majesty King George the Second, entitled *An Act for Amending, Explaining and Reducing into One Act of Parliament the Laws Relating to the Government of His Majesty's Ships, Vessels and Forces by Sea,* it is, among other things, enacted, 'that from and after the twenty fifth day of December, one thousand seven hundred and forty nine, no member of any court martial, after the trial is begun, shall go on shore till sentence be given, but remain on board the ship in which the court shall first assemble, except in case of sickness to be judged of by the court, upon pain of being cashiered from His Majesty's service; nor shall the proceedings of the said court be delayed by the absence of any of its members, provided a sufficient number doth remain to compose the said court, which shall and is thereby required to sit from day to day (Sunday always excepted) until the sentence be given:' and whereas it hath been found by experience that the confining members of courts martial to the ship in which such courts martial shall first assemble until sentence be given hath been attended with great inconveniences and prejudice to the healths of officers summoned to attend as members of courts martial; and it is highly necessary and expedient that such inconveniences should be prevented in future, may it therefore please your Majesty that it may be enacted and be it enacted by the King's most excellent majesty, by and with the advice and consent of the lords spiritual and temporal and commons in this present Parliament assembled, and by the authority of the same that so much and such part of the said recited Act as directs that no member of any court martial, after the trial is begun, shall go on shore till the sentence be given, but remain on board the ship in which the court shall first assemble, except in case of sickness to be judged of by the court, upon pain of being cashiered from His Majesty's service and that the proceedings of the said court shall not be delayed by the absence of any of its members provided a sufficient number doth remain to compose the said court, which is thereby required to sit from day to day (Sunday always excepted) until the sentence be given, shall be and the same is hereby repealed and made void to all intents and purposes whatsoever.

II. Provided always, and be it enacted, that the proceedings of any court martial shall not be delayed by the absence of any of its members, provided a sufficient number doth remain to compose such court, which shall and is hereby required to sit from day to day (Sunday always excepted) until the sentence be given, anything herein before contained to the contrary thereof in anywise notwithstanding; and no member of the said court martial shall absent himself from the said court during the whole course of the trial upon pain of being cashiered from His Majesty's service, except in case of sickness or other extraordinary and indispensable occasion to be judged of by the said court.

III. And whereas by two clauses in the said Act passed in the twenty second year of the reign of His late Majesty King George the Second, it is enacted and declared, that 'every person in the fleet, who through cowardice, negligence, or disaffection, shall in time of action withdraw or keep back, or not come into the fight or engagement, or shall not do his utmost to take or destroy every ship which it shall be his duty to engage, and to assist and relieve all and every of His Majesty's ships, or those of his allies, which it shall be his duty to assist and relieve, and being convicted thereof by the sentence of a court martial, shall suffer death'; and also that 'every person in the fleet, who through cowardice, negligence, or disaffection, shall forbear to pursue the chase of any enemy, pirate, or rebel, beaten or flying; or shall not relieve or assist a known friend in view, to the utmost of his power; and being convicted of any such offence by the sentence of a court martial, shall suffer death': And whereas the restraining of the power of the court martial to the inflicting of the punishment of death in the several cases recited in the said clauses may be attended with great hardship and inconvenience; be it enacted, that, from and after the passing of this Act, it shall and may be lawful in the several cases recited in the said clauses for the court martial to pronounce sentence of death or to inflict such other punishment as the nature and degree of the offence shall be found to deserve.

3. *Chapter on Courts Martial in Regulations and Instructions of 1731*

[*Regulations and Instructions Relating to His Majesty's Service at Sea*, 1st edn, pp. 3–6]

Of Courts Martial

Article I

All courts martial are to be held, offences tried, sentence pronounced and execution of such sentence to be done according to the Articles and Orders contained in an Act of Parliament made in the thirteenth year of the reign of King Charles the Second, entitled *An Act for the Establishing Articles and Orders for the Regulating and better Government of His Majesty's Navy, Ships of War and Forces by Sea*, which Act all officers concerned are duly to peruse for their instruction herein.

II

All commissions or general powers for holding courts martial are to be understood to be in force no longer than during the expedition.

III

Courts martial shall always be held in the forenoon and in the most public place of the ship, where all who will may be present; and the captains of all His Majesty's ships in company, which take post, have a right to assist thereat.

IV

All complaints at sea or in foreign parts, upon which the summoning a court martial is to be grounded, shall be made in writing to the commander in chief (unless where the said commander in chief shall see cause of himself to call the same) in which are to be set forth the particular facts, with the place, time, and in what manner they were committed. And if any captain, who is entitled by his rank to sit in the court, be personally concerned in the matter to be tried, he shall not be admitted to sit at the said trial.

V

The judge advocate is to examine the witnesses upon oath, take down their depositions in writing, and show the same to the commander in chief, who is to order him to send timely before the trial an attested copy of the charge or accusation to the party accused in order to his being the better prepared for his defence.

VI

When the court is sitting, the judge advocate is to take minutes of their proceedings and to advise them of the proper forms when there shall be occasion, and to deliver his opinion in any doubts or difficulties in their methods that may arise in the course of the trial.

VII

When the court shall have gone through the examination and heard all parties, the person accused shall be removed and the standers by ordered to withdraw; after which the matters being fully considered and debated by the court, the president is to state and put the several questions agreed by them, in which the youngest officer shall vote first, proceeding in order up to the president, who, having delivered his own opinion, is to collect the numbers and settle the determination of the court according to the majority of voices.

VIII

The judge advocate is to draw up in writing the sentence of the court, which being approved and signed by them, all persons shall be admitted; and the party accused being present, the judge advocate, by direction of the president, is to pronounce the same.

IX

When sentence of death is to be executed upon any criminal, notice is to be first given from the ship by a signal and firing a gun, upon which, the captains of all the ships present shall summon their companies upon deck to be spectators thereof and shall make known to them the crime for which the punishment is inflicted.

X

The judge advocate is always to send the original sentence and affidavits, as also the minutes which he has taken of the proceedings of the court to the Secretary of the Admiralty.

4. *Chapter on Courts Martial in the Regulations and Instructions of 1806*

[*Regulations and Instructions Relating to His Majesty's Service at Sea*, 1806 edn, pp. 404–10]

Chapter II
Of Courts Martial

ARTICLE I.

Courts martial are to be assembled and held, offences tried, sentence pronounced, and execution of such sentence to be done, according to the articles and orders contained in an Act of Parliament made in the 22nd year of the reign of King George 2nd, intituled, *An Act for Amending, Explaining, and Reducing into One Act of Parliament, the Laws Relating to the Government of His Majesty's Ships, Vessels, and Forces by Sea* and also an Act made in the 19th year of the reign of His present Majesty, intituled *An Act to Explain and Amend the Foregoing Act*. In addition to the Articles and rules contained in the said acts, the following regulations are to be observed.

II.

All representations, or complaints, intended as the foundation of a court martial, are to be made in writing, setting forth the particular facts, when and where, and in what manner the same were committed.

III.

When a court martial is appointed to be held, the officer, who is to preside thereat, is to take care that a copy of the charge or complaint be delivered to the person accused, as soon as may be, after he shall have received the order to hold such court martial, and not less than twenty-four hours before the trial.

IV.

Courts martial are to be assembled and held in the most convenient and public place of the ship; and all persons, excepting such as are intended to give evidence, are to be admitted.

V.

If any officer, entitled by his rank to sit at a court martial, be personally concerned in the matter to be tried, he is not to be permitted to be of the number of members, by whom the court shall be composed.

VI.

A junior officer commanding a post ship, shall, in sitting at courts-martial, take precedence of his senior officer commanding a sloop.

Captains and commanders appointed to the temporary command of His Majesty's Ships shall be considered as liable to sit on courts-martial, in the same manner as if they were actually the captains or commanders of such ships. Lieutenants shall not be permitted to sit as members at a court martial, although they may be in the temporary command of ships by order.

VII.

When a court is assembled, the person to be tried, as also the accuser, if any, are to be brought before them; the judge advocate is to read the warrant or power authorizing the court to assemble; and immediately after to administer to the members, and to take himself, the oath prescribed by the Act first mentioned; he is next to read the charge, or complaint against the person to be tried, and thereupon the court may proceed to call witnesses: but they are not to question the said witnesses until an oath hath been administered by the judge advocate in the words following, which the witness is to repeat:

> 'I, A. B., do most solemnly swear, that in the evidence I shall give before the court, respecting the present trial, I will, whether demanded of me by question or not, and whether favourable or unfavourable to the prisoner, declare the truth, the whole truth and nothing but the truth; So help me God.'

VIII.

In the examination of witnesses the following method is to be observed: first, to call such as are in support of the charge, who are to be questioned by the accuser, if any, the court, or judge advocate, and afterwards by the party upon trial. Such as are produced to invalidate a charge are next to be examined, and the party accused is to begin with his interrogatories, if he shall think fit. If a question proposed is objected to, the opinion of the court is to be admitted or dropt as the majority shall agree.

IX.

A witness may be called in, as often as the court, or judge advocate, with the consent thereof, shall think proper; and they may call for and examine any person as a witness, whom they think can give information, though not desired by the accuser, or accused; it being the duty of the court to attain the fullest insight they possibly can into the matter before them.

X.

The judge advocate is the take down in writing the evidence given by each witness and read the same to the Court in his hearing, that, in case of a mistake, it may be corrected.

XI.

When the evidence is closed, the accused person is to be removed, and the accuser and standers-by are to withdraw; the court is then to consider the matter in evidence before it, and the judge advocate, by the direction of the court, is to draw up such questions as shall be agreed upon, whereon to form a determination in regard to the innocence or guilt of the person upon trial. If the party be found guilty of a breach of any of the Articles of War established by law, the court is to consider and to determine on the punishment proper to be inflicted conformably thereto. The judge advocate is to draw up the sentence accordingly, being careful to specify therein the charge, or substance of it, and the same is to be signed by every member of the court by way of attestation, notwithstanding any difference of opinion there may have been among them.

XII.

In taking the opinion of the court upon all questions, the youngest officer shall vote first, proceeding in order up to the president, and should the members of the court disagree upon any previous question, and upon a division the votes be equal, the point is to be re-considered; but if an equality of votes still continues, the matter in debate must remain as it stood before the question was put. If there should be an equality upon the main question, whether the charge or charges be proved, or not, and it continues so after re-consideration, the favourable construction is to take place.

XIII.

The judge advocate is to take minutes of the proceedings of the court; he is to advise the court of the proper forms, when there shall be occasion, and to deliver his opinion in any doubts or difficulties that may arise in the course of the trial.

XIV.

After the sentence is drawn up and signed, all persons are to be re-admitted; and, the party accused being also present, the judge advocate is, by direction of the court, to pronounce the same.

XV.

The judge advocate is to send the original sentence, and an attested copy of the minutes of the evidence and proceedings of the court, to the Secretary of the Admiralty, by the first opportunity.

[X]VI.

When sentence of death is to be executed, or other public punishment to be inflicted, upon any criminal, notice is to be first given from the ship by a signal and firing a gun, upon which the captains of all the ships present are to summon their companies upon deck, to be spectators thereof, and to make known to them the crime for which the punishment is inflicted.

5. *Court Martial of Joseph Piper*

[ADM 1/5330]

Minutes of the proceedings of a court martial assembled and held on board His Majesty's Ship *St. George* in Hamoze the 11th January 1793 for the trial of Joseph Piper, alias John Joseph Pearson, a Seaman belonging to the *Charon*, for desertion.

Captains Robertson and Keats, being unable to attend thro' illness, and the same being certified on oaths, the court proceeded to trial.

Mr. W. H. Read, Clk. of the *Lowenstoffe*, sworn.

Court:

Q. – Have you the *Lowenstoffe's* ship's books?

A. – Yes, here they are.

Q. – Do you know the prisoner?

A. – Yes, he entered for the *Lowenstoffe* in the name of John Joseph Pearson.

Court to the prisoner:

Q. – Have you any question to ask this evidence?

A. – None.

John Miles, a Seaman belonging to the *Charon* and left at the hospital, sworn.

Q. – Do you know the prisoner?

A. – Yes.

Q. – Under what name?

A. – Piper, I do not recollect his Christian name.

Q. – Was you on board the *Charon* at the time she was paid the two months advance?

A. – Yes.

Q. – Was the prisoner on board when the two months was paid?
A. – Yes.
Q. – Do you know whether he did or did not receive the two months advance?
A. – I was ill and do not.
Q. – How long did you remain on board after the two months advance was paid before you went to the hospital?
A. – I went to the hospital the day after.
Q. – Had the desertion taken place before you went to the hospital?
A. – Not as I know of.
Court to the prisoner:
Q. – Have you any question to ask this evidence?
A. – None.

Morris McLaughlin, another Seaman from the hospital, sworn.

Court:
Q. – How long did you belong to the *Charon* before she sailed?
A. – Five weeks.
Q. – Do you know the prisoner?
A. – Yes. I saw him on board the *Charon*; he belonged to her.
Q. – Under what name did he go on board the *Charon*?
A. – I don't know.
Q. – Was you on board the *Charon* at the time the two months advance was paid?
A. – Yes.
Q. – Was the prisoner on board at the time?
A. – I don't know.
Q. – How long were you at the hospital before the desertion of the five men took place?
A. – I don't know. The two months advance was paid on the Saturday and I went to the hospital on the Sunday.
Court to the prisoner:
Q. – Have you any question to ask this evidence?
A. – None.

Mr. Bleech [?], Boatswain of the *Magnanime*, called to the prisoner's character.

Court:
Q. – Do you know the prisoner?
A. – Yes, he was with me about three years and a half, as a servant, in the *Magnanime*; during which time he was honest, and I had no fault to find with him, which is all I have to say.

Prisoner threw himself on the mercy of the court.

5A. *Report of the Court Martial of Joseph Piper*

[ADM 1/5330]

At a court martial assembled and held onboard His Majesty's ship *St George* in Hamoze the 11th day of January 1793.

Present

Sir Thomas Rich, Bar^{t}, Captain of His Majesty's ship *Culloden* and second officer in the command of His Majesty's ships and vessels at Plymouth, President.

Captains

Thomas Hicks	Richard Boger
William Wolseley	Thomas Byard
Joseph Ellison	Willm Hancock Kelly
Willm Alb^{y} Otway	Edward Buller

The court, in pursuance to an order from the Right Honourable the Lords Commissioner of the Admiralty dated the 7th instant and directed to Sir Thomas Rich, Bar^{t}, Captain of His Majesty's ship *Culloden* and second officer in the command of His Majesty's ships and vessels at Plymouth, proceeded to try Joseph Piper (alias John Joseph Pearson) belonging to His Majesty's ship *Charon*, for desertion and the court, having accordingly heard the evidence produced in support of the charge as well as what the prisoner had to offer in his own defence and very maturely and deliberately considered the same, is of opinion that the charge is proved and therefore adjudge him to receive one hundred lashes on his bare back with a cat o' nine tails onboard of, or alongside, such ship or ships in Hamoze at such time, or times, and in such manner and proportion as the commander in chief of His Majesty's ships and vessels at this port shall direct; and the said Joseph Piper (alias John Joseph Pearson) is hereby sentenced to receive the same accordingly. …

6. *Report of the Court Martial of William Clark and John Rolfe*

[ADM 1/5330]

At a court martial assembled and held onboard His Majesty's Ship *Alfred* at Chatham on Tuesday the 26th day of March 1793.

Present

Thomas Pasley, Esqr, Captain of His Majesty's ship *Bellerophon* and second officer in the command of His Majesty's ships and vessels in the River Medway and at the buoy of the Nore, President.

Captains

The H^{ble} Geo Keith Elphinston	James Pigott
Henry Harvey	William Parker
John Bazely	Peter Rainer
The Honble Hugh S. Conway	Horatio Nelson
Charles Cotton	John Nich Inglefield
R^{t} Honble Lord Cranstown	Thomas Drury

The order for assembling the court martial being read and the oath directed by the Act of Parliament administered, the books of the *Medusa* and *Audacious* and the surgeon of the hospital's report were produced; and on examining them, it appeared that no such man as William Clark was upon the books of the *Audacious*, and that no such man as John Rolfe appeared upon the books of the *Medusa*, the court was thereupon cleared, and they were unanimously of opinion that the prisoners so described in their Lordships' order could not be tried. …

7. *Commander Thomas Archibald Orrok to Sir Peter Parker, Bar^{t}.*

[ADM 1/5331] *Orestes*. Portsmouth.
July 4, 1794

… Whereas in the night of the 20th & 21st of June last the bread room of His Majesty's sloop under my command was broke open and a considerable quantity of slops stolen from thence, and as I have every reason to apprehend that the offence above mention'd was committed by the persons whose names hereafter follow, viz. Samuel Mose, Thomas Jones, Samuel Powdrill, William Todd (Marines), John Bonny, George Hall and James Cains (Seamen), I have therefore to request that you will be pleased to order the three Marines whose names are first mentioned to be tried by a court martial and to allow the four others to be admitted as witnesses on the trial, not having otherwise evidence sufficient to convict them. …

8. *Court Martial of William Walker*

[ADM 1/5331]

Minutes of the proceedings of a court martial held on board His Majesty's ship the *Britannia* in Leghorn Road, the 13th day of September 1794.

Present

William Hotham, Esqr., Vice Admiral of the Red, President
Robert Linzee, Esqr., Rear Admiral of the White

Captain	Robert Man	Captain	Samuel Reeve
"	Horatio Nelson	"	Thomas Lenox Frederick
"	John Holloway	"	John Knight
"	Benjamin Hallowell	"	Edward Cook
"	Robert Gambier Middleton		

The prisoner was brought into court and the evidence and audience admitted.

The order was then read from the Right Honourable Lord Hood, Admiral of the Blue and Commander in Chief, &c, &c, &c, dated the 11th instant and directed to William Hotham, Esqr., Vice Admiral of the Red, to try Lieutenant William Walker of the *Rose* cutter on a representation 'of his having been guilty of practices highly disgraceful to His Majesty's navy, by taking money for giving protection to the trade between Bastia and this port.'

The members of the court and judge advocate then respectively took the oaths prescribed by Act of Parliament.

The charge against the prisoner was read and all the witnesses ordered to withdraw, the first to be sworn excepted, and the court proceeded to trial.

Captain John Gore of *La Fleche* was then sworn.

Court — Please relate to the court what you know respecting the charge against the prisoner.

Answer — The only circumstance I know relative to the charge against the prisoner proceeds from a conversation between the prisoner and myself.

Court — Please relate to the court what that conversation was.

Answer — Upon my taxing the prisoner with a supposition I had of his being guilty of the charge, he informed me he had been ignorant of the consequences and supposed there was no harm in receiving a present from foreigners for a convoy, that he had not received anything, but was told when the vessels arrived safe at Leghorn, he was to be recompensed for his trouble by a handsome present.

Court — What reason had you for that supposition?

Answer — Merely from repeated applications from the merchants to order the prisoner to take those vessels under his convoy from Bastia to Leghorn and the prisoner's applying himself also to me for an order for that purpose.

Court — Do you know whether the prisoner ever did receive money for any convoy between Bastia and this port?

Answer — I do not.

Court — Might not the application from the merchants have proceeded from the prisoner's care and attention to convoys?

Answer — I know not whether the prisoner ever did convoy vessels from Bastia before, having always ordered the cutters not to do so, as they mostly went from Bastia with dispatches.

Court — Had you ever any complaint from merchants or masters of their having paid money to the prisoner for taking their vessels under convoy?

Answer — None from any person whatever.

Prisoner to evidence — At what time did I apply to you for an order to convoy vessels of any kind?

Answer — To the best of my recollection, about the 27th or 28th of last month.

Neither the court or prisoner having any further questions to ask this evidence, he was ordered to withdraw.

Captain William Shield of the *Sincere* was then called in and sworn.

Court — You will please to relate to the court what you know relative to the charge against the prisoner?

Answer — In conversation with Captain Gore, he told me the prisoner had been making an agreement with some masters of tartans[1] to give him money for convoying them to Leghorn.

Court — Do you, from your own knowledge, know that the prisoner ever did receive money for convoy?

Answer — I do not.

Court — Did you ever hear any person say they had given him money for that purpose?

Answer — Never.

[1]According to the 1815 edition of Falconer's *Universal Dictionary of the Marine* edited by William Burney, a tartan was 'a small coasting vessel navigated in the Mediterranean Sea and having only one mast and a bowsprit …' [s.v. tartan].

Neither the court or prisoner having any further questions to ask this evidence, he was ordered to withdraw.

The evidence in support of the charge being finished, the prisoner was called upon to make his defence, when he produced a written deposition from Salvator Arbib and Co., merchants in Leghorn, stating that he had never convoyed any vessels belonging to them between Bastia and Leghorn, nor had they ever paid him any money or made him any present whatever for convoys.

The master of the *Rose* cutter (Mr. Edward Older) was then called in and sworn.

Court Relate to the court whether you know that the prisoner ever gave convoy between Bastia and Leghorn.

Answer Never to any other vessel than a Danish ship from Bastia to Leghorn, which was our prize.

Neither the court or prisoner having any further questions to ask this evidence, he was desired to withdraw and here the prisoner rested his defence, when the court proceeded to deliberate upon the sentence, the audience being directed to withdraw.

8A. *Report of the Court Martial of William Walker*

[ADM 1/5331]

… And the court, having heard the evidence in support of the charge, as well as what the prisoner had to offer in his defence and having maturely and deliberately weighed and considered the same, is of opinion that the charge is not proved and do therefore acquit the said Lieutenant William Walker of the whole and every part thereof.

And he is hereby acquitted accordingly. …

9. *Captain Edward James Foote to Evan Nepean*

[ADM 1/1795]

Niger at St. Helens,
Tuesday, May 19th 1795

… Daniel Roy, Seaman of His Majesty's ship *Niger* under my command, having manifested the utmost contrition for his improper conduct, I am induced to hope in consequence of the sense he has of his guilt and the length of his confinement their Lordships will be pleased to allow me to withdraw my letter of the 21st of last month requesting he might be tried by a court martial.

It is but justice in me to mention that Daniel Roy wrote to me, when the *Niger* had a skirmish on the French coast, to beg I would allow him to go to his quarters. …

[Adm Note]
20 May. Orders to withdraw the w[t]. for court martial. Let Cap[t]. Foote know it. NB – The order for this c. martial (owing to the *Niger*'s going to sea) had not been dispatch'd before this letter was rec[d] requesting it might be withdrawn and there was therefore no entry made of it.

10. *Courts Martial of Patrick Tarney, William Perkins, Henry Perkins, Patrick Morgan and John M[c]Laughlin*

[ADM 1/5333]

Minutes of a court martial assembled and held on board His Majesty's ship *Assistance* in S[t] John's Harbour, Newfoundland, the 26 day of August 1795, for the several trials of Pat., alias Phil., Tarney, W[m] Perkins, Henry Perkins, Pat. Morgan, John M[c]Laughlin, Seamen, belonging to His Majesty's ship *Romney*, for desertion, *viz.*

Present

Henry Mowat, Esq[r], Captain of His Majesty's ship *Assistance* and senior captain of His Majesty's ships and vessels in St John's Harbour, Newfoundland, President.

Captains

Henry D. Darby	Frank Sotheron
Thomas Wolley	Ambrose Crofton

John Hall, deputy judge advocate

The prisoners being brought into court and audience admitted, the order of Vice Admiral Sir James Wallace, Kn[t]., Commander in Chief of His Majesty's ships and vessels employed, and to be employed, at and about the island of Newfoundland, dated the 24 inst., directed to Henry Mowat, Esq[r], Captain of His Majesty's ship *Assistance* and senior captain of His Majesty's ships and vessels in St John's Harbour, Newfoundland, for the several trials of Pat, alias Phil. Tarney, William Perkins, Henry Perkins, Patrick Morgan and John M[c]Laughlin, seamen of His Majesty's ship *Romney*, for desertion, was read; the members of the court and deputy judge advocate then, in open court and before they proceeded to trial, respectively took the oath enjoined by Act of Parliament. The letter of Captain Sotheron of His Majesty's ship *Romney*, enclosing one from Thomas Hand, first Lieutenant of the same ship, to Vice Admiral Sir James Wallace (containing the charges against the prisoners) were both read and all the witnesses, being ordered to withdraw and attend the examination separately, together with all the prisoners, except Pat., alias Phil. Tarney and the first witness to be sworn, they withdrew accordingly and the court proceeded to trial as follows:

The evidence in support of the charge, Thomas Rotherford, Seaman of His Majesty's ship *Romney*, sworn and examined.

Court	Do you know the prisoner?
Evidence	I know the man.
Court	Was you coxswain of the boat in July last?
Evidence	Yes.
Court	Did the prisoner belong to that boat at that time?
Evidence	Yes.
Court	Did he absent himself from duty whilst on shore?
Evidence	He left the boat.
Court	Did he since return to the boat or ship till brought on board a prisoner?
Evidence	No.

The prisoner was asked by the court if he had any questions to put to the witness, which he answered in the negative.

William Balcombe, Clerk to Captain Sotheron, was then sworn, who produced the muster book of His Majesty's ship *Romney*, by which it appeared the prisoner was run[1] the 14th July last.

The evidence in support of the charge being finished, the prisoner was called upon for his defence, but having none to offer, he called the prosecutor, Lieutenant Hand, to speak to his character, who said he always behaved well and very regular and, as a reward for his good behaviour, he had removed him from the waist to the main top.

Minutes of a court martial assembled and holden [*sic*] on board His Majesty's ship *Assistance* in St John's Harbour, Newfoundland, the 26th day of August 1795, for the trial of William Perkins and Henry Perkins, two Seamen belonging to His Majesty's ship *Romney* for desertion, *viz*.:

… The prisoners being brought into court, William Learson, Boatswain of His Majesty's ship *Romney*, was sworn.

[1]If a mariner in the Royal Navy was absent from three consecutive musters, an R, signifying 'run' or 'runaway', was placed on his line in the muster book.

Court	Do you know the prisoners, William and Henry Perkins?
Evidence	I do.
Court	Was you ashore in the launch a day or two before the *Romney* last sailed?
Evidence	I was.
Court	Did the prisoners belong to the boat?
Evidence	They did at the time.
Court	Was the boat on duty?
Evidence	It was.
Court	Did they return in the boat?
Evidence	They did not.
Court	Have they since returned to the boat or ship till brought on board as prisoners?
Evidence	They have not.
Court	How often have the Articles of War been read on board the *Romney* since you left England?
Evidence	Every month.

The prisoners asked by the court if they had any questions to put to the evidence, who answered in the negative.

Robert Pierce, Master of His Majesty's sloop *Lutin*, sworn.

Court	Do you know these men?
Evidence	Yes.
Court	Did you know them to belong to the *Romney* when you apprehended them?
Evidence	No.
Court	Why then did you apprehend them?
Evidence	I went on shore with Captain Crofton to attend at the jolly boat at the wharf to stop all seamen, who should attempt to go from the wharf. After remaining there a quarter of an hour, Captain Crofton came down on the wharf and hailed me; in consequence of that, I landed and went with Captain Crofton to Mr McCormack's stores, one of the doors was open and, in a cot, he found the prisoners stowed away. The captain's coxswain went up and got them out of the cot, and Captain Crofton desired me to take them on board in the jolly boat; I took them on board the *Lutin*.
Court	Did you know they were deserters?
Evidence	He knew they were deserters, but from what ship, he did not know.
Court	Did the prisoners give themselves up as deserters from a man of war?

Evidence Not to me, but they said they belonged to a brig alongside the wharf.
Court Were they confined on board the *Lutin*?
Evidence They were in irons.
Court Were they in liquor when you took them up?
Evidence They did not appear so to me.
Court Do you recollect what day of the month they were taken up?
Evidence No, the day after the *Romney* sailed.

It appear'd the Romney sailed the 28th July. Here the witness closed his evidence and the court asked if the prisoners had any questions to put to him, which they answered in the negative.

The muster book was produced in court by William Balcombe, Captain's Clerk, by which it appeared the prisoners were run 22 July last on the *Romney*'s books.

The court asked the prisoners if they had anything to say in their defence, which they answered in the negative, but wished to call the boatswain and prosecutor to give them a character.

Wm Learson, the Boatswain, gave them a good character; whilst on board, he had no fault to find with them.

Court to the prosecutor What do you think of them?
Prosecutor They have been regular, sober, orderly, well behaved men.

Minutes of a court martial assembled and held on board His Majesty's ship *Assistance* in S[t] John's Harbour, Newfoundland, the 26 day of August 1795, for the trial of Patrick Morgan, a Seaman belonging to His Majesty's ship *Romney* for desertion, *viz.*:

… The prisoner being brought into court; James Ayscough, Midshipman of His Majesty's ship *Romney*, was sworn and examined.

Court Do you know the prisoner?
Evidence Yes.
Court Does he belong to the *Romney*?
Evidence Yes.
Court Was he ever employed in a party on shore under your direction?
Evidence Yes.
Court Do you recollect, some time in the month of July last, his having left that party?
Evidence Yes.
Court Did he ever since return, to your knowledge, until brought on board a prisoner?

Evidence Not to his knowledge.

Here the evidence closed on the part of the prosecution, when the court asked the prisoner if he had any questions to put to the evidence, who answered in the negative, or if he could bring any officer to give him a character; the prisoner called upon the prosecutor, who said that he always behaved well.

The prisoner then called upon William Learson, Boatswain of His Majesty's ship *Romney*, who said, 'He always behaved very well.'

The muster book was produced in court by William Balcombe, Clerk to Captain Sotheron of His Majesty's ship *Romney*, by which it appeared the prisoner was Run 18 July last.

Minutes of a court martial assembled and held on board His Majesty's ship *Assistance* in S[t] John's Harbour, Newfoundland, the 26th day of August 1795, for the trial of John M[c]Laughlin, Seaman belonging to His Majesty's ship *Romney,* for desertion, *viz.*

… The prisoner being brought into court, Lieutenant William Shippard of His Majesty's ship *Romney* was sworn and examined.

Court Do you know the prisoner?

Evidence Yes I do.

Court Do you recollect his having left the boat in July last?

Evidence I remember one of the boat's crew was missing; I do not know that he was the man.

Court Do you know the prisoner to have belonged to the *Romney*?

Evidence Yes I do.

The witness, having delivered his evidence, the prisoner was asked by the court if he had any questions to put to the witness, which he answered in the negative. The evidence then withdrew and John Sewell, Seaman of His Majesty's ship *Romney*, was sworn and examined.

Court Do you know the prisoner by the name of John M[c]Laughlin?

Evidence Yes.

Court Does he belong to the *Romney*?

Evidence Yes.

Court Do you recollect in July last the prisoner having left the boat when you steered the boat with Lieutenant Shippard on board on shore?

Evidence I do.

Court Did he ever return to the boat or ship till brought on board a prisoner?

Evidence I never saw him.

Here the evidence closed on the part of the prosecution, when the court asked the prisoner if he had any questions to put to the evidence, which [he?] answered in the negative; the court desired to know if he would call upon anyone for a character. He called upon the prosecutor, who said, 'He has always conducted himself with peculiar satisfaction to me; when fitting out the ship at Plymouth, he was mentioned to me by the gunner, in whose crew he was, as a very sober, deserving man.'

The muster book was then produced by William Balcombe, Clerk to Capt. Sotheron of His Majesty's ship *Romney*, by which it appeared the prisoner was Run 20th July last.

There being no other witness to examine, either in support of the charge against the present, or the prisoners before tried, viz.: Pat., alias Phil., Tarney, Wm Perkins, Henry Perkins, Patrick Morgan, and John McLaughlin, the court was cleared and, having maturely considered the whole, agreed that the charges against the several prisoners were fully proved, when the court was again opened, audience admitted and the sentence hereunto annexed was delivered by the deputy judge advocate accordingly.

10A. *Report of the Courts Martial of Patrick Tarney, William Perkins, Henry Perkins, Patrick Morgan and John McLaughlin*

[ADM 1/5333]

… having heard read the charge exhibited against them in a letter from Lieutenant Hand of His Majesty's ship *Romney* to Vice Admiral Sir James Sotheron as well as the evidence in support of the said charge and also what the prisoners had to offer in their own defence respectively, and, having maturely and deliberately considered the whole and every part thereof with the minutest attention, the court is of opinion that the charge is fully proved against them, do adjudge the said Patrick, alias Phil, Tarney, William Perkins, Henry Perkins, [and?] Patrick Morgan to receive eighty lashes only on their bare backs with a cat with nine tails in consequence of their former good behaviour and to John McLaughlin forty lashes only in consideration of his particular good character, the said lashes to be received alongside such ships and at such times as the commander in chief shall think proper. And the court does further recommend the said John McLaughlin to the clemency of the commander in chief.

10B. *Hand to Sotheron*

[ADM 1/5333] *Romney*, St John's,
August 24th 1795

… I beg leave to inform you that the seamen as p. margin [Pat^{k}., alias Phil., Tarney, Wm Perkins, Hen^{y} Perkins, Pat. Morgan, Jno McLaughlin], belonging to His Majesty's ship *Romney* under your command (and who were lately sent on board as prisoners from His Majesty's ship *Adamant*) did in the month of July ult. severally absent themselves from their respective duties when employed on shore. …

11. *Members of the Court Martial of the mutineers of the* Defiance *to Evan Nepean*

[ADM 1/5334] HMS *Jupiter*, Sheerness Harbour
February the 11th, 1796

… We, the members of the court martial, who have sat on the trial of the mutineers belonging to His Majesty's ship *Defiance*, beg permission particularly to recommend Joseph Flint (from his extreme youth) to their Lordships as an object for mercy. …

12. *Members of the Court Martial of the Mutineers of the* Defiance *to Nepean*

[ADM 1/5334] Sheerness,
12 February 1796

… We, the members of the court martial on the mutineers of the *Defiance*, considering the great length of the trial, the extra trouble and expense as well as the unremitting attention of the judge advocate, beg leave to recommend to their Lordships that he may be paid for the trial of each individual separately. …

12A. *Enclosure in the Court Martial of the Mutineers of the* Defiance *Members of the Court to Nepean*

[ADM 1/5334]

These are to certify that Mr. Benjamin Stow officiated as judge advocate at a court martial at which I presided, held on board His Majesty's Ship, the *Jupiter* in Sheerness Harbour for the separate and respective trials of William Parker 1st, Robert McLawrin, George Wythick, Martin Ealey, William Froud, John McDonald, John Sullivan, William Handy, George Harden, John Prime, Joseph Flint, Michael Cox, John Lawson, William Morrison, John Graham 1st, Charles Pick, and William Avery belonging to His Majesty's ship *Defiance* for mutiny, which court continued sitting from the 20th January 1796 to the 11th February following, Sundays excepted.

Given on board His Majesty's ship *Sandwich* at the Nore, the 9th March 1796 …

12B. *Nepean's notes to Lords of the Admiralty*

[ADM 1/5334]

Courts Martial

12 Jan^ry 1793 – M^r. Greetham paid 30. 5. 0. for the minutes of the trial of the mutineers of the *Bounty*, being 25 Guineas in addition to the established 4 –.

The minutes consist of 166 pages; and the trial lasted from the 12 Sept. to the 18 Sept. 1792

23 Jan^ry 1795 – M^r. Greetham paid for 18 days at the rate of 8/s for the minutes of the court martial held on the mutineers of the *Culloden*

The minutes consisted of 129 pages; and the trial continued from the 14th to 20 December 1794

Deputy judge advocates who have not yet been p^d.

M^r. Brown for the trial of Captain Bridges and Lieut^t Crooke. It was a reciprocal prosecution.

The minutes occupy 144 pages, including both trials and the court sat from the 4 to 20 March 1795 (one Sunday included).

M^r. Greetham for the trial of Captain Molloy

The minutes extend to 290 pages close writing; and the trial lasted from the 28 April to 15 May 1795 (two Sundays included).

M^r. Stow for the trial of the mutineers of the *Defiance*.

The minutes fill 250 pages, each of which page occupies the entire surface of the sheet in the manner of a lawyer's brief; the trial continued from the 20

January to 11 February 1796 (three Sundays included).

…

It is however proper to observe that in many instances their Lordships have considered the sum of four Pounds for each court martial as an averaged compensation. Mr. Greetham was paid only £4 Pounds for the minutes of the trial of Captain Dawson, which was very bulky and continued from the 7th to the 20th Nov. 1788; and the like reward was paid for the minutes on Lieut. Hill, which filled 100 pages. The trial lasted from the 12 to the 16 March 1795. Mr. Greetham was Dep. Jud. Adv. in both the preceding trials.

13. *Court Martial of John Styles*

[ADM 1/5335]

Minutes of the proceedings of a court martial assembled and held on board His Majesty's ship *Cambridge* in Hamoze on Tuesday the 23d of February 1796 to enquire into the conduct of Lieutenant John Styles, late commanding the *Castor*, a tender hired into His Majesty's service, respecting the escape of twenty three pressed men from the said ship tender on the morning of the 18th of November last whilst he, the said Lieutenant Styles, was on shore at Liverpool and to try him for the same.

Present

Smith Child, Esqr., Captain of His Majesty's ship *Le Commerce de Marsailles* and third officer in the command of his Majesty's ships and vessels at Plymouth, President.

Captains	Captains
Thomas Taylor	John Manley
Joseph Ellison	Richard Grindall
Geo. Martin	Maurice Delgarno
Honble. Robt. Stopford	Wm. Lechmere
John Oakes Hardy	Joseph Sidney Yorke
Hble. Arthur Kaye Legge	Frank Sothoron

The surgeons of His Majesty's ships *Magnificent*, *Cambridge* and *Tremendous* attended to certify the inability of Captains Squire, Boger and Aylmer to attend through ill health.

M^{r}. W^{m}. Johns, Midshipman, swn.

C. Relate to the court what you know respecting the charges you have heard against the prisoner.

Answer On the 18th of November last in the morning between 7 & 8 o'clock, M^{r}. W^{m}. Hutton, Mid., having charge of the deck, James Powell, sentinel, with a cutlass in his hand over the hatchway, M^{r}. Walter Wylie, the Mate, being in the after hold, & myself in bed ill, I heard a noise and jumped out of bed and found the pressed men in possession of the tender. For some time till they got into the boat, I was kept below by the pressed men; but so soon as I got upon deck, I presented a pistol at them in the boat. I could not get a pistol to go off and then took a musket and fired at them, but they got off.

C. Who was commanding officer at the time?

A. I considered myself as commanding officer over the pressed men, but not over the ship.

C. Have you ever before been left as commanding officer of the tender?

A. Yes.

C. Did Lieutenant Styles leave his orders with you when he went ashore himself?

A. Yes.

C. What were those orders?

A. To keep a good lock over these men.

C. Were the sentinels placed by you or by Lieutenant Styles before he went out of the ship?

A. They were placed by me that morning.

C. Were they placed in the same manner as when Lieut. Styles placed them?

A. Yes, as usual.

C. Relate in what manner.

A. One at the main hatchway.

C. Where were the pressed men, in general, kept?

A. In the pressed room.

C. Was the sentinel at the main hatchway at the time these men rose and made their escape?

A. I believe he was.

C. As commanding officer was any report made to you of the pressed men having forced the sentinel from his post?

A. No report; I heard them myself.

C. At any time before, do you know of the pressed men on board the *Castor* having attempted to run?

A. Many times.

C. Was there a sentinel placed there in consequence of these attempts, or was it usual to have one there?

A. It was usual to place one there.

C. Was there any additional sentinels in consequence of these attempts?

A. At night, there were two or four, agreeable to the number of men on board.

C. Who was considered as officer of the watch at the time those men rose and run?

A. M^{r}. W^{m}. Hutton, Acting Midshipman.

C. I think, sir, you've said that Lieutenant Styles left orders with you; at what time did he leave his last orders?

A. Between 3 and 4, the evening before.

C. Was the master of the tender on board at the time?

A. I cannot tell.

C. What number of men belonged to the tender?

A. I cannot possibly say.

C. How happens it you do not know the number of men belonging to the *Castor*?

A. I understand 14 to be the complement besides the gang, but I do not know what number was on board at that time.

C. Was it not customary for the lieutenant to muster the people?

A. Sometimes he did so. The last time they were mustered by Captain Uzuld.

C. When was the last time you remember their being mustered?

A. It was the day before the men run.

C. Do you recollect if the number was on board that ought to be?

A. There was not.

C. Do you know the number of men the gang ought to consist of?

A. Two midshipman & 8 men.

C. Was that number on board?

A. No, there was not.

C. What number was on board?

A. I cannot tell.

C. Were any of the gang on board?

A. I believe two.

C. Do you know the cause why your lieutenant was absent on shore that night?
A. He complained that he was ill.
C. Was it usual for your lieutenant to sleep on board the tender?
A. It was when there was volunteers or pressed men on board.
C. When the pressed men deserted, had you any other boat on board than the one they went away with?
A. We had one astern.
C. You've said you endeavour'd to fire a pistol at the deserters and, afterwards, you discharged a musket at them with two balls; did those balls appear to wound any of them?
A. I cannot tell. I saw one go by the side of the boat and one right amongst them.
C. At what distance was the main hatchway from the pressed room door?
A. Almost close to it.
C. Was there any regular watch bill in the tender?
A. No, there was not.
C. Was the lieutenant frequently absent from the vessel?
A. More on shore than on board.
C. How long has Lieutenant Styles commanded the *Castor*?
A. About a twelvemonth.
C. What number of men has deserted from the *Castor* since Lieutenant Styles commanded her?
A. I cannot tell, but there has been many.
C. The charge states that a good number have deserted before the 23 that run away on the 18th; is that true?
A. It is.
C. During the time you've been in the tender, did the pressed men run away before with the boat?
A. Yes, once, but not during Lieut. Styles' command.
C. You've said many men have deserted before those 23 since Lieutenant Styles commanded the tender, inform the court by what means they effected their escape?
A. By force.
C. Were the sentinels taken from the men belonging to the tender or from the gang immediately under the command of the lieutenant?
A. In turn from both.

Thomas Paul, Steward & Coxswain, swn.

C. Who checked the men when they absented themselves from the tender?

A. I did, by the master's orders.

C. Do you know from your own knowledge that all the men that are mark'd run deserted from the tender?

A. I cannot to all, but can to the greater part.

C. Were you on board the 18th of November?

A. Yes.

C. Relate what you know respecting the desertion that took place on that day?

A. In the morning, just after I got out of bed, I went into the cabin. The cabin boy was lighting the fire when I heard a great noise upon deck; and, when I went to go upon deck, the boy told me there was one of the pressed men standing over the scuttle. I then went back. After the men had got into the boat, I went upon deck and saw them in the boat about 20 yards from the ship.

C. Were all the men in one boat.

A. Yes, in the cutter.

C. Do you recollect M^r^. Johns, the Midshipman, firing at them?

A. Yes, I do.

C. Do you know the reason of the lieutenant being on shore?

A. Yes, he complained of being ill.

M^{r}. Walter Wylie, Mate, sworn.

C. Relate to the court what you know respecting the charge you have heard against the prisoner.

A. About 8 o'clock in the morning of the 18th of Novr. last, I went down to clear the hold and send up a cask of beer. Whilst I was below, I heard a noise and came out of the hold betwixt deck to go upon deck and found two men, one with a cutlass and the other with a handspike, over the hatchway; and I was obliged to stay below till they got into the boat. When I got upon deck, they were gone off. The lieutenant and master being on shore, one boat, being over the stern, was lowered down to send on shore for the long boat; and the man that was lowered in her cut the painter and went on shore to acquaint the lieutenant and master with what had happened and the master and the man immediately came off.

C. Do you know the reason why the lieutenant was on shore that night?

A. No, I do not.

C. Was he frequently on shore?

A. Sometimes.

C. How long have you belonged to the *Castor*?

A. Ever since she was taken into the service.

C. Have you ever known the pressed men to make attempts to escape from the ship before the 18th Nov[r].?
A. Yes.
C. Did you consider one sentinel sufficient to guard the men in the press room, provided they were inclined to go away?
A. No, I do not.
C. How was the sentinel arm'd?
A. With a cutlass only.
C. Do you recollect that one sentinel was at the hatchway when the men before that time escaped?
A. Yes.
C. Do you think that there was sufficient care taken on the part of the officers to hinder the press men from running away?
A. No, I do not.
C. During the time you have been in the tender, do you know of any press men before these effecting their escape from the press room?
A. No, I do not.
C. In what manner did the great number of people run effect their escape?
A. In general, jump overboard and swim on shore, one or two at a time.
C. Is there a regular watch kept when the ship is in harbour?
A. Yes.
C. How was the press room secured?
A. Lock'd down with bars.
C. Was the sentinel placed in charge of those locks?
A. Yes, over the hatchway.
C. Had he any authority to open them without orders from the commanding officer?
A. No.
C. Was you not the principal officer on board on the 18th of November when the men ran?
A. Yes, but I had no command over the hatchway; the midshipmen had the charge.
C. Who generally kept the keys?
A. The midshipman.
C. What was the name of the midshipman who had the keys that day?
A. Mr. Hutton.
C. Do you know how the hatchway happened to be opened so early as 8 o'clock?

A. I do not.

James Powell, Sentinel, sworn.

C. Was you the sentinel at the scuttle of the press room on board the *Castor* tender on the 18th of November last when the press men made their escape?

A. I was.

C. What time was it?

A. About ½ past 8 in the morning.

C. Who placed you there?

A. Mr. Wm Hutton, the officer of the watch.

C. Had you the keys of the bars of the hatchway in your possession?

A. No, I had not.

C. Relate to the court what you know respecting the charge you have heard against the prisoner.

Answer Mr. William Hutton, Midshipman, placed me sentinel on the 18th of November about 7 o'clock in the morning, at which time, according to his orders, I let up two men. They walked the quarter deck a considerable time; and there was a cutlass left behind the companion by the morning watch, and one of those two men got the cutlass in his hand. One of the men below, wanting to come up, cried out for the rope and, as I stood over the hatchway telling him I wou'd not give him the rope, one of the men on deck catched hold of me behind and pinioned me. The other held the cutlass up to me and told me he would run it through my heart, by which means they both wrenched the cutlass out of my hand and then drove me aft and the officer of the watch forward. The men belonging to the ship were stowing the after hold. By the time they got up out of the hold, to the best of my knowledge, there were 10 or 12 of the pressed men on deck and got to the hand spikes. Some of them let down the ladder and one stood over the hatchway, flourishing a cutlass until such time as they'd lower'd the boat and, to the best of my knowledge, 22 or 23 got into the boat. While they were shoving off the boat, we got arms out of the cabin; some of them wou'd, some wou'd not go off and no person was hurt by them. We detected 6 of them going down the side and put them in the press room again. Those in the boat made their escape to Chester Side.

C. You've said that when the press men broke loose, the men belonging to the ship were stowing the after hold; where were the men belonging to the lieutenant's gang?

A. They were asleep in the forecastle.
C. Do you know how many of them were on board?
A. They were all on board, but none on deck but me.
C. Was it customary for part of them to keep watch?
A. Yes, it was.
C. What number in each watch?
A. Two of the gang and two of the ship's company.
C. Had you a surgeon or surgeon's mate belonging to the *Castor*?
A. No.
C. Do you know the cause of Lieutenant Styles being on shore the night before the desertion?
A. No.

Prosecution closed.

The prisoner read the following defence:

I beg leave to offer to the court the following particulars relative to that affair, for which my conduct is now called in question:

On the afternoon of the 17th of November last, in consequence of a severe hurt I received on the 28th of October (by particular advice of the Surgeon and Agent of the Sick and Hurt at Liverpool), I went on shore for the better administering of medicines &^{c}. prescribed by him.

Previous to my leaving the *Castor*, I gave charge of her to the master and left strict orders with him to take care of the impressed men, as I did also to M^{r}. Johns, the Midshipman, and to William Hutton, a volunteer (who acted in that capacity).

On the said 17th of November, in consequence of my very bad state of health, I wrote to the Lords Commissioners of the Admiralty, representing to them my inability to proceed to sea in the *Castor*, and requested their Lordships to supersede me.

M^{r}. Charles Sims, Master, sworn.

Prisoner Did I not on the afternoon of the 17th of Novr. last just before I went on shore desire you to take charge of the tender and take all possible care of the pressed men?
A. No.
Court Relate to the court what Lieutenant Styles did say to you at the time.
A. 'I am going on shore,' and then spoke to the mid. about the pressed men.
Prisoner Do you know the reason of my going on shore?

A. M^{r}. Styles had been complaining before some days of his being unwell.

C. Had you any surgeon on board?

A. No.

W^{m}. Johns, Midshipman.

Prisoner On my leaving the *Castor* on the 17th of Novr. to go on shore, what orders did I leave with you?

A. To keep the best look out.

P. Did I not always give strict orders to this purpose whenever I quitted the ship?

A. You always did.

P. When on board, do you not think I always paid strict attention to my duty?

A. Yes.

Sentence

'The court is of opinion that Lieutenant John Styles is not reprehensible on account of the desertion of these men and do therefore fully acquit him from any culpability therein; and he is therefore fully acquitted accordingly. It appearing to this court that the state of Lieutenant Styles' health was such as to make it absolutely necessary for his going on shore, there being no medical assistance to be had on board the tender.'

. . .

14. *Court Martial of Henry Hone Haviland*

[ADM 1/5337]

Minutes of the proceedings of a court martial assembled on board His Majesty's ship *Barfleur*, in Mortilla Bay, the twentieth day of October, one thousand, seven hundred and ninety-six.

Present

The Honourable William Waldgrave, Vice Admiral of the Blue, &c^{a}, &c^{a}, &c^{a}, President.

Captain	Robert Calder Captain of the Fleet	Captain	Thomas Lenox Frederick
	John Pakenham		Sir Charles Henry Knowles, Bar^{t}.
	James Richard Dacres		Thomas Troubridge
	Thomas Southby		Samuel Hood
	Thomas Foley		Benjamin Hallowell
	George Grey		Shuldham Peard

The prisoner being brought into court and audience admitted, the order from Sir John Jervis, Knight of the Bath, Admiral of the Blue, and Commander in Chief of His Majesty's ships and vessels employed, and to be employed, in the Mediterranean, dated at four o'clock p. m. the eighteenth instant, and directed to the Honble. William Waldegrave, Vice Admiral of the Blue and second in command in the absence of Vice Admiral Sir Hyde Parker, Kn^{t} &c^{a}, &c^{a}, &c^{a}, for the trial of Lieutenant Henry Hone Haviland of the Marines of His Majesty's ship *Blanche* on the charges exhibited against him by Captain Sawyer, late commander of the said ship, for having been guilty of a breach of part of the twentieth Article of War and for having behaved disrespectfully towards him, the said Captain Sawyer, was read.

The members of the court and judge advocate then, in open court and before they proceeded to trial, respectively took the oaths directed by an Act of Parliament made and passed in the twenty second year of the reign of His late Majesty King George the Second, entitled *An Act for Amending, Explaining and Reducing into One Act of Parliament the Laws relating to the Government of His Majesty's Ships, Vessels, & Forces by Sea.*

Then a letter from Captain Sawyer to Admiral Sir John Jervis, K.B. &c^{a}, &c^{a}, &c^{a}, was read by the judge advocate as follows:

Blanche 5th September 1796

…

Lieutenant Henry Hone Haviland of the Marines of His Majesty's ship under my command, having been guilty of a breach of part of the 20th Article of War and having behaved himself disrespectfully towards me,

I have to request, sir, that you will be pleased to order a court martial to be assembled to try him for the several offences set forth against him.

…

The signal for assembling the court[1] having been made at eight o'clock and no prosecutor or evidences in support of the charges appearing at twelve o'clock, the court asked the judge advocate if he had summoned any evidences in support of the charges, who answered that he had not and assigned as his reasons for not having done so that the prosecutor had previously acquainted him that it was not his intention to prosecute the charges he had exhibited to the commander in chief against the prisoner.

[1]This signal was the Union Flag flying from the upper corner of the yard or gaff sloping from a mast (Timothy Wilson, *Flags at Sea: A Guide to the Flags Flown at Sea by Ships of the Major Maritime Nations from the 16th Century to the Present Day, Illustrated from the Collections of the National Maritime Museum* (Annapolis, MD: Naval Institute Press, 1999) p. 109).

The captain of the fleet produced a letter to the president to the same effect, which was read in open court by the judge advocate.[1]

Sincere 19 October 1796

On His Majesty's Service
… I beg to inform you that it is not my intention to prosecute the charges I have exhibited to the commander in chief against the three lieutenants, master and lieutenant of the Marines of the *Blanche*. …

The court was cleared.

No prosecutor having appeared in court or any evidences in support of the charges summoned, the court adjudged the said Lieutenant Henry Hone Haviland to be acquitted.

The court opened, audience admitted & sentence passed accordingly. …

15. *Court Martial of Peter Egan alias Peter Hugan*

[ADM 1/5337]

Minutes of proceedings at a court martial assembled on board His Majesty's ship *Brunswick* at Cape Nicola Mole in the island of Saint Domingo on the 19th day of November 1796, for the trial of Peter Egan, alias Peter Hugan, a Seaman belonging to His Majesty's ship *Dictator*, for the murder of —— Ludovick, Gunner in the Dutch artillery.

Present

Richard Rodney Bligh, Esqr, Rear Admiral of the Red and second officer in the command of His Majesty's ships & vessels employed, and to be employed, at and about Jamaica, President.

Commodore	Jno Thomas Duckworth	Captain	George Bowen
Captain	Edwd Tyrrel Smith	"	Eliab Harvey
"	James Bowen	"	Henry Jenkins
"	Thomas Western	"	Joseph Bingham
"	Man Dobson	"	William Gordon Rutherford
"	Robt. Mends		

The prisoner, Peter Egan alias Peter Hugan, was brought into court and the evidences & audience admitted.

[1]This letter is from Captain C. Sawyer to Robert Calder, Captain of the Fleet on the Mediterranean Station.

Read the order from Vice Admiral Sir Hyde Parker, Commander in Chief of His Majesty's ships & vessels employed, and to be employed, at and about Jamaica, dated the 18th instant and directed to Richard Rodney Bligh, Esqr, Rear Admiral of the Red and second in command, &c., &c., to try Peter Egan alias Peter Hugan, a Seaman belonging to His Majesty's ship *Dictator*, for the murder of —— Ludovick, Gunner in the Dutch artillery, on the afternoon of the 14th instant on shore at Presque Isle.

Then the members of the court and judge advocate, in open court and before they proceeded to trial, took the oaths directed by Act of Parliament.

The evidences were then called over and ordered to withdraw, *viz.*:

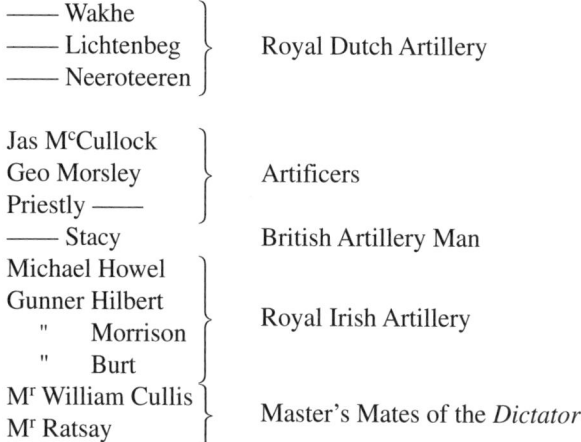

—— Wakhe —— Lichtenbeg —— Neeroteeren	Royal Dutch Artillery
Jas McCullock Geo Morsley Priestly ——	Artificers
—— Stacy	British Artillery Man
Michael Howel Gunner Hilbert " Morrison " Burt	Royal Irish Artillery
Mr William Cullis Mr Ratsay	Master's Mates of the *Dictator*

A doubt arising in the minds of some of the members whether or not Presque Isle, the place where the murder was said to be committed, is a part of His Majesty's dominions or not, the court was cleared.

The court came to the following resolution: 'That Presque Isle, the place where the murder is said to be committed, is a part of His Majesty's dominions; and that they are not competent to try the said Peter Egan, alias Peter Hugan, for the murder with which he stands charged.'

The prisoner, evidences & audience were then admitted, when the president informed them the court was dissolved and ordered the prisoner to be sent on board the *Dictator*.

Copy of the sentence transmitted by the court to Sir Hyde Parker.

At a court martial assembled on board His Majesty's ship *Brunswick* at Cape Nichola Mole in the island of St Domingo.

… But a doubt arising in the minds of some of the members whether or not Presque Isle, the place where the prisoner is said to have committed the murder, is a part of His Majesty's dominions and it being the opinion of the court that it is a part thereof, the court came to the following resolution: 'That they are not competent to try the said Peter Egan, alias Peter Hugan, for the murder with which he stands charged.'

Given under our hands on board His Majesty's ship *Brunswick* at Cape Nichola Mole, St Domingo, the 19th day of December [*sic*] 1796.

…

16. *Captain Henry Mitford to Rear Admiral Henry Harvey*

[ADM 1/5342] *Matilda*, Fort Royal Bay, Martinique
19th Decem^{r}. 1797

… The four seamen whose names are hereafter expressed, belonging to His Majesty's ship under my command, having been guilty of the crimes as are severally charged against them, vizt.:

James Morgan, Ordinary Seaman, for breaking from his confinement at English [Harbour] Antigua as a prisoner at large during the day on the 28th November last, to which he had been ordered as a further punishment after being flogged for behaving in an insolent, contemptuous and mutinous manner to the boatswain, his superior officer, and was brought back the next day by a sergeant of His Majesty's 59th Regiment of Foot.

William Holms, Able Seaman, for desertion, being absent from his duty without leave from the 17th August 1797 to the 8th Novem^{r}. following, and was brought back by the master at arms of His Majesty's ship under my command.

Alexander McLeach, Able Seaman, for attempting to swim from the ship while under weigh on the evening of the 14th instant off St. Pierre of Martinique, for insolence to and striking his superior officer in the execution of his duty after being brought on board, and refusing to go into confinement to which he was carried by force. Abraham Maddison, Able Seaman, for attempting to swim from the ship while getting under weigh on the evening of the 17th ins^{t}. in Kingston Bay of S^{t}. Vincent's, thereby forsaking his duty and interrupting the service the ship was then employed upon.

These, Sir, are charges I have to exhibit against the four men above mentioned, which I humbly submit to your serious consideration and request that if His Majesty's service will admit of the delay a court martial must necessarily occasion, you will be pleased to order them to be tried as early as possible for which purpose the evidences necessary to substantiate each man's charges are in readiness.

The numbers which have deserted from His Majesty's ship *Matilda,* during the time of my command, amount to such an alarming evil that I feel myself bound by duty to take this harsh step to endeavour in some measure to put a stop to it. …

17. *Court Martial of Daniel Brennan*

[ADM 1/5343]

Minutes of a court martial assembled and held on board His Majesty's ship *Madrass* in Fort Royal Bay, Martinique 22nd Feby. 1798.

Present

Thomas Macnamara Russell, Esqr., Captain of His Majesty's ship *Vengeance* and senior captain of His Majesty's ships and vessels in Fort Royal Bay, Martinique, President.

Captains

John Dilkes	Ja^{s}. Ross
Rich^{d}. Browne	Alex^{r}. S. Burrows

The prisoner was then brought into court and evidence and audience admitted. Read the order of Henry Harvey, Esqr, Rear Admiral of the Red and Commander in Chief of His Majesty's ships and vessels employed and to be employed at Barbados and the Leeward Islands and in the seas adjacent, dated the 21st ins^{t}., directed to Thomas Macnamara Russell, Esqr., Captain of His Majesty's ship *Vengeance* and senior captain of His Majesty's ships and vessels in Fort Royal Bay, Martinique to try M^{r}. Daniel Brennan, Gunner of His Majesty's ship *Madrass*, for having, in breach of the 23rd Article of War, violently struck Mr. George Dall, Captain's Clerk of that ship, using provoking speeches tending to make quarrel and disturbance.

The members of the court and judge advocate, in open court and before they proceeded to trial, respectively took the oaths enjoined by Act of Parliament.

The letter from Captain Dilkes of His Majesty's ship *Madrass*[1] (containing the charges) was then read as follows, vizt.:

[1] Dilkes's letter is to Rear Admiral Henry Harvey, Commander in Chief of the Leeward Islands Station.

Madrass, Fort Royal Bay, Martinique
7th Feby. 1798

… Mr. George Dall, Captain's Clerk of His Majesty's ship under my command, having complained to me that on the 25th August 1797, M^{r}. Danl. Brennan, the Gunner, in breach of the 23rd Article of War, did violently strike him, using provoking speeches tending to make quarrel and disturbance,

I am to request you will order a court martial to try and adjudge him for the offence. …

All the evidence ordered to withdraw, except M^{r}. George Dall, who was sworn.

Court asked:

Ques^{n}. Relate to the court what you know relative to the charge against the Prisoner.

The prisoner observed that the charge was improperly made, that the circumstance took place on the 15th and not on the 25th, which the witness admitted.

The court being cleared, it was agreed that the prisoner should be dismissed, as no trial could be proceeded on from the above circumstance. Court opened and the same was notified to the prisoner (by the president) and he was dismissed.

The following letter was written to the commander in chief upon the occasion, vizt.:

His Majesty's Ship *Madrass*
Fort Royal Bay, Martinique
22nd Feby. 1798

… We, whose names are hereunto subscribed, being the members of a court martial assembled according to your order of yesterday's date for the trial of M^{r}. Daniel Brennan, Gunner of His Majesty's ship *Madrass* (for having on the 25th of August last, in breach of the 23rd Article of War, violently struck Mr. George Dall, Captain's Clerk of the said ship, using provoking speeches tending to make quarrel and disturbance) beg leave to acquaint you that after the court was formed, the regular forms gone through and the first evidence for the Crown on the part of the prosecution called in for examination and sworn, the prisoner made the following statement that the circumstance took place on 15th, not on the 25th, of August, as stated in Captain Dilkes's letter to the commander in chief.

The same being admitted by the said first witness, M^{r}. George Dall, the court was cleared and, after having maturely and deliberately considered the said statement, is of opinion that it cannot proceed on the trial of M^{r}. Daniel Brennan, Gunner of His Majesty's ship *Madrass*, the crime exhibited against him having been committed at a period prior to the day whereon he is charged therewith, and that he should consequently be dismissed from confinement. We have therefore directed the provost martial to dismiss him from confinement accordingly. …

18. *Court Martial of Angus McMillan, Thomas Mack, and William Logan*

[ADM 1/5345]

Minutes of the proceedings of a court martial assembled and held onboard his Majesty's ship *Cambridge* in Hamoze the 26th June 1798 for the trial of Angus McMillan, Thomas Mack and William Logan, three seamen belonging to His Majesty's ship *Foudroyant*; the said Angus McMillan for having on or about the 19th inst^{t}. been heard to declare that so soon as the ship was got into the Sound, the ship's company wou'd rise and turn Lieutenant Conn, the First Lieutenant, out of the ship; the said Thomas Mack for having on or about the 14th ins^{t}. said he wished he was in Ireland amongst the rebels and that he wished them success; and the said William Logan on being ordered on Sunday the 17th inst^{t}. to go into the boat, for saying he wished the boat might sink with the first man that attempted to put his foot into her.

Present

Richard Boger Esqr., Captain of His Majesty's ship *Cambridge* and second officer in the Command of His Majesty's ships and vessels at Plymouth, President.

Captains	Captains
Jonathan Faulkner	Honble. Michael de Courey
Richard Goodwin Keats	Robert Carthew Reynolds
Charles Cunningham	William Pierrepont
Joshua Mulock	Thomas Twysden
Perry Fraser	George Byng

H.M. Stokes
D. J. A.

Angus McMillan arraign'd.

William Dixon, Qrmas, Sn.

Court Do you know the pris.?

A. Yes

C. Relate to the Court what you know of the charge against the prisoner.

A. I happened to be at the Sign of the Swan in dock on the 19th of this month drinking of a pint of beer when the prisoner came in very much intoxicated and some person told him that I was a shipmate of his. I ask'd him to drink with me which he did, after which I heard him say the ship's company were going to rise when the ship got into the Sound and turn M^{r}. Conn, the First Lieutenant, out of the ship. I asked him 'Why so?' And, he gave me no answer; but some person unknown to me who stood by, said it was for making them make points and gasket's for task. With that, I told the prisoner if he turn'd M^{r}. Conn out of the ship and search the Navy thro' he would not get a better. The prisoner made answer that he supposed I was one of his followers. I replied, if I was, 'twas nothing to him. The prisoner then said 'As for you, we will chuck you overboard.'

Pros^{r}. Did any of the ship's company tell you it was proper as an old shipmate to make this known to the captain?

A. I said to Owen Curry, if he did not represent it to the captain that I would.

C. Where had you this conversation with Owen Curry, at the public house or onboard the ship, & when?

A. In North Corner Street at the Sign of the Riggers Arms the same evening.

C. Was the prisoner present with you then?

A. No, he was gone onboard.

C. Was any other of the ship's company present with you at the Swan when you had the conversation you've mentioned with the prisoner?

A. No.

C. At what time was it you reported to Sir Thos. Byard or any officer of the ship the malicious words you had heard the prisoner make use of at the public house?

A. Between 9 & 11 o'clock the next day I told L^{t}. Conn of it in the foresheet.

Prosecution closed.

No defence.

James Dunbar Sn.

Prisoner Nº. 1 Was you with me all the time I was at the Sign of the Swan on the 19th of this month, and did you hear me make use of the following words – that the ship's company were going to rise when the ship got into the Sound and turn M^{r}. Conn, the First Lieutenant, out of the ship?

A. I was about ten minutes out of the room in the bar and left Dixon, the Quartermaster, with the prisoner. I did not hear any such words made use of.

C. Was the prisoner, while in conversation with Dixon, drunk or sober?

A. He appeared to me about half drunk.

C. What was the conversation that you heard pass between the prisoner and Dixon?

A. I heard no conversation pass between them.

C. Was there any other person present beside the pris^{r}., yourself, Dixon, & a young woman?

A. Yes, John Robinson.

John Robinson Sn.

Prisoner Nº. 1 Was you with me all the time?

A. No, I was not there a minute altogether and never heard any such words spoke.

Thomas Mack arraign'd.

C. Do you know the prisoner?

A. Yes.

C. Relate to the Court what you know of the charge against the prisoner.

A. I was standing on the larboard side of the lower gun deck one day in last week after twelve o'clock when the prisoner cross'd over the fore-grating, & said, 'Success to the Irish.' He then went into the wake of the capstern, and he or some other person said 'We wish we were among them.'

C. Did you hear the prisoner say he wished to be amongst the rebels in Ireland?

A. No, I did not.

C. Did you believe the prisoner in saying 'Success to the Irish' meant thereby the rebels in that country or the loyal subjects?

A. I cannot say which he meant.

C. Did you conceive it proper to make known as a subject of complaint to any officer of the *Foudroyant* the speech of wishing success to the Irish made by the prisoner?

A. I mention'd it to the Master at Arms but not as a complaint.

C. What has the general conduct, character & behaviour of the prisoner been?

A. But very indifferent, by always quarrelling and wrangling.

C. Was this the first time you ever heard the prisoner make use of the words?

A. Yes.

C. Are you under any apprehensions of improper treatment from any man or body of men from the evidence that you may give to this court?

A. No, I am not.

W. A. Duff, Sn.

C. Do you know the prisoner?

A. I have seen him once before only; I believe his name is Mack.

C. Relate to the Court what you know of the charge against the prisoner.

A. I never saw the prisoner but on the day he was call'd into Sir Thomas Boyard's cabin onboard the *Foudroyant*. He there, to the best of my remembrance, did not deny the mutinous expressions with which he was charged, but pleaded drunkenness as an excuse. I never heard the prisoner make use of any mutinous expressions.

Pros^r^. Did you make any remark to the prisoner when he said he wou'd not have made use of the mutinous expressions with which he stood charged by Corp^l^. Harper if he had not been drunk?

A. I observed to him that had he not hatch'd the idea when sober, he wou'd never have conceived it when drunk.

P. Did I observe to him at the same time when he beg'd for mercy on his knees that I had more than once given him his life and I could no longer forbear?

A. Yes, you did.

C. What were the words of the crime with which Corporal Harper charged the prisoner?

[A.] There were three men in the cabin at the same time. I cannot distinctly say what each was charged with. I know it was of a mutinous nature.

C. Was one of the three persons charged with wishing success to the rebels in Ireland?

A. There was one.

C. When you saw the prisoner in the cabin before his captain, did he, in your mind, appear at that time as a man injured by the accusation that was alleged or as a person feeling guilty?

A. By the supplicating posture he assumed, he appeared to me to be conscious of his guilt.

Prosecution closed.

No defence.

Pris. threw himself on the mercy of the court.

William Logan arraign'd.

M^r^. Henry Clarke Mid^n^. Sn.

C. Do you know the pris.?

[A.] Yes.

[C.] What orders did you receive from M^r^. Conn on the 17th inst^t^.?

[A.] To send the men from the *Bedford* onboard the *Foudroyant* at 7 o'clock in the morning; I accordingly order'd the hands to be turn'd up at that time but found that not a man wou'd go into the boat.

Robert Harper, Corp^l^., Sn.

C. Do you know the pris.?

A. Yes.

Pros^r^. Did you complain to me that the pris. on Sunday the 17th inst^t^. had declared in your hearing that he hoped the boat wou'd sink with the first man who should put his foot into her?

A. Yes, I did.

C. Did you hear the prisoner say that he hoped the boat wou'd sink with the first man that attempted to put his foot into her?

A. I heard the prisoner say so, but did not see him at the time.

C. Where was you & where was the prisoner at the time you say he made use of the expression?

A. I was in my hammock and the prisoner was passing either forward or aft from the forehatchway.

C. You say you did not see the prisoner at the time. Can you positively swear to his voice and that he made use of the expression aforemention'd?

A. I've known him sixteen months and, to the best of my belief, t'was the prisoner who made use of the expression aforemention'd.

C. Have you directly or indirectly had any converse or communication with the prisoner or with any other person touching the evidence you should give before this court?

A. I have not.

Prosecution closed.
No defence.

L^{t}. Conn Sn.

Prisoner Did I come on board the *Foudroyant* on Sunday morning the 17th inst^{t}. from the *Bedford* in the first boat with men?

A. I recollect seeing the prisoner on board the *Foudroyant* that morning but cannot say whether he came in the first of [*sic*] second boat; two only came a considerable time after they were first order'd by M^{r}. Clark & M^{r}. Jackson, Mid^{n}.

Were there any people left onboard the *Bedford* after the two boats with men went on board the *Foudroyant*?

A. Yes.

The prisoner call'd on Sir Thomas Byard for a character, who said 'I know nothing of the prisoner that entitles him to my recommendation in any degree'.

Extract of the sentence.

'Is of opinion that the charges against Angus McMillan and Thomas Mack are proved in part and that the charge against William Logan is not proved; the court doth therefore adjudge the prisoner Angus McMillan to receive sixty lashes with a cat of nine tails on his bare back onboard the *Foudroyant*, the said Thomas Mack in like manner to receive fifty lashes, each at such time as the Commander in Chief of His Majesty's ships and vessels at this port shall direct & afterwards that the said Thomas Mack be imprisoned in the Marshalsea and for the space of twelve months in solitary confinement, and do acquit William Logan. And the said prisoners are each of them hereby so sentenced accordingly.'

...

19. *Court Martial of John Kerr*

[ADM 1/5347]

Minutes taken at a court martial assembled on board His Majesty's ship *Gladiator* in Portsmouth Harbour on the 10th day of October 1798.

Present

John Holloway, Esqr., captain of His Majesty's ship *St. George* and second officer in the command of His Majesty's ships and vessels at Portsmouth and Spithead, President.

Captain	Theophilus Jones	Captain	James Hunt
	Francis Pickmore		William Lechmere
	Francis Fayerman		George Cockburne
	John Harvey		William Lukin
	Charles Ogle		Robert Larkan
	John West		James Stevenson

The prisoner was brought in and audience admitted. The order from the Right Honble Lords Commissioners of the Admiralty, dated the 6th October instant and directed to the president, setting forth that a court martial was holden on the 29th of last month on board His Majesty's ship *Gladiator* in Portsmouth Harbour for the trial of Lieut.^{t} Thomas Lawton Robins, commanding His Majesty's gun vessel the *Teaser*, on charges exhibited against him by M^{r}. John Kerr, Clerk and Steward of the said gun vessel, for having sent false muster books to the Navy Board, embezzled His Majesty's stores and delivered false weekly accounts to the admiral; and the said court martial, by their sentence transmitted to their Lordships, had declared their opinion that the said charges had not been proved against the said Lieutenant Thomas Lawton Robins, but were founded in malice and did thereby acquit the said Lieutenant Thomas Lawton Robins of the said charges accordingly. And, their Lordships thinking fit as much as in them lay to discountenance and prevent unjust, unfounded and malicious charges against officers in His Majesty's navy, did require and direct the said M^{r}. John Kerr might be tried by a court martial for maliciously, unjustly and without sufficient cause exhibiting the charges above mentioned against the said Lieutenant Thomas Lawton Robins and thereby unjustly and to the injury and prejudice of His Majesty's service causing him to be tried by a court martial for the same; and [the order?] for the trial of the said M^{r}. John Kerr for the above mentioned offences was read.

The president reported to the court that Captains Sir William Sidney Smith, Knt., and the Honble Courtney Boyle were absent on Admiralty leave.

M^{r}. Charles Boveard, Surgeon of His Majesty's ship *Sans Pareil*, being sworn, stated to the court that Captn. W^{m}. Browell had several complaints, especially a hurt in his loins occasioned by a bag of cotton falling on him and that he was informed by Captn. Browell that he could not therefore attend the court martial.

The members of the court and the judge advocate then, in open court and before they proceeded to trial, respectively took the several oaths enjoined and directed in and by an Act of Parliament made and passed in the 22nd year of the reign of His late Majesty King George the 2nd, entitled *An Act for Amending, Explaining and Reducing into One Act of Parliament the Laws Relating to the Government of His Majesty's Ships, Vessels and Forces by Sea.*

The judge advocate produced the minutes of the court martial that had been held on Lieutenant Robins.

Lieut.[t] Thomas Lawton Robins called in and sworn.

The Court asked:

Q. State to the court the reason that you apprehend induced the prisoner to bring you to a court martial.

A. About 10 weeks ago, being in want of a clerk and steward, I advertised for one accordingly. The prisoner met me at a place appointed by the advertisement and, having professed himself well versed in those two branches of duty, I accepted him; a very short time after he had joined the ship, he went on shore on duty, after I had rated him as clerk, and remained all night on shore without leave. I pointed out this impropriety of conduct to him, at which he seemed hurt; he appeared to be angry. Very shortly afterwards, he went on shore for fresh beef for the ship's company; he returned visibly in liquor and, on being admonished on this occasion, he told me that his being clerk with me should never prevent his taking his glass when he pleased. And, on several occasions which I have not noted down, he has behaved with disrespect and contempt, walking fore and aft the deck with very hasty steps on my admonishing him to act contrary. I have at different times pointed out many errors he has made in the course of his duty with respect to the books or accounts, which he has taken in very ill part and made unhandsome replies to. I have been under the necessity sometimes, particularly once when I was unwell to get the master of the brig to assist in copying the charges to be inserted in sick tickets when men have been going to the hospital; and therefore from all these circumstances, I gave orders in public that he should not be trusted again to go on duty, but that the midshipman should have the charge of bringing on board fresh beef and other duties; and I am therefore inclined from these reproofs to think he was induced to bring these charges against me as seems to be corroborated by a letter from him, which I have in my possession.

The letter, being produced, was read by the judge advocate and is hereby annexed marked no. 1.

Q. You have said when you have reproved him he has made use of very unhandsome replies, state such replies.

A. I cannot state them because they were not said in my hearing; with respect to faults in the books when I have reproved him, he has asked me if I was so correct a man as never to make faults.

M[r]. Kerr asked:

Q. When I met you at first on the Hard did I inform you that I was not completely informed of the purser's business?

A. I remember well while making the necessary inquiry to find out your abilities you pressed me hard to put my books before you, then I should see you knew your duty.

Q. At the time I made as you say unhandsome replies were we not in the habit of treating each other with great familiarity?

A. Entirely opposite to any assertion of the kind.

M[r]. George Read, Master of the *Teaser*, called in and sworn.

The Court asked:

Q. Do you know any act of the Lieut.[t] that could justify the prisoner in bringing him to a court martial?

A. I do not.

Q. Do you know if the prisoner prior to that time ever threatened to bring the Lieut[t]. to a court martial?

A. I recollect his saying he would bring him to a court martial.

Q. Have you ever heard him make use of any expressions of revenge against the lieut.[t]?

A. I have, he said he would ruin his commission; it was thro' some words that he had had with the lieut.[t] of being upbraided of being in liquor when coming on board from duty.

Q. Have you ever heard the Lieut.[t] admonish the prisoner to be correct in his conduct and to refrain from getting in liquor when on duty?

A. I have.

Q. Did you ever know the Lieut.[t] treat the prisoner with cruelty or oppression?

A. I never did.

The prisoner asked:

Q. On the night before I wrote the charges against the Lieutenant, in a conversation with you, did I complain to you that I thought it would be for the good of His Majesty's service to exhibit some charges that I had in my possession against Lieut.[t] Robins?

A. I very well recollect his speaking to me upon the subject, but there was nothing mentioned of its being for the good of the service.
Q. Did you ask me to let you look at the charges?
A. I do not recollect it.
Q. Did I show you the charges?
A. In a small memorandum book the next day, he showed me remarks he had taken of every person's conduct, who belonged to the ship, if anything went on shore in a basket or otherwise.
Q. Did you say that I should bring on the court martial, that it was no use to fall back as I had showed you the charges?
A. Not to my recollection, I know he had a great deal of to say upon it [*sic*]; he said he would ruin the lieutenant; he had him on all tacks, that everything was in his own favour.

M^{r}. George Howell, acting Midshipman belonging to the *Teaser*, called in and sworn.

The Court asked:

Q. How long have you known the prisoner?
A. Only since I have been on board, about 3 months.
Q. Did you ever hear the prisoner threaten to bring the lieut.^{t} to a court martial and say what reason he had for it?
A. Yes. When I was in M^{r}. Read's cabin, the prisoner said he would be damned if he would not bring Lieut.^{t} Robin's to a court martial; he would sweat his commission. M^{r}. Read desired him to hold his tongue.
Q. Did you ever see the lieut.^{t} treat the prisoner in a cruel or ungentlemanlike manner?
A. No.
Q. Did you ever hear the lieut.^{t} reprove the prisoner for misconduct and advise him to behave correct?
A. Yes, several times.
Q. How did the prisoner behave when the lieut.^{t} reproved him?
A. He said he had lived a number of years in the world; he was not a boy.
Q. Did you ever hear the prisoner use any expression of disrespect towards the lieut.^{t}?
A. Yes. I heard him say he was a damned rascal.

The prisoner asked:

Q. Where was I when I made use of such an expression?
A. In M^{r}. Read's cabin; I heard him say so several times before.
Q. Who was present?
A. I do not recollect who was present.

Q. When you first came on board the *Teaser*, did it appear to you that I was in a state of familiarity with Lieut.[t] Robins?

A. Yes. He dined with [you] very often; I believed [you] messed with him.

The prisoner, being called on for his defence, produced a paper writing containing the same, which was read by the judge advocate and is hereto annexed.

The court was cleared and agreed that the charge had been proved against the said John Kerr and did adjudge him to receive fifty lashes on his bare back with a cat o' nine tails on board of, or alongside, such of His Majesty's ships or vessels at Spithead, or in Portsmouth Harbour, at such times, or times, and in such manner and proportions as the commander in chief of His Majesty's ships and vessels for the time being at Portsmouth aforesaid should direct.

The court was again opened, the prisoner brought in, audience admitted and sentence passed accordingly. …

19A. *Kerr to Robins*

[ADM 1/5347]

His Majesty's Gun Vessel *Teaser*
Spithead, 22nd Sept. 1798

… From the general tenor of your conduct towards me since I have belonged to the *Teaser*, under your command, I feel myself hurt, my character at stake, & all my intentions of doing well disappointed by being so unfortunate as to engage with you and have been induced to exhibit some certain charges against you & have accordingly applied to the Admiralty for a court martial upon your conduct, of which I think it proper to give you this notice …

No 1

19B. *Defence of John Kerr*

[ADM 1/5347]

October 10th. 1798

I am extremely sorry to appear before you on this occasion. My chief reason for bringing L[t]. Robins to a court martial was that I look'd upon it as a duty incumbent on me for the good of His Majesty's service to bring to light all such transactions, as I had for some time before this look'd with abhorrence on his manner of proceeding, but the immediate instigation proceeded from M[r]. George Read, Q. Master & Pilot of His Majesty's gun vessel *Teaser*. On the night before I drew out the charges against Lt Robins, as M^{r}. Read & myself was conversing together, our discourse turned on L^{t}. Robins concerning the affair that happened some time ago between M^{r}. W^{m}. Murray, Surgeon's Mate at that time, & L^{t}. Robins, Comm^{dr}. of the *Teaser*; when I ask'd M^{r}. Read if ever there was such men on board the *Teaser* as John Gillam & Henry Jenkins, he reply'd he was sure there never was such men entered by L^{t}. Robins on board the *Teaser* & that he, M^{r}. Read, never heard from L^{t}. Robins or any other person that these men were enter'd on board the *Teaser*, until a long time afterwards in His Majesty's dockyard at Portsmouth, he was inform'd by L^{t}. Robins, & that L^{t}. Robins was afraid least M^{r}. Murray, at that time Surg^{n}'s Mate of the *Teaser*, should bring him to a court martial & would have done it had not he, M^{r}. Read put a stop to it. I inform'd M^{r}. Read I had made some remarks on Lt. Robins' conduct. M^{r}. Read asked me to let him look at them. I went to my cabin & bro^{t}. a small memorandum back & read some remarks to him, some of them M^{r}. Read objected to, as he thought he might be bro^{t}. in concerned. The others, he said, I might put down, which I did next morning accordingly, M^{r}. Read saying it was no use for me to fall back, that he would oblige me to bring the lieu^{t}. to a court martial, as I had shown him these remarks. This he said in the hearing of M^{r}. Hammond &, after I made L^{t}. Robins acquainted with my proceedings, M^{r}. Read quitted me and went to the opposite side. M^{r}. Read ordered me to write a letter to him to require him to appear as an evidence against L^{t}. Robins & to make use of these words in the letter to threaten him that if he perjured himself, that I would prosecute him, but I thought that improper to insert into the letter I wrote him. M^{r}. Read expressed himself that as L^{t}. Robins & M^{r}. Calloway were his friends, he would show this letter to them, that it might appear he was obliged to be an evidence against L^{t}. Robins. I humbly pray to state before this hon^{ble}. court my long servitude in the American war & this as well as I can recollect (being taken, all my papers were destroyed) on the later end of the year 1797 or beginning of 1798, I went on board the *Hydra*, Capt. Lloyd. My uncle, M^{r}. Thomas Anderson, was master of her; he got promoted to H.M. ship *Centaur*, Captain John Neal Pleydwell Nott. I went with him & my brother, Mark Kerr. I got into the office & rated Ab & assisted M^{r}. Alex Lang, Captain Nott's clerk. I was in the first action against Adm^{l} Count de Grass when he first arrived in the West Indies off Fort Royal, Martinique in April 1781 & Captn Nott was killed, when Mr Eastwood, 2nd lt., & my uncle recommended me to Ant^{y} Johnson, Esqr., President of St. Kitts & afterwards Governor of all the Leeward Islands. In the action the 12 April 1782, I understand my uncle, M^{r}. Thos Anderson, was put prize master on board the *Ville de Paris* & took my brother with him &, to my affliction, they were both lost in that ship & this was going out from this port in an hosp^{l} store ship in the year 1796 to Barbados, I was taken by the *Le Galatea*, a French national brig & carried prisoner to St. Martins; however I got clear of them in a short time, came up to St. Kitts & enter'd on board H.M. ship *Perdrix*, Wm Chas Fahie, Esqr, Captain, at St. Kitts in May 1796 was promoted on board the *Invincible*, Wm Cayley, Esqr, in Octr 1796 & on the 22nd Jany 1797 was rated Mid^{n} & did my duty in Captn. Cayley's office until my health declin'd & I was invalided in April 1798 at Martinique Hosp^{l} & Captn Cayley was never angry with me until he found I was invalided & going to quit him to come home. I assure you gentlemen that there is no person wishes the service better than I do, or I would not have entered so often. I can get a livelihood either at home or abroad on shore without going to sea for it. It is through inclination, & not necessity, as was insinuated in L^{t}. Robins defence, that I go to sea.

Therefore, if all that I have already expressed is not sufficient to convince the hon^{ble}. members of the court that I was not actuated by malice, I throw myself entirely on the mercy of the court, submitting to their candid consideration my long servitude, the misfortunes I have undergone in the service, my present bad state of health, unassisted & without a friend to help or direct me in my present critical situation.

Upon a serious review of my conduct, I cannot blame it in any respect, excepting that I did not pay due regard to my own safety in bringing my commander to trial in as much as I did not provide sufficient evidences to support the charges I brought against him & the chief one (M^{r}. Read) deserted me as I above stated.

I therefore humbly pray to his honour the president & the honble. members that compose this court that they will consider my distress & the unfortunate condition I now labour under …

20. *George Tripp to William Goddard*

[ADM 1/5349]

… Whereas the Right Honourable Lords Commissioners of the Admiralty have directed me to assemble a court martial to try James Graham (Boatswain), Christopher Atkinson (Gunner) and Willm. Brackenbridge (Carpenter), of His Majesty's Ship *Waaksamheid*, for uttering expressions highly improper and of a mutinous tendency, of embezzling several articles belonging to the said ship, and behaving in a manner unbecoming the character of officers, and whereas in the absence of the judge advocate and his deputy, the members composing the court martial are, by the Act of the 22nd of His Majesty King George the 2nd, empowered to appoint a person to execute the office of judge advocate;

I do therefore, with the approbation of the members who compose this court, hereby authorize and appoint you to officiate as judge advocate upon the occasion.

Given on board the *Agamemnon* at Blackstakes the 29th of May 1799.

…

21. *Court Martial of William Johnson*

[ADM 1/5349]

Minutes of proceedings at a court martial held on board His Majesty's ship *Cleopatra* in Halifax Harbour, the 11 June 1799.

Present

Robert Murray, Esqr., Captain of His Majesty's ship *Asia*, senior captain in Halifax Harbour, President.

Captains

John Oakes Hardy	Israel Pellew
Joseph Larcom	And. F. Evans
John Seater	

The prisoner, being brought into court, and the evidence and audience admitted, the order of George Vandeput, Esqr., Admiral of the Blue & Commander in Chief of H.M. ships & Vessels in the River St Lawrence, the coast of Nova Scotia & & &, dated the 1 June 1799 & directed to Robert Murray, Esqr., Captain of H.M. ship *Asia* & senior captain of H.M. Ships in Halifax Harbour, to try William Johnson, a Seaman, belonging to H.M. ship *St Albans* for charges stated in a letter from Captain Pender of His Majesty's ship *St Albans*, dated the 31 May 99, was read.

The members of the court and judge advocate, in open court & before they proceeded to trial, respectively took the oaths directed by Act of Parliament. The letter of Captain Pender to George Vandeput, Esqr., Admiral of the Blue & & &, was read as follows, vizt.:

His Majesty's ship *St Albans*
May 31, 1799

… William Johnson, a Seaman belonging to His Majesty's ship under my command, having been order'd in confinement for drunkenness and riotous behaviour on or about the 6th June last & having then resisted the ship's corporal & struck the sentinels, being in the execution of their office, and having on the night of the 28th inst. again resisted the ship's corporal and drawn a knife on him when in the execution of his office, I have to request that you will be pleased to order a court martial to be held on the said William Johnson for the said offences. …

All the evidences were ordered to withdraw out of court, except Terrence Connor, Ship's Corporal, who was sworn.

Court – You will relate to the court what you know respecting the charges against the prisoner.

Ans^r – On the 6th May

The court, being cleared to consider of an error in the charge, were of opinion that it appears to be an error in the first part of the charge, owing to it being wrong dated, and the 6 of June instead of the 6 May being inserted, & therefore the prisoner cannot be tried for the offences contained therein.

The court, being open'd, Terrence Connor was again called in & examined as follows:

Court – Relate to the court what happened on the 28 May last, respecting the charge against the prisoner.

Ans^r – About 9 o'clock in the evening, I was going out on the wharf to report the fire and lights to Mr Morris, the commanding officer. He asked me what noise that was on board. I told him I did not know. He said he was sure he heard Wm Johnson (the prisoner's) voice in the galley. He came with me to the galley & there found the prisoner, David Jones, the sentinel, & Wm Jones, the Ship's Corporal, endeavouring to get the prisoner to the place of his confinement, he being then a prisoner. Mr Morris ordered him down below. He seem'd inclined not to go. Lieut. Morris was obliged to take him by the breast & pull him down the fore hatchway & assisted in putting him in irons. M^r. Morris then left him. About 10 o'clock, the prisoner sent for me to let him go to the head, which he said he cou'd not stay from; I let him out of irons & ordered him to go to the head. When he return'd, he said he wou'd make his bed up before he wou'd go to it. After making it up, he wanted to go into it without being put in irons. Will Jones, the other Ship's Corporal, came to him, & desired that he wou'd go in irons; he swore he wou'd not, taking a knife out of his pocket. He swore he wou'd cut the first person's fingers, who wou'd attempt to put him in irons. On his drawing the knife, I went to the officers [*sic*] of the watch, M^{r}. Smith, & acquainted him with Johnson (the prisoner's) behaviour. He immediately came & assisted me in putting the prisoner by force in irons, then left him.

Court – Did the prisoner open the knife, and attempt to cut or stab any person?

Ans^{r} – He open'd the knife, but did not attempt to cut anybody.

Court – Was the prisoner sober or in liquor?

Answer – In liquor, but not very drunk.

William Jones, Ship's Corporal, sworn.

Court – Relate to the court what you know respecting the charge against the prisoner.

Answer – On the 28th in the evening between 9 & 10 the prisoner had occasion to go to the head; when he came down, he was obstreperous & said he wou'd not go in irons. He had a drawn knife in his hand & said he wou'd cut off the first person's fingers that offer'd to put him in irons. Terrence Conner, the Ship's Corporal, went for the officer of the watch, which was M^{r}. Smith, who came down; & by his assistance, we got the knife out of his hand, & by that means we got him in irons. We then left him in irons.

Court – Was the knife in his hand or did you see him draw it?

Answer – The knife was in his hand open, but I do not know where he got it from or who gave it him.

David Jones, sentinel, sworn.

Court – Relate to the court what you know respecting the charge against the prisoner.

Answer – On the 28th of May in the evening about 8 o'clock, I was sentry over the prisoner. I was assisting the ship's corporal (William Jones) to put the prisoner in irons and he wou'd not be put in irons by me or the ship's corporal; after that he told me if I came near him he wou'd knock me down. He afterwards drew his knife from his pocket, & said the first man that offer'd to put him in irons, he wou'd cut their fingers off. The ship's corporal went to the officer of the watch (M^{r}. Smith), who came back with him; & by his assistance, we got him in irons. M^{r}. Smith took the knife from the prisoner.

Court – Did he open the knife?

Ans^{r} – Yes, I saw him open it.

Court – Are you certain as to the time?

Ans^{r} – I was reliev'd at half past 8 and it was just before that.

J. W. Smith, Midshipman, sworn.

Court – Relate to the court what you know respecting the charge against the prisoner.

Answer – On the evening of the 28 May about 10 o'clock, the ship's corporal (Terrence Conner) came aft, and reported to me that the prisoner (Johnson) was out of irons, & had drawn a knife &, sworn that the first who laid his fingers on him, he wou'd cut them with it. I immediately went with the corporal & saw the prisoner sitting by the irons. I asked him the reason why he wou'd not go in irons; he told me he wanted to go to the head. The corporal (Conner) told me he had just been up twice before that; I immediately seized him &, with the assistance of the corporal, put him in irons by force. After I had secured him, I took the knife out of his pocket & left him. I heard no more of him that watch.

Court – Had he his knife in his hand when you went below?

Answer – No! He had not.

Court – Who was sentinel over the prisoner at that time?

Ans^{r} – I do not know.

William Jones, Corporal, was again called in.

Court – Who was sentry over the prisoner at the time this business happened?

Ans^{r} – I am certain it was David Jones and he assisted me in securing the prisoner.

Terrence Connor called in.

Court – Are you sure that David Jones was sentry over the prisoner when you went to bed?

Ans^{r} – Yes.

The evidence for the prosecution being closed, the prisoner was called on for his defence, who says that he knows nothing of the matter, & throws himself on the mercy of the court. The court was then clear'd & proceeded to deliberate upon a sentence.

The court, having carefully and deliberately consider'd the evidence produced, were of opinion that the charge was proved and, therefore, adjudged him to be hanged by the neck until he is dead at the yard arm of such one of His Majesty's ships as the commander in chief shall direct; but in consideration of circumstances which had appeared in the course of the trial, the court do most earnestly recommend him to mercy.

…

22. *John Dawson to Nepean*

[ADM 1/1721] *Diadem*, Downs,
Sept[r]. 30th, 1799

… In answer to yours of the 27th (which I but this day rec[d].), I beg leave to lay before their Lordships the following particulars relative to Matthew Stephens, a prisoner on board the *Diadem*. In my letter of the 25th I mention'd the mast[r]. at arms having made a complaint to me that a false and malicious story was industriously propagated in the ship in order to weaken his authority and injure him amongst the ship's company. The story was that when on board the *Cumberland*, doing duty as master at arms, he had falsely sworn away the life of a man. Matthew Stephens declared at the gangway that the man I was going to punish for spreading the above story was not the guilty person as he was then and there with him and to the truth of which he offer'd to take his oath, but would neither declare the person nor did he attempt to deny his knowledge of him. I therefore put him in irons as (in my opinion) coming under that part of the 20th Article of War, viz.: 'And if any person in the fleet shall conceal any traitorous or mutinous words spoken by any' &c, &c.

…

[Admiralty Note]
2 Octo. Own and acquaint him that if he has no farther grounds to exhibit against the man, their Lordships do not judge it advisable to bring him to trial by a court martial and that he is to discharge him into the *Sophie*.

23. *John Oake to Lords Commissioners of the Admiralty*

[ADM 1/3093] *Fury* gun vessel, off Lymington
20 November 1799

… I beg leave to represent to your Lordships that on Thursday the 7th of this inst. Nov[r]., I was sent by my commanding officer to Portsmouth to draw stores. I did everything [in?] my power to execute his orders, but was prevented from returning so soon as I should have done on account of the weather, for which he has confined me a close prisoner (this 9 days) as if I had been guilty of the greatest crime; neither my wife nor any of my friends are suffered to come near me.

Indeed, my situation has been altogether very unpleasant ever since Lieu[t]. Roberts has had the command and I conceive myself used very ill.

I have therefore to beg your Lordships will order a court martial that I may have an opportunity of justifying my conduct and releasing myself from my very unpleasant confinement.

…

[Admiralty Note]
21 Nov. Send to the lieut. directing him to state the circumstances.

24. *Roberts to Nepean*

[ADM 1/3093] His Majesty's gun vessel *Fury*, Needles Passage
November 22nd, 1799

… I am this day honoured with your letter of yesterday's date also enclosed a letter which M^{r}. Oake, Master of His Majesty's gun vessel under my command, has written to my Lords Commissioners of the Admiralty stating his grievances.

I have to inform their Lordships that on the 7th ins^{t}. I sent M^{r}. Oake to Portsmouth in the *Duke of Clarence*, hired cutter, to draw stores for the use of the *Fury*. The *Duke of Clarence* returned about the 10th instant without the master, which I found had remained behind to come here in a private boat belonging to Lymington. Instead of seeing the stores which he had drawn safe deliver'd on board his own vessel, they were left without any one person to take care of them. After M^{r}. Oake's return, I got only part for what the notes were made out for, in which case I judged it most proper to suspend him from his duty until I went to Portsmouth to see what stores has been deliver'd to him, but he has never been close confined as a prisoner and his wife has had intercourse with him every day. As I am in want of a master's assistance, he now does his duty as before and whatever deficiency of stores there is wanting from his negligence I shall beg leave to have it charged against his wages. I beg leave to add that Mr. Oake has thought it a grievance to assist in keeping His Majesty's gun vessel in order the same as any other gun vessel here,

…

25. *Ann Brasington to Lords of the Admiralty*

[ADM 1/5349]

The Humble Petition of Ann Brasington, wife of Thomas Brasington, late Boatswain of His Maj^{s} ship *Le Conquerante*.

Most humbly showeth:

That your petitioner's husband sometime since [he?] was dismissed from being a boatswain, he is now a midshipman on board His Maj^{s} ship *Saint Sodora*; my said husband has served His Majesty thirty three years, eleven years of which he was a boatswain. Your petitioner has a large family, three children and pregnant with the fourth; she humbly begs the favour of your Lordships, for the sake of herself and children, that you will be pleased to stand her friend in reinstating her husband in his former station, and to look over his faults. Your petitioner hopes this her petition will meet with a favourable reception and rests in hopes that your Lordships will be so well pleas'd to restore her husband to his former station as soon as your Lordships shall think proper.

Most humbly implores your Lordships, out of your great and bountiful goodness, to be pleas'd to take her case, and her husband's long servitude into your mature consideration and for the sake of her family to grant, if possible, this her request; and your Lordships' petitioner (and family) as in duty bound will ever most humbly pray for your health, wealth and prosperity.

Plymouth Dock
Dec. 19, 1799

26. *James Gomm to Nepean*

[ADM 1/2895] No. 6 Durham Place
Lambeth, April 22nd 1800

… Not knowing where to find the only essential witness to vindicate my injured cause while commander of His Majesty's gun vessel *Tickler* prevented me at that time from soliciting a court martial to enquire into my conduct as that obstacle is removed as you will perceive by the copy of the subjoined letter which I have just now received and willing my conduct should bear the test of the strictest scrutiny. Should it not be incompatible with the rules of the service, I request you will be pleased to move the Lords Commissioners of the Admiralty to order a court martial in order that I may have an opportunity of acquitting myself of those aspersions on my character which my uncommon treatment has subjected me to; my intention being to travel into different parts of Europe in which my connections are extensive is my urgent motive for my present request in order that I may receive that consideration which the injustice I have laboured under might tend to deprive me of. …

P.S. The copy of the subjoined letter is from my late clerk and steward onboard the *Tickler*

26A. *William Midgley to Gomm*

[ADM 1/2895] H.M. ship *Northumberland*
April 25th 1799

Copy

… Having heard from a friend of mine in England of some infamous aspersions having been cast on your character by some ill disposed persons indicating that the provisions were not regularly issued to the people of H.M. brig *Tickler* when under your command, I think it no more than the duty I owe to the credit of a deserving officer under whom at that time I had the honour to serve in a station where issuing the provisions fell immediately under my inspection to send you this testimony of my gratitude to the truth of which I am willing to make oath that during the time you commanded the *Tickler* the provisions of all species were issued to the ship's crew without any distinction in the same manner & proportion as I have seen in every other ship in the navy. I have known with this exception every man in the *Tickler* had the indulgence granted him of choosing to have his meat raw or boiled in the coppers which he liked best, whereas in all other ships in the navy it is given to the ship's cook and served out when boiled and I have frequently heard several of the oldest men in the ship declare that they had never seen finer pieces of meat onb^{d} of a ship in their lives.

That you was ever attentive to the welfare and happiness of the people under your command and conducted yourself to every individual on board the vessel with that affability and condescension which will ever denote the character of a worthy, just and humane officer was and ever will be the opinion of. …

Witness that this is the handwriting of W^{m}. Midgley
Joseph Ault, Purser
J^{no}. Smith, Surgeon

To prevent any doubts arising from the identity of my handwriting, I have thought proper to have it witness'd by the above gentlemen.

[Admiralty Note]
23 April Desire Mr. Bicknell to return the papers respecting this offence.

27. *Report of the Court Martial of William Connor*

[ADM 1/5355]

At a court martial assembled and held on board His Majesty's ship *Hydra* in Sheerness Harbour on Friday the 30th day of January 1801 in pursuance of an order from the Commissioners for executing the office of Lord High Admiral of the United Kingdom of Great Britain and Ireland &c., dated the 27th of the same month.

Present

James Robert Mosse, Esqr., Captain of His Majesty's ship *Monarch* and second officer in the command of His Majesty's ships and vessels in the River Medway and the buoy of the Nore, President.

Captains

William Mitchel	Richard Incledon
George Brisac	Sir Francis Laforey, Bart.
Charles Hare	Richard Lee
Henry Inman	William Hall Gage
John Mackellar	Robert Hall

The court, being sworn agreeable to Act of Parliament, proceeded to try William Connor, a supernumerary on board His Majesty's ship *Hydra*, for having behaved himself in a most insolent and contemptuous manner to Lieutenant Nathaniel Charles Jones of the said ship publicly on the quarter deck on the evening of the 17th of January 1801 and, having heard the evidence in support of the charge as also what the prisoner had to offer in his defence and very maturely and deliberately weighed and considered the same, is of opinion that it is proved and do adjudge the said William Connor to receive five hundred lashes on his bare back with a cat of nine tails alongside of such ships, at such times and in such proportions as the commander in chief at this port shall direct and afterwards to be confined in such solitary prison as the Lords Commissioners of the Admiralty shall think fit for the space of two years. And the said William Connor is hereby so sentenced accordingly, but as he has stated in his defence that 'he is at present under sentence of death, having been tried by a court martial in the West Indies when belonging to the *Gaite*,' the court do recommend this sentence not be put into execution until the same is ascertained, legal opinion taken and the said commander in chief shall receive directions from the Lords Commissioners of the Admiralty thereon. …

28. *Court Martial of Charles Burne*

[ADM 1/5361]

Minutes of a court martial, assembled on board His Majesty's ship *Neptune*, in Torbay the 8th day of April, 1802 for the trial of the Reverend Charles Burne, Chaplain of His Majesty's ship *Hercule* for sacrilegious, impious, drunken and ungentlemanly conduct.

Present

James Gambier, Esqr., Vice Admiral of the White and second in command, President.
Rear Admiral Sir Charles Cotton, Baronet
Rear Admiral Cuthbert Collingwood, Esqr.
Rear Admiral Sir Robert Calder, Esqr.
Captain William Domett, first captain to the Commander in Chief
Captain, The Earl of Northesk
Captain Thomas Wells
Captain Samuel Osborne
Captain John Child Purvis
Captain George Murray
Captain Sir Richard Strachan B^{t}.
Captain Edward Buller
Captain William Luke

The prisoner being brought into Court and the evidences and audience admitted, read an order for assembling the same as follows[1] viz.:

… Whereas Captain Luke of His Majesty's ship *Hercule* has transmitted to me in his letter enclosed, one from Lieutenant Hill of the said ship, dated the 4 instant, charging the Reverend Charles Burne, the Chaplain, with sacrilegious, impious, drunken and ungentlemanly conduct the evening of the 10th January 1802 on shore at Brixham and repeatedly on board. Captain Luke, having requested that a court martial may be held to try the said Reverend Charles Burne for the above charges, agreeably [*sic*] to the request of Lieutenant Hill, and whereas I think fit to comply therewith, I send you the before mentioned letters; and by virtue of the power and authority in me vested, do hereby require and direct you to assemble a court martial as soon as may be, for the trial of the Reverend Charles Burne, Chaplain of the *Hercule*, for the offences with which he therein stands charged, and try him for the same accordingly.

Given on board the *Ville de Paris*, Torbay, the 4th April 1802

[1]This letter is from Admiral William Cornwallis to Admiral James Gambier.

...

Then, the Court being sworn according to Act of Parliament, the following letters were read:[1]

Hercule, Torbay,
4th April 1802

... Since sealing my letter to you this morning requesting a court martial on Lieutenant William Hill of His Majesty's ship under my command on charges preferred against him by Lieutenant Collett and the Reverend Charles Burne, and, since Lieutenant Hill has been under arrest, I have received a letter from the said Lieutenant Hill, charging the Reverend Charles Burne with sacrilegious, impious, drunken and ungentlemanly conduct on the evening of the 10 of January 1802 on shore at Brixham and repeatedly on board, which I beg leave to enclose for your inspection and also beg that you will be pleased to order a court martial on the Reverend Charles Burne for the above charges agreeably [*sic*] to the request of Lieutenant Hill.

...

His Majesty's ship *Hercule*, the 4 April 1802

... I have to request that you will apply to the commander in chief for a court martial on Mr. Burne, Chaplain of His Majesty's ship under your command for sacrilegious, impious, drunken and ungentlemanly conduct on the evening of Sunday, January the tenth 1802 while on shore at Brixham and repeatedly on board.

...

The witnesses all withdrew out of Court.

The Prosecutor, having desired to call on a witness to prove that part of the charge said to have been committed onshore, the Court was cleared and came to the following resolution viz.:

'In the present case the Court do not think themselves competent to try the prisoner on that particular part of the charge which is stated to have been committed on shore.'

	Captain George Mortimer of the Marines, *Hercule*, sworn.
	Mr. William Hill, late Lieutenant of the *Hercule*, Prosecutor
Prosecutor	Did you ever see the prisoner drunk on board the *Hercule*?
Answer	I think I have, but cannot state any particular time.

[1]The first letter is from Captain William Luke to Cornwallis; the second is from Lieutenant William Hill to Luke.

Prosecutor	Have you ever seen the prisoner so drunk as either to stagger in walking or falter in his speech?
Answer	No, I don't recollect I ever have.
Court	Have you ever seen the prisoner in the state you have described him more than once?
Answer	I think I have seen him twice.
Court	What was your reason for supposing the prisoner to be drunk at those times?
Answer	He appeared as men usually do when they are in liquor. I judged so from his manner and countenance; there was a kind of vacant, absent look, he was totally silent and in that stupid way that men who have drunk too much liquor. He sat with the company and said nothing. I recollect it was once upon an occasion of some of the officers having friends on board; the other time was last Christmas evening. The prisoner is not generally a silent man.
Court	How long have you been shipmates with the prisoner?
Answer	About six or seven months.
Court	Were those the only occasions that you have observed the chaplain in that state you have described?
Answer	They are the only occasions.
Court	From your observation, does the prisoner generally go to bed early?
Answer	He generally does.
Court	Might not his stupid appearance have proceeded from his staying up unusually late?
Answer	No. I rather think it was in consequence of having drunk too much.
Court	Have you ever known any instance of impiety in the conduct, the language and reasoning of the prisoner since you have known him in the ship?
Answer	I have heard the prisoner swear repeatedly and he has been guilty of gross and ungentlemanlike conduct.
Court	State the circumstances of that conduct.
Answer	A great deal of indecent and improper language has been made use of at the mess table, which the prisoner has never in any one instance attempted to check or repress, which I conceive in a divine, it was his duty to have done.
Court	If the prisoner had interfered at those different times when ill language was going on, would his remonstrances have been attended to?
Answer	I should hope so. I am sure that some of the members of the

	mess would have attended to them, but cannot say that they all would have done so.
Court	State to the court any instance where in the prisoner's remonstrances were attended to in the *Hercule's* wardroom.
Answer	I never recollect his making use of any remonstrance except on the subject of improper women being admitted to the wardroom.
Court	In what instances was the prisoner's remonstrances attended to?
Answer	Mr. Hill, in consequence of Mr. Burne's first remonstrance, would not suffer the woman who was with him to come out of his cabin. The prisoner never made any other remonstrance in this instance it was attended to.
Court	When you had company on board on the day when you think the prisoner was in liquor, did you dine at the table?
Answer	I think I did. We sat till 6 at night, dined at 2, our usual hour. Port wine was drunk at table. The prisoner drank of it. The company was at last reduced to a small party; the prisoner remained amongst that number.
Court	Were those women of ill fame frequently introduced in the wardroom after the prisoner's remonstrance?
Answer	I only recollect one instance of their being introduced afterwards, which was the 31st March.
	Cross examined by the prisoner.
Prisoner	On the evening you allude to, who did you leave sitting at the table when you left?
Answer	M[r] Hill, M[r] Miln, M[r] Dymock (I think) was there and some friends of the gentlemen; I was myself there.
Prisoner	Did you leave the table before I did?
Answer	No, I believe not. I think we broke at the same time.
	Lieutenant Thomas Dering, Marines, sworn.
Prosecutor	Did you ever see the prisoner drink on board the *Hercule*?
Answer	Yes, I conceived so. I recollect that on Christmas eve or Christmas evening the gestures, actions and appearance of the prisoner indicated that he was in that state, by being vociferous and noisy, by striking his hand upon the table and by a wild and vacant stare in his countenance. I do not recollect any other circumstances.
Court	Did you ever hear the prisoner make use of any oaths in profanation of the name of God.

Answer — Yes, but the prisoner was not in the common habit of doing so.

Lieutenant Thomas Dymock, Marines, late *Hercule*, sworn.

Prosecutor — Were you in company with the prisoner and me on a Sunday evening in my cabin on board the *Hercule* drinking wine at 12 o'clock at night?

Answer — I was.

Prosecutor — Did you hear the prisoner several times call for more wine?

Answer — Yes, I did.

Prosecutor — Did you hear the prisoner express a wish that we should stay up till after 12 o'clock, that we might have a song?

Answer — I do not recollect it.

Prosecutor — What state was the prisoner in when he went out of my cabin?

Answer — I do not recollect.

Prosecutor — Did you ever hear the prisoner swear?

Answer — I never took notice that he did.

Prosecutor — Was the prisoner drunk on Christmas night last?

Answer — I do not recollect seeing the prisoner drunk then, nor can I positively say I ever saw him drunk. I was present at the table with the prisoner on Christmas evening.

Lieutenant Robert Milne, *Hercule,* sworn

Prosecutor — At the time when you were ill in bed, do you recollect M^{r}. Dymock, the prisoner and myself coming into your cabin and drinking some wine & the prisoner calling for more?

Answer — To the best of my recollection, a considerable time ago. I remember M^{r}. Hill and M^{r}. Dymock coming into my cabin. I am not certain whether M^{r}. Burne came in with them, but he came in the cabin and drank some wine with the other two officers; and after they had drunk some quantity of wine, I heard the prisoner say, 'We can take another bottle.' I cannot charge my memory whether that bottle was drunk or not.

Prosecutor — Did you ever hear the prisoner swear?

Answer — To the best of my recollection I never did.

Prosecutor — Did you ever see the prisoner drunk?

Answer — The only time I can be certain of it was the night he was in my cabin, as I have mentioned before, and he then appeared to me to be elevated with wine, but I cannot say he was drunk.

Court — Were you at the wardroom table on Christmas night?

Answer — Yes.

Cross examined by the prisoner.

Prisoner — At the time alluded to, was I not invited to spend the evening in your cabin?

Answer — I do not recollect. I do not know whether the prisoner was asked by M^{r}. Hill or M^{r}. Dymock.

Lieutenant Charles Touzeau, *Hercule,* sworn

Prosecutor — Were you in company a few evenings ago, before the 3rd instant, with the prisoner, M^{r}. Cairn and Lieutenant Collett in the after cockpit of the *Hercule*?

Answer — I was in the cockpit in the surgeon's cabin about 10 o'clock; I had not been there two minutes before the surgeon, the prisoner and Lieutenant Collett were sent for to come into the wardroom. During their stay there I stopped and read M^{r}. Burne's charges. He returned about 11 o'clock. I withdrew.

Court — At that time did you observe anything improper in the prisoner's conduct?

Answer — I never observed anything improper in the prisoner's conduct, either at this time or any other since he has been in the ship. (Here the prosecution closed.)

Prisoner's defence read by the judge advocate.

… As to the circumstances of the prosecution brought against me by M^{r}. Hill, I trust it will appear to every member of this honourable court to be solely the dictator of malice and revenge, for it cannot be supposed that after such a lapse of time he would ever have thought of arraigning my conduct, of his own atrocious behaviour and repeated insults to me, had not compelled me to bring my accusation against him; in proof of which I beg leave to point out, the contradiction in the evidence of Captain Mortimer and M^{r}. Dering, respecting me on Christmas day or eve, the former thinking me in liquor because I was silent and the latter believing me so because I was vociferous. The honourable court will therefore judge what credit is due a prosecution so instigated.

I will no longer trespass upon you by entering into any vindication of myself, as I have no doubt but the court will consider, that, as the character of every person is of the utmost importance, that of a clergyman is most essentially so. I shall now therefore beg leave to bring forward such testimony to the general tenor of my conduct, as may help to relieve me from the charges which have been brought against me.

...

Read a paper delivered by the prisoner as follows, viz.:

The character and conduct of Mr. Charles Burne, Chaplain of His Majesty's ship *Hercule,* (during the time of my being first Lieutenant of the said ship), has been at all times that of a good, moral, quiet, sober and inoffensive man.

(Signed) Jno. Warren

Paignton Hospital, April 7th 1802

Note: Mr. Jno. Warren is first Lieutenant of the *Hercule* at present sick in Paignton Hospital

Captain Luke declares the above to be Mr. Warren's handwriting.

The following letter was delivered into court by Captain Buller, one of the members.

... I had fully intended to be at the court martial this morning and should have been very ready (had it been thought necessary) to have borne testimony to the character of Mr. Burne, but, being prevented by indisposition, in justice to Mr. Burne, I think it is my duty to assure you and which I would solemnly assert that I have known him from his childhood, that his conduct has been uniformly correct and that he has ever been considered a very peaceful, prudent and deserving young man.

...

J. Rudall

Brixham, Wednesday morning

Mr. Rudall is said to be a clergyman of respectable character.

Captain Luke, being called on to the prisoner's character, declared that since he has been in the *Hercule*, he has conducted himself as a modest, sober, well-behaved man and quite consistent with the character of a clergyman.

Mr. William Thompson, Purser of the *Hercule*, sworn

Prisoner Do you think me at all addicted to swearing?

Answer Certainly not.

Prisoner Did you ever see me drunk since I belonged to the *Hercule*?

Answer I never saw him drunk.

Mr. James Cairn, Surgeon of the *Hercule*, sworn

Prisoner Do you think me at all addicted to swearing?

Answer Not at all.

Prisoner Did you ever see me drunk since I belonged to the *Hercule*?

Answer Never.

Prisoner What has been my general conduct on board the ship?

Answer Mild and inoffensive and perfectly consistent with the character of a gentleman and a clergyman.

Here the prisoner closed his defence.

The Court, after mature deliberation, were of the opinion that the charges are not proved and that the part thereof of which they thought proper to take cognizance appears to them to be scandalous, malicious and unfounded, and therefore adjudged the prisoner to be acquitted.

The court opened and sentence of acquittal was pronounced accordingly.

...

29. *Court Martial of Edward Nicholas Conner, Green Berry, Henry Keal and Thomas Hemmett*

[ADM 1/5366]

Minutes of proceedings at a court martial held on board His Majesty's ship *Theseus* in Port Royal Harbour, Jamaica on Friday the 6th day of July 1804.

Present

James Richard Dacres, Esqr., Rear Admiral of the White and second in command of His Majesty's ships and vessels at Jamaica &c., President.

Captains

H'ble John Murray — John Bligh

John Ayscough — Edmond Boger

Read the order of Sir John Thomas Duckworth, K.B., Rear Admiral of the Red and Commander in Chief &c., &c., dated the 5th day of July 1804 and directed to James Richard Dacres, Esqr., Rear Admiral of the White and second in command of His Majesty's ships and vessels at Jamaica, to try Edward Nicholas Conner and Green Berry for desertion, Henry Keal, Quartermaster, for uttering seditious and mutinous words tending to sanction the said desertion and Thomas Hemmett, Seaman, for striking his superior officer and afterwards using improper language, all of whom belong to His Majesty's sloop *Pelican*.

Then the members of the court and judge advocate, in open court and before they proceeded to trial, respectively took the oath enjoined them by Act of Parliament.

A letter from Lieutenant Foley, (at present) commanding His Majesty's sloop *Pelican*, to the commander in chief was read as follows:

H.M. Sloop *Pelican*, Port Royal
21st June 1804

… I have to request you will be pleased to grant an order to try by court martial the under mentioned persons, viz.:

Edward Nicholas Conner, Ab.	Desertion
Green Berry	
Henry Keal, Quartermaster,	for uttering seditious and mutinous words tending to sanction the said desertion
Thomas Hemmitt, Seaman,	for striking his superior officer and afterwards using improper language: all of whom belong to His Majesty's sloop *Pelican* (and sent by me on board His Majesty's ship *Theseus*).

…

All the witnesses were ordered out of court, except Daniel Button, a Private Marine, who was sworn.

Lieut^{t}. Foley, the Prosecutor	Was you doing duty as corporal of Marines by my order on or about the seventeenth of June last?
Ans^{r}.	I had no orders to do that duty; I did no duty. I had been captain's steward.
Ques^{t}.	Do you know the prisoners?
Ans^{r}.	Yes
Ques^{t}.	Did you see the prisoners leave the brig and go into a canoe?
Ans^{r}.	Yes.
Ques^{t}.	Relate to the court what you know further respecting the conduct of the prisoners.
Ans^{r}.	When I saw the prisoners leave the brig, I went on shore to the capstern house and told the quartermaster, John Roach, of it.

This witness asked nothing further and John Roach, Quartermaster, called & sworn.

Prosecutor — Were you quartermaster of the watch on or about the 17th of last month, when the two prisoners left the brig?

Ans^r^. — Yes.

Ques^t^. — Do you know the prisoners, Connor & Berry?

Ans^r^. — Yes.

Ques^t^. — At what time did you first understand the two prisoners leaving the brig and from whom?

Ans^r^. — From Button, who came and told me. I then informed the sergeant of Marines, who reported to Mr. Foley and I went to see that no boat left the wherry wharf.

Court — Did you see them return or were they brought in?

Ans^r^. — They were brought in.

Nothing further to this witness; he withdrew and Lieutenant Foley was sworn and examined.

Court — Relate to the court where you found the two prisoners; what state they were in; whether they had any clothes with them; and if they made any resistance at the time you saw them.

Ans^r^. — On the corporal of Marines reporting to me that the prisoners, Edward Nicholas Connor and Green Berry, had called a canoe alongside the brig and got into her and went to the wherry wharf, I immediately got my side arms and went to the capstern house and ordered a midshipman, corporal of Marines and a private to follow me into the town as soon as they possibly could get armed, at the same time went myself into the town and, on going up the through the market place, I saw the two prisoners crossing from the water side towards the middle of the town. I ran immediately to seize Connor; Berry, seeing me at the moment, made a short run, but was stopped by a black man. I immediately seized him and brought both into the dock yard and put them into confinement. Green Berry had some clothes under his arm, but Connor had none.

Ques^t^. by the prisoner, Connor — When you saw me, did I say, 'M^r^. Foley, I have no intention to desert from you?'

Ans^r^. — Yes you did.

Nothing further asked and M^r^. Foley returned to his proper place to proceed with the prosecution.

M^{r}. Butts, the Gunner, was examined on the part of the prosecution against the prisoner, Keal.

Prosecutor Do you know the prisoner, Keal?

Ans^{r}. Yes.

Ques^{t}. Relate to the court the conversation held by Keal in general, but to the quartermaster, Roach, in particular, a short time after the two prisoners had deserted and after the signal was made for the captain of the *Pelican*.

Ans^{r}. The prisoner, Keal, said, 'Damn my eyes, we have got no captain. M^{r}. Foley is no captain;' and said he wished Mr. Marshall, the First Lieutenant of the *Hercule*, would come and be captain of the *Pelican*; and, if he did not like him, he would make the best of his way.

Nothing further asked the witness, and Mr. Whittaker, Captain's Clerk, called and sworn.

Ques^{t}. Relate to the court the conversation held by Keal in general, but to the quartermaster, Roach, in particular, a short time after the two prisoners had deserted and after the signal was made for the captain of the *Pelican*.

Ans^{r}. I was in the capstern house when the prisoners were brought in. I heard the prisoner, Keal, asked Quartermaster Roach what business he had to inform the officers of the escape of the prisoners; Roach said, as quartermaster of the watch, if he had not done so, he himself would no doubt be punished for it and, if it had been his own brother, he would have done the same. I was standing close to M^{r}. Butts, the Gunner, when the signal was made for a captain. Keal said, 'We have no captain, M^{r}. Foley is not a captain,' or words to that effect. I said he was the commanding officer for the time and ought to be considered as such; he said if that man Marshall comes here and I do not like him, I will make the best of my way.

Ques^{t}. Do you recollect of Keal's reproaching Roach for his informing of the desertion of the two men, and did he mention anything about the boat they had deserted in?

Ans^{r}. He said they could not be tried for desertion, as they had not taken a King's boat, but a shore boat.

This witness asked nothing further and the prosecution against the three former was closed; and the prisoner, Hemmett was then tried for striking his superior officer, &^{c}.

Mr. Hogg, the Carpenter, called and sworn.

Prosecutor Relate to the court what happened between you and the prisoner, Hemmett, on or about the seventeenth of June last.

Ans^{r}. The prisoner, Hemmett, abused Button, a Marine, and called him an informer, and said he had not any business to complain of the prisoners for going away, and swore he would knock his head off; with that, I went to him and pushed him from Button. He turned round to me immediately and swore I was the bugger he wanted, and made a blow at me. I had a small stick in my hand, which I held up to fend off the blow; he immediately caught hold of the stick and hove me down. Button and M^{r}. Gordon, the Boatswain, came to my assistance and, when I was clear, I went and called M^{r}. Tudor, a Midshipman; and in the mean time another midshipman went to call M^{r}. Foley, who came and put the prisoner into confinement and, when in confinement, he swore and wished they would hang him. He was rather the worse for liquor at the time.

No further questions asked, the witness withdrew; and M^{r}. Gordon, the Boatsn., called and sworn.

Prosecutor Relate to the court what you saw on the seventeenth of June last in the capstan house between M^{r}. Hogg, the Carpenter, & Hemmett, the prisoner.

Ans^{r}. On Sunday in the afternoon, hearing a noise in the capstern house, I came down out of my room. M^{r}. Hogg had a large stick, which he used to walk with, being lame. I then heard the prisoner make a great noise. M^{r}. Hogg went up to him to demand silence; the prisoner then said, ‘You are the bugger I want.’ I saw M^{r}. Hogg and the prisoner fall in the capstern house together. I ran and called the officers for assistance, which officers and men came immediately and seized the prisoner. M^{r}. Foley came into the capstern house and ordered him into irons; he still made a noise, crying out, ‘Hang me! Hang me! That’s all I want.’ M^{r}. Foley then ordered the prisoner to be gagged and asked him if he would be quiet if he took the gag out of his mouth; his answer was yes. M^{r}. Foley then ordered the people to disperse from the prisoner.

Court You have said you saw the prisoner and M^{r}. Hogg fall together. Did you see the prisoner give M[r]. Hogg any blow?

Ans[r]. No, I saw him endeavouring to wrench the stick out of his hands.

Ques[t]. Was the prisoner drunk at the time?

Ans[r]. Yes.

This witness was asked no further questions and Dan[l]. Button, Marine, recalled.

Prosecutor Relate to the court what happened between you and Hemmett, the prisoner, and what you saw between M[r]. Hogg and the prisoner on or about the seventeenth of last month.

Ans[r]. The prisoner abused me for informing against the two prisoners for running away. M[r]. Hogg, hearing it, came to take my part. The prisoner tried to take the stick from M[r]. Hogg and have him down. I went and parted them; and the prisoner was put into confinement.

Court Did you see him strike Mr. Hogg or make use of any bad language?

Ans[r]. I did not see him strike or make use of any bad language.

Prosecutor Do you recollect after the prisoner was put in irons, his using any bad language to me? If you do, relate it to the court.

Ans[r]. He said he would be sooner hanged at once than be put into confinement and would not keep silence for any buggering officer belonging to the *Pelican*; with that, Mr. Foley gagged him with a pump bolt and kept him in that manner until he was quiet.

This witness retired, no further questions being asked him.

The evidence on the part of the prosecution being closed, the prisoners were asked severally for their defence.

The prisoners, Connor and Berry, requested M[r]. Foley might speak to their character.

Lieutenant Foley said. 'During the time I have been Lieutenant of the *Pelican*, something better than six months, I found Berry & Connor to be sober, quiet men and very willing to do their duty as seamen.'

M[r]. Tudor, Midshipman, also said, 'During the time I have known the prisoners, Berry & Connor, they have always behaved very well and very sober men.'

Mr. Butts, the Gunner, said, 'During the time I have known them, they have always behaved themselves very well, ever since they belonged to the brig, and are very sober men.'

The prisoner, Keal, requested Lieutenant Foley might speak to his character.

Lieutenant Foley said, 'The prisoner is a good seaman, a quiet man and very attentive to his duty. I have had no occasion to find fault with him until this present business.'

M^r^. Tudor said, 'He has always done his duty very well and was a quiet man until this business and very sober.'

The prisoner, Hemmett, left himself to the mercy of the court.

The court was then cleared to deliberate upon and form the sentence.

...

The court is of opinion the charge against the prisoners, Edward Nicholas Conner and Green Berry is not proved and do therefore acquit them; that the charge against Henry Keal is proved and the charge against Thomas Hemmett is proved in part and do therefore adjudge them to receive one hundred and fifty lashes each on their bare backs with a cat of nine tails alongside such of His Majesty's ships and vessels and at such times as the commander in chief shall think proper to direct; and they are all hereby sentenced accordingly.

...

30. *Byam to Heathcote*

[ADM 1/5367]

At a court of enquiry held on board His Majesty's ship *Galatea* in English Harbour, Antigua on the 2nd day of October 1804.

Present

Captain	Charles Richardson
"	Edw[d]. Woolcombe
	Byam

The court, in pursuance of orders from Commodore Hood, Commander in Chief, &[c]., &[c]., &[c]., to us directed, dated the 7th September 1804, proceeded to enquire into the conduct of Lieutenant Howard of His Majesty's ship *Centaur* on charges exhibited against him by John Baldwin, Private Marine of the said ship, and, having examined with attention the different witnesses, are of opinion that the charge is totally unfounded; and that there is not the least ground for a court martial.

Given under our hands on board the *Galatea* at English Harbour, Antigua this 2nd day of October 1804.

...

31. *Court Martial of Woodford Simms*

[ADM 1/5368]

Minutes of proceedings of a court martial held on board His Majesty's ship *Salvador del Mundo* in Hamoaze on Tuesday the fifth day of February 1805.

Present

Sir Thomas Graves, K.B., Rear Admiral of the Red and second officer in the command of His Majesty's ships and vessels at Plymouth, President.

John Sutton, Esqr., Rear Admiral of the Blue.

Captains

John Boyle	The Hble. Michael de Courey
John Lawford	The Hble. Alan Hyde Gardner
John Cooke (1)	Graham Moore
Charles John Moore Mansfield	William Bedford
William Prowse	Willoughby Thomas Lake
	Thomas Elphinstone

Robert Liddel
Deputy Judge Advocate

Being all the admirals and captains of post ships according to seniority.

The prisoner was brought into Court, and the evidences and audience admitted.

Read the order of the Right Honourable, the Lords Commissioners of the Admiralty, dated the 27th of January 1805, directed to Sir Thomas Graves, K.B., Rear Admiral of the Red and second officer in the command of His Majesty's ships and vessels at Plymouth to try Woodford Simms, a Seaman late belonging to His Majesty's ship *Doris*, for having made use of insolent and improper language to M^{r}. Maitland, Boatswain, and John Davis, Boatswain's Mate, late of the said ship, also for negligently performing his duty from the 12th to the 15th of January last.

Read the Warrant appointing a judge advocate.

Then the members of the court and judge advocate, in open court and before they proceeded to trial, respectively took the oaths directed by Act of Parliament passed in the twenty second year of the reign of King George the Second.

A letter from Patrick Campbell, Esquire, late Captain of His Majesty's ship *Doris*, to the Honourable Admiral Cornwallis, Commander in Chief, &ca., &ca., &ca., was then read as follows:

Le Tonnant, Jany. 23d, 1805

… I have to request you would be pleased to apply to my Lords Commissioners of the Admiralty to order a court martial on Woodford Simms, (Seaman) late of His Majesty's ship *Doris*, for making use of insolent and improper language to Mr Maitland (Boatswain) and to John Davis (Boatswain's Mate), late of the said ship, also for negligently performing his duty from the 12th to the 15th ins^{t}.

…

All the evidence being then ordered to withdraw and to attend their examinations separately, they all withdrew accordingly, except the first to be sworn, and the court proceeded to trial as follows:

Evidence in support of the charges.

M^{r}. Charles Maitland, late Boatswain of His Majesty's ship *Doris*, sworn and examined as follows:

Prosecutor	State to the court the language the prisoner made use of to you from the time the ship struck until the 15th of January last.
Answer	The first notice I took of him was on or about the 14th of January, being in the galley and then not employed as the rest of the ship's company was. I went on the forecastle and called Woodford Simms; he came. I desired him to turn too, to work with the rest of the forecastle men and, in a few minutes after, I saw him walk along the starboard gangway. M^{r}. Richards, the first Lieuten^{t}., being on the forecastle the same time, I pointed out to him the prisoner being so neglective and inattentive to his duty. M^{r}. Richards desired me to send for him; he came. I asked the prisoner what he was doing and why he did not attend to his duty. Lieut^{t}. Richards asked him what he had got to say for himself; he turned round and said to me, 'I have done my duty as well

as them as complained of me and that's M[r]. Boatswain.' I said, 'Simms you had better keep your tongue within your teeth.' He then stood by the foremast and told me that he had seen a man stand in better shoes than I did at present. I made no answer; then the prisoner went over to the starboard side of the deck and said, 'We all know that you are no great things.' I desired the men to stand round me to take notice what that man said; there was a deal more language which I could not properly hear as I went along with the people and employed them.

Prosecutor Did the prisoner call you a tale carrier and advise you not to carry tales of him or something to that purpose?

Answer Yes, I heard him say that I had been a tale bearer to the captain and first lieutenant.

Prosecutor Did the prisoner appear to you to have been attentive to his duty from the 12th to the 15th of January last or otherwise?

Answer The evening of the 12th he exerted himself extremely well in getting the spritsail over the bows in a boat under the bows which was very near swamped. He was there more than two hours; he was exceeding much so. I do not recollect seeing him the remainder part of that night; next day I took notice of him in different parts of the ship with 3 or 4 men at a time unemployed, who I dispersed. When I went on one side of the deck, he went over to the other in a careless manner. The evening of the 13th my mate came to me in regard of Simms' conduct, the same as what I had seen myself. I went to the prisoner and accused him of being the worse for liquor; he said he was not. At that time he went to the winches with the other people. I do not recollect any other instance of neglect. On the 15th, the prisoner came to me on the forecastle to make an apology; I told him to go about his business.

Court Did the prisoner appear to be drunk on the 13th?

Answer He appeared to be so, but spoke very sensible.

The witness withdrew.

Daniel Ross, a Seaman late of His Majesty's ship *Doris*, sworn and examined as follows:

Prosecutor State to the court the language you heard the prisoner make use of to the boatswain on the 14th of January last.

Answer When the prisoner came up, Lieut.[t] Richards asked him why he did not come when sent for; he said he did. He had not been five minutes off the deck to drink his grog and that he was as attentive to his duty as they that complained of him, which he supposed to be the boatswain, and that he was not more deficient than he, that he had seen as good a man wearing shoes before now.

Prosecutor Did you hear the prisoner tell the boatswain that he was a tale carrier and advise him not to carry tales of him?

Answer No.

Prosecutor Was the language which you have now given in evidence as uttered by the prisoner, spoken to Lieut.^{t} Richards or to the boatswain?

Answer To Lieuten^{t} Richards.

Prisoner After I came on the forecastle as you have stated on the 14th of January, did I remain there or go on the gangway?

Answer I saw him about half an hour before at his duty; after he came up, he remained there as long as I stayed. I was ordered away immediately to another place on duty.

The witness withdrew.

Lieutenant James Richards, late of His Majesty's ship *Doris*, sworn and examined as follows:

Prosecutor Did you hear the prisoner make use of any insolent or improper language to the boatswain on or about the 14th of January last?

Answer When I was employed on the afternoon of that day foddering[1] mats for the [hawser?], the boatswain informed me that the prisoner had not been there all the day. I ordered the boatswain to send for him, which he did, and soon after the prisoner came. An altercation took place between him and the boatswain, which I did not take notice of at first, as I was anxiously employed about the hawser. The first thing that I noticed the prisoner to say was telling the boats^{n} that he did not understand his duty and that he need not be telling tales about him (the prisoner) and many other words I do not recollect. This happened on the larboard side of the forecastle soon after the prisoner went round to the starboard side; and soon after I saw the prisoner going down the after ladder of the quarter deck, when he should have been employed on the forecastle. About three hours after I had seen the prisoner go down the quarter deck ladder, when we

[1]According to the *Oxford English Dictionary*, fodder is an obsolete form of the word fother, which means 'to cover . . . thickly with oakum, rope yarn or other loose material fastened on it with the view of getting some of it sucked into a leak …' [s.v. Fother].

were getting the hawser into the cabin window, I was on the forecastle, when I asked several times if the hawsers were in. The prisoner, then on the larboard gangway, called to me by name and said that one end of the hawsers was in, to the best of my recollection.

Prosecutor Did the prisoner appear to you to have been attentive to his duty or otherwise from the 12th to the 15th of January last?

Answer I saw no marks of attention; indeed I hardly saw anything of him until the circumstance before mentioned happened. He was not employed on the forecastle. The boatswain pointed out to me when the prisoner was going down the hatchway and said there he goes.

Court Did you suppose that was a mark of inattention in the prisoner to his duty?

Answer Undoubtedly.

Court Did you remark the prisoner's manner when speaking to the boatswain, as you have stated, and was it respectful?

Answer His manner was at that time entirely disrespectful.

Court Describe how it was disrespectful.

Answer The tone of his voice and his manner; he never touched his hat to the boats^{n}, as far as I observed.

Court Do you know of any other instance of the prisoner negligently performing his duty, than that you have stated, from the 12th to the 15th of January last?

Answer None other came under my observation.

Prisoner At the time you saw me going down the quarter deck ladder, were any of the people employed pumping at the winches?

Answer I presume they were, for one winch never was still to my knowledge.

The witness withdrew.

John Davis, late Boatswain's Mate of His Majesty's ship *Doris*, sworn and examined as follows:

Prosecutor State to the court the language the prisoner made use of to you respecting the charge between the 12th and 15th of January last.

Answer On the 14th when they served the forenoon's grog, every man was called by name to get his grog. I was waiting there with the rest; the prisoner said to me, 'Mr Davis, you complained of me.' I said, 'I have. I thought it proper to do so.' 'This is no time,' I said, 'to quarrel with anybody.' He had been quarrelling. 'You,' said the prisoner, 'are not as

	good as a barber's boy and you was the instigation of getting me punished.' I told him to hold his tongue; if he did not I would take him before Captain Campbell. 'Well,' says he, 'never mind; will you drink with us?' I said no. I had my pint of grog the same as he had. I did not want anymore.
Prosecutor	Did the prisoner make use of any other expressions or did he continue long abusing you?
Answer	I went away as soon as he asked me to drink.
Prosecutor	Was the prisoner attentive to his duty from the 12th to the 15th of January last as far as came within your observation?
Answer	He did not exert himself as he ought to have done.
Court	Relate any instance of neglect of duty in the prisoner within those days.
Answer	On the 13th and 14th, he did not come to the pumps when called to his spell readily; he shuffled about.
Prisoner	Did I go to the pump directly after I asked you to take some grog?
Answer	I do not know.

The witness withdrew.

The evidence in support of the charge being finished, the prisoner was called upon to make his defence, who said that he had nothing to offer but evidence, which he begged might be examined in his behalf, whereupon:

Lieutenant Henry Jones, late of His Majesty's ship *Doris*, was sworn and examined as follows:

Prisoner	Did I always answer my musters at the pumps within the time of the charge?
Answer	Always, he frequently worked his spells; he was not ever missing when I was there.
Court	What was the prisoner's general conduct during the time of the charge?
Answer	Very good as far as came within my knowledge.
Court	Were the forecastle men employed generally at the pumps?
Answer	Yes.

The witness withdrew.

The prisoner not having anything further to offer in his defence, the court was cleared and proceeded to deliberate upon and form the sentence.

The court, having heard the evidence in support of the charges, as well as the evidence adduced on the prisoner's behalf, he not having any other thing to offer in his defence, and very maturely and deliberately weighed and considered the same, was of opinion that the charges had been proved against the prisoner, Woodford Simms, and did in consequence thereof adjudge the said Woodford Simms to receive two hundred lashes with a cat of nine tails on his bare back alongside such of His Majesty's ships at such times and in such proportions as the commander in chief of His Majesty's ships and vessels at this port shall direct.

The court was opened, the prisoner brought in, the evidence and audience admitted, and the sentenced passed accordingly. …

32. *Court Martial of Captain Patrick Campbell, the officers and crew of the* Doris

[ADM 1/5368]

Minutes of proceedings at a court martial held on board His Majesty's ship *Salvador del Mundo* in Hamoaze on Wednesday the sixth day of February 1805.

Present

Sir Thomas Graves, K.B., Rear Admiral of the Red and second officer in the command of His Majesty's ships and vessels at Plymouth, President
John Sutton, Esq[r]., Rear Admiral of the Blue.

Captains

John Boyle	The Hble. Michael de Courcey
John Lawford	The Hble. Adam Hyde Gardner
John Cooke (1)	Graham Moore
Charles John Moore Mansfield	William Bedford
William Prowse	Willoughby Thomas Lake
	Thomas Baker

Robert Liddel
Deputy Judge Advocate

Being all the admirals and captains of post ships according to seniority, except Thomas Elphinstone, Esq[r]., Captain of His Majesty's ship *Diamond*, who is, by illness of body, prevented attending the court.

The prisoners were brought into court and the evidence and audience admitted.

The surgeon of His Majesty's ship *Diamond* appeared before the court and reported that Thomas Elphinstone, Esq[r]., Captain of the said ship, was afflicted with fever and that he could not attend the court without materially endangering his health and declared that he was ready if required to make oath to the truth of such report; whereupon the court thought proper to dispense with the attendance of the said Captain Elphinstone.

Read the order of the Right Honourable the Lords Commissioners of the Admiralty, dated the 28th of January 1805, directed to Sir Thomas Graves, K.B., Rear Admiral of the Red and second officer in the command of His Majesty's ships and vessels at Plymouth, to examine into the cause and circumstances of the loss of His Majesty's ship *Doris* and to try Captain Patrick Campbell, late Commander of the said ship, his officers and ship's company for their conduct on the occasion of her loss.

Read the warrant appointing a judge advocate.

Then the members of the court and judge advocate, in open court and before they proceeded to trial, respectively took the oaths directed by Act of Parliament passed in the twenty second year of the reign of King George the Second.

Captain Campbell's narrative of the circumstances of the loss of His Majesty's ship *Doris*, in a letter addressed to Sir Thomas Graves, K.B., &c[a]., &c[a]., &c[a]., was then read as follows:

Le Tonnant, Quiberon Bay, 19th January 1805

… It is with the greatest regret I acquaint you of the loss of His Majesty's ship *Doris*, late under my command, by striking on a sunken rock going thro' the Benequet Passage into Quiberon Bay at 6 p.m. on Saturday the 12th instant. After having reconnoitred the squadron of the enemy under Isle D'Aix on the 9th instant as I was proceeding to give you information of its state, I fell in with the *Felix* schooner; from her I learnt that you was in Quiberon Bay. I immediately made the best of my way for that anchorage and did not ascertain your having sailed until my arrival there on Friday night the 11th; owing to the thick weather and the wind at SE, it was too late to work out. In the morning we weighed and off Belle Isle spoke [to] an American, who informed me he had been boarded by one of the squadron the day before and had seen it at five that morning 7 or 8 leagues to the S.W. of Belle Isle. In the evening, the wind veered to the southward and began to blow with every appearance of bad weather. Judging (from your nearness to the land) you would swim if it proved unfavourable and, not being able to weather Belle Isle or the Cardinals, induced me to bear up to gain an anchorage; and, just as the pilot had assured me the ship was in safety, she struck, but so lightly that I had no idea of her having received any material injury. On sounding the well, found she made water fast and before we could anchor it had increased to four feet and continued gaining on us to 1½, though the people were instantly sent to the pumps. The guns, shot, spare anchors and everything heavy that could be got at thrown overboard, as well as having thrum'd sails under her bottom. At 3 a.m. Sunday, by the unremitting exertions of the people at the pumps & bailing, we began to gain on the leaks and by 8 got her clear, but it required both chain pumps to keep her so. At noon it began to blow extremely hard from the southw^{d}. The ship, driving, let go the other bower and veered to two cables. Soon after, the *Felix* schooner arrived and informed me by signal of the French squadron having put to sea from Rochfort on the 11th instant; at this time it was blowing a heavy gale. At night it moderated and continued so during the whole of next day, during which time we had succeeded in nearly stopping the leaks so that one pump forward and one aft kept her free. Being extremely anxious you should receive the earliest information of the squadron's sailing and having reason to believe the enemy were apprised of our distressed situation, as also, the fullest confidence in the ship's being able to reach England, at ½ past 5 p.m. I put to sea with a gentle breeze from the southward and every appearance of fine weather, intending if the leaks did not increase during the night to send the schooner in quest of you. At 12, it began to freshen, but no appearance of the leaks increasing. At ½ past 1 a.m., fresh gales with heavy squalls, close reefed the topsails; at 2, handed the fore and mizzen; at 3 wore to regain the bay, a heavy sea running; the ship laboured much; the leaks began rapidly to increase and the pumps in the coalhole were continually choking. The scuttles that had been made to let the water from the magazine to the pumps being stopped, the deck was scuttled and we began bailing, the leak still gaining fast. At 5, the magazine became full, the water forcing its way aft thro' the passages in alarming quantities; at ½ past 5 more moderate, but still a heavy sea running; set the fore and mizzen topsails, let three reefs out and made all sail possible for Quiberon Bay; ½ past 6 in a squall, the wind flew to the NW by W; soon after saw Hadie bearing NW by N, 5 or 6 leagues. The ship at this time was settling fast by the head and had nearly lost her steerage; finding it impossible to weather the force and the carpenter giving it as his opinion that the ship could not be kept longer above the water and my officers concurring in the same, I gave over all hopes of being able to save His Majesty's ship and was under the painful necessity a little after 9 of bearing up for an American schooner for the purpose of saving the people, who were worn down and exhausted with fatigue. The leaks still gaining rapidly notwithstanding every exertion to keep them under, at ½ past 9 came to with both bowers in 15 fathoms water, Croisic bearing N.E. 7 or 8 miles. Hoisted out the boats and began sending the people on board the *Felix* and American, but, owing to the heavy swell, could not get them all out of the ship before ½ past noon. At 3, the water being nearly up to the lower deck, I set her on fire and quitted;

soon after she blew up. I cannot conclude this painful subject without expressing how sensibly I feel the exertions of all my officers and ship's company which must ever reflect on them the highest credit …

The court then proceeded to trial as follows: Partick Campbell, Esqr., late Captain of His Majesty's ship *Doris*, sworn and examined as follows:

Court Is the narrative just read to the court a true statement of the circumstances of the loss of His Majesty's late ship *Doris*?

Answer It is as far as I can recollect.

Court Have you any complaint to make of any of the officers or company of the said ship on that occasion or any instances of neglect or disobedience to orders on that occasion to notice in any of your officers or ship's company?

Answer None, but what has been already taken notice of, unless any question may attach to the conduct of the pilot on that occasion.

Court To the officers and ship's company of the *Doris*.
Have you, or any of you, anything to object to the narrative you have heard or anything to lay to the charge of any officer or man for neglect or disobedience on the occasion of the loss of His Majesty's ship *Doris*?

Answer The first lieutenant, master and the officers generally answered that they had not any, that Captain Campbell's utmost exertions were used with those of every other officer and man (except as before excepted) for the preservation of His Majesty's late ship *Doris*.

The ship's company declared they had not any complaint to make of either officer or company.

All the officers and ship's company late of the *Doris*, except Captain Campbell, were then ordered to withdraw; they withdrew accordingly.

M^{r}. James Mayn, late Master of His Majesty's ship *Doris*, sworn and examined as follows:

The log book of His Majesty's ship *Doris* produced to the court.

Court Are the minutes of the log book of His Majesty's late ship *Doris* now before the court true minutes?

Answer They are to the best of my recollection.

Court When did you meet with the American schooner?

Answer On the 15th and the Danish brig on the same day.

Court Did you remove the company of the *Doris* into the Dane at the same time that you removed them into the American?

Answer No, we removed them from the American to the Dane.

Court Where was the *Doris* when you bore up for Quiberon Bay?

Answer The S.W. end of Belle Isle bore S.W. about 3 or 4 miles; it was on the 12th.

Court What day was it you had reconnoitred the French fleet?

Answer On the 9th.

Court Was the vessel that is stated in the narrative to have given you intelligence that which was used in saving the people?

Answer No.

Court What was the appearance of the weather on the evening you bore up to anchor in Quiberon Bay before the accident?

Answer It had every appearance that it would blow hard.

Court Had you any reason to suppose the *Doris* to be in danger before she struck on the sunken rock by which she was lost?

Answer I had not; I did not know of that rock.

Court Was it in your opinion necessary to quit the *Doris* at the time she was quitted and was every exertion used for her preservation?

Answer It was necessary to quit her when that measure was adopted and every exertion had been previously used for her preservation.

Captain Campbell
How soon after we came to anchor, after the ship had struck, did it begin to blow?

Answer In about two hours and half, to the best of my knowledge.

Captain Campbell
How did it then blow?

Answer S.W. by S. fresh and increasing in strength gradually, thick and dirty weather.

Captain Campbell
In whose charge did you consider the ship when going through the Benequet?

Answer In the pilot's charge.

Captain Campbell
When we bore up that evening for the passage, did the pilot take charge of her for the purpose of carrying her through that passage readily or not?

Answer He did readily.

Captain Campbell
Was every attention paid to the wishes and directions of the pilot on that occasion?

Answer There was.

Captain Campbell
Before the ship struck, did you hear the pilot assure me that the ship was thro' the passage and in safely?

Answer I did.

Captain Campbell
How soon after such assurance did the ship strike?

Answer Not above a minute, or a minute and half at the farthest. Captain Campbell, before he left the forecastle, asked the pilot whether she was clear; the pilot said she was clear. Captain Campbell went aft and in my opinion he could not have got on the quarter deck before the ship struck.

Witness withdrew.

Jean Legal, Pilot of His Majesty's late ship *Doris*, sworn and examined as follows:

Court Did you acquaint Captain Campbell at the time the ship was going thro' the Benequet passage and supposed by you to be in safety that the ship was clear and out of danger?

Answer Captain Campbell and the master was upon the forecastle; he asked me, 'Pilot is you think the ship is clear?' I says, 'I think she is clear;' after that, 2 or 3 minutes, the ship struck; one foot would have cleared the rock.

Court Was the ship close to the wind when she struck?

Answer Yes.

Court Was the light sufficient for you to see the marks for the passage?

Answer No. I could not see the Point le Marie of Belle Isle, nor the Petit Mont on the main land.

Court Under those circumstances, is it justifiable in a pilot to take charge of King's ship [*sic*] in so narrow and difficult a passage as the Benequet?

Answer The ship being close to the land and the weather appearing so bad that the captain wanted to get to an anchorage and there was no other way of getting into safety at that time, but by that passage.

Court Do you mean to say that there was greater danger in staying out that night than in venturing thro' that passage?

Answer Yes.

Court How was the tide at that time?

Answer I suppose two hours flood.

Witness withdrew.

Lieutenant James Richards, late of His Majesty's ship *Doris*, sworn and examined as follows:

Court Was it light enough for the pilot to see the danger in the Benequet passage in order to avoid it, when he undertook to take the *Doris* thro' on the evening on which she struck?

Answer It was light enough to see the rocks above water which we passed.

Court Had the pilot taken the *Doris* thro' that passage in which she struck before?

Answer Yes.

Court Was he esteemed a person to be trusted as a pilot on such an occasion?

Answer I presume he was, for he carried the *Doris* thro' the first time when no officer on board had any knowledge of that passage.

Court When Captain Campbell proposed to the pilot to carry the *Doris* thro' the Benequet passage on the night in which she struck, did he discover any reluctance to do so?

Answer None in the least.

Court From the appearance of the weather, did it appear to you that there was greater danger in keeping the sea than in attempting the Passage Benequet at the time she bore up?

Answer It looked dirty and likely to blow, and we could not weather Belle Isle or the Cardinals. In tacking under Belle Isle once on that evening, a battery fired at us.

Court Was it, in your opinion, necessary to quit His Majesty's late ship at the time she was quitted and was every exertion used for her preservation?

Answer Every exertion was used for her preservation. And, it was so necessary to quit her that I did not think she would swim till the people could be got out.

Captain Campbell

Did you hear me express great anxiety to acquaint Sir Thomas Graves of the French squadron having put to sea?

Answer Yes, several times, particularly on the night we put to sea from Quiberon after having stopped the leaks. Captain Campbell informed me about eleven o'clock that night that if the ship should continue in her then state, that he would in the morning, should the weather prove favourable, dispatch the schooner in quest of Sir Thomas Graves without the least hesitation. And, after having quitted the ship, on board the schooner he told me he would go off the Isle Dieu and cruise there as long as water and provisions would last, and that he would go on a pint of water a day each and called the people up and acquainted them with it, stating his reasons for so doing to which they cheerfully submitted. And, they were put to allowance accordingly; and we were proceeding for Isle Dieu when we met Sir Thomas Graves.

The witness withdrew.

Captain Campbell not having anything further to offer, the court was cleared and proceeded to deliberate upon and form the sentence.

The court, having heard Captain Campbell's narrative of circumstances and examined the officers and ship's company of the *Doris* and very maturely and deliberately weighed and considered the same narrative and evidence, was of opinion that no blame whatever is imputable to Captain Patrick Campbell, his officers or ship's company on account of the loss of His Majesty's late ship *Doris*.

And it appeared to the court that the exertions of Captain Campbell, his officers and ship's company after the accident, in attempting to bring the ship to England and in communicating the intelligence of the movements of the enemy to Sir Thomas Graves, were highly meritorious.

And further that His Majesty's said ship was lost through the ignorance or unskillfulness of Mr. Jean Legal, her pilot. And did in consequence thereof adjudge the said Captain Patrick Campbell, his officers and ship's company (except Woodford Simms, who was yesterday tried by court martial) to be acquitted.

And did adjudge the said Mr Jean Legal, late Pilot of the said ship, to be reprimanded for his conduct on the occasion.

The court was opened, the prisoner brought in, the pilot put into custody before the court, the evidence and audience admitted and sentence passed accordingly.

…

33. *Court Martial of George Marshall*

[ADM 1/5369]

Minutes of proceedings at a court martial assembled and held on board His Majesty's ship *Saint George* in Port Royal Harbour, Jamaica on Monday the 27th of May 1805.

Present

The Honble Michl de Courcy, Captain of His Majesty's ship St *George* and senior captain of His Majesty's ships and vessels in Port Royal Harbour, Jamaica, President.

Captains

Honble F. F. Gardner
John Bligh
Barrington Dacres
Henry Whitby
James Newman Newman
David Colby
Samuel Pym

Being all the captains of post ships in Port Royal Harbour, Jamaica, except Captain Gordon of His Majesty's ship *Diligent*, whose surgeon appeared in court and stated that the captain was so ill as not to be able to attend the court.

Read the order of James Richard Dacres, Esqr., Rear Admiral of the Red, Commander in Chief, &^{c}, &^{c}, dated the 24th day of May 1805 and directed to the Honble. Mich^{l}. de Courcy, Captain of His Majesty's ship *Saint George* and senior captain of His Majesty's ships and vessels in Port Royal Harbour, Jamaica to try Lieutenant George Marshall, first Lieutenant of Marines of His Majesty's ship *Princess Charlotte*, for using reproachful and provoking speeches to M^{r}. Joseph Knight, Purser of the said ship, tending to make a quarrel and disturbance in the ship.

For behaving in a scandalous and infamous manner, unbecoming the character of an officer and a gentleman.

Then the members of the court and judge advocate, in open court and before they proceeded to trial, respectively took the oath enjoined them by Act of Parliament.

A letter from Mr. Joseph Knight, Purser of H.M. ship *Princess Charlotte*, to the Honble. Captain Gardner, requesting his application to the commander in chief for a court martial to be held for the trial [of?] Lieutenant George Marshall, 1st Lieutenant of Marines of the said ship, was read as follows, viz.:

Princess Charlotte, Port Royal
12th May 1805

… I beg leave to inform you I was yesterday afternoon most grossly insulted by Lieutenant George Marshall, 1st Lieutenant of Marines of H.M. ship under your command, by snapping his fingers in my face and calling me before the officers and ship's company a kiss my arse fellow, that I would kiss any man's arse for a six pence, and that there were four in the mess against me and he would be damned if I did not march.

I have, therefore, to request you will be pleased, as soon as opportunity offers, to apply for a court martial upon him upon the following charges:

23 For using reproachful and provoking speeches tending to make a quarrel and disturbance in the ship,

33 For behaving in a scandalous and infamous manner, unbecoming the character of an officer and a gentleman.

…

All the witnesses were then ordered out of court, except Lieutenant Dorbresay of the Marines, who was sworn.

Mr Knight, Prosecutor. Did you hear the prisoner ask me on the quarter deck on the 11th of May last if I meant to turn Lieutenant Hawkes out of the ship?

Ansr. I do not recollect.

Quest. Do you recollect seeing the prisoner snap his fingers in my face, saying I was a kiss my arse fellow and that I would kiss any man's arse for a six pence?

Ansr. No.

Quest. Did you hear the prisoner say there were four in the mess against me and that he would be damned if I did not march?

Ansr. I do not recollect.

Cross questioned by the prisoner.

Prisoner During the time you have known me, did you ever know me to behave to the prosecutor or any other officer in the ship in a scandalous, infamous manner, unbecoming the character of an officer and gentleman?

Ansr. Never.

No further questions asked this witness; he withdrew and Mr Landergen, the Gunner, called and sworn.

Prosecutor Did you hear the prisoner ask me on the 11th of May last on the quarter deck if I meant to turn Lieutenant Hawkes out of the ship?

Ansr. I did not.

Quest. Did you see him snap his fingers in my face and say I was a kiss my arse fellow and would kiss any man's arse for a six pence?

Ansr. I did not see him snap his fingers in your face, but saw him hold his fingers up and say you was a kiss my arse fellow and would kiss any man's arse for a six pence.

Prosecutor Did you hear him tell me that there were four in the mess against me and he would be damned if I did not march?

Ansr. I heard him tell you that there are four of us against you, but the words 'mess' or 'march' I never heard.

Quest. Did you hear me tell him that I should take proper notice of such conduct?

Ansr. I did not, having gone out of the way after I heard there are four against you.

Court When you heard the prisoner say there [are?] four against you, did you understand he meant there were four of different sentiments against Mr Knight?

Ansr. I cannot say what he meant.

Quest. What officers were on the quarter deck at the time the altercation took place?

Ans^{r}. I did not observe any officer on the quarter deck, but the prisoner and Mr Knight & Mr Warner. Mr Cameron and Mr Waldren went forward along the gangway and I followed them.

Nothing further asked this witness and Mr Camplin, the Captain's Clerk, called and sworn.

Prosecutor Did you hear the prisoner ask me on the 11th of May last on the quarter deck if I meant to turn Lieutenant Hawkes out of the ship?

Ans^{r}. No.

Quest. Did you see him snap his fingers in my face and say I was a kiss my arse fellow and would kiss any man's arse for a six pence?

Ans^{r}. I did not see him snap his fingers in your face, but I heard him say you would kiss any man's arse for six pence.

Quest Did you hear him tell me that there were four in the mess against me and he would be damned if I did not march?

Ans^{r}. I did not.

Court Were the officers and ship's company present at the time?

Ans^{r}. There were several officers on the quarter deck, but do not recollect any of the ship's company; there were several seamen on the gangways.

Court You have said you did not hear the prisoner say he would be damned if the prosecutor did not march. If he had said so, was you near enough to have heard him?

Ans^{r}. I was not.

Court What are the names of the officers that were on the quarter deck?

Ans^{r}. Lieutenant Hawkes, Lieutenant Dorbresay (Marines), M^{r}. Cuthbertson (Surgeon), M^{r}. Henderson, Mr Lambert, and M^{r}. Waldren.

Quest Were these officers near enough to have heard any conversation between the prisoner and M^{r}. Knight?

Ans^{r}. They were.

This witness was asked nothing further and Mr. Henderson, Master's Mate, called and sworn.

Prosecutor Did you hear the prisoner ask me on the quarter deck on the 11th of May last if I meant to turn Lieutenant Hawkes out of the ship?

Ans^{r}. No.

Quest Did you see him snap his fingers in my face and say I was a kiss my arse fellow and would kiss any man's arse for six pence?

Ans[r]. I saw him hold his hand up and say, 'By God, Knight, you would kiss any man's arse for six pence.'

Quest Did you hear him say there were four in the mess against me and he would be damned if I did not march?

Ans[r]. No.

Quest Did you hear me say to him that I would take proper notice of his conduct?

Ans[r]. No.

Court What occurred previous to the expression made use of by the prisoner?

Ans[r]. I was coming from under the half deck to go into one of the boats that were alongside and heard the prisoner make use of those words, but heard nothing pass before.

Quest When M[r]. Marshall lifted his hand as you have already mentioned, did you suppose he snapped his fingers at the time?

Ans[r]. No.

Court Did it appear to you there were any degree of warmth at the time between the prisoner and M[r]. Knight?

Ans[r]. Yes it did.

Court Were there many or any officers or ship's company at the time on the quarter deck and what were the officers' names?

Ans[r]. I do not recollect as I went immediately to the boat.

No other questions asked and M[r]. Waldren (Midshipman) called and sworn.

Prosecutor Did you hear the prisoner ask me on the quarter deck on the eleventh of May last if I meant to turn Lieutenant Hawkes out of the ship?

Ans[r]. No.

Quest Did you see the prisoner snap his fingers in my face and say I was a kiss my arse fellow and would kiss any man's arse for six pence?

Ans[r]. Yes, I did.

Quest Did you hear him say there were four in the mess against me and he would be damned if I did not march?

Ans[r]. I did not, but I heard him say there were four.

Court What conversation took place between the

prisoner and Mr. Knight prior to the prisoner making use of those words?

Ansr. I cannot say; I had just come on the quarter deck.

Court When you heard the prisoner make use of the words, did you see him snap his fingers in his face and was there a great deal of warmth at the time between them?

Ansr. I did see him snap his fingers at the time, but it did not appear to me to have been any warmth at the time.

Quest What distance were they from one or other?

Ansr. I believe about five or six feet.

Quest Were any of the officers and ship's company on the quarter deck at the time?

Ansr. There were Mr. Trenholm (the first Lieutenant), Lieutenant Hawkes, Mr. Cuthbertson (Surgeon), Lieutenant. Dorbresay of the Marines, Mr. Camplin, Captain's Clerk, Mr. Henderson, Master's Mate, and Mr. Lambert, Midshipman. I cannot say if any of the ship's company were on the quarter deck, except a quarter master and signal man; there were several of the ship's company on the gangways.

Court Did Mr. Knight put any question or say anything to the prisoner?

Ansr. To the best of my judgement, he did not; I was on the quarter deck two minutes.

Court Did you at any time hear Mr. Knight say that Mr. Hawkes ought to be hung and the prisoner transported?

Ansr. I heard something about transportation, but I do not know who was meant by it.

Quest. Did Mr. Knight use that expression previous to the prisoners making use of the words 'you are a kiss my arse fellow?'

Ansr. Yes.

This witness withdrew, no further questions being asked him.

The evidence on the part of the prosecution was then closed and the prisoner called upon to make his defence, which he read in the following words, viz.:

...

Having ten years been honoured with a commission in His Majesty's service, and employed under many distinguished officers, to whom my conduct has afforded ample satisfaction not only in the discharge of my public duties, but also in the character of a gentleman, I cannot easily express how painfully

I feel and keenly I regret the cause that now compels me to address you.

Conscious of the attention that has been paid by this honourable court to the charges exhibited against me, as well as to the evidence adduced, it will not, I trust, be necessary for me to trouble the court with many remarks; some observations I must beg leave to offer, namely the motive of the present prosecution, which, I trust, will appear malignant, personal and originating in no view to promote the welfare of the service.

In extenuation of the expressions made use of to the prosecutor, permit me to advert to the enormity of the insult received, which I trust you will consider sufficient to excite the indignation and provoke the resentment of any person who has the honour to bear His Majesty's commission. Let me be further allowed that the tenor of my conduct towards the prosecutor, so far from being inimical, has been marked by a disposition to amity and good will, and that the present expression forming the charge on which I have been tried was in a particular degree extorted from me by the warm, offensive and petulant manner in which I was addressed by the prosecutor and which provoked me in that moment to concur in the coarse terms of reproach his own expressions furnished. How far my conduct has been reprehensible, I now with all humility submit to the decisions of this honble. court, feeling a full assurance that while they maturely deliberate upon the nature of the offence alleged, they will not decline taking into consideration the provocation that gave rise to it.

...

The prisoner requested his witnesses might be examined; M^r^. Cuthbertson, the Surgeon of the *Princess Charlotte*, called and sworn.

Prisoner Relate to the court the language made use of by M^r^. Knight to me, respecting Lieutenant Hawkes and myself on the eleventh of May last.

Ans^r^. I heard M^r^. Marshall mention to M^r^. Knight that he behaved in a very ungrateful manner; M^r^. Knight replied and said that M^r^. Marshall behaved in a mean, ungentlemanlike manner and that M^r^. Hawkes ought to be hung and M^r^. Marshall transported if they had their deserts; M^r^. Marshall then told him he must answer for his conduct to M^r^. Hawkes when he came on board. M^r^. Knight then went down below. They came up again after dinner. M^r^. Marshall said some words which I did not hear; then M^r^. Knight said, 'Do you suppose I would kiss any man's arse?'

Quest. Do you think that the expressions I am charged with by the prosecutor were extorted from me?
Ans[r]. It is my opinion they were extorted from you by the prosecutor making use of such language.
Quest. Do you think the opprobrious language made use of to me by the prosecutor the sole and immediate cause of the quarrel and disturbance complained of by him?
Ans[r]. I cannot say.
Court The prosecutor having charged the prisoner with making use of reproachful speeches to him tending to make a quarrel and disturbance in the ship, do you attribute that conduct to the prisoner?
Ans[r]. I think the language M[r]. Knight made use of provoked M[r]. Marshall to say what he did afterwards.
Court Did you observe M[r]. Marshall snap his fingers in M[r]. Knight's face?
Ans[r]. I did not.
Prisoner Since you have known me, did you ever find me deviate from the strict principles of an officer and gentleman?
Ans[r]. In my opinion, I never did.
No further questions asked, and Lieut[t]. Hawkes called and sworn.
Prisoner Relate to the court the expressions made use of by the prosecution to me on the eleventh of May last.
Ans[r]. They were, 'Do you suppose I would kiss any man's arse for six pence?' You answered, 'Yes, I am damned if I do not.'
Quest. Did the prosecutor appear to you to extort the expression from me for the purpose of taking an advantage?
Ans[r]. Yes.
Quest. Did you ever since you have known me, find me deviate from the strict principles of an officer and gentleman?
Ans[r]. Never.
Court Did you observe the prisoner snap his fingers in M[r]. Knight's face?
Ans[r]. No.
Quest. What was the occasion of the prosecutor's making use of that expression?
Ans[r]. I do not know, not being present.
Prisoner Did I immediately on your return from the dockyard tell you of M[r]. Knight's language respecting yourself and me, that you ought to be hung and myself transported and that we

deserved every appellation but that of gentlemen or words to that effect?

Ans[r]. Yes, you did.

No further questions asked this witness, he withdrew. The prisoner requested Captain Gardner might speak to his character.

Captain Gardner said, 'Mr Marshall has been with me about nine months, during which time I always found him a very good officer and obedient to all duties and orders.'

The prisoner having nothing further to offer in his defence, the court was cleared to deliberate upon and form the sentence.

…

… and having heard the evidence on the part of the prosecution as well as what the prisoner had to offer in his defence and very maturely and deliberately weighed and considered the same, is of opinion the words 'You are a kiss my arse fellow' are proved to have been made use of by the prisoner. Yet, as it appears that the expression was extorted by words which the prosecutor previously used, they do acquit the prisoner of any intention to excite a quarrel or disturbance in the ship and behaving in a scandalous and infamous manner unbecoming the character of an officer and gentleman and he is hereby acquitted accordingly. At the same time, the court cannot but bewail that His Majesty's quarter deck should have been made the scene of any altercation.

…

34. *Court Martial of Michael Raven*

[ADM 1/5406]

Minutes of proceedings at a court martial held on board His Majesty's ship *Dannemark* in Basseterre Roads, Guadeloupe, Saturday, the 9th day of June 1810.

Present

James Bissett, Esq., Captain of His Majesty's ship *Dannemark* and second officer in command of His Majesty's ships and vessels at Guadeloupe, President.

Captains

Joshua Rowley Watson	Norborne Thompson
Edward Scobell	Colin Campbell

William Balhetchet officiating as Judge Advocate

The court was opened, the prisoner brought in, the evidence and audience admitted.

Read the order of the Honble. Sir Alexander Cochrane, KB, Vice Admiral of the Blue, Commander in Chief of His Majesty's ships and vessels at Barbados, the Leeward Islands &c, &c, &c, dated the 1st day of June 1810, and directed to James Bissett, Esq., Captain of His Majesty's ship *Dannemark* and second officer in command of His Majesty's ships and vessels at Barbados, to assemble a court martial and try Lieu[t] Michael Raven of His Majesty's ship *Castor* for sleeping on his watch.

Read the warrant appointing a judge advocate.

Then, the members and judge advocate, in open court and before they proceeded to trial, respectively took the oaths directed by an Act passed in the 22nd year of the reign of King George the Second.

The following letter from Captain Roberts[1] was then read:

His Majesty's ship *Castor*,
off Guadeloupe, April 16, 1810

… I have the honour to request you will be pleased to direct a court martial to be held on Lieutenant Michael Raven, His Majesty's ship *Castor* under my command, for sleeping in his watch. …

The court was then cleared to deliberate whether, on the foregoing letter, it could proceed to trial and was of opinion that in consequence of the 2nd Article of the 2nd Chapter, Section 12, under the head of 'Courts Martial,' in the General Printed Instructions, the court was not authorized to proceed to trial, as it is there directed that 'All representations or complaints, intended as the foundation of a court martial, are to be made in writing, setting forth the particular facts, when and where and in what manner the same were committed.'

The court was again opened, the prisoner brought in, evidence and audience admitted, the opinion of the court (signed by the members and judge advocate) read and the prisoner remanded to the custody of an officer of the *Castor* appointed to receive him. The President then dissolved the court.

…

[1]Roberts's letter is to Admiral Sir Alexander Cochrane, Commander in Chief of the Leeward Islands Station.

35. *Court Martial of John Bathie*

[ADM 1/5419]

Minutes of proceedings at a court martial held on board His Majesty's ship *Salvador del Mundo* in Hamoaze on Tuesday the 1st day of October 1811.

Present

Thomas Alexander, Esqr. Captain of His Majesty's ship *Colossus* and second officer in the command of His Majesty's ships and vessels at Plymouth, President.

Captains

Sir Michael Seymour, Bart.	James Brisbane
George Mc Kinley	James Nash
Francis Holmes Coffin	Clotworthy Upton
William Ferris	Andrew King

George Eastlake, Junr. officiating Judge Advocate

Being all the captains of post ships then and there present, next in seniority to the president, except Captains Anselm John Griffiths and Charles Malcolm, who were absent on Admiralty leave.

The prisoner John Bathie, Coxwain of His Majesty's ship *Rhin*, was brought into court and the witnesses and audience admitted.

Read – The order of the Right Honble the Lords Commissioners of the Admiralty, dated the 21st day of February 1811, directed to the President to try the said John Bathie for his conduct on the occasion of the escape of the commander and two other persons belonging to the *Brocanture*, French letter of marque prize to the *Rhin*, in a boat belonging to the *Merope* on her arrival in Plymouth Sound on the 5th of the said month.

Read – The warrant appointing a judge advocate.

Then the members of the court and judge advocate, in open court and before they proceeded to trial, respectively took the oaths directed by Act of Parliament passed in the twenty second year of the reign of King George the Second.

Read – The annexed report from R^r^. Admiral Sir Edward Buller, K^t^., and Captains Richardson and Scobell to Admiral Sir Robert Calder, Bart, Commander in Chief at Plymouth.

All the witnesses, except the first to be sworn, being then ordered to withdraw and to attend their examinations separately, they all withdrew accordingly and the court proceeded to trial as follows:

Evidence in support of the charge.

Mr. William Netherwood, Master's Mate of His Majesty's ship *Rhin*, sworn and examined as follows:

Cot. State to the court everything you know respecting the charge against the prisoner.

A The *Brocanture* came to an anchor between the island and the main about half past 6 in the evening on the 4th of February last. I was ordered by Lieut. Hopkins, the Prize Master, to go on board the *Merope* brig and request her commanding officer to lend a boat to assist in mooring the *Brocanture* prize to the *Rhin*. The request was complied with and the boat sent manned and with a master's mate in her I directly informed Lieut. Hopkins that I had got the boat. He desired me immediately to get the boat forward, and run the hedge out, which I complied with. When it was done, I requested the master's mate of the *Merope* to allow the boat's crew to go up and assist our men in furling the sails, which was complied with in a short time. I heard the master's mate call down the men to man the boat. I then, being forward, seeing the service on the cable, heard the prisoner called for by some person abaft; the prisoner went aft to Lieut. Hopkins. The boat at this time was manned; in a short time after, I was called aft by Lieut. Hopkins, who asked me if I had seen anything of the ship's papers or the tin canister they came on board in. I told him they were over the ledge in his cabin, where he found them. He immediately took the canister down and said he believed there was something gone out of it and took the whole of the papers out and found a letter missing addressed to Lord Gambier. He immediately sent for the first and second French captain, supposing they might have taken them out at the time three privateers were in chase of us, nobody having been then present but the French prisoners. On being sent for, they could not be found and we directly made a search both on deck and below, but to no purpose. The prisoner was sent on shore in the *Merope*'s boat by order of Mr. Hopkins about half past 6 with a letter to Mrs. Malcolm and he was to return again in the morning. I did not see the boat shove off.

Cot. What was the last time you saw the prisoner?

A. About a quarter of an hour before Lieut. Hopkins sent for me.

Cot. Were there any other boats alongside?

A. None, but the pilot's boat. She left the *Brocanture* about half past 10; the prisoners were missed before.

Cot. Do you know whether the prisoner did aid or assist in the escape of the French prisoners?

A. I have reason to think not from his actions on the passage; he has sent for me several times, saying he was afraid the prisoners intended rising by their actions. The prisoner has requested me to desire M^{r}. Hopkins to let fire arms be kept under the man's care at the helm.

Co^{t}. Have you any reason to believe that M^{r}. Hopkins gave leave to the French prisoners?

A. No.

Co^{t}. Do you know that the prisoner was placed in his situation of coxswain from his good character?

A. Yes, I believe so; I know him to be a man of good character.

Co^{t}. Did the boat return?

A. Yes and stopped two hours.

Co^{t}. Did you see the prisoner hold any conversation with the French prisoners from your anchoring to the time the *Merope*'s boats left the prize?

A. I did not.

Co^{t}. Was it possible for a shore boat to have come under the stern and taken the prisoners away?

A. I think it is possible from the confusion on board.

Co^{t}. Was the construction of the *Merope*'s boat such as to enable the Frenchmen to have been hidden forward when the prisoner sitting in the stern might not have seen them from the darkness of the night?

A. She was a large boat; I think they might.

Co^{t}. When you came to an anchor, were any people placed on the lookout to see if anyone came alongside?

A. There were not, until the prisoners were missing.

The witness withdrew

Robert Row, Seaman belonging to His Majesty's ship *Rhin*, sworn and examined as follows:

Co^{t}. Relate what you know respecting the charge against the prisoner and did he aid and assist the escape of the French prisoners from the *Brocanture* prize on or about the 4th of February last?

A. I don't know. I was assisting to furl the sails. The prisoner was on deck.

The witness withdrew

John Cheater, Seaman belonging to His Majesty's ship *Rhin*, sworn and examined as follows:

Co^{t}. Did the prisoner aid and assist the escape of the French prisoners from the *Brocanture* prize on or about the 4th of February last?

A. I don't know.

The witness withdrew

Thomas Foley, Seaman belonging to His Majesty's ship *Rhin*, sworn and examined as follows:

Co^{t}. Did the prisoner aid and assist the escape of the French prisoners from the *Brocanture* prize on or about the 4th of February last?

A. I don't think he did. I know nothing of it?

Co^{t}. Did you see the prisoner converse with the Frenchmen that afternoon after you arrived?

A. No.

Co^{t}. Did you observe the prisoner at any time hold any secret conversation with the French prisoners?

A. No, but always very careful of seeing the prisoners down below, for he said he had every suspicion of their rising by what he could see in their manners and told me , 'Foley go and call all hands on deck, for those fellows are coming up pretty thick.' Immediately I did so and the men all came up and went abaft the man who was at the helm to stand by the arms. The prisoner said to me, go down and see what that fellow (the French boatswain) was doing with his hammock. I immediately went down and he was lying on his knees doing something with his hammock and clothes. I came over to him and asked what he was doing; he went away and I overhauled his hammock and found a large knife in a scabbard. I took that away and sent him on deck. I told the prisoner. 'Bathie,' says I, 'this fellow's pocket is very bulky; let us see what is in it.' I overhauled it and there was nothing but tobacco.

The witness withdrew

John Brown, Joseph Guiteres, Francis Germain, James Hickey, Michael Fitzgerald [and?] Richard Gaffney, Seamen belonging to His Majesty's ship *Rhin*, severally called in, sworn and examined as follows:

Co^{t}. Did the prisoner aid and assist the escape of the French prisoners from the *Brocanture* prize on or about the 4th of February last?

Ans^{r}. by all 'I don't know'.

The evidence in support of the charge being here closed, the prisoner was asked if he had anything to offer in his behalf, when he declared his innocence of the charge and called in Lieut. Robert Henley Rogers, 1st Lieut. of His Majesty's ship *Rhin*, to speak to his general character, who said:

'I have always found the prisoner a sober, steady, good man. He has been a long time with Capt. Malcolm, whom I have heard speak in the highest terms of him. The prisoner has been a prisoner at large since February.'

The prisoner having nothing further to offer, the court was cleared and proceeded to deliberate upon and form the sentence.

The court, having very maturely and deliberately weighed and considered the evidence in support of the charge as well as what the prisoner had offered in his behalf, was of opinion that the charge had not been proved against the prisoner, John Bathie, and the court do in consequence adjudge the said John Bathie to be fully acquitted.

The court was opened, the prisoner brought in, the witnesses and audience readmitted and the prisoner acquitted accordingly. …

35A. *Buller, Richardson and Scobell to Calder*

[ADM 1/5419] *Salvador del Mundo*, Hamoaze
18th February 1811

… Pursuant to your order of the 15th instant, directing us to make a most strict enquiry into the circumstances of the escape of the two persons belonging to the *Brocanture*, French letter of marque prize to His Majesty's ship *Rhin*, in a boat belonging to the *Merope* on her arrival in Plymouth Sound on the 5th instant and, after having most circumstantially enquired into the cause of their escape, are of opinion it proceeded from Lieutenant Hopkins', the Prize Master of the said letter of marque, great neglect of duty, which encouraged the prisoners in question to risk their escape and from circumstances that have come before us, we think that the captain's coxswain of His Majesty's ship *Rhin* must have aided and was accessory to the above men's getting away. …

36. *Court Martial of William Craig*

[ADM 1/5420]

At a court martial assembled on board His Majesty's ship *Astrea* in Port Louis (Isle of France) on Friday the 1st of November 1811.

Present

Captains Henry Heathcote, President
Philip Beaver
Samuel Warren
Charles Marsh Shomberg
James Johnston

The court having read an order from the Honourable Robert Stopford, Rear Admiral of the Red and Commander in Chief of His Majesty's ships and vessels employed and to be employed at the Cape of Good Hope and the seas adjacent, dated the 31st of October 1811, and directed to Henry Heathcote, Esquire, Captain of His Majesty's ship *Lion* and second in command of His Majesty's ships and vessels at Port Louis (Isle of France) to try M[r] William Craig, acting lieutenant and commander of His Majesty's gun brig *Staunch*, for drunkenness. The acting judge advocate stated to the court that he went on board the said brig yesterday afternoon to acquaint the said Acting Lieutenant William Craig thereof and that the commanding officer then on board reported that he had not been on board or heard of for three days past, that he then desired the commanding officer of the said brig to acquaint him should he receive any intelligence of the said acting lieutenant and that he had not received any such information, in consequence of which the court was dissolved.

…

37. *Orders for Executions of John Smith and Jean Tourney*

[ADM 1/5422]

Admy Office
Jan. 15, 1812

Minutes of two courts martial & sentences of death on John Smith, Private Marine, & Jean Tourney, Ordinary Seaman, belonging to His Majesty's ship *Kite*, for having committed an unnatural & detestable crime.

The proof being in their lamentable cases complete & decisive, Mr. Yorke most humbly submits that your R. Highness should be pleased to approve of the intention of the Lords of the Admy to give their warrant for the execution of the said offenders.

Approv'd
George P.R.

Court Martial on John Smith

The Lords Commissioners of the Admiralty have been pleased to direct the minutes and sentence of a court martial lately held on John Smith, a Private Marine belonging to His Majesty's sloop *Kite*, for an unnatural crime, to be laid before His Majesty's Attorney and Solicitor General and the Council for the Affairs of the Admiralty and Navy for their opinion

Whether any legal objection presents itself to carrying the sentence into execution.

We find no legal objection to carrying this sentence into execution. …

13 Jan[ry] 1812

Court Martial on Jean Tourney

The Lords Commissioners of the Admiralty have been pleased to direct the minutes and sentence of a court martial lately held on Jean Tourney, Ordinary Seaman belonging to His Majesty's sloop *Kite*, for an unnatural offence, to be laid before His Majesty's Attorney and Solicitor General and the Council for the Affairs of the Admiralty and Navy for their opinion

Whether any legal objection presents itself to carrying the sentence into execution.

We do not find any legal objection to carrying this sentence into execution.

. . .

13 Jan^{ry} 1812

38. *Court Martial of Charles Clark Dobson*

[ADM 1/5423]

Copy of minutes of the proceedings of a court martial held on board His Majesty's ship *Monmouth* in The Downs on the 20th day of Janry. 1812.

Present

John Ferrier, Esqre, Rear Admiral of White and third officer in the command of His Majesty's ships and vessels in The Downs, President.

Captains

George Byng	Joseph Bingham
James Walker	E. W. C. R. Owen
Richard Raggett	Francis Wm Austen
Philip Carteret	John Halsted

Being all the post captains in The Downs, except Captain Hyde Parker of the *Monmouth*, who certified to the president his inability to attend through sickness.

The prisoner was brought into court and evidence and audience admitted.

Read the order of the Right Honble the Lords Commissioners of the Admiralty, dated the 19th ins^{t}. and addressed to the president to try Lieut^{t}. Charles Clark Dobson, late Commander of His Majesty's Gun Brig *Brevdragerer*,[1] on the following charges, vizt.:

[1]In J. J. Colledge's *Ships of the Royal Navy: An Historical Index, Volume 1: Major Ships* (Newton Abbott: David and Charles, 1969), p. 88, this vessel is listed as the *Brevdraderen*.

1st For repeatedly attempting a very unnatural & indecent act upon several men and boys belonging to His Majesty's gun brigs *Censor* & *Brevdragerer*, between the month of April 1809 and the 12th day of Septr 1809.
2nd For absenting himself from His Majesty's gun brig *Brevdragerer* on the 12th day of Septr 1809.

Then the members of the court & judge advocate, in open court and before they proceeded to trial, respectively took the oaths enjoined by Act of Parliament.

A letter[1] from Lieutenant Joshua Latimer Rowe, late commanding His Majesty's gun brig *Censor*, was then read as follows:

Bristol, Octr 31st, 1811.

(Copy)
… By mere accident, I this day discovered that Lieutenant C. C. Dobson, who deserted from His Majesty's gun brig *Brevdragerer* in the month of Septr. 1809, when under my orders in the River Enis, to avoid answering in a court martial to the charge of an unnatural crime, is still on the list of Lieutenants of the Royal Navy. I have therefore the honour to request you will be pleased to submit the enclosed original correspondence official and private with copies of my answers there to on that occasion between the Right Honble Lord George Stuart, Captain of His Majesty's ship *L'Aimable* & senior off^{r}. at Heligoland, Lieutenant Dodson & myself to the consideration of the Lords C. of the Admy in the event of the said Lieutenant C. C. Dobson's having imposed a false statement of his case upon their Lordships, which the tacit acknowledgement of his crime particularly in his last letter to me will completely contradict. Humbly conceiving their Lordships were totally unacquainted with the real cause of Lieut. Dobson's desertion as well as convinced that his reinstatement must in some degree reflect upon my proceedings on that occasion, I feel strong in the hope their Lordships will perceive I am actuated by no other motive that a proper sense of duty to my country, their Lordships and myself as well as in vindication of a character which has some of the strongest testimonials to speak to its professional capacity and moral conduct. …

Another letter from the said Lt. Joshua Latimer Rowe[2] was also read to the following effect, *vizt*.:

[1]This letter was written to the Lords Commissioners' First Secretary, John Wilson Croker.
[2]This letter was addressed to Second Secretary John Barrow.

Bristol 17th Novr. 1811

… I have the honour to acknowledge the receipt of your letter of the 15th inst. And in conformity to their Lordships directions contained therein to prefer charges ags^t^. Lieutt. C. C. Dodson for desertion and for the improper conduct imputed to him in order to his trial by a court martial. I have therefore to request you will be pleased to submit to their Lordships the following charges preferr'd against L^t^. C. C. Dobson, late Comn^r^. of H.M. gun brig *Brevdragerer* 1st charge – for repeatedly attempting a very unnatural and indecent act upon several men and boys belonging to H.M. gun brigs *Censor* and *Brevdragerer* between the month of April 1809 and the 19th Septr 1809, knowing his conduct had been represented to the Right Honble L^d^. George Stuart, senior officer of His Majesty's ships and vessels at Heligoland. The under mentioned names are a list of witnesses in support of the charges (then follow their names).

…

Then was read the original correspondence above alluded to in L^t^. Rowe's letter to J. W. Croker, Esqre., of the 31st Octr. 1811 between himself, Lieut. Dobson & L^d^. G. Stuart.

The court was cleared & came to a resolution that if the prisoner could give proof that more than one year had elapsed between the time of his delivering himself up to the Admiralty and the preferring the present charges, he might by so doing put an end to the trial, upon which the prisoner produced letters and documents to the court, which were read as follows: 1st. A letter from the Secretary of the Admiralty to the offg. judge advocate, dated 13th Janry 1812, enclosing a certificate from Mr. Robert Carey King, surgeon at Saxmundham, respecting the prisoner, dated the 9th Octr. 1810, also a certificate from Major Frederick de Frane, also respecting the prisoner and bearing date 8 Octr. 1810, and a certificate from R^r^. Adm^l^. Sr J. S. Yorke, dated Admiralty 15th Octr. 1810. There were also read letters from R^r^. Adm^l^. S^r^. Joseph Sydney Yorke to the prisoner, dated Admiralty Novr. 3 & 5, vizt. Admiralty Novr. 3. 10:

… I have received your note of this day and, in order to put you out of suspense, acquaint you that the subject of your half pay is before the Navy Board, & when they make their report, the Admiralty will decide when you will immediately be acquainted. …

Also another letter from S^r^. J. S. Yorke,[1] dated 5th Novr. 1810, as follows:

[1]This letter is to Lieutenant Charles Clark Dobson.

Sr. Joseph Yorke's compliments to Lieut^{t}. Dobson and [he?] acquaints him in reply to his letter of this date that there certainly is not any necessity for his remaining in town, the only thing required being his place of residence where the report of the Navy Board, respecting his half pay now respited in consequence of unpass'd accounts will be forwarded to him, together with the decision of the L^{ds}. Commissioners of the Admy., on this subject. …

The court, being cleared, proceeded to consider the said documents, the dates thereof, and the date of the order for trying the prisoner in consequence of the charges preferred against him in Lieutenant Rowe's letter of the 17th Novr. 1811, when it appearing to the court that the said order had not been issued by the Lords Commissioners of the Admiralty within one year after the prisoner had reported to the Admiralty his return to Great Britain, resolved that they could not proceed to try the said Lieutenant C. C. Dobson, for the offences charged in the above letter of Lieutenant Rowe, agreeably to the provisions of the Statute 22 G. 2, C33, s23.

The court therefore was of opinion that it could not try the said p^{r}., L^{t}. Charles Clark Dobson, but that he should be discharged from custody.

The court was open'd, audience admitted & sentence pass'd accordingly. …

39. *Court Martial of William Kinder*

[ADM 1/5426]

Minutes of proceedings at a court martial held on board His Majesty's ship *Salvador del Mundo* in Hamoaze on Tuesday the 12th day of May 1812.

Present

Philip Charles Durham, Esqre., Rear Admiral of the Blue and third officer in the command of His Majesty's ships and vessels at Plymouth, President.

Pultney Malcolm, Esqr., First Captain to Admiral Lord Keith, K.B., Commander in Chief of the Channel Fleet.

Captains

Robert Barton	Samuel Hood Linzee
Willoughby Thomas Lake	Henry Hotham
Thomas Alexander	John Halliday
James Nash	The Honble. Duncombe Pleydell Bouverie
Francis William Fane	Samuel Pym
	John Surman Carden

George Eastlake, Junr., officiating Judge Advocate

Being all the captains of post ships then and there present next in seniority to the president, except Capt. Lord William Stuart, who was absent on Admiralty leave and Capt. Sir Michl. Seymour, Bt., who was the prosecutor.

The prisoner, William Kinder, Landsman of His Majesty's ship *Niemen*, was brought into court and the witnesses and audience admitted.

Sir Michael Seymour, Bt., Captain of the said ship appeared as prosecutor.

Read – The order of the Right Honble. the Lords Commissioners of the Admiralty, dated the 1st day of May 1812, directed to the president, to try the said William Kinder for having struck his superior officer.

Read – The warrant appointing a judge advocate.

Then the members of the court and judge advocate, in open court and before they proceeded to trial, respectively took the oaths directed by Act of Parliament passed in the 22d year of the reign of George the 2d.

Read – The annexed letter of charge from the said Capt. Sir Michl. Seymour to Adml. Sir Chas. Cotton, Bt.

All the witnesses, except the first to be sworn, being then ordered to withdraw and to attend their examinations separately, they all withdrew accordingly and the court proceeded to trial as follows:

The prosecutor desired to give evidence first himself, whereupon Capt. Sir Michl. Seymour, Bt., of His Majesty's ship *Niemen*, was sworn and examined as follows:

Cot. Relate what you know respecting the charge against the prisoner.

A. The prisoner joined the *Amethyst* under my command about 4 years since, when, from his strange conduct, Mr. John Bowen, then Surgeon of her, stated to me the propriety and necessity of sending him to be surveyed and invalided from the service; that could not be accomplished, the surveying officers not thinking he was a fit object to be discharged from the ship. Having occasion afterwards from his extreme filthiness and negligence of himself to punish the prisoner and, on expressing my regret at it to Mr. Bowen, he (Mr. Bowen) stated decidedly that he did not appear to be of perfect and sound mind.

Cot. When you wrote the letter for a court martial on the prisoner, did you consider him a proper object to be tried?

A. I knew it was impossible for me to punish him for such a crime and, as I could not get him discharged from the ship, I took that step, writing afterwards to Sir Robert Calder, Commander in Chief at Plymouth, to state the circumstances which I have now given in evidence in hopes the Admiralty might be pleased to order his discharge and withdraw the order for a court martial. I have received a letter from Sir Robt. Calder, stating that their Lordships wished the trial to take place to leave the court to judge of his sanity.

Co^{t}. Have you any particular instances of the prisoner's insanity to state about the time he is charged to have struck the lieutenant?

A. Not at that moment, he has always been extremely filthy and dirty, extremely quiet and indolent generally, except on three occasions when he has been punished – twice, while I was absent, for striking officers. I think there is something wrong in the prisoner's intellects.

Co^{t}. State any particular instance of insanity in the prisoner which has come within your notice.

A. I know of no instance, other than the general conduct I have mentioned.

Co^{t}. Was the prisoner considered a sober man in regard to drink?

A. Generally, very sober.

The witness withdrew.

Lieut. James Gledstanes Jacob, of His Majesty's ship *Niemen*, sworn and examined as follows:

Co^{t}. State to the court what you know respecting the sanity of the prisoner.

A. I have known the prisoner between three and four years, during which time his conduct on different occasions has been that of a man not in his right senses; and that has been the opinion of the surgeon and myself from his former conduct on different occasions.

Co^{t}. Do you think the prisoner a fit object to be brought to trial from the state of his mind?

A. At times the prisoner is sane, at other times not; therefore, I can't say.

Co^{t}. State any particular instance of insanity in the prisoner that has come within your own direct personal observation.

A. I have known the prisoner to have offered all his clothes for sale; and, at other times, he has refused to eat.

Co^{t}. What has been his conduct since he was charged with this offence?

A. He has been punished since he has been prisoner at large for striking a seaman on board.

Co^{t}. Has the prisoner, at any time, been under the care of the surgeon for insanity, or has he been suspended from his duty on that account?

A. Not to my knowledge.

Co[t]. Do you know if any officer has been directed to watch the actions of the prisoner?

A. He has been given in charge to the master at arms and sergeant of Marines to take charge of his clothes and see he eats his provisions. The prisoner never sleeps in a hammock, washes himself or takes off his clothes, except when compelled to.

Co[t]. Is the prisoner, to your knowledge, considered by the officers of the ship as well as by yourself in an unsound state of mind?

A. Yes.

Co[t]. Is the prisoner considered a sober man in regard to drink?

A. I never saw him drunk in my life.

Co[t]. Does he keep his watch regularly at sea.

A. Generally, but there is difficulty to get him up to keep his watch.

The witness withdrew.

M[r]. Robert Wiley, Assistant Surgeon of His Majesty's ship *Niemen*, sworn and examined as follows:

Co[t]. Do you know the prisoner?

A. Yes; I have been shipmates with him about two years and half.

Co[t]. Do you consider the prisoner to be of sound mind?

A. Not always; I have never seen him at any times when he has been insane and I believe that he is so at times.

Co[t]. Has the prisoner been in the sick list, and, if so, for what complaint?

A. He has been in the sick list, I think, two or three times for a cold. I have never seen any symptoms of lunacy in the prisoner at any time.

Co[t]. What was his conduct when under your care?

A. The same as it is at all other times, not like any other man – stupid, paying no attention to what was said to him. He always answered sensibly.

The witness withdrew.

James Wade, Master at Arms on board His Majesty's ship *Niemen*, sworn and examined as follows:

Co[t]. Are you of opinion that the prisoner is in a sound state of mind?

A. No, I don't think he is.

Co[t]. How long have you been shipmates with the prisoner?

A. Better than four years.

Co[t]. State to the court any particular instance of madness you have yourself observed in the prisoner?

A. By his childish actions, by picking up crumbs and bits of meat from the ashes and cinders, and by laughing to himself without any meaning. He will lie on the bits and never mind his victuals or grog, unless his messmates bring it [to?] him, and he as often feeds out of the dirt basket as anywhere else.

Co[t]. Has the conduct you have described been visible in the prisoner during the whole of the 4 years?

A. Yes, ever since I knew him first.

The witness withdrew.

Lieut. Jacob again called in and examined as follows:

Co[t]. Were you struck by the prisoner on the 17th of January last?

A. Yes, frequently about the body between the hours of 5 & 6 o'clock. It was dark. John Ball, a marine, was present.

The witness withdrew.

John Ball, Private Marine of His Majesty's ship *Niemen*, sworn and examined as follows:

Co[t]. Did you see the prisoner strike Lieutenant Jacob on the evening of the 17th January last?

A. I did not.

The witness withdrew.

Andrew Gray, seaman on board His Majesty's ship *Niemen*, sworn and examined as follows:

Co[t]. Did you see the prisoner strike Lieut. Jacob on the evening of the 17th January last?

A. Yes, about the face with his fist.

Co[t]. Were the people at quarters at the time?

A. No.

Co[t]. Where did it happen?

A. On the fore part of the main deck, Lieut. Jacob was giving orders to clue up the fore top sail.

Co[t]. What appeared to you to be the cause of the prisoner's striking his officer?

A. I don't know; I was not there at the beginning.

Co[t]. Did the prisoner appear in a state of madness at the time he struck Lieut. Jacob?

A. He did not appear worse than he is used to be; he used to be out of his head at times.

The witness withdrew.

Richard Bourne, Private Marine serving on board His Majesty's ship *Niemen*, sworn and examined.

Co^{t}. Do you know the prisoner?

A. Yes.

Co^{t}. Did you see the prisoner strike Lieut. Jacob?

A. Yes, with his fist in the galley.

The witness withdrew.

The evidence in support of the charge being here closed, the prisoner was asked if he had anything to offer in his defence, when he said he had not.

Whereupon the court was cleared & proceeded to deliberate upon & form the sentence.

The court, having very maturely and deliberately weighed and considered the evidence in support of the charge, was of opinion that the charge had not been proved against the prisoner, William Kinder; he being insane and the court did, in consequence, adjudge the said William Kinder to be acquitted.

The court was opened, the prisoner brought in, the witnesses and audience re-admitted and the sentence pronounced accordingly. …

39A. *Seymour to Cotton*

[ADM 1/5426] His Majesty's ship *Niemen* off Maumasson Pass
January 18th, 1812

… William Kinder, Landsman of this ship, having yesterday afternoon, Friday the 17th instant, struck Lieutenant James Gledstanes Jacob, his superior officer, whilst on duty on the fore part of the main deck, I have to request you may be pleased to apply to the Lords Commissioners of the Admiralty for an order to try the said William Kinder, Lm, for a breach of the 22d Article of War accordingly.

…

40. *Court Martial of James Scaby*

[ADM 1/5426]

Proceedings of a general court martial held pursuant to a warrant from the Lords Commissioners of the Admiralty, bearing date the 19th May 1812, at the Royal Marine Barracks Woolwich, May 22nd 1812, for the trial of Private James Scaby, 167 C. Royal Marines, for desertion.

President
Major General James Meredith

Lt Colonel Wm Binks
B^{v} Major Wm Barry
Capt R. P. Boys
Capt John Wright
1st Lt Edward H. Stewart
1st Lt Frederick Layton
1st Lt James R. Moriarity

B^{v} Major Paul Hunt
B^{vt} Major Wm M. Combe
Capt M. Wybourne
1st Lt Wm Henry Robinson
1st Lt George B. Berry
1st Lt Lewis Robley
2nd Lt Charles Rinker

Capt George Varlo, acting Judge Advocate

The president & members being seated according to seniority, the prisoner was brought into court; the court opened and the audience admitted. The divisional order for assembling the court martial was read. Major General Bane's letter to the Lords Commissioners of the Admiralty read. Their Lordships' warrant for assembling the court martial &, after it, the acting judge advocate's warrant was read.

The members' names called over & the prisoner asked if he objected to any one, answered in the negative.

The witnesses summoned, their names called over, the court sworn by the judge advocate & the judge advocate sworn by the president.

The charge read to the prisoner, to which he pleaded guilty & throws himself on the mercy of the court & trusts the court will take his long confinement into consideration, and, having been only a fortnight in the service, has no person to call on for a character.

Sentence

The prisoner having acknowledged himself guilty of a breach of the Articles of War, the court do sentence him to receive four hundred lashes in the usual manner. …

41. *Vice Admiral Herbert Sawyer to Commodore A. F. Evans*

[ADM 1/5426] His Majesty's ship *Africa*, at Bermuda
the 25th of May 1812

… Captain Bastard of His Majesty's ship *Africa*, having by my order inquired into the circumstances attending the charges preferred against Lieutenant Henry Walker, commanding the *Cuttle* schooner, and thereby rendered himself unfit to sit as a member of the court martial you are directed to assemble for his trial,

I have to acquaint you that I have ordered him to carry on the prosecution against that officer, if the court think fit. …

42. *Court Martial of Simon Thomas*

[ADM 1/5427]

Proceedings of a general court martial held pursuant to a warrant from the Lords Commissioners of the Admiralty, bearing date the 5th day of June 1812, at the Royal Marine Barracks Woolwich, the 12th day of June 1812, for the trial of 165th Company Simon Thomas, Private Marine, for desertion.

Major General James Meredith, President

Lieu^{t}. Col^{l} Willm Binks	B^{t} Lieu^{t} Col^{l} Hro^{t} Pimins
B^{t} Major Jno Lovington	B^{t} Major Paul Hunt
B^{t} Major Wm Barry	B^{t} Major Wm M. Combe
B^{t} Major Edwd Nicolls	Captn Hen^{y} Sherman
Captain Jno Maughan	1st Lieu^{t} Edwd H Stewart
1st Lieu^{t} Fred^{k} Layton	1st Lieu^{t} James R. Moriarity
Lieu^{t} Ge^{n} Pt Puddicembre	2d Lieu^{t} Wm Hagarly

Captain George Varlo, acting Judge Advocate

The president and members being seated according to seniority, the prisoner was brought into court; the court was opened and audience admitted. The Divisional order for assembling the court martial was read; Major Genl Burns' letter to the Lords Commissioners of the Admiralty was read, as also their Lordships' warrant for assembling the court martial, and, after it, the acting judge advocate's warrant.

The members' names call'd over and the prisoner asked if he objected to anyone, he answered in the negative. The witnesses summon'd, their names call'd over, the court sworn by the judge advocate and the judge advocate sworn by the president.

The charge against the prisoner read, to which he pleaded not guilty, having delivered himself up to a serg^{t} of the Derby Militia.

Serg^{t} Smith, Clerk in the Adjutant's office, produced the furlough book and sworn.

Ques^{n} by Court	Point out to the court the particulars respecting his furlough.
Ans^{r}	On the 16th of August 1811, his furlough began and expired the 17th October 1811; his furlough was for Denbighshire.

162d C. Thomas Lowbridge, Serg^{t}, call'd into court and duly sworn, gives the following evidence:

Que^{s} State to the court what you know of the prisoner's case.

Ans^{r} The prisoner went on furlough the 16 August 1811; I never saw him until the 4th June 1812.

Que^{s} Was the barracks the first place you saw him in, when he was brought in as a prisoner?

Ans^{r} Yes.

The prisoner states in his defence that it was not his intention to desert and he gave himself up to a sergeant in the Derby Militia, a Serg^{t} Kerr, and calls on Serg^{t} Wm Polsom to prove that the sergeant of the militia told him to give himself up.

172 Co. Serg^{t} Willm Polsom call'd into court and duly sworn, gives the following evidence:

Ques^{n} Do you know Serg^{t} Kerr of the Derby Militia?

Ans^{r} Yes. I was in company with him.

Ques^{n} What conversation had he with you respecting the prisoner?

Ans^{r} He call'd me when first I went to Wrexham and said that Simon Thomas had given himself up to him as a deserter at Wrexham; he was sworn in as such and lodged in Wrexham gaol, from whence I received him.

Que^{s} Had he his uniforms on at the time you took him from Wrexham?

Ans^{r} He had not them on but he had his uniforms, knapsack and side arms with him, which I brought to quarters.

Que^{s} How did he behave on the march?

Ans^{r} He behaved very well indeed; no man could behave better.

The prisoner calls on Serg^{t} Pimmins for a character.

Serg^{t} Saml Pimmins call'd into court and duly sworn.

Que^{s} What do you know of the general conduct of the prisoner?

Ans^{r} I kncw thc prisoncr from 16th Dcc^{r} 1810 and, while doing duty on the Parade with me for about three months, he conducted himself as a good soldier, always sober, clean and fit for duty at any time.

Saml Strees, Serg^{t}, call'd into court by the prisoner and duly sworn, gives the following evidence:

Que^{s} What do you know of the prisoner's general conduct?

Ans^{r} Since I have known him about Decr 12 month, he always behaved himself in a respectful and soldier-like manner in the room to which he belonged and which I had charge of; he was employed as bricklayer's labourer in the barracks.

The prisoner calls on Serg^{t} Dungey for a character and, being duly sworn, gives the following evidence:

Ques^{n} What do you know of the prisoner's general conduct?

Ans^{r} He worked with me as bricklayer's labourer at the barracks for about 5 months; during that time, he behaved himself in a steady, sober manner.

Sentence

The court, having duly considered the evidence for & against the prisoner & what he alleged in his defence, is of opinion that the prisoner, Simon Thomas, is guilty of the crimes laid to his charge & of a breach of the Articles of War and do sentence him to receive only three hundred lashes in the usual manner, in consideration of his former good character and it appearing by evidence that he repented of his crime and gave himself up and had also taken care of his uniforms & side arms. …

43. *Court Martial of Thomas Harris*

[ADM 1/ 5434]

Minutes of the proceedings of a court martial held onboard His Majesty's ship *Hibernia* at Port Mahon on Saturday the 9th day of January 1813.

Present

Sir William Sidney Smith, Knight, Commander and Grand Cross of the Royal Military Orders of the Sword and S^{t}. Ferdinand, Vice Admiral of the White and second officer in the command of His Majesty's ships and vessels employed in the Mediterranean, President.

Francis Pickmore, Esqre, Vice Admiral of the Blue

Israel Pellew, Esqre, Rear Admiral of the White and Captain of the Fleet

Captains

Josias Rowley
John Erskine Douglas
Sir Edward Berry, Bar^{t}.
Patrick Campbell
Charles Grant
Robert Plampin
Robert Rolles
Richard Hussey Moubray
Edward Stirling Dickson
William Henry Dillon

The prisoner being brought into court and audience admitted, M^{r}. W^{m}. Donald, Surgeon of His Majesty's ship *Tremendous*, stated that Captain Robert Campbell could not attend in consequence of ill health. M^{r}. Jas. Cragie, Surgeon of His Majesty's ship *Berwick*, stated the same respecting Captain Edward Brace.

Read the order from Sir Edward Pellew, Bar^{t}., Vice Admiral of the Red and Commander in Chief of His Majesty's ships and vessels employed in the Mediterranean dated the 7th instant and directed to Sir William Sidney Smith, Vice Admiral of the White and second officer in the command of His Majesty's ships and vessels employed in the Mediterranean, to try Thomas Harris (2d), Seaman belonging to His Majesty's ship *Elizabeth*, for a breach of the second Article of War on or about the 3d instant.

Read the judge advocates warrant.

Then the members of the court and judge advocate, in open court and before they proceeded to trial, respectively took the oaths enjoined by Act of Parliament. The letter from Captain Gower[1] containing the charge against the prisoner was then read as follows:

H.M.S. *Elizabeth*, Mahon, 6 January 1813

… I request you will be pleased to order a court martial to be held on Thomas Harris (2d), Seaman belonging to His Majesty's ship under my command, for a breach of the second Article of War on or about the 3d ins^{t}.

…

Witnesses ordered to withdraw

James Duell, Boy H.M.S. *Elizabeth*, called and sworn.

Question – Relate what passed between you and the prisoner on or about the night of the 3d. instant.

Answer – On Sunday night after the lights were put out, the prisoner came to my hammock and endeavoured to pull the blanket off me. I bid him go away and he told me he would not go away. I bid him go again and he went away; nothing more passed.

Q The lights being put out, how did you know it was the prisoner?

[1]This letter is to Edward Pellew.

A By his voice.

Q At any other time on or about the third, did anything pass between you and the prisoner?

A No. The prisoner declined asking the witness any questions.

Witnesses ordered to withdraw.

William Lee, Boy H.M.S. *Elizabeth*, called and sworn.

Q Relate what passed between you and the prisoner when you were on the main deck with a number of other boys, telling stories on or about the 3d instant.

A Nothing passed between us at that time.

The prisoner declined asking this witness any questions.

The witnesses withdrew.

Thomas Harris, Boy H.M.S. *Elizabeth*, called and sworn.

Q Did anything pass between you and the prisoner on or about the 3d instant?

A No. The prisoner declined asking this witness any questions.

Witness ordered to withdraw.

The prosecutor declined calling any more witnesses and the prosecution closed. The prisoner was called upon for his defence; he declined making any. The court was then cleared to deliberate upon and form sentence and, having maturely and deliberately weighed and considered the evidence in support of the charge, is of opinion that the charge has not been proved and doth therefore adjudge the prisoner, Thomas Harris, to be acquitted. The court was opened, audience admitted and sentence passed accordingly.
…

44. *Bicknell to John Wilson Croker*

[ADM 1/3704] Spring Garden Terrace
1st March 1813

… In obedience to the commands of my Lords Commissioners of the Admiralty signified to me in M[r]. Barrow's letter of the 25th instant (enclosing a letter from Vice Admiral Foley, accompanied with one from Captain White of the *Vigo* reporting the result of an enquiry he had been directed to make into a complaint made to their Lordships by the crew of the *Dwarf* of the harsh and unjust treatment they experienced from the commander and acting master of the said cutter and it appearing that the said complaints were unfounded and that Arthur Johnstone, a seaman and one of the crew of the *Dwarf*, was the writer of the letter of complaint and was active in procuring the sanction of the crew to the same) that I should report whether this man could be tried by a court martial for this offence, I take the liberty to acquaint you for their Lordships' information that, having perused and considered the said papers and the Act of the 22nd Geo 2nd ch 33 for the government of His Majesty's forces by sea, I am humbly of opinion that the said Arthur Johnstone's offence, in writing the said unfounded letter of complaint and procuring the sanction of the crew to the same, falls within the meaning of the 21st Article of War contained in the said Act and that he may be tried by a court martial for the same accordingly if their Lordships shall think fit.

Herewith I return the papers abovementioned. …

[Admiralty note]
Mar. 2. Order for a court martial

45. *Court Martial of Edwin Henry Chamberlayne*

[ADM 1/5440]

Minutes of the proceedings of a court martial held onboard His Majesty's ship *Hibernia* in Port Mahon on Monday the 3d day of January 1814.

Present

Sir William Sidney Smith, Knight, Commander and Grand Cross of the Royal Military Orders of the Sword and S^{t}. Ferdinand, Vice Admiral of the White and second officer in the command of His Majesty's ships and vessels employed in the Mediterranean, President.
James Pickmore, Esqre., Vice Admiral of the Blue
Israel Pellew, Esqre., Rear Admiral of the White and Captain of the Fleet
Sir Richard King, Bar^{t}., Rear Admiral of the Blue

Captains

George Burleton	Sir Josias Rowley, Bar^{t}.
Robert Plampin	John Erskine Douglas
Robert Rolles	Sir Edward Berry, Bar^{t}.

Edward Brace
Charles Grant

Norborn Thompson

The prisoner being brought into court and audience admitted.

Read the order from Sir Edward Pellew, Bar[t]., Vice Admiral of the Red and Commander in Chief of His Majesty's ships and vessels employed in the Mediterranean dated the 27th of December 1813 and directed to Sir William Sidney Smith, Vice Admiral of the White and second officer in the command of His Majesty's ships and vessels employed in the Mediterranean, to try Captain Edwin Henry Chamberlayne of His Majesty's ship *Unite* on charges exhibited against him by Lieutenant A. Crozier of the Royal Marines serving onboard the said ship. Read the judge advocate's warrant. Then the members of the court and judge advocate, in open court and before they proceeded to trial, respectively took the oaths enjoined by Act of Parliament. The letter and charges were then read (Nos. 1, 2 and 3); Witnesses ordered to withdraw.

The prisoner submitted to the court that the offence stated in the first charge preferred against him by Lieutenant Crozier had taken place above twelve months previous to the application now before the court and that Lieu[t]. Crozier had had an opportunity of making such application before, the ship having been at Malta in August 1812.

Lieutenant Joseph William Crabb, H.M.S. *Unite*, called and sworn.

He produced the log of H.M.S. *Unite*, which he stated to be correct to the best of his belief. It appeared by the log that H.M.S. *Unite* anchored in Malta harbour on Friday August 14th, 1812 and sailed from thence on Thursday September 24th, 1812. The court is therefore of opinion that it cannot take cognizance of the first charge, the time prescribed by Act of Parliament having elapsed previous to its being produced.

The prosecutor requested to produce a copy of a letter he stated he had sent to Rear Admiral Freemantle containing charges against the prisoner.

The court was then cleared and, on being reopened, the following minute was read:

Upon the prosecutor's application to produce a copy of [the?] charges, which he says he had transmitted to Rear Admiral Freemantle, the court have decided that it cannot receive any charge but those which are stated in the commander in chief's order under which it is assembled.

The prisoner stated to the court that he had written for a court martial on Lieutenant Crozier for the offences which induced him to put Lieu[t]. Crozier under an arrest on the 21st of June and that he, Lieutenant Crozier, had been tried by a court martial and been severely reprimanded for the same; and therefore he submitted to the court that he, the prisoner, was not liable to be tried on the second charge.

M[r]. Richard Spear sworn.

He produced the sentence passed on Lieutenant Crozier at the court martial held on board the *Hibernia* on the 29th of December 1813, which was read No. 4.

The court was then cleared and decided that the prosecutor is at liberty to call evidence on the second charge; the prosecutor declined calling any witnesses. Here the prosecution closed and the prisoner was called upon for his defence; he declined stating anything or calling any witnesses, leaving the whole to the consideration of the court. The court was then cleared and proceeded to deliberate upon and form the sentence and, having maturely and deliberately considered the whole of the circumstances, determined the following sentence:

'The first charge being decided by the court to be out of date under the Act of Parliament, the court did not enter upon examination of witnesses.'

'Upon the second charge, the prosecutor having declined to produce any witnesses in support thereof, the court is of opinion that such mode of proceeding of the prosecutor in preferring such charges against his commanding officer without attempting to establish their foundation is vexatious, highly improper and prejudicial to the discipline of His Majesty's service; the court doth therefore acquit the prisoner, Captain Edwin Henry Chamberlayne of His Majesty's ship *Unite*. The court was opened, audience admitted and sentence passed accordingly.' …

45A. *Crozier to Pellew*

[ADM 1/5440]

His Majesty's ship *Unite*
Port Mahon, December 26, 1813

No. 1
… Feeling myself to have been treated in a degrading, cruel and oppressive manner on frequent occasions by Captain Chamberlayne,

I trust you will think proper to grant a court martial on Captain Chamberlayne on the charges which I beg leave to transmit. …

45B. *Crozier's Charges*

[ADM 1/5440]

No. 2
First

On or about the 13 of July 1812, having been threatened to be sent aft on the quarter deck of His Majesty's ship *Unite* for volunteering to go on service in the boats of His Majesty's ship to attack some of the enemy's vessels,

All the other officers being allowed to go and, on my respectfully making a second application, being threatened to be put in arrest and gag'd.

…

45C. *Crozier's Charges*

[ADM 1/5440]

No. 3
Second

On or about the 21 of June 1813 I made an application to M[r]. Crabb, the First Lieutenant, for leave of absence to go onshore when I was informed by him it was the captain's orders that I should not quit the ship.

On my receiving this order, I addressed, I trust, a respectful letter to Captain Chamberlayne begging I might be informed why I was deprived the indulgence which extended from him to the other officers of His Majesty's ship, but received no answer.

The following day I went to the quarter deck to see the captain out of the ship when Lieutenant Crabb was sent for by the captain and received orders to put me in arrest.

…

45D. *Report of the Court Martial of Acheson Crozier*

[ADM 1/5440]

No. 4

At a court martial assembled and held on board His Majesty's ship *Hibernia* in Port Mahon on Wednesday the 29th day of December 1813.

Present

Sir William Sidney Smith, Knight, Commander and Grand Cross of the Royal Military Orders of the Sword and S^{t}. Ferdinand, Vice Admiral of the White and second officer in the command of His Majesty's ships and vessels employed in the Mediterranean, President.
Francis Pickmore, Esqre., Vice Admiral of the Blue
Israel Pellew, Esqre., Rear Admiral of the White and Captain of the Fleet
Sir Richard King, Bar^{t}., Rear Admiral of the Blue

Captains

George Burlton	Sir Josias Rowley, Bar^{t}.
Robert Rolles	Sir Edward Berry, Bar^{t}.
Edward Brace	Norborn Thompson
Charles Grant	Thomas Francis Charles Mainwaring
Charles Thurlow Smith	

Captain Douglas of His Majesty's ship *Prince of Wales*, who is senior to Captain Rolles, and Captain Graham of His Majesty's ship *Caledonia*, who is senior to Captain Mainwaring, having certified the president of their inability to attend through ill health, the court, in pursuance of an order from Sir Edward Pellew, Bar^{t}., Vice Admiral of the Red and Commander in Chief of His Majesty's ships and vessels employed in the Mediterranean, dated the 27th of December 1813 and directed to Sir William Sidney Smith, Vice Admiral of the White and second officer in the command of His Majesty's ships and vessels employed in the Mediterranean, proceeded to enquire into the conduct of Lieutenant Acheson Crozier of the Royal Marines serving onboard His Majesty's ship *Unite* and try him for having behaved in an unofficer-like manner on the 20th of June 1813 as specified in a letter from Captain Edwin Henry Chamberlayne of the said ship stating that 'Lieutenant A Crozier of the R.M. of His Majesty's ship under his command behaved in an unofficer-like manner by entering the palace appropriated to Her Majesty the Queen of Sicily in the Island of Zante on or about the forenoon of Sunday the 20th of June, while he, as the officer in command of the Sicilian Squadron and in attendance on Her Majesty, was present. He felt it his duty to reprehend the said Lieutenant Crozier R.M. for such unofficer-like conduct and that on the morning following on the quarter deck of His Majesty's ship under his command having remarked to the said Lieutenant Crozier that such conduct on his part as above stated would subject him (Captain Chamberlayne) to reprimands from Her Sicilian Majesty and Prince Leopold and that it was his directions he (the said Lieutenant Crozier R.M.) did not again so deviate from the conduct of an officer. Lieutenant Crozier R.M. replied to him that if he meant what he said to him as a reprimand, he would not receive it, that he was on shore and that he had nothing to do with him when on shore, that he was introduced by a friend, or words to that effect, and on his insisting on the name of the friend, who he (Lieutenant Crozier stated as having introduced him); Lieutenant Crozier again repeated in the same positive disrespectful way which marked his first reply to him that he would not inform him who he, the person to whom he alluded, was and, on his further stating that he should write for an enquiry into his (Lieutenant Crozier's) conduct, he replied to him that he might do so, that he was quite ready for enquiry and then repeated part of his former assertions as above stated.' And the court having heard the evidence in support of the charge as well as what the prisoner had to offer in his defence and, having maturely and deliberately weighed and considered the same, is of opinion that the charges have been proved in part. The court doth therefore adjudge the prisoner Lieutenant Acheson Crozier R.M. to be severely reprimanded and the said Lieutenant Acheson Crozier is hereby severely reprimanded accordingly.

…

46. *Rear Admiral T. W. Martin to the Principal Officers and Commissioners of His Majesty's Navy*

[ADM 1/835]

Salvador del Mundo
Hamoaze, 14th Octr 1814

… I forward a letter from the officiating judge advocate at this port and request you will give directions for his being supplied with the copies of the Acts of Parliament therein requested.

…

[Admiralty Note]
18 Oct. Let them be supplied. There being several copies in Mr. Winchester's possession of this Act, he has been directed to send down the necessary supply. Inform the admiral.

46A. *George Eastlake to Martin*

[ADM 1/835]

… I request you will be pleased to make the necessary application for my being furnished with fourteen copies of the Act of Parliament (22 Geo. 2 c. 33) for the use of members assembled at courts martial at this port, those in present use being so much worn as to be illegible. …

47. *John Jefferson to Croker*

[ADM 1/4782] 47 Portsmouth Street
Lincolns Inn Fields, Jany 7th 1815

… I transmit herewith to be laid before the Lords Commissioners of the Admiralty the minutes of a court martial held on the 31st August last on the person named in the margin [Lt Henry Davis (3) *Myrtle*] at which I officiated as judge advocate together with the charges enclosed in their Lordships directions to Vice Admiral Sir Thomas Williams to order the assembling of such court martial and the defence of the prisoner.

Having been discharged from His Majesty's naval service on the 2d Sep^{t}., two days subsequent to the court martial, it is only until this moment thro a series of events equally unforeseen by me as unexpected that I have been enabled to transmit the enclosed for their Lordships' information.

Under the general outline which I have given, I trust their Lordships will not be inclined to consider the very unofficial delay which has taken place in any other light than unavoidable and I most respectfully hope that they will in consequence be pleased to put a favourable construction on this protracted business.

The circumstances already alluded to have caused the loss or mislaying of the certificate given by Captain Maitland. However as the minutes now sent and the sentence previously transmitted will sufficiently substantiate the fact of my having officiated, I again beg leave to hope their Lordships' goodness will induce them to give me an order in the letter acknowledging the receipt of this for the Navy Board to pay me the amount of my advocacy. …

[Admiralty Note]
Jan. 9. Remit & let him be paid.

48. *Charles Martyn, Secretary to Rear Admiral Griffith, to Croker*

[ADM 1/4910] *Bermuda* 23rd April 1815

… I take the liberty of acquainting you that in various instances of late strong doubts have arisen and much discussion taken place at courts martial where I have officiated as judge advocate upon the propriety of permitting to sit as members commanders who from being on the Admiralty list for promotion have been appointed by the commander in chief on this station where vacancies have occurred to command post ships until the pleasure of the Lords Commissioners of the Admiralty be known.

By the 6th article of the 2 section of the printed Naval Instructions, page 40, it would distinctly appear 'that a commander, or where there is no commander a lieutenant appointed by the commander in chief to act as captain of such ship of war, shall during his continuance in such command be considered to all intents and purposes as a captain with the exception of being allowed to sit as a member at a court martial.' This in my humble opinion bears directly to the case in question and it does also appear to me that this prohibition to officers thus situated from sitting is supported by the tenor of the 6th article of the chapter under the head of courts martial, page 46, which 'directs a junior officer commanding a post ship, when sitting at courts martial, to take precedence of his senior officer commanding a sloop;' whence it must be concluded that this part of that article refers solely to cases where, from a want of captains, commanders are obliged to sit. It has, however, repeatedly occurred that the latter part of this article, 'rendering captains and commanders appointed to the temporary commands of His Majesty's ships liable to sit on courts martial in the same manner as if they were actually the captains or commanders of such ships,' has induced courts composed of more than five post captains to permit commanders acting in post ships to sit as post captains; although I beg leave respectfully to give it as my opinion that this refers only to cases where *confirmed* captains or commanders are in the temporary command of ships and the authority thus given for commanders sitting is only to be extended to cases where officers of that rank are required as members.

Indeed this inference appears absolutely necessary in order to reconcile the latter part of this article to its preceding paragraph and to the article before quoted from the 40th page of the Naval Instructions.

I confidently trust that their Lordships will pardon the liberty I take in requesting to have their opinion or decision on this subject when they learn that in many instances of late, and I believe in more than one where the prisoner has been adjudged to suffer death, commanders acting in post ships by the commander in chief's order, *till their Lordships' pleasure should be known*, have been allowed to take their seats at courts martial although the opinion of the court has almost invariably been divided as to its propriety. …

[Admiralty Note]
June 6. Refer to Mr. Bicknell.

49. *Bicknell to Croker*

[ADM 1/3707] Spring Garden Terrace
8th June 1815

… In obedience to the commands of my Lords Commissioners of the Admiralty signified to me in Mr. Barrow's letter of yesterday's date (inclosing one of the 13th April from Mr. Martyn, Secretary to Rear Admiral Griffith at Bermuda, stating that in various instances of late strong doubts have arisen and much discussion has taken place at courts martial where he has officiated as judge advocate upon the propriety of permitting to sit as members commanders who, from being on the Admiralty list for promotion, have been appointed by the commander in chief on the Halifax Station where vacancies have occurred to command post ships, until the pleasure of their Lordships should be made known), that I should report my opinion on the subject in question; I take the liberty to acquaint you for the information of their Lordships that by the 14th section of the Act of the 22d. Geo. 2d. ch. 33, it is provided in cases of courts martial appointed to be held where there are not less than three and not so many as five officers of the degree and denomination of post captain or of a superior [rank?] to be found, it shall be lawful for the officer who is to preside at the same to call to his assistance as many commanders under the rank and degree of post captain as together with the post captains present will make up the number of five to hold such court martial; and upon the authority of this section, I am humbly of opinion that is the case provided by the Act, namely where there are only three post captains present two officers of the rank of commander may be called in and legally sit as members of a court martial, but this provision will not extend to authorize commanders in the situation mentioned by Mr. Martyn to sit as post captains on any such court martial nor to authorize any commanders whatever to sit where five officers of the rank of post captain or of a superior rank can be procured. …

[Admiralty Note]
June 9. Send copy to the judge advocate.

50. *Bicknell to Croker*

[ADM 1/3707] Spring Garden Terrace
17 August 1815

… In obedience to the commands of my Lords Commissioners of the Admiralty signified to me in M^{r}. Barrow's letter of the 13th June last, inclosing one of the 19th February preceding from M^{r}. Greetham, Deputy Judge Advocate of the Fleet, upon the subject of a court martial assembled at Portsmouth for the trial of Captain Samuel Butcher late of the *Antelope* on charged [*sic*] preferred against him by the committee at Lloyds and at which he conducted the prosecution, that I should lay the same before the King's Advocate, the Attorney and Solicitor General, the Advocate of the Admiralty, and the Counsel for the Admiralty for their opinion whether in cases in which no prosecutor appears or no prosecutor is specially appointed, it does not become the duty of the judge advocate to conduct the prosecution on the part of the crown; I take the liberty to transmit herewith for the consideration of their Lordships a case laid before the said counsel with their opinion on the point in question. And I likewise return herewith M^{r}. Greetham's letter …

2

SOCIAL CRIMES

This chapter contains the transcripts of courts martial for the various types of social crime. For the present purpose the term 'social crime' can be defined as a transgression against either the conventions or morality of eighteenth-century British society ashore. Therefore, included here are trials dealing exclusively with alcohol [51–6], property [57–64], violence [65–73], disturbances of the peace [74–5] and sex [76–80].

Social crimes constituted only about a quarter of the alleged offences tried by naval courts martial. A preliminary survey of the charges listed in 22 of the 118 volumes of transcripts for the period under consideration reveals that 22 per cent of these transgressions were of this nature.[1] Some were combined with other offences. Mariners tried solely for social offences constituted just 15.8 per cent of the total.[2]

By comparison, naval crimes amounted to nearly 78 per cent of all the offences in the sample. Given that social crimes adjudicated by naval courts martial were far fewer, how can a chapter pertaining to these offences that is roughly the same length as that on naval crimes be justified? The answer to this question is straightforward. It is only through the inclusion of multiple examples of trials for social offences that a clear picture emerges of the legal standards used to determine guilt or innocence in such cases. For example, from the transcripts of proceedings for drunkenness it is evident that those found guilty of this offence had to have been too intoxicated to do their duty. Similarly, the minutes of enquiries involving indictments for buggery reveal that the criterion for conviction was anal penetration.

Of the social offences mentioned in the sample, alcohol-related crimes were the most common, comprising almost a third of the charges. The second most frequent type of accusation involved transgressions against property (theft, plunder, embezzlement, fraud, and so on), which constituted about 28 per cent. These were followed by offences involving violence (homicide, fighting, striking an officer, self-mutilation), which

[1]Of the 1,596 charges listed in these volumes, 352 were social offences. For a list of the volumes comprising the sample, see 'Documents and Sources'.

[2]Of the 1,149 men tried, 182 were charged exclusively with social crimes.

made up 21 per cent of the total. Sexual offences were next, amounting to a little more than 9 per cent of the aggregate. And disturbances of the peace (rioting, quarrelling) were the least frequent cause for indictment, coming to only about 8 per cent of the allegations in this category.[1] These social offences are dealt with here in the same order.

[1]The raw numbers are:

Crimes involving alcohol	117
Property crimes	100
Violent crimes	74
Sexual offences	33
Disturbances of the peace	28
Total social offences	352

ALCOHOL-RELATED OFFENCES

51. *Court Martial of James Flanagan*

[ADM 1/5355]

Minutes of proceedings at a court martial held on board His Majesty's ship *Abergavenny* on Monday the 9th day of March 1801.

Present

Edward Tyrrel Smith, Esqr., Captain of His Majesty's ship *Carnatic* and senior captain of His Majesty's ships and vessels in Port Royal Harbour, Jamaica, President.

Captains

Chas. Vinicombe Penrose	Robert Minds
George Ross	John Child

The prisoner was brought into court and the evidence and audience admitted.

Read the order of the Right Honble Lord Hugh Seymour, Vice Admiral of the Blue and Commander in Chief, &^{c}., &^{c}., &^{c}., dated the 5th instant and directed to Edward Tyrrel Smith, Esqr., Captain of His Majesty's ship *Carnatic* and senior captain of His Majesty's ships and vessels in Port Royal Harbour, Jamaica, to try James Flanagan, Sergeant of Marines on board His Majesty's ship *Abergavenny*, for having been repeatedly drunk and incapable of duty, particularly on or about the 20th and the 24th of February last.

Then the members of the court and judge advocate, in open court and before they proceeded to trial, respectively took the oaths directed by Act of Parliament made and passed in the 22d. year of the reign of His late Majesty King George the Second, entitled, *An Act for Amending, Explaining and Reducing into One Act of Parliament the Laws relating to the Government of His Majesty's Ships, Vessels and Forces by Sea.*

A letter from Captain Henry Vansitart of His Majesty's ship *Abergavenny*, to the Right Honble Lord Hugh Seymour, Vice Admiral of the Blue and Commander in Chief, &^{c}., &^{c}., &^{c}., was read as follows:

H.M. ship *Abergavenny*
Port Royal, February 26th, 1801

… James Flanagan, Sergeant of Marines on board His Majesty's ship under my command, having been repeatedly drunk and incapable of duty, particularly on or about the 20th and 24th instant,

I request your Lordship will be pleased to order a court martial to be assembled for the trial of the said James Flanagan on the above written charge. …

All the evidence were ordered to withdraw out of court, except Lieutenant Baily, who was sworn.

Prosecutor Have you seen the prisoner repeatedly drunk and incapable of duty?

Ans^{r}. I have.

Prosecutor Can you point out any particular instance?

Ans^{r}. On the 20th of Febry last, between the hours of seven and eight in the evening, I sent for Sergeant Flanagan to give him orders respecting the sentinels; the corporal whom I sent told me he could not come, being so much intoxicated. As I had often spoken to him on that subject and to beware of it [*sic*], he still repeated it. I ordered the corporal and Sergeant Neal of the *Surprize* to bring him on deck; the situation he was then in Captain Vansitart saw, the prisoner not being able to speak.

Court Has the prisoner ever been in the Sick List to your knowledge?

Ans^{r}. Not that I can recollect.

This witness was asked no further questions; he withdrew and Mr. Lamb, the Master, was called and sworn.

Prosecutor Do you know the prisoner to be sergeant of Marines?

Ans^{r}. Yes.

Prosc^{r}. Have you seen the prisoner repeatedly drunk and incapable of duty?

Ans^{r}. I have seen him drunk several times and incapable of duty from drunkenness.

Pros^{r}. Can you remember any particular instances?

Ans^{r}. One evening between four and five o'clock, previous to the prisoner's confinement, he was not able to attend to see or serve the wine out.

Pros^{r}. Could he have taken charge of the guard, relieve the sentinels or otherwise have done his duty as a sergeant?

Ans^{r}. He was not capable of doing his duty.

Court From what cause was the prisoner incapable of doing his duty?

Ans^{r}. Being in liquor.

Court Was he drunk?

Ans^{r}. It is my opinion he was drunk.

Court Has he been in the Sick List any time to your knowledge, any time since he belonged to the ship?

Ans^{r}. No.

Court For what length of time has he attended issuing of wine to the ship's company?

Ans^{r}. He has acted as purser's steward about three or four months.

Court Did he do the duty of sergeant of Marines as well as purser's steward during that time?

Ans^{r}. Not to my knowledge.

Court Do you know of any other instance of the prisoner's drunkenness besides the one you have already ment^{d}.?

Ans^{r}. No.

Prosecutor You have said you do not know any particular instance, excepting the one specified in your evidence; do you mean that you do not exactly remember the time?

Ans^{r}. No, I do not remember the time.

Cross questioned by the prisoner.

Prisoner How long have I been in the ship?

Ans^{r}. About five months to the best of my knowledge.

Prisoner During that time, did I do duty as a purser's steward continually?

Ans^{r}. Not to my knowledge.

Prisoner Have I done my duty as sergeant of Marines all the time I have been in the ship?

Ans^{r}. I never saw you do duty as sergeant of Marines.

Prisoner When Sergeant Hale was confined, who did the duty of sergeant?

Ans^{r}. I do not know.

Prisoner Have you ever seen me exercise the Marines on the quarterdeck?

Ans^{r}. I never have.

Prisoner Did I ever report to you my putting the lights out when you was commanding officer?

Ans^{r}. Not to my knowledge.

Prisoner Did you call upon me as sergeant when you and Sergeant Hale had a difference?

Ans^{r}. I did.

Court Have you ever sent for the prisoner to give him orders at any time and was he ever incapable of executing those orders from drunkenness?

Ans^{r}. No, I never did.

Court How do you know the prisoner was drunk the evening he was serving out the wine?

Ans^{r}. I was on deck and saw him so and Mr. Fitten sent for another person to serve out the wine.

No further questions was asked this witness; Corporal Wood of the Marines was called and sworn.

Prosecutor Do you know the prisoner to be James Flanagan, Sergeant of Marines?

Ans^{r}. Yes.

Prosecutor Have you seen the prisoner repeatedly drunk and incapable of duty?

Ans^{r}. Yes I have, particularly on the 20th and 24th of February last.

Pros^{r}. Can you remember any other instances?

Ans^{r}. No, I cannot exactly remember as to the day.

Pros^{r}. Do you remember a particular instance, when, in consequence of the prisoner's drunkenness, the prisoners were let loose and drinking and making a riot with him about the decks?

Ans^{r}. Yes I do, but cannot remember the time.

Prosecutor Was he then doing duty as sergeant of Marines?

Ans^{r}. Yes, he was.

Pros^{r}. Were two men confined as mutineers of the *Hermione* among the prisoners that were released?

Ans^{r}. No, they were not; they were in irons.

Pros^{r}. Was there two sentries, one having particular charge of the mutineers, the other with the rest of the prisoners?

Ansr. Yes, there were two.

Prosecutor Is it customary when lights are put out, the sergeant or corporal of Marines having the watch, to return the keys of the prisoners' irons to the commanding officer?

Ans^{r}. No, the person who has the watch always carries them in his pocket.

Prosecutor The night that the prisoners were let out of irons, was it at that time the prisoner's watch?

Ans^{r}. Yes, it was.

Prosecutor Had he charge of the keys?

Ans^{r}. Yes, he had.

Prosecutor Did he release the prisoners or, in consequence of his drunkenness, were they taken from him?

Ans^{r}. It is the rule of the ship to put the prisoners in irons at eight o'clock at night, but the prisoner neglected doing it at eight o'clock; and they remained out of irons until half past eleven.

Prosecutor Are the prisoners kept in irons on the poop during the day time?

Ans^{r}. No, they are not.

Court You say that the prisoner was drunk on the 20th and 24th of February last; relate to the court any particulars you can recollect of the situation of the prisoner on those days?

Ans^{r}. The prisoner on the twentieth was ordered at eight o'clock at night to appear before the captain; he was so drunk that Corporal Foot and myself were obliged to carry him up on the quarterdeck before the captain. And on the 24th at eight o'clock at night, Lieutenant Fitten went to see whether the prisoners were well secured in irons; he found the sergeant laying on his chest drunk and I was present at the time.

Court At either of the above mentioned times, had the prisoner charge of the keys of the prisoners' irons or was it his watch?

Ans^{r}. He had not charge of the keys nor had he the watch.

Court Did you know the prisoner's performing any parts of a sergeant's duty on either of those days and what were they?

Ans^{r}. He did not.

Court How many prisoners were there under the sergeant's care on the night he neglected putting them in irons?

Ans^{r}. To the best of my knowledge, about six or seven.

Court In what part of the ship were they confined during the day?

Ans^{r}. The two mutineers of the *Hermione* were constantly in irons under the half deck; and the rest were on the poop, but not in irons.

Court Has the prisoner ever done duty as a sergeant independent of purser's steward?

Ans^{r}. He did sergeant's duty before he acted as purser's steward.

Court Did you ever see the prisoner drunk and incapable of duty while doing duty as sergeant of Marines only?

Ans^{r}. Yes, the time he neglected putting the prisoners in irons.

Court Do you know at whose request or by whose order he assisted the purser?

Ans^{r}. I do not.

Cross questioned by the prisoner.

Prisoner — You say I was drunk on the night the prisoners were out of irons! Who put the lights out and to whom was it reported?

Ans^{r}. — I do not know who reported it, but I know you was drunk.

No further questions asked this witness, and Lieutenant Bayley was again called by the court.

Court — Did you consider the prisoner, upon the 20th of February last, doing duty as sergeant of Marines?

Ans^{r}. — I did.

Court — In the double capacity of the prisoner as sergeant of Marines and doing the duty to assist the purser, did he do his duty, in general, as sergeant of Marines?

Ans^{r}. — I considered him as such.

Court — Have you given him orders as sergeant of Marines in the execution of your duty?

Ans^{r}. — I have at times.

Court — For what purpose was the prisoner wanted when you sent for him the night of the 20th? You say he was so drunk he could not come up?

Ans^{r}. — I wanted him to caution the sentries to be very particular that no communication should be had with the shore boats in order to prevent desertion.

Court — To your knowledge, did the prisoner ever do duty as sergeant of Marines independent of purser's steward.

Ans^{r}. — He has done duty as sergeant of Marines and purser's steward at the same time.

Cross questioned by the prisoner.

Prisoner — Have you since the 20th of February called upon me to take an account of any business transacted in the ship in the purser's concerns?

Ans^{r}. — Yes.

The witness withdrew, having no further questions put to him.

The evidence in support of the charges being finished, the prisoner was called upon to make his defence; he said he had no defence to make or witnesses to call. The court was cleared and proceeded to deliberate upon and form the sentence. …

The court is of opinion that the charges are proved, but in consideration of circumstances and the various duties with which the prisoner has been charged, they do only adjudge him to be broke as sergeant and reduced to serve as Private Marine in the ranks, and he is hereby sentenced accordingly.

...

52. *Court Martial of David Lawson*

[ADM 1/5363]

Minutes taken at a court martial assembled on board His Majesty's ship *Gladiator* in Portsmouth Harbour the 27th day of June 1803.

Present

John Holloway, Esq[r]., Rear Admiral of the Red and second officer in the command of His Majesty's ships and vessels at Portsmouth and Spithead, President.

Captain	Captain
Albemarle Bertie	The Right Honble. William, Earl of Northesk
William Henry Jervis	Philip Charles Durham
The Honble. Henry Blackwood	James Bowen
W[m] Gordon Rutherford	Thomas Baker
The Honble. Courtney Boyle	Henry Heathcote
Thos Gordon Caulfield	Thomas Manby

The prisoner was brought in and audience admitted.

The order from the Right Honourable Lords Commissioners of the Admiralty, dated the 25th June 1803 and directed to the president for the trial of Mr. David Lawson, Carpenter of His Majesty's ship *Nemesis*, for repeated drunkenness between the 24th of December last and the 14th of May, was read.

The members of the court and the judge advocate then, in open court and before they proceeded to trial, respectively took the several oaths enjoined and directed in and by an Act of Parliament made and passed in the 22d. year of the reign of His late Majesty King George the 2nd, entitled *An Act for Amending, Explaining and Reducing into One Act of Parliament the Laws relating to the Government of His Majesty's Ships, Vessels and Forces by Sea*.

Then the letter from Captain Philip Somerville, Commander of His Majesty's ship *Nemesis*, dated 15th May 1803 and directed to Sir Evan Nepean, Bar[t]., containing the charge, was read and the witnesses were ordered to withdraw and attend their examinations separately, which they did as follows:

Lieutenant Thomas Bright, First Lieutenant of His Majesty's ship *Nemesis*, called in and sworn.

Captain Somerville asked:

Q Relate to the court the general conduct of the prisoner between the 24th of December and the 14th of May last as to sobriety.

A He was drunk on the 24th of December when on duty at the yard and on the second of January and 29th of April, when the ship was at sea, and very often at other times, the particular dates I do not recollect.

The court asked:

Q Do you recollect sending for the carpenter at any time on duty when he was incapable of coming to you from drunkenness?

A On the night of the 2nd of January, he was sent for on the quarterdeck to repair the binnacle; he was so drunk that two of the after guard were obliged to bring him up.

Mr. Elias Symes, Master of the *Nemesis*, called in and sworn.

Captain Somerville asked:

Q Relate to the court the general conduct of the prisoner between the 24th of December and the 14th of May last as to sobriety.

A On the evening of the 2nd of January, something was the matter with the binnacle; I requested the officer of the watch to have it altered as the helmsman could not see the compass. I was directed by Captain Somerville to send for the prisoner; after some time finding he did not come up, I sent for him the second time. He was reported to me that he was not able to come upon deck, owing to being in liquor; I was requested by Mr. Bright to go down into his cabin to see if it was so or not. I found the prisoner in liquor and incapable of duty; I have frequently seen him in the same state. I cannot speak to particular days, I have seen it so often, even when he has been at the dockyard on duty.

The prosecution being closed, the prisoner was called on for his defence; he said that he recollected being so drunk as to be incapable of duty but once and that was at nine o'clock at night.

The court was cleared and agreed that the charge had been proved against the said David Lawson and did adjudge him to be dismissed from his office of carpenter of His Majesty's said ship *Nemesis* and to serve on board such ship or ships of His Majesty and in such situation as the commander in chief of His Majesty's ships and vessels for the time being at Portsmouth aforesaid should direct.

The court was again opened, the prisoner brought in, audience admitted and sentence passed accordingly. …

52A. *Somerville to Nepean*

[ADM 1/5363] *Nemesis*, Plymouth Sound
May 15th, 1803

… I have to request that you will be pleased to move my Lords Commissioners of the Admiralty for an order to try by a court martial Mr David Lawson, Carpenter of His Majesty's ship under my command for repeated drunkenness between the 24th December last and the 14th of this month. …

53. *Court Martial of John Farrel and John Barry*

[ADM 1/5372]

Minutes of the proceedings at a court martial assembled and held onboard His Majesty's ship *Dreadnought* off Cadiz the 7th March 1806.

Present

The Right Honble, the Earl of Northesk, Rear Admiral of the Red, &c., &c., &c., Presid^{t}.

Captains

The Right Honourable
Lord Amelius Beauclerk
Charles Rowley
John Giffard
Thomas Harvey
John Conn
Richard Thomas

Chas. Jno. Moore Mansfield
Charles Ogle
W^{m}. Gordon Rutherford
Charles Bullen
James Hillyar

Thomas Tait appointed judge advocate by the court.

A.M. at 8, the court assembled and, being opened by the president, the prisoners, John Farrell and John Barry, Corporals of His Majesty's ship *Neptune*, were brought in and the witnesses and audience admitted.

Read the order from the Right Honble Cuthbert Lord Collingwood, Vice Admiral of the Red and Commander in Chief of His Majesty's ships and vessels on the Mediterranean station, dated the 6th day of March 1806 and directed to the Right Honourable, The Earl of Northesk, Rear Admiral of the Red and second officer in the command of His Majesty's ships and vessels off Cadiz, for assembling the court.

The court and judge advocate then, and before they proceeded to trial, respectively took the oaths appointed agreeable to Act of Parliament.

Read the following letter[1] from Thomas Francis Fremantle, Esqr., Captain of His Majesty's ship *Neptune*, in application for the court martial, vizt.:

Neptune at sea, 6 March 1806

… John Farrell and John Barry, Corporals onboard His Majesty's ship *Neptune*, having been guilty of drunkenness on the evening of the 5th instant,

I am to request your Lordships will be pleased to direct a court martial may be assembled to try them for that offence.

…

All the witnesses being withdrawn out of court except M^r^. Richard Hurrill, Clerk of the *Neptune*, and him being sworn, the prosecutor put the following question to the witness:

Prosecutor Qust — Have you the ship's books? See and inform the court what John Farrell and John Barry are rated.

Ans. — John Farrell, Ship's Corporal; John Barry, Ship's Corporal.

The witness then ordered to withdraw.

Lieutenant Acklam of the *Neptune* sworn.

Prosecutor Qust 1 — Relate to the court the circumstances that occasioned the reporting the prisoners to me on the evening of the 5th instant.

Ans. — I had occasion to send for the prisoner, Barry, between 7 and 8 o'clock and, after sending several messages to him without his coming, I desired the sergeant of Marines of the watch to go for the other corporal, Farrell; he returned to me soon afterwards and reported that Farrell was too drunk or incapable of receiving orders, upon which I desired him to be put on the poop under charge of the sentinel. Upon his going over the quarterdeck, I observed that he was too drunk to walk without some difficulty. The other prisoner, Barry, came up soon afterwards and I directed him also to be put on the poop under charge of the sentinel, as he appeared to be in the same state with Corporal Farrell; in the course of the evening, I reported this to Capt. Fremantle.

[1]This letter is addressed to Vice Admiral Collingwood.

Sergeant Purcell, Royal Marines, sworn.

Prosecutor

Ques^{t}. 1st — Was you sent by Lieut. Acklam to bring the prisoner, Farrell, on deck on the evening of the 5th instant?

Ans. — Yes.

2nd — Where did you find him and in what situation?

Ans. — I found him in his own berth with his hand on his head in a state of intoxication.

3d. — What time of evening did this happen?

Ans. — To the best of my recollection, it was half past seven.

Court

Ques^{t}. — How do you know he was in a state of intoxication?

Ans. — I put my hand on his shoulder, roused him, told him M^{r}. Acklam wanted him on deck; when he stood on his legs, he was incapable of walking to the quarterdeck.

Lieut^{t}. George Westal Hooper sworn.

Prosecutor

Ques^{t}. 1st — Was you officer of the watch between the hours of 6 and 8 on the evening of the 5th instant?

Ans. — Yes.

2nd — Did you see the prisoner, John Barry?

Ans. — Yes.

3d — Was he drunk or sober?

Ans. — He appeared to be drunk.

Court

Ques^{t}. 1 — Where did you see the prisoner?

Ans. — I saw him going on the poop.

2nd — What was your reason for supposing him to be drunk?

Ans. — By his staggering and almost falling on the ladder as he went up.

Lieutenant Westroppe sworn.

Prosecutor

Ques^{t} 1st — Did you report the people at your quarters were all sober about half past five on the evening of the 5th instant?

Ans. — I did.

2nd — Did you particularize John Barry at that time?

Ans. — I did and he was then sober.

3d — Is it not usual for him to carry a candle and lantern when the ports are lowered down and the people at quarters?

Ans.	Yes and he did so on the evening of the 5th instant and walked along the starb^{d}. side with me so that if he had been drunk at that time, I must have seen it.
Court Ques^{t}	Did you see the prisoner afterwards, when he was brought on the quarterdeck?
Ans.	No.

Lieut. Shaw sworn.

Prosecutor Quest. 1st	Is the prisoner, John Farrell, at your quarters?
Ans.	Yes.
2nd	Did you report him, with others, sober on the evening of the 5th ins^{t} at half past five?
Ans.	I did.
3d	Did you see him in particular?
A.	Not in particular.
Court Qus^{t}.	Did you see the prisoner, Farrell, any time afterwards on that evening?
Ans.	I did not see him until the next day.

Mr. Smith, Mids^{n}., sworn.

Prosecutor Ques^{t}. 1st	Did you see the prisoner, Farrell, at his quarters on the evening of the 5th instant about half past five?
Ans.	I did.
Q. 2nd	Was he then perfectly sober and did you report him so?
Ans.	I did not see he was any ways intoxicated; he ans^{d}. his muster very well.
Q. 3d	Did you not report him sober?
Ans.	Yes.
Q. 4th	Did you see the prisoner afterwards, when he was brought on the quarterdeck?
Ans.	No, I did not.

The evidence on the part of the prosecution being closed, the president called on the prisoners to enter on their defence; they gave into court a written paper signed by themselves, which was read as follows:

… It is with great concern that we, John Farrell and John Barry, have heard the charge of drunkenness substantiated against us and should think it an aggravation of our offence to offer anything in vindication of our conduct, which, with much contrition, we confess has been very bad; but as it is the only time we ever offended, we humbly entreat the court for mercy, with a perfect assurance of doing everything in future to merit it. We will not trespass longer on the time of the court; only beg leave to call upon Cap[t]. Fremantle, the officers of the *Neptune* now in court and Sergeant Anderson, who has acted as master at arms these two years, to speak to our character during the whole time we have served under them (except in the unfortunate circumstance for which we have been tried). …

Capt[n]. Fremantle gave the prisoners a general good character, except in the instance for which they were now tried.

The court was then cleared and the members proceeded to deliberate; and on being again opened, the following sentence was read by the judge advocate:

'The court is of opinion that the charge is fully proved against the prisoners, but, in consideration of their good characters, does only adjudge them to receive sixty lashes on their bare backs, with a cat of nine tails, onboard His Majesty's ship *Neptune* at such time as the commander in chief shall think proper to direct.'

…

54. *Court Martial of Joseph Fountain*

[ADM 1/5399]

Minutes of the proceedings at a court martial assembled on board His Majesty's ship the *Polyphemus* at Port Royal, Jamaica, on Saturday the 23d September 1809.

Present

Charles Dashwood, Esquire, Captain of His Majesty's ship the *Franchise* and second officer in the command of His Majesty's ships and vessels at Port Royal, president.

Captains

John Serrel
William Pryce Cumby
Samuel Hood Inglefield

Commander

William Henry Shirreff

Being all the post captains commanding His Majesty's ships at Port Royal and the senior commander.

The court being opened and the prosecutor, prisoner and witnesses present, read the order from Bart. Bartholomew Samuel Rowley, Esq[re].,

Vice Admiral of the White and Commander in Chief of His Majesty's ships and vessels at Jamaica &c., &c., &c., dated the 22d day of September 1809, directing the aforesaid Captain Charles Dashwood to assemble a court martial (he being president thereof) to try Joseph Fountain, Master at Arms of His Majesty's ship the *Polyphemus*, for having on the 20th instant, when officiating as provost marshal, permitted Thomas Green, a prisoner in his charge under the sentence of a court martial, to drink to such excess immediately before his punishment was to have commenced as to render it improper for the said punishment to take place.

Read the warrant from the president, with the concurrence of the court, appointing Mr George Maude to execute the office of judge advocate on the occasion.

Then the members of the court and judge advocate respectively took the oaths directed by Act of Parliament.

Read the documents constituting the charge as follows:[1]

HMS *Lily*, Port Royal Harbour
September 20th, 1809

... I beg leave to acquaint you that in compliance with your orders relative to the punishment of Benjamin Taylor and Thomas Green, Marines belonging to His Majesty's sloop under my command, the boats were assembled this morning for that purpose; but in consequence of the former having been sent to the hospital in a fever and the latter, when brought on board by the provost marshal this morning, being extremely intoxicated, I judged it proper, from the opinion of the surgeon, not to proceed with the punishment.

...

Polyphemus, Port Royal, Jamaica
21st September 1809

... I beg to state in obedience to the direction contained in your letter of yesterday's date that being unable this morning from ill health to quit the ship, I ordered the first lieutenant (Edmund Denman) to proceed on board the *Lily* and make all possible inquiry into the circumstances therein referred to.

I herewith transmit to you his statement together with the enclosure of your letter.

...

[1]The first of these letters is from Commander W. H. Shirreff to Vice Admiral B. S. Rowley; the second and third are from Captain William Pryce Cumby to Rowley; and the fourth is from Lieutenant Edmund Denman to Cumby.

Polyphemus, Port Royal, Jamaica
21st September 1809

… In obedience to your directions, I have been on board His Majesty's sloop *Lily* and find from the testimony of M[r]. Justice Hall, Boatswain, and Patrick Burns, Boy, that the prisoner, Thomas Green, did, on the morning of the 20th instant, procure from Johnston, Purser's Steward of that sloop, about a pint of spirits, which was given to and drank by him in presence [*sic*] of Joseph Fountain, Master at Arms of this ship then doing duty as provost marshal, who repeatedly urged the said prisoner to bear a hand as the boats were coming alongside.

It also appears from the testimony of W. Prideaux, Surgeon of the *Lily*, that the provost marshal said to the prisoner, 'You had some grog on board the *Polyphemus*;' but on the strictest inquiry on board here, I am unable to procure any proof of this fact. As I apprehend the circumstance of the provost marshal having allowed the prisoner, Green, to drink to excess immediately before the punishment was to have commenced can be clearly proved before the court martial by the abovementioned evidence, I beg leave humbly to submit to your decision the propriety of his being tried for so gross a neglect of his duty by which the punishment awarded by a court martial and ordered by the commander in chief to be inflicted was shamefully evaded.

…

Then all the witnesses withdrew by direction of the court, except Lieutenant John Love Hammick of the *Polyphemus*, who was sworn and examined as follows:

Question by Lieutenant Edmund Denman, as prosecutor: Do you recollect being sent on board the *Lily* on the morning of the 20th instant with the prisoner, Fountain, as provost marshal and a man named Green, a prisoner under his charge, for the purpose of receiving the punishment adjudged on the said Green by a court martial?

Ans[r]) Yes.

Pros[r].) Did the said Green appear to be intoxicated when carried on board the *Lily* and what state was he in when ordered to be tied up?

Ans[r].) He did not appear to be in the least intoxicated on our way to the *Lily*; but when sent from her into the boat to be seized up, he appeared perfectly drunk and vomited while it was attempted to seize him up.

Court) What time did he then remain on board the *Lily*?

Ans[r]) I think about three quarters of an hour.

Lieutenant Hammick withdrew and Mr. Justice Hall, Boatswain of the *Lily*, was called and sworn.

Pros[r].) State to the court what you know respecting the charge against the prisoner.

Ans^{r}.) On the morning of the day appointed for the punishment, I heard Green say to the prisoner that Johnstone was the only man that could do it. The prisoner answered, 'Bear a hand with it. I don't care; I shall not see it.' I then returned from the head and heard Green reply that he was hurried away so quick; the prisoner said, 'it was a pity.' Green said, 'Never mind, I have taken a good drink; and if I had time, I would have drank the whole.' On my return below, I saw the boy, Patrick Burns, with a white basin in which there appeared to be liquor, but I am not sure; he delivered it to Green.

Pros^{r}.) Did Green drink it in your presence?

Ans^{r}.) I did not see him drink it.

Court: Was the prisoner present when the boy gave the basin to Green.

Ans^{r}.) He was.

Court) Did you hear any conversation between them at the time?

Ans^{r}.) No.

Court) Was the prisoner in a situation to see, or must he have known, that Green took the basin?

Ans^{r}.) He must have certainly have seen and known it.

Prisoner) Was I at that time in the head or on the forecastle?

Ans^{r}.) The prisoner was standing on the forecastle by the night heads, close to Green.

> Mr. Justice Hall withdrew and Patrick Burns, Boy belonging to the *Lily*, was called and, after being examined touching his knowledge of the nature of an oath, was sworn according to the Romish mode.

Prosecutor) State to the court what you know relative to the charge against the prisoner.

Ans^{r}.) Green, being in charge of the prisoner, was going from the gangway to the head when he saw the purser's steward and I heard him (Green) ask him if he was the man to get him some liquor. The purser's steward went down and handed the liquor to me up the fore hatchway: I gave it to Green in the head, which the prisoner saw and told him to bear a hand with it, as the boats were coming alongside. There was about a pint of rum in a blackjack,[1] which I saw Green drink. He then gave me the jack and I carried it down the fore hatchway.

Pros^{r}.) Did the prisoner offer to taste it before Green drank?

Ans^{r}.) No.

Court: Are you sure it was spirits that was given to Green?

Ans^{r}.) Yes.

Court) Did you give Green any liquor in a basin?

[1]A tankard.

Ans^{r}.) No.

The witness withdrew and William Johnstone, Purser's Steward of the *Lily*, was called and sworn.

Prosecutor) Did you on the morning of the 20th instant give the Boy, Patrick Burns, spirits and what quantity and to whom did you direct him to deliver it?

Ans^{r}.) I gave him about a gill and a half of spirits in a large blackjack, which stood on the gunner's table with some water in it, and I told him to give it to Green.

Court) Did you measure it?

Ans^{r}.) No.

Court) Who asked you for it?

Ans^{r}.) Green did; I then asked the prisoner if he would allow me to do it and he said, 'Yes, bear a hand and bring it up.'

Court) Do you know if any other liquor was given to Green?

Ans^{r}.) No.

The witness withdrew and M^{r}. Justice Hall was again called.

Court) Are you sure it was a white basin that you saw the boy have in his hand and how far were you from him?

Ans^{r}.) Yes; I was about two yards from him.

Court) Did this happen before the punishment was to have commenced?

Ans^{r}.) It happened about a quarter of an hour after they came on board.

The witness withdrew and Mr. Robert Prideaux, Surgeon of the *Lily*, was called and sworn.

Court) What state was Thos. Green in on the morning of the 20th instant, when ordered to be tied up for punishment?

Ans^{r}.) So extremely intoxicated that two or three men were not able to tie him up.

Court) Had you seen him at any previous time on that day?

Ans^{r}.) Yes, about 10 minutes before on the *Lily*'s gangway when he appeared very stupid and became worse & worse.

Court) Did it appear to you that his intoxication proceeded from his having drank spirits?

Ans^{r}.) I am quite positive it was from rum; he threw up, as I believe, above a pint of rum on the *Lily*'s quarterdeck, after coming out of the launch.

Court) When you first saw him that morning, did he appear sober?

Ans^{r}.) It did not, at the time, appear to me that he was not sober; he appeared rather stupid, which I then attributed to his apprehension of the impending punishment, but, from what afterwards occurred, I imagine he must have been in liquor to a certain degree.

The prisoner was then informed that the prosecution was closed; and the court was cleared to allow him time to consider of what he might have to offer in his defence, which (on the court's being re-opened) was read as follows:

… Never having before officiated as provost marshal at a punishment nor having orders not to let the prisoner have any refreshment, I did not know that I was culpable in so doing. I regret that I forgot to taste the contents of the pot given him, having no idea that it was anything at most but a little weak grog. I trust that from the character I hope to produce from my captain and the late first lieutenant, Captain Grove, the court will favourably consider my case and therefore depend on your clemency. …

Captain Cumby of the *Polyphemus* then stated that prior to the present offence the prisoner's conduct as ship's corporal was such as to induce him to recommend him to the commander in chief as a fit person for the office of master at arms and he was accordingly, about a month ago, appointed to that situation.

Captain Groves of the *Shark* stated that, during the time of his being first lieutenant of the *Polyphemus*, the prisoner was uncommonly attentive and his conduct as ship's corporal perfectly correct.

Lieutenant Denman (first of the *Polyphemus*) stated that he was induced by the prisoner's general good conduct while ship's corporal to recommend him to Captain Cumby on the dismissal of the former master at arms as a fit person to succeed him.

The court was then cleared and proceeded to deliberate on the sentence and, having very attentively considered the evidence produced in support of the charge and what the prisoner had offered in his defence, the court was of opinion that the charge was proved; but, in consideration of his general good character, did only adjudge the said Joseph Fountain to be dismissed from his situation as master at arms of His Majesty's ship *Polyphemus* and to receive fifty lashes on his bare back with a cat of nine tails alongside such of His Majesty's ships or vessels and at such time as the commander in chief shall direct.

The court was opened and sentence was passed accordingly.

…

55. *Court Martial of Samuel Pike*

[ADM 1/5436]

Minutes of a court martial assembled and held on board His Majesty's ship *Theseus* off West Capel the 24th day of June 1813.

Present

Wm Bedford, Esqr, Rear Admiral of the Blue, Captain of the Fleet and second officer in the command of His Majesty's ships and vessels off West Capel, President.

Captain Jno Sprat Rainier
Captain Wm Hall Gage
Captain Ge^o^ Char^s^ Mc Kenzie
Captain William Prowse
Captain H^y^ Edwd Regin^d^ Baker

John White, officiating Judge Advocate

The prisoner was brought into court and the evidence and audience admitted. Read the order of William Young, Esqre., Admiral of the White and Commander in Chief of a squadron of His Majesty's ship and vessels to be employed on a particular service, dated the 23d of June 1813 and directed to William Bedford, Esqre., Rear Admiral of the Blue, Captain of the Fleet and second officer in the command of His Majesty's ships and vessels off West Capel, to try Mr Samuel Pike, Carpenter of His Majesty's sloop *Drake*, for having been guilty of repeated drunkenness between the 28th of April 1812 and 6th of June 1813. Read the order for Mr John White to officiate as judge advocate upon the occasion. Then the members of the court and judge advocate, before they proceeded to trial, respectively took the oaths directed by Act of Parliament made and passed in the 22d year of the reign of His late Majesty George the 2d, entitled *An Act for Amending, Explaining and Reducing into one Act of Parliament the Laws relating to the Government of His Majesty's Ships, Vessels and Forces by Sea*.

Read a letter from Captain Gregory Grant to Admiral Wm Young, Commander in Chief &^c^., as follows, viz.:

His Majesty's Sloop *Drake*
Off the Scheldt, the 16 of June 1813

… M^r^. Samuel Pike, Carpenter of His Majesty's sloop *Drake* under my command, having been guilty of repeated drunkenness between the 28th of April 1812 and 6th of June 1813,

I have to request he may be tried by a court martial for the above offence. …

All the evidences were ordered to withdraw out of court, except Lieutenant Edward Reding, belonging to His Majesty's sloop *Drake*, who was sworn:

Captn G. Grant, Prosecutor	Had the prisoner been repeatedly drunk between the 28th of April 1812 & the 6th instant?
Answer	He has.
Prosecutor	Do you consider the prisoner to be an habitual drunkard?
Answer	Completely so.
Prosecutor	State any particular instance of his drunkenness.
Answer	I cannot recollect the exact time.
Prosecutor	When the ship was at Sheerness on, or about, the 20th July 1812, was he drunk when he returned from the dockyard?
Answer	He was to the best of my knowledge.
Court	Was he returning from duty at the time?
Answer	He was.
Court	Have you found the prisoner drunk when wanted on duty in any instance you can recollect?
Answer	I have so, but cannot say as to the particular time.
Court	In what state was the prisoner at those times you stated he was drunk; was he perfectly incapable of doing duty?
Answer	Quite incapable.
Court	Was it a general practice when he went on shore on duty that he got in that state?
Answer	It was.
Court	Has the prisoner ever been punished in any way for being drunk at any of the times you have specified?
Answer	He has been suspended from duty till he was sober.
Prisoner	Have you ever seen me come off sober from my duty?
Answer	I cannot say I have.
	Evidence withdrew
Mr. Robert Gillespie, Surgeon of the *Drake*,	Sworn and examined as follows, *vizt*.

Prosecutor	Have you ever seen the prisoner drunk between the 28th of April 1812 and 6th of June 1813?
Answer	I have seen him frequently drunk and so much so that I would not have put any trust in him.
Prosecutor	Do you consider the prisoner to be an habitual drunkard?
Answer	I have seen him repeatedly drunk.
Prosecutor	While you have been attending the prisoner when he was sick, have you found him in a state of intoxication?
Answer	I have found him so once, certainly.
	The prisoner asked this witness no questions; the latter withdrew.

M^{r}. Ja^{s} Wharton, Midshipman of the *Drake*, sworn.

Prosecutor	Have you ever been sent frequently to the dockyard with the prisoner between the 28th of April 1812 and 6th of June 1813?
Answer	I have.
Prosecutor	Has he repeatedly returned to the ship drunk when with you during the above time?
Answer	He has, more than once.
Prosecutor	Do you conceive that the prisoner will get drunk when he has an opportunity?
Answer	I think he will.
Court	When you have been on duty with the prisoner, were you under the necessity of looking sharp after him to prevent his getting drunk?
Answer	I have been under such necessity.
	The prisoner asked this witness no questions, the latter withdrew.

David Botherwicke, Seaman, sworn and examined as follows:

Prosecutor	Have you seen the prisoner repeatedly drunk between the 28th of April 1812 and 6th of June 1813?
Answer	Yes.
Prosecutor	During that time has he been repeatedly drunk when returning from duty at the dockyard?
Answer	Yes.

The prisoner asked this witness no question, the latter withdrew.

Mr. Robert Gillespie, Surgeon, was again called.

Prisoner — You will be pleased to certify to the court whether I have suffered from the gout and a lightness in my head.

Answer — The prisoner has been labouring under a complaint which I believe to be the gout but know nothing of the lightness of his head.

Witness was ordered to withdraw.

The prisoner was called upon to make his defence, which he did in the following words, *viz*[t]:

… I most humbly beg leave to apologize to the honourable court for the trouble imposed upon them in consequence of my being arraigned before them, which devolves upon me one of the most painful of duties. I shall not trespass upon your time by any futile comments on the charge prefer'd against me any more than a great debility arising from long service in the North Sea, a rheumatic gout with which I am frequently afflicted and the excruciating pain that attends the malady have caused me to enter into that excess which has been produced in evidence against me. I cannot omit making mention of my distressed situation when I was apprehended on suspicion of being one concerned in the dreadful crime that was perpetrated on board the *Hermione* and sent from Spithead to Yarmouth Roads for trial, during which period I remained twenty eight days with my legs in irons before an opportunity offered for me to frustrate so base an attempt against my life, when it was proved that I, at the time, was carpenter's mate on board the *Success* and had never been on board the *Hermione*, the effects of which circumstance show themselves at intervals by a derangement of mental faculties and to which may be imputed a manifest change in my deportment at various periods.

This small narrative with the testimonials, now before this honourable court, of my former good conduct will, I trust, cause that lenity to be observed towards me which is the characteristic of the English navy. …

The prisoner having nothing further to offer in his defence, the court was cleared and proceeded to deliberate upon and form the sentence. The court, having carefully and deliberately weighed and considered the evidence produced and what the prisoner alleged in his defence, was of opinion that the charge had been proved and in consequence thereof adjudged the said M[r]. Samuel Pike to be broke from the situation of carpenter of His Majesty's sloop *Drake* and to serve in the carpenter's crew on board any of His Majesty's ships that the commander in chief might direct.

The court was then opened, audience admitted and sentence passed accordingly. …

56. *Court Martial of William Robson*

[ADM 1/5442]

Minutes taken at a court martial assembled on board His Majesty's ship *Gladiator* in Portsmouth Harbour on the eighteenth day of April 1814

Present

Edward James Foote, Esquire, Rear Admiral of the Blue and third officer in the command of His Majesty's ships and vessels at Spithead and in Portsmouth Harbour, President

Captains	Robt. Dudley Oliver	Captains	John Halliday
	Benjn. Willm. Page		George Fowke
	Francis Willm. Austin		Sir Mich^{l} Seymour, Bar^{t}.
	Charles Dashwood		Edward Hawker
	William Wooldridge		John Davie
	John Martin Hanchet		Willm. Elliott

The prisoner was brought in and audience admitted.

The order from the Right Honourable Lords Commissioners of the Admiralty, dated the 16th day of April 1814 and directed to the president, setting forth 'that Admiral Sir Richard Bickerton, Bart. had transmitted to their Lordships a letter, dated the 13th of April 1814, from Edward Saurin, Esquire, Commander of His Majesty's sloop *Hope*, requesting that M^{r}. William Robson, Boatswain of that sloop, may be tried by a court martial for being drunk on the evening of the 20th of the preceding month and to try the said M^{r}. William Robson, Boatswain, for being drunk on the aforesaid evening as represented by Captain Saurin in his said letter,' was read.

The president reported to the court that Captain George Parker was absent on Admiralty leave.

The members of the court and the judge advocate then, in open court and before they proceeded to trial, respectively took the several oaths enjoined and directed in and by an Act of Parliament made and passed in the twenty second year of the reign of His late Majesty King George the Second, entitled *An Act for Amending, Explaining and Reducing into one Act of Parliament the Laws relating to the Government of His Majesty's Ships, Vessels and Forces by Sea*.

Then the abovementioned letter from the said Captain Saurin, containing the charge as set forth in the abovementioned order, was read and is here to annexed and the witnesses were ordered to withdraw and attend their examinations separately, which they did as follows:

Lieutenant Charles Pollard, first Lieutenant of His Majesty's sloop *Hope*, called in and sworn.

Captain Saurin asked:

Q. Do you recollect having seen the prisoner on the evening of the seventeenth of March last?

A. Yes.

Q. Was he drunk or in a fit state or capable of doing his duty?

A. In my opinion he was so drunk as to be incapable of doing his duty. The hands were turned up to hoist the gig in about six o'clock in the evening.

Q. State to the court the conversation that passed between you and him on the afternoon of that day relative to his being then in a state of intoxication.

A. I went upon deck about half past four o'clock when the grog was serving out and saw the boatswain (the prisoner) drinking at the tub. I then called him on one side and spoke to him of the impropriety of what he was doing and cautioned him against doing the like; he said very well he would take warning.

Q. What else did you say to him?

A. I warned him to be cautious of what he was doing and that he then appeared to be rather forward in liquor.

The court asked:

Q. Where was the *Hope* on the evening of the twentieth of March?

A. In Dartmouth Harbour.

Q. When the hands were turned up to hoist the gig in about six o'clock was the prisoner more intoxicated than he was when you admonished him at half past four o'clock?

A. Much more so.

Q. Did he pipe and attend the hoisting the boats in?

A. He did.

Q. Had you occasion to find fault with the manner of his carrying on the duty at that time?

A. Yes, he piped in such a way that it was of no use; the captain and myself were obliged to hoist the boat in by word.

James Grace, a Seaman belonging to His Majesty's sloop *Hope*, called in and sworn.

Captain Saurin asked:

Q. Do you recollect having seen the prisoner on the evening of the twentieth of March last?
A. Yes.
Q. Was he drunk and in a fit state to do his duty?
A. He had been drinking, but not incapable of doing his duty.

The court asked:

Q. Was you on deck when the gig was hoisted in about six o'clock?
A. Yes.
Q. Was she hoisted in by the boatswain's pipe?
A. Yes.
Q. Were you near him?
A. I was standing aft by the mainmast.
Q. Did he pipe in the same manner he usually does?
A. I cannot say exactly; I did not see any odds with regard to the piping but what he did it as usual.
Q. Did you hear the prisoner give any order or speak at the time?
A. No, I did not.
Q. Did you see him walk?
A. Yes.
Q. Did he walk perfectly steady?
A. Yes, he walked steady.
Q. Did you hear anybody else at the time the gig was hoisting in interfere or give any orders relative to the hoisting her in?
A. No.
Q. Did you hear any officer speaking at the time?
A. No, I was not taking particular notice.
Q. Why did you suppose the prisoner had been drinking when he carried on the duty perfectly well and walked without reeling?
A. I could tell by the look of him that he had been drinking.
Q. Did you see him drink that afternoon?
A. No.
Q. Had you been drinking that afternoon with the prisoner?
A. No.
Q. Were you perfectly sober that afternoon yourself?
A. Yes, I was myself.

William Boyce, a Seaman belonging to His Majesty's sloop *Hope*, called in and sworn.

Captain Saurin asked:

Q. Do you recollect having seen the prisoner on the twentieth of March last?
A. Yes.
Q. Was he drunk or in a fit state to do his duty?

A. He was not sober; he was intoxicated. He was not fit to do his duty.

The court asked:

Q. Why did you think him intoxicated?

A. I saw the captain when he called him aft and told him he was drunk and not in a fit state to do his duty. Mr. Robson asked the ship's company if he was drunk. I told him then that he was not sober and soon afterwards the captain sent him below.

Q. Did you observe yourself that he was drunk?

A. No, not until the captain called him aft.

Q. Was that after the gig was hoisting?

A. Yes, it was whilst they were squaring yards.

Q. Were you on deck when the gig was hoisted in?

A. Yes.

Q. Did you observe the boatswain carry on the duty then?

A. Yes.

Q. Where was the prisoner when he asked the ship's company if he was drunk and in what manner did he ask the question?

A. He went round the deck, between decks; he asked them, 'Am I drunk?' first to one, then to another.

The prisoner asked:

Q. Did I go round betwixt decks to ask all the ship's company before the captain confined me?

A. No, it was when he was sent below to be confined.

The prosecution being closed, the prisoner was called on for his defence. He produced a paper writing containing the same [*sic*], which was read by the judge advocate and is hereto annexed.

Alexander Gilmore, a Seaman belonging to His Majesty's sloop *Hope*, called in and sworn.

The prisoner asked:

Q. Did you see me on board the *Hope* on the evening of the twentieth of March about the time the gig was hoisted in?

A. Yes.

Q. Did you think that I was then drunk or not?

A. No, he was not drunk to the best of my knowledge.

Q. Did I do my duty in hoisting the boat in?

A. Yes, he did to the best of my knowledge. I was present.

Q. Did I square the yards afterwards?

A. Yes.

The court asked:

Q. Did he perform the duty in his usual manner?

A. Yes.
Q. Did you hear any officer besides the prisoner give directions as to hoisting the boats, the captain or lieutenant?
A. No, I did not.
Q. Did you hear the captain speak to the prisoner about that time?
A. Yes.
Q. What did he say to him?
A. He told him to get the boat in smart. I was busy at the time and did not take notice of anything else.
Q. If the prisoner had been drunk, must you have observed it from the situation you were in?
A. Yes, I think I must.
Q. Did you see him walk backwards and forwards?
A. Yes.
Q. Did he walk steady?
A. Yes, perfectly steady.
Q. How near was you to him?
A. I was on one side of the brig and he on the other.
Q. You state that the prisoner was sober, how do you judge of a person's being drunk?
A. When not capable of doing duty.

Captain Saurin asked:
Q. Did you tell me on the evening of the twentieth of March that the boatswain was not sober?
A. I said to Captain Saurin that he was not drunk to the best of my knowledge. I said that he was sober to the best of my knowledge.

John Thompson, a Seaman belonging to His Majesty's sloop *Hope*, called in and sworn.

The prisoner asked:
Q. Did you see me on the evening of the twentieth of March last about the time the gig was hoisted in?
A. Yes.
Q. Was I then drunk or sober?
A. Sober.
Q. Did I hoist the gig in and square the yards?
A. Yes.

The court asked:
Q. How near were you to the prisoner?
A. On the opposite side of the deck.
Q. Did he pipe and carry on the duty exactly in his usual manner?
A. Yes.

John Hailey, a Seaman belonging to His Majesty's sloop *Hope*, called in and sworn.

The prisoner asked:

Q. Did you see me on the evening of the twentieth of March about the time the gig was hoisted in?
A. Yes.
Q. Was I then drunk or sober?
A. He was not drunk; he might have drank more than his allowance.
Q. Did I carry on the duty of hoisting the boats in, in my usual manner?
A. Yes.

The court asked:

Q. Was the prisoner completely sober?
A. He was sober and capable of doing his duty.
Q. What induced you to think at that time that he had drank more than his allowance?
A. Because I had been talking to him a little before and it appeared to me that he had been drinking rather more than his allowance.
Q. How does that answer tally with your former answer that he was sober?
A. He was not drunk; he was sober enough to do his duty.
Q. When the prisoner was sent below by the captain, did he ask you if he was sober and if so, what was your answer?
A. I answered yes.

Edward Elback, a Seaman belonging to His Majesty's sloop *Hope*, called in and sworn.

The prisoner asked:

Q. Did you see me on the evening of the twentieth of March about the time of hoisting the boat in?
A. Yes.
Q. Was I drunk at this time?
A. No.
Q. Did I hoist the gig in and square the yards in my usual manner?
A. Yes.

The court asked:

Q. Did you hear the captain or lieut[t]. give any orders while the boatswain was carrying on that duty?
A. No.
Q. How near were you to the prisoner at the time?
A. I was hoisting the boat in; I was at the main stay.
Q. Did you hear the captain call the boatswain aft and speak to him?

A. No, I was not present at that time.
Q. Had you any conversation with the boatswain that afternoon or evening?
A. No, I had not.
Q. Did you hear him speak to anyone?
A. No, I did not.

John Stevens, a Seaman belonging to His Majesty's sloop *Hope*, called in and sworn.

The prisoner asked:
Q. Did you see me on the evening of the twentieth of March last about the time the gig was hoisted in?
A. Yes, I was in the main top.
Q. Did I hoist the gig in as usual and square the yards?
A. Yes.
Q. Was I drunk?
A. No.

The court asked:
Q. Was you present when the captain called the prisoner?
A. I heard the captain order him to his cabin.
Q. Did you think the prisoner was perfectly sober?
A. Yes.
Q. Had you any conversation with him either before or after the gig was hoisted in?
A. No.
Q. Did you hear him speak to anyone?
A. No.

The court was cleared and agreed that the charge had not been proved against the said William Robson and did adjudge him to be acquitted.

The court was again opened, the prisoner brought in, audience admitted and sentence passed accordingly. …

56A. *Defence of William Robson*

[ADM 1/5442]

… I beg leave to lay my case before the members of the court and with my feelings much wounded to think [I should] ever be accused of that dreadful crime drunkenness; I further beg leave to inform the honourable members that I've been nearly sixteen years in His Majesty's navy and have sailed with some of the strictest officers in the service and during the whole of my servitude was never accused of insobriety before. Knowing how Captain Saurin was down on me, I took every precaution to pay the strictest attention to my duty and I am sorry to say I've not had the same indulgence of late as other officers of the same rank. On Sunday the 20 of March no officer being on deck, I went to the gun room and ask'd the first lieutenant if the grog should be mix'd as it was the usual time; his answer was yes and when mix'd. I was to pipe. After the people had their time, he then sent for me and order'd me to turn the hands up in gig, hoist'd her in, squar'd the yards. When done, the first lieutenant then told me I was drunk; I told him I was not. The captain immediately ordered me to my cabin; he then told me he would try me by a court martial as sure as I had a head upon my neck. I obey'd the captain's orders and went below and, before I went to my cabin, I ask'd the ship's company then remaining on board if they thought me drunk; their answer was no and they are ready to come forward and make oath if requir'd that what I've now stated to be correct and likewise to take my case into consideration that I've an aged and an infirm mother to support from my earnings and what I am now accus'd of, I am quite innocent. Likewise I hope the honourable gentlemen of the court will consider me worthy of the station I have occupied these few years and take my servitude into consideration. In the first place to sail with Captain James Padgett, *Pennelope*, and the Hon^{er}. Henry Blackwood, Captain Brauton, H Majesty's ship *Arrow,* with Richard Bird Vincent of Mahoan in the action when sunk, *Hamphatrite*,[1] Captain Robert Corbert, and the Hon^{er}. Courtney Boyle, the *Belona*, Captain Dudley Pater, Captain John Erskine Douglas and being at Rochford in the *Belona* and belong to a gig then with a fire ship destroying the fleet in that port. And now to be accused of that which I know myself innocent of, therefore I hope the court will take my case into consideration as being a poor man …

56B. *Saurin to Bickerton*

[ADM 1/5442]

His Majesty's sloop *Hope*
Spithead, April 13, 1814

… M^{r}. William Robson (Boatswain of His Majesty's ship under my command) having been drunk on the evening of the 20th of March, I have to request you'll be pleased to move their Lordships to order a court martial to try him for the same. …

[1]The word 'mahoan' probably refers to Port Mahon. There was no ship named the *Hamphatrite* in the Royal Navy at this time; thus *Hamphatrite* is probably a misspelling of *Amphitrite* (see Colledge, *Ships of the Royal Navy*, vol. 1, p. 40).

PROPERTY CRIME

A. Theft and Plunder

57. *Court Martial of Thomas Beecher and George Delany*

[ADM 1/5349]

Minutes of the proceedings of a court martial assembled and held on board His Majesty's ship *Cambridge* in Hamoze, the 10th and by adjournment to the 11th June 1799, for the trial of Mr. Thomas Beecher and Mr. George Delany, Midshipmen late belonging to the *Ambuscade* and now Supernumeraries on board His Majesty's ship *Cambridge*, on a complaint preferred against them by Captain Thomas Hawker, Superintendent of the Gun Vessels at this port, for having on the night of the 25th May last, between the hours 12 and 1 o'clock committed great acts of violence and plunder on board the *Anna Theresa* gun barge, or suffered Magnus Groundwater, Robert Blake & Patk Gill, Seamen, and Thomas Hearn, Marine, the boat's crew of His Majesty's sloop *Voltigeur*, to commit the same.

Present

Thomas Totty, Esqr., Captain of His Majesty's ship *Saturn* and third officer in the command of His Maj's ships and vessels at Plymouth,

President.

Captains	Captains
Robt Carthew Reynolds	Sir Char^s Hamilton, B^t
Viscount Renelagh	William Taylor
Thomas Byam Martin	Ja^s Newman Newman
The Hble. Charles Herbert	Frederick Watkins
George Fowke	

H.M. Stokes
DJA

Captain Martin, having received his orders and going to sea immediately, his attendance was dispensed with.

Lieutenant Abel Ferris of His Maj'^s sloop *Voltigeur* sworn.

Court – Are you Lieutenant of the *Voltigeur*?

Ans^r – Yes.

Court – Relate to the court the circumstances of the prisoners getting a boat from the *Voltigeur* and whatever you know of the proceedings respecting the charge.

Ansr – About 5 o'clock in the evening of the 25th May last the prisoners came on board the *Voltigeur*'s hulk & went below with some of the midshipmen of the ships; they stayed some time with them, and then went into the gunroom and there drank wine. I left them there about ½ past 10 when I went to bed; after giving leave for a boat to put some gentlemen on shore at six in the morning, the officer of the watch came and informed me that the cutter was returned. I asked him what cutter; he told me, the cutter that put the gentlemen on shore last evening and that they had brought a binnacle & two oars in the boat that they had taken out of some gun boat. I desired them to hand it in and I'd enquire where it came from; I made enquiry & found it had been taken from the *Anna Theresa* gun barge. I immediately sent for the officer of the *Anna Theresa* & he owned the things & which he took away with him.

Saml Philpot, Q^{r} Mas^{r}, of the *Anna Theresa*, sworn.

Court – Do you know the prisoners?

Ans^{r} – Yes.

Court – Were you on board the *Anna Theresa* gun barge on the 25th of last month?

Ans^{r} – Yes.

Court – Relate to the court what you know respecting the charge against the prisoners.

Ans^{r} – The prisoners came on board the *Anna Theresa* gun barge about gun firing in the morning; and the man that had the first watch gave me a call, when somebody was knocking the shot about. I got up and came upon deck; and the prisoners asked me who had charge of the vessel; I told them I had. They then asked me where the commander was, I told them he was on shore at his lodging; the Prisoner Delany said the commander was on board and that he saw him on board in the day time. I said, 'You may depend upon it he is not on board;' then they desired me to look up to the masthead and see where the pendant was. I looked up and said that I saw the pendant was down; they then went into the boat, and I went down below. They pulled off a short distance with the boat & returned with the pendant again. I never saw any more of them.

Court – Was it at gun firing in the morning the first time you saw the prisoners on board the *Anna Theresa*?

Ans^{r} – Yes.

Court – Did you keep any watch on board the gun barge?

Ans^{r} – Yes.

Court – Who had the watch?

Ans^{r} – The man was asleep that had the watch.

Court – When were you first informed that there were some things missing out of the *Anna Theresa*?

Ans^{r} – At 4 o'clock in the morning.

Richard Finn (Seaman) of the *Anna Theresa* sworn.

Court – Do you know the prisoners?

Ans^{r} – Yes.

Court – Do you belong to the *Anna Theresa* gun barge?

Ans^{r} – Yes.

Court – Were you on board the 25th of last month?

Ans^{r} – Yes.

Court – What watch had you that night?

Ans^{r} – The middle.

Court – Relate to the court what you know respecting the charge against the prisoners?

Ans^{r} – I had been on shore on liberty, returned about 11 o'clock; I had the middle watch, was in liquor and fell asleep. In the morning, I found some things were lost; but I don't know who took them. I saw the prisoners come alongside with a pendant in the morning.

Court – Did the prisoners ask for liquor on board?

Ans^{r} – Yes.

Court – When?

Ans^{r} – I believe 'twas after gun firing.

Miles Hall (Seaman) belonging to the *Anna Theresa* sworn.

Court – Do you belong to the *Anna Theresa* gun barge?

Ans^{r} – Yes.

Court – Do you know the prisoners?

Ans^{r} – Yes.

Court – Relate to the court what you know respecting the charge against the prisoners.

Ans^{r} – About ½ past 2 o'clock on Sunday morning (I don't know the day of the month) in May last, I came upon deck and saw the prisoners on the deck; and the Prisoner, M^{r}. Beecher, told me he had been at the masthead and took the pendant down. He said he had watch over the man that had the watch & that he was asleep; he said, 'How pretty you look without a pendant' and said he should report it to the admiral, and he had a good mind to send us all on board the *Cambridge* in irons & take charge of the vessel himself. They asked if the commander was on board; I told them he was not, but the Prisoner Delany would insist upon it that he was. The prisoners then ordered the men into the boat and put off; and when they had got a little way off, they backed their oars & came alongside and returned the pendant to me and I delivered it to the man that got the watch. The men in the boat said I ought to thank the gentlemen for returning the pendant, which I did and they went away.

Court – Was there anything found missing in the morning?

Ans^{r} – Yes.

Court – State what you found missing in the morning.

Ans^{r} – A bucket, a pair oars, a p^{r}. stockings, a carpenter's nail box, part of a hawser (9 turns), a deck tackle, a binnacle (with a scraper & marlinspike in it).

Court – When did you first find that the things were gone?

[Ans^{r}] – About 6 o'clock in the morning we found the binnacle gone, which induced us to search further and found the other things missing.

Court – What time did the commander of the *Anna Theresa* come on board?

Ans^{r} – About 9 o'clock.

Court – Had you any boat astern of the gun barge?

Answer – Yes, but the oars were on deck.

Thos. Hearn, (Marine) belonging to the *Voltigeur*, sworn.

Court – Do you know the prisoners?

Ans^{r} – Yes.

Court – Was you one of the boat's crew in pulling the prisoners on board the *Anna Theresa* on the night of the 25th May last?

Ans[r]	–	I don't know the day of the month; 'twas last Saturday fortnight.
Court	–	Inform the court of all the circumstances that you know from leaving the *Voltigeur* that night to your return to her again.
Ans[r]	–	I was sent in the boat about 12 o'clock at night to curry some gentlemen on board the *Magnanime* with orders to return immediately; the two prisoners was also in the boat. After putting the gentlemen on board the *Magnanime*, we did not know where to curry the prisoners, who remained in the boat; they desired us to row up the harbour, which we did. We passed by a gun boat, which the prisoners hailed 8 or 9 times, but did not receive any answer. We then went alongside of her; and no one being upon deck, one of the boat's crew took the binnacle and hove it into the boat, also 2 oars, a piece of an hawser, & a tackle. We then rowed up the harbour & hailed several vessels as we passed. We were absent about an hour, when we returned again to the *Anna Theresa*, hailed her and not being answered, one man went to the mast head to haul the pendant down. Then we put off and returned the pendant and abused the people for not keeping a better look out. We then went on shore to North Corner. I was boat keeper; Patrick Gill came to me with a waterman & said he was ordered by one of the officers to take the tackle & hawser out of the boat, which they did.
Court	–	Was there anything else taken out of the boat?
Ans[r]	–	No. After this, the prisoners came to me to the boat with two of the boat's crew and asked what was become of the other man (meaning Gill); I told them he went such away and taken the tackle & hawser with him. They went after him and soon after returned with Gill, when we all went up to a public house together, facing the beach, where all of us had two glasses of gin each; but I don't know who paid for it. I, with the boat's crew, returned to the boat when the prisoners left us & then returned to the *Voltigeur*.
Court	–	In whose charge was the boat when you left the *Voltigeur*?
Ans[r]	–	I don't know; I believe Blake, the Q[r]. M[r].

Court – By whose order was the things handed out of the *Anna Theresa* gun vessel into your boat?

Ans^{r} – By the prisoners; they remained in the boat with me and I heard them tell the boat's crew to hand anything into the boat that was loose upon deck.

Court – Did the prisoners see those things handed into the boat?

Ans^{r} – Yes, they must have seen them handed in.

Court – Did you or any of the boat's crew object to the things being handed into the boat?

Ans^{r} – No, I did not.

Court – Did you consider the prisoners as officers of the boat at the time?

Ans^{r} – Yes, and I was bound to obey them.

Court – Did one of the prisoners appear to be more forward than the other in giving orders?

Ans^{r} – No, both alike.

Court – Were they sober or in liquor?

Ans^{r} – In liquor.

Pris^{r} Beecher – Did Mr Delany & myself meet you going up Queen Street with a sailor and ask you if you were going off that morning?

Ans^{r} – Yes.

Pris^{r} Beecher – Did you go off in the boat at that time?

Ans^{r} – No, not till the boat return'd a second time at twelve o'clock.

Pris^{r} Delaney – Did I tell you to take a great deal of care of that man (Gill) and see him safe on board?

Ans^{r} – Yes.

Partick Gill (Seaman), belonging to the *Voltigeur*, sworn.

Court – Do you know the prisoners?

Ans^{r} – No, I was very drunk the night I went into the boat.

Court – Inform the court all the circumstances that happened in the *Voltigeur*'s boat on the night of the 25 May last, when you was one of the boat's crew in putting some gentlemen on shore.

Ans^{r} – There were 4 gentlemen in the boat when we left the *Voltigeur*, two of whom we put on board some frigate, the other two gentlemen carried us up the harbour to some gun boat. They went on board of her, stayed a considerable time and then came into the boat again; they made us pull down the harbour and go alongside another gun boat & the prisoners went on board first and then we (the boat's crew) were called in to get a glass of grog each. After getting a glass of grog each, we went into the boat again; and soon after, the prisoners followed. The grog took such an effect that I don't know what gun vessel next we went on board of, but the prisoners hailed one which did not answer & we went on board. We from her went on shore at North Corner, and I went up to a house to get something to eat; the prisoners followed me with two of the boat's crew. One of the gentlemen, the tallest of the two, desired me to go down with a strange man (a waterman) to take the tackle & hawser out of the boat. I took it out of the boat with the waterman & brought it up to the end of North Corner Street and threw it into an old house. The prisoners, with two of the boat's crew, followed me up and came to where this man and I stood and ordered the tackle and hawser to be taken down to the beach near high water mark which the two men (with the strange man) took down. I then went away and did not see anything more till I returned and had two glasses of gin at a house opposite the landing place at N^{o}. Corner.

Court – Relate what you heard pass between the waterman, the officers, and boat's crew respecting the deck tackle and the hawser.

Ans^{r} – The strange man said to all, 'If you wish to sell it, I know where to sell it' and it was then carried down to the beach with the assistance of the waterman. When I drank the two glasses of gin, the gentlemen told me 'twas for the rope sold.

Court – Do you, as you hope for salvation hereafter, know that the prisoners standing before the court were the officers in the boat that night?

Ans^{r} – I believe they are to the best of my knowledge.

Robert Blake (Seaman), of the *Voltigeur*, sworn.

Court – Do you know the prisoners?

Ans^{r} – Yes.

[Court] – Relate to the court what you know respecting the charge against the prisoners.

[Answer] – When we went from the ship between 11 and 12 o'clock at night, we put two gentlemen on board the *Magnanime*; then we rowed up the harbour by order of the prisoners, who remained in the boat, and returning down again, the prisoners hailed some of the gun boat [*sic*]. I don't recollect their names. We went alongside different gun boats & we took out of one a binnacle & two oars out of a boat astern. We hauled the pendant of one down. Then we went on shore and we all went up from the boat, except the marine, who was left boat keeper. Patrick Gill and the two prisoners went up first and myself and Magnus Groundwater went up after them. The two prisoners stopped for us; in the meantime, Patrick Gill went away. When we returned to the boat, the marine told us that Gill had been down & got things out of the boat, not mentioning what things; we went up to find Gill and he took us up to where the things were lying in an old building. There was a tackle and cordage of some sort, but I did not go nigh enough to particularize. It was taken from that place by Gill (a waterman & we all following) and lodged in a house opposite North Corner facing the water; the prisoners desired the boat to wait for them, but I went down and, with Groundwater, took the boat off.

Court – Who ordered the binnacle into the boat?

Ans^{r} – The prisoners ordered anything to be handed in that they could find loose.

Court – Did you know that the tackle & cordage you saw at North Corner came out of the boat?

Ans^{r} – No.

Court – Did you not ask Gill what he was going to do with the cordage?

Ans^{r} – No, I did not.

Court – Who was the officer of the boat?

Ans^{r} – There was none, but the two prisoners; I considered myself the officer after landing the prisoners, who did not belong to the *Voltigeur*.

Court – Did you hear any proposal made to sell this cordage?

Ans^{r} – Yes, Gill offered to sell it and the woman offered 4p for it.

Court – Were the prisoners present at the time this offer was made?
Ans[r] – Yes.
Court – Did the prisoners agree to the selling of the cordage?
Ans[r] – They did not object to it.
Court – What reply did Gill make to the woman, when she offered 4p for the cordage?
Ans[r] – That she should have it & carried it into the house.
Court – Did either of the two prisoners seem to be more forward than the other in those transactions?
Ans[r] – Yes, the tallest (meaning Mr. Beecher).
Court – Was the prisoner (Mr. Beecher) sober?
Ans[r] – He was not sober.
Court – Was Mr. Delany sober?
Ans[r] – He was in the same state as the other.

Prosecution closed.

The court adjourned to tomorrow morning, 9 o'clock, June 11th, 1799.

The court met agreeable to adjournment.

Court – Mr. Beecher have you any certificates?
Pris[r] – No, I was turned out in the middle of the night to take charge of a prize and left them behind in the *Ambuscade*.

Defence, as annexed, read by the judge advocate

No witnesses called.

Charge proved in part.

Extract of the sentence:

'The court doth therefore adjudge the said Thomas Beecher and George Delany to be disqualified to receive or hold a commission in the naval or military service of His Majesty, his heirs or successors for three years to be computed from this 11th day of June 1799, and also to be severely reprimanded; and the said Thomas Beecher & George Delany are hereby sentenced to be disqualified to receive or hold a commission in His Majesty's naval or military service for three years, to be computed from this 11th day of June 1799 and to be severely reprimanded accordingly.

'And it appearing to the court that Patrick Gill, a Seaman belonging to His Majesty's sloop *Voltigeur*, who was produced as a witness, sworn and examined on the said trial, did in the course of his examination prevaricate in his evidence, the court doth order him to be imprisoned in the Marshalsea for the term of three months.'

…

57A. *Defence of Thomas Beecher and George Delany*

[ADM 1/5349]

… The situation in which we stand presses too heavily on our minds to allow us to address you in the manner we could wish and, feeling as we do most acutely the very great impropriety of our conduct, we cannot deliver to this honourable court the few observations that now occur to us, respecting the evidence adduced against us, with that confidence we otherwise might experience. But whilst we acknowledge ourselves truly culpable in boarding the *Anna Theresa* at such an unreasonable hour and in the very intoxicated state we then were, yet at the same time, when we avow in the most sacred and solemn manner, that we were truly ignorant of any plunder having been committed on board her. We hope that such intoxication, considering our youth, will in some measure induce this honourable court to judge our case with lenity and compassion.

Gentlemen:

Altho' it has been alleged by the boat's crew of the *Voltigeur* that this plunder on board the *Anna Theresa* was committed by our orders, yet we firmly trust that the court will give no credit whatever to the evidence of men of that description, men who must have known that such orders were not only illegal but highly criminal and, as such, had those men been of characters, entitled to any, the smallest, credit at this bar, they would not only have refused obedience to such orders, but likewise have used their utmost endeavours to bring us to shame for this proposal.

Gentlemen:

Altho' we may have been guilty of many of the follies and excesses incident to youth, yet we thank God nothing criminal was ever yet attached to us; we therefore shrink with horror at the charge of theft now brought against us by the boat's crew of the *Voltigeur* (no doubt with a view to screen themselves). It is an action our nature spurns at. The stigma of it is truly dreadful; but it will be for you Gentlemen either to affix that stigma to us forever or clear our fame from so foul a charge. It is your decision that will render our names ever infamous or clear them in the eyes of mankind.

We, therefore, await your sentence with a dreadful anxiety, yet not without a firm hope that in judgement you will remember mercy. …

58. *Court Martial of John Hazlehurst, William Wilson and Richmond Norton*

[ADM 1/5352]

Minutes of proceedings at a court martial assembled on board His Majesty's ship the *Lancaster* in Table Bay, Cape of Good Hope, the 4th of February 1800.

Present

John Osborn, Esquire, Captain of His Majesty's ship the *Tremendous* and second officer in the command of His Majesty's ships and vessels in Table Bay, president

Captains

Samuel Hood Linzee	William Hotham
Thomas Larcom	John Lee

The prisoners were brought into court and the evidence and audience admitted.

Read the order of Sir Roger Curtis, Baronet, Vice Admiral of the White and Commander in Chief of His Majesty's ships and vessels employed, and to be employed, at the Cape of Good Hope and the seas adjacent, dated the 3d. instant and directed to the president to try John Hazlehurst, William Wilson and Richmond Norton, Seamen, belonging to His Majesty's ship the *Tremendous*, who were under the command of M^{r}. Harty, Master's Mate of the said ship, in a Prussian ship seized for prize lying in Simon's Bay 'for stealing several articles of the cargo of the said ship on or about the 24th of July 1799, some of which were taken on shore by the said John Hazlehurst and sold.'

Then the members of the court and judge advocate, in open court and before they proceeded to trial, respectively took the oaths directed by Act of Parliament made and passed in the 26th year of the reign of His late Majesty King George the 2d., entitled *An Act for Amending, Explaining and Reducing into one Act of Parliament the Laws relating to the Government of His Majesty's Ships and Vessels and Forces by Sea.*

A letter from John Osborn, Esquire, Captain of His Majesty's ship the *Tremendous*, to Sir Roger Curtis, Baronet, Vice Admiral of the White & Commander in Chief &^{c}. &^{c}. Cape of Good Hope, was read as follows:

Tremendous, Table Bay, C. Good Hope
The 2nd February 1800

… M^{r}. Harty, Master's Mate of His Majesty's ship which I command, having represented to me that John Hazlehurst, William Wilson and

Richmond Norton, Seamen belonging to the said ship, and who were under his command in a Prussian ship seized for prize, lying in Simon's Bay, had stolen several articles of the cargo of the said Prussian ship on or about the 24th day of July 1799 and that John Hazlehurst had carried on shore some of the said articles and sold them, I am to request you will be pleased to order a court martial to try the abovementioned seaman for the said robbery. …

All the evidences were then ordered to withdraw out of court, except Derk Franson, Mate of the *Three Brothers*, Prussian ship, sworn and examined by the prosecutor.

	Question	Did you on or about the 24th of July last complain to me that some of the people under my command had broke through the bulkhead and taken from thence a part of the cargo of the ship?
	Answer	Yes, I did.
Court	Question	Relate to the court all you know respecting the charge against the prisoners, committed either at that time or any other.
	Answer	On the 24th of July last, the boatswain came to me and told me the people belonging to M^{r}. Harty had brought some ladies' shoes on shore; and I then went and told M^{r}. Harty and we both went down below together and saw a hole in the bulkhead under the forecastle on the larboard side and a case of shoes opened and some of them taken there from.
Prosecutor	Question	Which of the prisoners lay nearest the hole next to the bulkhead?
	Answer	I think it was John Hazlehurst.
	Question	Was you present when I questioned the prisoner, John Hazlehurst, concerning the theft?
	Answer	Yes.
	Question	Relate to the court what you heard him say at that time?
	Answer	He said he had taken the shoes out of the case.
	Question	What did he say he had done with them?
	Answer	He said he had sold them on shore.
	Question	Did he at that time say in your hearing that he knew others had taken shoes also and who they were?
	Answer	He did say that Wilson and Norton were guilty also.

Clements Riegs of the Prussian ship sworn & examined by the prosecutor.

Question — Did you on the 24th of July last observe any of the people under my command in possession of goods part of the ship's cargo and who were they?

Answer — Yes, I saw John Hazlehurst with a green shoe in his bosom; it came out as he was rowing on shore, when I was in the boat going for fresh beef.

Question — Did you, at any time, say to Hazlehurst, the prisoner, that the shoes were part of the cargo?

Answer — I said nothing but 'take care.'

Question — Did you, on coming on board, complain to the mate of what you had seen?

Answer — Yes, I told the chief mate that I had seen some shoes, which I thought belonged to the cargo.

Question — Was you present when the mate and myself examined the bulkhead?

Answer — Yes, I was and there saw a hole in the bulkhead on the larboard side.

Question — Did you examine the hole and find that any of the shoes was taken?

Answer — I did not take particular notice whether any shoes were taken or not.

Court Question — Have you any reason to believe that the shoe you said you saw was part of the cargo, or did you ever see the three prisoners at the bar at any time with any other property that you knew to be part of the ship's cargo?

Answer — I supposed it part of the cargo. I never saw any thing in the possession of the others.

Paul Canfield, Seaman of the *Tremendous*, sworn & examined by the prosecutor.

Question — Did you, at any time on or before the 24th of July last, receive from any of the prisoners at the bar any goods? And if you have, relate for what purpose you received them.

Answer — I received a pair of shoes from the prisoner, Norton, to sell.

Question — What did you do with them?

Answer — I gave them to Hazlehurst to sell.

	Question	Do you know if they were sold and what became of the money they fetched?
	Answer	I do not know anything further than what I have related respecting them.
Court	Question	What did the prisoner, Norton, say to you, when he gave you the shoes to sell?
	Answer	He told me to sell them.
	Question	Did you ask him how he came by them?
	Answer	I did and he told me not to mind.
	Question	Was the shoes that were given you to sell part of the prize's cargo that you was in charge of?
	Answer	To the best of my belief, they were.

The prosecution here closed and the prisoners entered on their defences.

The prisoner, John Hazlehurst, called on Mr. Harty, the Prize Master, for a character and he reported him as a diligent, sober and attentive man & exerted himself much on the passage.

The prisoner, Richmond Norton, called also on Mr. Harty for a character and he reported him as a quiet, good man and never had any cause to complain of him till the present. He also called on his captain for a character and he said he did not recollect he was ever complained of before the present time and belonged to the ship two years and a half.

The prisoners having nothing further to offer in their defences, the court was cleared and the members proceeded to deliberate upon and form the sentence.

The court, having carefully and deliberately weighed and considered the evidence produced in support of the charge and what the prisoners had to allege in their defences, is of opinion that the charge has been proved against Richmond Norton and that it is not fully proved against John Hazlehurst and William Wilson, doth therefore adjudge the said Richmond Norton to receive one hundred lashes on his bare back with a cat-o-nine tails alongside of such ship or ships of the squadron and at such time or times as the commander in chief shall direct and to forfeit his share of prize money in case the Prussian ship, *The Three Brothers*, should be condemned; and he is hereby sentenced so to suffer as aforesaid accordingly, and the court doth acquit John Hazlehurst and William Wilson and they are hereby acquitted accordingly. …

59. *Court Martial of Solomon Barnett and Robert Dent*

[ADM 1/5370]

Minutes taken at a court martial assembled on board the *Gladiator* in Portsmouth Harbour on the eighth day of July 1805.

Present

Sir Isaac Coffin, Bar[t]., Rear Admiral of the White and second officer in the command of His Majesty's ships and vessels at Portsmouth and Spithead, President.

Captain	John Oakes Hardy	Captain	Edward Codrington
	George Byng		Robert Dudley Oliver
	John Irwin		Henry Heathcote
	Charles Adam		John Stiles
	Adam Drummond		Robert Hall
	William Selby		John Wentworth Loring

The prisoners were brought in and audience admitted.

The president reported to the court that Captain Henry Hill of His Majesty's ship *Orpheus* was absent on Admiralty leave.

The order from the Right Honourable Lords Commissioners of the Admiralty, dated the seventh day of July instant and directed to the president, setting forth that Admiral Montagu, Commander in Chief of His Majesty's ships and vessels at Portsmouth and Spithead, had transmitted, with his letter to their Lordships's secretary, one which he had received from Captain George Hope, Commander of His Majesty's ship *Defence*, dated the fourth instant, representing that the spirit room of the said ship had been broken open on the proceeding evening, during the first watch, when Solomon Barnett (a Marine) was placed as sentinel in the after cockpit and it appeared that Robert Dent (Marine) was aiding and assisting the said Solomon Barnett by relieving him on his post during the time he was down in the spirit room broaching the wine casks, was read.

The members of the court and the judge advocate then, in open court and before they proceeded to trial, respectively took the oaths enjoined and directed in and by an Act of Parliament made and passed in the twenty-second year of the reign of His late Majesty King George the Second, entitled *An Act for Amending, Explaining and Reducing into one Act of Parliament the Laws Relating to the Government of His Majesty's Ships, Vessels and Forces by Sea.*

Then the letter from Captain George Hope, Commander of His Majesty's ship *Defence*, dated the fourth day of July instant and directed to Admiral Montagu, Admiral of the Blue and Commander in Chief of His Majesty's ships and vessels at Portsmouth and Spithead, containing the charge was read and is hereto annexed and the witnesses were ordered to withdraw and attend their examinations separately, which they did as follows:

Benjamin Body, a Private in the Royal Marines embarked on board His Majesty's ship *Defence*, called in and sworn.

Captain Hope asked:

Q. Was you sentry in the after cockpit of the *Defence* between the hours of six and eight o'clock in the evening of the third of this month?

A. Yes.

Q. Who relieved you?

A. Solomon Barnett.

Q. Who was the non-commissioned officer who planted the sentries?

A. Corporal Jervis.

Q. Was the hatch to the spirit room properly secured when you was relieved?

A. Everything was secured when I was relieved, to the best of my knowledge.

The court asked:

Q. Did you see that the lock was on?

A. Yes, the lock and bar were on; I did not try the lock.

Jervis Jervis, a Corporal of the Marines embarked on board the *Defence*, called in and sworn.

Captain Hope asked:

Q. Did you see the sentry relieved in the after cockpit of the *Defence* at eight o'clock in the evening of the third of this month?

A. Yes.

Q. Who did you place as sentry in the after cockpit at that hour?

A. The prisoner, Solomon Barnett.

Q. Did you observe whether the hatch of the spirit room was properly secured when you placed the sentry?

A. Yes.

M[r]. Thomas Stoddart, a Midshipman belonging to the *Defence*, called in and sworn.

Q. Relate to the court all you know of the charge against the prisoner.

A. On the night of the third of July, when I was going to bed in the cockpit, between nine and ten o'clock, I knocked my foot against the spirit room hatch, which was partly opened. I called immediately to M^{r}. Robinson, another midshipman, and told him that the spirit room was broken open. The sentry that was then in the cockpit, Robert Dent, one of the prisoners, said that he had relieved the other prisoner, Solomon Barnett, about ten minutes before, to go to the head and that he did not know how it was done. I left M^{r}. Robinson at the hatchway and went on deck to inform M^{r}. Hosie, the commanding officer, of it. He came down with me and Mr. Robinson and I lifted the hatch off entirely; the lock and bar were hove abaft the hatchway a considerable distance, a few feet. When I opened the hatch, I saw the prisoner, Barnett, standing between the casks in the spirit room with a pot in his hand. I immediately collared him and took the pot from him, which had some wine in it, which appeared to be red and smell like wine. The prisoners were then ordered into confinement and I drove the staple down (which had been driven up) again and fastened the hatchway.

The court asked:

Q. Did you examine the casks in the spirit room?

A. I looked at two or three of them, but was afraid to go far with a light. I saw one with a spoil hole open in it and I spoiled it up. The wine appeared to have been running out; it was wet round the spoil hole.

Q. Did you find any gimblet?[1]

A. No.

Q. Do you know how much had been drawn out?

A. No.

Q. Where was the *Defence* at the time?

A. In dock.

Q. Did the prisoner give any reason for his being there?

A. Barnett said he did it and that none else was concerned in it; he told the lieutenant so.

Mr. William Robinson, a Midshipman belonging to the *Defence*, called in and sworn.

Captain Hope asked:

Q. Relate to the court what you know respecting the charge against the prisoners.

A. I was in the after cockpit going to bed about half past nine o'clock on Wednesday night, the third instant. M^{r}. Stoddart observed the hatch of the spirit room was broken open, upon which he went to

[1] 'Gimblet' probably means gimlet, which is a device used to drill holes.

acquaint Lieutenant Hosie of it. While he was gone, I lifted the hatch and saw a man down in the hold. I laid the hatch over again. I asked the sentry, Robert Dent, who was in the hold? He said he did not know, that he relieved Barnett to go to the head. When Lieutenant Hosie came down, I told him there was a man in the hold; and Mr. Stoddart and I lifted the hatch and the prisoner, Solomon Barnett, came out with half a pot of red wine in his hand. I saw the cask with a spoil hole in the bilge, then running with red wine.

Q. Was there a light in the after cockpit at the time and where was it hanging up?

A. Yes, it was a lamp hanging on the stanchion before the spirit room hatch.

Q. Was it possible for any person to go down that hatchway without the sentry in the after cockpit seeing him?

A. It was impossible.

The court asked:

Q. When you found the prisoner, Barnett, in the hold, did the other, Robert Dent, account to you for the other's being there?

A. No, he said nothing, except that he did not know who was there and that he had relieved the other to go to the head.

Q. Did either Dent or Barnett appear to be disguised with liquor?

A. No, they appeared to be sober.

Q. Did Barnett say anything?

A. Yes, when he came out of the hold, he said he had nobody to blame but himself.

Q. Did you observe where the hatch bar was?

A. It was on the starboard side of the cockpit, laying with the lock and the staple which had been drawn out.

Lieutenant William Hosie of the *Defence* called in and sworn.

Captain Hope asked:

Q. Relate to the court what you know of the charge against the prisoners?

A. On the third of the month about half past nine o'clock in the evening, I was walking the quarterdeck, when M^r^. Stoddart, one of the mates, came up and told me that the spirit room was broken open. I immediately went down to the cockpit and saw that the hatch bar was wrenched open. We took off one of the hatches and saw the prisoner, Solomon Barnett, in the spirit room with a tin pot in his hand nearly half full of wine, one of the casks of wine spoiled at the bilge and running out. I then asked the sentry, Robert Dent, the other prisoner, how the other had got into the spirit room; he told me he did not know, he relieved him to go to the head. I then desired Sergeant Pigley to relieve Robert Dent and sent them both to the quarterdeck. I asked Corporal Jervis, in the presence of the prisoners, if he had placed Dent sentry at eight o'clock; he told me he had placed Solomon Barnett and he had relieved Robert Dent at eight o'clock. I then ordered them into confinement.

Q. Was there a proper light for the sentry on the cockpit?
A. Yes, hanging at the mid ship stanchion before the spirit room.
Q. Was it possible for any person to break open that spirit room or go down into it without the knowledge of the sentry?
A. I should think not, unless he was asleep.

The court asked:

Q. Where did you find the bar?
A. On the starboard side with the lock and staple, which was drawn.
Q. Did the prisoner, Barnett, account for his situation?
A. No, he said that nobody knew anything of it but himself.
Q. Did Dent express any surprise that Barnett was not gone to the head?
A. He said that he did not know he was there; he relieved him to go to the head.
Q. Where was he standing?
A. He was standing near the hatchway when I went down.

Sergeant Charles Pigley of the Royal Marines, belonging to the *Defence*, called in and sworn.

Captain Hope asked:

Q. Was you sergeant of the party of marines on board the *Defence* during the time she was in dock?
A. Yes.
Q. What were the orders you gave to the sentries in the after cockpit?
A. To see that no person broke open the spirit room or went down to it without a master's mate or by the orders of the lieutenant.
Q. Do you know who was the proper sentry in the first watch in the after cockpit on the third instant?
A. Solomon Barnett, one of the prisoners.
Q. Who was the non-commissioned officer of the watch?
A. Corporal Jervis.
Q. Did you know of any of the proper sentries being relieved there in the first watch?

A. No.
Q. Was it ever allowed for the sentries to relieve each other without a non-commissioned officer being with them?
A. No.

Corporal Jervis called in again.

Q. Was you non-commissioned officer of the first watch on the third instant on board the *Defence*?
A. Yes.
Q. After you placed Barnett sentry at eight o'clock, did you relieve him by Robert Dent for any purpose whatever?
A. No.
Q. Were the marines on board of the *Defence* ever allowed to relieve each other without a non-commissioned officer?
A. No.

The court asked:

Q. Who did Barnett relieve at eight o'clock?
A. Benjamin Body.
Q. What orders did you give Barnett when you put him on sentry?
A. To take charge of the store rooms, spirit room and the lights, and to see that no naked lights went about the tier or cockpit; no one to have a light out of his lantern, without an order from the quarterdeck.
Q. At what intervals do the non-commissioned officers visit the sentries?
A. Every hour.
Q. When did you last visit them?
A. I had not got round to him.

The prosecution being closed, the prisoners were called on for their defence.

Solomon Barnett said he had nothing to say, but left it to the mercy of the court.

Robert Dent said he had relieved Barnett to go to the head and did not think it any harm to do it without the corporal; that he went to the marine store room to get some oil to trim the lamp and, in the mean time, Barnett got into the spirit room; that when he came down, he observed that the bar and staple were up and he called out to him as he was going up the ladder, but he made no answer.

Captain Cox of the Royal Marines was requested to speak to Solomon Barnett's character, who said:

That he had behaved himself in general pretty well since he had been in the *Defence*, which was about eight months; that he had never known anything particularly against his character, except the present offence.

That Robert Dent embarked at the same time; during which time, he had never known anything bad attached to his character and he had that opinion of him as to believe him incapable of his present offence.

Sergeant Pigly called in again.

The court asked:

Q. Could the sentry obtain oil from the marine store room to trim the lamp without your or some other person's attendance?

A. No.

Q. Was the marine store room locked?

A. Yes.

Q. Who had the key?

A. Corporal Jervis.

Q. Is the oil kept in the marine store room?

A. No, Corporal Jervis had the custody of it.

Corporal Jervis called in again.

Q. Where was the oil for the lamp on the evening of the third of July?

A. It was by the lamp in a tin case; the jar was in the marine store room. I had the key of it.

Q. Could the prisoner, Dent, get to the store room without your attendance?

A. No, I had the key and found the door locked the next morning.

Q. Was there any oil in the tin case?

A. Yes, enough for the night.

The court was cleared and agreed that the charge had been proved against the said Solomon Barnett and Robert Dent and did adjudge the said Solomon Barnett to receive three hundred lashes and the said Robert Dent to receive two hundred lashes on their bare backs with a cat o' nine tails on board of or alongside such of His Majesty's ships and vessels at Spithead or in Portsmouth Harbour, at such time or times and in such manner and proportions as the commander in chief of His Majesty's ships and vessels (for the time being) at Portsmouth aforesaid should direct.

The court was again opened, the prisoners brought in, audience admitted and sentence passed accordingly. …

59A. *Hope to Montagu*

[ADM 1/5370] His Majesty's ship *Defence*
Portsm^{o}. Harbour, 4 July 1805

… The spirit room of His Majesty's ship under my command having been broken open last night during the first watch, when Solomon Barnett,

Marine, was placed as sentry in the after cockpit and it appearing that Robert Dent (Marine) was aiding and assisting the said Solomon Barnett by relieving him on his post during the time he was down in the spirit room broaching the wine casks,

I have to request you will be pleased to apply to my Lords Commissioners of the Admiralty to order a court martial on them for the above offence. …

60. *Court Martial of John Goodridge*

[ADM 1/5389]

Minutes of proceedings at a court martial held on board His Majesty's ship *Trident* in the harbour of Valletta, Malta on the 6th October 1808.

Present

Sir Alexander John Ball, Bar[t]., Rear Admiral of the White and senior officer in the command of His Majesty's ships and vessels at Malta, president.

Captains

James Dunbar — Richard Budd Vincent
Henry Hope — Robert Elliot

The prisoner was brought into court and the evidence and audience admitted.

Read the order of Edward Thornbrough, Esquire, Vice Admiral of the White and commanding a squadron of His Majesty's ships in the Mediterranean, & dated the 10th ultimo, directed to Sir Alexander John Ball, Bar[t]., Rear Admiral of the White, &c., &c., &c., to try John Goodridge, Corporal of Marines belonging to His Majesty's ship *Porcupine*, for having on or about the 9th of August last, when at sea, stole from on board *La Conception* (prize to the said ship) a handkerchief containing one or more Dollars, which on his return alongside the ship he gave thro' one of the main deck ports to a Marine, who was sentinel there, to prevent anything being handed in, thereby enticing him to betray his trust, and that the said John Goodridge having (while searching for the above Dollars) been found with articles in his possession which he must have stole or known to have been stolen from *La Nouvelle Entreprize*, French schooner taken by the said ship on the 25th June last.

Then the members of the court and judge advocate, in open court and before they proceeded to trial, respectively took the oaths directed by Act of Parliament, made and passed in the 22d year of the reign of His late

Majesty King George the Second, entitled *An Act for Amending, Explaining and Reducing into One Act of Parliament the Laws relating to the Government of His Majesty's Ships, Vessels and Forces by Sea.*

The letter from the Honourable Henry Duncan, late Captain of His Majesty's ship *Porcupine*, (containing the before recited charges against the prisoner) was then read; and all evidences were ordered to withdraw out of court, except Mr. John Wilkes, Midshipman of the *Porcupine*, who was sworn.

Q. by Prosecutor	Do you know the prisoner?
	Yes.
	Did you on or about the 9th of August last see a handkerchief thrown in at one of the main deck ports from a boat then alongside?
	Yes.
	Who threw the handkerchief in?
	The prisoner.
	What did it appear to contain?
	One or more Dollars.
	Do you know how many Dollars?
	I saw one, but no more.
	Might there have been more?
	I heard one, but it sounded like more.
	Did the handkerchief fall on the deck?
	It did.
	Did it sound as if it contained more than one Dollar?
	No.
Court	Where were you standing?
	Under the half deck.
	At what time of day was it?
	About eleven in the forenoon.
Court	Was the port, thro' which the handkerchief was thrown, near to where you was standing?
	I was about two yards abaft it.
	Did you see any of the articles which were stolen from the schooner?
	Yes, they were shown to me by captain clerk.
	Do you know anything of the circumstances of their being stolen and, if you do, relate it?
	No.
	After the handkerchief fell upon deck, did you see it taken up and opened?

No, the sentinel, who was stationed under the half deck to prevent anything being passed thro' the port, brought the Dollar to me.

Ellis Evans, Private Marine of the *Porcupine*, sworn.

Q. by Prosec[r]. Was you sentinel on the main deck of the *Porcupine*, on or about the 9th August last, to prevent anything being handed in at the port?

I was.

Was there a handkerchief thrown in to you?

Yes.

What was in it?

One Dollar.

Who threw it in?

The prisoner.

What did you do with it afterward?

I showed it to M[r]. Wilkes directly; he told me to keep it, that it was a matter of no consequence.

Did the prisoner ever speak to you about it?

When I was in irons, he asked me what I was confined for. I told him I picked up a Dollar on the main deck and a handkerchief; he asked me for it and said it was him that hove it thro' the port, when I told him I would not give it to him.

What did you do with the handkerchief?

I left it on the gun and I saw Mitchell, one of the Marines, take it away.

Court You say in your evidence that the prisoner threw the handkerchief thro' the port; did you see him throw it?

No.

Do you know of his having stolen that handkerchief?

No.

Do you know of his having stolen any goods or articles from the *Conception*?

No; I do not.

What orders did you receive upon your post, respecting things not being thrown into the port?

I was ordered to see that nothing was thrown into the port.

Did the prisoner, either directly or indirectly, invite you to connive at anything being thrown in?

No.
Who planted you sentinel there?
Sergeant Summers.
Did the prisoner make any proposal or terms with you, concerning the Dollar or handkerchief?
No.

Mr. Geo. Anderson, Captain's Clerk, sworn.

Q. by Prosecr. Did I send you, on or about the 9th August last, to examine the prisoner's knapsack and chest?
Yes, with the Sergeant of Marines.
What was found there?
Four small parcels of combs.
Do you know that part of the cargo of *La Nouvelle Entreprize* consisted of combs?
I do not.

Court Do you know of the prisoner having stolen any articles from *La Conception* or *Nouvelle Entreprize* (prizes)?
I do not know.

Sergeant Charles Summers, Marines, sworn.

Q. by Prosr. Did you, on or about the 9th August last, examine the prisoner's knapsack, chest, &c., and what you find there?
I examined them and found four bundles of combs.
Previous to that day, was there a box of combs (the head of which had been damaged) brought on board the *Porcupine* for its better security from *La Nouvelle Entreprize*, prize?
Yes there was.
Who did you give the combs to, to carry to the boatswain's store room?
I carried them down myself.
Had the prisoner them ever in his possession or in his charge?
Yes, he had.
Were the combs found in his chest of the same kind and quality as those you saw brought from *La Nouvelle Entreprize*?
They were.
Were the parcels made up in the same was [*sic*] as those brought on board, except being a little damaged from wet?
They were.

The evidence for the prosecution closed here and the prisoner was put upon his defence, who stated that he was conscious of never having stolen anything in his life. He did not wish to call any witnesses, but begged his captain and officers would speak as to his general conduct.

Captain Duncan

In general, he behaved well till this circumstance, but has been sometimes in liquor.

Lieut. Ja[s]. Renwick, Royal Marines

Gave the prisoner a very good character, who had served with him four years and one of the first to serve in the boats, &c.

Lieut. Price

said the prisoner was a very good man.

The court was then cleared and, having considered the evidence produced and what the prisoner had offered in his defence, were of opinion that the charges had not been proved and did, therefore, adjudge him to be acquitted.

The court was opened, audience admitted and sentence passed accordingly. …

B. Embezzlement

61. *Court Martial of Mark Moore*

[ADM 1/5335]

Minutes taken at a court martial assembled on board His Majesty's ship *Pegasus* in Portsmouth Harbour on the tenth day of March one thousand seven hundred and ninety-six.

Present

Sir Roger Curtis, Bar[t]., Rear Admiral of the Red and second officer in the command of His Majesty's ships and vessels at Portsmouth and Spithead, President.

Rear Admiral	Richard Rodney Bligh	Captain	John Thomas
Captain	Robert Montagu		Sir James Saumarez
	William Cayley		Theophilus Jones
	Charles Stirling		Henry D'Esterre Darby
	Francis Pickmore		Thomas Peyton
	Edmund Crawley	The Honble. Lord Augustus Fitzroy	

The prisoner was brought in and audience admitted.

The order from the Right Honble. Lords Commissioners of the Admiralty, dated the fifth of March instant and directed to the president, setting forth that M^r^. J. Shipman, Second Master and Pilot of His Majesty's fire vessel the *Nancy*, had acquainted their Lordships by his letter of the eighteenth of February last that a quantity of brandy, fresh beef and beer, received from His Majesty's stores at Portsmouth for the use of the said fire vessel, had been sent on shore by order of M^r^. Mark Moore, her commander, and sold to different persons at Portsea and also for keeping a false muster and for the trial of the said Mark Moore, was read.

The president reported to the court that Captains Charles Edmund Nugent, Charles Powell Hamilton, Sir Andrew Snape Douglas and William Brown were absent on Admiralty leave.

A lieutenant, from His Majesty's ship *Assistance*, reported to the court the inability of Captain Henry Mowat, her commander, to attend as a member of the court martial.

Mr. Robert Cinnamond, Surgeon of His Majesty's ship *Assistance*, being sworn, said that Captain Henry Mowat, her commander, was so ill from the effects of a fit of the gout and a cold that his attendance as a member of the court martial would endanger his health.

The members of the court and the judge advocate then, in open court and before they proceeded to trial, respectively took the several oaths enjoined and directed in and by Act of Parliament made and passed in the twenty-second year of the reign of His late Majesty King George the Second, entitled *An Act for Amending, Explaining and Reducing into One Act of Parliament the Laws relating to the Government of His Majesty's Ships, Vessels and Forces by Sea.*

Then the letter from the said J. Shipman, dated the eighteenth of February last, to the Lords Commissioners of the Admiralty, containing the charge was read and the witnesses were ordered to withdraw and attend their examinations separately, which they did as follows:

Mr. Thomas Grant, Junr., Clerk to the Clerk of the Cheque, called in and sworn.

The court asked:

Q. Produce the muster book of the *Nancy*, which being produced, turn to the name of William Irwin and acquaint the court how it there stands.

A. It appears on the sixteenth of January, twenty-third January, twenty-ninth of January, fifth February and the twelfth of February that M^r^. Irwin was answered for at the musters of the *Nancy* as being on the spot and which musters were noted on the books by a particular mark, which I usually make for that purpose when the person is reported to be on the spot, but not present. On my succeeding muster of the twentieth of February, I was informed by the prosecutor, then commanding officer, that M[r]. Irwin had been a considerable time absent; on my desiring him to fix, with as much precision as could be, the time of such absence, he informed me a month or five weeks as near as he could recollect. I understood from him that William Irwin had originally gone on leave, but that for some time past he believed him to be without leave; from that information and finding by my book that he had not been present on several prior musters, I run him back on the fourth of February, which I considered myself justified in doing. I should have added that finding he had been off the spot, which had not been represented to me before that, I checked him with leave from the eighteenth of January, about the time, to the best of the prosecutor's recollection, that he had been off the spot.

Q. At the times of the dates before mentioned, who was it that answered for Irwin's being on the spot?

A. I cannot, with any precision, state to the court who may have been commanding officer on any of the dates that I have mentioned, but I well remember seldom to have seen M[r]. Moore, the commander, frequently and generally the prosecutor and sometimes I have mustered the vessel when neither was on board.

Q. Was the prosecutor ever commanding officer at any of the musters that Irwin was absent and did he answer for his being on the spot?

A. I have not a doubt but that must have been in the case at one or more, but I cannot positively speak to it.

The prosecutor asked:

Q. Do you recollect on the twelfth of February M[r]. Moore told you that Irwin had been absent three days?

A. I have no recollection of any such thing.

John Morgan, Gunner's Mate of the *Nancy*, called in and sworn.

The court asked:

Q. Did you know M[r]. Irwin belonging to the *Nancy*?

A. Yes, by sight.

Q. Was you present at the muster on the twelfth of February?

A. I was.

Q. Did you hear Mr. Moore tell the clerk of the cheque on that day that he had been only absent three days?

A. Yes.

Q. Do you recollect the time when Irwin did absent himself from the *Nancy*?

A. I do not know the day, but, at that time, he had been absent a month or better.
Q. Was he on board at any time between those periods?
A. Not to my knowledge.
Q. Do you know what became of the man when he went away?
A. I do not know.
Q. Did Mr. Moore ever desire you in case the clerk of the cheque came to muster to say that Irwin was upon the spot?
A. He has told me to say if he happened to come that he was absent, either on liberty or duty.
Q. Did the prosecutor, M^r. Shipman, ever desire you to answer for Irwin to the clerk of the cheque if he should come in the same way?
A. Not to my knowledge.
Q. How long may you have been absent from the vessel at any one time?
A. Not above a day.

George Kinneer, a Seaman belonging to the *Nancy*, called in and sworn.

The court asked:

Q. Do you remember a man by the name of Irwin on board the *Nancy*?
A. Yes.
Q. Do you remember when the clerk of the cheque mustered that M^r. Moore told him that Irwin had been absent only three days?
A. Yes.

William Smith, Carpenter's Mate of the *Nancy*, called in and sworn.

The court asked:

Q. Do you remember on the sixth of December last a cask of beer being taken from the *Nancy* by M^r. Moore's order and carried to a ship at Spithead?
A. Yes, we carried it to the Mother Bank on board a transport called the *Pomona*, I think; M^r. Moore went in the boat with us. Twenty seven gallons was marked upon it.

The prisoner acknowledged taking the beer on board that ship, which he said was in lieu of wine.

Q. Do you remember, on the twenty eighth of December last, a quantity of spirits being brought on board the *Nancy* from the Victualling Office?
A. I remember the spirits being brought, but do not recollect the day.

Q. Do you know what became of these spirits?

A. We carried some on shore to the King's Stores in a stone bottle betwixt two gallons and a half or three gallons by M^r^. Moore's order. He was in the boat with us; M^r^. Moore went away and came down again and brought a man to whom it was delivered by his order.

Q. What was in the bottle?

A. Brandy. We carried brandy on shore at the Common Hard,[1] about four gallons in two stone bottles by M^r^. Moore's order; either he or M^r^. Moore was in the boat; Ryan, belonging to the vessel, carried it up. At another time, some more brandy was carried on shore, but I do not recollect the quantity by M^r^. Moore's order; it was carried to the Common Hard, but I do not know where it went to.

Q. Do you know if any of the brandy that was so carried on shore came out of the cask that came from the Victualling Office?

A. I cannot say.

The prisoner acknowledged that it was taken out of the cask.

Q. Do you remember on the second of January a fore quarter of beef coming on board from the Victualling Office?

A. Yes.

Q. Was any of it carried on shore?

A. Yes, to the Hard. Mr. Moore told us that he was going to have it in a house to carry it to the *Amity*, another fire vessel; there was fifty pounds weight of it in two pieces.

Q. Who took it up from the Hard?

A. Either Ryan or Gill, but I do not recollect which.

Q. Was you ever abridged of your allowance of any provisions on board?

A. No.

John Ryan, a Seaman belonging to the *Nancy*, called in and sworn.

The court asked:

Q. Do you remember on the twenty eighth of December a quantity of brandy being brought on board the *Nancy* from the Victualling Office?

A. Yes.

Q. Do you know if any of that brandy was drawn from the cask and carried on shore?

[1]The Common Hard is a section of Portsmouth (Jonathan G. Coad, *The Royal Dockyards, 1690–1850: Architecture and Engineering Works of the Sailing Navy* (Aldershot: Scolar Press, 1989) p. 53).

A. Yes, I drew off one jar better than two gallons by M^{r}. Moore's order and carried it to the King's Stairs and delivered it there to a man I do not know by his orders; he was present at the time. I had filled another jar with brandy and a few days afterwards carried that also on shore to M^{r}. Morgan at the Sign of the Leopard, four gallons by M^{r}. Moore's order.

Michael Morgan, a publican at Portsea, called in and sworn.

The court asked:

Q. Did you receive any quantity of beef about the second of January last from M^{r}. Moore, the prisoner, or any person in authority under him?

A. It was sometime in January Mr. Moore brought me a piece of beef in a sack and put it down in my kitchen and told me he had brought some fresh beef on shore that he could spare and desired me to sell it for him. I told him to fix his price; he told me four pence half penny per pound. I sent for a man and he thought it rather too much, but M^{r}. Moore would not let it go under and I bought it at that price and it weighed about forty-nine pounds, as the man told me who weighed it. I paid M^{r}. Moore eighteen Schillings and four Pence half penny for it.

Q. Did you lend M^{r}. Moore a gallon measure for the purpose of measuring some spirits?

A. Yes.

Q. Did you buy any spirituous liquors about the twenty-eighth of December or beginning of January of M^{r}. Moore?

A. M^{r}. Moore had borrowed some liquor of me and told me at his outfit he would repay me, which he did, to the best of my knowledge, it was eight gallons that I received of him. I lent him one gallon and a quart. There was a small bill owing in the house and he said he had a little more to spare and asked me if I would take more brandy in payment. I asked him what he would take per gallon; he said sixteen Schillings, which I gave him for it by out setting it against the bill.

The prisoner, being called on for his defence, said, 'I gave Irwin a fortnight's liberty with a ticket, when it was out, the clerk of the cheque came on board, I told him his liberty had been out three days; as to the beef the master of the *Amity* had borrowed of me, a score of beef which I sent ashore to Morgan's and a score for my own use. The master of the *Amity* said he had got some provisions and would rather have some cash than the beef. I sold it therefore to Mr. Morgan; I sent the brandy ashore for payment of brandy I had borrowed for the use of the vessel.'

The court was cleared and agreed that the charge had been in part proved against the said Mark Moore and did adjudge him to be dismissed from the command of His Majesty's said fire vessel, the *Nancy*, and to be incapable of serving in His Majesty's naval service again.

The court was again opened, the prisoner brought in, audience admitted and sentence passed accordingly. …

61A. *Shipman to Lords Commissioners of the Admiralty*

[ADM 1/5335] Portsmouth, Feb[y]. 18th, 1796

… A quantity of brandy, fresh beef and beer received from H.M. stores at this place for the use of H.M. fire vessel the *Nancy* having been sent on shore by the order of M[r]. Mark Moore, Commander of the said fire vessel, and sold to different persons at Portsea, Your Lordships will therefore be pleased to order an enquiry to be made into the conduct of the said Mr. Mark Moore respecting the above mention'd provisions, as likewise for keeping a false muster. …

62. *Court Martial of Jonathan Sturdy*

[ADM 1/5344]

Minutes taken at a court martial assembled onboard His Majesty' ship *Bellona* in Portsmouth Harbour on the 27th day of April 1798.

Present

George Wilson, Esq[r]., Captain of His Majesty's ship the *Bellona* and second officer in the command of His Majesty's ships and vessels at Portsmouth and Spithead, President.

Captain	Charles Hawkins Whitshed	Captain	Sir Richard Bickerton, Bar[t].
	Robert Montagu		Sir Henry Trollope, Kn[t].
	Francis Pickmore		Charles Tyler
	William Hargood		Francis Fayerman
	Sir Francis Laforey, Bar[t].		George Cockbourne
	George Henry Tourey		Ross Donelly

The prisoner was brought in and evidence admitted.

The order from the Right Honble. Lords Commissioners of the Admiralty, dated the 25th instant and directed to the president, setting forth that Admiral Sir Peter Parker, Bar[t]. had transmitted to their Lordships a letter, dated the 23rd of April 1798, which he had received from Captain

Thomas Rogers, commander of His Majesty's ship *Mercury*, representing that about four o'clock in the afternoon of the 2d proceeding a quantity of gun powder and oil was found in a wherry alongside the said ship and requesting, as he had reason to believe the articles above mentioned had been embezzled from onboard the *Mercury* by M^r^. Jonathan Sturdy, her Gunner, that he (the said gunner) might be tried for the same at a court martial and for the trial of the said Jonathan Sturdy for embezzlement of the stores, with which he is charged by Captain Rogers in his above mentioned letter, was read.

The president reported to the court that Captn. John Willett Payne was ill and not able to attend his duty as a member of the court martial and that Sir Richard John Strachan Bar^t^. was absent on Admiralty Leave.

The members of the court and the judge advocate then, in open court and before they proceeded to trial, respectively took the several oaths enjoined and directed in and by an Act of Parliament made and passed in the 22d year of the reign of His late Majesty King George the Second, entitled *An Act for Amending, Explaining and Reducing into One Act of Parliament the Laws relating to the Government of His Majesty's Ships, Vessels and Forces by Sea.*

Then the letter from the said Captain Thomas Rogers to Sir Peter Parker, Bar^t^., dated the 23rd April last containing the charge was read and the witnesses were ordered to withdraw and attend their examinations separately, which they did as follows:

James Bloom, Master at Arms belonging to His Majesty's ship *Mercury*, called in and sworn.

Captain Rogers asked:

Q. Did you find a quantity of gunpowder and oil in a wherry alongside the *Mercury* about 4 o'clock in the afternoon of the second of this month?

A. Yes.

Q. Relate to the court what happened in consequence of this discovery.

A. I went on the gangway and I saw the wherry lay alongside. I looked into her and saw there was nothing in the wherry at that time. Afterwards, I went down below and may have been there about ten minutes; I came up again and saw a large open basket in the boat, which seemed to be stowed very snug with things. I asked the waterman who that basket belonged to; he said to M^r^. Sturdy, the Gunner. I told him I thought proper to look at the basket before it went on shore; I went down into the wherry and examined the basket and there found a quantity of loose powder, about twenty pounds in a bag in the after part of the boat. I saw a jar of oil, containing about six quarts stand. I took the bag of powder onboard with me and the waterman handed out the jar of oil and quart bottle filled with oil also. I took them on the quarterdeck, in a moment after M^{r}. Sturdy came up from below with a letter, telling the waterman to carry it on shore and give it to some person. The waterman began to tell him that the master at arms had taken the things out of the boat. M^{r}. Sturdy immediately came on the quarterdeck to me and asked me what I had taken out of the boat. I told him oil and powder; he asked me what business I had to stop his things. I told him I thought I had a great right to stop such things as they were; he said he would insist on their going on shore and catched hold of the jar of oil, in which we had a tussle on the quarterdeck and spilt some of the oil there. After he found he could not have it in the boat, he gave it up; and I sent down the quarter master for the gentleman of the watch and he came up. I told him I had stopped some things, which M^{r}. Sturdy was sending out of the ship and desired him to acquaint the commanding officer. He went down and M^{r}. Sturdy with him. M^{r}. Sturdy came up a little time afterwards, before the gentleman of the watch, and said he would take charge of the powder. I told him he should not; I would keep charge of it myself, until the commanding officer should give orders what it should be done with. M^{r}. Sturdy asked would I insist on stopping his things from going on shore. The commanding officer came on deck and told M^{r}. Sturdy to take the things below again, which he did.

Q. Were the gunpowder and oil of the kind made use of in His Majesty's navy?

A. Yes.

The prisoner asked:

Q. Are you sure there was so much powder as 20lbs.?

A. I am sure there must have been 20lbs. weight.

Q. Are you sure there were six quarts of oil?

A. I am sure in the jar and bottle, there were six quarts.

Q. Was the oil in the bottle such as is used in His Majesty's service?

A. It was.

Richard Prince, Ship's Corporal belonging to His Majesty's ship *Mercury*, called in and sworn.

Captn. Rogers asked:

Q. What do you know respecting the quantity of gunpowder and oil found in a wherry alongside the *Mercury* about 4 o'clock in the afternoon of the second of this month?

A. I was present with the master at arms on the gangway when he asked the waterman what things were in the boat. He said they were Mr. Sturdy [*sic*]. He went down and searched it and at the bottom of the basket was a bag containing powder. He brought it up and left it with me; we both returned to the gangway and asked the waterman what he had got in the jar and told him to hand it up, a jar and a quart, which he did, and they were found to contain oil. Mr. Sturdy came up with a letter and gave it to the waterman and told him to carry it to some person. The waterman then told him that the master at arms had taken his things and he asked him what business he had to take his things, who said it was not lawful for such things to go out of the ship. M[r]. Sturdy made a catch at the quart bottle of oil and spilt some of the oil on the quarterdeck. M[r]. Sturdy collared the master at arms and called him a damned rascal for not letting his things go out of the ship. The master at arms sent for the officer of the watch, who came up and sent to the lieutenant. M[r]. Sturdy went down with him; M[r]. Sturdy came up and the gentleman of the watch. M[r]. Sturdy took hold of the powder and said he would secure it and he carried it down. He abused the master at arms very much indeed.

The prisoner asked:

Q. Can you judge how much powder there was?

A. I think about 20lbs.

Richard Quinton, a customs house officer belonging to the *Mercury*, called in and sworn.

Captain Rogers asked:

Q. Did you see a quantity of gunpowder in a wherry alongside the *Mercury* about four o'clock in the afternoon of the second of this month?

A. I saw a bag brought up from the boat, but what was in it, I cannot tell; and about the oil, the master at arms brought it out of the boat and from there it was carried down below.

Lieut[t]. Henry Frederick Woodman, Second Lieut[t]. of the *Mercury*, called in and sworn.

Capt[n]. Rogers asked:

Q. What do you know concerning the quantity of gunpowder and oil being found in a wherry alongside the *Mercury* about 4 o'clock in the afternoon of the second of this month?

A. The gunner came to me in my cabin, requested I would allow him to send a little powder and oil out of the ship as the master at arms had prevented him. I spoke hastily and told him the master at arms did perfectly his duty and asked him how he could request such a thing, that he was not aware of what he was doing and to send it below instantly and was proceeding to reprimand him, when I observed [him?] muddled apparently from being drunk the day before. I told him to go out of the cabin and go on deck and see the powder put below immediately. I went out of my cabin and the midshipman of the watch came down a minute or two afterwards and told me the master at arms had stopped some things going into the wherry; I immediately went on deck and told the midshipman of the watch I had ordered them below. I saw then standing there a bag of powder and a small jar of oil.

The prisoner, being called on for his defence, said that the powder was intended to get himself instructed to prepare rockets; that he had a son in the volunteers at Gosport and the oil was intended to keep his musket clean; that the quantity was exaggerated, there was not so much of powder or oil as stated.

Lieut[t]. Robert Baylis, First Lieut[t]. of His Majesty's ship *Mercury*, called in and desired to speak to the prisoner's character.

During the time that I have belonged to the *Mercury*, about five months, he has been generally attentive to his duty and I have always found him diligent in executing the orders I have given to him.

Lieut[t]. Woodman called in again and desired to speak to the prisoner's character, who said:

I, in generally [*sic*], found him eagerly attentive to his duty, interestingly so when anything was going on.

Captain Rogers was desired to speak to the prisoner's character, who said:

That he had generally found him attentive to his duty when at sea, but, in harbour, drunken and negligent.

The court was cleared and agreed that the charge had been proved against the said Jonathan Sturdy and did adjudge him to be dismissed from his office as Gunner of His Majesty's ship *Mercury*.

The court was again opened, the prisoner brought in, audience admitted and sentence passed accordingly. …

62A. *Rogers to Parker*

[ADM 1/5344] *Mercury*, Spithead 23rd April 1798

… I beg leave to acquaint you that on the 2nd ins[t]., about 4 o'clock in the afternoon, a quantity of gunpowder and oil was found in a wherry alongside His Majesty's ship under my command and, as I have reason to believe the said gunpowder and oil was embezzled from on board the *Mercury* by M^{r}. Jonathan Sturdy, Gunner of the said ship, I have to request you will be pleased to apply to the Right Honble the Lords Commissioners of the Admiralty for a court martial to be held upon him for the said offence. …

63. *Court Martial of William Henry Brown Tremlett*

[ADM 1/5354]

Minutes taken at a court martial assembled on board His Majesty's ship *Gladiator* in Portsmouth Harbour on the 9th day of September 1800.

Present

John Holloway, Esqr., Rear Admiral of the White and second officer in the command of His Majesty's ships and vessels in Portsmouth and Spithead, President.

Captain	Eliab Harvey	Captain	Francis Pickmore
	Joseph Sidney Yorke		Thomas Francis Freemantle
	Edward James Tode		John Loring
	James Macnamara		William Prouse
	George Fowke		George Clark

The prisoner was brought in and audience admitted.

The order from the Right Honble. Lords Commissioners of the Admiralty, dated the 25th day of August last and directed to the president, for the trial of Lieutenant William Henry Brown Tremlett, commander of His Majesty's gun vessel *Tigress*, for having frequently embezzled part of His Majesty's provisions and stores, was read.

The president reported to the court that Captains Sir Charles Hamilton, Bar^{t}., William Lukin and Jemmett Mainwaring were absent on Admiralty Leave and that Captain Philip Charles Durham, commander of His Majesty's ship *Anson*, was performing quarantine at Spithead.

The members of the court and the judge advocate then, in open court and before they proceeded to trial, respectively took the several oaths enjoined and directed in and by an Act of Parliament made and passed in the 22d year of His late Majesty King George the 2nd, entitled *An Act for Amending, Explaining and Reducing into One Act of Parliament the Laws relating to the Government of His Majesty's Ships, Vessels and Forces by Sea.*

Then the letter from Mr. James McIntosh, Second Master and Pilot of the said gun vessel *Tigress* to Admiral Milbank, dated the 28th of July last, containing the charges, was read and the witnesses were ordered to withdraw and attend their examinations separately, which they did as follows:

The prosecutor, M^{r}. Ja^{s}. McIntosh, 2nd Master and Pilot, did not appear; and Lieut^{t}. Tremlett informed the court that he had left the gun brig on the 31st day of July last or the 1st of August with 6 days leave and had not since returned and was therefore run on the books of the gun brig.

M^{r}. John Wilson, a Marine belonging to His Majesty's gun brig *Tigress*, called in and sworn.

The court asked:

Q. How long have you been servant to Lieut^{t}. Tremlett?

A. About 9 months.

Q. Have you constantly attended upon him during that time?

A. Yes, I have.

Q. Are you likewise steward of the gun brig and have you charge of the provisions?

A. Yes, I have.

Q. Do you know anything of Lieutt. Tremlett during the time you have been his servant and the ship's steward making use of the ship's provisions for the benefit of his family or sending any ashore for public sale?

A. I know he has made use of very little in his own family, but, at different times, he has sent some oatmeal and peas by me on shore to exchange for fresh provisions, sometimes I have taken 3 or 4 gallons or 4 or 5 gallons of different articles. I cannot say exactly how much the provisions I brought on board in lieu, sometimes mutton, sometimes greens, were used in M^{r}. Tremlett's cabin.

Q. Was any of it ever applied to the use of the ship's company or for the benefit of the sick?

A. Yes, greens were once or twice a week, when there were fresh provisions in the broth. Some part were applied to the use of the ship's company and some part to his own table.

Q. Did you ever, during the time you have been his servant, sell or dispose of the ship's provisions or King's stores for money or goods (not for other provisions) which were applied for the benefit of Lieut^{t}. Tremlett?

A. No, no other, except when the value of the provisions sold was greater than the value of the provisions or greens bought. The overplus money was given to me; he agreed to give me two Guineas a year for my extra duty and I kept it a [*sic*] that account, informing him what it was.

Q. Do you recollect if any kegs of rum were ever sent from the vessel to M^{r}. Tremlett's house?

A. No, I recollect one went out of the vessel, which I understood came from another vessel to him.
Q. Do you keep a mess book on board?
A. I am not able to keep it myself; I tell the Captain what it is and he writes it down.
Q. How many people are there in the Lieut[t].'s mess?
A. Nobody, but him and me.
Q. Did the provisions you sent out of the brig exceed the allowance that was due from government to the Lieut[t]. and you?
A. I cannot tell exactly; I do not know whether it did or not.
Q. Do you know anything of a boat being sent from the *Tigress* by the Lieut[t]. to his friends at Torbay?
A. There was a boat went away that the Lieut[t]. said he had lent to a cousin of his.
Q. Do you know if the boat belonged to the gun brig?
A. I do not.
Q. How many boats had the brig on board at the time?
A. Two besides that one.
Q. How many has she now?
A. Two.
Q. Do you know if any new boat came on board or any other boat when this boat was sent away?
A. I cannot recollect that there was. It was, I think, in June last.
Q. Do you recollect giving any rum, biscuit or junk to the master of the vessel, who took the boat from the *Tigress*?
A. I gave him a couple of bottles of rum and about 20lb. or 30lb. of biscuit.
Q. Do you know what the rum and biscuit were given him for?
A. I do not. I heard the man begging of the Captain to give it him.
Q. What size boat was it?
A. A small boat, I think about 4 oars.
Q. Was it a King's boat or a merchant ship's boat?
A. I think it was a merchant ship's boat.
Q. Had the boat been mostly used as the King's business or was it privately used as the property of the Lieutenant?
A. The Captain mostly used it himself; I heard him say it was his private property, that the former commander left with him.
Q. Did the former commander leave it with him as a present or did he pay him any money for it?
A. I heard the former commander say that he left it with him as one more than was on charge.
Q. How long is it since the master left the *Tigress*?

A. I think about 5 or 6 weeks ago.
Q. Do you know why he left the *Tigress*?
A. I do not.
Q. Did you ever hear that he never intended to return to her?
A. No, I heard the captain complain that his duty was very hard on account of his being away.
Q. What terms did the Lieut[t]. and Master live on?
A. I never heard them dispute much. I have sometimes heard the Captain complain of his living on too familiar terms with the people.
Q. Did you weigh out the provisions of the ship?
A. Yes.
Q. Do you know the allowance of oatmeal to each man during the week?
A. Three pints, I think.
Q. How often did you carry oatmeal on shore during the week?
A. Sometimes, I have carried oatmeal on shore twice a week, but it was only for about 3 weeks I did it at all.
Q. What quantity during that three weeks did you carry?
A. I think I carried altogether about 15 or 16 gallons on shore.
Q. Do you recollect from whence the boat was sent?
A. Out of Portsmouth Harbour from alongside the vessel.
Q. When you went on shore with oatmeal or peas, did you take as much as you chose or did the commander direct you what to take?
A. The commander told me that when the cask was out, then in use, I was not to dispose of any more. It was about half down when I broke into it and I served the ship's company out of it at the same time.
Q. Upon the oath you have taken, how much money have you taken for provisions since you have been servant to Mr. Tremlett?
A. I do not think it amounted altogether to 2 Guineas.
Q. Do you know of any person belonging the *Tigress* having disposed of His Majesty's stores otherwise than for the King's service by Lieut[t]. Tremlett's permission or for his benefit?
A. No, except what I have stated before.

Lieut[t]. Tremlett asked:

Q. Did you hear Lieut[t]. Acton say that he had a boat, which was of no use to him and not on charge, that he would give me?
A. Yes.
Q. Did you hear me tell Lieut[t]. Stapleton, to whom I lent the boat, that I would lend her when I could spare her?

A. Yes, I did.
Q. Have I told you that I did not mean to dispose of more than my allowance of provisions due to me.
A. Yes, he has.
Q. Have you heard me say that I gave the man, who carried the boat round, 2 Guineas for the carriage of her?
A. I saw him pay it to him.
Q. Did I tell the master of the vessel if he would take care of the boat in her passage, I would give him 2 bottles of liquor for his trouble?
A. Yes, he did and desired me to go to the master and get it drawn off at the same time.
Q. Did you hear the man beg that I would give him some biscuit as the wind was then fair and he could not get any on shore?
A. I heard him beg some, but did not hear him say anything about the wind.
Q. Did you know that I have frequently bought kegs of liquor and brought them to the ship?
A. I remember 4 kegs coming in.
Q. Have I brought more liquor into the ship than I gave away?
A. It is impossible for me to say, but I think he has full as much.
Q. Do you know that I make use of any myself?
A. He very seldom drinks spirits; he drinks wine in general.

Thomas Brown, Boatswain's Mate of the *Tigress*, called in and sworn.

The court asked:
Q. Was you in the *Tigress* before Lieutt. Tremlett commanded her?
A. No.
Q. Do you recollect how many boats the *Tigress* had when you came to her?
A. A cutter, a pleasure boat and the jolly boat at the boathouse.
Q. What was the jolly boat?
A. I believe she might be a five oared boat.
Q. Did you conceive that boat belonged to the *Tigress* or the lieut^{t}.'s private property?
A. I conceived her to be the lieut.'s boat by the form she was knocked up in.
Q. Has the *Tigress* the same number of boats now that she had then, independent of the pleasure boat?
A. Yes.
Q. Do you know how that boat was sent from the *Tigress*?
A. She was sent away by the Lieut^{t}. and I do not know to whom she was delivered.

Q. Do you know whether the Lieut[t]. sold her or gave her away or lent her?
A. I cannot say.
Q. Do you know anything of the Lieut[t]., since you have been in the ship, selling any of the provisions or stores?
A. No.
Q. Have you always had your full allowance of provisions since you have been in the ship?
A. Yes.
Q. Did you ever hear any of the ship's company complain that they had not their proper allowance of provisions or that they were discontented at not having what was allowed by government?
A. No.
Q. How long has the master been gone from the *Tigress*?
A. It is a month ago good.
Q. What did he go away for?
A. I cannot tell.
Q. Did he say he did not intend to return to the ship again?
A. Not to my knowledge.
Q. Did you know anything of his having written for a court martial against the Lieut[t]. before he went away?
A. Yes, I did.
Q. Did you think the master would return again?
A. I did not think anything at all about it.

William Weeks, Corporal of Marines belonging to the *Tigress*, called and sworn.

The court asked:

Q. Do you recollect how many boats the *Tigress* had when the last commander left her?
A. To the best of my knowledge 3; I think there were 3.
Q. How many has she now?
A. Two.
Q. Do you know anything of a boat being sent from the *Tigress* by Lieut[t]. Tremblett to his friends in the country?
A. No.
Q. What became of the other boat?
A. I know not.
Q. Did you hear that Lieut[t]. Tremlett sent a boat away from the ship?
A. I heard that he had a boat which he was going to send away, but where it went to, I know not.

Q. Do you know anything of Lieut[t]. Tremlett bringing liquor into the ship as his own private property that did not come from the King's stores?

A. Yes, I saw, at different times, as much as 3 kegs come into the vessel.

Q. Do you know anything of Lieut[t]. Tremlett's having sent provisions out of the ship to dispose of?

A. No, at no time.

Q. Did you suppose all 3 of the boats belonged to the King?

A. I do not know; all of them did as far as I know.

Q. Have you, at any time, any reason to complain of your allowance of provisions?

A. No.

Lieutenant Tremlett, being called on for his defence, said:

When I joined the *Tigress* Lieut[t]. Acton told me that he had a boat, which was not on charge, and that he would give her to me and did so, and I looked on her to be my private property. As to the provisions, as I have nothing but my pay and did not use oatmeal and peas, I thought there was no impropriety in exchanging it for fresh provisions and never sent away more than my allowance amounted to, and I rely on the mercy of the court. I have been 14 years in His Majesty's service and once had the good fortune to save the crew of the *Reunion* at a time when I was only a passenger and volunteered it, which the letter of Captain Bayntun, her commander, will show, which was read. I once jumped overboard in the North Sea to save a man's life, for which Captain Dixon gave me his public thanks and recommended me to Lord Duncan and Lord St. Vincent. I was sent with a party by Captain Dixon to board a vessel, one party having been beat off, and all the men were killed or wounded, except myself and 3 others. I had the handle of my sword shot away and several shot through my hat and coat and was knocked down by the butt end of a blunderbuss and, at length, beaten off again and I have, at all times, volunteered whenever any service of that sort was getting on.

Captain Foot said he had heard Captain Dixon speak very highly of the conduct of Lieut[t]. Tremlett.

Captain Loring said that he heard a lieut[t]. of the *Hannibal* state that Lieut[t]. Tremlett was the means of saving the people of the *Reunion*.

The court was cleared and agreed that the charges had not been proved against the said Lieutenant, William Henry Brown Tremlett, and did adjudge him to be acquitted.

The court was again opened, the prisoner brought in & audience admitted, and sentence passed accordingly. …

63A. *McIntosh to Milbank*

[ADM 1/5354] H.M. gun brig *Tigress*, July 20th, 1800, Spithead

… I have to request you will be pleased to apply to my Lords Commissioners of the Admiralty for a court martial on Lieut. Wm Henry Brown Tremlett, commander of His Majesty's gun brig *Tigress* for frequently embezzling part of His Majesty's provisions & stores, such as fresh beef, oatmeal & peas, &c, which he has at different times sent the said provisions on shore for public sale by his servant. The stores above mentioned was a five oar'd cutter, which Lieut. Tremlett converted into a pleasure boat & sent her away in a Torbay vessel for his own private use, for which he gave a strand of His Majesty's junk, two bottles of rum & some biscuit in part of payment of the carriage of the said five oar'd cutter & as Lieut. Tremlett sent some kegs of H.M. rum to his private friends, at different times, & other things, which I can clearly prove on a court martial. As my being master of the said gun brig, I think it my duty to apply for a court martial to prevent any further embezzlement. I hope their Lordships will excuse my not knowing better of the service in applying for a court martial, but I hope their Lordships will grant me a court martial, as the number of times Lieut. Tremlett has sent provisions & spirits on shore for sale is too long to mention. But being he prepared to prove the said charges, such as embezzlement of stores, selling of provisions &c, I hope their Lordships will grant me my request. …

64. *Court Martial of David Richards*

[ADM 1/5440]

Minutes of the proceedings of a court martial held onboard His Majesty's ship *Hibernia* in Port Mahon on Monday the 17th day of January 1814.

Present

Sir William Sidney Smith, Knight, Commander and Grand Cross of the Royal Military Orders of the Sword and S^{t}. Ferdinand, Vice Admiral of the White and second officer in the command of His Majesty's ships and vessels in the Mediterranean, President.

Francis Pickmore, Esqr., Vice Admiral of the Blue

Israel Pellew, Esqre., Rear Admiral of the White and Captain of the Fleet

Sir Richard King, Bar^{t}., Rear Admiral of the Blue

Captains

George Burlton
John Erskine Douglas
Sir Edward Berry, Bar[t].
Edward Brace
Charles Grant
Robert Plampin
Robert Rolles
William Hall Gage
Edward Stirling Dickson

The prisoner being brought into court and audience admitted, M[r]. Ross, Surgeon of His Majesty's ship *Repulse*, stated that Captain Moutray could not attend in consequence of ill health. Read the order from Sir Edward Pellew, Bar[t]., Vice Admiral of the Red and Commander in Chief of His Majesty's ships and vessels employed in the Mediterranean, dated the 15th of January 1814 and directed to Sir William Sidney Smith, Vice Admiral of the White and second officer in the command of His Majesty's ships and vessels employed in the Mediterranean, to try Mr. David Richards, Boatswain of His Majesty's sloop *Philomel*, for having on or about the evening of the 13th of January 1814 attempted to embezzle a quantity of canvas from His Majesty's store under his charge. Read the Judge Advocate's warrant. Then the members of the court and judge advocate, in open court and before they proceeded to trial, respectively took the oaths enjoined by Act of Parliament. The letter from Captain Shaw containing the charge against the prisoner was read (N[o] 1). Witnesses ordered to withdraw.

John Chapple, Carpenter's Mate, H.M.S. *Philomel*, called and sworn.

Question — State to the court everything that came within your knowledge from the time of leaving off work on board the *Philomel* which led to the discovery of the canvas found in the carpenter's berth on board the *Neptune* hulk.

Answer — When I left off work at 5 o'clock in the afternoon on Thursday the 13th to go on board the *Neptune*, I stood by the water's edge waiting for a boat to go on board. I saw the prisoner come through the archway at the dock with a bundle wrapped up in old canvas. He went down to the water's edge and hailed a shore boat. The shore boat came about half way to the shore when our jolly boat came round the ship's bows. The two armourers came in it. One armourer came out of the boat; the prisoner, myself, John Jerratt, William Fowler and M[r]. Patten went in the boat and went on board the *Neptune*. When we got on board, I went to my berth and sat down a little while and afterwards went forward into the carpenter's berth to exchange some Spanish money for English money, the sum of half a Dollar. While I was in the berth, I saw the Spanish carpenter take the bundle I had seen the prisoner with and put it behind his chest. To be sure, I sat down on the chest and felt the bundle which I judged to contain new canvas. I went out of the berth and returned to my own and sat down and asked the advice of my messmates what to do. They told me to discover it or else it would be laid to other people. I went up immediately on the main deck to the wardroom and then went up to the cabin to Mr. Hannay, the Master's Mate, and called him out and told him there was some canvas in the Spanish carpenter's berth behind the chest and told Mr. Hannay if he would go along with me, I would seize it. He immediately went down with me and looked over the screen and saw the Spanish carpenter and the prisoner handling the canvas, which I saw at the same time. Mr. Hannay pushed in and took it away from them and we went up to the cabin and the commanding officer asked who saw it. Mr. Hannay answered, John Chapple. Lieut. Crosdale then told me to go and I went and met the prisoner who called me 'a curry favouring bugger.' I then went into the cabin again and told the commanding officer of it and the commanding officer told him to be quiet. I then went away to my berth.

Some new canvas was produced, which the witness stated to the best of his belief to be the canvas he had seen in the Spanish carpenter's berth, it being marked the same way with the King's mark.[1]

Court Is that canvas now produced before the court the same, to the best of your knowledge and belief, that you saw the prisoner handling with the Spanish carpenter in the berth of the latter?

A. Yes.

Court Did you see the new canvas in the possession of the prisoner when he was in the boat going on board the *Neptune* or what did you see?

[1]According to the 1815 edition of Falconer's *Universal Dictionary*, 'the mark in canvas is distinguished by a blue thread being woven in it and a serpentine line, painted black, down the centre of each breadth' (Falconer, *A New Universal Dictionary*, s.v. Marks).

A. I saw a bundle wrapped up in old canvas and afterwards saw the same bundle in the Spanish carpenter's berth.

Court Did you see the Spanish carpenter offer the prisoner any money or anything else in exchange for the canvas?

A. No.

Court Where are the boatswain's stores of the *Philomel* kept?

A. They are kept under old sails at the end of a store in the dockyard.

Court When you saw the prisoner and the Spanish carpenter handling and examining the canvas, what did it appear to you they were doing that for?

A. They appeared to be measuring it.

Court Was you near enough to hear any expression pass between them?

A. I heard the Spanish carpenter speaking Spanish, but I did not understand it.

Court Did they appear to you to be bargaining for it.

A. I have no other suspicion.

The prisoner declined asking this witness any questions. Witness ordered to withdraw.

M^{r}. Peter Hannay, Master's Mate H.M.S. *Philomel*, called and sworn.

Q. State to the court what you saw pass between the prisoner and the Spanish carpenter after you had been apprised by John Chapple that he suspected an embezzlement of stores and offered to show you where you might detect it?

A. About half past seven on Thursday the 13th ins^{t}., I was called from the mess room table of the *Neptune* by one of the servants and told that John Chapple, the Carpenter's Mate, wished to speak with me. When I came out, he accosted me by saying if I would go down with him to the old Spanish carpenter's berth, I should find there behind the Spanish carpenter's chest a quantity of canvas which he had seen deposited there. I consequently went down to the lower deck on the starboard side forward and in the screen cabin I found the prisoner in conversation with the Spanish carpenter. On my making my appearance, the prisoner in a confused manner called me by name and asked me what was the matter. I made reply nothing, that I was come down to take some canvas that was lodged there; and, in the Spanish carpenter's cot, I found some new canvas with the King's mark, which I believe to be the canvas now before the court. The Spanish carpenter was in the act of measuring or folding it up in his cot. I laid hold of the canvas and hauled it out. The prisoner replied that he knew nothing of the canvas and that he would take it on deck himself. I said no, I would do it and took it up to the mess room of the *Neptune* before Mr. Crosdale, the 1st lieutenant, the 2d. lieu^{t}. and master. The prisoner followed close up and said he had given the canvas to the Spanish carpenter to make a cot and repeated several times that he had done so. Afterwards Lieu^{t}. Crosdale ordered the prisoner to leave the cabin and he would enquire into it tomorrow morning.

Q. Had any of the *Philomel*'s stores been, to your knowledge, ever deposited onboard the *Neptune*.

A. No.

Court Did you look over the screen before you went into the berth to search for the canvas and, if so, what did you see or hear relative to the charge before the court?

A. No; I went straight in.

Court Was John Chapple with you at the time and did he enter the berth at the same moment?

A. He had hold of me by the arm and said, 'There, sir.'

The prisoner declined asking this witness any questions. Witness ordered to withdraw.

William Clements, Sailmaker, H.M.S. *Philomel*, called and sworn.

Q. Where is the store canvas belonging to the *Philomel* stowed and in what is it contained?

A. On shore at the dockyard in a tent along with the sails.

Q. Is it in a bag?

A. Yes.

Q. Have you seen the new canvas which was brought upon the quarterdeck and said to be found in the Spanish carpenter's berth on Thursday the 13th ins^{t}.?

A. I saw some canvas on the 14th on the quarterdeck which I was told had been found the evening before in the Spanish carpenter's berth and which I measured by Captain Shaw's order and there were about nine yards.

Q. Did you know that to have been about the quantity of canvas and of that quality in the bag which contains the store canvas belonging to the *Philomel*?

A. Yes, both as to quantity and quality.

Q. In what state did you find the bag which contains the store canvas upon your going to the dockyard on the morning of the 14th ins^{t}.?

A. I found it had been opened; I immediately searched the bag and missed the canvas and reported it immediately to Mr Crosdale, the 1st Lieutenant, and to the master.

Q. Has there ever been any spare canvas belonging to the *Philomel* stowed on board the *Neptune* to your knowledge?

A. None. The witness stated to the best of his belief the canvas before the court was the canvas that had been in the bag, being N° 6 with the King's mark and about nine yards.

Court Do you know of any orders being given for a cot to be made and had you any reason to suspect the canvas had been taken for that purpose?

A. Not that I know of.

Q. Who besides yourself is in the habit of going to the store for canvas?

A. Nobody but myself and the prisoner.

The prisoner declined asking this witness any questions. Witness ordered to withdraw.

Here the prosecution closed and the prisoner was called upon for his defence. The prisoner stated that the Spanish carpenter had asked him for some canvas to make a cot and that he gave him the canvas now before the court for that purpose and that he was not to receive anything in return.

Captain Shaw called upon by the prisoner for a character respecting the care of his stores.

Captain Shaw I had no reason to suspect any embezzlement before and the prisoner has conducted himself well in action and been wounded.

The prisoner gave in a paper which was read (N° 2).

Here the defence closed; and the court was cleared and proceeded to deliberate upon and form the sentence and, having maturely and deliberately weighed and considered the evidence in support of the charge as well as what the prisoner had offered in his defence, is of opinion that the prisoner, Mr David Richards, did very improperly attempt to give away nine yards of canvas from His Majesty's stores under his charge, but, in consideration of the length of time the prisoner has been in His Majesty's service and his having been wounded when behaving gallantly in action, the court doth only adjudge the prisoner to be severely reprimanded and to be admonished to be more correct respecting the stores entrusted to his charge in future.

The court was opened, audience admitted and sentence passed accordingly.

…

64A. *Shaw to Pellew*

[ADM 1/5440] His Majesty's ship *Philomel*
No 1 Port Mahon, January 14th 1814

… Mr David Richards, Boatswain of His Majesty's sloop under my command, having on or about the evening of the 13th of January 1814 being found in an attempt to embezzle a quantity of canvas from His Majesty's stores under his charge,

I have to request that you will be pleased to order a court martial to try him for the same.

…

64B. *Richards's Paper*

[ADM 1/5440]
No 2

… The unfortunate prisoner which stands before you most humbly begs your humanity will show him some lenity, having been twenty one years in His Majesty's service and fifteen years of that time a petty officer, and was never guilty of any such misconduct before. I have a wife and four children to support beside to help an aged father of ninety two years of age.

Your prisoner shall and will in duty bound ever pray to the Almighty for your humanity. …

VIOLENT CRIMES

A. Homicide

65. *Court Martial of Edward Smith*

[ADM 1/5331]

Minutes taken at a court martial assembled on board His Majesty's ship *Stately* in Portsmouth Harbour on the 29th day of December 1794.

Present

The Honble. William Cornwallis, Vice Admiral of the Blue and second officer in the command of His Majesty's ships and vessels at Portsmouth and Spithead, President.

Rear Admiral John Colpoys
Captain
Francis Parry
The Right Honble. Hugh Seymour
Charles Edward Nugent
Sir Erasmus Gower, K^{t}.
Sir Andrew Snape Douglas, K^{t}.

Rear Admiral Sir George Keith Elphinstone, K.B.
Captain
Sir John Orde, Bar^{t}.
Christopher Parker
Charles Powell Hamilton
The Honble. Thomas Parkenham
The Right Honble Lord Charles Fitzgerald

The prisoner, Edward Smith, was brought in and audience admitted.

The order from the Right Honble. Lords Commissioners of the Admiralty, dated the 23rd day of December instant and directed to the president setting forth that Admiral Sir Peter Parker, Bart., Commander in Chief of His Majesty's ships and vessels at Portsmouth and Spithead, had transmitted to them a letter of the proceeding day's date, which he had received from Captain Edmund Dod of His Majesty's ship *Dictator*, representing that whilst the said ship lay in Madeira Road, Edward Smith, a Private Marine who had been placed sentinel over a prisoner, was insulted on his post by Patrick Ryan, a Seaman, and provoked, after several repetitions of abusive language, to strike him, the said Patrick Ryan, with the hilt of his cutlass and lightly wounded him on the elbow, which wound it was supposed was the occasion of throwing him into a fever, of which he died and for the trial of the said Edward Smith for what is represented in the said letter, was read.

The president reported to the court that Captains Molloy, Poole and Rodney were absent on Admiralty Leave.

The members of the court and the judge advocate then, in open court and before they proceeded to trial, respectively took the several oaths enjoined and directed in and by an Act of Parliament made and passed in the 22d year of His late Majesty King George the Second, entitled *An Act for Amending, Explaining and Reducing into One Act of Parliament the Laws relating to the Government of His Majesty's Ships, Vessels and Forces by Sea.*

Then the said letter from Captain Edmund Dod, containing the charge, was read and the witnesses were ordered to withdraw and attend their examinations separately, which they did as follows:

David Creighton, a Seaman belonging to His Majesty's ship *Dictator*, called in and sworn.

Captain Dod asked:

Q. Relate to the court what you know of the charges ag[st]. the prisoner.

A. I was laying badly in the master at arms' berth with my finger, in Madeira Roads. The ship's butcher was in irons and he asked the prisoner, who was sentry, leave to go to the head with him; and when he fetched him down, Ryan, a seaman, the deceased, had got into the prisoner's berth and the prisoner asked him to get up and he said he would not, neither for him and no bloody bugger like him. With that the sentinel took hold of the blade of his cutlass and struck Ryan over the elbow with the hilt of it. Ryan took the sentry to the quarter deck to the first Lieut[t]., who ordered him to go to his post and say no more about it.

The court and the prisoner asked the witness no questions.

Edward Sheppard, a Seaman belonging to the *Dictator*, called in and sworn.

Captain Dod asked:

Q. Relate to the court what you know of the charge against the prisoner?

A. The prisoner, who was sentry over the man on board the *Dictator*, went up with him to the head. When he came down, he asked Ryan to get up off the shot-box for the prisoner to set down; he told him he would not get up for him, for he was in his own berth and no such bloody buggers like him. The prisoner, Smith, then up with the hilt of the cutlass, taking hold of the blade and hit Ryan on his arm. There were a good many angry words passed and Ryan shoved Smith, the sentinel, out of the berth.

Mr. Jeremiah Swithers, Surgeon of His Majesty's ship *Dictator*, called in and sworn.

Captain Dod asked:

Q. State to the court what, in your opinion, was the cause of Ryan's death.

A. Fever.

The court asked:

Q. Do you know of his having received a wound in the elbow?

A. Yes, it was a small scratch. He was intemperate and had been drunk for three or four days, laying about the deck, from the intelligence I could collect, which produced a fever of which he died. I do not consider the scratch to be of the least consequence or in any degree the occasion of the man's death. We had 40 in our sick list ill of fevers at the time.

Captain Dod asked:

Q. Did you report to me that the wound had festered and afterwards mortified?

A. Yes, a partial mortification, which would have separated if the man had recovered of the fever.

The court asked:

Q. Is it your opinion that the wound occasioned the fever?

A. Not in the least, for if he had not been attacked with a fever, it would have healed in a day, I believe.

The court was cleared and agreed that it appeared to the court that the death of the said Patrick Ryan was caused by a fever, which was not occasioned by the slight wound in his elbow given to him by the said Edward Smith, and did therefore adjudge him to be acquitted.

The court was again opened, the prisoner brought in, audience admitted and sentence passed accordingly. …

66. *Court Martial of Richard Probert*

[ADM 1/5334]

Minutes of proceedings at a court martial held onboard His Majesty's ship the *Isis* in The Downs, the 4th day of January 1796.

Present

Henry Trollope Esq[r]., Captain of His Majesty's ship the *Glatton*, third officer in command and senior captain of His Majesty's ships and vessels in The Downs, president.

Captains

William George Fairfax	Herbert Sawyer
John Dilkes	Velters Cornewall Berkeley
William Swatfield	William Carthew
James Bissett	John Bazely

The prisoner was brought into court and the evidence and audience admitted.

Read the order of the Right Hon'ble the Lords Commissioners of the Admiralty, dated 1st January 1796, directed to Henry Trollope, Esqr., Captain of His Majesty's ship the *Glatton*, third officer in command and senior captain of His Majesty's ships and vessels in The Downs to try Richard Probert, alias James Probert, a landsman belonging to His Majesty's ship the *Isis*, for having attempted to take away the life of John Kell, a Quartermaster's Mate of the said ship, by firing at and wounding him with a pistol, on the 22d of last month.

Then the members of the court and judge advocate, in open court and before they proceeded to trial, respectively took the oaths directed by Act of Parliament. The letter from Captain Robert Watson, commander of His Majesty's ship the *Isis* (containing the charge against the prisoner) was then read; and all witnesses being ordered to withdraw and attend their examination separately, they all withdrew accordingly, except the first to be sworn. And the court proceeded to trial as follows:

Evidence in support of the charge. John Kell, Quartermaster's Mate of His Majesty's ship the *Isis*, sworn and examined as follows:

Court – Did you hear the charge against the prisoner read?

Ans. – Yes.

Court – You will relate to the court what you know relating to the charge.

Ans. – The prisoner and myself were in the larboard watch. We had the watch from four to eight on the morning of the 22d of December 1795. I ordered the prisoner to go to the wheel at 12 o'clock when he came on deck; he neglected going until it struck one bell. I then called to him on the main deck and asked the reason he did not go to the wheel; he said he did not know it was his turn. I told him it was and desired him to go there directly; he did not offer to go. I took him by the shoulder and shoved him towards the gangway; he then went to the wheel and said no more to me at that time. A short time after 8 o'clock on the evening of the same day, on coming off the deck from our watch, I was standing by my hammock making ready to take off my clothes to go to bed; I heard the voice of Rich^{d}. Probert say, 'Where do Kell lie?' I heard the voice of one Peter Reading say, 'He lies in that birth.' Richard Probert said, 'Do he lie in that inside hammock?' One answered yes, but I do not know who it was. Then I looked about and saw Probert standing at the after part of the pump dale; and he said, 'Kell,' beckoning to me,

'I want to speak to you.' I told him I was going to bed and desired he would do the same. He came to the fore part of the pump dale and said, 'Kell, what have I done that you insulted me so at 12 o'clock?' I told him I had nothing to say to him at that time; I would speak to him at some other time. The prisoner said, 'I suppose you have been cobbing[1] them tonight;' I told him I had cobbed five, and if he had been there, he would have made six. He said there were more deserved cobbing as well as him; he also said one had as well be at the devil as be in the after guard. I said, 'No, not that neither.' By this time I had got off my jacket and waist coat; going to bed, I turned my back towards the prisoner and sat down on a chest with my face toward the larboard side of the ship, pulling my trousers off. I had the left leg out of them when immediately a pistol was fired. I found myself wounded on my right breast under my arm. I looked toward the report of the pistol and saw Probert shake the pistol in his hand; and he said, 'there's for you, I thought I would do you.'

Court – Was it a ship's pistol the prisoner held in his hand?

Ans. – No, it was not.

Court – Was there a light in the birth at the time?

Ans. – Yes, the corporal's lantern was hanging between me and the prisoner.

Court – Were there any other persons present besides Probert?

Ans. – Yes, John Murray was standing close by me and James Rozier lying in his hammock slung between the two trains of the guns. Several others were there, but I do not recollect their names.

Court – Was this the pistol, now produced in court, found on the prisoner?

Ans. – I cannot swear to it, but it was one like it.

The prisoner asked this witness no questions; the latter withdrew.

John Murray, acting Ship's Corporal of the *Isis*, was next called into court and sworn.

[1]Cobbing was a punishment that was very similar to starting. According to Falconer, it was 'performed by striking the offender a certain number of blows on the breech with a flat piece of wood called a cobbing-board' (Falconer, *A New Universal Dictionary*, s.v. Cobbing).

Court – You will relate to the court what you know respecting the charge against the prisoner.

Ans. – On the 22d of last month, I think about ¼ past 8 o'clock in the evening, I came down between decks with a lantern in my hand and went into my birth. I sleep alongside John Kell. The prisoner came up and asked Kell to go and speak to him; he told him he would not speak to him then and told him to go to his bed. The prisoner said 'You have been cobbing some people of the after guard this afternoon, four or five;' and I heard him say there were several not there that deserved cobbing as well as those that were. He asked him why he insulted him at 12 o'clock. Kell told him to go to bed about his business; he wanted no more discourse with him that night. The prisoner said a man might better be at the devil than belong to the after guard. 'No,' replied Kell 'You had better be of the after guard than go to the devil.' The prisoner was leaning on the pump dale, his right hand in his left side pocket. I heard a pistol go off; the powder came into my face. If the prisoner had not said, 'I told you I would do for you,' I had not known it was him that fired the pistol, shaking it in his hand at the same time. I turned about to Kell and said, 'Are you shot?' He answered, 'I believe I am.' I immediately went after the prisoner, who was two yards before me. I spoke to Timothy Tool and desired him to get out of his hammock as I did not like to go to the prisoner by myself. I was afraid he had another pistol about him. I looked behind and saw Tool coming to me. I then seized hold of the prisoner and said, 'You have shot the man; where did you get the pistol?' The prisoner said, 'I will not run away.' I put my hand into his side pocket and took out a pistol; it was not loaded. I put it into my jacket pocket. I felt if he had any more about him, but did not find any. Then the master at arms came and I delivered the pistol to him.

Court – Is the pistol now in court, the one you took from the prisoner?

Ans. – I cannot swear particularly to it, but it was just such another.

Court – Did the pistol appear to have been lately fired?

Ans. – Yes.
Court – How did it appear to have been lately fired?
Ans. – The powder was moist in the pan.
Court – Was you between the prisoner and Kell when the pistol was fired?
Ans. – Yes, rather a little on one side of him.
Court – Do you know the position Kell was in when the prisoner fired at him?
Ans. – I think he was stooping.

The prisoner asked this witness no questions; the latter withdrew.

James Rozier, an Ordinary Seaman of the *Isis*, was called into court and sworn.

Court – You will relate to the court what you know respecting the charge against the prisoner.
Ans. – About a fortnight ago, I was in my hammock near John Kell's when the prisoner came to the after side of the pump dale on the larboard side. Kell said to the prisoner he did not wish to have anything to say to him and desired him to go to his hammock. The prisoner then got on the other side of the pump dale and asked Kell how he came to insult him in the way he did. Kell said he would not have anything to say to him then, but desired him to go to his hammock; and he would speak to him another time. The prisoner said to Kell, 'You have been cobbing some of the after guard.' Kell replied, 'I have, five of them, and some told me you was in liquor or I would have cobbed you.' The prisoner said he had better go to the devil than be in the after guard. He stepped about a foot further near my hammock and fired a pistol at Kell, saying, 'That's for you. I thought I would do you.'
Court – How near was you to Kell at the time?
Ans. – Not two yards.
Court – How far from the prisoner?
Ans. – Close to him; he touched my hammock at the time he fired the pistol.
Court – Was there light sufficient to distinguish the person of the prisoner?
Ans. – Yes, there was a lantern hanging between Kell and me.
Court – Did you see the pistol in the prisoner's hand?
Ans. – I saw something glitter, which he put into his pocket.

The prisoner asked this witness no questions; the latter withdrew.

Lieutenant William Lamb of the *Isis* was called into court and sworn.

Court – You will relate to the court what you know respecting the charge against the prisoner.

Ans. – On the 22d of last month, about half past 8 o'clock in the evening, I heard a noise at the wardroom door and, on my going out, I found the ship's corporal, John Murray, with the prisoner. He informed me the prisoner had shot John Kell. I asked the prisoner if it was true. He answered that what he had done, he should suffer for, after which the people were dispersed from the wardroom and I brought the prisoner on the quarter deck, when he was ordered to be confined.

Court – In what station in the ship do John Kell do duty?

Ans. – As captain of the after guard.

Court – In what station did Probert, the prisoner, do duty?

Ans. – In the after guard.

Court – By whom was the prisoner ordered into confinement?

Ans. – By the captain.

Court Quest. – Was a pistol delivered to you?

Ans. – Yes, by the master at arms.

Court – Is the pistol now produced in court, the one delivered to you by the master at arms?

Ans. – Yes.

Court – Do you know to whom the pistol belongs?

Ans. – I have always understood it belonged to the prisoner.

The prisoner asked this witness no questions; the latter withdrew.

M[r]. Edward Bell, Surgeon of the *Isis*, called into court and sworn.

Court – You will please relate to the court what you know respecting the charge against the prisoner.

Ans. – On the 22d of last month about half past 8 o'clock in the evening, I was called to a man, who I was told was shot. When I came on the lower deck, I met the surgeon's mate, who told me the man was not hurt. I then enquired what had happened and he informed me that James Probert, the prisoner, had discharged a pistol at James Kell. John Kell came below to the cockpit and upon examination, I found a slight wound, or rather a graze, which gave me reason to believe it was that of a pistol ball.

Court – On what part of the body was the wound?

Ans.	–	On the right side, a little below the armpit.
Court	–	Did you observe any hole in the shirt, as if done by a pistol ball?
Ans.	–	No.
Ques.	–	Did you examine the shirt?
Ans.	–	Yes, I saw a small mark, which might have been occasioned by a ball.

The evidence for the prosecution being ended, the court, at ¼ past 12 o'clock, was cleared and the prisoner told he might retire to prepare his defence. At ¾ past 12, the prisoner and audience were again admitted into court and the prisoner, being asked what he had to offer in his defence, desired to call Charles Goddard, a Seaman belonging to the *Isis*, to his character. Charles Goddard said he had known him for eleven months, and that, during that time, he bore a good character.

The prisoner was then asked if he wished to call any other witnesses to his character or otherwise; he answered no.

The prisoner then begged to throw himself on the mercy of the court.

The court was then cleared and proceeded to deliberate upon and form the sentence.

The court, having carefully and deliberately weighed and considered the evidence produced, were of opinion that the charge had been fully proved, that the punishment to be inflicted on him for his offence be capital, and that therefore, the court adjudges the prisoner to be hanged by the neck until he is dead at the yard arm of such of His Majesty's ships, and at such time as the Right Honble the Lords Commissioners of the Admiralty shall direct.

The court was then opened, audience admitted and sentence passed accordingly. …

67. *Court Martial of James Smith*

[ADM 1/5390]

Minutes of proceedings at a court martial held on board His Majesty's ship *Salvador del Mundo* in Hamoaze on Monday the 19th day of December 1808.

Present

John Sutton, Esqr., Rear Admiral of the Red and second officer in the command of His Majesty's ships and vessels at Plymouth, President.
The Honble. Robert Stopford, Rear Admiral of the Blue.

Captains

	Matthew Henry Scott
John Tremayne Rodd	Michael Seymour
Philip Bowes Vere Broke	Thomas Briggs
Clotworthy Upton	Sir William Bolton, Knight
John Quilliam	Thomas Smyth

(George Eastlake, Jun[r]., officiating Judge Advocate)

Being all the admirals and captains of post ships then and there present, next in seniority to the president, except Capt. Lord Amelius Beauclerk of His Majesty's ship *Saturn* and Capt. Thomas Wolley of His Majesty's ship *Salvador del Mundo*, who were absent on Admiralty leave.

The prisoner, James Smith, Seaman of His Majesty's sloop *Parthian* was brought into court and the witnesses and audience admitted.

Read – The order of the Right Honourable the Lords Commissioners of the Admiralty, dated the 15th day of December 1808, directed to the president to try the said James Smith for having shot John Bassett Balderston, Esquire, late Commander of His Majesty's said sloop *Parthian*, and thereby occasioned his death.

Read – The warrant appointing a judge advocate.

Then the members of the court and judge advocate, in open court and before they proceeded to trial, respectively took the oaths directed by Act of Parliament passed in the 22d. year of the reign of King George the 2d.

Read – The annexed letter of charge from Lieut. Thomas Steventon of His Majesty's said sloop *Parthian* to Admiral Young, Commander in Chief at Plymouth.

All the witnesses, except the first to be sworn, being then ordered to withdraw and to attend their examinations separately, they all withdrew accordingly and the court proceeded to trial as follows:

Evidence in support of the charge.

The prosecutor, Lieut. Thomas Steventon of His Majesty's sloop *Parthian*, sworn and examined as follows:

Court Relate to the court all the circumstances you know respecting the charge against the prisoner.

Ans[r]. On the 12th of the present month, between the hours of 12 and 4, I was sent for by Capt. Balderston, late Commander of the *Parthian*, to know why the prisoner was not on deck; I told him I believed he was unwell, as I had not seen him for some time. Capt. Balderston then told me to send for the prisoner. I did so, and left Capt. Balderston and went below, having duty to perform. In about 5 minutes, I was sent for by Capt. Balderston again, when I was ordered to station the prisoner in any part of the ship I thought proper to do his duty for that he had disrated him, or words to that effect. I went below again, and in the course of 10 minutes or a quarter of an hour, Capt. Balderston sent for me on the quarterdeck, told me not to mind the duty I was then performing below, but to get the booms stowed, the boatswain being then sick. Between one & three o'clock (it did not exceed three), as I was standing forward on the starboard bitts and looking aft, I saw the prisoner rush across the quarterdeck pass [*sic*] the capstern towards the larboard gangway with a pistol in his hand. I instantly ran aft towards the larboard gangway, but by the time I got half way, I heard the report of a pistol or musket. On my coming to the larboard gangway, I perceived that Capt. Balderston was wounded; I then ordered the prisoner to be seized and Capt. Balderston conducted down to his cabin, which was done. In about 5 or 10 minutes, after Capt. Balderston was taken to his cabin, he sent for me and ordered me to take the ship back. I did so. I did not see Capt. Balderston again till after he expired. At about half past 3, the surgeon came on deck and reported to me officially that the capt. had expired.

Co^{t}. At the time the prisoner was missed from the deck by Capt. Balderston, what was the duty then performing on board?

A. Bracing the yard about, there being little wind to get the ship out of the sound.

Co^{t}. Did you know that the prisoner was wanting in his station at that time?

A. When Capt. Balderston enquired where he was I did not see him on deck at that time or for some time before, but being in a hurry to get the ship under way, I did not miss him at the moment.

Co^{t}. Were all hands on deck when the prisoner had a duty to perform?

A. When the hands were turned up to unmoor the ship, it was the prisoner's duty to attend the coiling away of the cables below, but, at the time Capt. Balderston enquired for the prisoner, the ship must have been unmoored and under way half or ¾ of an hour. Part of the ship's company were then down at their dinners.

Co^{t}. Do you know for what reason you was directed by Capt. Balderston to order the prisoner to do his duty in any part of the ship you thought proper?

A. Because he was not on deck, which it was his duty to have been after the anchors were up and the ship under way.

Co^{t}. When you saw the prisoner, as you were standing forward by the bitts, rush across the quarterdeck with a pistol in his hand, had you any reason at that time for supposing the intention of the prisoner then was to discharge it at Capt. Balderston?

A. I had scarce time to imagine what were his intentions, but, seeing him with a pistol, I suspected that his intentions were to shoot himself or Capt. Balderston or anybody that might oppose him; whatever his intentions might be, I thought it my duty to prevent it, if possible, which was the occasion of my running towards him. I don't know, but I rather suspected it was Capt. Balderston he meant to shot, seeing him run across the quarterdeck and I know that Capt. Balderston was somewhere in that direction, leaving him about there when last I saw him.

Co^{t}. Did you consider at the time Capt. Balderston so manifested his displeasure towards the prisoner, by those directions he had given you, that it was caused not alone by his being wanting in his station to discharge his duty, but as well as from the answer you describe, in your letter, him to have given to the captain in a most contemptuous manner?

A. From both.

Co^{t}. At the time you came aft from the bitts, did you pass the starboard or the larboard side of the booms?

A. I am not clear which; I think the starboard. Had I passed on the larboard, I think I should have seen the prisoner shoot the captain.

Co^{t}. Have you ever discovered in the prisoner any appearance of so malignant a disposition as to give you reason to suppose him capable of shooting an unarmed person in the back?

A. No.

Co^{t}. Why did you order the prisoner to be seized?

A. As suspecting it was him that shot the captain.

Co^{t}. Did you see the prisoner with a pistol in his hand when you ordered him to be seized?

A. To the best of my recollection, he had a pistol in his hand. When I ordered him to be seized, he hove it down on deck.

Co^{t}. Did you see any other person with a pistol in his hand before the captain was shot?

A. To the best of my recollection, I did not.

Co^{t}. When you came to the spot where Capt. Balderston was after being wounded, were there many people about him?

A. Some 3 or 4: Mr, Snape the Purser, the surgeon, 2d. lieut. and the master.

Co^{t}. Did you cause the pistol to be examined?

A. I did not, the 2d. Lieut., Mr. Schultz, took charge of the pistol which he has in his possession at this time.

Co^{t}. Do you know if that pistol belonged to the prisoner?

A. It was a ship's pistol.

The witness resumed his place as prosecutor.

Mr. Stephen Love Hammick, First Surgeon of the Royal Naval Hospital at Plymouth, sworn and examined as follows:

Co^{t}. Was you present at the opening the body of Capt. Balderston?

A. Yes, I opened him myself.

Co^{t}. Describe to the court with what implement the wound given was, in your opinion, the cause of his death.

A. On the back part, I found a wound the size of a Dollar through the back bone; on the fore part about 2 inches below the navel, there was an opening thro' which a ball or slug had passed apparently; and within the abdomen, I found three other slugs or cut balls.

Slugs or cut balls produced by the witness and examined by the court.

The intestines were wounded in several places and those slugs were the cause of his death. I should suppose a whole ball had passed through, as there was a round opening near the navel.

Co^{t}. On which part of his body was the first impression of the wound received?

A. Certainly from behind, as the bone was driven in in that direction.

Co^{t}. How long might it be after the wound was given that you saw the body?

A. I examined the body 2 days after, but I saw the body on board about half an hour after it was said to have been dead.

The witness withdrew.

Mr. William Coombes, Midshipman of His Majesty's sloop *Parthian*, sworn and examined as follows:

Pros^{r}. Relate to the court all you know relative to the charge against the prisoner and mention the part of the ship you were in at the time.

A. On Monday the 12 of Decr. ins^{t}. between 12 and 4 o'clock, Capt. Balderston sent for the prisoner and likewise the midshipmen on the quarterdeck; he told the prisoner he was to do no more duty as an officer, for that he was not to be played with. The prisoner made answer to Capt. Balderston, 'No more was he.' The prisoner then walked off the quarterdeck and went down the fore hatchway; and I saw him go to his chest, close to the berth near the gun room in the after part of the ship, and take a ship's pistol out and carry it into the berth. Then he came out of the berth again and asked me what I was looking at. He told me he did not want me there, on which I went on the quarterdeck. When I came down again in about 10 minutes, I saw him in the berth sitting, leaning on his elbow. He spoke to himself and said, 'What am I broke for?' He said he would be revenged, knocked his hand on the table, took the pistol from the side of him close to the bulkhead and ran up the after ladder. I followed him and had hold of the tail of his coat as he was getting up the ladder and told him to stop. He made no answer. I let his coat go when he got to the ladder and he ran up. I followed him close round the companion and saw him present the pistol at the captain and fire it. He shot the captain through the back. Then there was a cry out, 'Seize him. Seize him;' the pris^r^. replied, 'Aye, seize him, seize him.' The prisoner's hands were then tied behind him and he was taken below.

Co^t^. You say you saw the prisoner take a pistol out of his chest; what time of day was it?

A. Near two o'clock.

Co^t^. Did you see the prisoner load or prime the pistol?

A. No.

Co^t^. Do you know that the pistol was loaded?

A. No.

Co^t^. What occasioned you to follow the prisoner below?

A. He ran down in a hurry and I ran after him to see what he was going to do.

Co^t^. You have said you saw the prisoner fire the pistol at the back of Capt. Balderston, relate to the court every part of that act.

A. He had the pistol by the side of him in his right hand. He presented the pistol to the captain, as the captain was leaning over the larboard gangway, and fired it at him. He was about 4 paces from him, as near as I can guess. I might be about 3 yards from the prisoner when he fired.

Co^t^. What was Capt. Balderston doing at the time?

A. Leaning over the larboard gangway, looking at the ship; his back was towards the prisoner.

Co^t^. What time lapsed between your following the prisoner off the quarterdeck down to the chest, where he took the pistol from, and the moment when you saw the prisoner fire it at the back of the captain?

A. About half an hour. He went below immediately when the captain said he should do no more duty as an officer. Capt. Balderston did not fall; he was caught. He hollowed and put his hand to his stomach.

Co[t]. Did you see the pistol in the prisoner's hand after he fired it?

A. I saw it after the prisoner was secured, lying on the quarterdeck.

Co[t]. Can you positively swear that it was the prisoner, whom you now have in view, who discharged that pistol in the back of Capt. Balderston and that it could not be any other person?

A. Yes.

Co[t]. Did you keep sight of the prisoner constantly after quitting your hold of the prisoner, as he was going up the hatchway with the pistol in his hand, until you saw that pistol discharged by him in the back of Capt. Balderston?

A. Yes.

Co[t]. Did you see Capt. Balderston after he was taken from the quarterdeck?

A. Yes, on his sofa in his cabin before he expired and afterwards.

Co[t]. How long have you been in the *Parthian* with the prisoner?

A. Three months.

Co[t]. Did you ever know him to have been reprimanded by his captain?

A. No.

Co[t]. What passed between the captain and the prisoner before the captain told him he would not be trifled with?

A. Only told him he was to do no more duty as an officer, that was all I heard.

Co[t]. What duty was going on when the capt. sent for the prisoner?

A. They were coiling cables below.

The witness withdrew.

M[r]. John Snape, Purser of His Majesty's sloop *Parthian*, sworn and examined as follows:

Pro. Relate to the court all you know relative to the charge against the prisoner.

A. On Monday the 12 of Dec[r]. ins[t]., about 1 o'clock, I was walking on the starboard side of the quarterdeck, when I heard Capt. Balderston enquire for the prisoner, requesting to know why he was not on deck and desired he might be immediately sent for. In the course of 2 or 3 minutes, the prisoner came up, saying, 'Did you send for me, Sir.' Capt. Balderston replied, 'Why was you not on deck at a time like this when the ship is getting under way?' The prisoner replied, 'I was never told.' When Capt. Balderston replied that was no excuse and for his general bad conduct since he had been in the ship, he would disrate him, as neglect of duty was a thing he never forgave in any officer; at the same time saying to me, who was on the other side of the quarterdeck, 'M^r^. Snape, disrate him.' The prisoner then, in a most contemptuous manner, crossed his hands over his body, saying, 'Very well, Sir, you may do so if you please.' I went below and ordered the clerk to disrate him at the captain's request. In the course of about 10 or 15 minutes, I went on deck and reported that I had desired the clerk to disrate the prisoner, but did not see the prisoner at that time. About ½ or ¾ of an hour after I was standing on the poop, Capt. Balderston was then standing with his back towards me on the larboard gangway, looking at the sails. I, at that time, was looking forward, when I observed the prisoner run round the capstern and, when at a distance of 5 to 6 feet from Capt. Balderston, I observed him present a pistol at the back of Capt. Balderston, I rushed from the poop with intent to seize him, but before I had reached him, he had discharged the contents in the back of Capt. Balderston. I then flew to the assistance of my captain, who, turning round with one hand hold of the stanchion, exclaimed, 'I am shot, I am shot. Who has shot me?' and fell in my arms. Many flew to his assistance and I rushed from him, in the agitation of my mind, to have put an end to the prisoner, when M^r^. Stevenson, the First Lieutenant, requested I would not do anything to the prisoner, as he was then secured. I then assisted in carrying Capt. Balderston to his cabin and continued with him for about 15 minutes, when I thought from his speaking so sensibly there might yet be hopes; and the first lieutenant immediately gave me a boat to go to D^r^. Beattie and his friends. I found D^r^. Beattie at home, who immediately went off, but unfortunately Capt. Balderston had expired 5 minutes before he reached the ship.

Co^t^. Do you, upon your oath, declare it was the prisoner whom you saw present the pistol at the captain and discharge it?

A. I do.

Co^t^. Do you know any of the instances of misconduct in the prisoner, alluded to by Capt. Balderston, at the time he ordered him to be disrated?

A. I do; 5 or 6 days after the prisoner had joined the ship, about the 5 of September last, the prisoner was taken from the quarterdeck by 4 men in a state of insensibility from drink.

Co[t]. Was Capt. Balderston ever made acquainted with the person who had killed him?

A. He was; when the captain was lying on his sofa, he looked round and asked who had shot him, saying, 'Was it a great gun?' The 2nd Lieut., Mr. Schultz, told him it was the prisoner, on which he replied, 'I know; I know; I know' and, looking round, said, 'If I have injured any of you, God forgive me.' I requested to know if he had anything particular to say, when he replied, 'I have 2 sisters; tell them I am sorry for the trouble I have given them.'

The witness withdrew.

M[r]. George Galbraith, Surgeon of His Majesty's sloop *Parthian*, sworn and examined as follows:

Pro[r]. Relate to the co[t]. what you know relative to the charge against the prisoner.

A. On Monday last, a little after the ship was under way, I think between 12 & 1 o'clock, Capt. Balderston asked me on the quarterdeck if the prisoner was sick; I told him not that I knew of; a few minutes after, I went below and, when near the foot of the ladder, I heard the captain speak in a loud tone to some person on deck. I listened for a few seconds and understand he was speaking to the prisoner, but did not hear what he said. I did not see or hear anything farther till about ¾s of an hour after. When I was walking the quarterdeck on the starboard side. I heard some person coming hastily up the companion ladder and, on looking that way, perceived the prisoner coming up. He seemed to trip his foot, but immediately recovered himself. At the same time, I observed a pistol under his left arm or in his left hand. I was then walking aft and proceeded a few paces and was considering where the prisoner could be going with a pistol. I formerly heard he intended to shot himself and the first reflection that struck me was that he was coming on deck for that purpose. I turned hastily round and, by the time the prisoner had got on the quarterdeck on the same side where I was and ran hastily along between the capstern and the gun room skylight, I followed him. While he was crossing the quarterdeck, he presented the pistol gradually as he went along at Capt. Balderston, and, at the distance of about 3 paces, fired it. Capt. Balderston was then standing on the larboard gangway ladder with his back towards the prisoner. He turned partly round and gave a shriek. I don't know correctly what he said. Some person then called out, 'Seize him,' meaning the prisoner. I laid hold of his arm, but instantly let it go to attend to the captain and told the first lieut. that the capt. must immediately go on shore. He was then carried aft the quarterdeck, where I examined his wound. I found that a ball had entered the lower part of his back a little to the right side and passed out at his belly about 3 inches below the navel, near the last wounds under the integuments. I could feel 2 hard substances, which I supposed to be slugs. I then reported to the 1st lieut. that Capt. Balderston was mortally wounded. He was then carried below to his cabin where I stayed by him nearly the whole time till he expired, about an hour an half [*sic*].

Co^{t}. You are positive that it was the prisoner you saw discharge a pistol in the back of Capt. Balderston at the moment you describe and no other person?

A. I am perfectly certain it was the prisoner that fired at Capt. Balderston, who was standing with his back towards the prisoner.

Co^{t}. Do you declare the death of Capt. Balderston was occasioned by the wound he received?

A. Yes, I am positive his death was occasioned by the wound he then received.

Co^{t}. Do you know the implements that made the wound?

A. The wound on the belly seemed to have been the effect of a pistol or musket ball passing out. He was then standing above the bulwark and the ball (if it was one) must have passed overboard. The wound on his back was more irregular, but could be accounted for from a ball and slugs carrying in pieces of his clothes along with it. It was a ship's pistol.

The witness withdrew.

Lieut. George Augustus Schultz of H.M. sloop *Parthian* sworn and examined as follows:

Co^{t}. Did you see the prisoner shoot Capt. Balderston?

A. I did not see it.

Co^{t}. Describe to the court what passed.

A. On the 12th instant, about 2 o'clock in the afternoon, I was busily employed on duty and was alarmed at the explosion of a pistol. I turned round and saw the prisoner with a pistol in his hand. I heard a voice call out, 'Seize him.' I immediately laid hold of the prisoner myself and from thence went to the captain, whom I attended down below.

Co^{t}. Did you see the pistol in the hand of the prisoner made use of in any way?

A. No, I laid hold of the pistol on the quarterdeck and sent it down below by one of the youngsters into my cabin. I then went down below attending Captain Balderston till I was ordered on shore by Lieut. Steventon to inform Admiral Young of what had happened.

Co^t. When you took up that pistol, had it been recently fired?

A. I did not examine it; I concluded it to be the pistol, which had just been fired.

Co^t. How near was the pistol to Capt. Balderston when you took it up?

A. About 11 or 12 feet.

Co^t. Did the prisoner show any signs of contrition or remorse afterwards or what was his conduct?

A. I thought his conduct inclined to be vindictive more than otherwise.

The witness withdrew.

Lieut. Steventon was then asked:

Co^t. Are the relative bearings & distances as set forth in your letter of charge against the prisoner, those given you by the master of the *Parthian* at the time, and, as such, upon record.

A. They are the bearings and distances given me by the master.

The evidence in support of the charge being now closed, the president now acquainted the prisoner thereof and asked him if he had any defence to make. The prisoner said, 'I have no witnesses and I don't see what use it will be for me to make any defence. I leave it to the court to judge as they think proper.'

On which, the court was cleared and proceeded to deliberate upon and form the sentence.

The court, having very maturely and deliberately weighed and considered the evidence in support of the charge (the prisoner not offering anything in his defence), was of opinion that the charge had been fully proved against the prisoner, James Smith, and did in consequence thereof adjudge him to be hanged by the neck until he is dead at the yard arm of such one of His Majesty's ships and at such time as the Right Honourable, the Lords Commissioners of the Admiralty shall direct.

The court was opened, the prisoner brought in, the witnesses and audience re-admitted and the sentence pronounced accordingly. …

67A. *Steventon to Young*

[ADM 1/5390] H.M. sloop *Parthian*
Plymouth, the 13th Dec[r]. 1808

… I beg leave to acquaint you of the death of Captain J. B. Balderston, late commanding His Majesty's sloop *Parthian*, who was yesterday shot by James Smith, one of the crew and late Master's Mate on board, the melancholy circumstances of which are as follows, viz[t].:

At one P.M., Captain Balderston, not perceiving M[r]. James Smith, Master's Mate, on deck, sent for him to know the reason why he was not attending his duty while getting under way; his answer was, in a most contemptuous manner, that he had not been told, on which Captain Balderston replied that was no excuse and said he would disrate him, on which he replied, in a most contemptuous manner, he might do so if he pleased and immediately went below. At 2:10 P.M., His Majesty's sloop being in the following situation, the buoy of the Panther, bearing SW by W distance a cable's length and being at that time forward attending the duty there, I observed M[r]. James Smith, Master's Mate, going across the quarterdeck with a pistol in his hand. I immediately ran towards him, but before I could get to him, he had discharged the contents in the back of Captain Balderston, who was then standing on the larboard gangway ladder. On my coming to the gangway, I perceived that Captain Balderston was mortally wounded, when I ordered M[r]. Smith to be immediately seized. Captain Balderston was then carried below and sent for me and ordered me to take the sloop back. I did not see Captain Balderston afterwards until he expired, as I was attending the duty of the ship.

At 3:40 P.M., the white buoy of the Shovel bearing N NE distance a cable's length, the surgeon reported Captain Balderston had expired in consequence of the wound he had received from M[r]. James Smith, Master's Mate; and I beg leave to inform you that previous to Captain Balderston expiring, he exclaimed he had two sisters, which it is surmised were depending on him.

With heart-felt pain, I am sorry to say that in this young and gallant (and) much to be regretted officer, the country will feel a loss. His father, also an old officer, and two brothers lost their lives in the service. …

68. *Court Martial of William Mason, Stephen Rolls and John M^c^Carthy*

[ADM 1/5430]

Minutes of proceedings at a court martial held on board His Majesty's ship *Salvador del Mundo* in Hamoaze on Thursday the 24th day of September 1812.

Present

Sir Edward Buller, Bart., Vice Admiral of the Blue and second officer in the command of His Majesty's ships and vessels at Plymouth, President.

Captains

James Nash	Sir Thomas Cochrane, Kn[t].
William Augustus Montague	George Harris
Robert Forbes	Donald Campbell

George Eastlake Jun[r]., officiating Judge Advocate.

Being all the captains of post ships then and there present next in seniority to the president, except Capt. William Charles Fahie of His Majesty's ship *Abercrombie*, who was the prosecutor.

The prisoners, William Mason, Stephen Rolls and John M[c]Carthy Seamen of His Majesty's said ship *Abercrombie*, were brought into court and the witnesses and audience admitted.

Read – The order of the Right Honourable, the Lords Commissioners of the Admiralty, dated the 10th day of September 1812, directed to the president to enquire into the circumstances which occasioned the death of John Driskill, Seaman of the *Abercrombie*, and to try the said William Mason, Stephen Rolls and John M[c]Carthy respectively for their conduct on that occasion.

Read – The warrant appointing a judge advocate.

Then the members of the court and judge advocate, in open court and before they proceeded to trial, respectively took the oaths directed by Act of Parliament passed in the 22d. year of the reign of King George the 2d.

Read – The letter annexed from the said Capt. Fahie to Adm[l]. The Right Honble Lord Kieth (No. 1).

All the witnesses, except the first to be sworn, being then ordered to withdraw and to attend their examinations separately, they all withdrew accordingly and the court proceeded to trial as follows:

Evidence in support of the charge.

James Mitchell, Seaman of His Majesty's ship *Abercrombie*, sworn and examined as follows:

Pro. Were you in the main top of the *Abercrombie* about 6 P.M. on the 31st of August last?

A. Yes.

Pro. Did you see the deceased, John Driskill, & the prisoner, Mason, fight?

A. Yes, when I went up in the top at 6, I found the prisoner Mason sitting there and also the deceased, John Driskill, and many others. I lay down my head against Mason's leg and Driskill began to pull me about and ask me some questions. I desired him to let me alone; Driskill then asked Mason who he was. Mason told him he was a man. 'Yes,' says Driskill, 'you are a play actor, but you shan't come with your play acting tricks over me.' Mason said he was and could act a play that would astonish him. By this time the hands were turned up to reef topsails. When the topsails were reefed, I came down into the top again. I sat down on the larboard side. I had not been there long before I saw Mason & Driskill coming round the fore part of the top, Mason with his mouth bleeding. He and Driskill then stripped off their jackets and began to fight, when Driskill knocked Mason down in the fore part of the top and struck him after he was down. I told Driskill that was not fair, and. if he struck him so again, I would strike him. They fought 4 or 5 rounds; afterwards when they shook hands and made it up to fight another time, I left them then. Salter, Webster and the prisoner were there when I came away, which was about 10 minutes after the fight began. About 5 minutes after, I heard Salter cry out, 'There is a man overboard.' I asked who it was; he said it was Driskill. I went to the larboard side and found Mason sitting upon the studding sail, crying.

Pro. Did you hear Stephen Rolls or McCarthy urge them to fight it out at that time?

A. No.

Co^{t}. Can you take upon yourself to say that Driskill fell out of the top overboard in consequence of any violence of either of the prisoners?

A. No.

Co^{t}. Do you know that any ill will existed between the deceased and either of the prisoners previous to the fighting?

A. None.

Co^t^. Was Driskill drunk or sober?
A. I don't think he was sober.

The witness withdrew.

David Roberts, Seaman on board His Majesty's ship *Abercrombie*, sworn and examined as follows:

Pro. Were you in the main top of the *Abercrombie* about 6 P.M. on the 31st of August last?
A. Yes.
Pro. Did you see the deceased (Driskill) & the prisoner Mason fighting there?
A. Yes, Driskill said to Mason, 'Don't think to come with any of your play acting tricks over me.' Said Mason, 'I didn't come with my play acting tricks, so let me alone.' Then they challenged one another. Mason wanted him to come on the lower deck to fight and not in the top. Then Driskill struck Mason and knocked him against the stay sail. Mason returned the blow; then they both went down the lee side and stripped, and they fought about 15 minutes. Then Driskill was getting quite tired; he was making a blow at Mason and missed it. Then Mason struck him and he fell right down through the lubber's hole; and, when Mason saw that the man had fallen, he sat down in the stay sail and cried and said he would never fight another battle as long as he lived. I then came down.
Pro. Where was Driskill struck when he fell?
A. Upon the side of the head.
Pro. Did you hear either of the other prisoners, Rolls & M^c^Carthy, urge them to fight it out in the top?
A. No.
Co^t^. Was the deceased drunk or sober?
A. He was not sober.
Co^t^. Do you think if he had been sober that the blow was so violent as to have knocked him out of the top?
A. No, I don't think it was.
Co^t^. What was the disposition of the deceased?
A. He was a quarrelsome man always, drunk or sober.

The witness withdrew.

Aaron Holson, Seaman of the *Abercrombie*, swn & ex^d^. as follows:

Pros^r^. Were you in the main top of the *Abercrombie* about 6 P.M. on the 31st of August last?

A. Yes.

Pro. Did you see the deceased (Driskill) and the prisoner Mason fighting there?

A. Yes; after reefing the topsails, I came down into the top and saw the deceased and Mason quarrelling. Driskill wished to go down below. Mason refused and Driskill turned himself round and struck Mason. They fought a few blows and then went to the lee side of the top, where they fought a few rounds and Driskill sat down and did not wish to fight any more. When the prisoner, John M^c^Carthy, made answer to fight it out, Driskill said, 'So I will.' They fought 2 or 3 rounds when Driskill fell down through lubber's hole, but whether he was struck, I don't know.

Pro. Did you hear the prisoner Rolls urge them to fight it out?

A. No, he was present.

Co^t^. Did you hear Mason use any aggravating language to the deceased?

A. No, they shook hands and agreed to fight it out another day.

Co^t^. Was Driskill sober?

A. No.

The witness withdrew.

William Arthur, Seaman on board His Majesty's ship *Abercrombie*, sworn and examined as follows:

Pro. Were you in the main top of the *Abercrombie* about 6 P.M. on the 31st of August last?

A. Yes.

Pro. Did you see the deceased (Driskill) and the prisoner, Mason, fighting there?

A. Yes, when I came down the rigging they exchanged 2 or 3 blows to windward; then they came over to the lee side and fought 3 or 4 rounds there. Driskill said he would fight no more till they went below and he shook hands with Mason. The prisoner [*sic*], McCarthy & Webster, were standing up on the cross piece and one of them, but which I can't say, said, 'Have it out now,' upon which Driskill got up and began to fight again. He made a blow at Mason and missed him and shied round and stumbled. Mason caught him by a blow somewhere about the head and the deceased fell down through lubber's hole. Then Mason began to cry and clasped his hands and said, 'Oh my God; what shall I do.'

Co^t^. Was Driskill drunk or sober?

A. He was not sober.

Co^t^. What was the temper of the deceased?

A. Quarrelsome when in liquor.

Co[t]. Do you know the cause of the quarrel?

A. No.

The witness withdrew.

Lloyd Owen, Seaman on board His Majesty's ship *Abercrombie*, sworn and examined as follows:

Pro. Were you in the main top of the *Abercrombie* about 6 P.M. on the 31st of August last?

A. Yes.

Pro. Did you see the deceased, John Driskill, and the prisoner, Mason, fighting?

A. Yes, when I came out of the topmast rigging into the top, after reefing the topsails, I heard Mason say to Driskill, 'This is no place to fight, let us go on the lower deck or in the galley.' Driskill answered something; I don't recollect. Driskill said, 'Because I have been but a short time in the top, you think to tread upon me, but I'll be damned if you do.' With that, Driskill struck Mason somewhere about the face, which made Mason stagger back against the mizzen top gallant stay sail. If he had been a little farther forward, it is my opinion he (Mason) would have gone through lubbers hole. They exchanged 5 or 6 blows on the starboard side of the top, it being the weather side at the time; they then went to leeward, where they fought for some time till Driskill tore Mason's shirt. Mason pulled his shirt off and they fought again. Driskill struck Mason a foul blow. James Mitchell said if he did that again, he would strike him. I told Driskill, 'You had better pull your shirt off, or you will have it torn.' Driskill said, 'Damn the shirt.' They knocked one another down 2 or 3 times and then dropped it. I ran to the after part of the top to see if the hammocks were all down, as mine was not below at the time. I turned round and saw a blow exchanged between the prisoner, Mason, and the deceased, just at the same moment. Driskill staggered back and I believe his foot caught the carlings of the top and he fell through lubber's hole. I ran down the rigging, got into the white cutter on the larboard side to save him, but I saw no more of him.

Pro. Did you hear either of the other prisoners urge them to fight it out?

A. No, I don't recollect seeing them.

Co[t]. Was Driskill drunk or sober?

A. I think he was a little in liquor; he was a very cross man and quarrelsome when in liquor.

The witness withdrew.

Robert Salter, Seaman on board His Majesty's ship *Abercrombie*, sworn and examined as follows:

Pro. Were you in the main top of the *Abercrombie* about 6 P.M. on the 31st of August last?

A. Yes.

Pro. Did you see the deceased & the prisoner, Mason, fighting?

A. Yes, Driskill and Mason were quarrelling. Driscoll called Mason a play acting son of a bitch. Mason said if he said that again, he would knock him down; then Driskill up with his fist and hit Mason. Then they began to fight. They fought 2 rounds there and then said they had better go below to fight it out. Then they fought to leeward, about 4 or 5 rounds. Mason said they had better knock it off and fight on the lower deck. Rolls said it was best to have it out at once. Then they got up and began to fight again and Mason knocked Driskill down. Then, as he was getting up again Driskill was hitting Mason a blow, when received a blow himself from Mason, which knocked him down through lubber's hole.

Pro. Did you near M^c^Carthy say, 'fight it out?'

A. No.

Co^t^. Do you think the dec'ed fell in consequence of the blow he received from Mason?

A. I cannot say. The man was in liquor; he was falling down before the blow was given.

The witness withdrew.

The evidence for the prosecution being here closed, the prisoners were asked if they had anything to offer in their behalves, when they called upon the prosecutor to speak to their general character.

Capt. Fahie said, 'Mason, I have known two years. I have never heard any complaints against him; he has never been before me. The other two have been but a short time in the ship.' The pris^r^., Mason, gave in the annexed written paper (no. 2), which was read to the court.

The prisoner [*sic*], Rolls and McCarthy, denied having urged the deceased and Mason to fight.

The prisoners having nothing further to offer, the court was cleared & proceeded to deliberate upon and form the sentence.

The court, having very maturely and deliberately weighed and considered the evidence that had been adduced, as well as what the prisoners had offered in their behalves respectively, was of opinion 'That the death of the said John Driskill was occasioned by his drunkenness and fighting with the said William Mason, who was provoked to fight from having been first struck by and received the most insulting and aggravating language from the deceased; and although the court must express its strong disapprobation of the conduct of the three prisoners in fighting or encouraging others so to do, yet taking into consideration the conduct of the deceased towards the said William Mason, the court doth acquit the said William Mason, Stephen Rolls and John McCarthy, at the same time charging them to be more attentive in future to the 23d Article of War.'

The court was opened, the prisoners brought in, the witnesses and audience re-admitted and the prisoners acquitted accordingly. …

68A. *Fahie to Keith*

[ADM 1/5430] H.M.S. *Abercrombie* at sea, Septr. 3d, 1812

(No. 1)

At 6:30 P.M. of the 31st ultimo, the man named in the margin [John Driskill, Ordinary Seaman, aged 23] fell from the main top overboard. The ship was instantly thrown in the wind and the boats lowered down with the utmost promptness to save him, but without success.

On the following morning it was represented to me by one of the ship's corporals that it was rumoured that the deceased had been knocked out of the top; an inquiry was immediately made and it appears that he was fighting with William Mason, another main top man, from whom he received a blow in consequence of which he fell through lubber's hole overboard as above stated. It further appears that the fighting was urged and promoted by Stephen Rolls and John McCarthy, two other main top men, who with William Mason, are in confinement.

I deem this unhappy event to be of a nature which renders it my duty to state it with all its circumstances to your Lordship that such further investigation may be made as to your Lordship may appear expedient.

68B. *Mason to Court*

[ADM 1/5430] [No Date, No Place]

… It is the prisoners' wish that the learned gentlemen will request of Capt. Fahie to state our different characters before the learned jury. …

68C. *Defence of William Mason*

[ADM 1/5430]

(No. 2)

Prisoner's Defence

… At 6 P.M., I went up into the top, it being my watch there, and laid myself down in the studding sail with the witness Mitchell. I had not lay long in conversation with Mitchell before the deceased came up into the top and began to pull Mitchell about and Mitchell desired him to let him, the witness, alone. I then asked him why he did not let the witness alone and not to trouble his head with those that did not concern themselves with him. He made answer, 'Who the hell are you?' I said I was a man; he made answer, 'What am I?' & I said he acted like a boy. 'You are a play acting bugger, but you shan't come your play acting tricks over me.' I then said I should not play act with him. He then said, 'I am but a short time in the top and you wish to impose upon me;' I said I did not. The hands were turned up to reef top sails and the top sails were reefed. When he said to me, 'Do you want to fight,' I said no, I would not fight in the top. He said, 'There is room enough here, come.' I said no, but if he wanted to fight, come down below and I would have it out; he said he would not, but there is room enough in the top stave and then struck me and knocked me down against the mizzen top gallant staysail. I then got up and said, 'Is that what you are up to?' He was in a posture to strike me again. We then fought on the larboard side of the top for some time, till he said he would give it in for the present and would fight me some other time. I was going to shake hands with him, when McCarthy and Stephen Rolls, as well as I remember, said, 'Don't give it in; fight it out now.' There was 3 or 4 in all that prompt [*sic*] him on to fight again, but I do not recollect who they were. He then got up and struck me and knocked me against the rigging and we began again till the last blow was struck by me. We both struck at one another, but my blow hit him, which stagger'd me on one side. I did not see him go overboard, nor so knew of it till the men sang out in the top, 'The man is overboard.' …

B. Striking an Officer

69. *Court Martial of Edward Patton*

[ADM 1/5330]

Minutes of the proceedings of a court martial held onboard His Majesty's ship *Cambridge* in Hamoaze the 15th day of April 1793 for the trial of Edward Patton, Seaman belonging to His Majesty's ship *Porcupine*, on a charge exhibited against him by Captain Edward Buller, commander of the said ship, of having on the 9th day of March, when all hands were on deck to hoist the boats in at sunset, stabbed Mr. Andrew Gilmore, Boatswain of the said ship.

Francis Watson, Surgeon, certified sickness to be the cause of Captain Roger of the *Cambridge* not attending the court.

Mr. Francis Megson, Master of the *Porcupine*, sworn.

Court – Relate to the court what you know respecting the charge you've heard against the prisoner.

Ans. – On the ninth of last month at Waterford, after the boats were hoisted in, Mr. Hibbs, Midshipman, came and informed me in the gunroom that the boatswain was struck by the prisoner. I immediately went upon deck and was told by the boatswain that the prisoner had stabbed him with a knife; I desired to see the place where he was stabbed. He took his shirt out of his breeches and I saw it, and then went and acquainted Captain Buller of it, who ordered me to put the prisoner in irons.

C. – What was the nature of the wound?

A. – It was a small wound about an inch long, no blood issuing from it, but an appearance of blood.

C. – Are you convinced that the wound was a fresh one?

A. – Yes.

C. – What examination took place previous to the confinement of the prisoner?

A. – I asked the boatswain if he was sure he was stabbed and he told me he was. I asked by what? He told me by a knife, he believed.

C. – What examination took place to make you believe it was the prisoner, [who?] had stabbed the boatswain?

A. – The boatswain saying he was sure 'twas the prisoner that had stabbed him.

C. – At what hour of the night was the complaint made to you?

A. – About nine o'clock, when it was dark.

C. – At what part of the ship was the boatswain, when he says he was stabbed?

A. – The quarterdeck.

C. – Were all hands upon deck?

A. – Yes.

C. – How long do you apprehend the wound had been given before you saw it?

A. – From the report given me, it must be near a minute.

C. – Had you any reason to doubt the prisoner was not the person that stabbed the boatswain?

A. – Not in the least.

Mr. Andrew Gilmore, Boatswain of the *Porcupine*, sworn.

C. – Relate to the court what you know respecting the charge you have heard against the prisoner.

A. – On the 9th of March last about half past seven in the evening, I went aft upon the quarter deck and struck the prisoner some strokes with my stick; he was stooping down at the time and rose and struck me in the belly. I found myself pricked, and took him by the shoulders and forced him against barracudo rail, and called for assistance, when Hugh Drougherty took the prisoner from me.

C. – At the time you found yourself pricked, did you see the stroke or the instrument by which it was given?

A. – I did not see the instrument but I saw the prisoner make the blow.

C. – You are very certain as to the person?

A. – Yes, I am very certain.

C. – Was it dark when this happened?

A. – It was dusky, not quite dark.

C. – Was the prisoner alone, or were there other men near him?

A. – To the best of my memory, I saw no person near him.

C. – Was there no other man at the time near enough to have struck the blow?

A. – Not to the best of my knowledge.

C. – When you seized the man that struck you, did you seize him by the hand that struck the blow?

A. – No, by the shoulders.

C. – Why did you strike the prisoner those blows with your stick?

A. – Through his neglect of getting the starboard main yard tackle down and partly from his giving a short answer.

C. – Were the hands upon the quarterdeck for the purpose of getting the boats in?

A. – Yes.

C. – And can you speak with certainty, when so many men were on the quarter deck, there was not any other man than the prisoner near enough to strike the blow you received?

A. – To the best of my knowledge, there was not.

C. – Was there any knife or other weapon found in the prisoner's hand or on the deck near where the blow was given?

A. – Not to my knowledge.

C. – Did the prisoner make use of any words at the time you say he struck you?

A. – Not that I know of.

C. – Was there any search made for the instrument by which the wound was given?

A. – Not to my knowledge.

C. – Describe the wound and say by what instrument you suppose it was given.

A. – The wound is in the belly, near the navel about a quarter of an inch long and I suppose it to have been given by a sharp-pointed knife.

C. – Had the blow been given with violence by a sharp-pointed knife, do you not suppose it wou'd have penetrated further?

A. – I have reason to believe from my waist coat that the knife was turned askance.

C. – On what part of the quarter deck was the prisoner standing at the time and what was he about?

A. – He was stooping down by the fore brace on the quarter deck; I do not know what he [was?] about.

C. – Was the blow given immediately upon your striking him?

A. – I believe it was.

C. – Do you think that the prisoner cou'd be employed there about anything to occasion his having a knife in his hand?

A. – I do not know.

C. – How long after the prisoner had neglected getting down the yard tackle was it that you struck him?

A. – Shortly after the boats were hoisted in.

Here the clothes were produced in court.

C. – Court do you believe that the holes in that jacket and shirt were made by the instrument at the time you received the wound?

A. – Yes.

C. – You say that the prisoner was stooping and that he rose up suddenly on your striking him; do you believe that the blow you received was given intentionally as a blow or that he struck accidentally by swinging of his arm as he rose up suddenly?

A. – I believe intentionally.

C. – After receiving the blow, how long before you found you were wounded?

A. – Immediately.

C. – Do you wish, prisoner, to ask any questions of the evidence?

Pris. – No.

Hugh Drougherty, Seaman belonging to the *Porcupine*, sworn.

C. – Relate to the court what you know respecting the charge against the prisoner.

A. – When the *Porcupine* was lying at the Passage of Waterford, I believe in the month of March after sunset, I saw the boatswain strike the prisoner with a stick. The prisoner bid him not strike him any more; the boatswain said he would. Then the prisoner took hold of the boatswain and, soon after, they both fell. Then the boatswain call'd for assistance, saying the prisoner had a knife in his hand and I went and took hold of the prisoner, but did not see any knife.

C. – When you saw the scuffle between the boatswain and the prisoner and heard the former declare that he was struck with a knife, did you see any knife or other sharp instrument in the hands of the prisoner or near him?

A. – No, I did not.

C. – Did you see any other person, besides the prisoner, near the boatswain that might have given him a blow?

A. – No.

C. – Did you see the prisoner direct any blow at the boatswain?

A. – No.

C. – Do you believe yourself to have been the person nearest to the prisoner and the boatswain at the time?

A. – Yes, I do.
C. – What degree of light was there?
A. – 'Twas darkish, after sunset.
C. – Do you know of any search being made for a knife or other weapon at that time?
A. – No.
C. – You say the boatswain and the prisoner fell; did the prisoner make use of violence to throw the boatswain down?
A. – I do not know.
C. – What was the prisoner doing when the boatswain struck him and in what position was he?
A. – He was stooping, doing something about the main yard tackle.
C. – What did the prisoner do when the boatswain struck him?
A. – He got hold of the boatswain.
C. – Cou'd you see what part of the boatswain he caught hold of?
A. – I do not recollect what part.
Prosecutor – Did you not hear the prisoner say that he had not stabbed the boatswain, but only struck him?
A. – Yes, only struck him with his hand.
C. – When you heard the boatswain call for assistance did you not hear him say he was stabbed?
A. – I do not recollect.
C. – Prisoner have you any questions to ask this evidence?
A. – No.

Jn°. Farrier, Marine belonging to the *Porcupine*, sworn.

C. – Relate to the court what you know respecting the charge you've heard against the prisoner.
A. – About a month ago onboard the *Porcupine* after sunset when I was sentry upon the starboard gangway, I saw the boatswain come aft on the quarter deck and began beating the prisoner; he left off for a [*sic*] about a minute and then began beating him again. Then the prisoner said. 'For God's sake, don't strike me about the head;' then he stopped about a minute more, call'd him 'a worthless old bugger,' and then began beating him a third time. I took a turn on the gangway and then saw the prisoner on his back, the boatswain having hold of him. The boatswain cried out to the people, who were round to catch hold of

the prisoner, for he had stabbed him with a knife, but I saw no knife. I saw the gentlemen looking about the chains with a lantern for the knife, but none cou'd be found.

C. – When the boatswain call'd for assistance, who went to his assistance?

A. – I don't recollect I saw any person.

C. – Did you see the prisoner strike the boatswain?

A. – I did not.

C. – Did you hear him say anything by which you might judge he had done so?

A. – No, I did not.

C. – When you heard the boatswain say he was stabbed, did he say it was done by the prisoner?

A. – Yes.

C. – Did you hear the prisoner make any answer to that charge?

A. – I heard the prisoner say he had no knife.

C. – Do you know of [*sic*] any search was made about the person of the prisoner for a knife?

A. – Yes, but none was found.

C. – When the boatswain call'd for assistance and said he was stabbed, did you go to his assistance?

A. – No.

C. – How far was you from the boatswain at the time this happened?

A. – About three or four yards.

C. – Were you within three or four yards of an officer, stabbed and calling for assistance, and not go to his assistance?

A. – Many men were nearer and several between the boatswain and myself.

C – You say you saw the prisoner search'd to find a knife and that no knife was found on him?

A. – Yes, and no knife was found.

C – If you was three or four yards off and several men [were?] between you and the prisoner, how do you know that no knife was found on him?

A. – I was near enough myself to see.

C. – You say the boatswain beat the prisoner three different times?

A. – Yes.

C. – In what position was the prisoner the first time the boatswain beat him?

A. – He was standing upright, with his side towards him.
C. – Was he standing upright the other two times?
A. – I cannot say.
C. – Are you very sure the prisoner was beaten three times?
A. – Yes, I'm positive of that.
C. – Did you see the prisoner stooping down at any of the times the boatswain beat him?
A. – I did not.
C. – You saw the person of the prisoner search'd for the knife; did you see any other search made for a knife?
A. – I saw the gentlemen looking for one sometime after with a lantern & candle.
C. – Was it before the boatswain & prisoner left the quarterdeck that the search was made with a lantern?
A. – It was after the prisoner was in irons.
C. – When the boatswain call'd for assistance, did you see Hugh Drougherty go to him?
A. – No.
C – Did you see any person go?
A. – No.
C. – Were there any people near the prisoner when he was struck by the boatswain?
A. – Several.
C. – How near?
A. – Almost a yard.
C. – When you saw the boatswain holding the prisoner, was there any person joined in the scuffle?
A. – No.
C. – At the time you have been speaking of were the boatswain and the prisoner quite sober?
A. – I do not know; I believe they were sober.
C. – Did you see the wound?
A. – I did not.

William Ryan, Marine belonging to the *Porcupine*, sworn.

C. – Relate to the court what you know respecting the charges against the prisoner.
A. – Some time in March last on board the *Porcupine* in the dusk of the evening when getting the boats in, the prisoner, being at work near the main lifts, or there abouts, coming aft, I saw the boatswain run and strike the prisoner, who desired him not to strike him about the head; the boatswain made answer that he would strike the worthless old bugger across

the face or any place he cou'd. Then, the prisoner made his escape amidships by the fife rail and stooped down, I suppose, to save his head from the blows; but the boatswain continuing to strike him, the prisoner rose up and shoved against him; with that, the boatswain sung out that the prisoner had stabbed him, and desired the people to lay hold of him for he had a knife. The boatswain then collar'd the prisoner and got him down against the ship's side, after which he was taken into custody and put into irons.

C. – Did you see any person go to the boatswain's assistance on his calling for it?

A. – No.

C. – Did you see any search made about the person of the prisoner for a knife or any other weapon that might be supposed to give the wound?

A. – The boatswain made the search when he got the prisoner down under him; but I know of no other search.

C. – Was anything found in consequence of the search?

A. – Not to my knowledge.

C. – Was any search made with a candle & lantern?

A. – None that I saw.

C. – Was it dark enough to require a light to make the search?

A. – No, it was not.

C. – If a search had been made on the quarterdeck with a candle and lantern must you not have seen it?

A. – Yes.

C. – Did you see the boatswain beat the prisoner more than once?

A. – Yes, three times.

C. – Did the prisoner strike the boatswain?

A. – No, but, to the best of my recollection, he shoved him.

C. – In what manner did he shove him?

A. – He put his hands against him as he was getting up and immediately the boatswain collar'd him.

C. – Did you see against what part of the boatswain the prisoner put his hands?

A. – As well as I can remember, 'twas about the breast?

C. – Was it by throwing his hands forward or swinging them round that he shoved him?

A. – I can not say positively as the man was getting up but I am positive as to his shoving.

C. – Did it appear to you that the prisoner intended to shove the boatswain or that he shoved him by accident?

A. – I cannot say.

C. – Could the prisoner have got up and gone away without shoving the boatswain?

A. – I don’t think he could, on account of the prisoner’s being between the boatswain and the fife rail.

C. – When the prisoner was stooping, was his head towards the boatswain or towards the fife rail?

A. – His head was towards the fife rail and he was singing out to the boatswain not to strike him over the head.

C. – Were there any men near the prisoner when the boatswain was beating him?

A. – Yes, there were many.

C. – Was there any person so near the prisoner when the boatswain was beating him as to have been able to strike and wound the boatswain without his being enabled to judge who it was?

A. – I am certain there might.

C. – Prisoner, do you wish to ask this evidence any questions?

Pris.^{r} – No.

M^{r}. Robert John Hibbs Mid.^{n} sworn.

C. – Relate to the court what you know respecting the charge you’ve heard against the prisoner.

A. – On the ninth of March last about half past seven in the evening, the boatswain came aft to ask the prisoner why he did not get the starboard yard tackle down; the prisoner reply’d it was none of his fault. The boatswain said you [*sic*] a petty officer and captain of the after guard and [did?] not see it done? The prisoner said he did not care if he was captain’s swabber in the ship; the boatswain reply’d, ‘Is that what you tell me?’ and then struck him, then leaved of [*sic*] about a minute and struck him again. The prisoner desired him not to strike him over the head. The boatswain called him a damn’d old rascal, and said he’d strike him over any part of the body; he then struck him again and called him an old bugger. The prisoner was stooping down, coiling the starboard fore brace at the time, and rose up and made a shove at the boatswain with both his hands, saying he would not be used that way, [and?] he should not strike him any longer. They then fell down together against the fife rail; then the boatswain cried out that he was stabbed, when Hugh Drougherty ran to his assistance, and I went down to tell the master that the prisoner had shoved the boatswain. The master came on deck and the boatswain lifted up his shirt and showed that he was cut in the belly; it bled. M^{r}. McKellar then came on deck and the boatswain showed him that the prisoner had stabbed him. The boatswain call'd the prisoner a worthless old rascal and M^{r}. McKellar reply'd he was as good a man as there was onboard the ship.

C. – Did you see the prisoner strike the boatswain or aim a blow at him?

A. – I don't know what you mean by striking; I saw the prisoner put out both his hands and shove the boatswain.

C. – Did you see anything in either of his hands?

A. – I did not.

C. – You say the boatswain complained of being stab [*sic*] and call'd for assistance; was any search, to your knowledge, made about the prisoner's person?

A. – I don't remember whether his pockets were searched or not.

C. – Do you remember any search to be made at that moment or afterwards?

A. – Afterwards the gunner and carpenter came up with a lantern and candle and look'd about the brink of the quarter deck and the main chain, but nothing was found.

C. – Was you very near the prisoner at the time you say he shoved the boatswain?

A. – Yes, very near, within a yard of him.

C. – Do you suppose the prisoner could have had a weapon in his hand without your seeing or knowing of it?

A. – He might, as the boatswain was between me and the prisoner.

C. – When the boatswain complain'd of being wounded, did he or any other person search the prisoner?

A. – Not that I remember.

C. – Did the boatswain complain of being stabbed immediately on being shoved by the prisoner?

A. – Not immediately.

C. – Do you recollect how long after it was before he complained?

A. – About a minute.

C. – Did you see the prisoner strike or shove the boats^{n} after the first time of doing it?

A. – No, I did not.

C. – Do you recollect on what part of the boatswain the prisoner put his hands when he shoved him?

A. – About his breast.

C. – Did you see the wound yourself?

A. – Yes, I did.

C. – Did you see the hole in the boatswain's jacket while the boatswain had it on?

A. – Yes, I did.

C. – Did the hole in the jacket seem to correspond with the part of the body that was wounded?

A. – Yes, it did.

C. – Did the boatswain complain of being stabbed after or before he fell with the prisoner?

A. – A short time after.

C. – Did you see the hole in the boatswain's jacket or the wound before you went down to the master?

A. – Afterwards.

C. – When you went to the master what did you inform him?

A. – I informed him the prisoner had shoved the boatswain.

C. – Did you understand the boatswain was stabbed before you went down to the master?

A. – Yes, he said he was before I went down.

C. – Were there any men near the prisoner when the boatswain was beating him?

A. – Yes, there were a great number of men.

C. – Was there any person so near the prisoner or the boatswain that either by design or accident the boatswain might have been struck and wounded without his being able to know who it was?

A. – Not in that place.

C. – Prisoner do you wish to ask any questions of the evidence?

Pris.^{r} – No.

Here the evidence for the prosecution closed. And, the prisoner, on being call'd upon in his defence, denied the charge by saying he had no knife or any other weapon about him at the time to stab the boatswain with; that his duty call'd upon him to carry a knife, but it so happen'd that he had none all that day. And, having no witnesses to call, he had nothing further to advance, but to refer to his officers for a character. Captain Buller, Lieutenant McKellar [and?] Mr. Francis Megron, Mas., were then called on, who severally declared the prisoner ever since they knew him to have always behaved as a sober, orderly, well disposed man. …

69A. *Report of the Court Martial of Edward Patton*

[ADM 1/5330]

At a court martial, assembled and held onboard His Majesty's ship *Cambridge*, in Hamoaze, the 15th day of April 1793:

Present

Samuel Reeve, Esq.[r], Captain of His Majesty's ship *Captain* and second officer in the command of His Majesty's ships and vessels at Plymouth,

President.

Captains	Captains
William Young	Charles Morice Pole
Cuthbert Collingwood	Andrew Sutherland
Robert Montagu	Charles Carpenter
William O'Brien Drury	Thomas Lewis
William Hancock Kelly	Henry Nicholls

The court, in pursuance of an order from the Right Honorable the Lords Commissioners of the Admiralty, dated the eleventh instant, and directed to Samuel Reeve, Esq[r]., Captain of His Majesty's ship *Captain* and second officer in the command of His Majesty's ships and vessels at Plymouth, being first duly sworn, proceeded to try Edward Patton, Seaman, belonging [to?] His Majesty's ship *Porcupine*, for having on the ninth day of March, when all hands were on deck to hoist the boats in at sunset, stabbed Mr. Andrew Gilmore, Boatswain of the sd ship, and the court, having accordingly heard the evidence produced in support of the charge, as well as what the prisoner had to offer in his defence, and maturely and deliberately considered the same is of opinion that the charge is not proved and doth therefore acquit the prisoner Edward Patton and he is hereby acquitted accordingly. …

70. *Court Martial of Thomas Brown*

[ADM 1/5350]

At a court martial assembled & held on board His Majesty's ship *Royal Sovereign* in Torbay on the 23^{d} day of August 1799.

Present

Sir Alan Gardner, Bar^{t}., Admiral of the Blue, President.

Vice Admiral Lord Keith, KB		Rear Adm^{l}. C. M. Pole	
Rear Adm^{l}. Sir C. Cotton B^{t}.		Rear Adm^{l}. J. H. Whitshed	
Rear Adml. Sir J. B. Warren, B^{t}., KB		Captains	Sir H^{y} Trollope, K^{t}.
Captains	Edwd Thombrough	"	Sampson Edwards
"	Geo. Campbell	"	Sir W^{m} G Fairfax K^{t}
"	Thos. Totty	"	Sir Ja^{s}. Saumarez K^{t}.

The prisoner was brought into court and the evidence & audience admitted.

Read the order from the Right Honourable the Lords Commissioners of the Admiralty, dated the 18th ins^{t}. and directed to Sir Alan Gardner, B^{t}., Admiral of the Blue & second officer in the command of His Majesty's ships & vessels in Torbay, to try Thomas Brown, a Seaman belonging to His Majesty's ship *Atlas*, on a charge exhibited against him by Captain Theophilus Jones, commander of the said ship, in his letter of the 1st ins^{t}. to Captain Totty of His Majesty's ship *Saturn*, for having on the preceding day struck Mr Peter Loney, the Boatswain, while on duty.

The warrant appointing Mr George Grant to officiate as judge advocate on the occasion was then read. Then the members of the court and judge advocate, in open court & before they proceeded to trial, respectively took the oaths directed by Act of Parliament made and passed in the 22d year of His late Majesty King George the 2d, entitled *An Act for Amending, Explaining & Reducing into One Act of Parliament the Laws relating to the Government of His Majesty's Ships, Vessels & Forces by Sea.*

A letter from Captain Theophilus Jones, Comm^{r}. of His Majesty's ship *Atlas* to Captain Totty of His Majesty's ship *Saturn* was then read as follows, *vizt.*:

Atlas, Torbay, August 1st, 1799

… I request you will be pleased to apply to the Lords Commissioners of the Admiralty to direct a court martial to try Thomas Brown, a Seaman belonging to His Majesty's ship under my command, for having struck M^{r}. Peter Loney, the Boatswain, yesterday evening while on duty. …

The evidences were then ordered to withdraw except M[r]. Peter Loney, Boatswain of the *Atlas*, who was sworn & examined as follows:
Pros[r]. – Do you know the prisoner?
A. – Yes.
Pros[r]. – What is his name?
A. – Brown, but do not know his Christian name.
Pros[r]. – Do you know he belongs to the *Atlas*?
A. – Yes.
Pros[r]. – State to the court his conduct on the evening of the 31st July last.
A. – On the 31st July last, I went upon the middle deck in order to hoist the boats in betwixt the hours of 7 & 8 in the evening and I saw two men scuffling together by the galley on the starboard side and I went forward to know who they were. And, finding one of them was the prisoner and the other was one Avery, a Ship's Corporal, and I interfered & ordered the prisoner to go upon deck to hoist the boats in. He said it was not his watch & I left him & went upon deck & I enquired whether it was his watch and I ordered John Hardy, a Boatswain's Mate, to go down & send him up. The prisoner was coming along the main deck grumbling and said he would not be shoved. With that I ordered him to go aft; he told me he would not be shoved and, as he was coming up the ladder, I took a bit of rope out of my pocket & struck him twice or three times. With that he came upon the gangway & was arguing along with me in the room of going aft. And, upon my pushing him in order to send him aft, he said he would not be shoved and turned round and struck me upon the breast with his fist. With that, I got hold of him & collared him and he collared me; and I was getting him along the quarterdeck aft and Lieu[t]. Ley & M[r]. Wilson & M[r]. Crawley, Mid[n]. came over to assist me to get him along aft. With that, Lieu[t]. Hoy came out of his cabin & interfered in it; with that, I left him and went upon the larboard gangway to hoist boats in.
Court – When you *saw* the prisoner & the other person scuffling in the galley, did they appear to you to be in anger?
A. – Yes, and when I interfered, I struck him with my fist & ordered him to go upon deck.
C. – Was you in the act of shoving the prisoner at the time he struck you on or near the larb[d]. gangway?
A. – Yes.
C. – Did he strike you more than once?
A. – I do not recollect that he did.
C. – Did the prisoner appear to you to be in his sober senses or drunk?
A. – Drunk.
C. – Where is the prisoner watched?

A. – I believe in the afterguard or mizzentop and it was his watch upon deck.

Withdrew.

Mr. John Wilson, Midshipman of the *Atlas*, sworn.

Prosr. – Do you know the prisoner & that he belongs to the *Atlas*?

A. – I do.

Prosr. – State to the court his conduct on the 31st July last in the evening respecting the charge.

A. – Being on the larboard gangway between the hours of 7 & 8 in the evening, I observed John Hardy, a Boatn. Mate, endeavouring to force Thomas Brown, the prisoner, aft by pushing him along to assist hoisting in the boats; the said Thomas Brown said he would not be forced or shoved to his duty. Mr. Loney, the boatswain, then called to him from the gangway to come aft & hoist in the boats. Then the prisoner came upon the larboard gangway. Mr. Loney, the Boatswain, struck him twice with a small rope; then Thomas Brown, turning round, struck Mr. Loney in the breast with his right hand. Mr. Loney then laid hold of him to send him aft; Thomas Brown then took hold of Mr. Loney and endeavoured to throw him, but on my coming forward and assisting Mr. Loney & throwing Brown down on the quarterdeck, Mr. Loney returned to his duty.

Court – Was the prisoner perfectly sober at this time?

A. – I think not.

C. – Did you hear any other conversation pass between the boatswain & the prisoner than what you have related?

A. – Nothing

C. – When Hardy, the Boatswain's Mate, was shoving the prisoner along the waist, did he, the prisoner, appear to be refractory or riotous?

A. – Yes he did.

C. – You have said you saw the prisoner strike the boatswain at the time Mr. Loney, the Boatswain, was shoving the prisoner upon the larboard gangway; are you sure that it was a direct blow, not the effect of a defence when two persons were scuffling or to prevent his being beaten?

A. – I think it was an intended blow.

C. – Did the prisoner make use of any abusive language at the time?

A. – Not that I heard.

C. – Did he strike the boatswain immediately after the boatswain had struck him twice with the bit of rope he had in his pocket?

A. – Yes he did.

C. – Are you sure that the prisoner endeavoured to overthrow the boatswain or might not the boatswain have fallen by accident?

A. – I never saw the boatswain fall.

C. – Are you positive that the prisoner endeavoured to throw the boatswain down?

A. – I think he did.

C. – When the boatswain ordered the prisoner aft, did the prisoner obey that order with alacrity or did he go up in a backward, reluctant manner?

A. – He came very reluctantly up the ladder.

C. – What did the boatswain say to him as he was coming up the ladder?

A. – I think he said, 'Go aft & hoist in the boats.'

C. – Was he going aft when he was ordered?

A. – He stopped upon the gangway.

C. – What do you suppose was the provocation that caused the boatswain to strike him?

A. – His not coming aft so smart as he wished when he ordered him.

Withdrew.

John Hardy, Boatswain's Mate of the *Atlas*, sworn.

Pros[r]. – Do you know the prisoner & that he belongs to the *Atlas*?

A. – Yes.

Pros[r]. – Relate to the court his conduct on the 31st July last in the evening respecting the charge.

A. – The watch & idlers was turned up in boats. Mr. Loney, the Boatswain, asked me whether Brown, the prisoner, was in the watch upon deck. I told him I did not know what watch it was upon deck; one of the boatswain's mates said it was his watch upon deck. M[r]. Loney sent me down for the prisoner to fetch him up to him on the gangway. When I came down, I found him in the galley very groggy; smoking his pipe, he told me he would go upon deck, but he would not be shoved. He went upon the gangway and M[r]. Loney took a small rope out of his pocket and struck the prisoner three times. Brown took hold of M[r]. Loney's jacket and I did not see any more of it.

Pros[r]. – Did you see the prisoner strike the boatswain?

A – No, I did not.

Pros[r]. – Did you immediately go away from the gangway when the prisoner got up the ladder?

A. – Yes, I went over from the larboard side to the starboard to man the falls.

Court – From your finding the prisoner in the galley till he got aft to the gangway, did he go with that readiness & alacrity that a man ought to go when he was ordered upon deck or was you as boatswain's mate obliged to make him go?

A. – No, he did not go with that readiness but said he would not be shoved.
C. – What was the reason he said he would not be shoved?
A. – I don't know.
C. – Did you shove him?
A. – No.
C. – Was you not obliged to take hold of him to bring him aft when the boatswain ordered you to bring him up to the gangway?
A. – No, I did not take hold of him.

Withdrew.

William Bodley, Ship's Corporal of the *Atlas*, sworn.
Pros^{r}. – Do you know the prisoner & that he belongs to the *Atlas*?
A. – Yes I do.
Pros^{r}. – Relate to the court his conduct on the 31st July last in the evening respecting the charge.
A. – On Wednesday the 31st July last between the hours of 7 & 8 in the evening, I was standing on the main gratings on the main deck; I saw the prisoner go up the larboard ladder to go on the gangway. M^{r}. Loney, the Boatswain, struck him with a piece of rope twice just as he was at the top of the ladder. When some words passed between M^{r}. Loney & the prisoner and Brown took M^{r}. Loney by the collar with one hand and struck him with the other, I went up to M^{r}. Loney's assistance and by the time I got up, they was got part of the way on the quarterdeck, when I laid hold of Brown by the collar to make him loose his hold from M^{r}. Loney and by the assistance of others that was there at the time, threw him on his back, where I held him until I was ordered to confine him by Lieutenant Hoy, the first Lieutenant. The prisoner appeared to me to be very drunk.
Court – When you were standing upon the main gratings, did you hear any of the conversation that passed between the boatswain & the prisoner?
A. – I could not distinctly hear it.
C. – Were there any persons near you at the time that might have heard the conversation?
A. – None in particular that I can name.
C. – What was the position of him, Brown the prisoner, and M^{r}. Loney, the Boatswain, when they were upon the larboard gangway?
A. – M^{r}. Loney's back was towards me and Brown's face.
C. – Did you positively see Brown, the Prisoner, strike M^{r}. Loney, the Boatswain?
A. – I did not see where the blow fell.
C. – What reason have you to believe there was a blow struck at all?

A. – Because he lifted up his fist and threw it down quite sharp and, to the best of my belief, he struck the boatswain, but, his back being towards me, I could not see where the blow fell.
C. – Are you sure that the prisoner might not have lifted up his hand for any other purpose, but that of smiting the boatswain?
A. – It did not appear to me to be for any other purpose.
C. – Was it possible for the blow to miss the boatswain at the time you saw the prisoner's hand fall?
A. – They was too close for the blow to miss.

Withdrew.

Lieu^{t}. Robt. Hoy, first Lieutenant of the *Atlas*, sworn
Pros^{r}. – Do you know the prisoner & that he belongs to the *Atlas*?
A. – Yes.
Pros^{r}. – State to the court the prisoner's conduct on the evening of the 31st July last respecting the charge.
A. – On Wednesday evening the 31st July last between the hours of 7 & 8, I gave the boatswain's mate directions to turn the watch & idlers up to hoist the boats in and, on going on the quarterdeck myself, I saw M^{r}. Loney, the Boatswain and the prisoner, Thomas Brown, struggling together on the quarterdeck. I saw the prisoner, Thomas Brown, strike the boatswain and the boatswain fell; I immediately rushed in to separate them. M^{r}. Loney had fallen on his back. It was with great difficulty I could extricate the prisoner from the boatswain and I immediately ordered him in charge of the ship's corporal, who was on the spot.
Court – Did you see the blow given on the quarterdeck and on what part of the quarterdeck?
A. – I did see the blow given on the larboard side of the quarter deck, nearly in the midway between the fiferail and the after part of the quarterdeck.
C. – Did you hear any conversation pass between the prisoner and the boatswain previous to your coming on the quarterdeck?
A. – None.
C. – Did any conversation pass afterwards?
A. – Yes, I heard the prisoner frequently make use of the words 'damn your blood,' which I conceived to be addressed to the boatswain & threatened to be revenged.
C. – Who else was present upon the quarterdeck at that time?
A. – M^{r}. Wilson & M^{r}. Crawley, Midshipman, & Bodley, the Ship's Corporal; I saw no person else that I suppose could have seen the prisoner's behaviour.
C. – Do you know of any blow having been struck on the gangway previous to what you have stated?

A. – Only by hearsay.
C. – Do you know when Bodley, the Corporal, came aft upon the quarterdeck?
A. – I do not.
C. – Was it the effect of the blow given by the prisoner or accident that occasioned the boatswain's fall?
A. – I can't say. The deck was very slippery & the boatswain's foot might have slipped in the struggle; it had been raining all day. Both parties seemed very much agitated.
C. – Was the prisoner perfectly sober?
A. – No, he was not; he appeared to me to be in liquor.

Withdrew.

Mr. Edmund Crawley, Midshipman of the *Atlas*, sworn.
Pros[r]. – State to the court what you know of the prisoner's conduct on the evening of the 31st July last respecting the charge.
A. – On Wednesday the 31st July last, I was on the quarterdeck between the hours of 7 & 8 in the evening and saw M[r]. Loney, the Boatswain, & the prisoner struggling together on the break of the quarterdeck on the larboard side. I saw the prisoner strike the boatswain on the breast and I saw M[r]. Wilson (Midship[n].) assist M[r]. Loney and got the prisoner down on his back on the quarterdeck. I saw Lieutenant Hoy come out of his cabin & lay hold of the prisoner. I went on the other side of the quarterdeck & saw no more of it.

Withdrew.

The evidence on the part of the prosecution closed here and the prisoner was put on his defence. Prisoner said: 'I had a fall from the mizzentop sail yard, when handing the mizzentop sail about two years ago, coming to an anchor at S[t] Helens of an evening. I struck the top & fell down upon the netting; my head was cut and I was carried into the sick bay speechless. Since that accident, I have been disordered in my senses after taking a little too much liquor and, being in liquor at the time, it has been said that I struck the boatswain. I do not recollect anything at all about it nor who was present.'

Lieutenant Hoy called into court.
Pris[r]. – Do you recollect my having fallen off the mizzentop sail yard some time ago and being, in consequence, much hurt & carried down into the sick bay?
A. – I have heard of it & that he was in sick bay a week in consequence of it.
Court – Do you know any person now in the ship who was in her at the time the prisoner fell?
A. – There are a great many, but I cannot particularize any.

Withdrew.

Thomas Crump, Seaman of the *Atlas*, sworn.
Pris^r^. – How long have you belonged to the *Atlas*?
A. – About four years.
Pris^r^. – How long have you known me?
A. – About four years.
Pris^r^. – Did you know from your own knowledge that I have had any fall on board the ship?
A. – I heard he had a fall and was sentry in the sick bay when he was brought in.
Pris^r^. – How long did I continue in the sick bay?
A. – About six days, but he came to the surgeon every day for some time after and did not do duty.
Pris^r^. – Did I not appear speechless & insensible when you saw me carried into the sick bay?
A. – He appeared insensible.
Pris^r^. – Do you recollect at any time since that accident that I have appeared to be disordered in my senses and not to know what I have been about?
A. – Yes, I have seen you out of your mind when you have been in liquor and, at times, when you have not been in liquor and he is reckoned among the ship's company as a man not in his senses and, at those moments, he does not mind who he kills, officers or other persons.

Withdrew.

James Gill, Seaman of the *Atlas*, sworn.
Pris^r^. – Do you know of my having had a fall from the mizzentop sail yard of the *Atlas* about two years ago?
A. – Yes, I saw him fall and was close by him; he was taken to the sick bay.
Pris^r^. – Do you know where I fell to?
A. – He struck the topbrim & fell into the quarterdeck netting
Pris^r^. – Do you know how long it was after the accident before I returned to my duty?
A. – No, I can't tell.
Court – Have you at any time seen the prisoner behaving himself in a riotous & extravagant manner when in liquor previous to the 30th July last?
A. – I have seen him singing about the decks when in liquor
C. – Have you at any time seen the prisoner behaving himself in a riotous & extravagant manner when sober previous to the 30th July last?
A. – No.
C. – Have you observed since his falling off the mizzentop sail yard anything different in his conduct to what you observed before?

A. – I was not long enough in the ship before the accident happened to say whether his conduct was different or not.

Withdrew.

The court found upon inquiry that the surgeon who belonged to the ship at the time the prisoner received his fall had been since drowned.

The prisoner called upon Captain Jones for his character:

Captain Jones said he does not recollect any other complaint against the prisoner but the one with which he now stands charged since he has commanded the *Atlas*.

The prisoner having no other evidence to call in, the defence rested here; the court was cleared and proceeded to deliberate upon & form the sentence.

The court, having carefully & deliberately weighed and considered the evidence produced and what the prisoner had to offer in his defence, came to the following determinations:

1st. That the charge against the prisoner is proved.

2d. That the crime is capital.

3d. That the prisoner, the said Thomas Brown, shall suffer death by being hanged by the neck until he is dead at the yard arm of such of His Majesty's ships at such time & at such place as the Right Honourable the Lords Commissioners of the Admiralty shall think proper to direct.

The sentence being drawn up agreeably to the above resolutions and signed by the court, the court was opened and all persons were again admitted and the prisoner brought in. The judge advocate, by direction of the president, pronounced the same and the court broke up. …

71. *Court Martial of Richard Gaff*

[ADM 1/5355]

Minutes of the proceedings of a court martial assembled and held on board His Majesty's ship the *Royal Sovereign* in Torbay, the 26th day of December 1800, to try Richard Gaff, a Marine belonging to His Majesty's ship the *Royal George* on a charge exhibited against him by Captain Robert Waller Otway, commander of that ship, for striking his superior officer on, or about, the 18th instant.

Present

Sir Henry Harvey, K. B., Vice Admiral of the White and second officer in the command of His Majesty's ships and vessels in Torbay, President.

Sir Andrew Mitchell, K. B.,
Vice Admiral of the Blue

Sir Chas. Cotton, B^{t}.,
Rear Admiral of the Red

James Hawkins Whitshed, Esqr. Rear Admiral of the White	Capt. Thos. Graves (1st)
Captain Thomas M. Russel	Capt. Sir H. Y. Trollope
Captain John Knight	Capt. Edwd. Thornbrough
Captain Sir Willm. G. Fairfax	Capt. the Earl of Northesk
Captain James Vashon	Capt. John C. Purvis

The prisoner, having been brought into court attended by the provost martial, and all the witnesses and every other person that thought proper being admitted, the court was sworn, agreeable to the Act of Parliament; the order for their assembling, being first read, together with a warrant appointing Mr. John Smith Tracey to officiate as judge advocate on the occasion, the following letter containing the charge was then read:[1]

Royal George in Torbay
the 23d December 1800

… I have the honour to request your Lordships will be pleased to order a court martial to assemble for the trial of Richard Gaff, a Marine in His Majesty's ship under my command, for striking, on or about the 18th instant, his superior officer. …

All the witnesses were now desired to withdraw, except Mr. Alford Hughes, who was sworn and examined as follows:

Prosecutor — Were you on or about the 18th instant struck by the prisoner?

Answer — Yes.

Question — Relate the manner in which it was done and the circumstances attending it.

Ans^{r}. — I was going forward into the head and the prisoner coming out of the head; I touched him on the arm and told him to stand aside and he said he would not. Thomas Cleave (who was close by) then spoke to him and told him to take care of what he said. The prisoner then said he did not care a damn, for he was as much an officer as he was. He then took me by the collar and shook me and pushed me out of the head and struck me on the shoulder with his hand. I then immediately brought him aft on the quarter deck.

Court — What time of day was it?

Answer — At three o'clock in the afternoon.

[1]This letter is from Robert Waller Otway to the Earl of St Vincent.

Court	On what occasion was you going forward into the head?
Ans^{r}.	On my own private occasions.
Quest^{n}.	Was the place crowded?
Ans^{r}.	No.
Quest^{n}.	What dress had you on?
Ans^{r}.	Jacket and trousers (not uniform).
Quest^{n}.	What duty did you do on board?
Ans^{r}.	Midshipman's duty.
Quest^{n}.	Are jackets commonly worn by the midshipman of the *Royal George*?
Ans^{r}.	Yes.
Quest^{n}.	Did you remonstrate with the prisoner and tell him who you was, when he struck you?
Ans^{r}.	I told him he must take care of what he was about.
Prosecutor	Was it perfectly clear and light when he struck you?
Answ^{r}.	Yes, it was perfectly clear and light; the butcher, Thos. Cleave, was killing a sheep at the time.
	This witness was now desired to withdraw and Charles Stone called, sworn and examined as follows:
Prosecutor	Did you see the prisoner on or about the 18th instant strike Mr. Hughes?
Answer	No, I saw the prisoner, with both his hands, shove him from him and said to M^{r}. Hughes, 'Don't shove me into the dirt, for I must keep myself as clean as you.' Then the prisoner took M^{r}. Hughes by the collar and shook him and told him he was as good an officer as he was.
Quest^{n}.	Did it appear to you to be a blow?
Answer	It appeared a shove (explaining the manner by the motion of his arms).
Question	How far was you from the prisoner when you saw this?
Answer	Quite close to him.
Court	What was the dirt you allude to that the prisoner desired he might not be shoved into?
Answ^{r}.	I did not see any dirt, except a tub that stood by his legs that receives the water that runs out of the hog sty; the head was very clean.
Quest^{n}.	If you had been shook in the manner you describe the prisoner to have shook M^{r}. Hughes, should you have conceived it an equal insult to a blow?
Ans^{r}.	Yes, he shook M^{r}. Hughes very hard.
Court	Was M^{r}. Hughes dressed in such a manner as for you to have known him to be an officer?

Ans^{r}. Yes.

Quest^{n}. Have you any reason to suppose whether the prisoner knew M^{r}. Hughes to be an officer or not?

Answer No, I have no reason to suppose but what the prisoner knew him to be an officer.

Prosecutor When you saw the prisoner shove M^{r}. Hughes, was his fist open or shut?

Ans^{r}. I don't know.

Quest^{n}. Did you admonish the prisoner for his improper conduct towards M^{r}. Hughes?

Answ^{r}. Yes, I asked him if he knew who he was shaking of at the time. The prisoner said yes, he did know who he was shaking of at the time?

There being no farther questions to ask this witness, he was desired to withdraw and Matthew Long called, sworn and examined as follows:

Prosecutor Relate to the court what you know about the prisoner's striking M^{r}. Hughes on or about the 18 instant.

Answ^{r}. Thomas Cleave was killing a sheep on the 18th instant and I was looking on. I saw the prisoner come out of the head, and M^{r}. Hughes was going into the head, and they met. M^{r}. Hughes gave the prisoner a small shove and the prisoner returned it by taking hold of Mr. Hughes's collar and shook him. I asked the prisoner if he knew what he was about, that he was shaking an officer; he told me that he was as good an officer as he was. It happened about 3 in the afternoon.

This witness was now desired to withdraw and Thomas Cleave called, sworn and examined as follows:

Prosecutor Relate to the court what you know respecting the prisoner's striking M^{r}. Hughes on, or about, the 18 instant.

Answer It appeared to me that the prisoner had been to the head to make water and, coming back, he passed M^{r}. Hughes, who put his hand to the prisoner's shoulder. The prisoner asked him if he meant to shove him into the dirt. 'I am ordered to keep myself as clean as you,' & with the same, looking M^{r}. Hughes in the face, he catched him by the collar and shook him very hard. I said to the prisoner, 'Shipmate, do you know who you are shaking of?' He answer'd, 'Yes, I do. I am as good an officer as he is; I have as much business here as he has. You mind your own duty.'

Quest^{n}. What happened after this?

Answ^{r}. M^{r}. Hughes asked the prisoner his name; he answered, Gaff. M^{r}. Hughes then took him aft on the quarterdeck.

Question Was it quite light?

Answ^{r}. Yes, as good as it is now.

There being no further questions to ask this witness or any other to examine, the prisoner was called on for his defence, which was as follows:

I was coming out of the head on the 18th, and M^{r}. Hughes met me and shoved me, and desired me to stand out of the way, but I did not know who he was by his dress, having been only three months in the ship; and my reason for saying I was as good an officer as he was, I thought Thomas Cleave was joking when he told me I was shaking an officer. I thought he was one of the men, nor did I know he was an officer till I was brought aft on the quarterdeck.

John Mc Douall called and sworn and examined as an evidence for the prisoner as follows:

Prisoner Did you, at the time this happened between M^{r}. Hughes and me, conceive that I knew whether he was an officer or not?

Ans^{r}. Not before he shoved him, but afterwards he did by being told so.

Court When he did know it, did he appear sorry for it or say so?

Answ^{r}. There was nothing passed after.

Quest^{n}. Did you hear the prisoner say he was as good an officer as he was (M^{r}. Hughes)?

Answer Yes, he said he was as good an officer as he was, speaking to the butcher.

Quest^{n}. Why do you think the prisoner did not know M^{r}. Hughes?

Answer I believe M^{r}. Hughes had a brown great coat on, but I know t'was a long one, and an oilskin over his hat at the time.

Question Was the coat buttoned?

Ans^{r}. Yes, I believe, but I saw the white patch on the jacket under it.

Quest^{n}. How long have you been in the ship?

Ans^{r}. Ever since Sir Hyde Parker joined.

Quest^{n}. Did you know M^{r}. Hughes to be an officer?

Ans^{r}. Yes.

The court was now cleared, but after a few minutes deliberation, it was determined to be opened again to ask the following question of the witnesses for the prosecution. M^r^. Hughes called into court.

Question Had you a great coat on when this affair happened between the prisoner and you?

Answer No, but the jacket and trousers, as I have already said.

He withdrew and Chas. Stone called.

Question Had M^r^. Hughes a great coat on when this affair happened between the prisoner and him?

Answer He had not, but the jacket he usually wears.

Chas. Stone withdrew and Matthew Long called and asked the same question as the last.

Answer He had not; he had a round blue jacket on.

Matthew Long withdrew and Thomas Cleave called and asked the same question as before.

Answer He had not; he had a round blue jacket on with anchor buttons.

The court was again cleared, and, having maturely & deliberately considered the evidence in support of the charge & the prisoner's defence, was of opinion it was proved, and, therefore, adjudged the said prisoner, Richard Gaff, to suffer death by being hanged by the neck until he is dead at the yard arm of such ship as the commander in chief should direct.

The sentence being drawn up in the usual form and signed by the court, all persons were again admitted and the prisoner brought in; the judge advocate, by the direction of the president, pronounced the same and the court broke up. …

71A. *Harvey to the Earl of St. Vincent*

[ADM 1/5355] *Royal Sovereign*, Torbay
26th December 1800

… I am requested by the members of the court to recommend the prisoner, Richard Gaff, to mercy, it being their unanimous opinion that the offence was committed without any premeditation in the galley, but being confined by the first part of the 22nd Article of War to convict capitally or acquit, we were obliged to condemn him to suffer death; I, therefore, request your Lordship will be pleased to transmit to the Lords Commissioners of the

Admiralty this our recommendation of the prisoner to mercy accordingly. …

C. Fighting and Self-mutilation

72. *Court Martial of Robert Pring*

[ADM 1/5358]

Proceedings of a court martial held on board His Majesty's ship *York* in The Downs, the 3rd of September 1801.

Present

John Ferrier, Esq[r]., Captain of His Majesty's ship *York* and third officer in command of His Majesty's ships and vessels in The Downs, President.

Captains

William Edward Cracraft	John Bazely, Jun[r].
Samuel Sutton	Tho[s]. Masterman Hardy

The court, being duly sworn, proceeded to try M[r]. Robert Pring, Boatswain of His Majesty's ship *Alkmaar*, 'for having on the 23 of August last aided and abetted two men to fight and otherwise excited them by threats if they did not decide who was the strongest, instead of preventing the affray.'

Richard Poulden, Esq[r]., Captain of His Majesty's ship *Alkmaar*, Prosecutor.

Thomas Bookless, First Lieut. His Majesty's ship *Alkmaar*, sworn.

Prosecutor Question. You will please to relate the complaint lodged against the prisoner on Sunday the 23d of August last by some of the people when you was commanding officer.

Answer. On Sunday the 23d of August last about 5 o'clock, Rich[d]. Roebottom (Seaman) came to me on the quarterdeck and said the boatswain (the prisoner) was threatening to thrash him and was then going for a stick for that purpose. I enquired of Roebottom what he had done to cause the boatswain to threaten him. He said he had done nothing, but was sitting in his own berth. I desired him to stay where he was till I enquired into the business. The same time, John Simmonds came with a complaint and said the boatswain had beat him on the face with his fist; I asked Simmonds what he had been doing. He said that the boatswain's mate, James Stuart, and

Joseph Gilbert were fighting forward between decks and the prisoner was there present and in consequence [of?] some words that he said caused the boatswain to strike him. I sent for the two men that had been fighting, and found them disguised in liquor, and sent them upon the poop, and they were not fit to answer any questions. I saw a boat coming with Cap. Poulden and related the whole circumstance to him.

Ques. Did the two men that had been fighting appear bruised or beat?

Ans. Yes, both on the face.

Lieut. Bookless ordered to withdraw & John Simmonds, Sail Maker, sworn.

Prosecutor Ques. Relate to the court the circumstances of the fight between James Stuart and Joseph Gilbert on the 23 of August last and of the conduct of M^r^. Pring, the prisoner, on that occasion.

Answer. M^r^. Pring and James Stuart and Joseph Gilbert came to the starboard bay and the two men fell a fighting and the prisoner was laying some money on one man's head. I told the prisoner I thought it was a shame he should be then seeing the men fight. He told me directly he would get a man to fight me. He brought Daniel Madden to fight me and I would not fight, upon which the prisoner knocked me down. He struck me twice with his left fist in the face. I went aft and made a complaint.

Ques^t^. Do you recollect the name of the man in whose favour the boatswain (prisoner) laid the wager?

Ans^r^. James Stuart.

Court Ques^t^. Were Stuart and Gilbert in liquor?

Ans. They appeared so to me.

Ques^t^. Was you in the bay before they began to fight?

Ans. Yes, I was in my own berth.

Ques^t^. Did the two men and the prisoner come forward together and did Stuart and Gilbert begin to fight immediately?

Ans. Yes, they did.

Ques^t^. What were the words the prisoner made use of when laying the wager upon the man that was fighting?

Ans. Two Pound or five Pound on James Stuart's head.

Quest. What number of people were there present and did they appear to be looking on to see the fight?

Ans. About thirty standing round.

John Simmonds ordered to withdraw; Richard Roebottom, Seaman, sworn.

Prosecutor Question. Relate to the court the circumstances of the fight between James Stuart and Joseph Gilbert on the 23d of August last and the conduct of M[r]. Pring, the prisoner, on that occasion.

Ans. I saw Stuart and Gilbert fighting; Mr. Pring, the prisoner, was with them when they were fighting. The prisoner said he would lay five Pound on Stuart's head. When they left off fighting, the prisoner told Stuart to go and fight again. Stuart did not fight any more at that time. The prisoner struck John Simmonds with his left hand and cut him in the face.

Court Ques[t]. Did you see Gilbert and Stuart begin to fight?

Ans. I did.

Ques[t]. Was the prisoner there at that time?

Ans. I don't know that he was at the beginning.

Ques[t]. What was the reason that the prisoner struck John Simmonds?

Ans. I don't know.

Ques[t]. How many men were present at the fight?

Ans. More than twenty.

Ques[t]. Did you see the prisoner come into the bay?

Ans. I did not.

Ques[t]. Did you hear the prisoner bet more than once on Stuart's head?

Ans[r]. Yes, several times.

Richard Roebottom ordered to withdraw; Thomas Robbins, Quartermaster, sworn.

Prosecutor Quest. Relate to the court the circumstances of the fight between James Stuart and Joseph Gilbert on the 23d of August last and of the conduct of M[r]. Pring, the prisoner, on that occasion.

Answer. I saw Stuart and Gilbert fighting. The prisoner came forward and took Stuart's part and said he should fight him for five Pound and, if he did not beat him, he would break his back.

Court Questn. How long had Stuart and Gilbert been fighting before the prisoner came forward, & how long did they continue fighting afterwards?

Answ. Between 4 and 5 minutes and they continued fighting for 20 minutes after the prisoner came.

Quest. Did you hear the prisoner say to Simmonds he would bring a man to fight him.

Ans. I did; he said Madden should fight him.

Thomas Robbins ordered to withdraw.

Lieut. Edmund Sykes, H. Maj. ship *Alkmaar*, sworn.

Prosecutor Quest. Did you hear the prisoner express himself anything relative to the fight between Stuart & Gilbert on Sunday the 23d of August last?

Ans. I heard the prisoner say to Simmonds that he would lay five Pound that his mate, Stuart, would beat the man he was fighting with and likewise beat Simmonds too, &, if he could not, he would himself.

Court Quest. Where was you when the prisoner offered the bet?

Ans. On the main deck.

Quest. Where was the prisoner?

Ans. At the fore hatchway, talking to Simmonds.

Quest. Was there a great noise at the fore part of the ship at that time?

Ans. Only what the prisoner made himself.

Quest. Did the noise the prisoner was making occasion you to go forward?

Ans. Yes, it did. I wanted the prisoner to attend the side for the captain.

Quest. Had the prisoner been sent for before to attend the side?

Ans. Yes, he was piped once and ran away to the fore hatchway.

Lieut. Sykes ordered to withdraw.

The prosecution being closed, the court adjourned to allow the prisoner time for his defence.

At ¼ past eleven the court met and the prisoner presented a written defence.

Defence

(Copy)

… I beg leave to represent to you the cause of my being so unfortunate as to be brought to a court martial. Hearing a noise upon deck when I was in my cabin, I immediately went up and found one of the ship's company fighting with my mate. I asked the man what business he had to fight with the boatswain's mate, saying at the same time if my mate did not give him a good beating, I would, for fighting, thinking it my duty to preserve quietness in the ship. I observed John Simmonds wishing to take the man's part against my mate, observing at the same time that he would beat any boatswain's mate in the ship, upon which I struck him, as I thought it was stirring the people to disobey their officers.

Having been 25 years in the service and being in possession of certificates of my behaviour during that time, I trust the court will consider my case as I have always endeavoured to preserve good order in my department and, in this case, acted to the best of my judgement to prevent their fighting by taking my mate to his own berth, which I will prove by the witnesses I shall call.

Daniel Madden, Boatswain's Mate, sworn.

Prisoner Quest. Do you recollect where I was at the beginning of the battle between Stuart and Gilbert?

Ans. On the starboard side of the gun deck.

Ques. What did I do on going to where the affray was?

Ans. I was [in?] the galley at the same time. The Sail Maker, Jack Simmonds, said he would lick every a boatswain's mate in the ship. I, being standing by at the same time, you must allow there is a boatswain's mate in the ship, but it was a foolish nonsense for you to mention such a word, which, if you give the same to me you did to the prisoner, I would have taken you aft, but my duty is not to fight, my duty is to bring you aft. The prisoner then struck Simmonds.

Quest. Did I take my mate, James Stuart, from fighting Joseph Gilbert?

Answer. Yes, you did directly.

Daniel Madden ordered to withdraw.

James Stuart, Boatswain's Mate, sworn.

Question. Do you recollect my saying [I?] would lay five Pound upon your head if you were on the sod?

Ans^r. I do.

James Stuart ordered to withdraw.

Mr. John Waller, Master's Mate, sworn.

Question. What was my conduct during the fight on the 23d of August last?

Ans^r. I know nothing of your conduct, as I was not present at the time.

The prisoner, having closed his defence, called upon Mr. Yarrow, the Master of His Majesty's ship *Alkmaar*, who informed the court he had belonged to the *Alkmaar* about 22 months, during which time the prisoner's character was an honest and diligent officer.

Sentence The court, having heard the charges against the prisoner and what the prisoner had to say in his defence and having very maturely and deliberately considered the whole, are of opinion that the charges are proved and doth therefore sentence him to be dismissed as boatswain of His Majesty's ship *Alkmaar* and to serve in any of His Majesty's ships in a subordinate situation the commander in chief shall think proper and he is hereby so sentenced accordingly.

…

73. *Court Martial of John Wheeler*

[ADM 1/5420]

Minutes of proceedings at a court martial held on board His Majesty's ship *Salvador del Mundo* in Hamoaze on Friday the 8th day of November 1811.

Present

Sir Edward Buller, Bart., Rear Admiral of the Red and third officer in the command of His Majesty's ships and vessels at Plymouth, President.
Sir Richard King, Bart., first Captain of His Majesty's ship *San Josef.*

Captains

	Henry Richard Glynn
James Brisbane	George Mc Kinley
Philip Somerville	Anselm John Griffiths
James Nash	Francis Holmes Coffin
George Tobin	Edward Galway
Clotworthy Upton	William Ferris

George Eastlake, Junr., officiating Judge Advocate

Being all captains of post ships then and there present, next in seniority to the president, except Capt. Sir John Gore, Kn^t., who was the prosecutor.

The prisoner John Wheeler, Private Marine serving on board His Majesty's ship *Tonnant*, was brought into court and the witnesses and audience admitted.

Read – The order of the Right Honble the Lords Commissioners of the Admiralty, dated the 1st day of November 1811, directed to the president, to try the said John Wheeler for having on the morning of the 5th of September last attempted to disable himself by cutting his left arm across the wrist.

Read – The warrant appointing a judge advocate.

Then the members of the court and judge advocate, in open court and before they proceeded to trial, respectively took the oaths directed by Act of Parliament passed in the 22d. year of the reign of King George the 2d.

Read – The annexed letter of charge from the said Capt. Sir John Gore to Admiral Sir Charles Cotton, B[t].

All the witnesses, except the first to be sworn, being then ordered to withdraw and to attend their examinations separately, they all withdrew accordingly and the court proceeded to trial as follows:

Evidence in support of the charge

Corp[l]. David Pinnegar of the Royal Marines serving on board His Majesty's ship *Tonnant*, sworn and examined as follows:

Pro. Relate to the court all you know respecting the charge against the prisoner.

A. On Thursday the 5th of September last, I saw the prisoner sitting on a stool in his berth with a knife in his hand; he had his face towards the ship's side. I saw him several times making wry faces, as if something was the matter with him. John Merrafield then looked over the table and said, 'Don't Wheeler, don't. You will ruin yourself.' I turned round to see what was the matter and the prisoner had made a cut across his wrist with a penknife, which he had in his hand. I asked him for the knife and he gave it to me. I took the knife to the sergeant major and he sent me to the surgeon for him.

Co[t]. Did you see him absolutely give himself the wound?

A. No, it was done when I turned round; it must have been done by the prisoner himself.

Co[t]. Did he give any reason for his conduct?

A. No.

Co[t]. What state of health had the prisoner been in?

A. He came out of the List that morning or the day before.

Co[t]. Do you think at the time the act was committed that the prisoner was in his right senses?

A. Yes, I saw nothing of anything else.

Co[t]. How long have you known the prisoner?

A. Fourteen months.

Co[t]. Did you in that time ever see him disturbed in his mind?

A. No.

Co[t]. Did you ever hear the prisoner express a wish to be rid of the service?

A. No.

Co^{t}. Was the prisoner at work at the time the wound was made?

A. I did not see him about anything at all.

Pro. State the time of day it happened.

A. It was one bell after 8 in the morning.

The witness withdrew.

John Merrafield, Private Marine serving on board His Majesty's ship *Tonnant*, sworn and examined as follows:

Pro. Relate all you know respecting the charge against the prisoner.

A. I saw the prisoner's arm bleeding and I saw a knife in his right hand and I said, 'Shame, shame Wheeler; don't go to destroy yourself.' He looked at me and put a dish cloth over his arm. I told Corporal Pinnegar the prisoner was doing something wrong. Corporal Pinnegar turned round and saw the knife in his hand and told him to give it to him, which he did, and the corporal carried it to the sergeant major. The prisoner said, 'I am undone.'

Pro^{r}. Did you see the prisoner cut himself?

A. No, I saw the knife to his arm and the arm bleeding.

Pro. Why did you tell him not to destroy himself?

A. I thought he was cutting the sinews of his hand.

Pro. When and where was it.

A. He was sitting on the corner of the stool against the ship's side; it was about a quarter past 8 in the morning on the 5th of September.

Co^{t}. Are you a messmate of the prisoner?

A. I am in the same berth.

Co^{t}. How long have you been shipmates?

A. Two years and 8 months.

Co^{t}. Did you ever see the prisoner out of his senses or deranged?

A. No.

Co^{t}. What state of mind was he in when he attempted to commit this act?

A. I thought he seemed in trouble.

Co^{t}. Did he ever express to you any cause of his being so?

A. No.

Co^{t}. Was he apparently in good health?

A. He appeared so.

Co^{t}. Was the prisoner under the idea of any punishment at the time?

A. I believe he was in the master at arms's list.

The witness withdrew.

M^{r}. William Stenhouse, Surgeon of His Majesty's ship *Tonnant*, sworn and examined as follows:

Pro. Had the prisoner been under your care previous to the 5th of September last?

A. Yes.

Pro. Was there anything in the nature of his complaint that showed symptoms of mental derangement?

A. No.

Pro. Describe the nature of the wound the prisoner received on the 5th of September last.

A. I was called between 8 and 9 o'clock in the morning of that day to the prisoner and found that he had received a wound with some sharp instrument about two inches in length across the left wrist, dividing the integuments and slightly wounding the tendons of the wrist. There were several slight scratches alongside the wound.

Pro. Was there anything in the nature of the wound to lead you to suppose it was done by accident?

A. Nothing, from several scratches alongside, it appeared to be made by repeated applications of the instrument.

Pro. Had it nearly disabled the prisoner from doing his duty?

A. From the direction of it, if it had been applied with more force, it might have had that effect.

Co^{t}. From the nature of the wound, had it not been for the early application to you, would he have been rendered unfit for His Majesty's service?

A. As there was little bleeding, which is generally the most urgent symptoms in wounds, immediate assistance was hardly necessary, other than applying common dressings and, as none of the tendons were divided, it was not likely he would have been rendered unfit for the service.

Co^{t}. What was the state of the prisoner's mind on the 4th of September, when you discharged him from your list?

A. Neither his mind or his bodily health seemed to be at all affected.

Co^{t}. What was the state of the prisoner's mind and health on the 5th when you went to his assistance?

A. In a state of great trepidation from the wound he had received, not deranged in his mind.

Co^{t}. How long was the prisoner incapable of doing his duty in consequence?

A. From the 5th of September to the 7th of October, but during the latter part of the time in consequence of a boil in the axilla.

Co^{t}. Did the prisoner say anything to you when you went to examine him?

A. He seemed much agitated; I could not make out what he said.

Co[t]. Did he at any time assign a cause for committing such an act?
A. He once told me it was done by accident in cutting the slings for his great coat. This was several days after.
Co[t]. Had you asked him before?
A. Yes, he would give no answer.

The witness withdrew.

The evidence in support of the charge being closed, the prisoner was asked if he had anything to offer in his behalf, when he delivered to the judge advocate the annexed written paper, signed by himself, which was read to the court and, having nothing further to offer, the court was cleared and proceeded to deliberate upon and form the sentence.

The court, having very maturely and deliberately weighed and considered the evidence in support of the charge as well as what the prisoner had offered in his behalf, was of opinion that the charge had been proved against the prisoner, John Wheeler, and did in consequence adjudge him to receive two hundred lashes with a cat of nine tails on his bare back alongside such of His Majesty's ships, at such times and in such proportions as the commander in chief of His Majesty's ships and vessels at Plymouth should direct, and to be mulcted of all pay which might be then due to him.

The court was opened, the prisoner brought in, the witnesses and audience re-admitted and the sentence pronounced accordingly. …

73A. *Gore to Cotton*

[ADM 1/5420]

His Majesty's ship *Tonnant*
Off the Black Rocks, September 5th, 1811

… John Wheeler, Private of the Royal Marines embarked on board His Majesty's ship under my command, having this morning attempted to disable himself by cutting his left arm across the wrist,

I have to request you will be pleased to apply to the Lords Commissioners of the Admiralty to order the said John Wheeler to be tried by a court martial for the above offence. I subjoin a list of evidences for the prosecution. …

List of evidences in support of the prosecution.

William Stenhouse, Esq[r]., Surgeon
David Pinnegar, Corporal Roy[l]. Marines
John Hughes
John Merrifield [*sic*] Privates of the Royal Marines
John Kerrigan

73B. *Defence of John Wheeler*

… On the morning of the fifth of September, I was sitting inside of my berth near the ship side, endeavouring to make a pair of great coat straps out of some old canteen straps, and, in cutting one of the ends of the straps in order to place an [*sic*] buckle on it, the knife I made use of, I borrowed, I not having one of my own, and it being much sharper than I expected, slipped through the [ ] and cut the wrist of my left hand. I then took up an [*sic*] piece of the cloth to wipe the blood off my wrist and the corporal came and took up the knife. If I was inclined to do it purposely, I would take an [*sic*] more secret place to do such a thing, not in the face of fifteen or sixteen people that was in the berth. Therefore gentlemen, I have nothing more to say, but throw myself to the mercy of the honable. court.

…

DISTURBANCES OF THE PEACE

74. *Court Martial of Thomas Nelson*

[ADM 1/5353]

Minutes taken at a court martial assembled on board His Majesty's ship *Gladiator* in Portsmouth Harbour on the 30th day of July 1800.

Present

John Holloway, Esq[r]., Rear Admiral of the White and second officer in the command of His Majesty's ships and vessels at Portsmouth and Spithead, President.

Captain	Eliab Harvey	Captain	Charles Tyler
	Robert Carthew Reynolds		Edward Riou
	Joseph Sidney Yorke		George Grey
	Thomas Boys		John Talbot
	James Hardy		Robert Redmill
	James Wallis		George Clarke

The prisoner was brought in and the audience admitted.

The order from the Right Honble. Lords Commissioners of the Admiralty, dated the 24th inst[t]. and directed to the president, for the trial of Thomas Nelson, a Supernumerary Seaman belonging to His Majesty's ship *Royal William*, for having on or about the 14th inst[t]. used reproachful and provoking speeches to a man who had given evidence before a court martial held for the trial of one of the mutineers of the *Hermione*, was read.

The president reported to the court that Captains Henry D'Esterre Darby, Sir Charles Hamilton, Joseph Larcoin & William Lukin were absent on Admiralty leave.

The members of the court and judge advocate then, in open court and before they proceeded to trial, respectively took the several oaths enjoined and directed in and by an Act of Parliament made and passed in the 22d year of the reign of His late Majesty King George the 2nd, entitled *An Act for Amending, Explaining and Reducing into One Act of Parliament the Laws relating to the Government of His Majesty's Ships, Vessels and Forces by Sea*.

Then the letter from Captain Francis Pickmore, Commander of His Majesty's ship *Royal William*, to Admiral Milbanke, containing the charge was read, and the witnesses were ordered to withdraw and attend their examinations separately, which they did as follows:

John Jones, late Captain's Steward of H.M.S. *Hermione* now belonging to the *Puissant*, called in & sworn.

Captain Pickmore asked:

Q. Did you give evidence at a court martial held for the trial of one of the mutineers of the *Hermione*?

A. Yes.

Q. Do you know the person of the prisoner?

A. Yes.

Q. Was you passing by the *Gladiator* in a boat towards your ship on or about the 14th inst[t]?

A. Yes.

Q. Was you abused by anyone from the *Gladiator* at that time?

A. Yes.

Q. Relate the circumstance.

A. As I passed the *Gladiator* under her bow, a woman on the starboard side of the forecastle called out, 'There goes bloody Jack Catch belonging to the *Hermione*; you bloody bugger, you hung the man the other day. If ever I catch you on shore, I will have your bloody life taken from you.' She still kept calling after me as far as I could hear her. I ordered the waterman to turn back to take me alongside the *Gladiator*. When I got alongside, I asked for liberty to speak to the commanding officer and the officer of the watch told me to come on board. When I came on board, I related everything to him how the woman had served me. He got a candle and lantern and went to search for the woman, but she could not be found. I came up again and went down into the wherry and was going away; and the prisoner was sitting down on the top of the head chock forward and said, 'You bugger, who are you going to hang now? That is the bloody bugger belonging to the *Hermione*, who hangs all the men. You bugger, if I had my will of you, I'd hang you. I'd make a swab of you upon the beach.' He still kept abusing me as far as I could hear him. As I was passing along to go on shore, I could not understand what he was then saying, but he kept his eyes on me all the time. I then went on shore, and made my complaint to my captain; he gave me a letter to carry on board the *Gladiator* to the commanding officer and ordered me to attend the next day at 10 o'clock.

Q. Did you go on board the *Gladiator* with me the next day?

A. Yes.

Q. On mustering the people, did you point out to me the prisoner as one of the persons who had abused you?

A. Yes.

The prisoner asked:

Q. Did M^r^. Harding, the Boatswain, first bring me aft before you picked me out?

A. I saw him coming aft with the boatswain, and I immediately said he was one of the men. I did not know the boatswain was bringing him aft at the time as a prisoner; I am certain he is the man.

Q. Did M^r^. Harding say I heard this man speak before you declared me to be the man?

A. I did not hear him say a word before I said to a midshipman that is the man.

M[r]. W[m]. Harding, Boatswain of the *Gladiator*, called in and sworn.

Captain Pickmore asked:

Q. Was the prisoner lent from the *Royal William* to the *Gladiator*?

A. He came with a draft; he was one of the men.

Q. Do you know Jones, who lately belonged to the *Gladiator*?

A. Yes.

Q. Did he come on board the *Gladiator* on the 14th inst[t]. and complain to you that he had been grossly abused in passing by the ship?

A. Yes, he did.

Q. Did you go forward in the forecastle and take the prisoner by the collar for abusing him?

A. Not at that time; after we came up from below, Mr. Jones was going into the boat and we said we could not do anything in it tonight and I advised him to go to the admiral's office. He did and brought an order, signed by Captain Symes, not to let any person out of the ship; before that he was passing the head of the ship. The prisoner was the foremost man on the head when I came forward and he said, 'Good morning or good morrow morning,' I do not know which. I supposed it was to the waterman or Jones. I asked him how he dared call after any boat passing the ship; he asked my pardon and said he did not think any hurt.

Q. Did you take the prisoner at that time by the collar?

A. Yes, when he came off the head.

Q. Did you say anything to him about his being liable to be tried at a court martial for his conduct?

A. Yes, I did. He said he did not mean any harm.

Q. What did you mean that he was liable to be tried at a court martial for, when you spoke to him?

A. For calling after Jones.

Q. When I examined you the next day and the prisoner was present, did you not inform me that you heard the prisoner abusing Jones and seized him in consequence?

A. Yes, I told Captain Pickmore that I heard him calling after him.

Q. Did you not inform me that you heard him using abusive language to Jones, relative to his giving evidence, but that you could not tell what the words were?

A. Yes, but I could not tell what he said, as there was a great number of people on the forecastle and the people were very merry.

Q. Are you sure that at the time the boat was passing with Jones in it that the prisoner was calling to him in a reproachful manner?

A. I am not certain; there was so much noise.

The court asked:

Q. What was it that you heard the prisoner say that induced you to tell him he was liable to be tried at a court martial for?

A. For calling after any person passing the ship, particularly Jones. I observed he was speaking something to the man, which I could not distinguish. On the next morning after Captain Pickmore came on board, I informed him I could point out the prisoner in particular. Captn. Pickmore ordered me to go and get him. Just abaft the fore bits, I met the prisoner and he begged of me that I would not acquaint Captn. Pickmore of his conduct the night before. He kept on begging I would not point him out to Captn. Pickmore, but I took him up.

Q. When you brought him upon the quarterdeck and when he was mustered, did Jones point him out as one of the persons, who had grossly abused him?

A. Yes, he did as soon as he saw him.

The court asked:

Q. Since this court martial has been held or the prisoner put into confinement, have you received any threatening letter or been threatened in any manner, as to the evidence you should give on this trial?

A. No, I have not.

Q. What was the manner in which he spoke the words 'good morning' or 'good morrow morning' to you?

A. He swung his arm.

Q. Was it in a friendly manner or not?

A. It was in a friendly manner.

Q. After Jones came on board and complained to you of the improper language that was given to him by the woman, did you remain on deck till the boat put off?

A. We went below and made a search. After I put the candle away, I came up and he was at the foot of the ladder going into the wherry.

Q. When you went forward to seize the prisoner, did you see M[r]. Jones in the wherry at that time?
A. Yes, she was rowing ahead of the ship.
Q. Did Jones say anything to you when you went out to seize this man?
A. No, I did not hear him; he was looking back towards the ship and the wherry was rowing towards Gosport.
Q. Was there any other man on the ship's head at the time?
A. Yes, a good number sitting all round the head and forecastle; the prisoner was standing up and pointing his hand towards Jones. I thought it was in an unbecoming manner.
Q. Did you know any other man on the ship's head abusing Jones at the time?
A. No.
Q. If any other man had done it, should you have heard it?
A. I might not.

M[r]. George Belam, Surgeon's Mate of the *Gladiator*, called in and sworn.

Captain Pickmore asked:

Q. Did you see Mr. Harding the Boatswain, take the prisoner by the collar on the 14th of this month on the forecastle in the head?
A. Yes.
Q. What did he say to the prisoner at that time?
A. He said he had heard the prisoner say something, but he could not understand what he said and he would put him in irons.
Q. Did he accuse the prisoner of abusing Jones or making use of improper language to him in the wherry?
A. He went up to the prisoner and asked him what business he had to be calling after the man in the boat; the prisoner said he did not call after him, that he was standing on the head and said nothing to him.
Q. Was you present the next day when I examined the man on the quarterdeck?
A. I was.
Q. Did he deny the charge of abusing Jones at that time?
A. I do not recollect.

The court asked:

Q. Did you hear the boatswain say at any time on that day, or since, that the prisoner made use of threatening language to Jones?
A. I have heard the boatswain say that he heard the prisoner say 'good morrow morning' to you or words to that effect.
Q. When was it?

A. Within these 3 or 4 days past.
Q. What do you suppose the boatswain seized the prisoner by the collar for?
A. I supposed it was for saying something to him as he passed by.
Q. Was you on board when Jones came alongside to ask for the commanding officer?
A. I was.
Q. Did you hear him make his complaint to the commanding officer?
A. Yes.
Q. How long did you remain on deck after he went away & where was you?
A. I was about the gangway when Jones put off; I heard a woman abuse him, calling him a 'hanging bugger.'
Q. Did you then hear any man's voice abusing him?
A. I did not. There was a great noise at the time when Jones came up from below; a great number of men hooted and hissed him.
Q. Do you recollect the prisoner being among those men?
A. I do not.
Q. Were you on the forecastle before the boatswain?
A. No, I was behind him.
Q. Did you see the prisoner on the head?
A. I did.
Q. Did you hear him say anything?
A. I did not.
Q. Did you see him point or make any gestures towards the boat?
A. I did not.
Q. Might he have spoken or made any gestures without your seeing him?
A. Yes, he was standing up; I believe there were one or 2 standing up.
Q. When the boatswain collared the prisoner, did you hear him say he had made use of any improper expressions?
A. Yes, he did.
Q. At what time was it?
A. Nearly 8 o'clock in the evening or betwixt 7 & 8 o'clock.

The prisoner, being called on for his defence, produced a paper writing containing the same, which was read by the judge advocate and is hereto annexed.[1]

[1] This defence is not bound with the transcript of the trial.

John Hunter, a Seaman late belonging to H.M.S. *Bellerophon*, now in the *Royal William*, called in & sworn.

The prisoner asked:

Q. Was you on the head on the night of the 14th ab[t]. 8 o'clock?

A. I was.

Q. Did you see me there?

A. I did not take notice of him. I did not see him; he might have been there, for there were a great many there.

Q. Did you see a wherry go by?

A. I saw it after it was passed.

Q. Was you so situated on the forecastle as to have heard any person on the head abusing another going by at the time?

A. There were a great many calling out to people passing by, but I did not take notice what was said.

The court:

Q. Was it not possible for the prisoner to have made use of indecent or improper expressions to the people in the boat without your hearing it?

A. He might.

Captain Pickmore asked:

Q. How far was the wherry from the ship when you saw her?

A. About 50 yards.

William Newman, a Marine, called in & sworn.

The prisoner asked:

Q. Was you on the forecastle on the 14th day of this month about 8 o'clock?

A. I was; I saw the prisoner on the head.

Q. Did you hear me say anything to any person passing in a wherry?

A. I heard him say 'good morrow morning' to you, or some word like that.

Q. Did you see me come on the forecastle?

A. Yes, I saw him step on the forecastle on the larboard side.

Q. Did I at any time sit down on the head?

A. I cannot say, for my back was towards him. When I saw him, he was standing up.

Q. Could I have spoke or said anything to the persons in the wherry without your hearing it?

A. I cannot say for that, for there were many persons standing round.

Q. Did you see any person sit down before me?

A. There were 3 or 4 sitting down on the head further out than the prisoner was.
Q. How long was I from coming up till the boatswain collared me?
A. I cannot rightly say; I did not take particular notice.
Q. Was there time for me to have spoken any other words than those you have stated?
A. He was not long there. There may have been time; he was about a minute there.

The court asked:

Q. Did you hear the boatswain call to the prisoner to curse [*sic*] to him?
A. I did not.
Q. Did you hear the boatswain say to the prisoner, 'You are liable to be tried by a court martial for what you have said,' or words to that effect?
A. Yes, I did.
Q. What did you hear the prisoner say that should occasion the boatswain to have made use of that speech, or any other man that the boatswain may have mistaken for him?
A. I did not hear the prisoner say any other words than what I have related.

Captain Pickmore asked:

Q. Did the prisoner appear to go on the head for the purpose of speaking to the wherry passing by?
A. I cannot say; he went very quietly by me when he went on the head.

John Drummond, a Seaman late belonging to the *Bellerophon*, called in & sworn.

The prisoner asked:

Q. Was you on the head on the evening of the 14th inst[t]. when a wherry passed by?
A. No, I was in the larboard fore chains.
Q. Did you see the prisoner on the head?
A. I did not.

William Batt, a Seaman belonging to the *Bellerophon*, called in & sworn.

The prisoner asked:

Q. Was I sitting forward in the larboard bay at the time the boatswain and a waterman came forward?
A. Yes.
Q. How long had I been sitting there before?

A. I cannot rightly recollect; he was below when the woman came down to shift herself and she demanded a gown of him. She was in the ship with him. The prisoner afterwards came down and said the boatswain accused him of saying something to M^r^. Jones, and all he said was, 'Good morrow morning to you.'

Lieut[t]. John Haddiway, late of the *Bellerophon*, now of the *Spencer*, called in and sworn.

Q. What has been the general character of the prisoner?

A. I know nothing against him; he is a quiet, sober lad. For nearly the last 2 years, he has been in the cockpit.

M[r]. Ja[s]. Rose, Master's Mate late belonging to the *Bellerophon*, now of the *Spencer*, called in and sworn.

Q. What has been the general character of the prisoner?

A. He waited on us for ab[t]. 18 months and behaved very well indeed. I never knew him guilty before. Since I belonged to the ship, he was very obedient and attentive, and a very sober young man.

The court was cleared and agreed:

That the charge had been proved against the said Thomas Nelson and did adjudge him to be imprisoned in solitary confinement in His Majesty's prison called the Marshalsea, or such other of His Majesty's prisons as the Lord Commissioners of the Admiralty or any three of them for the time being should direct, for the space of two years from the date hereof and to be mulcted or to forfeit all the pay or wages due to him for his services done as a seaman in the Royal Navy.

The court was again opened, the prisoner brought in & audience admitted, and sentence passed accordingly. …

74A. *Pickmore to Milbanke*

[ADM 1/5353] *Royal William*, Spithead
17 July 1800

… Thomas Nelson, a Supernumerary Seaman belong to His Majesty's ship under my command, having, on or about the 14th instant, used reproachful & provoking speeches to a man who had given evidence before a court martial held for the trial of one of the mutineers of the *Hermione*, I think it my duty to request he may be tried at a court martial for the above offence. …

75. *Court Martial of William Downes*

[ADM 1/5395]

Minutes of the proceedings at a court martial assembled on board His Majesty's ship the *Diamond* in Port Royal Harbour, Jamaica on Friday the 28th of April 1809.

Present

Stephen Thomas Digby, Esqr., Captain of His Majesty's ship *Argo* and second officer in the command of His Majesty's ships and vessels at Port Royal, President.

Captains

George Argles | The Honourable Edward Rodney
Rowland Bevan

Commander
Lewis Shepheard

Being all the post captains of His Majesty's ships at Port Royal and the Senior commander.

The court being opened and the prosecutor, prisoners [*sic*] and witnesses admitted.

Read the order from Bartholomew Samuel Rowley, Esqre., Vice Admiral of the White and Commander in Chief of His Majesty's ships and vessels at Jamaica &c., &c., &c., dated the 26th instant directing the aforesaid Captain Stephen Thomas Digby to assemble a court martial (he being President thereof) to try William Downes, a Seaman belonging to His Majesty's sloop the *Avon*, on a charge exhibited him by Captain Thomas Thrush of the said sloop of having on or about the 12th day of March last behaved in a riotous and insubordinate manner.

Read the warrant from the president appointing (with the concurrence of the court) M^{r}. George Maude to execute the office of judge advocate on the occasion.

Then the members of the court and judge advocate respectively took the oaths prescribed by Act of Parliament.

Read letters from Captain Thomas Thrush, commanding His Majesty's sloop the *Avon*, and M^{r}. Robert Mills, Purser of the said sloop, containing the charges against the prisoner as follows:[1]

[1]The first letter is from Captain Thrush to Vice Admiral Rowley; the second is from Mr Mills to Captain Thrush.

Avon, Port Royal, Jamaica
19th April 1809

… William Downes, a Seaman belonging to His Majesty's sloop under my command, having, on or about the 12th day of March last, behaved in a riotous and insubordinate manner (as will appear by the enclosed letter from Mr. Mills, the Purser) and having, on or about the 17th instant, been guilty of similar misconduct on board His Majesty's sloop *Shark*, I have to request you will be pleased to order a court martial to be assembled to try him for the same.

…

Avon, Port Royal, Jamaica
13 March 1809

… William Downes, a Seaman belonging to His Majesty's sloop *Avon* under your command, having on the night of the 12th inst. said, 'give me a knife and I will stab the bloody purser, the bloody bugger, and then I shall die happy at the yard arm,' I beg, Sir, to acquaint you therewith.

…

After which all the witnesses withdrew by direction, except M^{r}. Robert Lewis, Midshipman of the *Avon*, who was sworn and examined as follows:

Prosecutor	Ques^{n}.)	Relate to the court what you know relative to the charge against the prisoner.
	Answer)	On the 12th March after 9 p. m., it being my watch, the prisoner being in irons, I heard a noise and demanded what it was and I heard the prisoner say, 'Give me a knife till I stick the bloody purser, the bloody bugger, and I hope I'll die happy at the yard arm for him yet.' I immediately went down with the Sergeant of Marines, and told the commanding officer and purser of it.
Court	Ques^{n}.)	Where was the prisoner at the time you heard him make use of these expressions?
	Ans^{r}.)	In the between decks by the main hatchway on the larboard side
	Court)	Describe your own situation at that time.
	Ans^{r}.)	I was walking the deck by the main hatchway on the starboard side.

C^{t}.) Did you see the prisoner at the time, or how do you know that those words proceeded from him?

Ans^{r}.) I did not see him, but I knew his voice and am positive it was the prisoner.

C^{t}.) Do you know the crime he was put in irons for?

Ans^{r}.) No.

The witness withdrew, and Sergeant Alexander Lyons, of the *Avon*, was called and sworn.

Prosc^{r}.) Relate to the court what you know relative to the charge against the prisoner.

Ans^{r}.) On the 12th of March about a quarter past 9 at night, the prisoner was making a very great noise (he was then in irons). M^{r}. Mills asked me if I would tell the prisoner to make less noise, as he had to get up early in the morning. The prisoner sung out, 'The bloody purser, give me a knife that I may stick him; then I'll die happy at the yard arm for him, the bloody bugger.' I desired the sentry to keep him silent and went on deck. I did not hear any more of his discourse.

Co^{t}.) Where was the prisoner at the time you heard him make use of these expressions, and describe your own situation at that time?

Ans^{r}.) The prisoner was in irons on the larboard side of the main hatchway in the between decks. I was sitting in my berth on the same side within sight of him.

Co^{t}.) Was the prisoner in liquor at the time?

Ansr.) I do not think he was perfectly sober, but he was not what could be called a drunken man.

C^{t}.) Do you act as master at arms?

Ans^{r}.) Yes.

Court) Do you know why he used these expressions, particularly against Mr. Mills, the purser?

Ans^{r}.) No.

The witness withdrew. Mr. Robert Marshall, Master of the *Shark*, called and sworn.

Prosecutor) Relate to the court what you know relative to the charge against the prisoner.

Ans[r].) On Monday night the 17th instant about 8 o'clock, I was sitting in the cabin with one of the gentlemen. I heard a noise and desired the sentry to keep less noise; the sentry sung out, 'Keep less noise' and the prisoner made answer he did not care for any bloody officer on board the *Shark*. He said, 'I know I shall be hung and I don't care how soon.' I perceived the prisoner in a state of intoxication, the corporal having previously taken a bottle of rum from him.

C[t].) How do you know it was the prisoner that uttered these words?

Ans[r].) I knew his voice and went out to speak to him.

C[t].) Who was the officer with you?

Ans[r].) M[r]. Sharp.

C[t].) What passed between you and the prisoner when you went out to speak to him?

Ans[r].) I desired him to be quiet; he muttered something. I don't recollect what.

The witness withdrew and M[r]. Reuben Sharp was called and sworn.

Prosecutor) Relate to the court what you know relative to the charge against the prisoner.

Ans[r].) I was sitting in the cabin on the main deck with M[r]. Marshall at 8 o'clock the 17th instant in the evening. I heard a noise in the steerage and desired the sentry to keep silence. The prisoner then said he did not care a damn for any bloody officer in the ship, as he knew he would be hung.

C[t].) How do you know it was the prisoner that uttered these words?

Ans[r].) Because I was coming out of the cabin door when he uttered them and saw him.

C[t].) Where was the prisoner confined?

Ans[r].) On the larboard side of the main deck, under the main hatchway, near the cabin door.

C[t].) Did he appear to be in liquor at the time?

Ans[r].) He certainly was.

The witness withdrew and M[r]. William Owen, Midshipman of the *Shark*, was called and sworn.

Prosecutor) Relate to the court what you know relative to the charges against the prisoner.

Ans[r].) On the 17th instant a little after 8 p. m., while sitting in the gun room of the *Shark*, I heard a great noise on the main deck and some ill language made use of. I requested the sentry to keep less noise. He told me that the prisoner was the person who made it and he could not keep him quiet. I then desired the prisoner to recollect his situation and hold his tongue. He replied he did not care a damn for any bloody officer on board. He knew he should be hung and the sooner, the better. M[r]. Marshall, the Master, then came out from the wardroom and likewise desired him to hold his tongue and, on his return to the wardroom, the prisoner said, 'What bloody old fool is that?' The prisoner seemed rather intoxicated, but, when I spoke to him, he said he knew very well what he was about.

The witness withdrew and M[r]. Robert Mills, the Purser of the *Avon*, called and sworn.

He was shown the letter purporting to be that which he wrote to Captain Thrush, respecting the charge against the prisoner.

C[t].) Is that your letter and, if so, state motives for having written it.

Ans[r].) It is. On the night of the 12th instant, after I had gone to bed between 9 and 10 o'clock, I heard a great noise in the between decks. I called to know who was making it; I was answered by the sergeant of Marines that it was Downes. I desired the sergeant to pacify him and then heard the prisoner exclaim, 'Oh there is the bloody purser, the bloody bugger. Give me a knife, and I'll stick him.' There was a great deal more which I could not distinctly hear. I thought it my duty to acquaint Captain Thrush of this conduct on the part of the prisoner and therefore wrote the letter.

C[t].) Are you quite positive that the language you have just stated proceeded from the same person you had before heard making a noise?

Ans^r^.) I am.

The witness withdrew and the prisoner was informed that the prosecution was closed and he might have a reasonable time for his defence.

The prisoner stated that he had only to say that he was much affected in consequence of wounds received in his head, which prevent him from knowing always what he is about.

M^r^. Robert Lewis was again called.

C^t^.) How long have you known the prisoner?

Ans^r^.) To the best of my recollection, between eight and nine months.

C^t^.) Did you ever know him evince symptoms of insanity or derangement of intellect?

Ans^r^.) No.

The witness withdrew, and Alexander Lyons was again called.

C^t^.) How long have you known the prisoner?

Ans^r^.) From his joining the *Avon* till he went to the *Shark*; I suppose about two or three months.

C^t^.) Did you ever know him evince symptoms of insanity or derangement of intellect?

Ans^r^.) No.

The defence rested here, and the court was cleared and proceeded to deliberate on the sentence and, having very maturely considered the evidence produced on the part of the crown in support of the charges and what the prisoner had to offer in his defence, the court was of opinion that the charges were fully proved and did therefore adjudge the said William Downes to receive three hundred and fifty lashes on his bare back with a cat of nine tails alongside of such of His Majesty's ships and vessels in Port Royal Harbour, in such proportions, and at such times, as the Commander in Chief of His Majesty's ships and vessels at Jamaica shall direct.

The court was then opened, the prisoner, witnesses, &c admitted and sentence passed accordingly. …

SEX CRIMES

76. *Court Martial of William McMaster and John Callaughan*

[ADM 1/5350]

Minutes of the proceedings of a court martial assembled and held on board His Majesty's ship *Unite*, Fort Royal Bay, Martinique, the 29th day of July 1799, for the trial of William Mc Master (Seaman) and John Callaughan (Marine), belonging to His Majesty's ship *Invincible*, for having been caught in the act of buggery on the evening of the 8th of July 1799.

Present

John Poo Beresford, Esq[r]., Captain of His Majesty's ship *Unite* and third officer in command of His Majesty's ships and vessels employed in Fort Royal Bay, Martinique, President.

Captains

Thomas Leeth Goselin
Thomas Harvey
Adrian Renou
Thomas Western
Richard Matson

The prisoners brought into court and the evidence and audience admitted.

Read the order of the Right Honourable Lord Hugh Seymour, Vice Admiral of the Blue and Commander in Chief of His Majesty's ships and vessels employed and to be employed at Barbados, the Leeward Islands and the seas adjacent, dated the 28th instant, and directed to John Poo Beresford, Esq[r]., Captain of His Majesty's ship *Unite* and third officer in command of His Majesty's ships and vessels employed in Fort Royal Bay, Martinique to try William Mc Master (seaman) and John Callaughan (marine), belonging to His Majesty's ship *Invincible,* on a charge exhibited against them by Captain William Cayley of the said ship for having been caught in the act of buggery on the evening of the 8th instant.

Then the members of the court and judge advocate, in open court and before they proceeded to trial, respectively took the oaths directed by Parliament, made and passed in the twenty second year of the reign of His late Majesty King George the Second entitled *An Act for Amending, Explaining and Reducing into One Act of Parliament the Laws Relating to the Government of His Majesty's Ships, Vessels and Forces by Sea*. The letter from William Cayley, Esq[r]., Captain of His Majesty's ship *Invincible* (containing the charge against the prisoner [*sic*]) was then read; and all the witnesses being ordered to withdraw and attend their examinations separately, they all withdrew accordingly, except the first to be sworn and the court proceeded to trial as follows:

Evidence in support of the charge, William Murray, Sergeant of Marines of the *Invincible*, sworn and examined as follows:

Court – Relate to the court what you know respecting the charge against the prisoners.

Answer – At or near half past 9 o'clock at night on Monday, July 8th, 1799, being in my hammock, I heard a noise alongside of me; not knowing who the people were by their voices, I went to the gunroom sentinel, begged his light and that he would accompany me for a few minutes. Seeing John Huson standing by, I desired him to come with me also at the same time, calling out, 'Is there anybody else awake,' to which I got no answer. The two people before mentioned went with me to the berth where the prisoners were laying, where by the help of the light I found William Mc Master and John Callaughan (the prisoners) laying upon their sides, very close together. I desired the two men, who came with me, to take notice what they saw. I then gave the prisoners a shake and saw the one's privates (to the best of my knowledge, John Callaughan) come out of the fundament of the other. I then went and called for the master at arms, whom I found under the half deck, and made a report to him of the situation in which I found the prisoners. At the time I was speaking to the master at arms, John Callaughan (one of the prisoners) was standing by me, who said, 'Murray, I hope it is not me you mean,' to which I made no answer, but went on the quarterdeck and reported the circumstances to the officer there, who immediately ordered them into confinement. Mc Master (one of the prisoners) was found and directly confined; John Callaughan (the other prisoner) was not found until 12 o'clock at night.

Prisoner Mc Master:

Which side were we laying upon?

Answer – On your left sides.

Question – Which of the two was nearest the ship's side?

Answer – John Callaughan.

Prisoner Callaughan:

When writing the charge against me and the other prisoner, did you call any person into the berth where you was writing (by order of Captain Cayley) and say, 'Do you think this is sufficient?'

Answer – Not that I recollect. Ordered to withdraw.

William Smith, a Seaman belonging to the *Invincible*, was next called into court and sworn.

Court – Relate what you know respecting the charge against the prisoners.

Answer – At half past 9 o'clock in the evening of the 8th of July 1799, Sergeant Murray came to me at the gunroom door, where I was sentinel, and asked me for my light and to go with him; I went with him and found the prisoners in their berth laying on their left sides very near to each other. Sergeant Murray said, 'Let us see, you rascals, what you are doing,' on which he took hold of Mc Master (one of the prisoners) and hauled him from Callaughan (the other prisoner). Mc Master had no trousers on; Callaughan had his trousers below his haunches.

Question – Did the prisoners appear to be sober?

Answer – They did to me.

Question – Did you see the prisoners in the act with which they stand charged?

Answer – No.

Prisoner Mc Master:

Did you, on the 9th of July, when pumping off the water on the starboard side of the main deck, say that you saw nothing indecent pass between me and the other prisoner on the night that you was called by Sergeant Murray?

Answer – I do not recollect.

Question – Had you any conversation with Edward Dilliforce on the subject of the charge against us?

Answer – No. Ordered to withdraw.

John Huson, belonging to the *Invincible*, was next called into court and sworn.

Court – Relate to the court what you know respecting the charge against the prisoners.

Answer – After three bells in the first watch on the 8th July, Sergeant Murray came and took the light from the sentinel at the gunroom door and called me, saying, 'Come with me and I'll show you something.' I went with him and the sentinel from the gunroom door. The sergeant, holding the light over the prisoner, said, 'Here's two buggers buggering themselves.' The prisoner Callaughan's backside was very close in to Mc Master's lap; they lay both on their left sides and both their heads aft. Mc Master had his trousers off;

Callaughan's trousers were half way down and the flap hauled up on his privates. The sergeant said, 'Come let us see whether you are males or females or what you are,' directly laying hold of Mc Master's right shoulder and hauling him round on his back from the other man; he took up Mc Master's frock and his yard was standing. I cannot tell whether he was in him or no. The sergeant said, 'I'll report them.'

Court – In what part of the ship were the prisoners?

Answer – In Sergeant Murray's berth on the larboard side, the next berth but one to the gunroom.

Court – On which side of the ship was the sentinel's light at the gunroom door.

Answer – The larboard side. Ordered to withdraw.

Sergeant Murray called into court again.

Court – Did you see the prisoners in the act with which they stand charged?

Answer – Yes.

Court – Were their faces to the ship's side.

Answer – From the ship's side. Ordered to withdraw.

The evidence in support of the charge being finished, the prisoners were called upon to make their defence, when they requested to be allowed half an hour, which was granted and the court cleared.

The court was again opened; and the prisoners deliver'd a written paper into court as their defence and requested permission for its being read by the judge advocate, which was granted and was as follows:

> … We humbly beg to submit to you that being both of us in a very high state of intoxication at the time we are charged with the having committed the foul and detestable sin of buggery, it is impossible for us to have the smallest recollection of what then passed or what persons were near us so as to enable us to call upon them as witnesses on our part.
>
> We beg to state to the court that in our opinion but one of the three evidences called in support of the charges has made out that he saw us in the act with which we stand charged, the other two positively denying the having seen us in such situation and we humbly conceive that the testimony of two witnesses is necessary on a charge of so very serious a nature.
>
> We also beg to state that in a climate like this, where it is common for men on board ship to lay about the decks as they can make it most convenient to themselves, even when sober, how easy it may be for a

man to be deceived in the conclusion he draws from the situation in which he finds two men in a high state of intoxication without the least knowledge of their situation or actions. We beg to assure the court that we have a very proper abhorrence of the foul crime with which we are charged; and we trust from the characters we shall receive from the officers of the *Invincible* that the court will be inclined to believe that our then state of intoxication was the cause of our being found in the situation we were and not any intention of committing the detestable sin of sodomy. We rely entirely on the mercy of the court.

Prisoner Mc Master request Lieutenant Burnby, of the *Invincible*, to speak to his character. Lieut. Burnby said, 'that he had been his servant for near twenty months during which time he had behaved himself so as to give him satisfaction and that he had discharged him about five months ago.'

Prisoner Callahaughan requested Lieutenant Abbot, of the Marines on board the *Invincible*, to speak for his character, who said he could give him a good character previous to the time of the charge.

The prisoners, having nothing further to offer in their defence, the court was cleared and proceeded to deliberate upon and form the sentence.

The court, having carefully and deliberately weighed and considered the evidence produced and what the prisoners alleged in their defence, were of opinion that the charge had been fully proved and that they fell under the twenty-ninth article of an Act passed in the twenty-second year of His late Majesty King George the Second *for Amending, Explaining and Reducing into one Act of Parliament the Laws relating to the Government of His Majesty's Ships, Vessels and Forces by Sea.*

In consequence thereof, the court adjudged the prisoners, William McMaster (Seaman) and John Callaughan (Marine), to be hanged by the neck until they are dead at the yard arm of such of His Majesty's ships and at such time as the commander in chief shall direct.

The court was opened, audience admitted and sentence passed accordingly. …

77. *Court Martial of John Harrison, William Harris, John Ware and John Douglas*

[ADM 1/5355]

Minutes of proceedings at a court martial held on board His Majesty's ship *Trident* in Back Bay, Trincomallee, ye 14th June 1800 & continued till the 16th of June 1800 inclusive for the separate trials of Jno. Harrison

& William Harris, & Jno. Ware & Jno. Douglas, Seamen belonging to His Majesty's ship *Trident*.

Present

Wm. Clark, Esqre., Captain of His Majesty's ship *Victorious*, President.

Captains

Wm. Hargood	Henry Lidgbird Ball
Thos. Alexander	Charles Adam

The prisoners were brought into court & evidence & audience admitted.

Read the orders from Peter Rainier, Esqre., Vice Admiral of the Blue & Commander in Chief of His Majesty's ships & vessels in the Asiatic Seas, dated the 29th day of May 1800, directed to Wm. Clark, Esqre., Captain of His Majesty's ship *Victorious,* to try Jno. Harrison, William Harris, Jno. Ware & Jno. Douglas, Seamen of His Majesty's ship *Trident* on complaints alleged against them by Randl. Blake and others belonging to that ship of having committed the unnatural & detestable sin mentioned in the first part of the 29th Article of War.

Then the members of the court and judge advocate, in open court & before they proceeded to trial, respectively took the oaths directed by Act of Parliament, made & passed in the 22nd year of the reign of His late Majesty King George the 2nd, entitled *An Act for Amending, Explaining and Reducing into One Act of Parliament the Laws Relating to the Government of His Majesty's Ships, Vessels & Forces by Sea.*

A letter from Captn. John Turnor[1] was read as follows, vizt.

His Maj's ship *Trident*
Negapatnam Roads, May 4th, 1800

… I beg leave to inform you that Jno. Harrison was confined on or about the 6th of March last & Wm. Harris on the 8th, Seamen belonging to His Majesty's ship *Trident* under my command, on complaints alleged against them by Randal Blake, belonging to the said ship, of having committed the unnatural and detestable sin mentioned in the first part of the 29th Article of War; and on the 3rd inst. Jno. Ware & Jno. Douglas likewise were confined for the same crime.

I have therefore to request you will be pleased to order a court martial to be held the first opportunity on the said Jno. Harrison, Wm. Harris, Jno. Ware & Jno. Douglas, Seamen, for the detestable crime express'd in the first part of the above mention'd Article of War.

…

[1]This letter is to Vice Admiral Rainier.

All the evidence were order'd to withdraw & attend their examinations separately; they all withdrew accordingly, and Jno. Harrison & W^{m}. Harris were first brought to trial.

Randal Blake was first call'd & sworn.

Quest^{n}. by the Prosecutor: Did you on the 8th of March, or about that time, make a public complaint to me on the quarterdeck of the two prisoners, Jno. Harrison & W^{m}. Harris, of their having frequently committed the unnatural sin of buggery?

Ans^{r}.: Yes, I did on the 6th of March to Lieut. Rutherford of Jno. Harrison & on the 8th of W^{m}. Harris to the captain.

Q^{n}. Pros^{r}.: Relate to the court what you know respecting the two prisoners relative to the complaint.

Ans^{r}.: I know nothing of them. I done it out of spite & malice, because young Harrison struck me & the other persuaded him to do it. That's all I got to say on it.

Q^{n}. Pros.: Did you tell me, in the presence of Lieut. Rutherford & others, that both of them had committed the before mention'd crime *on you* at different times, particularly in the main chains?

The court retired on this question, which was admitted to be put to the evidence. He did not reply to it, but fell into a fit. The surgeon was sent for, who reported that it was really an epileptic fit, and he was taken below.

Sergeant Burke, of the Marines, sworn on the Cross, being a Roman Catholic.

Q^{n}, Pros^{r}.: Relate to the court what you saw & heard, on a particular night, of the two prisoners & their conversation & transactions.

Ans^{r}.: I was laying on the poop in the netting; Harrison lay down on the deck outside me. A little after, Harris lay down alongside him. Harrison desired Harris to quit him, as he had already gain'd him a very bad name in the ship; the answer the other made was that he loved him, & would not hurt him. That is the purport of what I heard; there was several things of the same nature said, but I can't now positively recollect them.

Q^{n}. Pros.: Were you on your guard, knowing the two men, to keep awake to seize them if any improper transactions took place?

Ans^{r}.: I was, from the report there was in the ship of the two prisoners.

Q^{n}. C^{t}.: Did you observe any improper transactions take place between the prisoners?

Ans^{r}.: No, I observed nothing improper.

Q^{n}. C^{t}.: Would you have taken notice of the conversation that you say pass'd between the prisoners had you not heard that report against them?

Ans^{r}.: No.

M^{r}. John Burosse, Surgeon, sworn.

Q^{n}. C^{t}.: In your opinion, will the health of the evidence, Randal Blake, admit of his being further examined this afternoon, respecting the charges alleged against the prisoners, Jno. Harrison & W^{m}. Harris?

Ans^{r}.: From the health of Randal Blake at this time, I do not think he will be capable of giving a proper evidence today.

In consequence of the surgeon's report respecting the health of Randal Blake, the court adjourn'd to Monday morning, the 16th June.

Monday, the 16 June.

Randal Blake again call'd.

Q^{n}. Pros^{r}.: Did you tell me, in the presence of Lieut. Rutherford & others, that both the prisoners had committed the before mention'd crime on you at different times, particularly in the main chains?

Ans^{r}.: I don't remember saying any such thing.

Here the prosecution closed, & the prisoner, Jno. Harrison, called Robt. Gardiner, who was sworn.

Q^{n}. Pris^{r}.: Was you in the sick bay at the time that Randal Blake said 'twas thro spite he complain'd on us?

Ans^{r}.: Yes.

Q^{n}. C^{t}.: In what manner did this confession come forward?

Ans^{r}.: I can't exactly say; I only came in promiscuously.

Q^{n}. C^{t}.: How long was it after the alleged crime against the prisoners that you heard this said by Randal Blake?

Ans^{r}.: I don't recollect.

Q^{n}. C^{t}.: Were the prisoners in confinement at the time?

Ans^{r}.: Yes.

Lukis Kanivis call'd & sworn.

Q^{n}. Pris^{r}.: Was you in the sick bay at the time Randal Blake said 'twas thro' spite he complain'd of us?

Ans^{r}.: Yes.

Q^{n}. C^{t}.: In what manner did this confession come forward?

Ans^{r}.: At the time he came to his senses from a fit, he said that it was thro' spite & malice that he had done it, & that he was very sorry for it, & that he wou'd go to Capt. Turnor & tell him the same; & I told him if he know'd they were innocent, he ought to do it.

Q^{n}. C^{t}.: Do you know if he went to Capt. Turnor at that time, or any other time, to make that declaration?

Ans^{r}.: I don't know; he went out of the sick bay & had his hammock hung up under the half deck. I know nothing more.

Q^{n}. C^{t}.: How long was it after the alleged crime against the prisoners that you heard this said by Randal Blake.

Ans^{r}.: I don't recollect.

Q^{n}. C^{t}.: Was anyone present when he said this?

Ans^{r}.: Yes, there was Branham, who is now sick, and several others, but it's so long ago, I don't remember their names.

Andrew Foley call'd & sworn.

Q^{n}. Pris.: Did you hear Randal Blake say in the gunroom that he know'd nothing of us & cou'd not hurt us without taking a false oath & that he wou'd not do for all the captains in the navy?

Ans^{r}.: Yes.

Qn. Ct.: In what manner did this confession come forward?

Ans.: 'Twas the first or second night after he (Randal Blake) was confined below in the gunroom; he said he did it out of spite & malice, because Jno. Harrison had struck him & for Captain Turnor, nor all the captains in the navy, he wou'd not take a false oath; & to keep their hearts up, that they shou'd not be hurt, & that he was sorry for it half an hour after he had made the complaint.

Q^{n}. C^{t}.: Do you recollect how long it was after the prisoners were confined that you heard Randal Blake say this?

Ans^{r}.: I do not.

W^{m}. Harris in his defence call'd on Ja^{s}. Brown, who was sworn.

Q^{n}. Pris^{r}.: Did you hear Randal Blake say in the galley that we were both innocent & what he had related against us was thro spite & malice?

Ans^{r}.: Yes.

Q^{n}. C^{t}.: In what manner did this confession come forward?

Ans^{r}.: I came by when they were under the sentry's charge & heard Randal Blake say so.

Q^{n}. C^{t}.: Do you know how long after the prisoners were confined you heard Rand^{l}. Blake say this?

Ans^{r}.: I don't recollect.

Jno. Harrison call'd on Captain Turnor for his general character in the ship; Capt. Turnor said, 'As far as I know of him, he has always had a very good character & I never heard a complaint against him before the present one.'

Wm. Harris also call'd on Capt. Turnor for a character, who said, 'I cannot speak to his character.' Here the prisoners closed their defence. The court was clear'd & again open'd, & proceeded to the trials of Jno. Ware & Jno. Douglas.

Jno. Cook was call'd & sworn.

Q^{n}. Pros^{r}.: Relate to the court what you know of the transactions of the two prisoners on, or about, the night of the 2nd of May last?

Ans^{r}.: I was asleep on the forecastle on the 2nd of May at night in the first watch; between 9 & 10 p. m., Thos. Smith came & asked me if I would go below & see the transactions that were going on between Jno. Ware & Jno. Douglas. I went below directly with him & I saw what was going on between them & I came on deck again & I acquainted the master at arms of what the two were about. He & I went with his lantern & saw the condition they were both in & he went and acquainted M^{r}. Maggs & I stood by the light till M^{r}. Maggs came down. That is all I know.

Q^{n}. Pros^{r}.: You have said you found them in a situation, what situation were they in?

Ans^{r}.: Jno. Douglas with his privates naked & Jno. Ware with his backside naked.

Q^{n}. Pros.: What were they about?

Ans^{r}.: When I came down with Thos. Smith, I really did see Jno. Douglas on the top of Jno. Ware.

Q^{n}. Pros.: Were they then in the naked situation you have already described?

Ans^{r}.: They had their trousers down, but they were not off.

Q^{n}. Pros.: Were they asleep in that situation?

Ans^{r}.: They were as much awake as I am at present.

Q^{n}. Pros.: You say you saw them on the top of one another, what were they doing?

Ans^{r}.: I cannot rightly say what they were about; they was making motions.

Q^{n}. Pros.:	What were the motions? Were they connected? Had they carnal knowledge of each other?
Ans^{r}.:	I cannot say; I had that suspicion.
Q^{n}. Pros.:	Was it light or was it dark?
Ans^{r}.:	It was dark.
Q^{n}. C^{t}.:	Where was it?
Ans^{r}.:	Abreast the bitts on the lower deck between the 2nd & 3rd gun.
Q^{n}. C^{t}.:	When you saw the prisoners making the motions you have related, what distance was you from them?
Ans^{r}.:	I was leaning over the hammocks that was hung betwixt the guns & they lying in the middle of the berth betwixt the 2 guns.
Q^{n}. C^{t}.:	Did you positively see the private parts of Jno. Douglas in the body of Jno. Ware?
Ans^{r}.:	I did not.
Q^{n}. C^{t}.:	By what light were you enabled to make the observations you have related to the court?
Ans^{r}.:	'Twas from the light that came thro' the ports.
Q^{n}.:	Was it moonlight?
Ans^{r}.:	Yes.
Q^{n}. C^{t}.:	Did you make any observations to the prisoners at the time you saw them in that situation or did they remain there any time after?
Ans^{r}.:	I did not speak a word to them.
Q^{n}.:	Did you find them when you came down with the mast^{r}. at arms in the same situation you left them in?
Ans^{r}.:	No, they were both asleep.
Q^{n}.:	Did you go to the mast^{r}. at arms immediately after you made those observations & what length of time elapsed till you return'd with him?
Ans^{r}.:	I walk'd the forecastle near half an hour after.
Q^{n}. C^{t}.:	What induced you to admit of such a length of time passing before you went to the mast^{r}. at arms?
Ans^{r}.:	I can't tell; I did not know what to do.
Q^{n}. C^{t}.:	Did you consult any of your ship mates in what manner you ought to proceed?
Ans^{r}.:	Yes; when I came on the forecastle, I consulted with W^{m}. Pritchard & Jno. Johnson what I shou'd do.
Q^{n}.:	What advice did they give you?
Ans^{r}.:	They told me it was best to acquaint the master at arms, which I did immediately.

Q^{n}. C^{t}.:	What did you relate to the mast^{r}. at arms?
Ans^{r}.:	I told him to go into our berth & see what Jno. Douglas & Jno. Ware were about.
Q^{n}. C^{t}.:	Had the sentry at the bitts a light?
Ans^{r}.:	Yes.
Q^{n}.:	On which side the deck?
Ans^{r}.:	On the starboard side.
Q^{n}.:	On which side the deck did the transaction you have related take place?
Ans^{r}.:	On the starboard side.
Q^{n}. C^{t}.:	You have said when you went with the mast^{r}. at arms, you found both the prisoners asleep. What steps did the mast^{r}. at arms take?
Ans^{r}.:	After he saw the situation they was in, he laid down his light & went on the quarterdeck.
Q^{n}.:	What was the situation you found them in, when you went down with the mast^{r}. at arms?
Ans^{r}.:	Jno. Douglas with his privates naked & Jno. Ware with his backside naked.
Q^{n}.:	Were they asleep in that situation?
Ans^{r}.:	Yes, they appear'd to be.
Q^{n}. C^{t}.:	At the time you say you saw them in motion, did they appear to be drunk or sober?
Ans^{r}.:	They were groggy, I believe, but I can't rightly tell.
Q^{n}. C^{t}.:	Were they messmates of yours?
Ans^{r}.:	Jno. Ware was.
Q^{n}.:	Did Douglas mess near your berth?
Ans^{r}.:	He mess'd abreast the jeer capstern.
Q^{n}.:	When had you last seen your messmate, Ware, prior to your going to sleep on the forecastle?
Ans^{r}.:	I saw him in the berth at four o'clock, when the grog was served. I did not see him after, till I saw him in that situation.
Q^{n}. C^{t}.:	Did he appear in liquor at that time?
Ans^{r}.:	No.
Q^{n}.:	You have said you supposed both the prisoners were groggy at the time you found them in this situation. What reason have you for supposing so?
Ans^{r}.:	I heard Jno. Ware call Jno. Douglas a bloody rascal.
Q^{n}.:	Are you so well acquainted with the voice of Jno. Douglas as to know from his speech whether he was drunk or sober?

Ans^{r}.: Yes, I know by his speech when he is drunk.

Q^{n}.: When the master at arms return'd with Mr. Maggs, what steps were then taken with the prisoners?

Ans^{r}.: I came on deck & was call'd aft.

Q^{n}.: Did you see either or both prisoners after that period during the night?

Ans^{r}.: No.

Q^{n}.: Had there been any quarrel or disputes between you & the prisoners previous to this transaction?

Ans^{r}.: A week or two before, I quarrel'd with Jno. Douglas for keeping Jno. Ware, my messmate, out of his company.

Q^{n}. What was the nature of the quarrel, did you fight?

Ans^{r}.: We fought & the master at arms bro^{t}. us aft.

Q^{n}.: What were your motives for keeping your messmate from Jno. Douglas?

Ans^{r}.: Because I thought Jno. Douglas a quarrelsome man. He used to come to the berth every time he got a drop of grog & through our striving to keep him out, he used to quarrel with us.

Q^{n}.: Did you ever see anything improper pass between the prisoners before the night of the 2nd of May?

Ans^{r}.: No.

Q^{n}.: Did you take any other method to ascertain the truth of the charge against the prisoners than that you have related to the court?

Ans^{r}.: No.

Thos. Smith call'd & sworn.

Q^{n}. Pros.: Relate to the court the situation you saw the prisoners in on the night they were confined on, or about, the 2nd May.

Ans^{r}.: I went down to my hammock after 8 o'clock, & I saw them both in one hammock together. I saw a great motion with Jno. Douglas the prisoner. I went to the hammock & haul'd him out from Jno. Ware; his trousers were unbutton'd, & his privates naked. I did not know the consequence, but went up & told my messmate, Jno. Cook, & we went both down together; & when we came down, they was both under the hammocks & I saw then Jno. Douglas in great motion, the same as before by the light of the lamp at the bitts.

Q^{n}. Pros.: When you haul'd Jno. Douglas out of the hammock, what position was Jno. Ware laying in?

Ans^{r}.: I don't know; as soon as I haul'd Jno. Douglas out of the hammock, I went up to Jno. Cook.

Q^{n}.: When you came down with your messmate, Jno. Cook, & found them laying under the hammocks, was Jno. Douglas on the other?

Ans^{r}.: Yes, he was.

Q^{n}.: What were they about?

Ans^{r}.: I can't tell what they were about; they were in great motion that's all I saw.

Q^{n}.: Did you see the privates of Jno. Douglas at that time?

Ans^{r}.: No.

Q^{n}.: Was his privates in the body of the other?

Ans^{r}.: I can't tell.

Q^{n}. C^{t}.: What induced you to haul Jno. Douglas out of the hammock from Jno. Ware?

Ans^{r}.: Seeing great motion in the hammock & knowing he had no business there.

Q^{n}.: After you haul'd Jno. Douglas out of the hammock, did he make you any excuse for having been found in that situation?

Ans^{r}.: No, he layed as tho' he was asleep.

Q^{n}.: When you saw the prisoners laying on the deck making the motions you mention, were their private parts exposed?

Ans^{r}.: I can't tell.

Q^{n}.: Did you, either at the time you saw the prisoners in the hammock or under the hammock or at any time during that night, see the private parts of Jno. Douglas in the body of Jno. Ware?

Ans^{r}.: No, I did not.

Q^{n}.: Had you ever any dispute with the prisoners prior to this evening?

Ans^{r}.: No.

Q^{n}.: Had you ever observed any great intimacy between the prisoners before this night?

Ans^{r}.: No.

Q^{n}.: Do you recollect Cook fighting with the prisoner Douglas & what was it about?

Ans^{r}.: Yes, I recollect their fighting, but don't recollect what about.

Q^{n}.: Were the prisoners drunk?

Ans^{r}.: I can't tell.

Q^{n}.: Did you see the prisoners that night after they were confined?

Ans^{r}.: No.

Ja^{s}. Holland call'd & sworn.

Q^{n}. Pros.: Relate to the court what you know respecting the charge against the prisoners.

Ans^{r}.: All I know is Jno. Douglas was a messmate of mine at the same time this affair happen'd. I know he was groggy the afternoon this affair happen'd & I knew likewise that he was in Ware's berth. So I went forward at night, as near as I can guess about 8 o'clock, & expecting that he might be quarrelsome, being groggy & that I might fetch him away from it, I went forward. I saw he was not quarrelsome, but that him & Jno. Ware were very quiet; & with that, I sat opposite to them on the cable. I stop'd there for a few minutes till they got into the hammock & Jno. Ware went into the hammock first, Douglas got in after him; & I seeing they were very peaceable & their two hands were across one another's neck, when I see that, so I went aft on the poop.

Q^{n}. C^{t}.: Did it not appear to you a very extraordinary circumstance seeing two men get into the same hammock together?

Ans^{r}.: No, I can't say it did 'cause I see'd nothing, but that of being in the hammock together.

Q^{n}. C^{t}.: Did you see the private parts of either or both of the prisoners when they were in the hammock together?

Ans^{r}.: No, I did not.

Q^{n}. C^{t}.: Did you know that Jno. Douglas & Jno. Ware had both hammocks?

Ans^{r}.: I don't know that every man in the ship had a hammock.

The court was clear'd to consider of the behaviour of this evidence, & are of opinion that he has behaved contemptuously to the court; they, therefore, adjudge him to one month's imprisonment wherever the commander in chief shall direct.

W^{m}. Allen, Master at Arms, sworn.

Q^{n}. Pros^{r}.: Relate to the court what you know respecting the charge against the prisoners.

Ans^{r}.: On a Saturday night on or about the 3rd of May last, at about ½ past ten o'clock, Jno. Cook came & asked me to be so kind to step into their berth to see the transactions going on there betwixt Jno. Douglas & Jno. Ware. I then took my lantern & went with Jno. Cook to his berth, but there being two hammocks hung up from gun to gun, I could not get properly into his berth. I then went round to the next berth & went in under the breast of the gun. I there found Jno. Ware laying with his trousers as far down as his knees, & likewise Jno. Douglas with the flap of his trousers down, & his shirt & privates out of his trousers. I said to Cook, 'Remain here with my lantern till I go to the quarterdeck & make a report of it.' I then came to the quarterdeck, & acquainted the officer of the watch, who was M^{r}. Maggs & wished him to go below & see the state the prisoners were then laying in. M^{r}. Maggs went with me &, after looking at them, we return'd to the quarterdeck.

Q^{n}.: Were they laying near each other?

Ans^{r}.: At about 18 inches distance.

Q^{n}.: Did you see any bags or anything else near them?

Ans^{r}.: I saw a pillow; the case was given to me the next morning, all bloody.

Q^{n}. C^{t}.: At the time you saw the prisoners with their private parts exposed, were they asleep?

Ans^{r}.: They apparently were.

Q^{n}. C^{t}.: Did you see the prisoner, Douglas, on top of Jno. Ware at any time?

Ans^{r}.: No.

Q^{n}. C^{t}.: Did you make any observation on the pillow case that night or in the morng.?

Ans^{r}.: Not till the morning, when I think W^{m}. Pritchard gave it to me.

Q^{n}.: Were the prisoners allowed to remain in the situation you saw them in?

Ans^{r}.: They did till M^{r}. Maggs came down, when I was ordered to put them in irons.

Q^{n}.: At the time you put the prisoners in irons, did it appear they were in a state of intoxication?

Ans^{r}.: Ware was very much so, but Douglas was not so, from the answers he made me.

Q^{n}.: What questions did you put to Douglas that made you certain he was not intoxicated?

Ans^{r}.: I said to him, 'Douglas you are not in liquor.' He answer'd me he knowed that he was not. 'Well,' says I, 'go along' & he went before me to the gun room, & sat himself down alongside the irons that were there. I unlocked the lock; he took one of the shackles, & put it on his leg himself. I then locked the lock again & went away & brought Ware. When Ware came to the gun room, Douglas said, 'Never mind Jack.' The ship's corporal then put Ware in & we left them.

Q^{n}.: Did you say anything to Douglas about the situation in which he was found?

Ans^{r}.: I did not.

Q^{n}.: Was Ware so drunk as to be insensible to any violence (which relates to the charge) offer'd to him?

Ans^{r}.: I think he was.

Q^{n}.: Did he make any reply to you or the corporal while you were confining him?

Ans^{r}.: No, he was so drunk the ship's corporal was obliged to carry him on his back.

M^{r}. Maggs, Master's Mate, sworn.

Q^{n}. Pros.: Relate to the court what you know respecting the charges against the prisoners.

Ans^{r}.: On or about the 3rd of May, I had the 1st watch on deck. The master at arms came & said he had something very particular to show me, if I wou'd go below with him. I went down & when I came into the berth there was a lantern burning. I saw the prisoners laying in the middle of the berth. Jno. Ware, with his trousers down, lay on his back & Douglas with his trousers unbutton'd, & his privates naked & his left leg over Ware. I immediately return'd on deck & acquainted the officer of the watch with what I had seen.

Q^{n}. C^{t}.: Were the prisoners asleep at the time you saw them in that situation?

Ans^{r}.: They appear'd to me to be asleep, because then I desired the master at arms to rouse them [*sic*], which he tried to do & cou'd not wake them.

Q^{n}. C^{t}.: Did you, at any time that night, see the prisoner Douglas on top of Jno. Ware?

Ans^{r}.: No.

Q^{n}. C^{t}.: Did you see the prisoners after they were order'd to be put in irons?

Ans^{r}.: No.

Q^{n}.: Did you see the prisoners awake that night?

Ans^{r}.: No.

M^{r}. Borasse, the Surgeon, sworn.

Q^{n}. Pros^{r}.: Did you examine the prisoners a few hours after they were confined, by my orders, for the crime alleged against them?

Ans^{r}.: I did on the morn^{g}. of the 4th May between the hours of 8 & 9 o'clock.

Qn. Prosr.: Relate the situation you found them in.

Ans^{r}.: I told Douglas to let down his trousers & draw his foreskin back; the head of his yard was bloody & inflamed. I ask'd him how he came in that situation; he was sullen & gave me no answer. I put the question to him a second time; he was still silent. I gave in charge of the mast^{r}. at arms [*sic*], & sent for Ware. I examined his posteriors, but found nothing but what was natural. M^{r}. McGoring, the Surgeon's Mate, was present.

Q^{n}. C^{t}.: Is it possible for the private parts of Jno. Douglas to be in the state you have described them by entering the body of Ware without apparently injuring the anus of Ware?

Ans^{r}.: I am clearly of opinion it might be.

Here the prosecution closed & prisoners put on their defence.

Both the prisoners said they wou'd not give the court further trouble & beg'd to thro' themselves on the mercy of the court.

The court, having heard the evidence in support of the prosecution & what the prisoners had to offer in their defence & having maturely & deliberately consider'd the whole & every part thereof with the most minute attention, are unanimously of opinion that the charge is not proved against the prisoners, Jno. Harrison and William Harris, but that the complaint made to Captain Jno. Turnor of His Majesty's ship *Trident* by Randal Blake, the principal evidence, is wicked, infamous, malicious & totally unfounded; the court do therefore acquit Jno. Harrison & W^{m}. Harris, & they are hereby acquitted accordingly.

The court is further of opinion that the conduct of the prisoners, Jno. Douglas and Jno. Ware, has been highly indecent, infamous, scandalous, unmanly, unworthy of British seamen, in derogation of God's honour & corruption of good manners.

But as the charge exhibited against the said Jno. Douglas & Jno. Ware is not fully proved, the court do acquit them & they are hereby acquitted accordingly. …

The court was open'd, the audience admitted, & the sentence passed accordingly. …

78. *Court Martial of Thomas Hubbard and George Hynes*

[ADM 1/ 5355]

Minutes taken at a court martial assembled on board His Majesty's ship *Gladiator* in Portsmouth Harbour on the 10th day of December 1800.

Present

John Holloway, Esq[r]., Rear Admiral of the White and second officer in command of His Majesty's ships and vessels at Portsmouth and Spithead, President.

Captain	Captain
Thomas Totty	William Dormett
John Sutton	Richard Grindall
Francis Pickmore	The Right Honble Lord Viscount Garlies
Philip Charles Durham	The Right Honble Lord Henry Paulet
John Monkton	James Bowen
Charles Clark Searle	Sir. Edward Berry, Kn[t].

The prisoners were brought in and audience admitted.

The order from the Right Honble Lords Commissioners of the Admiralty, dated the 6th day of December instant and directed to the president for the trial of Thomas Hubbard and George Hynes, Seamen belonging to His Majesty's ship *Saint George*, for having committed the unnatural crime of sodomy with each other on the night of the 12th of November 1800, was read.

The president reported to the court that Captains Alan Hyde Gardner, Sir Thomas Williams, Kn[t]., Stephen George Church, and George Parker were absent on Admiralty leave.

The members of the court and the judge advocate then, in open court and before they proceeded to trial, respectively took the several oaths enjoined and directed in and by an Act of Parliament made and passed in the 22d year of the reign of His late Majesty King George the 2nd, entitled *An Act for Amending, Explaining and Reducing into One Act of Parliament the Laws relating to the Government of His Majesty's Ships, Vessels and Forces by Sea*.

Then the letter from Captain Sampson Edwards, commander of His Majesty's ship *Saint George*, dated the 14th of November last, to Admiral the Earl of St. Vincent, K.B., Commander in Chief of a squadron of His Majesty's ships and vessels employed and to be employed in the Channel Soundings, &c., containing the charge, was read, and the witnesses were ordered to withdraw and attend their examinations separately, which they did as follows:

Thomas White, Master at Arms belonging to His Majesty's ship *Saint George*, called in and sworn.

Captain Edwards asked:

Q. Have you heard the charges read?

A. Yes.

Q. Do you know the prisoner?

A. Yes.

Q. Are those the two men mentioned in the charge?

A. Yes, Thomas Hubbard, the young man, and George Hynes, the black man.

Q. Relate to the court what made you go to the prisoner's hammock on the night of the 12th November last and what you saw when you came there.

A. On the 12th of November, I was in my berth about three quarters after 9 o'clock in the evening. Peter Melville, the Marine, came to me, and said, 'Mr. White, I want you.' I immediately took my lantern to go with him; he said, 'You must come in the dark.' I said I would not. I went a little way out of my berth and asked him what was the matter. He said he believed there was sodomy committing under the forecastle. I put my lantern down and went with him in the dark; as soon as I got to the top of the ladder, he said, 'Now keep a soft foot and I'll lead you to the place.' Accordingly, he led me to the hammock where the prisoners both were. I and he remained there for the space of half a minute, as near as I can speak, and then we both stole away as easy as we could. I came down below my berth and took my lantern, and put it in a bag; we went up together again and I hid the light as much as I possibly could and came on the upper deck and I told him to go to the starboard side. Accordingly, he did, and I went the larboard. The hammock hung abaft the foremast, right a mid ships. When I got there, I got under the hammock, with my lantern concealed in my bag. I remained there about half a minute and heard some people in the hammock and put my hand up and felt a great moving, but could not tell whether it was man or woman at first. Then, immediately, I got the mouth of my bag open, ready to haul my lantern out and, with my right hand, held it up to the hammock. I immediately fastened Thomas Hubbard by the neck. I called for assistance immediately; he tried to get away and I then found that George Hynes was under him, naked on his belly. On his trying to slue himself on one side in the hammock, I saw Thomas Hubbard's yard come from between the backside of George Hynes. I held him fast by the neck and got him out and made him button his trousers up. At that time George Hynes had made his escape out of the hammock; I immediately took Thomas Hubbard on the quarterdeck and related to my officer the situation I caught him in and he ordered him to be confined and I put him in irons.

Q. Who was with you besides?

A. Peter Melville, at the latter part of the business; Foster McDonald and Thomas White came to my assistance.

The court asked:

Q. When you discovered the prisoners in the situation you have described, did any person come immediately to your assistance so as fully to discover the unnatural act they were committing?

A. Yes, Peter Melville.

Q. You have said that George Hynes made his escape from the hammock, do you upon your oath solemnly swear that the black man, the prisoner, was the person you have described to be committing that horrid and abominable crime?

A. Yes, I positively swear that is the man.

Q. What reasons have you for saying he is the man?

A. Because he spoke to me, saying 'No, Mr. White No;' and I said, 'Oh! You rascal,' saw his face, and cut him over the eye with the bottom of my lantern.

Peter Melville, a Private Marine belonging to the *Saint George*, called in and sworn.

Captain Edwards asked:

Q. Do you know the prisoners?

A. Yes, and he pointed them out.

Q. Are those the 2 men named in the charge?

A. Yes.

Q. Relate to the court what you saw on the night of the 12th of November and your reasons for going down to the master at arms?

A. I was up under the forecastle, standing there in the dark. I heard something crack. Then I heard a whisper, but what it was I did not know. Then I drew very softly towards it. Then I heard one say to the other, 'You did not do it so well to me as I do it to you.' I stood there for some considerable minutes. Then I went down for the master at arms and he came up with me with a lantern in a bag. Then he told me to go to the starboard side and he would go on the larboard. Then we came under the same hammock where I had heard the noise and speaking. He pulled his lantern out of the bag; and then I saw Hubbard fall off from the top of George Hynes, as tho' he was intoxicated with liquor. Then I saw his tool come out of his fundament.

Q. Did either of the prisoners attempt to get away?

A. Yes, George Hynes got away on the starboard side.

Q. Could he afterwards be found?

A. No, he was not found till the next morning.

The court asked:

Q. In what situation was the light held and by whom, that you discovered the prisoners in the unnatural crime you have described?

A. By the master at arms, who held the light up over the hammock.

Q. Do you positively swear that you did plainly see the prisoners in the act you have described?

A. Yes.

Q. Was any other person, but the master at arms, so near as to have been witness of the same?

A. He sung out for people to come and see, saying, 'Come and look, come and look.' Tho[s] White (3rd) came and Alexander McDonold, Quarter Master.

Q. Were either of them so near as to enable them to see what you say?

A. I cannot say; I was at the foot of the hammock and they were at the head of the hammock.

Q. Were the prisoners naked?

A. George Hynes was naked all to his frock; Hubbard had his jacket and waistcoat on and his trousers down to his heels.

Q. Were any bed clothes covering them?

A. No.

Q. What was their position?

A. One lay flat on his belly, who was George Hynes, and the other on top of him.

Q. How come you to discover his yard come out of his fundament?

A. I was close to the hammock and saw it.

Q. Did you see the faces of both the prisoners, so as to know them?

A. Yes, without any doubt.

Joseph Foster, Ship's Corporal of the *Saint George*, called in and sworn.

Captain Edwards asked:

Q. Have you heard the charge?

A. Yes.

Q. Do you know the prisoners?

A. Yes.

Q. Are those the two men named in the charge?
A. Yes, Hubbard and Hynes.
Q. Relate to the court what you saw respecting those 2 men on the night of the 12th of November.
A. I was sitting on the lower deck by the fore ladder with my light. I saw the master at arms go up from the starboard side seemingly in a hurry. I thought something was amiss on deck. I followed him shortly. Afterwards, when I came under the forecastle, I saw him standing alongside of the hammock, with his lantern over the hammock, and I stepped to the hammock and held my lantern up and looked into the hammock. I saw Hubbard & Hynes in the hammock, Hubbard lying on his side, Hynes lying inclining more on his belly. I stood back and Hubbard got out of the hammock and his trousers were down and he appeared to be in liquor.
Q. What became of Hynes?
A. While I was looking at Hubbard, he got out of the hammock. I did not see him turn out.
Q. What became of him?
A. He ran off. We could not find him all night; he was found the next morning in the cable tier.

The court asked:

Q. When you saw Hynes in the hammock, do you recollect what dress he had on?
A. I do not; he was very black and dirty.
Q. Do you positively swear the two prisoners were the persons you saw in the hammock together, to which the master at arms had gone to?
A. Yes.
Q. How long had the master at arms exposed his light before you went?
A. I cannot say.
Q. Did you hear the master at arms accuse the two persons of an unnatural crime at that time?
A. Yes.
Q. Did either of them make any reply?
A. No, I did not hear either of them say anything. Hubbard was leaning against the partition and appeared to be in liquor. His trousers were down.
Q. When you went to the hammock, who was there?
A. The master at arms, Thomas White, and McDonold.
Q. When you went to the hammock, which part of it did you go to?
A. To the after side of it; it hung athwart ship.

Alexander McDonold, Quarter Master of the *Saint George*, called in and sworn.

Captain Edwards asked:

Q. Have you heard the charge read?

A. Yes.

Q. Are the prisoners the two men named in the charge?

A. Yes.

Q. Relate to the court all you know respecting the prisoners on the night of the 12th of November.

A. I was going forward to strike the bell about 10 o'clock; coming back again, I met the master at arms, running forward with a lantern in a bag. I went the opposite side and, by the time I got there, the master at arms had the lantern out of the bag, holding it up over the hammock and had hold of the man by the back of the jacket and hauled him out. Hubbard was the man.; he had his trousers down. He made him button his trousers and carried him aft on the quarterdeck.

Q. Did you see Hynes?

A. No, he was got away; I did not see him.

The court asked:

Q. Was there any other hammock near the one the master at arms hauled Hubbard out of?

A. Not that I saw.

Q. Who was with the master at arms?

A. Melville, the Marine.

Q. Can you positively swear that you saw Melville, the Marine, with the master at arms at the time he hauled Hubbard out of the hammock?

A. Yes.

Q. Did you hear the master at arms accuse Hubbard of committing the unnatural crime he is charged with?

A. Yes, when he got hold of his back, he said, 'Damn you. I have catched you at last.' He made no answer.

The prisoners being called on for their defence, Thomas Hubbard said he had nothing to say to the court. He was very much in liquor and knew nothing about it and he gave himself up to the court.

George Hynes denied the charge that the master at arms came down the next morning and asked him if he did not see him in the hammock naked; he said no. The master at arms said he saw him and would take a false oath against him at any time.

Francis Browning, a Seaman belonging to the *Saint George*, called in and sworn.

George Hynes asked:

Q. Was I in the galley on the evening of the 12th?

A. Yes.

Q. Was I intoxicated?

A. Yes, about 6 o'clock.

Q. What is my general character?

A. I know nothing of him, except seeing him in the ship. I can say nothing to his character.

The court asked:

Q. How long have you been shipmate with Hynes?

A. I do not know how long he has belonged to her; I have ever since she has been in commission.

Q. Do you positively swear that you know nothing of his character?

A. I know nothing of him, except seeing him in the ship, frequently a drunken man.

Q. Do you know anything of the prisoner after 6 o'clock?

A. No, not till I saw him in irons the next morning.

Captain Edwards said that, except in this instance, the character of Thomas Hubbard had been very good, a very quiet lad.

William Edwards, a Seaman, called in and sworn.

The prisoner, Thomas Hubbard, asked:

Q. Produce to the court a letter received from my mother, which was produced and read by the judge advocate.

The lad messed with me; he was a good lad till in Torbay last, when he several times got away and got drunk. I enquired why it was and found that one Ferrara gave him liquor. I enquired of Ferrara why he gave him liquor; he said he knew him in the West Indies, but he would not do so any more. He afterwards sent for him again and he got again in liquor and he said he would take him aft to the quarterdeck, but he was persuaded not to do so.

Q. Did you see any intimacy between Hubbard & Hynes?

A. Not until the last time of coming in, when I saw him frequently calling him away.

The court was cleared and agreed that the charge had been proved against the said Thomas Hubbard and George Hynes and did adjudge each of them to suffer death by being hanged by the neck on board such ship of His Majesty at Spithead or in Portsmouth Harbour and at such time as the commissioners for executing the office of Lord High Admiral of Great Britain and Ireland, &c. or any three of them for the time being should direct.

The court was again opened, the prisoners brought in, audience admitted and sentence passed accordingly. …

78A. *Greetham to Nepean*

[ADM 1/5355] Portsmouth, 12th Decr. 1800

… I beg leave to enclose to you the minutes of a court martial assembled at this port for the trial of Thomas Hubbard and George Hynes, Seamen belonging to His Majesty's ship *Saint George*, and also the letter containing the charge. …

[Nepean's Note]
17 Decr. Own to order their execution next Monday.

78B. *Edwards to St. Vincent*

[ADM 1/5355] *Saint George*, Torbay
14 November 1800

… Thomas Hubbard and George Hynes, two Seamen belonging to His Majesty's ship under my command, are accused of committing the unnatural crime of sodomy with each other on the night of the 12th instant and, as the accusation appear'd to me to be true, I am to request your Lordship will be pleased to apply for a court martial on them that they may be tried for the said unnatural crime of sodomy. …

78C. *Greetham to Nepean*

[ADM 1/5355] Portsmouth, 14th Decr. 1800

… The enclosed letter was produced by Thos. Hubbard in his defence at the court martial holden [*sic*] for the trial of him & Geo. Hynes for an unnatural crime, and, by mistake, was not annexed to the minutes. I now transmit it that it may be accompany [*sic*] them. …

78D. *Sarah Hubbard to Thomas Hubbard*

[ADM 1/5355] Sept. the 4

… My dear child, it makes me very happy for to hear that you are safe arrived to Plymouth, but oh what happiness it would be for me to see you once more. Your two poor brothers join in love to you and is so happy to hear that you are alive and well and, poor things, they may well be happy for to hear of you, for, if it was not for what you allow me out of your pay, we must all starve for provisions of all kind is so very dear that we can hardly live. My dear, I went to your master and he told me no, he did not desire anything of you at all, but he is glad for to hear that you are so good to me, and hopes that you will remain so and take care, and save your money against you come home to your poor mother. My dear child, what you desired me to send you, I must not send it. Your aunt and cousins and all friends desires their kind love to you and wishes you safe home again to me. I have not heard anything of your poor cousin Harry since he sail out of Plymouth, which is ever since you went first aboard the *Saint George* and I be glad if you will let me know if the *Athemena* [?] should arrive there before you leave it. I heard of you by the paper, but I do not hear anything of him. I hear that your cousin George is gone with his regiment to Weymouth on account of the Royal Family being there. So I have no more to say now, but my prays to God for to protect you all and send you all safe home to me again and soon. From your loving mother till death. …

79. *Court Martial of Isaac Wilson*

[ADM 1/5395]

Minutes of proceedings at a court martial held on board His Majesty's ship *Salvador del Mundo* in Hamoaze on Saturday the 1st day of April 1809.

Present

John Sutton Esqr., Rear Admiral of the Red and second officer in the command of His Majesty's ships and vessels at Plymouth, President.

Captains

Thomas Wolley	Henry Hotham
John Bligh	Sir Thos Masterman Hardy, Bart.
Zachary Mudge	John Serrell
The Hon. George Poulett	

George Eastlake Junr.
officiating Judge Advocate

Being all the admirals and captains of post ships then and there present, next in seniority to the president, except Capt. Charles Worsley Boys of His Majesty's ship *Statira* who was absent on Admiralty leave.

The prisoner, Isaac Wilson, Seaman of His Majesty's sloop *Orestes*, was brought into court and the witnesses and audience admitted.
Read – The order of the Right Hon. the Lords Commissioners of the Admiralty, dated the 27th day of March 1809, directed to the president to

try the said Isaac Wilson for having committed the unnatural crime of sodomy on a goat.
Read – The warrant appointing a judge advocate.
Then the members of the court & judge advocate, in open court and before they proceeded to trial, respectively took the oaths directed by Act of Parliament passed in the 22d year of the reign of King George the Second.
Read – The letter of charge from Capt. J R Lapenotiere of His Majesty's ship *Orestes* to Admiral Young, Commander in Chief at Plymouth, as follows:

HMS *Orestes*, Plym°. Sound, 24 Mch 1809

… I am to beg you will be pleased to apply to the Lords Commiss^{rs}. of the Admiralty to order a court martial to be held on Isaac Wilson, (Seaman) belonging to the sloop I have the honour to command, for having committed the unnatural crime of sodomy on a goat in the goat house on the evening of 31st of January 1809. …

All the witnesses, except the first to be sworn, being then ordered to withdraw and to attend their examinations separately, they all withdrew accordingly and the court proceeded to trial as follows:

Evidence in support of the charge

Thomas Blinkhorn, Corporal of Marines serving on board His Majesty's ship *Orestes*, sworn & examined as follows:

Pro. Relate what you know respecting the charge against the prisoner.

A. On the evening of the 31 of Janry last, about 10 minutes before 8 o'clock, I was standing at the main hatchway and, hearing a goat making a noise, I thought that she was dying. I went up on deck on the starboard side and opened the goat house door, where I found a man lying down all his length in the goat house and with his trousers unbuttoned and his shirt out before and behind. I told the sentry there was a man in the goat house and told the sentry to take charge of him while I went to get a light. And as soon as I found it was the prisoner, I went down the main hatchway and reported it to the sergeant, but I did not see the prisoner in the fact of having any connexion with the goat.

Pro. Did you find the prisoner's shirt and hands all over blood?

A. Yes.

Pro. Was his private parts all over blood?

A. Not that I know of; his shirt was bloody before.

Pro. Was the goat's private parts bleeding?

A. No, very much swelled.

Pro. Did it appear as if violence had been made use of very shortly before?

A. Yes, it did appear such to me.

Pro. Was the prisoner examined soon after you discovered him in that situation and by whom?

A. He was examined by Mr Hewitt, the first Lieutenant.

Co^{t}. When you discovered the prisoner in the goat house, did you take particular notice of the posture that he was found in?

A. Yes, he lay flat on his belly; the goat was standing up in the corner about a foot distant.

Co^{t}. Did you speak to the prisoner then?

A. Yes. I said, 'Who is here?' The prisoner made no answer. The goat house was underneath the booms; it was about 8 feet in length and 3 feet broad. It has a bottom off the deck. I believe it was built purposely for 2 goats.

Co^{t}. By what light did you first see the prisoner?

A. The prisoner hauled himself out before I got a light and the sentry on the gangway (Samuel Smith) said here is the man; it is Isaac Wilson. And then I went back and laid hold of the prisoner by the collar and said, 'It is you, is it' He said nothing.

Co^{t}. How long after the first time you saw the prisoner was he examined?

A. About an hour after.

Co^{t}. Why was he so examined?

A. Because Mr. Hewitt thought he had been guilty of the crime laid to his charge.

Co^{t}. What was the nearest light to you at the time you first saw the prisoner?

A. Nothing but the stars. The prisoner went down the hatchway with his trousers underneath his shirt which was out before and behind.

Co^{t}. What is the prisoner?

A. He was the captain's cook. He mostly looked after the goat to feed it.

Co^{t}. What was the state of the prisoner at the time?

A. He seemed as if he had been drinking, but no wise intoxicated.

The witness withdrew.

Lieut. William Hewitt of His Majesty's sloop *Orestes* sworn & examined as follows:

Pro. What time was it on the 31 of January last that you were informed of the prisoner's being taken out of the goat house?

A. Between 8 and 9 in the evening.

Pro. What steps did you take in consequence?

A. I went on deck and found the prisoner on the starboard side of the main deck. I found his hands and shirt all blood. I asked him how his shirt came so; he said he had the pox. I ordered the goat to be taken out and examined by Taylor, one of the men. The goat was taken out and her private parts appeared to be swelled very much and to be bleeding. By that, I ordered the prisoner in irons, which was done. I ordered the sergeant to strip him of his shirt and bring it to me, which he did.

Pro. Did you order the prisoner's private parts to be examined?

A. I don't recollect.

Pro. What is the height, breadth and length of the goat house?

A. About 7 feet long, 3 feet or more high, a solid bottom and about 4 feet broad. A man can get in, but not to lie his whole length as there is a partition between.

Co[t]. What was the state of the prisoner when you saw him?

A. He appeared to be intoxicated.

Co[t]. Was there a surgeon on board?

A. Yes, but neither the prisoner nor the goat were examined by him as I did not know of his being on board.

Pris. Did I say to you at the time that I had cut my finger?

A. I do not recollect.

The witness withdrew.

Joseph Lilley, Boatswain's Mate belonging to His Majesty's sloop *Orestes*, sworn & examined as follows:

Pro. Did you see the situation of the prisoner after he had been discovered in the goat house on the evening of the 31 of January last?

A. I did; I saw the prisoner after the sergeant had got him in charge between decks and the sergeant took him aft. I went aft also. His trousers were loose at the time. The prisoner was confined, both legs in irons. Afterwards the sergeant, Scantling and myself went on deck to examine the goat; we found her in a very bad state, all blood in her private parts. On coming down again, the prisoner began to tear off the flap of his shirt. We took it off from him at M[r]. Hewitt's request. Afterwards, we seized him with his hands over his head to the cable. The prisoner then asked Scantling to cut his head off.

Pro. Is it customary for any person to go into the goat house to feed the goat?

A. No.

Co^t^. Did you see any blood about the prisoner's hands?

A. Yes, he cut his finger between 4 and 5 o'clock in the afternoon. I saw it bleeding afterwards.

Pro. Was the prisoner's hands bleeding when he was seized?

A. No, the blood was cold upon his hands.

Co^t^. Do you think the blood on his shirt proceeded from the cut of his finger?

A. I cannot think it could come from so small a cut.

The witness withdrew.

James Scantling, Gunner's Mate of His Majesty's sloop *Orestes*, sworn & examined as follows:

Pro. Did you see the prisoner soon after the prisoner was taken out of the goat house?

A. Yes, about 8 o'clock. The sergeant came down and asked if there were any men in the ship to lend him a hand to secure the prisoner; I said there was and went with him. We found the prisoner in the galley; he was going to make his escape by getting up the fore scuttle with his trousers unbuttoned. We seized him and brought him aft under the sentry's care. He was trying to tear the fore part of his shirt and we seized his hands to the cable. After this, he asked me to cut his head off. Then I asked the sergeant to go on deck with a lantern to examine the goat, which he did with Joseph Lilley, Boatswains Mate. We found the goat lying down; she was not cut but swelled and running a stream of blood behind and had every appearance as if some person had had connexion with her. The goat remained in that way for two days or more. The prisoner's hands were bloody; he had cut his finger that afternoon about 5 o'clock. There was a deal of blood, but I did not examine whether his finger was bleeding or not. The prisoner was in the habit of looking after the goat. He is an American Negro.

Pris. Did my finger bleed, when it was cut, pretty much?

A. It did at first.

The witness withdrew.

M^r^. John Callan, Surgeon of His Majesty's sloop *Orestes*, sworn & examined as follows:

Pro. Did you receive my instructions a few days after the confinement of the prisoner to examine and let me know whether he had any venereal complaint?

A. I did and on examining him found there was a small discharge from the penis, but I am not positive that it was venereal. The prisoner was not in the Sick List for that complaint, nor did I give him any medicine.

Pro. Did you report to me that the prisoner had no venereal, but that his complaint was occasioned from filth.

A. I have every reason to believe that the prisoner's complaint was occasioned by filth, but I cannot positively swear it was not venereal. I examined the goat about 12 o'clock on the day following the transaction. I thought the goat's parts appeared irritated.

The witness withdrew.

The evidence in support of the charge being here closed, the prisoner was acquainted thereof and asked if he had anything to offer to the court. The prisoner said: 'On the evening of the 31 of January last about 6 o'clock, I went on deck to dance. When we had done dancing about half past 6, we began skylarking and playing with sticks on deck. I was on Scantling's back; Gibson came behind me and flung me down on a broken caisson by the gun, which cut my finger. I tied my hand up in my shirt. About half after 7, I was making a bed of fresh straw in the goat house for the goat and afterwards I lay down there. Then the goat began trampling on me and I beat her and put her up in one corner. I was in liquor at the time.'

The prisoner having nothing further to offer, the court was cleared and proceeded to deliberate upon and form the sentence.

The court, having very maturely and deliberately weighed and considered the evidence in support of the charge as well as what the prisoner had offered in his behalf, was of opinion that the charge had not been proved against the prisoner, Isaac Wilson, and did in consequence adjudge him to be acquitted.

The court was opened, the prisoner brought in, the witnesses and audience re-admitted and the prisoner acquitted accordingly. …

80. *Court Martial of John Sherwood*

[ADM 1/5426]

Minutes of proceedings at a court martial held on board His Majesty's ship *Argo* in Palermo Bay, the 15th May 1812.

Present

Thomas Francis Fremantle, Esqr., Rear Admiral of the Blue, President.

Captains

Frederick Warren
The Honble. George Heneage Lawrence Dundas
Edward Augustus Down
Benjamin Crispin

Being all the captains of post ships in Palermo Bay, except Captain Markland of His Majesty's ship *Milford*, whose surgeon certified the court (upon oath) his inability to attend through ill health.

The prisoner was brought into court and the evidence and audience admitted.

Read the order of Sir Edward Pellew, Bart., Vice Admiral of the Red and Commander in Chief of His Majesty's ships and vessels employed in the Mediterranean, dated the 25th day of March 1812 directed to Thomas Francis Fremantle, Esqr., Rear Admiral of the Blue, commanding His Majesty's ships and vessels on the coast of Sicily, to try John Sherwood, Seaman belonging to the *Milford*, for having, on the night of the 6th March 1812, been guilty of uncleanness, being detected in an indecent posture with his trousers down in the sheep pen.

Then the members of the court and judge advocate, in open court and before they proceeded to trial, respectively took the oaths enjoined by Act of Parliament.

Read Captain Markland's letter containing the charges against the prisoner.

All the evidence were then ordered to withdraw, except:

Peter Dobbins, who was sworn.

By the court. Relate to the court all you know concerning the charge against the prisoner.

On Friday evening, the 6th of March last, at 7 bells in the first watch. I was ordered to go down with the watch to freshen hawse; after it was done, I was coming up the main ladder. Seeing the grating was laid on very carelessly, I took it off and put it betwixt two guns on the starboard side, and, in going over to the larboard side with my lantern, I observed the sheep pen door open. I went to the sheep pen with the lantern in my right hand; looking in, I saw a man laid upon a sheep with his arm round the sheep's neck, his trousers unbuttoned and partly down his thighs. In looking, I observed his privates close under the sheep's tail. I asked him what he was doing there. He looked at me in the face, but gave me no answer. I told him to get up and come out, for I would take him on the quarter deck. The time he was coming out of the sheep pen, he wanted to speak to me twice. I told him no; if he had anything to say, to speak to the officer of the watch. I immediately took him on the quarter deck, and reported him to M^{r}. Campbell, the officer of the watch.

You are positively certain that the person you saw in the sheep pen, as you have described, was the Prisoner?

An. Yes.

How long have you known the prisoner?

An. About 2 years and a half.

Did you actually see him haul his breeches up?

An. I did not, Sir.

John Merrell sworn.

Relate to the court all you know concerning the charge against the prisoner.

On the night of the 6th or 7th of March last, I was coming along the deck from the head. I perceived something in the sheep pen, which appeared very bulky, and, upon closer examination, perceived a man to be laying down. Immediately, Peter Dobbins came with a lantern. I perceived a man to be laying upon a sheep, with his arms resting on the back of the sheep's neck and his head laying upon his arms. Peter Dobbins immediately told him to come out, and asked who he was. He rose up his head, and got upon his knees. I perceived his trousers to be unbuttoned. He buttoned his trousers, and begun to ask Peter Dobbins what was the matter. He replied, 'Come aft on the quarter deck, and I will tell you.' He immediately came out of the sheep pen and appeared before M^{r}. Campbell on the quarter deck and I was afterwards called for a witness to what I saw.

Did you see the prisoner in the sheep pen before Dobbins?

An. Yes, I did.

Did you speak to the prisoner before Dobbins came up?

An. I did not.

You are positive as to seeing the prisoner in the situation you describe?

I did, Sir.

How long have you known the prisoner?

An. To the best of my knowledge, three years.

Was it your watch upon deck at the time?

Yes, Sir, it was.

What watch are you in?

An. 2nd part, starboard watch.

Is the prisoner in the same watch?

An. Yes, Sir.

Lieutenant John Campbell, sworn.

By the court. Had you the 1st watch on the night of the 6th of March last?

An. Yes.

Relate to the court what you know on the subject of the charge against the prisoner.

About 12 o'clock on Friday night, the 6th of March last, Peter Dobbins (then B^{o}. Mte.) came aft and reported to me having seen the prisoner in the sheep pen, laying fore and aft on the sheep. I sent for the master at arms and ordered the prisoner under the sentinel's charge at the gun room door. I asked Peter Dobbins who else had seen the prisoner in this state; he told me John Merrill. I sent for him and asked him what he had seen of the business. He told me he had seen the prisoner by the light of the boatswain mate's lantern laying fore and aft the sheep with his arms round the beast's neck. I made the 1st lieutenant acquainted with the circumstances, who ordered the prisoner in irons.

What state was the prisoner in, when he was brought aft?

An. He was perfectly sober, but very much confused. He had his clothes on, but his feet were all over sheep's dung.

The prosecution being closed, the prisoner was allowed to make his defence, which he did in the following words:

Friday, 6th March

… I was drinking greatest part of the afternoon, being my birthday. I saved my wine on purpose. At night I took my wine up amidships on the forecastle and was drinking till it came to rain very hard. I came down in the galley; there I was drinking till near 10 o'clock. I went then and lay myself down between two guns on the half deck, the starboard side. The place where I lay was very wet. I was very cold, all of a shiver, for that reason I could not sleep. I was that way about a quarter of an hour. I then got up, and tried to walk backwards and forwards on the main deck. I staggered about, and fell down several times in the wet and dirt, then was afraid the master of arms would see me and take me aft. I rested myself against one of the guns, and considered within myself where I should go to to get out of his way. I did not like to go below because it was my watch on deck. On being near to the sheep pen, I thought of getting in there. Accordingly, I went in, laid my head on one of the sheep and went to sleep. When I waked, I wanted to make water very bad. I had begun to make water in my trousers, which I suppose waked me. I unbuttoned my trousers and made water. The while I was making water a man came to the sheep pen and looked in, which I suppose was Dobbins. Now if I had attempted to do such a thing or had such thoughts in my head, I had plenty of time to be on my guard, for he went away; but me thinking no harm and having no ill thoughts in my head, I kept on making water. And I had hardly done before Dobbins came with a light, and spoke to me. Just as I was with my trousers unbuttoned, I was on my knees with my one hand on the sheep, keeping myself up, for my head was very heavy indeed, and being half asleep and stupid, I could scarce keep myself up. I was going to lay down again, and I dare say, I should have been there till morning had he not disturbed me. That was the situation he found me in and him, seeing me in that posture and not knowing me to be drunk, thought immediately that I was doing a thing I ought not to do. But as for my doing anything to the sheep or attempting so to do, I had not. By Him that made me, I am entirely too fond of a woman ever to have such thoughts in my head. I have had a woman several times on board since we have been in Palermo and I had a Dollar given me that same day and I certainly should have taken a girl in that night, if I had not been intoxicated. 'Tis a thing I detest, and if I was guilty, it would be of little use me saying anything. But as I know myself innocent and clear of the crime that is laid against me, I don't think of myself wrong in speaking in my own defence. Now gentlemen, if I was to say I was guilty or attempted to do such a thing, I should belie myself and that I don't suppose you would wish me to do. …

At the request of the prisoner, the following persons were called in and examined:

Richard Williams, Seaman, sworn.

By the prisoner. Did you see me on the night of the 6th March?

An. Yes; at 9 o'clock on the forecastle, I asked him to come below, seeing him in liquor. It was his watch on deck and my watch below. He told me he would, for he had been in the head to make water. I went below then and did not see him afterwards.

James Irvine, Seaman, sworn.

What time did you see the prisoner on the 6th of March?

An. The last time I saw him was about 10 o'clock; he appeared to me to be very much in liquor.

How long have you known the prisoner?

An. About 2½ years now.

Do you mess with him?

An. No, Sir.

Jeremiah McCarty, Seaman, sworn.

How long have you known the prisoner?

An. About twelve month.

Where does he do his duty?

An. In the foretop.

What is his character and what is your opinion of the man as far as you have been able to judge of him?

An. Always very sober and attentive to his duty.

Didn't he belong to one of the boats?

He belonged to the barge.

Have you ever heard anything to the prejudice of the prisoner before the charge that is now laid against him?

An. I have not.

M^{r}. W^{m}. Scarth, Boatswain, sworn.

What was the last time you saw the prisoner on the night of the 6th March last?

An. Betwixt 8 and 9 o'clock, he appeared to me to be drunk.

Lieutenant Othuel Mawdesly sworn.

Is the prisoner in your division?

An. Yes.

What is his character as far as it has come under your inspection?

An. I have known him for 10 months, during which time I know of no complaint whatever against him.

Joseph Gibson, Master at Arms, sworn.

How long have you known the prisoner?

An. About 2 years and 9 months, or thereabout.

What is his character in the ship?

An. I never knew him to be guilty of anything, except getting groggy sometimes.

When you took charge of the prisoner on the 6th of March at 7 bells, was he drunk or sober?

An. I considered him sober.

The prisoner having no further evidence to call on, the court (being cleared) proceeded to deliberate on the sentence, which, after some deliberation, was formed as follows:

'The court, having heard the evidence on the part of the prosecution, and what the prisoner had to offer in his defence and maturely and deliberately considered the whole, is of opinion that the charge against the said John Sherwood is proved, and doth adjudge him to receive one hundred lashes on his bare back with a cat of nine tails on board His Majesty's ship *Milford*, at such time and in such proportions as the senior officer of His Majesty's ships and vessels (for the time being) in Sicily may think proper; and he is hereby sentenced accordingly.'

. . .

3

NAVAL CRIMES

As its title suggests, the present chapter is devoted to naval crimes. Naval crimes amounted to the lion's share of the offences tried by the courts martial in the volumes in the sample. Of the 1,596 violations of the Articles of War mentioned in these volumes, 1,241, or almost 78 per cent, fall within this category. At the same time, of the 1,149 defendants named in the sample, 533, or slightly more than 43 per cent, were tried exclusively for naval infractions.

It is all well and good to say that 43 per cent of the men tried by courts martial in the volumes in the sample were arraigned exclusively for naval infractions, but what were naval crimes? Naval crimes can be defined as those offences that were illegal only in the context of a maritime fighting force. Thus the transcripts in this chapter deal with transgressions such as desertion and absence without leave [81–94], mutiny [95–8], mutinous expressions and sedition [99–101], disobedience of orders [102–3], contempt, insolence and disrespect [104–5], neglect of duty [106–7], loss of ship and grounding [108–12], unofficerlike conduct [113–14] and brutality [115–16].

Charges of desertion or absence without leave were the most frequent naval crimes mentioned in the sample, amounting to 28 per cent of all offences in this category. Mutiny constituted almost 16 per cent of the allegations, with mutinous expressions accounting for approximately 4 per cent more. This percentage for mutiny is a bit misleading because three-quarters of the indictments for the said offence resulted from just nine incidents. Contempt, insolence and disrespect made up 13.6 per cent of the total, disobedience of orders 11 per cent and neglect of duty another 9.4 per cent. Loss of ship or grounding came to approximately 10 per cent of the aggregate, with unofficerlike behaviour being 4.7 per cent of the sum and brutality constituting a little more than 3 per cent.[1]

Trials for breaches of the Articles of War such as failure to join battle, collisions between ships and cowardice are not included in this chapter because the few cases to be found between 1793 and 1815 either exceed the limitations established in the Introduction or are more appropriate in another chapter.[2] For example, the transcript of the court martial of Lieutenants William Forbes Leith and Robert F Atkins, who were tried jointly on 7 May 1812 for the collision of the *Repulse* and the *Bombay*, is 45 pages long.[3] Similarly, there is no adjudication en masse resulting from a mutiny aboard a large ship because the transcripts generated by such courts martial commonly surpass 100 pages. The inquiry into the conduct of the seventeen men accused of the mutiny on board the *Defiance*, which took place from 20 January to 11 February 1796, is 273 pages long.[4] Still, despite these restrictions, the documents which follow provide the reader with a sense of the meaning of the majority of naval crimes.

[1]The raw numbers are:

Desertion/absence	349
Mutiny	196
Mutinous expressions	44
Contempt, insolence, disrespect	170
Disobedience of orders	136
Neglect of duty	110
Loss of ship/grounding	121
Unofficerlike behaviour	59
Brutality	39
Miscellaneous	17
Total naval offences	1,241

[2]See document 8.

[3]ADM 1/5426.

[4]ADM 1/5334.

DESERTION AND ABSENCE WITHOUT LEAVE

81. *Court Martial of Michael Jenking*

[ADM 1/5330]

Minutes of proceedings at a court martial held onboard His Majesty's ship the *Vengeance* in Carlisle Bay, Barbados on the 27th day of January 1794.

Present

Charles Thompson, Esq[r], Commodore and second officer in command &c, &ca., President

Captains

John Henry	George Grey
Henry Powlett	Sanford Tatham

The prisoner was brought into court and the evidence and audience admitted.

Read the order of Sir John Jervis, K.B., Commander in Chief, &c[a]., &c[a]., &c[a]., dated the 26th January 1794, directed to Charles Thompson, Esq[r] & second officer &c[a]., &c[a]. to try Michael Jenking, who went on shore upon leave on the 16th Oct[r] last, but did not return to the ship altho' he was ordered not to absent himself as she was under sailing orders.

Then the members of the court & judge advocate, in open court and before they proceeded to trial respectively took the oaths, directed by Act of Parliament made & passed in the 22d year of the reign of His late Majesty King George the Second entitled an *Act for Amending, Explaining and Reducing into One Act of Parliament the Laws Relating to the Government of His Majesty's Ships, Vessels & Forces at Sea.*

A letter from Captain J. Markham, Commander of His Majesty's ship the *Blonde* to Sir John Jervis, K.B., Vice Admiral of the Blue, Commander in Chief, &c[a]., &c[a]., &c[a]. was read as follows:

Blonde, Carlisle Bay, Barbados
Jan[ry] 26th 1794

… In consequence of the letter which I had the honour of writing to you on the 26th of October 1793, at Spithead, stating that M[r]. Michael Jenking, Master of His Majesty's ship the *Blonde* under my command, went on shore upon leave on the sixteenth of the said month, but did not return to the ship, altho' he was ordered not to absent himself, as she was under sailing orders, and that thereby His Majesty's service was delayed; I now find that he is thereupon sent out a prisoner and now [is?] in confinement on board His Majesty's ship *Blonde*, I request you will be pleased to order a court martial upon him as soon as it may be convenient. …

All the evidences were ordered to withdraw out of the court, except Ant[y] Ponsonby, Lieutenant, who was sworn.

Court. Did you give the prisoner leave to go on shore?

Answer. I did.

Pros[r]. What leave did you give him?

Ans[r]. I don't recollect that I mentioned any particular time, but I expected him onboard next morning.

Pros[r]. Was not the ship known to be under sailing orders at the time?

Ans[r]. She was.

Pros[r]. Did Mr. Jenking make his appearance on board from that time 'till the ship sailed?

Ans[r]. He did not.

Court. What time did he go on shore?

Ans[r]. To the best of my recollection, it was on Tuesday evening, the 15th Oct[r] last.

Pros[r]. On what day did the ship sail?

Ans[r]. On the Sunday following.

Court. Did you during that time hear anything of or from the prisoner?

Ans[r]. No.

Court. Why did you expect the prisoner on board next morning?

Ans[r]. I always understood that I had no power to give leave for more time than twenty four hours.

Court. Did the officers in general understand that also?

Ans[r]. I do not know that there was any particular written order to that effect, but it had been generally custom in the ships that I have served in for officers not to stay longer on shore than twenty four hours without leave from the captain.

Court. Had that been the custom in the *Blonde*?

Ans[r]. No officer belonging to the *Blonde* after we left Long Reach ever slept on shore at all before this, except the third Lieut[t], who went on duty, and myself once by Captain Markham's particular leave.

Court. How long had the master been on board?

Ans[r]. About six weeks or two months, but I don't recollect the exact time.

Pros[r]. Whither [*sic*] at this time the ship, being under sailing orders, it was not considered as a particular indulgence granted to the master to sleep out of the ship at all, on account of his long absence from his wife & family the [*sic*] residing at Portsmouth?

Ans[r]. In consequence of his long absence from his family, I always gave him leave to sleep on shore when the duty of the ship would permit it.

Court. Did you give him leave by the captain's desire in consequence of his long absence?

Ans[r]. To the best of my recollection Capt. Markham told me I might let him go on shore when he could be spared from the ship or words to that effect.

Court. Did you conceive that as an indulgence to the master?

Ans[r]. I did not conceive it an indulgence further than his having a family.

Court. Do you know or have you sufficient reason to suppose that the prisoner conceived the general regulation or custom of the ship that no officer should remain on shore more than twenty four hours, without leave from the captain?

Ans[r]. I cannot positively say that he did.

Court. Do you know that the prisoner knew positively that the ship was under sailing orders?

Ans[r]. It was generally known in the ship.

Rich[d] Symons, Purser, being sworn.

Pros[r]. What time was M[r]. Jenking absent from the ship or on what day?

Ans[r]. To the best of my recollection, he went out of the ship about 4 o'clock [in the] afternoon of the 16th October 1793 on Wednesday.

Pros[r]. Did he make his appearance on board at the any time after that before the ship sailed?

Ans[r]. Not to my knowledge.

Court. What time did the ship sail?

Ans[r]. She sailed on the morning of the 20th [of] the same month.

Captain Carpenter sworn.

Court. Please relate what you know respecting the prisoner's being brought on board the *Boyne*.

Ans[r]. He was brought on board the *Boyne*, then lying at Spithead, by some person from the Admiralty and delivered into my charge as a prisoner. Immediately on Captain Otway's coming on board, I informed him of it; in answer to which, he said that it was the master of the *Blonde* and, whilst he remained on board, was to be a prisoner at large.

Court. Did the person, who brought the prisoner on board, say why he took him and when?

Ans[r]. He showed me his authority for taking him up, but nothing further.

Court. Has the prisoner been considered as a prisoner ever since?

Ans[r]. As a prisoner at large.

Court. You don't recollect the day he was brought on board the *Boyne*?

Ans[r]. I cannot say positively, but I think it was the latter end of October.

John Harris, Master, being sworn.

A logbook being produced and [the witness?] asked by the court if it was the logbook of the *Boyne*.

Ans[r]. The logbook of the *Boyne* kept by me.

It appears by the said logbook that the prisoner went on board the *Boyne* the 28th October as a prisoner.

The prisoner being called upon to make his defence, he called on Captain Markham to say to his behaviour while on board the *Blonde*.

Cap[t]. Markham. During the time that M[r]. Jenking was under my command, his behaviour & conduct were highly meritorious, and he filled his station very much to my satisfaction & his own credit, and I regretted the loss of him very much.

M[r]. Willet being called by the prisoner and asked what he knew of his behaviour while on board the *Scorpion*.

M[r]. Willet. I was on board the *Scorpion* from the 21st of Sept[r] 1791 to the 4th of April following from England to the coast of Africa and to the West Indies with Captain Holwell and never knew a man behave with more propriety as an officer, and correctness as a man – so much so that Captain Holwell always asked him into the cabin to breakfast, dine & sup with us.

Barth[w] James, Lieutenant, being sworn.

Prisoner. Do you recollect our meeting near the Minories in London on the afternoon about the 19th of October 1793?

Ans[r]. I did meet the prisoner about that time.

Prisoner. Do you recollect the conversation that then passed between us?

Ans[r]. He told me he was going to Portsmouth to join his ship, and asked if I had any commands to M[r]. Moss, that he had passed for a fourth rate and was very anxious to get down as he was apprehensive he should otherwise be left behind.

The court, having very maturely considered the evidence produced and what the prisoner alleged in his defence, are of opinion that the charge has been fully proved. In consequence thereof the court do adjudge him to be dismissed as Master of His Majesty's ship the *Blonde* and to serve as master in a sloop of war for such time as the commander in chief shall be pleased to direct.

The court was opened, audience admitted and sentence passed accordingly. …

82. *Court Martial of Robert Tillford*

[ADM 1/5334]

Minutes of the proceedings at a court martial held onboard His Majesty's ship *Britannia* the 25th day of January 1796.

Present

Sir Hyde Parker, Kn^{t}., Vice Admiral of the Red, etc., President

V.A. Robert Linzee	V.A. Honble W^{m}. Waldgrave
Captn. Robert Caulder, 1st Captain of the Fleet	Captain T. L. Frederick
Captain Jno. Pakenham	Captn. Cuthb^{t}. Collingwood
Captn. Ja^{s}. Richd. Dacres	Captn. Jno. Saml. Smith
Captn. Jno. C. Purvis	Captn. Thos. Sotheby
Captn. Thos. Foley	the Rt. Honble. Lord Garlies

The prisoner was brought into court & the evidence and audience admitted.

Read the order of the commander in chief directed to Sir Hyde Parker, Kn^{t}., Vice Admiral of the Red, &c. to try Robert Tillford for deserting from His Majesty's ship *Egmont* at Leghorn, the 28th day of October 1794.

Then the members of the court & judge advocate, in open court, and before they proceeded to trial, respectively took the oaths prescribed by Act of Parliament, made & passed in the 22d year of the reign of George the Second, entitled, *An Act for Explaining, Amending and Reducing into One Act of Parliament the Laws relating to the Government of His Majesty's Ships, Vessels and Forces by Sea* [*sic*].

A letter from Captain John Sutton, Commander of His Majesty's ship *Egmont*, to Sir Jno Jervis, K^{nt}. Bth., Admiral of the Blue and Commander in Chief of His Majesty's ships and vessels employed and to be employed in the Mediterranean was read as follows:

Egmont 24th January 1796
St Fiorenzo Bay

… Robert Tillford, Seaman belonging to His Majesty's ship *Egmont*, having left the launch on duty at Leghorn on the 28th day of October 1794 and deserted from the *Egmont* & not having made his appearance again until the 14th day of January 1796, when he gave himself up (a deserter from the *Egmont*) on board His Majesty's ship *Captain*, I have to request that the said Robert Tillford, Seaman, may be tried by a court martial for the crime exhibited against him. …

All the evidences were ordered to withdraw out of court, except Lieutenant Samuel Folville of the *Egmont*, who was sworn.

Prosecutor – Can you swear to the identity of the person of Robert Tillford? Is the prisoner the man?

Answer – He is the man.

Prosecutor – Relate to the court the circumstances of the prisoner's absenting himself when he was under your orders on duty.

Answer – Robert Tillford was one of the crew who went in the launch watering; before it came to our turn to till, Robert Tillford was absent from the boat. I went and looked for him, found him, brought him back to the boat. Before the boat was full, he had absented himself again. I saw no more of him till onboard the *Captain*, when I was sent to fetch him on board the *Egmont*.

Prosecutor – Do you know of the prisoner being in the *Egmont* at any time since his leaving the launch?

Answer – He never was.

Prosecutor – Do you recollect the time that has elapsed since his desertion?

Answer – To the best of my recollection, he deserted last October twelve months.

Lieutenant Folville ordered to withdraw.

Lieutenant Geo. Burdett was next called into court and sworn.

Prosecutor – Can you swear to the identity of the person of Robert Tillford? Is the prisoner the man?

Answer – He is the man.

Prosecutor – Did you not by my order receive Robert Tillford on board the *Egmont*, a prisoner from His Majesty's ship *Captain*, and was directed by me to put him into confinement?

Answer – No; the officer of the watch (Lieu^{t}. Hanwell). I was at dinner in the cabin. I heard you order Lieut. Hanwell to confine him.

Prosecutor – Do you know that the prisoner, Robt. Tillford, had been absent at every muster day from the time of his leaving the launch to the time of his appearing as a prisoner onboard the *Egmont*?

Answer – Yes; I do know that he has been absent at every muster.

Lieu[t]. Geo. Burdett ordered to withdraw.

Jn[o]. Clarke, Captain's Clerk, was next called into court & sworn.

Court – Do you deliver these books into the court as an accurate and correct account of musters, discharges and entries of His Majesty's ship *Egmont*?

Answer – Yes, I do.
Robert Tillford's entry 8 January 1793 from H.M. ship *Cambridge*; deserted 28th October 1794 Leghorn. Re-entered 15 Jan[y] 1796 from the *Captain*.

Court – Is the prisoner the man who has always answered to the name of Robert Tillford, when the ship's company were mustered?

Answer – Yes, he is the man.

M[r]. Jn[o]. Clarke was ordered to withdraw.

M[r]. Thomas Stevens was next called into court and sworn.

Prosecutor – Can you swear to the identity of the person of Robert Tillford? Is the prisoner the man?

Answer – Yes, he is the man.

Prosecutor – Have you seen the prisoner onboard the *Egmont* at any time, or do you know of his being on board since he left the launch at Leghorn in October 1794 until the time of his returning a prisoner onboard the *Egmont*?

Answer – No.

The evidence withdrew.

The Prosecution is closed.

The Prisoner to Capt. L. Smith

Did I not deliver myself up a prisoner on board the *Captain*, immediately she came to an anchor here and say I would have done it before but I was afraid of being put in confinement?

Answer – Yes, you did deliver yourself up immediately upon anchoring.

The prisoner having nothing further to offer in his defence, the court was cleared and proceeded to deliberate upon and form the sentence.

The court, having carefully and deliberately weighed and considered the evidence produced and what the prisoner alleged in his defence, are of opinion that the charge is fully proved; and, they do therefore adjudge the said Robert Tillford to receive two hundred lashes on his bare back, with a cat of nine tails, alongside such of His Majesty's ships at such times and in such proportions as the commander in chief shall think proper to direct; & he is hereby sentenced accordingly. …

83. *Court Martial of John Maloney*

[ADM 1/5337]

Proceedings of a court martial assembled and held on board His Majesty's ship *La Minerve*, this 30th day of December 1796, by order of Horatio Nelson, Esqr., Commodore of a squadron of His Majesty's ships &^{c}., &^{c}., &^{c}., to try John Maloney, Seaman belonging to His Majesty's sloop *Speedy* for charges exhibited against him by Captain Thomas Elphinstone, Commander of the said sloop, for frequent desertion and attempting to desert from the said sloop at Naples on the 15th day of November 1796.

Present
Horatio Nelson, Esqr., Commodore &^{c}., &^{c}., &^{c}., President.
Captain George Cockburn
Captain D'Arcy Preston
Captain Philip Wodehouse
Captain Richard Retalick
John P. Castang appointed to officiate as Deputy Judge Advocate.
Being all duly sworn, according to Act of Parliament.

Lieutenant William Vosper sworn.

Quest^{n}. Court Relate to the court what you know respecting the charges against the prisoner.

Answ^{r}. I recollect that the prisoner deserted from the *Speedy* once at Leghorn, once at Bonifaccio, and left the boat once at Civita Vechia. When he left the sloop at Naples, I was not on board.

Quest^{n}. Do you recollect in what manner the prisoner deserted from the *Speedy* at Leghorn?

Answ^{r}. He took the boat with, I believe, two other seamen, and he was found on board the *Austrea* privateer some time after.

Quest^{n}. How do you know that the prisoner took a boat from the *Speedy*?

Answ^{r}. To the best of my recollection, he said after he was taken that he took away the launch with other seamen, or words to that purpose.

Quest^{n}. Did the *Speedy* loose her launch in the night when you supposed the prisoner deserted?
Answ^{r}. Yes.
Quest^{n}. When did you see the prisoner last on board the *Speedy* before his desertion, and what was the time between your having last seen him and the time he was missing from the *Speedy*?
Answ^{r}. I do not recollect when I saw the prisoner last before his desertion, but at daylight after the launch was missing, the prisoner was not on board.
Quest^{n}. Did you take him out of the *Austrea* privateer?
Answ^{r}. Yes.
Quest^{n}. Relate to the court what you know of the prisoner's desertion at Bonifaccio.
Answ^{r}. I know that he did desert from the sloop when the launch was missing; he was not to be found on board.
Quest^{n}. How long afterwards was it that you saw the prisoner?
Answ^{r}. I believe only a few days before he was taken by a Corsican guard.
Quest^{n}. Are you sure that the prisoner might not have been left on shore by accident?
Answ^{r}. If he had been left by accident, he might have hailed for a boat, or have come off in a shore boat, as there are plenty of them at Bonifacio, and the ship was laying close to the shore.
Quest^{n}. Do you know of any other time that the prisoner deserted from the *Speedy*?
Answ^{r}. He left the boat when on shore at Civita Vechia on duty, and was taken up by myself, I believe on the next day or the day after.
Quest^{n}. Where was he taken up?
Answ^{r}. He was laying drunk and asleep without the town.
Quest^{n}. Do you think that the prisoner intended to desert from the sloop at Civita Vechia?
Answ^{r}. It might probably have been from his being drunk that he left the boat.
Quest^{n}. Do you know anything of the prisoner's having attempted to desert at Naples on the 15th of Novr. last?
Answ^{r}. No, I was on shore at that time.
Quest^{n}. Was the *Speedy*'s launch run away with at Bonifacio?
Answ^{r}. Yes, she was missing in the morning.

Quest. Are you sure that she was moored to the ship the night before?

Answ^{r}. I can not be positive, but I have reason to suppose she was.

Quest^{n}. Do you recollect the time from the prisoner's being missing to the time of his being brought on board again?

Answ^{r}. I believe it was two or three days; I went on shore to the governor, by the captain's orders, to request that a guard might be sent to look after him.

Quest^{n}. Did you ever hear where the guard took him up?

Answ^{r}. I have heard that he was taken at Porto Vechio.

M^{r}. Thomas Sheraton sworn.

Court Relate to the court what you know respecting the charges against the prisoner.

Answ^{r}. On the 22nd of May 1795 at Bonifaccio when the prisoner was one of the sentinels, he took away the boat, and was brought back by a Corsican guard. And on the 1st of Octr. at Leghorn, he was one of five that took away the boat. Thereafter that, we took him out of the *Austrea* privateer at Vado; he likewise left the launch at Civita Vechia, and was taken by Lieutenant Vosper. On the 15th day of November when at Naples, I was commanding officer, and, when at dinner, the prisoner with four more went from the sloop in a shore boat without my knowledge. I heard some people on deck say that some men had deserted from the ship; I immediately ran on deck and ordered the sentinels to fire at them. I likewise hailed a merchant ship near to us and ordered them to fire and to go after them, as we had no boat, which they did and brought them back.

Quest^{n}. How do you know that the prisoner took away the boat on the 22d of May 1795.

Answ^{r}. He was missed in the morning when the launch was missed, and I therefore supposed he had taken the launch.

Quest^{n}. In what manner did he return to the ship again?

Answ^{r}. He was brought on board by a guard of soldiers and delivered up as a prisoner.

Quest^{n}. How long was he absent at Bonifaccio from the sloop?

Answ^{r}. I believe he was brought on board the next day.

Quest^{n}. When you lost your launch at Leghorn, did you understand that she was taken away from the sloop or that she might have broke adrift?

Answ^{r}. As there was five men missing from the sloop, we were certain that the launch was taken by them.

Quest^{n}. Are you sure that the prisoner was one of the five men missing after the launch was taken away?

Answ^{r}. Yes, I am.

Quest^{n}. Was the prisoner brought out of the *Austrea* privateer as a deserter?

Answ^{r}. Yes.

Quest^{n}. Did the prisoner receive any punishment for having deserted at Leghorn?

Answ^{r}. Yes.

Quest^{n}. What punishment?

Answ^{r}. I do not recollect, but I believe three dozen.

Quest^{n}. Are you perfectly sure that the prisoner was punished?

Answ^{r}. Yes.

Quest^{n}. Did you fire at the boat from the *Speedy*?

Answ^{r}. Yes.

Quest^{n}. Did you hail the boat from the *Speedy*?

Answ^{r}. Yes, before we fired.

Quest^{n}. What orders did you give to the people who had taken the shore boat?

Answ^{r}. To come back, or I would fire at them.

Quest^{n}. Was the prisoner one of those people?

Answ^{r}. Yes.

Quest^{n}. What answer did they make you and what was their proceedings?

Answ^{r}. They gave me no answer; they pulled toward the shore. I then ordered the sentinel to fire.

Quest^{n}. Did the firing induce them to come back?

Answ^{r}. I believe not; the merchantman threatened to fire at them and sent his boat, who brought them back.

Quest^{n}. When the merchantman's boat was rowing after them, did the prisoner and others in the boat make any effort to escape from them?

Answ^{r}. I cannot say; the merchant ship was between me and the shore.

Quest^{n}. When the boat was brought back in which the prisoner was, had he any of his clothes with him?

Answ^{r}. I cannot say; they came back in the merchantman's boat.

Quest^{n}. Do you know any further particular circumstances relative to the prisoner's going away with the boat at Naples than what you have related?

Answ^{r}. No.

M^{r}. George Day sworn.

Quest^{n}. How long have you been in the *Speedy*?

Answ^{r}. I came on board on the 12th day of Feby 1796.

Quest^{n}. Court Relate to the court what you know of the prisoner's having attempted to desert from the *Speedy* at Naples on the 15th day of November last?

Answ^{r}. On the 15th of November last, I was lying below asleep in my cabin. I heard a boy call out at the hatchway; I then ran upon deck, and seeing a boat go from under the bows, the master then ordered the sentinel to fire at the boat, but his musket would not go off at the time. I then went to arm chest [*sic*] on the quarter deck, and loaded a musket and fired at the boat. Mr. Sheraton, the Master, then hailed a merchant brig that was lying alongside of us and ordered him to bring the boat too; he immediately did so, and brought them on board.

Quest. Was the prisoner one of the people brought on board by the merchantman's boat?

Answ^{r}. Yes.

Quest^{n}. Do you know if the prisoner had his clothes with him?

Answ^{r}. I don't know; I did not see any. I supposed he had not.

Quest^{n}. Did you hear the boat hailed and ordered to come back?

Answ^{r}. Yes.

Quest^{n}. Did the boat return, or what did she do?

Answ^{r}. They did not offer to come back till they stopped them from the merchantman.

Quest^{n}. Was the prisoner drunk or sober?

Answ^{r}. I don't think he was drunk.

Quest^{n}. Did the prisoner say anything when he was brought on board by the merchantman's boat?

Answ^{r}. No, he never spoke.

The prosecution being closed, the prisoner could not call upon any person to speak to his character.

The court, having heard all the evidence in support of the charges, as well as what the prisoner had to offer in his defence, is of opinion that all the charges are most fully proved, and do therefore adjudge the said John Maloney to suffer death by being hanged by the neck at the fore yard arm (till he is dead) of such one of His Majesty's ships as the commander in chief of His Majesty's fleet in the Mediterranean shall direct.

And the said John Maloney is hereby sentenced to be hanged by the neck till he is dead accordingly. …

83A. *Elphinstone to Nelson*

[ADM 1/5337]

Speedy, Port Ferrero
December 26th 1796

… I have to request you will be pleased to order a court martial on Jno. Maloney, Seaman belonging to His Majesty's ship under my command, for frequent desertion and attempting to desert from the said sloop at Naples the 15th day of Novem^{r}. last. …

84. *Court Martial of John Jacobs*

[ADM 1/5338]

Minutes of the proceedings of a court martial held on board His Majesty's ship *Bellona*, Fort Royal Bay, Martinique, 27th day of March 1797, for the trial of John Jacobs, Seaman belonging to His Majesty's ship *Eurus*, for desertion from that ship on or about the 5th of December last by going from the boat when sent to the dockyard on duty, vizt.:

Present

George Wilson, Esqr., Captain of His Majesty's ship *Bellona* and senior captain of His Majesty's ships and vessels in Fort Royal Bay, Martinique, President.

Thos. M. Russel	Thos. Totty
W^{m}. Caley	John Dilkes
Chas. Sidney Davers	Thos. Harvey

The prisoner being brought into court, and evidence and audience admitted, read the order of Henry Harvey, Esqr., Rear Admiral of the Red and Commander in Chief of His Majesty's ships and vessels employed and to be employed at Barbados and the Leeward Islands and in the seas adjacent, dated 25th instant., directed to George Wilson, Esqr., Captain of His Majesty's ship *Bellona* and senior captain of His Majesty's ships and vessels in Fort Royal Bay, Martinique. The members of the court and judge advocate, in open court and before they proceeded to trial, respectively took the oaths enjoined by Act of Parliament. The letter from Captain James Ross[1] containing the charges was read as follows, viz[t].:

Eurus, Fort Royal Bay,
Martinique, 22d March 1797.

… John Jacobs, Seaman belonging to His Majesty's ship under my command, having on or about the 5th December last, deserted from the boat when sent to the dockyard on duty and, having since entered into His Majesty's service, and taken part of the new levied Bounty for the town of Portsea, was sent in a draught of men to complete the complement of the *Eurus* under the name of John Francis; he was however immediately recognized and put in confinement. I have therefore to request that you will be pleased to order a court martial may be held to try the said John Jacobs for the said offences.

…

All the evidences ordered to withdraw, except M[r]. James Milner, Clerk, who was sworn.

Pros[r]. – Do you know the prisoner?

Ans. – I do.

Pros[r]. – Produce the books, a copy of his enrolment and turn to his entry.

M[r]. Milner did so and the prisoner appeared to be entered the 22d Sept. and received 2.10.0 Bounty, to be chequed the 5th December and returned the 13th following from His Majesty's ship *Royal William* under the name of John Francis and by an attested copy of his enrolment at Portsmouth to have received part of the new levied Bounty of that parish 6th Dec.

Court – Are those produced, the original books kept by you as clerk of the *Eurus*?

Ans[r]. – They are.

Court – Do you know that the enrolment produced is a true copy of the original?

Ans[r]. – It is.

Witness withdrew, and M[r]. Andrew Webster called in and sworn.

[1]This letter is to Rear Admiral Henry Harvey, who was Commander in Chief of the Leeward Islands Station at the time.

Pros[r]. – Do you know the prisoner?
Ans[r]. – Yes.
Pros[r]. – Did he go on shore with you to Portsmouth yard on duty for stores on or about the 5th December 1796?
Ans[r]. – Yes.
Pros[r]. – Did he return on board in the boat?
Ans[r]. – No.
Pros[r]. – Did you see the prisoner on board the *Eurus* at any time between the day of his leaving the boat and his coming on board in the draft of men from the *Royal William* to complete the complement of the ship?
Ans[r]. – No.
Court – You were the officer of that boat?
Ans[r]. – No.
Court – Had the prisoner, to your knowledge, leave to go out of the yard?
Ans[r]. – No, not to my knowledge.
Court – Was there any pains taken to find him about the yard?
Ans[r]. – Yes, by the officer in the boat, who went to look for him.
Court – Was there any other man deserted from the boat at the same time?
Ans[r]. – One man.
Court – How long did the ship stay in port after his desertion?
Ans[r]. – I don't exactly know, about a fortnight.

M[r]. Edward Hunt called in and sworn.

Court – Do you know the prisoner?
Ans[r]. – Yes.
Pros[r]. – Did you go on shore from the *Eurus* on duty to Portsmouth dockyard on or about the 5th December 1796.
Ans[r]. – Yes.
Pros[r]. – Was the prisoner in the boat at the time?
Ans[r]. – Yes.
Pros[r]. – Did he leave the boat whilst on duty?
Ans[r]. – Yes.
Pros[r]. – Did you see the prisoner on board the *Eurus* at any time between the day of his leaving the boat and his coming on board in a draught of men from the *Royal William* to complete the complement of the ship?
Ans[r]. – No.
Court – Had the prisoner to your knowledge leave to go out of the yard?
Ans[r]. – No.

Court – Is the prisoner the same person who belonged to the *Eurus* by the name of John Jacobs and who returned with a draft of men as a volunteer from the *Royal William* by the name of John Francis?

Ans^{r}. – Yes.

M^{r}. Francis Wemyss, the Master, called in and sworn.

Pros^{r}. – Do you know the prisoner?

Ans^{r}. – I do.

Court – Did you go on board the *Royal William* for a draft of men to complete the *Eurus*'s complement on the 13th of December 1796?

Ans^{r}. – I did.

Pros^{r}. – Relate to the court what happened on board the flag ship.

Ans^{r}. – When I came on board the *Royal William*, there were five men ready; the sixth could not be found. He was called several times by the name of Francis. I then observed to the lieutenant that, as the boats were coming very thick on board, the signal for all lieutenants being made, it would be better for me to go on board and send the boat again for the man and I went on board with the five men.

Court – Is the prisoner the same person who belonged to the *Eurus* by the name of Jno. Jacobs and who returned with a draft of men as a volunteer from the *Royal William* by the name of John Francis?

Ans^{r}. – He is.

M^{r}. McKenzie, Midshipman, called in and sworn.

Pros^{r}. – Do you know the prisoner?

Ans^{r}. – Yes, I do.

Pros^{r}. – Did you go on board the *Royal William* in the afternoon on the 13th of December 1796 in order to bring a man from thence under the name of John Francis, who could not be found in the forenoon?

Ansr. – Yes, I did.

Pros^{r}. – What was told you by the officer of the *Royal William* concerning the said John Francis?

Ans^{r}. – That he was found in the morning.

Pros^{r}. – On the prisoner being produced, did you know him to have belonged to the *Eurus* before?

Ans^{r}. – Yes, I did.

Pros^{r}. – Under what name did he pass on board the *Eurus* before?

Ans^{r}. – Under the name of John Jacobs

Pros^{r}. – Did you report the circumstances that occurred on board the *Royal William* on your return to the *Eurus*?

Ans^{r}. – Yes, I reported it to the commanding officer.

Witness ordered to withdraw, and Robert Luke, Lm.,[1] called in and sworn.

Pros^{r}. – Do you know the prisoner?

Ans^{r}. – Yes.

Pros^{r}. – Were you in the boat on or about the 5th Decr. 1796 when sent on shore on duty to Portsmouth dockyard?

Ans^{r}. – Yes.

Pros^{r}. – Was the prisoner one of the boat's crew?

Ans^{r}. – Yes.

Pros^{r}. – Did he leave the boat while on duty?

Ans^{r}. – Yes.

Pros^{r}. – Did the prisoner return on board in the boat?

Ans^{r}. – No.

Pros^{r}. – Had the prisoner to your knowledge any leave from the officer to quit the boat?

Ans^{r}. – I don't know.

Court – Was any search made for the prisoner before the boat went off?

Ans^{r}. – We searched for him and waited about an hour.

Court – Is the prisoner the same person who belonged to the *Eurus* by the name of John Jacobs and who returned with a draft of men as a volunteer from the *Royal William* by the name of John Francis?

Ans^{r}. – He is the same man, but I don't know the name he returned with from the *Royal William*.

Witness ordered to withdraw, and John Lynn called in and sworn.

Pros^{r}. – Do you know the prisoner?

Ans^{r}. – Yes.

Pros^{r}. – Were you in the boat on or about the 5th Decr. 1796 when sent on shore on duty to Portsmouth dockyard?

Ans^{r}. – Yes.

Pros^{r}. – Were you one of the boat's crew on that day?

Ans^{r}. – Yes.

Pros^{r}. – Did he leave the boat whilst on duty?

Ans^{r}. – Yes.

Pros^{r}. – Did the prisoner return on board in the boat?

Ans^{r}. – No.

[1]Landsman.

Pros^r. – Had the prisoner to your knowledge any leave from the officer to quit the boat?

Ans^r. – I don't know.

Court – Did the prisoner assist in carrying any of the stores from the yard that day?

Ans^r. – Yes.

Court – Is the prisoner the same person who belonged to the *Eurus* by the name of Jno. Jacobs and who returned with a draft of men from the *Royal William* by the name of John Francis?

Ans^r. – Yes.

Pros^r. – Was any search made for the prisoner in the yard, when found to be absent?

Ans^r. – I don't know.

Witness ordered to withdraw, and Anto^y. Ferara called in and sworn upon the cross.

Pros^r. – Do you know the prisoner?

Ans^r. – Yes.

Pros^r. – Were you in the boat on or about the 5th Decr. 1796 when sent on shore on duty to Portsmouth dockyard?

Ans^r. – Yes.

Pros^r. – Was the prisoner one of the boat's crew on that day?

Ans^r. – Yes.

Pros^r. – Did the prisoner return on board in the boat?

Ans^r. – No.

Court – Is the prisoner the same person who belonged to the *Eurus* by the name of Jno. Jacobs, and who returned with a draft of men from the *Royal William* by the name of John Francis?

Ans^r. – Yes.

Court – Did the prisoner assist in bringing any of the stores down to the boat?

Ans^r. – Yes.

Prosecution closed and the prisoner having no defence to make, the court cleared and, when again opened, sentence was pronounced.

84A. *Extract of the Report of the Court Martial of John Jacobs*

[ADM 1/5338]

… The court, … having heard the evidence for the Crown in support of the charge as well as what the prisoner had to offer in his defence and maturely and deliberately considered the whole and every part thereof, is of opinion the charge is fully proved and therefore adjudge him to be mulcted of five Pounds, nineteen Schillings of his pay to reimburse the Parish of Portsea, of which parish he fraudulently received that sum as part of a gratuity for entering into His Majesty's service, belonging at the time to His Majesty's ship *Eurus* and to receive three hundred lashes upon his bare back with a cat of nine tails at such time and in such proportion and alongside such ships as the commander in chief may please to direct and he is hereby sentenced accordingly. …

85. *Court Martial of John McKinley and Robert Smith*

[ADM 1/5349]

Proceedings of a court martial held on board His Majesty's ship *Hannibal* in Port Royal Harbour, Jamaica on the 24th day of April 1799 for the trial of John McKinley and Robert Smith, seamen belonging to His Majesty's ship *Maidstone*, for desertion.

Present
Edwd Tyrrel Smith, Esqr, President

Captains	George Eyre	Man Dobson
	Samuel Peter Forster	Wm Sanderson

The prisoners brought in; evidences present.

The order for assembling the court read:[1]

> By Sir Hyde Parker, Kn^t, Vice Admiral of the Red and Commander in Chief of His Majesty's ships and vessels employed at and about Jamaica, &c^a, &c^a, &c^a.

Captain Donnelly of His Majesty's ship *Maidstone*, having in his letter of the 18th instant, requested I would order a court martial to be held to try John McKinley, a seaman belonging to the said ship, for having deserted on or about the second of December last while upon duty in one of the boats and Robert Smith, also a seaman belonging to the said ship, for having deserted on or about the first of December while upon duty in one of the boats and who, being by profession a crimp, there is every reason to believe enticed many of the ship's company away.

You are hereby authorized and directed to assemble a court martial as soon as possible and try John McKinley and Robert Smith, seamen belonging to the said ship, for desertion while upon duty in the boats of the said ship, agreeable to the charges exhibited against them in Captain Donnelly's letter before mentioned, which is herewith enclosed for your information and guidance.

[1]This order was sent by Sir Hyde Parker to Captain Edward Tyrrel Smith.

And for so doing this shall be your order.

Given under my hand on board His Majesty's ship *Queen* in Port Royal Harbour, Jamaica, the 19th day of April 1799.

...

The court duly sworn.

The charge against the prisoners read:[1]

HMS *Maidstone*, P. Royal, Jamaica
18th April 1799

... John McKinley, a Seaman belonging to the ship I command, having deserted on or about the 2d of Decem^{r} last while upon duty in one of the boats, and Robt Smith, also a Seaman belonging to the said ship, having deserted on or about the 1st of Decr last while upon duty in one of the boats, and who, being by profession a crimp, I am sorry to add, we have every reason to believe, enticed many of the ship's company away

I have therefore to request you will be pleased to order a court martial to be held upon them accordingly.

...

All the evidences withdrew, except:

Mr Joseph Reed, Captain's Clerk, sworn.

Court – Do you know the prisoner, John McKinley?

Answer – Yes.

The ship's books produced in court by Mr Reed.

Prosecutor, Captn Donnelly – Is this the complete book of the *Maidstone*?

Answer – It is.

Prosecutor – Do you recollect having received orders to cheque the prisoner for having absented himself without leave on, or about, the 2d December last?

Answer – To the best of my knowledge, I do.

Prosecutor – In the subsequent weekly musters by the open list did the prisoner answer to his name when called?

Answer – He did not.

Prosecutor – Do you recollect how and when he returned?

Answer – I can't exactly say the day when. (Withdrew)

Mr Thomas Martin, Gunner, sworn.

Prosecutor – Do you recollect the prisoner having gone on shore upon duty with you on, or about, the 2d Decem^{r} last?

[1]The charge was contained in a letter from Captain Ross Donnelly to Admiral Parker.

Answer – Yes.

Prosecutor – Did he absent himself from that duty without leave?

Answer – He had no leave from me.

Prosecutor – Did he return to the boat, when she was ready to come off?

Answer – No. (Withdrew)

M[r] John Burnett, Midshipman, Sworn

Prosecutor – Relate to the court the circumstances you know relative to the prisoner McKinley's return to the ship after his desertion.

Answer – On the 2nd of April between the hours of 7 & 8 o'clock as near as I can recollect, I was sitting in Taton's Coffeehouse, dressed in a plain blue jacket & white trousers. The prisoner McKinley and two other men, all genteelly dressed, came into the box where I was sitting. The prisoner tapped me on the shoulder and exclaimed, 'Damn my eyes; Burnett is this you?' I told him he had the advantage of me, as I did not know him, being dressed in long clothes. The prisoner asked me if I did not know McKinley; upon which I rose and shook hands with him. I asked the prisoner to sit down alongside of me, which he did. He then asked me if I had brushed, or some such expression. I told him no; he then enquired what brought me there, as he knew the frigate was at sea. I told him the frigate was at sea, but that I had come up in a prize. He asked me what prize. I told him a schooner privateer, which had the same long gun on board that was fired at the *Maidstone* off Cape Antonio; and that it would be well worth his while to come and see it. He enquired what officer came up, I said none. He then said, 'I suppose you are prize master.' I answered yes. He then asked if I had been made an officer. I told him I did not know, but at any rate he was not afraid of me, I supposed. No, he said; he was not. He enquired what people came up with me; I told him their names, and that Douglas was then on board the schooner, who I was sure would be happy to see him. After sitting a little while, I enquired after some other deserters; he told me he had fell in with three of them, two of which died of a fever, and the other was at Green Island. One of the persons, who came in company with him, rose from his seat and expressed a wish that the prisoner would go home with him, on which the prisoner told him to go home and he would follow him. They went away and left the prisoner with me. After some conversation nearly to the same purpose as above, I asked the prisoner if he would go on board the prize with me. We came down to the waterside, where I borrowed a boat from an American vessel and invited the 2d mate of the said vessel to go on board with me. On our getting on board, I asked them down to the cabin and told Douglas, in a low tone of voice, to hand the irons up from forward, which he did. After drinking a glass of grog with the prisoner and the mate, the prisoner expressed a wish to go on shore. I told him to make himself easy on that head, for he was my prisoner. After collecting himself a little, he told me he believed I was only joking. I said 'twas a very serious joke, of which I would soon convince him and that he must prepare to go in irons immediately. I put him in irons without his making any resistance. In the morning, I went on shore and acquainted the harbour master, who promised to send the first man of war's boat that came up. I went on board again and let the prisoner out of irons. I returned on shore about 9 o'clock, leaving the prisoner in charge of Douglas. I there met with Captain Rolls and acquainted him that I had a deserter on board and wish'd to send him down to Port Royal. He sent his boat and took the prisoner; and, in her, he was conveyed to Port Royal.

Court – Was you in the ship at the time the prisoner deserted?

Answer – Yes (Withdrew)

Lieutenant John Payne, *Maidstone*, sworn.

Prosecutor – Do you recollect the Prisoner McKinley having deserted from the *Maidstone*?

Answer – He stayed on shore when watering at Rock Fort.

Prosecutor – Do you recollect how long after he deserted the ship remained in harbour? And how often the ship came into this port before the prisoner returned to her?

Answer – About a week, I believe and the ship has been, I think, three or four times in harbour since.

Prosecutor – How was the prisoner returned to the ship?

Answer – Brought on board by an officer of the *Abergavenny.*

Evidence for the prosecution of John McKinley closed.

The Prisoner McKinley, having no defence to make nor any evidence to produce, calls on Captain Donnelly for his general character.

Captain Donnelly – During the time the Prisoner McKinley was under my command, I thought him a well behaved man and I verily believed he was enticed away with some other men by the other prisoner, Smith, who was by profession a crimp.

Lieutenant Payne to McKinley's character.

Lieut[t] Payne – He has always done his duty very much to the satisfaction of all the officers, and has been considered as a good man.

M[r] Andres, the Master, to the prisoner's character.

M[r] Andres – While he has been in the ship with me, about fifteen months, he has always behaved very well, has been very willing, and very attentive to his duty.

Trial of McKinley closed.

Trial on Robert Smith commenced.

M[r]. Joseph Reed, Clerk, again called in & sworn.

Prosecutor – Do you recollect having received orders to cheque the prisoner for having absented himself without leave on, or about, the 1st of December last?

Answer – To the best of my recollection, I do.

Prosecutor – In the subsequent weekly muster by the open list, did the prisoner answer to his name when called?

Answer – He did not. (Withdrew)

John Orr, Coxwain, sworn.

Prosecutor – Do you recollect the Prisoner Smith having belonged to the boat that carried me on shore upon duty to Greenwich on, or about, the 1st Decem[r] last?

Answer – Yes.

Prosecutor – Do you recollect my telling him when we landed that he should have leave to go to Kingston the next day and every time we came into the harbour?

Answer – Yes.

Prosecutor – Did he absent himself from that boat without your leave?

Answer – Yes.

Prosecutor – Was he drunk or sober?

Answer – Sober. (Orr withdrew)

Lieutenant Payne again sworn.

Prosecutor – Do you recollect the Prisoner Smith having absented himself from the ship on, or about, the 1st of December last?

Answer – I do.

Prosecutor – Did any men desert from the ship at Rock Fort the next day and how many?

Answer – Yes; I think three.

Prosecutor – Was it generally believed, & that by the officers, that the prisoner, as having been a crimp before, enticed those men to desert?

Answer – Yes.

Prosecutor – In what manner was he returned to the ship?

Answer – As a prisoner brought on board by an officer of the *Abergavenny*. (Withdrew)

M^r^. Andres, Master, sworn

Prosecutor – Do you know anything of the Prisoner Smith's keeping a crimping house in West Street, Kingston?

Answer – I have heard that he did, but I cannot certify that he did.

The prisoner, having no defence to make nor any evidence to produce in his behalf, calls on M^r^. Andres and Lieut^t^ Payne for his general character.

M^r^. Andres – He has always done his duty with cheerfulness and alacrity and considered [*sic*] as a good man.

Lieutenant Payne – I have always known [him?] to [be] very willing and attentive to his duty.

Trial of Robert Smith closed.

The court retired to deliberate & came to the following resolutions: that the charge of desertion is proved against the said prisoners;

That they be adjudged to receive each two hundred & twenty lashes with a cat of nine tails on their bare backs.

The court opened, prisoners brought in, evidences all present, the following sentence read by the judge advocate:

… And, having heard the evidence produced in support of the charge against the said prisoners, as well as in their behalf and what they had to offer in their own defence, and very maturely and deliberately weighed and considered the whole, the court is of opinion that the charge of desertion is proved against the said prisoners, John McKinley and Robert Smith; and do therefore adjudge them to receive each two hundred and twenty lashes on their bare backs with a cat of nine tails, alongside such of His Majesty's ships and vessels at this port, at such times, and in such proportions, as the commander in chief of His Majesty's ships and vessels shall think proper to direct.

And, they are hereby sentenced to be respectively so punished accordingly. …

The court dissolved. …

86. *Court Martial of Henry Carey*

[ADM 1/5362]

Minutes taken at a court martial assembled on board His Majesty's ship *Neptune* in Portsmouth Harbour, the eighteenth day of October one thousand eight hundred and two.

Present

William O'Brien Drury, Esquire, Captain of His Majesty's ship *Neptune*, and second officer in the command of His Majesty's ships and vessels at Portsmouth and Spithead, President.

Captain	Sir Richard John Strachan Bar^{t}.	Captn.	Solomon Ferris
	Edward James Foote		Joseph Bingham
	James Hardy		William Robert Broughton
	James Athol Wood		Thomas Elphinstone
	Robert Williams		Thomas Masterman Hardy
	William Cumberland		Peter Turner Bover

The prisoner was brought in, and audience admitted.

Then the order from the Right Honourable Lords Commissioners of the Admiralty, dated the 16th instant and directed to the president for the trial of Henry Carey, a Private Marine belonging to His Majesty's gun brig *Furious*, for having deserted from her (being then a corporal) was read.

The president reported to the court that Captain the Honble. Charles Paget was absent on Admiralty leave.

The members of the court and the judge advocate then, in open court and before they proceeded to trial, respectively took the several oaths enjoined and directed in and by an Act of Parliament made and passed in the 22nd year of the reign of His late Majesty George the Second, entitled: *An Act for Amending, Explaining and Reducing into one Act of Parliament the Laws Relating to the Government of His Majesty's Ships, Vessels and Forces by Sea.*

Then a letter from Major General Barclay of the Royal Marines at Chatham to their Lordship's secretary of the 16th August 1802 and also one from the Commissioners of the Navy, dated the 2d of September 1802, were severally read by the judge advocate, and are hereto annexed.

The witnesses were then ordered to withdraw and attend their examinations separately, which they did as follows:

Mr. James Lance, a Clerk in the Ticket Office of the Navy Office, being sworn.[1]

The court asked:

Q. Produce the book of His Majesty's gun brig *Furious*, and acquaint the court how the entry of Henry Carey, the prisoner, there stands.

A. No. 34, Marine list – Henry Carey, entered 1st July 1801, Corporal, from former books. He appears chequed on the 15th April 1802 without leave; the ship was paid off on the 22nd April last.

Lieutt. William Troth, late commander of His Majesty's gun brig *Furious*, called in & sworn.

The court asked:

Q. Do you know the prisoner?

A. I do.

Q. State to the court what you know of the charge against him.

A. To the best of my recollection, sometime in April last about the 6th or 8th, I am not certain to the day, he had my leave of absence for a few days; I am certain for not more than a week. The vessel being then ready to be paid off, he did not return to his leave and I immediately gave orders for him to be pricked on the books. I beg leave to mention that it was owing to his very good behaviour

[1]The Ticket Office inspected the pay tickets of discharged, disabled and deceased mariners (*Public Record Office Guide*, part 1: *Administrative Histories* (1998) p. 703/3/1).

while he belonged to the ship that I granted him the indulgence of leave of absence. He was nearly a year and half with me, and I never had occasion to find fault with him; part of the time, he acted as sergeant. The ship was paid off on the 23d of April, I believe, and the prisoner did not return before that time and I have not seen him since until this day.

Q. Can you speak positively whether it was the 6th or 8th that you gave him leave?

A. I cannot; all I go by is that immediately his leave was out and he did not return. I ordered him to be pricked on the books.

Q. Can you say positively that it was before the 10th of April that you gave him leave of absence?

A. I cannot, but I believe it was.

Q. Can you swear he was chequed on the 15th?

A. I ordered him to be chequed on the 15th, and, to the best of my recollection, I ordered the books up at the next muster day, and saw that he was chequed.

Q. Was he run on the books before the ship was paid off?

A. He was not.

Q. Did you report him as a deserter to quarters?

A. Yes. I sent a sergeant, I believe.

Q. When you gave him leave, on what occasion was it?

A. He said he wanted to see his wife and family. I understood from the prisoner, they lived near Chatham.

The prisoner, being called on for his defence, said:

When Lieutenant Troth gave me leave of absence, I gave myself up to Mr. Richard Fielding, a Magistrate, near Sittingbourne, on the 13th of April, for a misdemeanour I had committed before I was in the service and had not been happy afterwards, and was sent by him to Canterbury gaol, where I remained until the 4th of August and was removed from thence to Maidstone, from whence I was sent to Chatham barracks, and was broke from a corporal to a private and afterwards sent on board the *Clyde* as a private.

The court was cleared, and agreed that the charge had not been proved against the said Henry Carey and did adjudge him to be acquitted.

The court was again opened, the prisoner brought in, audience admitted and sentence passed accordingly. …

86A. *John Barclay to Nepean*

[ADM 1/ 5362] Royal Marine Barracks, Chatham
16th August 1802

… Be pleased to acquaint the Lords Commissioners of the Admiralty that Henry Carey, a private who deserted from His Majesty's gun brig *Furious* (being then a corporal) and who was only saved at the last assizes for this county in consequence of turning evidence against the party which he led himself (from every information I am able to obtain) in various felonies, has been brought to headquarters and from hence sent onboard His Majesty's ship *Clyde*, where he remains until their Lordships' pleasure is known respecting him. It will be unnecessary for me to observe how fit he is to be made an example of. You will also please to inform their Lordships that George Goodwin, private, has been brought from Nottingham a deserter from His Maj^s^. Ship *St. Albans*. …

[Admiralty Note]
7 Aug. Acquaint him that means will be taken for bringing Henry Carey to a court martial and that as the desertion of George Goodwin has not been attended with any circumstances of aggravation & that as he conducted himself to the satisfaction of his officers previous to his desertion; their Lordships will not bring him to trial and that he must therefore be taken on in duty.

Navy Board to report how Carey appears on the books of the *Furious*.

Please Sir to signify your directions respecting the bringing Carey to a court martial.

Direct the senior officer at the Nore to send this man by the first opportunity to Spithead where it is intended to bring him to trial by a court martial.

Acquaint Adm^l^. Milbanke accordingly & that he may be secured.

86B. *H. Duncan, J. Winslow and W. Palmer to Nepean*

[ADM 1/5362] Navy Office, 2nd Septem^r^ 1802

… In answer to your letter of the 31st ultimo signifying to us the directions of the Right Honourable the Lords Commiss^rs^ of the Admiralty to report how Henry Carey, a Private Marine who deserted from the *Furious* gun brig, appears on the books of that vessel.

We desire you will please to acquaint their Lordships he is borne as follows, viz:

Furious

Henry Carey No 34 Ent[d] 21st Decem[r] 1800 Corporal of Marines Open on last book ending the 23d April 1802 Noted absent without leave from 15th April 1802

. . .

[Admiralty Note]

3 Sep Lieu[t]. J Troth at Cork to take the first opportunity that may offer of a King's ship to proceed to Spithead for the purpose of bringing to trial Henry Carey, a Corporal of Marines who deserted from the *Furious* in the month of April last & apply to the senior officer for a passage.

Navy Board to send the book to Portsmouth to be ready to be produced on the trial.

Senior Officer at Cork to give the Lieu[t]. a passage in the first ship bound to Spithead.

87. *Court Martial of John Biggs*

[ADM 1/5368]

Minutes of proceedings at a court martial held on board His Majesty's ship *Hercule* in Port Royal Harbour, Jamaica on Wednesday the 23d day of January 1805.

Present

James Richard Dacres, Esq[r]., Rear Admiral of the Red and second in command of his Majesty's ships and vessels at Jamaica &[c], &[c], President.

Captains

Henry Vansittart — Richard Dalling Dunn
Charles Dashwood — Henry Whitby

Read the order of Sir John Thomas Duckworth, K.B., Vice Admiral of the Blue, Commander in Chief &[c], &[c], &[c], dated the 21st day of January 1805 and directed to James Richard Dacres, Esq[r]., Rear Admiral of the Red and second in command of His Majesty's ships and vessels at Jamaica &[c], &[c] to try John Biggs, Private Marine belonging to His Majesty's sloop *Penguin* for having deserted from her at Port Antonio on the 14th instant and been since apprehended.

Then the members of the court and judge advocate, in open court and before they proceeded to trial, respectively took the oath enjoined them by Act of Parliament.

A letter from Captain George Morris, commanding His Majesty's sloop *Penguin*, to the commander in chief was read as follows, viz.:

His Majesty's sloop *Penguin*
Port Royal Harbour, 20th Jany 1805

… John Biggs, Private Marine belonging to His Majesty's sloop *Penguin* under my command, having deserted at Port Antonio when on shore on duty on the 14 instant and being since apprehended, I have to request you will be pleased to order a court martial to try him for the said offence. …

All the witnesses were then ordered out of court, except M^{r}. Alex^{r}. Smellie, Captain's Clerk, who produced the ship's books and was sworn.

Court — Do you know the prisoner and are these the books of His Majesty's sloop *Penguin*?

Ans^{r}. — Yes.

Prosecutor — Were you on shore on duty at Port Antonio on Sunday the 14th instant by log?

Ans^{r}. — Yes.

Quest. — Did the prisoner desert from the party you were doing duty with at the time?

Ans^{r}. — Yes.

No further questions asked this witness and Lieutenant Franklin called and sworn.

Prosecutor — Do you know the prisoner?

Ans^{r}. — Yes.

Quest. — Was he one of the party sent on shore on duty at Port Antonio on Sunday the 14th inst. by log?

Ans^{r}. — Yes.

Quest. — Did he quit the station where you planted him and desert from thence?

Ans^{r}. — Yes.

Quest. — Relate to the court the circumstances attending his being brought on board on the 17th instant?

Ans^{r}. — When on shore with a watering party, I was informed by a planter that the prisoner was taken up by a party of the sixteenth regiment; the planter had seen him with me at the time of his deserting and said he knew him again very well. When I went on board, I acquainted the commanding officer who sent me with the sergeant of Marines to the guardhouse, where I found the prisoner; he would not acknowledge to me to belong to the *Penguin*, but wanted to pass as belonging to the 85th regiment. I then took him on board.

This witness asked nothing further and Sergeant Gibb called and sworn.

Prosecutor — Do you know the prisoner?

Ans^{r}. — Yes.

Quest. — Was he sent on shore on duty with you at Port Antonio on Sunday the 14th inst. by log and did he desert from that duty?

Ans^{r}. — He was sent on shore and did desert.

Quest. — Was you sent on shore to the guardhouse understanding he was there and did you bring him on board as a prisoner?

Ans^{r}. — Yes.

Nothing further asked this witness, he withdrew; the prisoner was then called upon for his defence. He threw himself on the mercy of court and requested Captain Morris might speak to his character.

Captn. Morris said, 'He is a very good man.'

The court was then cleared to deliberate upon and form the sentence.

…

And having heard the evidence on the part of the prosecution and very maturely and deliberately weighed and considered the same (the prisoner having nothing to offer in his defence, but threw himself on the mercy of the court) is of opinion the charge is fully proved and do therefore adjudge him to receive three hundred lashes on his bare back with a cat of nine tails alongside such of His Majesty's ships and vessels at such times and in such proportion as the commander in chief shall think proper to direct; and he is hereby sentenced accordingly. …

88. *Court Martial of Thomas Lee and Robert Jackson*

[ADM 1/5383]

Minutes taken at a court martial assembled on board His Majesty's ship *Gladiator* in Portsmouth Harbour on the tenth day of August 1807.

Present

John Irwin, Esq[r]., Captain of His Majesty's ship *Puissant* and second officer in the command of His Majesty's ship's and vessels at Portsmouth and Spithead, President.

Captain	The Honble Courtenay Boyle	Captain	James Walker
	George Scott		Thomas Manby
	Andrew Sproule		Robert Howe Bromley
	Robert Scott		

The prisoner was brought in and audience admitted.

The president reported to the court that Captains Sir Charles Hamilton, Bar[t]., Sir F Laforey, B[t]. and William Hoste were absent on Admiralty leave.

The order from the R[t]. Honble. Lords Commissioners of the Admiralty, dated the eighth day of August instant and directed to the president, to assemble a court martial for the trial of Thomas Lee and Robert Jackson, Seamen belonging to His Majesty's surveying vessel the *Sorlings*, for having on Friday night (the 24th of July last) forced the lock off their irons and made their escape, was read.

The members of the court and judge advocate then, in open court and before they proceeded to trial, respectively took the several oaths enjoined and directed in and by an Act of Parliament made and passed in the twenty second year of the reign of His late Majesty King George the Second, entitled: *An Act for Amending, Explaining and Reducing into one Act of Parliament the Laws Relating to the Government of His Majesty's Ships, Vessels and Forces by Sea.*

Then the letter from Lieutenant John Murray, commanding the said vessel *Sorlings*, dated the 26th day of July last, and directed to the Honourable W. W. Pole, containing the charge was read, and is hereto annexed and the witnesses were ordered to withdraw and attend their examinations separately, which they did as follows:

Lieutenant John Murray, commanding His Majesty's surveying vessel *Sorlings*, called in and sworn.

The court asked:

Q. Produce the muster book of the *Sorlings*, and turn to the prisoners' names, and acquaint the court how they there stand.
N[o]. 3. Thomas Lee, A.B. His entry is not on the book, an R appears against his name.

Q. Does the prisoner belong to the *Sorlings*?

A. He does; he has belonged to her for above eighteen years. (The witness produced a certificate of his good behaviour for fourteen years and two months in the vessel.)

Q. Is the prisoner the person so described?

A. Yes. No. 35. Robert Jackson, Ordinary, entered fourth June last from the *Gladiator*; there is an R against his name of the twenty sixth of July last.

Q. Is the prisoner the person so described?

A. Yes.

M^{r}. George John Henry Speed, a Midshipman belonging to the *Sorlings*, called in and sworn.

Lieutenant Murray asked:

Q. Relate what you know of the charge against the prisoners.

A. We were scrubbing her bottom in Little Hampton Harbour and Jackson was put into confinement for drunkenness, mutinous expressions and disobedience of orders and Thomas Lee was confined for theft about a fortnight ago. They were put into irons both feet together; Jackson was nearest the lock. They remained about two days in irons. About half past twelve o'clock at night, between Friday the twenty fourth day of July and the Saturday, they escaped. I went to the irons, and found a chisel, with which the lock appeared to have been broken open. I informed Mr. Murray of it and he ordered me to go to Lieutenant Spry at the rendezvous. I was afterwards sent to Arundel with two men to stay till day light. About five o'clock in the morning, I went to the barracks and afterwards saw the adjutant of the third Dragoons and he sent a man with me to pursue them to Chichester, where another trooper was ordered to join me and we continued the pursuit and we overtook them eight or nine miles from Portsmouth. They were seized and I heard them grumbling, but did not hear what they said. They submitted and we walked on to Portsmouth, as we were nearer to it than to Little Hampton and they were sent on board the *Gladiator* as prisoners.

The court asked:

Q. Where was the vessel when they were in irons?

A. Alongside the wharf at Little Hampton.

M^{r}. John Brown, a Midshipman belonging to the *Sorlings*, called in and sworn.

The court asked:

Q. Were the prisoners in irons on board the *Sorlings*?

A. Yes. I believe on Friday, I saw them about eight o'clock. They were let out of irons to make their hammocks up; I saw them put into irons again. About twelve o'clock, I was called up, but did not go to the place where they were confined and did not see them until today.

The prosecution being closed, the prisoners were called on for their defence.

Thomas Lee stated that if he had not been in liquor, he should never have thought of leaving the service. He had been frequently offered his discharge, but refused it, as he did not wish to quit the service. He produced a letter from M^r^. Graeme Spence, formerly Commander of the *Sorlings* and it was read and a copy whereof is hereto annexed.

Robert Jackson said he was badly ruptured in the service and trusted to the mercy of the court.

Lieutenant Price, Commander of the *Gladiator*, said that Jackson behaved very well while in the *Gladiator*, was a trusty man and always sent in the boats, and was considered an exemplary character.

The court was cleared, and agreed that the charges had been proved against the said Thomas Lee and Robert Jackson and did adjudge the said Thomas Lee to receive one hundred lashes and the said Robert Jackson one hundred and fifty lashes on their bare backs with a cat o' nine tails on board of, or alongside such of, His Majesty's ships or vessels at Spithead, or in Portsmouth Harbour at such time or times and in such manner and proportions as the commander in chief of His Majesty's ships and vessels for the time being at Portsmouth aforesaid should direct.

The court was again opened, the prisoner brought in, audience admitted, and sentence passed accordingly. …

88A. *Murray to Pole*

[ADM 1/5383] *Sorlings* in Little Hampton Harbour
26th July 1807

… I had the honour of receiving your letter of yesterday's date this morning, and regret being under the painful necessity of representing to their Lordships the behaviour of two of the seamen belonging to this vessel, who yesterday deserted. I had confined Thomas Lee for repeated theft and insolence, and Robert Jackson for mutinous expressions, disobedience of orders, and very frequent drunkenness. On Friday night between 12 and two o'clock, they forced the lock of their irons, and made their escape, although there was a regular watch on deck, but they were men I had from on board the *Gladiator*, and from whom, I have experienced the most hardened behaviour. On being informed of their escape, I immediately sent Lieu^t^. Spry's gang in different directions after them, and dispatched a midshipman and two men to Arundel Barracks to report their desertion to the commanding officer, who immediately mounted the midshipman and a dragoon. They took the Chichester Road, and having gained intelligence of them, were joined by another trooper. Eight miles from Portsmouth, they overtook them both, and, on being stopped, they told the midshipman they would have resisted had he been accompanied by only a single dragoon. They were conveyed to Portsmouth, reported to Rear Admiral Coffin, who ordered them in confinement on board the *Gladiator* to abide their lordships' pleasure. Lee's behaviour for years past has been so bad, I can say nothing in his favour; and Jackson is a very abandoned character. …

[Admiralty Note]
27 July – Orders for trying them by a court martial; acquaint L^{t}. Murray that they are to be tried at Portsmouth.

88B. *Spence to Lee*

[ADM 1/5383] No. 3 Isabell Row, Palace Street, Pimlico, Westminster, 29th July 1807

… I am very sorry to hear of your running away, as it will most likely subject you to the punishment which the law inflicts on all deserters; nor do I expect that anything I can say in your favour will avail you, but, as you say you have lost the certificate I once gave you, I have no objection or hesitation to give that character of you, which I *once* knew you deserved. What your character has been since I left the survey, I cannot tell; that is a question for others to answer. I can only certify that you was with me in H.M. surveying sloop *Sorlings* upwards of 14 years, during which time I found you a very useful and trusty man upon the survey and the *best walker* and *best leadsman* I ever had; nor was you ever punished by my desire during the whole time you was with me. As to moral character or rectitude of conduct, I never expect it from a sailor, though perhaps you had as much of that as most of your shipmates. …

89. *Court Martial of William Downes*

[ADM 1/5391]

Minutes of proceedings at a court martial held on board His Majesty's ship *Princess of Orange* in The Downs, the 12 January 1809.

Present
Sir Joseph Sidney Yorke, Knight, Captain of His Majesty's ship *Christian the 7th* and third officer in the command of His Majesty's ships and vessels in The Downs, President.

Captains

James Newman Newman	John Harvey
Edward Codrington	Honble. Henry Blackwood
Ross Donnelly	Charles Ekins
William Robert Broughton	William Cuming
Edward William Campbell Rich Owen	Brian Hodgson
Francis Beauman	Andrew King

The prisoner was brought into court, and the evidence and audience admitted.

Read the order of the Lords Commissioners of the Admiralty, dated the 11th instant., directed to Sir Joseph Sydney Yorke, Knight, Captain of His Majesty's ship *Christian the 7th* and third officer in the command of His Majesty's ships and vessels in The Downs, to try William Downes, Landsman belonging to His Majesty's sloop *Fly*, for having been guilty of a breach of the 16th Article of War by endeavouring to entice two other men belonging to the said sloop to desert and for having also formed a plan to run away with one of the boats of the said sloop for the purpose of aiding the said attempt on or about the eve of the 19th of November last.

Then the members of the court and judge advocate, in open court and before they proceeded to trial, respectively took the several oaths directed by Act of Parliament made and passed in the 22 year of the reign of His late Majesty King George the Second, entitled: *An Act for Amending, Explaining and Reducing into one Act of Parliament the Laws Relating to the Government of His Majesty's Ships, Vessels and Forces by Sea.*

A letter from Captain Thompson of the *Fly* to Vice Admiral Campbell, Commander in Chief, &c., &c., was read as follows, vizt.:

His Majesty's sloop *Fly*
Downes, the 7th Jany. 09

… William Downes, Landsman belonging to His Majesty's sloop under my command, having been guilty of a breach of the 16th Article of War by endeavouring to entice two other men belonging to the said sloop to desert and for having also formed a plan to run away with one of the boats of the said sloop for the purpose of aiding the said attempt on or about the eve of the 19th of Novr. last, I have to request you will be pleased to take the necessary steps that the said William Downes may be tried by a court martial for the above named crime.

…

Read a letter from Vice Admiral Campbell acquainting the court that Cap[t]. Kent of the *Agincourt* is absent on Admiralty leave.

All the evidences were ordered to withdraw out of court, except Lieut. Jacob Jones, who was sworn.

Pros[r]. Repeat the substance of the complaint you made to me on the morning of the 20 Nov[r]. last respecting the prisoner and others.

Ans[r]. On the evening of the 19 Nov[r]. the Corporal (Sykes) reported to me the sentry on the starboard gangway had overheard William Downes, the prisoner, swear he would go, at which time Joseph Hall was heard to say, 'Hush.' I examined Joseph Hall, who told me the prisoner had enticed him to desert with the jolly boat.

Richard Clist (Marine) called and sworn.

Pros[r]. Did you, on the evening of the 19 November last, hear the prisoner swear that he would go on shore?

Ans[r]. Yes.

Court Relate to the court what he said.

Ans[r]. I was walking sentry on the starboard gangway when I heard the prisoner say he would go on shore, which I reported to the corporal of Marines.

Court Did you hear him entice any other person to go with him?

Ans[r]. Drake stood by the prisoner's side and said he would go on shore too.

Court Did he say anything about a boat?

Ans[r]. I did not hear him say anything about a boat.

John Drake called and sworn.

Pros[r]. Did the prisoner on the 19th of Nov[r]. last endeavour to entice you with Joseph Hall to run away with the jolly boat, which was left out for the purpose of rowing guard, whilst laying at Guernsey?

Ans[r]. He enticed me to go with him on shore, but never mentioned anything about Hall.

Pros[r]. Did you, in consequence of his having so persuaded you, go into the jolly boat and endeavour to persuade the boat keeper to leave her?

Ans[r]. No.

Court How did you mean to go on shore?

Ans[r]. He (the prisoner) said the jolly boat was astern.

Court What did you understand by his saying the jolly boat was astern?

Ans[r]. I suspected he was going to take her.

Court What time was this?

Ans[r]. Between six and seven in the evening.

Court Do you recollect how the wind was at that time?

Ans[r]. It blew off the town.

Court Where did you propose landing?

Ans[r]. He did not mention anything about landing.

Court Do you recollect the story you told to your captain when you was punished for this offence? If you do, relate it.

Ans[r]. I told the captain I was between decks when the prisoner asked me if I would bring him off some liquor, and, before I had time to make him my answer, he told me that was not what he wanted of me. He said there was two or three of them who were going to make off and asked me if I would join with them or not. I told him I would not. He then desired me not to say anything about it.

Court By the oath you have taken, was what you related to your captain true or false?

Ans[r]. The whole of it was true.

Joseph Hall called and sworn.

Pros[r]. Did the prisoner in the evening of the 19th of November last endeavour to entice you with John Drake to run away with the jolly boat, which was left out for the purpose of rowing guard whilst laying at Guernsey?

Ans[r]. Yes, he endeavoured to entice me away with the jolly boat.

Pros[r]. Did you, in consequence of his having so persuaded you, go into the jolly boat and endeavour to persuade the boat keeper to leave her?

Ans[r]. Yes, he persuaded me to go into the jolly boat and persuaded me to tell the boat keeper (Atkinson) that the boatswain's mate had sent me to keep the boat.

Pros[r]. Could you prevail on Atkinson to leave the boat?

Ans[r]. No, he would not go out of the boat.

Court What words did the prisoner make use of to entice you to go away?

Ans[r]. He told me to go into the boat and drop her astern and that he and Drake would jump into her.

Court Did he make known his intention to you and what was it?

Ans[r]. He said he wanted to go on shore at Guernsey in the boat, that he knew the place.

Court Did the officers know he wanted to go on shore?

Ans[r]. They did not before they found it out.

Court In what words did the prisoner ask you to go in the boat?

Ans[r]. He said to me go into the boat and drop her astern and Drake and himself would jump into her.

Here the prosecution closed.

The prisoner had nothing to offer in his defence, and threw himself on the mercy of the court.

The court, having carefully and deliberately weighed and considered the evidence produced, were of opinion that the charge was fully proved against the said William Downes and did therefore adjudge him to receive three hundred lashes on his bare back with a cat of nine tails alongside such of His Majesty's ships at such times and in such manner as the commander in chief at The Downs should direct; and the said William Downes was thereby sentenced to receive three hundred lashes on his bare back with a cat of nine tails accordingly.

The court was opened, audience admitted and sentence passed accordingly. …

90. *Court Martial of John Hyde*

[ADM 1/5437]

Minutes of proceedings at a court martial held on board His Majesty's ship *Vigo* on the 16th day of August 1813 off Rostock

Present

Graham Moore, Esquire, Rear Admiral of the Blue and second officer in command of H.M. ships & vessels in the Baltic

Captains

Robert Williams	Richard Raggett
Thomas White (1)	William Hill, Comm[r]

Being all the admirals, captains and commanders according to seniority, except Thomas Alexander, Esquire, Captain of H.M. bomb vessel *Devastation*, who is prosecutor upon this occasion.

The prisoner was brought into court; the evidence and audience admitted.

Read the order from Rear Admiral Hope, Commander in Chief in the Baltic, dated the 22d day of July 1813 addressed to Graham Moore, Esquire, Rear Admiral of the Blue and second officer in command of H.M. ships and vessels in the Baltic, to try John Hyde, late Boatswain of His Majesty's bomb vessel *Devastation*, for a breach of the sixteenth Article of War on the 19th day of January 1813.

Read the warrant appointing M[r]. Emeric [?] Essex Vidal judge advocate.

Then the members of the court and judge advocate, in open court, respectively took the oaths as directed.

A letter from Captain Thomas Alexander of H.M. bomb vessel *Devastation*[1] was then read as follows:

H.M. sloop *Devastation*
Off Sprae, 22 June 1813

… I have to request you will be pleased to move the commander in chief to give the necessary directions for a court martial to be held to try John Hyde, late Boatswain of His Majesty's sloop *Devastation* under my command, for a breach of the sixteenth Article of War on the 19th day of January 1813. …

All the witnesses, except the first to be sworn, were ordered to withdraw and the court proceeded to trial as follows:
Evidence in support of the charge
M^r^. Matthew Curran, Master of *Devastation*, sworn.

Prosecutor	Do you recollect being sent on duty from Galleons Reach to Woolwich Dockyard on the 19th day of January 1813?
Ans^r^	No, I recollect the second lieutenant going.
Q	Did you go in the boat on that day?
Ans^r^	I believe I did; I went in one of the boats.
Q	Did you go in the boat with the prisoner?
Ans^r^	I believe not.
Q	Were you on dockyard duty on that day?
Ans^r^	No, I was told by the second lieutenant when on shore to go back for the boatswain – on no other duty.
Q	Was the boatswain sent on duty on that day?
Ans^r^	Yes.
Q	Do you know the nature of the duty he was sent on?
Ans^r^	To draw the ship's boats.
…	
Q	How long after was it that you saw the boatswain?
Ans^r^	Not till last July.
By the court:	
Q	Did you see him on the 19th day of January?
A	Yes.
Q	Where was it you saw him?
A	Going on shore in the boat on duty with the second lieutenant; I will not positively say that boat, but I saw

[1]This letter is to Rear Admiral Moore.

him that day before he went on shore on the point of leaving the ship in a boat.

Q When did you see him again after that for the first time?

A Sometime last July when he was sent back to the ship.

Q. How long did the ship lay at Galleons after that?

A About a week.

Q Have you been doing duty as Master of the ship from that time till now?

Ans[r] Yes.

Q If the boatswain had been on board at any time between the 19 January … and July when he was brought back you must have seen him?

A Yes.

Q How long after did you leave England?

A About the 25th March.

Q Where had the ship been from the time she left Galleons to the 25th March?

A At the Nore to about the 20th, when she sailed to Yarmouth.

Q Had anybody been doing duty as boatswain during the time the prisoner was absent?

A I had charge of the stores; the boatswain's mates did the other duty.

Q You say you were sent by the second lieutenant in search of the boatswain on the 19th of January; did you see him?

Ans[r] No.

Q Are you sure the prisoner was sent on duty on that day?

Ans[r] Yes, I heard the first lieutenant give him part of the orders to that effect.

Q In what part of the day was you sent by the second lieutenant to find the boatswain?

Ans[r] About 2 in the afternoon.

Q Were you on shore on leave or duty?

Ans[r] On leave.

Prisoner had no questions to ask. Witness withdrew.

M[r]. Thomas Sonnerat, Captain's Clerk, called in & sworn.

Produced the muster books of the *Devastation*.

By the court:

Q Are those the ship's books and kept by yourself?

Ans[r] Yes.

John Hyde N°. 3 appears Run 18th January 1813, Woolwich from duty. Re-entry 22d June 1813.

Q What was your reason for running the man the day before?

Ans[r] I checqued him on the 19th and understood it was usual to run the day before.

Q Have you been clerk ever since the 18 January?

Ans[r] Yes.

Q Did you see the prisoner between the 18 Jan[y]. and 22d June?

Ans[r] No.

Q How did the prisoner return to the ship?

Ans[r] He appears to have been apprehended; £3 being charged against him as straggling money in the list that came with him from the *Insolent*.

Prosecution closed. Witness withdrew.

The evidence in support of the charge being finished, the prisoner was called on to make his defence. He accordingly put in a paper signed by himself, which was read to the court as follows:

Defence

… When I went out of the yard knowing the ship was to remain a little time at Galleons and being near London where I have a wife and family (the boats were gone off and I had to walk down to Galleons), I thought I might get back to Woolwich by next day and was tempted to go off to London. I am sorry to say that when I got there I delayed from time to time coming back until I was afraid of doing it altogether.

I had many good offers of places in the merchant service while on shore which I would not accept, being at the same time in doubt on account of my friends about giving myself up. At last, I was going to Rotherhithe to visit a friend when a press gang met me; I immediately gave myself up as Boatswain of the *Devastation*.

I humbly assure this honourable court I did not leave the ship with intention to desert His Majesty's service. I have served with Captains Boyle, Lee and Bissett, by the latter I was made a boatswain's mate and afterwards, I believe, given my warrant.

I always previous to this conducted myself well and may venture to appeal to Captain Alexander for a character before this happened.

I am aware that I have been guilty in leaving the ship, but under the circumstances I have stated, I beg to throw myself upon the mercy of the court, assuring them I have no desire but to continue in His Majesty's service in which I hope to retrieve the character I have forfeited.

I hope they will take … into consideration my long servitude between nine and ten years, four of which I have been a boatswain, and that the support of a wife and family entirely depends on me.

…

The prisoner then called on Captain Alexander for a character, who says – The prisoner was always a very sober, good man previous to his leaving the ship.

The prisoner not having anything further to offer, the court was cleared and proceeded to deliberate upon and form the sentence.

Then, the court, having examined the books of the *Devastation* and heard the evidence in support of the charge as well as what the prisoner had to offer in his behalf and very maturely and deliberately weighed and considered the same, was of opinion that the charge had not been proved against the prisoner John Hyde and did therefore adjudge the said John Hyde to be acquitted; and the court being reopened, the prisoner brought in, the prosecutor, evidence and audience admitted, sentence was passed accordingly.

91. *Court Martial of John Harland, Joseph Nicholes and Charles Robinson alias Dougherty*

[ADM 1/5444]

Minutes of proceedings at a court martial held on board His Majesty's ship *Tonnant* at Bermuda, the 22d July 1814

Present

Edward Codrington, Esquire, Captain of the Fleet and second officer in the command of His Majesty's ships and vessels at Bermuda, President
Commodore the Honourable Henry Hotham
Commodore Andrew Fitzherbert Evans, commanding His Majesty's ship *Ruby*

Captains

Richard Byron	Sir William Bolton Knight
The Honble Frederick William Aylmer	Samuel Jackson

The surgeon of His Majesty's ship *Hebrus* attended to certify that Captain Palmer was unable to attend from ill health.

The prisoners were brought into court and the witnesses and audience admitted.

Read the order of the Honourable Sir Alexander Cochrane, K.B., Vice Admiral of the Red & Commander in Chief of His Majesty's ships & vessels on the North American Station, dated the 19 July 1814 and directed to the president, to try John Harland, Landsman, Joseph Nicholes, Ordinary Seaman, and Charles Robinson alias Dougherty, Marine of the Third Class, belonging to His Majesty's ship *Tonnant*, for having on or about the 9 July instant absented themselves from their duty without leave when lent to His Majesty's ship *Ruby*.

Then the members of the court and judge advocate, in open court and before they proceeded to trial, respectively took the oaths directed by Act of Parliament made & passed in the 22d year of the reign of His late Majesty King George 2d., entitled *An Act for Amending, Explaining and Reducing into one Act of Parliament the Laws Relating to the Government of His Majesty's Ships, Vessels and Forces by Sea.*

A letter from Captain John Wainwright of His Majesty's ship *Tonnant* to the Honble Sir Alexander Cochrane, Vice Admiral of the Red, &c, &c, &c, was read as follows, *viz.*:

Tonnant, Bermuda
19 July 1814

... The men named in the margin [John Harland, Joseph Nicholes, and Charles Robinson], belonging to His Majesty's ship *Tonnant* under my command, having on or about the 9 instant absented themselves without leave from their duty when lent to His Majesty's ship *Ruby*,

I request you will be pleased to order a court martial to be assembled to try the said men for the offence herein set forth. ...

All the witnesses were ordered to withdraw out of court, except *Mr. John Armstrong*, Clerk of His Majesty's ship *Tonnant*, who was sworn.

The muster books of the *Tonnant* being produced, the following entry appeared:

593	John Harland Lm	Cheqd –	4 July lent to *Ruby*
169	Joseph Nicholes Ordy	Do	Do
126	Charles Robinson Marine 3d Class alias Dougherty	Do	Do

Pros^{r} – Is that a correct copy from the muster books?

Ans^{r} – Yes.

A list was produced from the *Ruby* by which it appeared that the prisoners before mentioned absented themselves without leave on the 9 July.

Prosecutor – Is that the list sent from the *Ruby*?

Ans^{r} – Yes.

Prose^{r} – Describe how it is signed.

Ans^{r} – Signed 'James Knight, Lieutenant.'

Witness withdrew

M^{r}. *John Shaw, Assistant Clerk*, sworn.

Pros^{r}. Are the prisoners the persons named in the charge?

Ans^{r} – Yes.

Witness withdrew

M^{r}. *Jeremiah Macdaniel, Master's Mate*, sworn.

Pros^{r}. – Are the prisoners the persons named in the charge?

Ans^{r} – Yes.

Pros^{r}. – Were you the officer sent in command of the party of men of whom the prisoners formed a part to His Majesty's ship *Ruby* for the purpose of assisting in work carrying on at the naval yard at Ireland?

Ans^{r} – Yes.

Pro^{s}. – Did they absent themselves from their duty without leave and, if yes, what time?

Ans^{r}. – They did between the hours of 9 & 10 o'clock on the morning of the 9 July. When I mustered the party to work after breakfast, I found the prisoners absent.

Pros^{r}. – Relate to the court any further circumstances that you may know respecting the charges against the prisoners.

Ans^{r}. – One of the midshipmen, M^{r}. Blewitt, under my orders, was ordered to go in search of them by Lieut. Knight, the commanding officer of the *Ruby*. When he returned in the course of an hour or two, he said he had not heard or seen anything of them. I then went in search of them myself and could not hear or see anything of them. On my return, Lieut. Knight ordered the corporal of my party to go in search of them; on his return, he said he had heard they were at the mast house and enquiring for some spirits or something to drink. The day following, Lieut. Knight sent a party of his marines in search of them with the corporal belonging to my party but could not hear or see anything of them.

Court – What time did the prisoners land from the *Ruby* on the morning of the 9?

Ans^{r}. – About 5 or ½ 5 o'clock.

Court – Was any petty officer in charge of the prisoners at the time they were allowed to breakfast?

Ans^{r}. – No, as they were in a tent near ours.

Witness withdrew

M^{r}. *Rob. Johnstone* sworn.

Pros^{r}. – Do you know the prisoners?

Ans^{r}. – I do.

Pro^{s}. – Were you in command of the party that apprehended them?

Ans^{r}. – I was.

Pros^{r}. – Relate to the court the time & circumstances at the apprehension of the said prisoners to the best of your knowledge.

Ans^{r}. – On Thursday morning 14 July after I had my breakfast, I went on board of a brigantine lying at Hamilton for intelligence. There was a black man on board who told me he had been in company with the prisoners on Wednesday evening and had known one of them when a prisoner in America. I then asked him if he had any idea where they were; he told me he believed they had gone down to enter on board of a brig lying at the ferry passage. I immediately went on shore and, after giving the men time enough to get something to eat, I crossed over to the wells where I met a man from whom I understood that a brig had passed about an hour. I returned again to Hamilton & went to a M^{r}. Fouso who I asked to lend me his boat to board a brig lying at the mouth of the harbour, which he granted. I took the sergeant with me & went out towards the mouth of the harbour where I saw the brig lying close to the rocks. I told the sergeant to lay close down in the boat, which I did likewise. When we got alongside, I went on board & told the master I wanted three men that had entered with him on Wednesday morning. He gave up Nicholes & Harland; on my telling him if he did not give the other man up, I would clear the vessel, he went below to his cabin & brought Robinson, the other prisoner, up. I then ordered them into the boat & lashed their hands together. When we got on shore at Hamilton, I gave them time to get some refreshment & then marched them down to Baileys Bay. I there left them in charge of the sergeant while I went up & reported my proceedings to Comm^{r}. Hotham, who ordered the signal to be made for a boat from the *Belvidera* to which ship I took them & delivered them in charge of the commanding officer as deserters.

Court – Were they concealed on board the brig?

Ans^{r}. – No, Harland & Nicholes were working on deck & Robinson was below.

Court – Have you reason to think that the master of the brig knew them to be deserters?

Ans^{r}. – I think he did not.

Court – What was the name of the vessel?

Ans^{r}. – The *Genl. Horsford*, I think Capt. Butterfield.

Court – Was the marine in his uniform?

Ans^{r}. – He was not.

The evidence in support of the charge being finished, the prisoners were called upon to make their defence, which they did in the following manner:

The prisoners have nothing to offer in their defence, but state that they deserted owing to the treatment they received from Lieutenant Knight of the *Ruby*, who often said he would give them four dozen before they went on shore to work, threw stones at them when heaving at the capstan getting up spars and, when they did desert, it was their intention to go to the ship. They say they complained of their treatment to M^{r}. Blewitt.

. . .

Witnesses for the defence

M^{r}. *John Blewitt, Master's Mate*, sworn.

Court – Did the prisoner Harland complain to you that himself and the pris^{r}. Nicholes had been ill-treated by Lieutenant Knight of the *Ruby*?

Ans^{r}. – To the best of my recollection, no. Harland & Nicholes conducted themselves very well while with me, particularly Harland. Robinson was always a volunteer to pull backwards & forwards to the ship. They complained to me they had not sufficient time to their meals, which I represented to Lieut. Knight & the time was increased.

Court – Did Lieut. Knight ever to your knowledge threaten to give the prisoners 4 dozen lashes before they went on shore in the morning?

Ans^{r}. – I have heard Lieut. Knight when the people showed an unwillingness to work threaten to flog them.

Court – Did either of the prisoners show an unwillingness to work when they were employed at Ireland?

Ans^{r}. – Only Robinson.

Court – Was the threat, which you know Lieut. Knight to have made, addressed to Robinson only or generally to the prisoners.

Ans^{r}. – To those only who were dilatory, it was general.

Court – Do you know of Lieut. Knight having at any time thrown stones at the working party when they were heaving at the capstan?

Ans^{r}. – No.

Court – What time did the work party usually go on shore in the morning?

Ans^{r}. – Seldom before 5 o'clock.

Court – At what time were they called to go away?

Ans^{r}. – Generally at 4.

Court – Did they take their breakfasts with them or did they breakfast before they went away?

Ans^{r}. – They took it with them.

Court – How were they employed in the intervening hour between 4 & 5?

Ans^{r}. – Lashing their hammocks up & getting their provisions for the day into the boats.

Court – At what time did they commence work on shore?

Answer – Generally at 6 o'clock.

Court – At what time did they go to breakfast?

Ans^{r}. – 8 o'clock.

Court – What time was allowed for their breakfast?

Ans^{r}. – Never less than 1 hour.

Court – How long were they allowed for dinner?

Ans^{r}. – Till the men complained, little better than an hour, aft^{r}. nearly two.

Court – Did they lay by at all in the heat of the day or were they employed immediately after dinner hour?

Ans^{r}. – They went to work immediately after dinner.

Court – How late did they work?

Ans^{r}. – They usually left of [*sic*] once in the course of the day for about 10 minutes to get lime juice & water & then worked till six.

Court – Did you ever hear Lieut. Knight complain of the party being very slack at their work & requiring a constant eye upon them to keep them together?

Ans[r]. – Frequently.

Court – Did you see any instances of cruelty and oppression towards the prisoners on the part of M[r]. Knight?

Ans[r]. – None.

Court – Were the working party generally during the time you state to have been allotted for their meals obliged to occupy a part of that time in dressing their provisions or were those provisions prepared for them before hand?

Ans[r]. – Two men were excused from all other work for the purpose of cooking their meals.

Court – Were there any other persons with the party belong[g]. to the *Ruby* than the working party?

Ans[r]. – Six and sometimes eight men from the *Ruby*.

Witness withdrew

Philip Connor, Seaman, sworn.

Court – Did you ever see Lieut. Knight of the *Ruby* throw stones at the prisoners while heaving at the capstan?

Ans[r]. – No, I never did.

Court – Did you ever hear Lieut. Knight threaten to give the prisoners 4 dozen lashes before they went on shore?

Ans[r]. – I have heard him make use of the words, but cannot say whether they were addressed to the prisoners or not.

Witness withdrew.

William Medley, Marine, sworn.

Court – Did you ever see Lieut. Knight of the *Ruby* throw stones at the prisoners while heaving at the capstan?

Ans[r]. – Yes.

Court – Did you ever hear Lieut. Knight threaten to give the prisoners 4 dozen lashes before they went on shore?

Ans[r]. – I have heard him say to the party that he would flog every man of them, but I did not hear him mention any particular number of lashes.

Witness withdrew.

Christopher Black, Marine, sworn.

Court – Did you ever see Lieut. Knight of the *Ruby* throw stones at the prisoners while heaving at the capstan?

Ans[r]. – I have.

Court – Did you ever hear Lieut. Knight threaten to give the pris[rs] 4 dozen lashes before they went on shore?

Ans[r] – I did hear him.

Witness withdrew.

Captain John Wainwright, the prosecutor, having obtained leave to inform the court of the nature of the duty upon which the prisoners were employed, stated as follows: Some days after the men were sent to Ireland to work at the naval yard, I had occasion to go there on duty and on enquiring what the people were about & how they had conducted themselves, I heard no complaints of misconduct from the officer in command of the party; on the contrary, the impression was full upon my mind that the men had behaved well. To the best of my recollection, Lieut. Knight was present when I made several enquiries relative to the men of M[r] M[c] Daniell, the officer who commanded them. The work the men were employed on was to haul up very heavy spars from the water on the side of a hill over very rough ground which had previously been cleared of cedar trees by the party. It was about 11 o'clock on the morning I saw them & I was informed that they had hauled up 14 spars that day; some of those spars were 89 feet long & 26 inches in diameter & I understood that the usual work performed by the men was 20 spars of various dimensions per day, none of which could be considered small spars. The heat the time I mention was so intense that I could hardly stand the rays of the sun without working and considering the small number of men employed being as appears in evidence never more than 31 in number & considering the circumstances of the intense heat and the rough ground over which the spars were conveyed, I was of opinion that the quantity of work performed could only have been effected by great attention and skill on the part of the officers and great bodily exertion on the part of the men.

Mr. James Brown, Carpenter of His Majesty's ship *Tonnant*, called upon to state what he knew relative to the character of Joseph Nicholes.

He was always a quiet, decent man, very attentive to his duty & was taken from the waist to do his duty on the forecastle in consequence of his good behaviour.

Thomas Graham also to state respecting the character of Nicholes.

Was shipmate with Nicholes four years & he always bore a good character & paid great attention to his duty.

I was Captain of the Forecastle the 4 years & he did his duty there all the time.

Joseph Foss states:

Nicholes was taken out of the waist for his good behaviour; always did his duty with great propriety & to the best of his power; had known him 4 years.

William Maccraken states:

I have been 3 years & ½ shipmates with Nicholes; he always bore a very good character in the ship & was taken prisoner with me off Sandy Hook lighthouse & behaved himself well in prison. The Americans offered him a situation of boatswain's mate & 18 Dollars p^{r}. month if he would enter in their service, but he refused it and said he would return home with his fellow prisoners.

Francis Gray to speak to the character of John Harland

Have known him about 5 months & since he has been in this ship, he has always attended to his duty. He does his duty in the forecastle & I am Captain of the Forecastle.

The prisoners having nothing further to offer in their defence, the court was cleared and proceeded to deliberate upon & form the sentence.

The court, having maturely and deliberately considered the evidence in support of the charge & what the prisoners had to allege in their defence, are of opinion that the charge of absenting themselves from their duty without leave when lent to His Majesty's ship *Ruby* is proved and doth adjudge the prisoners John Harland and Charles Robinson alias

Dougherty to receive one hundred and fifty lashes each with a cat o nine tails on the bare back at such times & in such proportions as the commander in chief shall direct; and the court in consideration of the good character of Joseph Nicholes and of the proof he has given of his former fidelity to his country by declining to receive a considerable sum of money from the American government, offered him as a bribe to forfeit his allegiance, doth adjudge him only to receive one hundred lashes with a cat o nine tails on his bare back at such times & in such proportions as the commander in chief shall direct. And the said John Harland and Charles Robinson alias Dougherty are hereby sentenced to receive one hundred and fifty lashes each and Joseph Nicholes one hundred lashes as before directed accordingly.

Signed by the court

The court was opened, audience admitted and sentence passed accordingly. …

92. *Court Martial of John Brown*

[ADM 1/5447]

Minutes of proceedings at a court martial held on board His Majesty's ship *Impregnable* in Hamoaze on Wednesday the 16th day of November 1814.

Present

Robert Hall, Esq[re]., Captain of His Majesty's ship *Impregnable* and third officer in the command of His Majesty's ships and vessels at Plymouth, President.

Captains

Alex[r]. Wilmot Schomberg	Thomas Briggs
Thomas Browne	James Hillyar
Gilbert Heathcote	Francis Newcombe
Charles Montagu Fabian	Henry Weir
Robert Bloye	

George Eastlake, Jun[r]., officiating Judge Advocate

Being all the captains of post ships then and there present next in seniority to the president.

The prisoner, John Brown (8), Able Seaman of His Majesty's ship *Centaur*, was brought into court, and the witnesses and audience admitted.

Thos. Gordon Caulfield, Esqr., Captain of the said ship, appeared as prosecutor.

Read – The order of the Right Honble the Lords Commissrs. of the Admiralty, dated the 11th day of November 1814, directed to the president, to try the said John Brown (8) for absenting himself without leave.

The court was then duly sworn.

Read – The annexed letter from the said Capt. Caulfield to Rr. Admiral Martin (No 1).

All the witnesses, except the first to be sworn, then withdrew.

Mr. Thomas Walker, Captain's Clerk on board the said ship, sworn and examined as follows:

The muster book of the *Centaur* produced to the court, whereby it appeared that John Brown (8), AB, No. 2292, was checqued without leave on the 5th day of November 1814 and his returned entry was the 9th day of November 1814 and there appeared a charge of £3 straggling against his growing pay.

Jud. Adv. Is the muster book of the *Centaur,* now before the court, kept by you?

A. Yes.

Jud. Adv. Are the records on the said book of the checque and re-entry of John Brown (8) true records?

A. Yes.

Jud. Adv. Is the prisoner now in court, the person designed by the name of John Brown (8) at No. 2292 on the said book?

A. Yes.

The witness withdrew.

Lieut. Henry Pryce of His Majesty's ship *Centaur*, sworn and examined as follows:

Pro. Relate to the court what you know respecting the charge against the prisoner.

A. On the morning of the 5th of November inst. the prisoner was reported absent out of the ship and, by enquiry, I found he had not been seen since the evening before at 5 o'clock.

Pro. Were you commanding officer on board the *Centaur* on Friday the 4th of November inst.?

A. Yes.

Pro. Had the prisoner your permission to go out of the ship or was he sent out of her on duty?

A. No.
Pro. When did you report his absence to me?
A. To the best of my recollection the next day (Sunday).
Pro. What steps were taken in consequence?
A. His description was sent to the different Rendezvous Admirals' Office and guardhouses.
Pro. When did you see the prisoner again?
A. He was brought on board in the captain's barge on Wednesday the 9th ins[t]. as a prisoner in charge of a sergeant of marines.

The witness withdrew.

Thomas Fice, Ship's Corporal on board the *Centaur*, sworn and examined as follows:

Pro. Do you know the prisoner?
A. Yes.
Pro. What was the latest hour you saw the prisoner on Friday evening the 4th ins[t].?
A. Between 2 & 3 in the afternoon.
Pro. When did you miss the prisoner from the ship?
A. A few minutes before 8 the same evening.
Pro. When did you see the prisoner again after having missed him?
A. On Wednesday the 9th; he was on board in the barge under charge of a man in a blue jacket. He was put in confinement in irons.

The witness withdrew.

M[r]. Thomas Walker again called in.

Co[t]. Is there any charge for straggling against the prisoner previous to this offence?
A. None.
Co[t]. Did you deliver to the person who brought the prisoner on board the *Centaur* a certificate of straggling money being charged against him?
A. I did to Serg[t]. Thomas Davie of the Royal Marines.

The witness withdrew.

The prosecution being closed, the prisoner was asked if he had anything to offer in his behalf, when he delivered in the annexed written paper (No. 2) signed by himself which was read to the court.

The prisoner having nothing further to offer, the court was cleared and proceeded to deliberate upon and form the sentence.

The court, having very maturely and deliberately weighed and considered the evidence in support of the charge as well as what the prisoner had offered in his behalf, was of opinion that the charge had been proved against the prisoner John Brown (8) and the court did in consequence adjudge the said John Brown (8) to receive fifty lashes with a cat-o'-nine-tails on his bare back on board His Majesty's ship *Centaur* to which he belongs.

The court was opened and the sentence pronounced accordingly. …

92A. *Caulfield to Martin*

[ADM 1/5447]

Centaur in Plymouth Sound
Nov[r]., 9th, 1814

[No. 1]

… John Brown (8), an Able Seaman belonging to His Majesty's ship under my command, having absented himself on Friday evening the 4th ins[t]. without leave and having been informed by the 1st lieutenant that he has been repeatedly guilty of so doing,

I have to request their Lordships will be pleased to order a court martial on him for the same. …

92B. *Defence of Brown*

[ADM 1/5447]

[No. 2]

… John Brown, the prisoner before your honours, begs humbly to offer the following few words in his defence, trusting to the lenity & goodness of a merciful court. On the ship's arrival in harbour, I once obtained liberty to go on shore & returned according to the time granted. I frequently asked afterwards, but was always denied, which I thought hard, seeing the rest of my shipmates obtain liberty as frequent has they applied [*sic*], which induced me to go without leave of an evening after work & return the following morning before daylight. The 1st lieutenant, finding me guilty of the same, ordered me into the black list & into irons every night and my grog to be stopp'd, which was for 14 days until Friday 4th instant. At 10 minutes past 5 o'clock in the afternoon, I called a shore boat alongside the *Centaur* & left her I believed unobserved, not with an intention, Hon[d]. Gent[n]., of deserting, that been [*sic*] far from my ideas.

I should have returned myself on Tuesday; but as coming from North Corner to Mutton Cove with an intention of coming on board, but was taken into custody & carried to the guardhouse until the following morning when I was taken to the admiral's office, from thence to the *Centaur*. Having nothing further, and in my defence, I humbly trust myself to the judgement, mercy and goodness of so honourable a court. …

93. *Court Martial of Robert Eccles and George Chapman*

[ADM 1/5447]

Minutes of proceedings at a court martial held on board His Majesty's ship *Impregnable* in Hamoaze at Plymouth on Wednesday the 7th day of December 1814.

Present

Thomas Gordon Caulfield, Esqre., Captain of His Majesty's ship *Centaur* and second officer in the command of His Majesty's ships and vessels at Plymouth, President.

Captains

Robert Hall (1)	Alexander Wilmot Schomberg
Thomas Browne	Charles Malcolm
James Hillyar	John Bastard
Francis Newcombe	John Tailour

George Eastlake Junr., officiating Judge Advocate

Being all the captains then and there present, except Capt. Henry Weir of His Majesty's ship *Thais*, who was from sickness unable to attend the court, and Captain William Fairbrother Carroll, who was the prosecutor.

The prisoners Robert Eccles, Quarter Gunner, and George Chapman (1), A.B., belonging to His Majesty's ship *Cyrus*, were brought into court, and the witnesses and audience admitted.

The said Captain Carroll appeared as prosecutor.

Read – The order of the Rt. Hble the Lords Commissioners of the Admiralty, dated the 3rd day of December 1814, directed to the president to try the said Robert Eccles & George Chapman (1) for having attempted to desert from leave.

The members of the court and judge advocate were then duly sworn.

Read – The annexed letter of charge from the said Captain Carroll to Rear Admiral Martin, Commander in Chief at Plymouth.

The witnesses, except the first to be sworn, then withdrew.

The muster book of His Majesty's ship *Cyrus* produced to the court, whereby it appeared that Robert Eccles, Q^{r}. Gunner, No. 36, & Geo. Chapman (1), A.B., No. 83, were checqued without leave on the 20th day of October 1814 and their returned entry was on the 21st day of the same month.

Mr. Thomas Chapman, Captain's Clerk on board the *Cyrus*, sworn and examined as follows:

Jud. Adv. Is the muster book of the *Cyrus* now before the court kept by you?

A. Yes.

Jud. Adv. Are the records on the said book of the checque and re-entry of Robert Eccles and George Chapman true records?

A. Yes.

Jud. Adv. Are the prisoners now in court the persons designed by the names of Robert Eccles and George Chapman at Nos. 36 and 83 on the said book?

A. Yes. There is a charge of £3 straggling against each of the prisoners growing pay on the complete book of the *Cyrus*.

The witness withdrew.

Lieut. Charles Lechmere of His Majesty's ship *Cyrus* sworn and examined as follows:

Pro. State the leave you gave the prisoners on or about the 20th of October last and whether they returned at the expiration of it.

A. They had leave on the evening of the 19th until 6 o'clock on the morning of the 20th.

Pro. At what time did they return and in what way?

A. They were brought off by the gunner in the gig about noon on the 21st.

Co[t]. Did you ask the prisoners what kept them beyond their leave?

A. I put some question of that sort to them and they said they merely meant to take a country walk.

The witness withdrew.

John Bedworth, Private of the Royal Marines and one of the look-out men stationed at Crabtree near Plymouth, sworn and examined as follows:

Pro. Do you know the persons of the prisoners?

A. Yes.

Pro. State where you apprehended them and when.

A. About the 20th of October last at 6 in the evening at Crabtree, about three miles from Plymouth on the London Road. They were walking on the road and I asked them what ship they belonged to; and they said, 'the *Cyrus*, 20 gun ship.' I then asked them if they were discharged; they told me no, they were upon leave. I asked them how far they were going; they said to Ivybridge. I asked them if they had any liberty tickets; they told me no, they told me the officers never gave any liberty tickets, but let them go where they liked. I then took them into custody and delivered them into the charge of Corporal Coates and William Willy, who conveyed them to Plymouth. The prisoners were dressed as sailors and not all disguised. Eccles had his pea jacket on.

Co^{t}. Had they any parcel or bundle of clothes with them?

A. No, nothing at all.

Co^{t}. Had you any person with you to assist you in taking them?

A. No.

Co^{t}. Did they make any resistance?

A. Not any at all.

Co^{t}. Were they sober at that time?

A. They appeared as if they had been drinking.

The witness withdrew.

Corp^{l}. Coates of the Royal Marines and one of the lookout men at Crabtree, sworn and examined as follows:

Pro. Do you know the prisoners?

A. Yes.

Pro. Did you apprehend them and where?

A. I went into the Crabtree Inn on the 20th of October last in the evening and found the prisoners there with John Bedworth, a Private Marine; he told me in the presence of the prisoners that he had detained them on the road. I then asked them where they were going; they said to Ivybridge to see a friend. I asked if they had any liberty ticket; they said no, they never had any from the *Cyrus*. I then went to Ridgway for assistance and took them to the admiral's office at Plymouth.

Pro. How were the prisoners dressed?

A. In seamen's great coats, both.

Co^{t}. Were the prisoners disguised or dressed as sailors?

A. As sailors.

Co^{t}. Had they any bundle or parcel with them?

A. No.

Co^{t}. Did they make any resistance?

A. No.

The witness withdrew.

William Mc Cullum, Seaman on board the *Cyrus*, sworn and examined as follows:

Pro. Did you offer the prisoners money for the purpose of paying their waterage[1] off the morning the ship last went out of Hamoaze?

[1]Waterage was a fee paid for the transportation of cargo by water (Falconer, *A New Universal Dictionary*, s.v. Waterage).

A. Yes and they told me they were going on board, for they took the money, which was one shilling.

The witness withdrew.

The evidence in support of the charge being here closed, the prisoners were asked if they had anything to offer in their defence, when they stated through the judge advocate that they had no intention whatever to desert and that they had been out to Ivybridge several times to see their friend, Susanna Brett, who lives at the inn there, and they never were stopped before. They farther called the attention of the court to the circumstance of their having told a true story and made no resistance upon being stopped.

The prisoners having nothing further to offer, the court was cleared and proceeded to deliberate upon and form the sentence.

The court, having very maturely and deliberately weighed and considered the evidence in support of the charge as well as what the prisoners had offered in their behalf, was of opinion that the charge had not been proved against the prisoners, Robert Eccles and George Chapman, and the court did in consequence adjudge them to be acquitted.

The court was opened, the witnesses and audience admitted and the prisoners respectively acquitted accordingly. …

93A. *Carroll to Martin*

[ADM 1/5447]

His Majesty's ship *Cyrus*
Plymouth Sound, Decr. 1, 1814

… The two men named in the margin [Robt. Eccles, Qr Gunner; Geo. Chapman (1) AB], seamen belonging to His Majesty's ship under my command, having attempted to desert from leave on or about the 20th of October 1814 at this port,

I request you will be pleased to move their Lordships to order a court martial to be held on the above men to try them for the said offence. …

94. *Court Martial of Major Reynolds*

[ADM 1/5448]

Minutes of proceedings at a court martial held on board His Majesty's [ship?] *York* in Hamoaze at Plymouth on Thursday, the 13th day of April 1815.

Present

Alexander Wilmot Schomberg, Esq[re]., Captain of His Majesty's ship *York* and third officer in the command of His Majesty's ships & vessels at Plymouth, President.

Captains

Henry Edward Reginald Baker	James Nash
Samuel Campbell Rowley	The Honble Henry Duncan
Thomas Brown	Matthew Smith
William Paterson	William Fairbrother Carroll
James John Gordon Bremer	

George Eastlake Jun[r], officiating Judge Advocate

Being all the captains of post ships then and there present next in seniority to the president, except Capt. James Richard Dacres, who was prosecutor, and Captains Gilbert Heathcote and George Rose Sartorius, who were sick.

The prisoner, M[r]. Major Reynolds, acting Gunner of His Majesty's ship *Tiber*, was brought into court and the witnesses and audience admitted.

The surgeons of the *Scamander* & *Slaney* appeared and severally certified on oath the illnesses of Captains Heathcote and Sartorius of those ships and their consequent inability to attend the court, whereupon the members thought fit to dispense with the attendance of the said Captains Heathcote and Sartorius.

Read – The order of the R[t]. Honble the Lords Commiss[rs]. of the Admiralty, dated the 9th day of April 1815 directed to the president, to try the said M[r]. Major Reynolds for having gone on shore on leave on or about the 29th of March 1815 for a few hours and not returning on board until the 5th of April 1815.

The members of the court and judge advocate were then duly sworn.

Read – The annexed letter of charge from the said Capt. Dacres to Adm[l]. Sir J. T. Duckworth, Commander in Chief at Plymouth.[1]

The witnesses, except for the first to be sworn, then withdrew.

Lieut. Henry Thomas Lutwidge of His Majesty's ship *Tiber* sworn & examined as follows:

Pros[r]. Did you give the prisoner leave to go on shore & when?

A. Yes, on Wednesday the 29th of March last in the afternoon.

Pros[r]. For what time?

A. To return for duty on the morning following.

Pro. Did he come on board voluntarily or was he brought on board?

[1]This letter is not bound with the transcript.

A. Brought on board by the sergeant of marines on Wednesday the 5th of April in the afternoon, which was the first time I had seen him since he left the ship.

Co^{t}. Did the prisoner appear in the same health when he was brought on board as he had enjoyed when he went on shore?

A. Yes.

Co^{t}. Where was the ship?

A. In Barnpool.

Co^{t}. Are you sure he did not come on board before the 5th of April?

A. Yes, for had he been on board I must have known it.

The witness withdrew.

Lieut. William Smith (5) of the *Tiber* sworn and examined as follows:

Pro. Did you see the prisoner on shore between the 29th of March last & the 5th of April ins^{t}.?

A. I did, on Friday the 31st of March in Fore Street Dock.

Pro. Did you speak to him?

A. Yes, I told him the ship was come up into Barnpool and that we were getting the powder out and that he must go on board immediately. He said he would.

Pro. Did he appear in health sufficient to enable him to go on board at the time you saw him?

A. He appeared perfectly well.

Pro. Was the fitting of the ship in his department delayed by his absence?

A. Certainly, I conceive so.

The witness withdrew.

Lieut. William Glascock of the *Tiber* sworn & examined as follows:

Pros^{r}. Did you see the prisoner on shore between the 29th of March last & the 5th of April ins^{t}.?

A. I did, on the 31st of March in Fore Street, Plymouth Dock. I spoke to him and advised him to go on board the ship and asked him whether he was aware of the ship having taken her powder out; he answered he was not and that he would go on board her. He did not go on board until (I think) the 5th of April ins^{t}.

Pros^{r}. Did he appear in health sufficient to enable him to go on board at the time you saw him?

A. He appeared to me to be in perfect health when I saw him on shore.

Co^{t}. On what day was the *Tiber*'s gunpowder sent on shore?

A. On the 31st of March, as well as I can recollect.

Co^{t}. Where was the ship when the prisoner went on shore on the 29th of March?

A. I believe in Plymouth Sound.

The witness withdrew.

Serg^{t}. Thomas Brooks of the Royal Marines serving on board the *Tiber* sworn & examined as follows:

Pro. Were you sent on shore to look for the prisoner and on what day?

A. I was, on Tuesday evening the 4th of April ins^{t}.

Pro. Did you find him & where and when?

A. Yes, at the Commercial Inn, New Passage Dock on Wednesday the 5th of April ins^{t}.

Pro. Was he well enough to come on board without assistance?

A. Yes.

Pro. Did you take him in charge and conduct him on board the ship?

A. Yes.

Co^{t}. State what passed on your first meeting the prisoner at the Commercial Inn.

A. I found him in the passage of the Inn talking to someone. I told him I was come for him; he told me that he was coming on board and that he had been sick.

Co^{t}. Did he say how long he had been sick?

A. No, he said nothing more.

Co^{t}. Do you know whether the prisoner was on board at any time between the 29th of March & 5th of April inst.?

A. Not to my knowledge.

Co^{t}. On your apprehending the prisoner at the Inn, did he appear to you to have been sick?

A. Yes, to appearance he had been sick.

The witness withdrew.

The evidence in support of the charge being here closed, the prisoner was acquainted thereof and asked if he had anything to offer in his behalf, when he stated:

That he had been upwards of 16 years in the service and that he wished to leave his case to the mercy of the court.

Capt. Dacres, the prosecutor, said he had received a very good character with the prisoner, but that he had known him himself but a very short time.

The court was then cleared and proceeded to deliberate upon and form the sentence.

The court, having very maturely and deliberately weighed and considered the evidence in support of the charge as well as what the prisoner had offered in his behalf, was of opinion that the charge had been proved against the prisoner M[r]. Major Reynolds and the court did in consequence adjudge the said M[r]. Major Reynolds to be dismissed his situation of gunner in His Majesty's navy and to serve before the mast on board such of His Majesty's ships or vessels as the commander in chief of His Majesty's ships and vessels at Plymouth shall direct.

The court was opened, the prisoner brought in, the witnesses and audience re-admitted and the sentence pronounced accordingly. …

CHALLENGES TO AUTHORITY

A. Mutiny

95. *Court Martial of Michael Goley, Robert Powell, Peter Wair and Robert Field*

[ADM 1/5335]

Minutes of the proceedings of a court martial assembled and held on board His Majesty's ship *Cambridge* in Hamoaze on Friday, the 29th of April 1796, for the trial of Michael Goley, Robert Powell, Peter Wair and Robert Field, 'for having mutinied on board His Majesty's hired tender *Castor*.'

Present

Arthur Phillip, Esq., Captain of His Majesty's ship *Alexander*, and second officer in the command of His Majesty's ships and vessels at Plymouth, President.

Captains	Captains
Richard Bogar	John Drew
Richard Gridall	Geo. Martin
Richard Rundle Burgess	Francis Cole
Robert Carthew Reynolds	John Osborn
Anthony Hunt	Israel Pellew
John Bazeley, Junr.	Geo. Byng

H.M. Stokes
D.J.A.

The surgeon of the *Indefatigable* appeared to certify the inability of Captain Sir Edward Pellew's attending through ill health.

Lieutenant Alexander Allen sworn

Court – Do you know the prisoners?

A. – Yes.

C. – Do you know that the prisoners, Michael Goley, Robert Powell, Peter Wair and Robert Field, were the four sentinels placed over you, when the mutiny was on board the *Castor* tender?

A. – Peter Wair was a sentinel, the other three were found under arms when we got upon deck.

C. – Relate the particulars of the mutiny on board the *Castor* tender, and what part all or either of the prisoners had in it.

A. – Between the hours of 4 and 5 P.M. on the fifth of December 1795, I left orders with the midshipman who had the watch to keep a good look out. The weather being favourable, I'd every reason to imagine we should be able to sail in the morning. I had not been down in the cabin at tea five minutes, when, very much to my surprise, the people rose, and confined me to the cabin. I immediately attempted to get on deck up the companion ladder, but was prevented by the prisoner, Peter Wair, who had a drawn cutlass in his hand, which obliged me to return down to the cabin, where I remained some time and then attempted to go out of the cabin window, which I accomplished, and got on deck; and when on deck, I was not permitted to stay, but the prisoner, Peter Wair, said I must go down to the cabin, which I was obliged to do, and went down the companion. Manacle [*sic*] Eagle came just after me, and we took a musket, and fired at the prisoner, Peter Wair, the sentinel, and the others upon deck, at which time the boatswain joined us in the cabin from below, and then we went upon deck, the sentinel having laid down his arms. When I got on deck, we put Peter Wair into confinement, and the other three the next morning, in consequence of being informed by the boatswain and midshipman that they had broke open the store room and plundered it of provisions &^{ca}. and also having been in arms during the mutiny.

C. – Did you meet with any resistance when you put Peter Wair in irons?

A. – None.

C. – Did you know that the prisoners were volunteers?

A. – Yes.

C. – How do you know it?

A. – By the list that was brought with them from the regulating captain at Chester.[1]

C. – Had you any prest men on board?

[1]According to Falconer, *A New Universal Dictionary*, a regulating captain was 'an officer stationed at the different naval ports in time of war to examine the seamen intended for the navy, whether pressed or volunteers, and to see that they are fit for His Majesty's service before they are sent on board a man of war' (s.v. Regulating Captain).

A. – No, not any.

C. – How long had the volunteers been on board the tender previous to the mutiny?

A. – About four days.

C. – Do you know that they had heard the Articles of War read?

A. – Yes.

C. – What, to all of them?

A. – Yes.

C. – Peter Wair, have you any questions to ask this evidence?

A. – No.

C. – Have any of you other prisoners?

Robert Powell – Why was I not confined when Peter Wair was?

A. – I was not informed until the next morning of your being one of the mutineers.

Mr. William Johns sworn.

C. – Do you know the prisoners?

A. – Yes, all of them.

C. – Relate the peculiars of the mutiny on board the *Castor* tender, and what part all or either of the prisoners had in it.

A. – I don't recollect the day, but it was between the hours of five and six o'clock in the evening when I came down to the steerage with the keys. I heard a noise upon deck; the people were forcing their away [*sic*] down to the steerage, insisting on me to tell them where the arms were. I answered, I had not the keys nor did I know where they were. They then forced the arms chest, and took all the arms upon deck, and placed sentinels over the steerage; by these means, I had no power to get up. By the firing of a musket or a pistol from the cabin, we got up of the steerage upon deck, and took those four men, who were pointed out to have been sentinels by some of the remaining volunteers, and put Michael Goley, Peter Wair and Robert Field into irons immediately, and Robert Powell was confined the next morning.

C. – Do you know what prevented the prisoners going on shore when the others did?

A. – I cannot say.

C. – Do you suppose all the volunteers meant to go on shore?

A. – I cannot tell.

C. – Had you any prest men on board?

A. – No.

C. – Were either of the prisoners employed in breaking open the arms chest?

A. – Yes, Michael Goley was; I saw him.

C. – Who was the officer of the watch?

A. – M^{r}. Hutton.

C. – Prisoners, have you any questions to ask this evidence?

All the prisoners – No.

M^{r}. Robert Powell, Boatswain, sworn.

Court – Do you know the prisoners?

A. – Yes.

C. – Relate what you know of the mutiny on board the *Castor* tender and what part all or either of the prisoners took in it.

A. – On the 5th December 1795, in the evening between 5 & 6 o'clock, I was just gone below, and I heard a great noise upon deck. The mate was going up to see what the noise was, and the people made a blow at him with a handspike & wou'd not let him or myself get up, telling him to stay below. Then a number of them came down in the steerage and broke the arm chest open, and handed all the arms up on deck, broke the storeroom open and handed up the provisions. Then they all went upon deck, excepting one man, who stood sentinel over us awhile. Not being able to get at any arms, I thought I could get through the after hold to the cabin, which I did, and got some pistols and powder, and returned back to the steerage again, and was going to fire on the sentinels when they made towards the cabin door where we cou'd not get the pistols to bear on them. Those that were in the cabin then fired on them and then they ran away and we got on deck. When we got on deck, we began to clue the sails.

C. – Did you observe either of the prisoners at the breaking open the arms chest, with arms in their hands?

A. – I saw Michael Goley with arms; he was the sentinel placed over us in the steerage with a musket and a bayonet.

C. – Cou'd you see the sentinel at the companion from below?

A. – I could see many people, but could not distinguish the sentinel.

C. – Did you see any of the prisoners break[g]. open the storeroom door or taking away any part of the provisions?

A. – I cannot say I saw either of them.

C. – Do you know when the prisoners were confined?

A. – Three were confined that night, Michael Goley and two others, but I cannot name the other two.

C. – Do you know the reason why Powell was confined?

A. – No, I do not.

C. – Did you ever make a complaint of him to Lieutenant Allen?

A. – No.

Meleken Eagle sworn.

C. – Do you know all the prisoners?

A. – Yes.

C. – Relate what you know of the mutiny on board the *Castor* tender, and what part all or either of the prisoners took in it.

A. – I was setting in the steerage (I do not recollect the day of the month) in the evening between 5 and 6 o'clock, and heard a noise on deck. The mate rose and went up the ladder, and asked what was the matter, but before he got up the ladder a blow was made at him with a handspike and then he cried out to me that there was a mutiny. We wanted to go up, but were obliged to remain below. Some of the volunteers came down in the steerage; we ran into the storeroom. Hearing no noise, I got on deck through the steerage hatchway and was followed by a man with a gun and bayonet, which made me jump down the companion into the cabin, where I found the Lieutenant. He ordered me to take a gun and fire up the companion at the man, who stood sentinel there. After firing the gun, they all ran away and we went on deck, where we found the rest of our ship's company & took possession. We then went down to the press room to see who was there and found many men, among who was Peter Wair and Robert Field. The other two we found between decks.

C. – Who were the men you saw armed?

A. – Wair and Goley I saw with arms in their hands in the steerage.

C. – Did you assist in putting those men into confinement and at what time?

A. – Yes, Wair and Goley was confined the same night.

C. – Do you know why the other two were confined the next day?

A. – On account of the mutiny; I saw them in the steerage.

Court – Did you see either of the prisoners take away any provisions from the storeroom? If you did, name them or point them out.

A. – Yes, Wair, Goley and Powell.

C. – Had you any prest men on board?

A. – Not that I know of.

C. – Prisoners have you any questions to ask this evidence?

All the prisoners – No, not any.

Prosecution closed

Robert Powell read the following defence:

… Since it has been my misfortune to be a prisoner and liable to be tried by the laws of my King and country, I think myself peculiarly happy to have the honour of submitting my situation and case to the impartiality and clemency of this honourable court. I hope the gentleman will hear me with patience whilst I make my defence.

Before the men mutinied in Liverpool, I was continually between decks; but on the evening of the mutiny, I happened to be dressing something for supper, where I was obliged to remain some time in preservation of my life, but crept down between decks as soon as I possibly could, where I remained until I was put in irons next morning on the quarter deck. I do solemnly declare I neither aided or assisted the mutineers in any respect, as I dreaded I should be complicated in the dreadful scene that was then going on. Now that this is the truth, I affirm before that tribunal that judgeth not as man judgeth, and do solemnly declare it before this august court to whose decision in mercy and justice I submit myself …

John Maurrin sworn.

Robert Powell – Before the mutiny was not I continually between decks?

A. – Yes.

P. – At the time the mutiny [*sic*], was not I obliged to remain upon deck to preserve my life?

A. – I cannot say.

P. – Did not I creep down between decks as soon as I cou'd with safety and remained there quietly until I was confined in the following morning?

A. – Yes, you came down within a few minutes after the mutiny began and remained there close by my side till the next morning.

P. – Did I assist the mutineers?

A. – You did not, to my knowledge.

C. – Was Powell with you when the musket was fired from the cabin?

A. – Yes.

James Runy sworn.

Court – What was you on board the *Castor* tender?

A. – A volunteer.

Peter Wair – Was not I down in the press room during the whole time of the mutiny on board the tender?

A. – I saw you there after many of the men had gone up, but cannot say how long you remained there after they had taken away the light.

Michael Goley – Was I not down in the press room during the whole time of the mutiny on board the tender?

A. – I saw you there part of the time.

Robert Field – Was I not down in the press room during the whole or any part of the time of the mutiny on board the tender?

A. – I do not recollect.

Court – After having entered a volunteer in the service, had you heard the Articles of War read & where?

A. – Yes, on board the *Actaeon* and the tender.

Patrick Mc Sharry sworn.

C. – What was you on board the tender?

A. – A volunteer.

Robert Field – Do you know that I was in the press room when the mutiny began and did not those on deck break off the grating, point the arms down the press room and threaten to kill every man that would not come on deck?

A. – You was in the press room when the mutiny began and those on deck did point the arms down and threaten to kill every man that would not come on deck.

Michael Goley – Was I not in the press room during the whole or any part of the time of the mutiny on board the tender?

A. – Yes, you, Field and Wair were there till a man came down with a cutlass and a pistol about ten minutes after the mutiny began.

C. – Did you see them go up?

A. – No.

C. – Did you hear the musket fired?

A. – Yes, I did.

C. – Did you know where Field, Wair and Goley were at the time?

A. – To the best of my knowledge, in the press room.

C. – From the time the shot was fired till the tender was in the possession of the lieutenant, were those men there?

A. – I cannot say they remained there, t'was from voice only I knew; there was no light.

The charge not proved against Robert Powell and Robert Field.

The charge fully proved against Michael Goley and Peter Wair.

Sentence

Robert Powell and Robert Field acquitted.

Michael Goley and Peter Wair to be hanged, but recommended to mercy. …

95A. *Members of the Court to Nepean*

[ADM 1/5335]

Cambridge in Hamoaze
29th April 1796

… The court martial assembled this day on board the *Cambridge* for the trial of the men named in the margin [Mich^{l}. Goley, Robt. Powell, Peter Wair, Robt. Field] having found themselves under the necessity of condemning Michael Goley and Peter Wair, the two prisoners against whom the mutiny was fully proved, from the ignorance of those men who had been only a few days raised and from the court being fully satisfied that they were not the ringleaders, but had arms put into their hands by those who escaped before they had time to reflect on the consequences, do therefore beg to recommend them to His Majesty's mercy. …

95B. *Stokes to Nepean*

[ADM 1/5335]

Cambridge in Hamoaze,
3d. May 1796

… Herewith I transmit the minutes of a court martial held on the men named in the margin [Michael Goley, Robert. Powell, Peter Wair & Robert Field] for mutiny on board the *Castor* tender, which you will be pleased to lay before my Lords Commissioners of the Admiralty. …

96. *Court Martial of James Dollard and Garrett Caine*

[ADM 1/5349]

Minutes taken at a court martial assembled on board His Majesty's ship *Gladiator* in Portsmouth Harbour on the 9th day of April 1799.

Present

Sir Roger Curtis, Bar[t]., Vice Admiral of the White and second officer in the command of His Majesty's ships and vessels at Portsmouth and Spithead, President.

Captain	Captain
Albemarle Bertie	John Sutton
Sir Richard John Strachan, Bar[t].	Francis Sickmore
Sir Thomas Williams, Kn[t].	Lawrence William Tealsted
Francis Hayerman	Alexander Fraser
George Burdon	Henry Bayntun
William Bedford	Charles John Moore Mansfield

The prisoners were brought in and audience admitted.

The order from the Right Honble Lords Commissioners of the Admiralty, dated the 8th of April inst[t]. and directed to the President, for the trial of James Dollard and Garrett Caine, two Seamen belonging to His Majesty's ship *Diana*, for a breach of the 19th Article of War in endeavouring to make a mutinous assembly on board the said ship, was read.

The President reported to the court that Captain E. L. Gower was absent on Admiralty leave.

The members of the court and the judge advocate, then, in open court and before they proceeded to trial, respectively took the several oaths enjoined and directed in and by an Act of Parliament made and passed in the 22nd year of the reign of His late Majesty George the 2nd, entitled: *An Act for Amending, Explaining and Reducing into one Act of Parliament the Laws Relating to the Government of His Majesty's Ships, Vessels and Forces by Sea.*

Then the letter, dated the 11th September last containing the charge was read, and the witnesses were ordered to withdraw, and attend their examinations separately, which they did as follows:

Lieut.[t] James Meares of the *Diana* called and sworn.

The court asked:

Q – Relate to the court what you know of the charge against the prisoners.

A – On Tuesday September 11th 1798, about a ¼ before noon, the officer of the watch sent the mate (M[r] Brown) to acquaint me in the gun room that several of the people had been aft on the quarter deck requesting leave to dine below, which Captain Faulknor had no objection to, if I thought proper, as it was contrary to the regulation of the ship for the people to dine below, when the between decks were cleaned, except in bad weather, and the surgeon (who was present) being of opinion it was highly improper they should dine there, the deck not being perfectly dry. I represented it to Capt[n] Faulknor, who ordered the men to dine upon deck. At this time several were between decks and had lowered their chests down. I immediately gave directions for the chests being tied up again, and the people to dine upon deck. A little past noon, having piped to dinner, I was informed by M[r] Trelore (Master's Mate) that the ship's company had refused taking their meat. I immediately acquainted Capt[n] Faulknor with it, and proposed going myself with two officers to see the meat served out, which he desired to be done, Lieut[t] Gibbons and M[r] Brown (Master) attended me at the coppers; M[r] Trelore (Mate) and the ship's steward was likewise present. When upon calling over the messes, beginning with the first mess, James Dollard and Garrett Caine (Seamen), belonging to the 1st mess, refused taking their meat, I called them separately and guarded them against what they were doing. Asking their reasons for not taking their meat, they replied they would not take it except the ship's company did. I immediately took them aft on the quarter deck, and represented their conduct to Captn Faulknor, requesting they might be confined. On my returning to the coppers the remaining man in the mess (Dennis Bryan) was called; he took his meat, as did every other mess, when they were called. After the prisoners were confined, I was told they said the cause of their refusing their meat was in consequence of the boatswain's mates and ship's company agreeing to it. Upon which, they were brought on the quarter deck in presence of the officers and told if they would impeach any of these men, they would be released. They objected doing it and spoke in general terms.

Q – Were the two prisoners the first named in the mess?

A – They were. The mess not answering, I took the mess book and called the first man on it, James Dollard and desired him to take his meat, and he said he would not. I asked him his reason, and he said he would take it if the ship's company would. I then referred to Caine and he would not take it.

Q – James Dollard asked the witness to speak to his character.

A – I have no fault to find with the prisoners in particular for anything before this.

Mr John Trelore, Master's Mate of the *Diana*, called in and sworn.

Lieut^{t}. Meares asked:

Q – Do you recollect the prisoners refusing to take their meat on the 11th of Septr last?

A – Yes.

Q – Relate to the court what you know respecting that circumstance.

A – I was upon the quarter deck and was called down along with Mr Meares. We went forward to the galley with the purser's steward to serve out the salt beef. The first mess refused, who were the two prisoners; they said they would not take it, because the rest would not. The two prisoners were sent aft on the quarter deck, and all the other messes then took their meat.

Q – Was there to your knowledge any cause of complaint ags^{t} the meat on account of the unwholesomeness of the victuals and did they make complaint thereof?
A – No.
Q – Was it customary for the ship's company to dine between decks when the decks were washed before they were dry?
A – No, unless it rained very hard.
Q – Were the decks dry at the time?
A – They were not.
Q – Did the prisoners or any of the ship's company state what their reasons were for refusing to take their meat?
A – I did not hear what they said. The boatswain's mate went aft and made a complaint (it was a cold day) to the captain. The lieut^{t} of the watch sent for me, asked me if it was done between decks; I told him it was hardly dry. The Captn had ordered the officer of the watch to lower the chests down; Lieut^{t} Meares came up and told the captain it was not dry between decks. And then orders were given to trice the chests up again, and the people were sent up. I was at the wine tub; the cooper came to me and said the people would not take their meat. I then went into the galley and then things happened as I have stated.
Q – When the prisoners refused their meat, did I guard them against such conduct?
A – Yes.
Q – What answer did they make?
A – I do not recollect; but they had before said they would not take it, because the ship's company would not, as they should be ill used for it.

Mr John Morgan, Purser's Steward of the *Diana*, called in and sworn.

The court asked:
Q – Relate to the court what you know of the charge ags^{t} the prisoner.
A – On Tuesday the 11th of September, I sent the coopers forward to serve the provisions out; they came and acquainted me that no messes answered. I went forward with Mr Trelore, Master's Mate, and called as far as the 13th mess, and nobody answered. I asked M^{r}

Trelore if he would acquaint Lieut[t] Meares, which he did. He, with others, came forward. I began with the first mess; and James Dollard and Garrett Caine were first named; and they refused to take their meat. Dennis Bryan of the same mess took it and so did the remainder of the ship's company.

M[r] John Buchan, the Surgeon, called in and sworn

Q – Do you recollect the mate of the watch acquainting me in the gun room on the 11th of September last that several of the ship's company had been aft requesting leave to dine below?

A – I recollect some person coming for that purpose, and M[r] Meares asked me if I thought the decks were sufficiently dry for the people to dine below, and I said they were not, which I told Capt[n] Faulknor of afterwards.

M[r] John Trelore called in again.

Q – Did you hear M[r] Meares tell the ship's company that the decks were too wet for them to dine below?

A – I do not recollect it.

Lieut[t] Meares was again called.

Q – When you ordered the chests to be triced up again and the people to go on deck, did you explain to the ship's company the reason for it?

A – I did not address them pointedly to that effect; many of the ship's company were aft on the quarter deck, and in the waist near enough to hear me represent the state of between decks to Captain Faulknor.

Q – Have the prisoners been in confinement since the 11th of September last?

A – They have been prisoners at large at sea, but, when in harbour, in irons. They have conducted themselves properly, since, I believe, they were led away by the ship's company.

The prisoners, being called on for their defence, delivered a paper writing to the court containing the same, which was read by the judge advocate and is hereto annexed.

William Barton, a seaman belonging to the *Diana*, called in and sworn.

Dollard asked:

Q – On the 11th of September last after the between decks had been washed, do you know that Capt[n] Faulknor gave the ship's company leave to dine below?

A – Yes.

John Reeve, a seaman belonging to the *Diana*, called in and sworn.

Dollard asked:

Q – On the 11th of September last after the between decks had been washed, do you know that Captn Faulknor gave the ship's company leave to dine below?

A – He did.

The court asked:

Q – What time had elapsed between Captn Faulknor's having given this leave and the subsequent order of the lieut^{t} to dine above?

A – The course of 3 or 4 minutes.

Q – Was there time for the 1st lieut^{t} to communicate with Captain Faulknor?

A – I do not know.

The court was cleared and agreed that the offence committed by the said James Dollard and Garrett Caine did not come within the meaning of the 19th Article of War stated in the charge, and that, therefore, it had not been proved against them, and did adjudge them to be acquitted.

The court was again opened, the prisoners brought in, audience admitted, and sentence passed accordingly. …

96A. *Meares to Faulknor*

[ADM 1/5349] *Diana* off Lugo Bay, Septr 11th 1798

… In consequence of the ship's company refusing to take their meat, having piped to dinner for that purpose, agreeable to your orders, I attended the coppers with Lieut Gibbons, Mr Brown, Master, and Mr Trelaw [*sic*], Master's Mate. When upon calling over the messes, beginning with the first mess, the men named in the margin [Jas Dollard, Garrett Caine], belonging to the first mess, refused taking their meat; upon my guarding them against what they were doing, they said they would not take it, except the ship's company did. The remaining man in the mess (Dennis Bryan) was then called; he took the meat, as did every other mess in their [ ][1] As I conceive this a species of mutiny, I have to request you will apply for a court martial on the said James Dollard and Garrett Caine, for a breach of the 19 Article of War, in endeavouring to make a mutinous assembly.

[1]There is at least one word missing here.

And, as the ship's company of the *Diana* have in many instances been very disorderly, I hope you will solicit the commander in chief for a speedy trial, as an example for the good of His Majesty's service. …

96B. *Defence of Dollard and Caine*

[ADM 1/5349]

As we have (thro ignorance) been so unfortunate as to be brought before a court martial, we most humbly entreat you to grant us so much indulgence as to condescend to look to us with an eye of mercy, and to take our case into consideration as for the charge against us, part of it we acknowledge, and part of it we deny. We acknowledge refusing the meat, but as for mutiny we deny it, as to the best of our knowledge there was not the least symptoms of mutiny in the case, which (we hope) you gentlemen will be better judges of when we will lay our case before you. …

It was customary thing [*sic*] in the ship when we did clean between decks to dine upon deck, if the weather permitted it, and the day that this unhappy accident happened was a cleaning day between decks, and consequently the hands were ordered upon deck, and sentinels placed on the hatchways to prevent the men from going down till the decks were dry, but that day happened to be severely cold. The ship's company thought proper to go aft on the quarter deck to the captain to ask his leave to dine below, which leave the captain was pleased to grant them. Then the ship's company went down between decks. The 1st L^{t}, hearing the bustle of lowering chests and placing them, rushed out of the gun room to enquire who ordered the ship's company down; he was answered the captain, at which he stamped and ordered them upon deck again, and ordered to pipe to dinner, and ordered them to dine on deck. The men accordingly went on deck, & passed the word not to take the meat till the captain would be upon deck, so as to let him know that they were upon deck by the said 1st L^{t}, contrary to his orders. Having piped to dinner, as before observed, the purser's steward came to serve out the meat; but as the captain did not come on deck, since we were ordered up by the 1st L^{t}., the ship's company would not take it. He (the purser's steward), having once called the mess, but none would take the meat, whereupon he went and acquainted the said 1st L^{t}. of it, who came accompanied by the master and more of the officers to see that the men did take their meat. We happened to belong to the 1st mess, were the first that was called upon to take our meat; but as the ship's company did not see the captain, since ordered up by the said 1st L^{t}., we refused the meat, and were immediately ordered into irons. But being called aft, and also the ship's company, the captain told us of the impropriety of our conduct. But the said 1st L[t] said, altho we were the only unfortunate two that had the misfortune to be taken in for the whole, he believed we were innocent, and that nothing but our ignorance would bring us into such trouble; and he further said that he had before observed some symptoms of disorder among the ship's company and therefore was determined to try by court martial the first he could lay hold on and said he was very sorry to have pitched upon us, as he knew we were innocent of any mutinous design. Therefore, gentlemen, we have nothing further to add, but our innocence; we most humbly entreat your mercy. …

97. *Court Martial of David Roach, Nicholas Harrison and Naiad Suare*

[ADM 1/ 5376]

Minutes of the proceedings of a court martial assembled and held on board His Majesty's ship *Seine* in Carlisle Bay, Barbados on Monday the 3d November 1806 for the trial of David Roach, Nicholas Harrison and Naiad Suare for having been concerned with 'that part of the crew of His Majesty's late armed sloop *Dominica,* while lying to off the town of Rousseau in the island of Dominica during the absence of Lieutenant William Dean, her commander, on shore on duty on the evening of the 21st May last, did mutiny and take forcible possession of the said armed sloop and carry her to an enemy port.'

Present

David Atkins, Esq., Captain of His Majesty's ship *Seine* and second officer in the command of His Majesty's ships and vessels in Carlisle Bay, Barbados,

President.

Captains	Ship	Captain	Ship
George Sayer	*Galatea*	Hugh Pigot	*Circe*
Nath[l] Day Cochrane	*Northumberland*	Isaac Ferrieres	*Melville*

Thomas Freeman Jessip
officiating Judge Advocate

The order for trial being read and the court sworn:

M[r] Richard Osborn, Acting Master, sworn.

Court — Do you know the prisoners David Roach, Nicholas Harrison and Naiad Suare and did they belong to the *Dominica* sloop?

A. Yes.

C. Were they on board the *Dominica* on the night of the 21st May last when the crew rose and took possession of her?

A. Yes.

Court Relate to the court the conduct of the prisoner David Roach on that evening.

A. About 6 o'clock in the evening, I saw him between decks sick. When the mutiny commenced at half past 9, the mutineers put me below in the between decks; I soon after took the names of everyone below and David Roach was not there. The next morning when Henry Proctor called me on deck, he took me down to the cabin and asked me in presence of the clerk, M^{r}. Nicholes, who was there, for the key of the writing desk. On looking round, I saw David Roach setting on one of the lockers.

C. Was David Roach assisting in putting you below?

A. I did not see him.

C. Did you hear him aiding and assisting hoisting the sails or active in the mutiny?

A. I did not.

C. Did you know him make any exertion either to prevent or stop the mutiny?

A. I did not.

C. What was his conduct in the cabin?

A. He was laying sick against one of the pumps and did not speak.

C. Was he armed in any manner or did you consider him a sentinel over the clerk?

A. He was not armed and [I?] could not consider him as a sentry.

C. If the prisoner David Roach had made any exertion either to prevent or assist the mutiny, do you think you would have heard him?

A. Yes.

C. Do you know on what occasion the prisoner David Roach went into the cabin or had you any conversation with him there?

A. I don't know; I had no conversation with him.

C. Has it come to your knowledge whether the prisoner David Roach was put down to the cabin or went there of his own accord?

A. No, it has not.

C. Did you see the prisoner David Roach on deck after you had seen him in the cabin?

A. No.

C. Was the sickly state of David Roach such as to prevent his taking an active part either for or against the mutiny?

A. He had been sick several days and appeared very sick at the time.

C. How long were you in the cabin with him?

A. Quarter of an hour.

C. Did you see any person speak to him?

A. No more than ask how he was.

C. Do you know if the prisoner David Roach went on deck from the between decks of his own accord or was forced up?

A. I don't know.

C. Relate to the court the conduct of Nicholas Harrison at the time of the mutiny.

A. About 9 o'clock, the prisoner Nicholas Harrison, when in irons by my orders as a deserter, asked leave to go forward to the head. In a short time he returned and spoke to me, saying he had come back. I told Antony Beluzer to put him in irons again. I can't say whether he did so or not. Just before the mutiny commenced, I saw him setting on the arm chest where the irons were. During the scuffle on deck, when I was abreast of the binnacle, I heard the irons thrown overboard and I did not again see him until the next morning when I put my head up the scuttle and saw him laying on his back on the tarpaulin over the main hatchway.

Court Was the prisoner Nicholas Harrison below when you were confined there?

A. No.

C. Did you hear the prisoner Nicholas Harrison giving any orders or see him aiding and assisting in the mutiny?

A. I did not.

C. At the time you saw him laying on the tarpaulin, was he armed?

A. I did not see him armed but there were cutlasses laying about the deck.

C. Did you know the prisoner Nicholas Harrison to make any exertion to quell the mutiny?

A. No.

Court	Did he come to you when you called for assistance?
A.	No.
C.	When you looked up the scuttle, do you think the prisoner seemed if he cared not about what was going on?
A.	He appeared quite careless with a number of armed men about him.
C.	Did you see the prisoner on deck at the time the sloop was going into Guadeloupe and was he armed?
A.	Yes, but not armed.
C.	When you saw the prisoner laying on the tarpaulin, did you hear any conversation between him and the men near him?
A.	No.
C.	When did you again see the prisoner Nicholas Harrison after you had seen him laying on the tarpaulin?
A.	When I was going aft to the cabin, I saw him walking in conversation with several men that I knew to be active in the mutiny, some armed and some not, on the larboard side of the deck abreast the main hatchway but I could not overhear the conversation.
C.	Relate to the court the conduct of the prisoner Naiad Suare during the mutiny.
A.	Between 6 and 7 o'clock, I saw him handling wood below and did not again see him until the next morning about 6 o'clock when he was making the fire, being the cook, and he continued about it until the arrival of the sloop at Guadeloupe.
C.	Did you see the prisoner at the time you were put below?
A.	No, I did not.
C.	Was he below when you counted the persons there?
A.	No, he was not.
C.	Did you see him when you was taken to the cabin in the morning?
A.	Yes, he was setting on the arm chest forward with a cutlass on.
C.	Was he armed when you first saw him in the morning?
A.	Yes. The cutlass was buckled on him and when we were going into Guadeloupe I saw him also armed.
C.	Was he in conversation with any of the men at the time you saw him in the morning and did you overhear it?
A.	He was in conversation with those I knew to be concerned in the mutiny, but I did not overhear it.

Naiad Suare	Did you hear Proctor, the Boatswain, threaten me if I did not take a cutlass?
A.	No.
Court	David Roach and Nicholas Harrison have you any questions to ask this evidence?
A.	No.
	Mr. James Nicholls, Clerk, sworn.
Court	Do you know the prisoners David Roach, Nicholas Harrison and Naiad Suare and did they belong to the *Dominica*?
A.	Yes.
C.	Were they on board her on the evening of the 21st May last when the crew mutinied and took possession of her?
A.	Yes.
C.	Relate to the court the conduct of the prisoner David Roach.
A.	When I was called on deck from below about 12 o'clock by Proctor, the Boatswain, and desired to go into the cabin, I found David Roach laying on the locker on the larboard side; he appeared very ill and had been so for some time before. I saw him go on deck once and return again. He appeared very ill; I offered him some wine and water, but he did not take it. When we arrived at Guadeloupe, I saw him on deck.
Court	Did you see the prisoner David Roach take an active part for or against the mutiny?
A.	I did not; he appeared so ill as to be unable to exert himself.
C.	Relate to the court the conduct of Nicholas Harrison.
A.	When I went on deck at 12 o'clock, I saw him setting on the main hatchway gratings, not armed; naked cutlasses were not far from him on the gratings and 2 or 3 in their scabbards.
C.	Was he among the people that took possession of the vessel and did you consider him as one of the party?
A.	Yes, I did.
C.	Did you hear him at any time aiding or assisting or making any effort to suppress the mutiny?
A.	No, I did not.
C.	Did you at any time see him armed?
A.	No.

C. Did the prisoner Nicholas Harrison go on shore with the rest of the mutineers at Guadeloupe?

A. The crew went together I believe.

C. At the different times you went on deck, did you perceive the prisoner in conversation with any of the mutineers?

A. No.

C. Did the prisoner during the night go below?

A. He did not to my knowledge.

C. Having given it as your opinion that he was one of the mutineers, what were your reasons for thinking so?

A. By seeing him among the mutineers and not making any effort to go below to join those that were there and, if he had wanted to go below, he might have spoken to me saying so, the same as William Knight did.

Court At what time was the prisoner Nicholas Harrison released from irons?

A. I don't know. He was in irons about ½ past 8 o'clock when I went below, but I did not see him in irons afterwards. I believe they were thrown overboard.

Court Relate to the court the conduct of the prisoner Naiad Suare.

A. When I came on deck about 12 o'clock, I saw him armed with a cutlass the belt round him, near the fireplace. I again saw him at day light; he was then armed as before. He was walking about the deck assisting in working the vessel and seemed very active in the mutiny. I saw him afterwards several times until he went on shore with the rest of the men.

Naiad Suare Did you hear me say I did not want to go to Martinique?

A. I heard him speaking in broken English and mention the word Martinique, but whether to go or not I can't say.

Court David Roach and Nicholas Harrison have you any questions to ask this evidence?

A. No.

Daniel Mc Lear, seaman, sworn.

Court Do you know the prisoners David Roach, Nicholas Harrison and Naiad Suare and did they belong to the *Dominique* [*sic*] sloop?

A. Yes.

Court Were they on board the *Dominica* on the evening of the 21st May last when the crew mutinied and took possession of her.

A. Yes.

C. Relate to the court the conduct of David Roach.

A. The last time I saw him before the mutiny was at dinner time and I did not again see him until we were going on shore at Guadeloupe. He had been sick some time before and I let him sleep in my hammock. He was a little better on the day of the mutiny, but not well enough to do any duty.

C. Do you know where he was during the night?

A. He was not below in the between decks where I was confined.

C. At what time was you put below and was the prisoner among the people you found there?

A. Almost 10 o'clock, he was not there.

C. Relate to the court the conduct of the prisoner Nicholas Harrison.

A. When I was awoke up from my sleep by the noise, as I was going to the other side of the deck, I tumbled over him in the place I had seen him in irons in the morning, but I do not know whether he was in irons at the time I tumbled over him or not. I desired him to be still and be quiet; he made no reply, but sat still. I did not again see him until we were going on shore. I was kept below and did not come on deck during the night.

Court Was the prisoner Nicholas Harrison below at any time of the night?

A. No.

C. Was the prisoner armed or were any cutlasses near him when you saw him?

A. I did not see him armed, nor any cutlasses near him.

Court Relate to the court the conduct of the prisoner Naiad Suare.

A. About 8 o'clock, I saw him forward near the fireplace; he was cook and I did not again see him until the next morning when we were going on shore.

C. Was the prisoner Naiad Suare below any part of the time you were there?

A. He was not.

Court Prisoners have you any questions to ask this evidence?

A. No.

Collin Campbell sworn

C. Do you know the prisoners David Roach, Nicholas Harrison and Naiad Suare and did they belong to the *Dominica*?

A. Yes.

Court Were they on board the *Dominica* on the evening of the 21st May when the crew mutinied and took possession of her?

A. Yes.

C. Relate to the court the conduct of the prisoner David Roach.

A. In the afternoon, I saw him sick below. He had not done any duty for some time before and I did not see him again until we were going into Guadeloupe. I was put below between 9 & 10 o'clock; the prisoner was not there, nor during the night. I came on deck about 7 o'clock in the evening, but did not see him.

C. Was he so unwell as to be unable to render you any assistance was he so inclined?

A. To all appearance I think he was, as he had been ill for some days before.

C. Had you at any time after the mutiny any conversation with the prisoner David Roach respecting it?

A. I had not.

Court Relate to the court the conduct of Nicholas Harrison.

A. When I was put below about 10 o'clock, I saw him setting on the arm chest in irons and I did not again see him till 7 o'clock the next morning. He was sitting on the main grating with his head on his arm and out of irons; he was not armed, but cutlasses were near him. When I returned from the head to go below, he was still sitting there. I asked him what he was doing there; he replied nothing. I then asked him if he had anything to do with the mutiny; he said he 'would be damned if he had.' I did not again see him until we were going on shore the next morning.

Court Did he make any effort to go down below with you?

A. No, he did not; there were sentries over the hatchway.

C. Had you any conversation with him after the mutiny respecting it?

A. Yes; in prison, he often said he had nothing to do with it. The mutineers wanted him to take a cutlass, but he would not and he remained near the main gratings the whole night.

Court Relate to the court the conduct of the prisoner Naiad Suare.

A. I saw him in the afternoon near the coppers. He was cook and I did not see him again until the next morning about 7 o'clock. He was putting wood in the grate; he had neither arms or belt on, but a cutlass was laying on the chest near him.

Court Had you any conversation with him at the time you saw him?

A. Yes; he said, 'Campbell it is too bad, for if my master was to catch me in a French port, he would hang me.'

Court Prisoners have you any questions to ask this evidence?

A. No.

Prosecution closed.

Nicholas Harrison offered in his defence that he was in irons at the time the mutiny commenced and he had no opportunity when let out to join the people below, that he never assisted in the mutiny.

Naiad Suare said the Boatswain Proctor threatened to kill him if he did not take up a cutlass.

Sentence

Charge not proved against David Roach, therefore acquitted.

Nicholas Harrison charge proved in part – to receive 300 lashes.

Naiad Suare charge fully proved – to be hung by the neck until dead.

…

97A. *Members of the Court to Cochrane*

[ADM 1/5376]

Seine, Carlisle Bay
3 November 1806

… It appearing in evidence at a court martial assembled this day for the trial of the 3 men named in the margin [David Roach, Nicholas Harrison and Naiad Suare], for having been concerned in the mutiny that took place on board His Majesty's late armed sloop *Dominica* on the night of the 21st May last, that Naiad Suare, who is found guilty of the charge alleged against him and sentenced by the court to suffer death, is a black man, a native of Martinique, was cook of the vessel at the time of the mutiny and appears ignorant of the magnitude of the crime and to have acted under the influence of fear from the threats made him by the boatswain of the vessel, since hung, and the rest of the mutineers, the court beg to recommend him to mercy. …

[Admiralty Note]
17 Dec[r]. His Majesty having been graciously pleased to grant a free pardon to this man, give directions accor[d].

S[r] Alex[r] Cochrane to account for the minutes not having been transmitted.

98. *Court Martial of John Mose*

[ADM 1/5376]

Minutes taken at a court martial assembled on board His Majesty's ship *Gladiator* in Portsmouth Harbour on the eleventh of December 1806

Present

Sir Isaac Coffin, Bar[t]., Rear Admiral of the Red and second officer in the command of His Majesty's ships and vessels at Portsmouth and Spithead, President

Captain	Edward Buller	Captain	George Losack
	John Laugharne		Sir Joseph Sidney Yorke, Kn[t].
	Edward Codrington		Thomas Le Marchand Gosselin
	John Irwin		The Honourable Courtnay Boyle
	Michael Seymour		George Astle
	Thomas James Maling		Charles Worsley Boys

The prisoner was brought in and audience admitted.

The president reported to the court that Captain William Hargood was absent on Admiralty leave.

The order from the Right Honourable Lords Commissioners, dated the ninth day of December instant and directed to the president, to assemble a court martial for the trial of John Mose, a Marine belonging to His Majesty's ship *Saint George*, for having conducted himself in a mutinous manner towards Captain Bertie, commander of the said ship *Saint George*, was read.

The members of the court and the judge advocate then, in open court and before they proceeded to trial, respectively took the several oaths enjoined and directed in and by an Act of Parliament made and passed in the twenty second year of the reign of His late Majesty King George the Second, entitled *An Act for Amending, Explaining and Reducing into One Act of Parliament the Laws relating to the Government of His Majesty's Ships, Vessels and Forces by Sea*.

Then the letter from the said Captain Bertie, dated the eighth day of December last and directed to Sir Isaac Coffin, Bar[t]., Rear Admiral of the

Red, &c, &c, &c, containing the charges was read and is hereto annexed and the witnesses were ordered to withdraw and attend their examinations separately, which they did as follows:

Lieutenant Edward Caulfield, First Lieutenant of His Majesty's ship *Saint George*, called in and sworn.

Captain Bertie asked:

Q On Monday the eighth instant were the Articles of War read onboard the *Saint George*?

A They were on the quarter deck.

Q After they were read, was the prisoner brought forward to be punished for theft?

A He was.

Q Relate to the court the expression and exclamation of the prisoner upon my ordering him to strip to be punished for the above crime?

A When Captain Bertie ordered him to strip, he answered, 'I'll see you damned first.' Captain Bertie repeated, 'Strip Sir immediately.' He answered again, 'I'll not by God' or 'By God, I will not. I have been flogged too often already. I'll be tried by a court martial; try me by a court martial.' When the master at arms and ship's corporal proceeded in obedience to Captain Bertie's orders to strip the prisoner, he resisted and held out his hands in a threatening posture towards the officers. Captain Bertie then hesitated and I said to Captain Bertie, 'I think it would be better to try that man by a court martial.' He was then ordered to be taken away and he was taken away in that posture.

Q Has the prisoner always been considered in sound mind?

A I have never known anything to the contrary.

Q Where was he taken to?

A He was taken below and confined.

Q Was he punished?

A No, he was not.

The court asked:

Q Did anybody close with the prisoner to strip him?

A Yes, the master at arms and ship's corporal.

Q Did he resist or strike anybody then?

A He resisted, but I cannot say, nor do I believe, that he struck anybody.

Lieutenant John Bucke of His Majesty's ship *Saint George* called in and sworn.

Q On Monday the eighth instant were the Articles of War read on board the *Saint George*?

A They were.

Q After they were read, was the prisoner brought forward to be punished for theft?

A He was.

Q Relate to the court the expression and exclamation of the prisoner upon my ordering him to strip to be punished for the above crime.

A Captain Bertie ordered him to strip to be punished for theft; he said he would not, that he had been punished so often that he could not bear it any more and he would be tried by a court martial. The ship's corporal at the time had taken hold of him to insist on his stripping; he then got struggling very much indeed and said he would be damned if he would and 'I'll see you damned first.' Addressing himself to Captain Bertie, he repeated that twice. Captain Bertie ordered him in irons.

The court asked:

Q In resisting, did he strike the master at arms or ship's corporal?

A I did not see it.

Q Has it fallen to your lot to see much of the prisoner in the course of his duty?

A I have ordered him to be punished twice during three months for theft. I have made no particular remark of him in the course of his duty. I have not seen much of him.

Q In the two punishments you saw inflicted upon the prisoner, what was his conduct?

A Quite hardened and said he was enticed to commit that act by other people.

Q Did it appear to you that his being hardened arose from a weakness of understanding and intellect or from a determination to persist in a course of crime?

A From being punished so frequently and, in my opinion, he persisted in committing the crime.

Captain Bertie asked:

Q Has the prisoner always been considered in his sound mind?

A Yes, in my opinion.

The court asked:

Q Do you know that the prisoner has at any time been put upon by the officers or ship's company?

A No.

Cornelius Leary, Master at Arms belonging to the *Saint George*, called in and sworn.

Q On Monday the eighth instant were the Articles of War read on board the *Saint George*?

A Yes they were.
Q After they were read, was the prisoner brought forward to be punished for theft?
A He was.
Q Relate to the court the expression and exclamation of the prisoner upon my ordering him to strip to be punished for the above crime?
A Captain Bertie ordered him to strip to receive his punishment for the crime he was guilty of, which was fully proved on the quarter deck. He told the captain he would see him damned first and repeated the same expression. I took him by the collar and threw him back on the skylight. I put my hand to his mouth to make him be silent. Captain Bertie ordered me to put him in irons again, which I did.
Q Has the prisoner always been considered to be in his sound mind?
A He always appeared to me to be as such.
Q Did he make any resistance to you and the corporal when I ordered him in irons?
A On the quarter deck, he did.
Q Do you recollect the prisoner saying upon my ordering him to strip, 'I have been punished so frequently, I'll see you damned first. I'll be tried by a court martial?'
A He did.
The court asked:
Q Do you think the prisoner to be a man of weak understanding?
A I do not think he is.
Q Have you ever known that he has been imposed upon or used in a way that you have often seen fools used on board ships?
A Never to my knowledge.
Q Do you know how long the prisoner has been a marine?
A I do not.
Q How long has he been embarked?
A I cannot exactly say; more than eight months I think.
Q Do you recollect he ever behaved in this way before when brought up for punishment?
A He never did.
Q Do you think that, while in your custody, he could have procured any liquor previous to his being brought up?
A He could not.

The prosecution being closed, the prisoner was called on for his defence. He said he was only sixteen years of age; he had been only two years in the service and was bred up a labourer's servant. He came into the service as a boy, that he had spoke the words unthinkingly, that he had been taught his bad habits by a black man, Peter Johnson, who told him to swear if brought up to the gangway, that he was sorry for what he had done and his messmates were sorry for him when he left the ship. He hoped the court would look over it and he would in future conduct himself well.

The court was cleared and agreed that the charge had been proved against the said John Mose and did adjudge him, in consideration of his youth, to receive fifty lashes on his bare back with a cat o nine tails onboard His Majesty's said ship *Saint George* at such time or times and in such manner and proportion as the said Captain Bertie should direct.

The court was again opened, the prisoner brought in, audience admitted and sentence passed accordingly. …

98A. *Bertie to Coffin*

[ADM 1/5376]

His Majesty's ship *St. George*
Spithead, 8th of December 1806

… Jn°. Mose, Marine serving on board His Majesty's ship under my command, having conducted himself in a very mutinous manner to me on the quarter deck of the said ship this day in consequence of his having been brought up to be punished for theft, of which he had been frequently guilty of,

I have therefore to request you will be pleased to apply to the Lords Commissioners of the Admiralty that the said Jn°. Mose may be tried at a court martial for the same accordingly …

B. Mutinous Expressions and Sedition

99. *Court Martial of William Morison and John Moral*

[ADM 1/5331]

Minutes of the proceedings of a court martial assembled and held on board His Majesty's ship the *Sandwich* at the Nore, the 9th day of July 1794.

Present

Christopher Mason, Esq[r]., Captain of His Majesty's ship *Zealous* and second in the command of His Majesty's ships and vessels in the River Medway and at the buoy of the Nore, President.

Captains

Sir Jn° Orde, Bart. Rich[d]. Fisher
Jon[a]. Faulkner John Manley

Edm^{d}. Nagle	George Lumsdaine
Ja^{s}. R^{t}. Mosse	Willm. Hargood
Israel Pellew	

Being all the captains of the post ships in the River Medway and at the buoy of the Nore, except Captain Sir William Sydney Smith, Kn^{t}., of His Majesty's ship *Diamond*, who is absent with leave from the Lords Commissioners of the Admiralty.

The prisoner was brought into court, and the evidence and audience admitted.

Having read the order of the Right Honourable the Lords Commissioners of the Admiralty, dated the 6th instant, directed to Chris^{r}. Mason, Esqr., Captain of His Majesty's ship *Zealous* and second officer in the command of His Majesty's ships and vessels in the River Medway and at the buoy of the Nore, to try M^{r}. William Morison, Boatswain, and John Moral, Seaman, of His Majesty's sloop the *Scourge*, 'for uttering word of mutiny to the company of the said sloop,' and the letter from Captain William Stap therein referred to; the members of the court and the judge advocate, in open court and before they proceeded to trial, then took the oaths directed by Act of Parliament, respectively.

All the evidences were ordered to withdraw out of the court, except Robert Watson, a Seaman belonging to His Majesty's sloop *Scourge*, who was sworn.

Prosecutor	Do you know the Prisoner [*sic*]?
Answer	Yes.
Prosecutor	Did you see them together on the first of July?
Answer	Yes.
Prosecutor	Relate to the court what conversation passed from the boatswain, M^{r}. Morison, to John Moral.
Answer	I heard M^{r}. Morison tell John Moral to desire the hands not to go upon deck when they were turned up, for that when he, the boatswain, came down again, he should not strike any one of them.
Prisoner	Was you (the evidence) sober or drunk at that time?
Answer	Sober.
Prisoner	Was not the ship's company that morning all in liquor?
Answer	I did not perceive any one of them to be in liquor.
Court	Where were you when you heard this conversation, and where was the boatswain?
Answer	I stood close to the sail room, immediately abaft the fore ladder.

Robert Watson ordered to withdraw.

Richard Carter, Seaman belonging to His Maj. sloop *Scourge*, next called in and sworn.

Prosecutor	Do you know the prisoners?
Answer	Yes, I do.
Prosecutor	Did you see the prisoner, M^r^. William Morison, below when the hands were at breakfast on the morning of the 1st of July?
Answer	Yes.
Prosecutor	Relate to the court what you heard him say to the ship's company.
Answer	He said that none of the ship's company were to come upon deck when he piped all hands, that he would not hurt anybody, but would make a noise for them to come up.
Court	When you say the ship's company, do you mean that the boatswain called all the people around him, or to whom or what part of them did he particularly address himself?
Answer	He was sitting on the starboard side of the deck, and called out loud enough to be heard by the ship's company between decks.

Richard Carter ordered to withdraw.

William Taylor, Seaman belonging to His Maj. sloop *Scourge*, next called and sworn.

Prosecutor	Do you know the prisoner, M^r^. W^m^. Morison?
Answer	Yes.
Prosecutor	Was you not ordered down to turn the hands up on the morning of the 1st July?
Answer	Yes.
Prosecutor	Did you see the boatswain below?
Answer	Yes.
Prosecutor	Relate to the court what you heard him say to the ship's company.
Answer	I heard him say when I was going down the main hatchway ladder, 'let the hands stand true, and not come upon deck.'
Court	Where was the boatswain at that time?
Answer	Standing by the armourer's bench.
Prosecutor	Was not this after the hands were piped up?
Answer	Yes.

Court	When the boatswain made use of those words, did he speak sufficiently loud to be heard by the ship's company?
Answer	Yes, I think he did.

The court having been cleared, upon the legality of a question put by Capt. Fisher, was, when again opened, overruled.

William Taylor ordered to withdraw.

John Spurry, Seaman belonging to His Maj. sloop *Scourge*, next called in and sworn.

Prosecutor	Do you know the prisoner, John Moral?
Answer	Yes.
Prosecutor	Did he not come to you while at your breakfast on the morning of the 1st July?
Answer	Yes.
Prosecutor	Relate to the court what he said to you.
Answer	When I was going forward to the ship's steward for my provisions, he told me not to go upon deck. I then sat down to my breakfast, and asked the Quartermaster, Patterson, what was the reason of it; he said he could not tell me.
Prosecutor	Do you mean that you were not to go upon deck when the hands were to be turned up after breakfast?
Answer	Yes.

John Spurry ordered to withdraw.

John Patterson, Quartermaster belonging to His Maj. sloop *Scourge*, next called in and sworn.

Prosecutor	Do you know the prisoner, John Moral?
Answer	Yes.
Prosecutor	While you were at your breakfast on the 1st July, did you not hear the prisoner, John Moral, desire the people to sit still, and not go upon deck when the boatswain should pipe the hands up?
Answer	Yes.
Court	Did he speak loudly so as to be heard by the whole of the ship's company or did he speak to any particular man?
Answer	He spoke to the whole of the ship's company.
Court	Did you see the prisoner, John Moral, in consultation with the boatswain previous to his addressing the people?
Answer	Not at that time.

John Patterson ordered to withdraw.

Thomas Webber, Seaman belonging to His Maj. sloop *Scourge*, next called in and sworn.

Prosecutor	Do you know the prisoner, John Morai?
Answer	Yes.
Prosecutor	Did he not desire you not to come upon deck when the boatswain should pipe the hands up after breakfast on the morning of the 1st July?
Answer	He did not.
Prosecutor	Did you hear him pass the word for the people not to come upon deck when the boatswain should pipe the hands up after breakfast?
Answer	Yes, I did.

Thomas Webber ordered to withdraw.

The evidence in support of the charge against M^{r}. Will. Morison, the Boatswain, being finished, the Prisoner was called upon to make his defence, which he did in the following words, vizt.:

'I have been in His Majesty's service fifteen years, and was wounded in the head, which deprives me of my senses at times, and renders me incapable of performing my duty as I would wish to do. I have not a certificate to show that I was so wounded, from the captain having shot himself.' He then desired that his witnesses might be examined. James Benning, Seaman belonging to His Majesty's sloop *Scourge*, was accordingly sworn.

Prisoner M^{r}. W^{m}. Morison	Did not you see me on the morning of the 1st July go close to the booms and swear that the first man who denied coming on deck, I would knock down?
Answer	Yes I did.
Prisoner	Did I not take a broomstick and endeavour to break it in order to use it as a weapon to hasten the men on deck?
Answer	Yes, I saw you do so.
Prisoner	Did I not then go down immediately, and use every possible method to get the men on deck?
Answer	You did, and they came up.
Prisoner	Have I not ever behaved as an officer while in the ship, and done everything in my power to support the discipline of her?
Answer	Yes, you ever did.
Prosecutor	You say the boatswain used every means to get the people upon deck; from your situation as sentinel on deck, could you see or hear what passed below?

Answer	No, I answer from what I saw and heard on deck.

James Benning ordered to withdraw.

Cornelius Turnbull, Carp[rs]. Mate of His Majesty's sloop *Scourge*, called in and sworn.

Prisoner	Did you hear me on the 1st July desire the people not to come upon deck?
Answer	I did not.
Prosecutor	Was you not at work under the forecastle the greater part of the morning?
Answer	Yes.

Cornelius Turnbull ordered to withdraw.

James Adamson, Seaman belonging to His Maj. sloop *Scourge*, next called and sworn.

Prisoner	Did you not see me on the morning of the 1st July go close to the booms and swear that the first man who denied coming on deck, I would knock down?
Answer	Yes.

James Adamson ordered to withdraw.

M[r]. Peter Walling, Master of His Maj. sloop *Scourge*, next called in and sworn.

Prisoner	Have I not behaved like a seaman & officer on board the ship?
Answer	You always did, and have frequently told me that your skull is fractured, which I have every reason to believe from your behaviour when in liquor.
Prosecutor	You say you have every reason to believe that his skull is fractured from his behaviour when in liquor.
Answer	I never saw him in liquor.
Prosecutor	What reason have you to believe so if you never saw him in liquor?
Answer	By the prisoner being stupefied.
Prosecutor	Do you conceive a man who is stupefied capable of doing his duty like an officer?
Answer	I do not.
Court	How long have you been in the ship with the prisoner (Morison)?
Answer	Two months.

M[r]. Walling ordered to withdraw.

Lieu[t]. John Bevins, second Lieu[t]. of His Majesty's ship *Squirrel*, next called in and sworn.

Prisoner	Did I not, while on board the *Scourge*, behave myself with diligence, care and sobriety?
Answer	Yes, you certainly did.
Court	Inform the court how long you were on board the *Scourge*.
Answer	A little more than a month.

Lieu^{t}. Bevins ordered to withdraw.

The prisoner requested Captain Step^{n}. G. Church to speak to his character.

Capt. Church	During the time the prisoner was under my command, he was particularly attentive to his duty and I always observed him doing his utmost to keep the people to the duty they were ordered upon and was so satisfied with his conduct that upon my leaving the ship I applied for him to be removed to the one I now command.

Capt. Church withdrew, and Lieu^{t}. Drummond of His Maj. sloop *Peterel*, was called upon for his character.

Lieu^{t}. Drummond	While I was lieutenant of the *Scourge*, Mr. Morison always did his duty becoming the character of an officer in his station, and I never knew him incapable of doing his duty during the time I belonged to the ship, and I was about four months on board her.

Lieu^{t}. Drummond withdrew, and Capt. Stap was requested by the prisoner to speak to his character.

Capt. Stap	When the prisoner was sober, I thought him anxious to do his duty, but when he was drunk, which was often the case, it left him in a state of madness, which I was informed by him was occasioned by his receiving a fracture in the skull in the service of his country, which occasioned me to request him to get into a ship less active than the *Scourge* was likely to be from her being employed much at sea.

Capt. Stap withdrew.

Lieutenant Hill on behalf of John Moral was called in and sworn.

Prisoner John Moral	Was I upon deck when all hands were called on the morning of the 1st July?
Answer	Yes, you were.
Prisoner	Did you not order me upon the main topsail yard to mend sails?
Answer	Yes, I did.

Prisoner Did I not stay there till I was ordered down again?

Answer You did.

Lieu[t]. Hill ordered to withdraw.

Robert Watson again called in.

Prisoner Did you not hear the boatswain desire me to tell the hands to stay below?

Answer I did.

Robert Watson ordered to withdraw.

William Taylor again called in.

Prisoner Did you not hear the boatswain desire me to tell the hands to stay below?

Answer No, I did not.

William Taylor ordered to withdraw.

John Spurry again called in.

Prisoner Did you not hear the boatswain desire me to tell the hands to stay below?

Answer No, I did not.

The evidence on the part of the prisoner (John Moral) being all examined, he was asked if he had any defence to make, which he said he had, and accordingly spoke in the following words, viz[t].: 'I have been in the King's service about three months and have endeavoured to discharge my duty as well as possible, and when I was ordered to tell the hands to stay below, I did not know what the reason of it was.'

The prisoners having nothing further to offer in their defence, the court was cleared and proceeded to deliberate upon and form the sentence.

The court, having carefully and deliberately weighed and considered the evidence produced and what the prisoners alleged in their defence, were of opinion that the charge against M[r] William Morison was proved, and that the charge against John Moral was not proved. The court therefore sentenced the said M[r] Will. Morison to be dismissed from His Majesty's sloop *Scourge* and acquitted John Moral. The court was then opened, audience admitted and sentence passed accordingly. …

100. *Court Martial of James Seymonds alias Simmons*

[ADM 1/5387]

Minutes of the proceeding of a court martial, assembled and held on board His Majesty's ship the *Roebuck* in Yarmouth Roads, the 27th day of June 1808, for the trial of James Seymonds, alias Simmons, a Seaman belonging to His Majesty's ship the *Majestic* for having on the 2d. of June 1808 made use of the following horrid expressions, and frequently repeating the same among the ship's company, viz[t].: 'If this is the King's service, damn the King, the service and half his subjects. If I had some of them on shore, I would shave them pretty close. Damn all his royal subjects.'

Present

The Hon[ble]. Alan Hyde Gardiner, Rear Admiral of the Blue, and third officer in the command of His Majesty's ships and vessels in Yarmouth Roads, President.

Captains

Benjamin Hallowell	Hon[ble]. Henry Blackwood
Robert Campbell	The Hon[ble]. Th[os]. Masterman Hardy
William Cumberland	Norborn Thompson
Richard Curry	Samuel Warren

The prisoner being brought into court and audience admitted, the order of the Right Honourable the Lords Commissioners of the Admiralty, dated the 23rd of June 1808 directed to the Honourable Alan Hyde Gardiner, Rear Admiral of the Blue, and third officer in the command of His Majesty's ships and vessels in Yarmouth Roads, for the trial of James Seymonds, alias Simmons, for having on the 2d. of June 1808 made use of the following horrid expressions, and frequently repeating the same among the ship's company, 'If this is the King's service, damn the King, the service and half his subjects. If I had some of them on shore, I would shave them pretty close. Damn all his royal subjects,' was read. The members of the court and judge advocate then in open court respectively took the oath enjoined by Act of Parliament. The letter from Captain Valentine Collard, Commander of His Majesty's ship the *Majestic* (containing the charge against the prisoner) was then read; and all the witnesses being ordered to withdraw and attend their examinations separately, they all withdrew accordingly, except the first to be sworn; and the court proceeded to trial as follows:

M[r]. Peter Anselm Le Neve, Midshipman of His Majesty's ship *Majestic*, sworn and examined as follows:

Prosecutor	On the 2nd of this month, did you hear the prisoner say, 'If this is the King's service, damn the King, the service and half his subjects. If I had some of them on shore, I wou'd shave them pretty close. Damn all his royal subjects?'
Answer	Yes!
Court	On what occasion was it that he made use of that expression?
Answer	On being ordered to be confined on the suspicion of theft.

Court When the prisoner made use of the expressions you have related, was he sober?

Ans[r]. Yes!

M[r]. Le Neve withdrew.

M[r]. William Henry Whitehead sworn and examined as follows:

Pros. On the 2nd of this month, did you hear the prisoner say, 'If this is the King's service, damn the King, the service and half his subjects. If I had some of them on shore, I would shave them pretty close. Damn all his royal subjects?'

Answer I did!

Court When the prisoner made use of the expressions you have related, was he sober?

Ans[r]. I believe perfectly sober!

Presd[t]. What drew from him such language?

Ans[r]. I believe his passion on being put in irons.

M[r]. Whitehead withdrew.

M[r]. Henry John Hall, Midshipman of the *Majestic*, sworn & examined as follows:

Pros. On the 2nd of this month, did you hear the prisoner say, 'If this is the King's service, damn the King, the service and half his subjects. If I had some of them on shore, I wou'd shave them pretty close. Damn all his royal subjects?'

Answer Yes!

Court When the prisoner made use of the expressions you have related, was he sober?

Ans[r]. I believe he was!

Court When the prisoner made use of these expressions you've related, did he address himself particularly to any one person?

Ans[r]. No!

M[r]. Hall withdrew.

Lieutenant John Baikie of the *Majestic* sworn and examined as follows:

Presd[t]. How long have you known the prisoner on board the *Majestic*?

Ans[r]. As near as I can recollect, from December last.

Pres[t]. What has been his general conduct on board the *Majestic*?

Ans[r]. A very great part of that time, he has been in confinement.

Lieutenant Baikie withdrew.

The prisoner had nothing to offer in his defence.

M^r^. William Henderson, Assistant Surgeon of the *Majestic* was sworn and examined as follows:

Presd[t]. How long have you known the prisoner?

Ans[r]. About five months!

Presd[t]. During that time, from your own knowledge, has the prisoner shown any symptoms of insanity?

Ans[r]. No!

Pres[t]. Have you heard that he has shown any symptoms of insanity?

Ans[r]. I have heard that he has been guilty of foolish actions, but not sufficient to deserve any notice from me.

Pres[t]. Can you particularize any one action which you call foolish?

Ans[r]. No!

Pres[t]. Has the prisoner been in your list during the time from any illness?

Ans[r]. Yes!

Pres[t]. State what.

Ansr. I believe there was nothing the matter with him during the time he was there.

Pris[r]. The Master at Arms (M[r]. Farrell) has known me five years, and at times I have not found myself so well in the head as I could wish. I have had a wound in the head, occasioned by a fall from a horse. When I made use of the expressions I am tried for, I did not mean any harm to my King and country. I am no ill wisher of his. It was entirely against myself, as I am tired of my life from ill usage!

M[r]. Henderson withdrew.

The master at arms of the *Majestic*, being called upon by the prisoner to speak with respect to his character &[c]., states as follows:

I have known the prisoner five years, the tenth of next month; with regard to his character, I can say nothing in his favour, but during the time he has been in irons he appeared fractious and was frequently dancing and singing.

Robert Elder, a Seaman belonging to the *Majestic*, sworn and examined as follows:

Pris[r]. Was I confined for stealing shirts, and have I been ill treated?

Ans[r]. I can't say!

Pres. Do you know the prisoner to have been ill treated on board the *Majestic*?

Ans[r]. I do not.

Pres. Do you know the prisoner to have been insane or foolish prior to the crime with which he is accused of?

Ans[r]. Since I have known the prisoner, he has appeared to be foolish in his speech at times!

Pres. How long have you known the prisoner?

Ans[r]. Four or five years!

Pres. Where has the prisoner done his duty nearly the whole of the 5 years?

Ans[r]. Attending the gentlemen!

Pres. What has been his character in the ship?

Ans[r]. He has deserted twice, and stole both times.

Pros. Since I have commanded the *Majestic*, has the prisoner had a deal of lenity shown him by me for the crimes which he has committed, such lenity as he had no right to expect from his general conduct?

Ans[r]. Yes!

Rob[t]. Elder withdrew.

Court cleared

The court, being cleared, and the judge advocate having read the minutes, and the court having maturely and deliberately considered the whole, agreed that the charge against the prisoner is fully proved, and adjudged him to receive two hundred lashes on his bare back with a cat of nine tails alongside of such of His Majesty's ships and vessels, at such times and in such proportions as Vice Admiral Russell shall think proper to direct and to be kept for the space of one year in solitary confinement in the Marshalsea Prison. The court was then opened, audience admitted, and sentence passed accordingly. …

101. *Court Martial of Thomas Taylor*

[ADM 1/5403]

Minutes of proceedings at a court martial held on board His Majesty's ship *Dannemark*, at anchor off Englishman's Head, Guadeloupe, Saturday, the 10th day of March 1810.

Present

James Bissete, Esqr., Captain of His Majesty's *Dannemark*, and second officer in command of His Majesty's ships and vessels at Guadeloupe, President.

Captains

Wm Chas Fahie
Joshua Rowley Watson
John Hayes
Sir Ja^{s} Athol Wood
Volant Vashon Ballard
Robert Preston

William Balhetchet
officiating as judge advocate

The court was opened; the prisoner brought in; the evidence and audience admitted.

Read the order of the Honble Sir Alexander Cochrane, K.B., Vice Admiral of the Blue, Commander in Chief of His Majesty's ships and vessels at Barbados, the Leeward Islands &c, &c, &c, dated the 28th day of February 1810 and directed to James Bissete, Esqr., Captain of the *Dannemark*, and second officer in the command of His Majesty's ships and vessels at Guadeloupe, to assemble a court martial and try Thomas Taylor, Purser's Steward of His Majesty's ship *Castor*, for having uttered seditious words on the 18th of October last.

Read the warrant appointing a judge advocate.

Then the members and judge advocate, in open court and before they proceeded to trial, respectively took the oaths directed by an Act passed in the 22nd year of the reign of King George the Second.

The following letter from Captain Roberts[1] was read:

H.M.S. *Castor* at sea, February 28th, 1810

… I have to request you will be pleased to direct a court martial to be held on Thomas Taylor, Purser's Steward, for having uttered seditious words in the presence of the ship's company on October 18th 1809. …

All the witnesses, except the first to be examined, withdrew.

Lieu^{t}. Saml. Hellard of the *Castor* was sworn and examined as follows:

Prosecutor – Were you senior lieutenant on the 18th. of October during the punishment of the prisoner?

– Yes.

[1]This letter is to Sir Alexander Cochrane, the Commander in Chief of the Leeward Islands Station at the time.

– When I directed the prisoner to be tied up, did he address himself to me before you and the ship's company, 'I demand a court martial,' putting a Shilling on the capstan at the same time?

– Yes.

– After I had punished him with 24 lashes and read the Article of War for drunkenness, did I enquire of the prisoner his reason for putting the Shilling on the capstan?

– Yes.

– What was his reply?

– For a court martial.

Court – Do you know of the prisoner's having made use of seditious words on the 18 of October last, if he did repeat them?

– Nothing further than requesting a court martial.

– Did it appear to you that the prisoner's manner was seditious and calculated to excite discontent in the ship's company?

Ans[r] – No, as he had his hat off, when he spoke to Cap[t]. Roberts.

The prosecution being closed, the prisoner was asked what he had to offer in his defence; he said he wished Cap[t]. Flin, R Navy, and Lieu[t]. Carter to speak as to his character.

Cap[t] Flin said that he knew the prisoner as purser's steward of the *Castor*; that he was a steady, sober, good man, that when he was ashore at the reduction of Guadeloupe, he entrusted him with the provisions and liquor and nominated him as sergeant of the party; that he behaved so well, he desired the midshipman to represent it, when he went on board.

Lieu[t]. Carter always thought the prisoner a very steady, sober, well behaved man.

The court was then cleared and proceeded to deliberate upon and form sentence, and having heard what had been alleged, was of opinion that the charge had not been proved, and did therefore adjudge the prisoner Thomas Taylor to be acquitted.

The court was then opened; the prisoner brought in; the evidence and audience admitted; and his sentence of acquittal read accordingly. …

C. Disobedience of Orders

102. *Court Martial of George Lumsdaine*

[ADM 1/5330]

Copy of the minutes of a court martial held onboard His Majesty's Ship the *Britannia*, in the outer road of Toulon, the 1st day of November 1793, for the trial of Captain George Lumsdaine of His Majesty's Ship the *Iris*, on a charge exhibited against him by Vice Admiral Lord Hood, Commander in Chief, &^{ca}., &^{ca}. &^{ca}., 'of not complying with his Lordship's orders,' in having neglected to deliver to M^{r}. Consul Magra at Tunis the letter which he was directed to do by his Lordship's order of the 27th of June last.

Present

William Hotham, Esqr, Vice Admiral of the White, President
Samuel Granston Goodall, Esqr, Rear Admiral of the Red
Sir Hyde Parker, Kn.^{t}, Rear Admiral of the White and First Captain of the Fleet

Captain	Skeffington Lutwidge	Captain	Archibald Dickson
"	Samuel Reeve	"	Charles Morice Pole
"	Robert Manners Sutton	"	John Holloway
"	John Knight	"	John Child Purvis
"	John Matthews	"	Benjamin Hallowell

The court, being duly sworn (after the order for assembling them and the charge were read), proceeded to examine the evidence.

Court to the prisoner – Do you acknowledge to have received the letter in question from the commander in chief for M^{r}. Consul Magra?

Ans.^{r} – I do.

The prisoner then requested that his reasons for not complying with the order might be read to the court, which were permitted, and are as follows, *Viz.*:

I beg leave to lay before the court my reasons why Lord Hood's letter was not delivered to M^{r}. Consul Magra at Tunis; on the evening previous to my going into Tunis Bay, I dispatched Captain Martin of His Majesty's sloop *Tisiphone* with his lordship's letter to M^{r}. Magra; the next morning he rejoined me, having discovered a French frigate under the land, upon which I immediately stood in with the hopes of cutting her off, but found she was at anchor in the Road of Port Ferine, and, perceiving a boat dispatched from her to Tunis, conjectured there were more of the enemy's ships there, and directly ordered Captain Martin to that port with his lordship's letters. A few hours afterwards, he returned & informed me that there were in Tunis Road a French ship of the line and four frigates; I therefore, after consulting on the occasion Captains Trigge & Martin of His Majesty's ships *Mermaid & Tisiphone*, thought it most advisable to dispatch one of the ships with this intelligence to his lordship, and that the others should proceed to Tripoli with the convoy.

Understanding there were no forts in Tunis Bay that could give any sort of protection to His Majesty's ships under my command, and well knowing how little respect the French paid to a neutral port, when, a civilized nation, they attacked Commodore Johnstone in Port Praya Bay, and what could be expected from them at this present juncture, particularly on the coast of Barbary in an open bay, where there are no regular fortifications and upwards of four leagues from the town of Tunis; at the same time I considered the risqué of the King's ships, if not attacked, of being blocked up and prevented from putting into execution the orders I was under from the commander in chief.

Here I beg leave to call the attention of the court to that part of his lordship's orders wherein he directs me only to call at Tunis in my way and deliver a letter to the consul there and without loss of time, to make the best of my way to Tripoli; and he also adds that I have no occasion to have communication with Tunis, as it must prevent my having communication with the shore at other places, and from the general tenor of that part of his lordship's order, I concluded that his letter to M^r^. Magra was not of that importance as to authorize me to risqué the loss of any of His Majesty's ships and the convoy; and I have to observe that his lordship must have had early intelligence by the *Mermaid*, which I had dispatched to him, that M^r^. Magra's letter had not been delivered, and also of the steps I had taken for the good of His Majesty's service. M^r^. Consul Lucas had also furnished me with intelligence that the French squadron had certain information of the *Hampden* being bound to Tripoli with presents for the Bey and Regency, and meant, if possible, to intercept her, which, there was reason to suppose, might be the case, not only from the French corvette in Port Ferine Road having dispatched a boat to Tunis immediately upon discovering us, but from her other manoeuvres, which clearly indicated that she was the look-out ship and expected the squadron from Tunis to follow us.

I do not think it necessary to enumerate the irregularities committed by the French in the different Italian ports for these twelve months past, and how little respect they have paid to neutrality, especially when they had a superior force, as the court are perfectly acquainted with all these circumstances.

What, therefore I must again repeat, could I have expected had I gone with such an inferior force into Tunis Bay, which I beg leave to observe, I took upon as widely different from that of entering the port of a civilized nation. I have only to add that I had always conceived a certain degree of discretionary power was vested in a commander of a King's squadron or any person holding a responsible situation; it must be very evident to every member of the court that orders delivered from a commander in chief do not provide against unforeseen events or accidents that may occur in the course of service.

Captain Martin of the *Tisiphone* was then called in and sworn.

Quest^{n} by prisoner – Captain Martin, after you rejoined me from looking into Tunis Bay and informed me there were a French ship of the line and four frigates in the road, was it not your opinion and Captain Trigge's that it was most advisable to dispatch one of the ships with this intelligence to Lord Hood and that the others should proceed to Tripoli with the convoy with all possible dispatch?

Answer – I was clearly of opinion that one of the ships ought to be dispatched to the commander in chief with the intelligence. Captain Trigge perfectly acquiesced in the opinion. I was also of the opinion that the other ships should proceed to Tripoli with the convoy with all possible dispatch.

Prisoner – When I had delivered Captain Trigge his orders to make the best of his way with this intelligence to the commander in chief, did he not advise me to keep the *Mermaid* that night in company, as he was clearly of opinion that the French squadron would slip and follow us?

Ans^{r} – He did, and strongly urged the necessity of keeping together in company during the night, from a supposition that the enemy would slip and intercept us.

Prisoner – Do you not imagine it would have been imprudent to have stood into Tunis Bay; and would it not have risked His Majesty's ships?

Ans^{r} – I did, and do believe it would have been very imprudent and extremely dangerous to have stood into Tunis Bay.

Prisoner	–	Did you not observe the French corvette in Port Ferine Road, immediately upon discovering us, dispatch a boat for Tunis Bay?
Ans[r]	–	I did.
Prisoner	–	Did you not observe two boats full of men go off from the shore onboard the corvette?
Ans[r]	–	I did.
Prisoner	–	Did you not, from her situation and manoeuvres, suppose her to be the look-out ship?
Ans[r]	–	I did; from her situation and manoeuvres, I was strongly induced to believe she was there as a look-out ship.
Prisoner	–	Did you not, at the time we were consulting what were the best steps to be taken for the good of His Majesty's service, apprehend the King's ships and convoy in danger?
Ans[r]	–	I did.
Court to prisoner	–	What reason had you to suppose there were no forts in Tunis Bay to afford protection to His Majesty's ships?
Ans[r]	–	The purser and the boatswain of His Majesty's ship *Iris* under my command were there a short time ago in His Majesty's sloop *Bulldog* and informed me it was very far from being a regular fortification and had hardly any guns mounted and those in such a situation that they took an hour and a half to salute the *Bulldog*.
Prisoner to evidence	–	To the best of your judgment, how far do you suppose the French squadron were laying from the shore?
Ans[r]	–	I supposed them to be four miles distant from Galetta Castle, as laid down in the chart; where we hauled up, Cape Carthage bore south west 3 miles. Unless the enemy had been four miles out, I do not believe we could have seen them so open.

Ordered to withdraw.

M[r]. David Spence, Master of the *Isis*, called in and sworn.

Prisoner to evidence	–	Do you not recollect when we were standing off and on in the Road of Port Ferine that I observed there were people in the shrouds and

		at the mast heads of the corvette, looking and pointing towards Tunis?
Ans[r]	–	Yes.
Prisoner	–	Do you recollect that shortly after, we perceived the *Tisiphone* with the signal flying for seeing an enemy of superior force?
Ans[r]	–	Yes, perfectly.
Prisoner	–	From the men onboard the corvette keeping a look-out towards Tunis, from her situation and manoeuvres, do you imagine she was a look-out ship?
Ans[r]	–	I did imagine then she was a look-out ship.
Prisoner	–	Do you imagine the corvette was within sight of the ships in Tunis Bay?
Ans[r]	–	No, certainly not.

Ordered to withdraw.

The court, having no further questions to ask, and the prisoner having finished his defence; the court was immediately cleared and they proceeded to pass their judgment.

102A. *Report of the Court Martial of George Lumsdaine*

[ADM 1/5330]

… And the court, having heard the evidence in support of the charge, as well as what the prisoner had to offer in his defence and having maturely and deliberately considered the same, is of opinion that the said Captain George Lumsdaine did not comply with the orders of the commander in chief, inasmuch as he did not deliver to M[r]. Consul Magra the letter in question; yet, from the testimony before the court, it clearly appears that his conduct upon that occasion did not proceed from any neglect, but, on the contrary, was owing to the information he had received of the superiority of the enemy's force in Tunis Bay, and the little dependence he could place upon their observance of the laws of nations; and for the reasons given, it satisfactorily appears to the court that it was more prudent in Captain Lumsdaine to give up the attempt of entering Tunis Bay than of running the risk which would otherwise have attended His Majesty's ships. From all which considerations, the court is of opinion that, however unjustifiable it is in an officer not strictly to comply with orders, yet circumstances may sometimes arise in which his discretionary conduct may be found necessary; and, in the present instance, it appears to the court that Captain Lumsdaine was justified in not delivering the letter to

M[r]. Consul Magra. The court do, therefore, adjudge the said Captain George Lumsdaine to be acquitted.

And he is, hereby, acquitted accordingly. …

103. *Court Martial of Corthine Parker*

[ADM 1/5383]

Minutes of the proceedings at a court martial held on board His Majesty's ship *Africa* off Montevideo on Wednesday the 26th day of August 1807.

Present

Henry William Bayntun, Esq[r]., Captain of His Majesty's ship *Africa* and second officer in the command of His Majesty's ships and vessels off Montevideo, President.

Captains
Peter Heynwood
Fran[s]. Mason
Jn[o]. Thompson
Fran[s]. Beaufort

The prisoner was brought into court and the evidence and audience admitted.

Read the order from George Murray, Esq[r]., Rear Admiral of the White, and Commander in Chief of a squadron of His Majesty's ships and vessels employed on a particular service, dated the 25 day of August 1807 and directed to the president, to try M[r]. Corthine Parker, Master of His Majesty's ship *Nereide* for presuming to inflict punishment on two of the crew of the said ship (one a petty officer), in direct disobedience of the most positive orders of his captain.

Read the warrant appointing a judge advocate. Then the members of the court and judge advocate, in open court and before they proceeded to trial, respectively took the oaths directed by an Act passed in the 22nd year of the reign of King George the Second.

A letter from Robert Corbet, Esq[r]., Captain of His Majesty's ship *Nereide*, to George Murray, Esq[r]. was read as follows, viz[t].:

His Maj[s]. ship *Nereide*
Off Montevideo 25 Aug[t] 1807

… Lieutenant Blight, commanding officer of this ship during my unavoidable absence last night, having reported to me on my return on board that Mr. Corthine Parker, Master, had presumed to order punishment to be inflicted on two of the crew (one a petty officer), in direct disobedience to my most positive orders and in all subversion of true discipline and the rules of the service. In support of such discipline, I feel it a duty to request that you will order a court martial to try him for such disobedience of orders. …

All the witnesses were then ordered to withdraw out of court, except Lieutenant William Blight, who was duly sworn.

Prosecutor Repeat to the court the report you made me on my return on board on Sunday morning last.

Ansr. Soon after Captain Corbet's return on board, I acquainted him that on the evening before, while setting at the gun room table, I heard a very great noise and immediately went upon deck, where I found James Flynn, one of the gunner's crew, seized to the fore and fore top sail braces and a boatswain's mate beating him, the man violently calling murder. I instantly order'd him to be cast off, and acquainted Lieutenant Tailour, who desired me to report it to the captain, also that the boatswain's mate had been beat, but I did not see it, as it was previous to my coming on deck.

Prosr. Do you know that it is my most positive order, and inserted in the order book, that no punishment is to be inflicted in the ship, but by my order?

Ansr. I do.

Prosecutor Did the prisoner assign any reason for such conduct?

Ansr. He reported to me that on his ordering the gunner's crew aft, he heard Flynn answer, 'Damn your eyes; what do you want?'

Prosr. From the discipline of the ship I command, do you suppose it possible that *that* answer could be address'd to an officer?

Ansr. Certainly not.

Mr. Blight order'd to withdraw, and Mr. George Slade, Midshipman, called in and sworn.

Prosr. Were you upon deck when the circumstance stated in my charge against the prisoner took place?

Ansr. Yes.

Prosr. State fully the occurrence from first to last.

Ansr. I was on deck and the prisoner order'd the gunners of the larboard watch on deck to stow the waist netting cloth. James Flynn was forward in the galley; the gunner's mate was coming up the gangway ladder and he sung out for the gunners of the larboard watch. Flynn made answer, 'What do you want?' The prisoner was on the same gangway and he order'd him up and order'd me to send a boatswain's mate to start him up. The prisoner then order'd the boatswain's mate to take the end of the fore brace and start him. He then struck him four or five times and he fell down. He then got up and run over to the starboard gangway. The prisoner order'd him to come back again and called the quarter master to seize him up to the fore brace and the prisoner then order'd the boatswain's mate to give him a dozen with the end of the fore brace. The prisoner said the boatswain's mate did not do his duty and took the end of the fore top sail brace and struck him over the head. He then made the boatswain's mate thrash him again; in the mean time M^{r}. Blight came on deck and order'd Flynn to be cast off.

Pros^{r}. Do you mean in your statement that the prisoner struck the b^{ns} mate?

Ans^{r}. Yes.

Pros^{r}. Have you read my written orders?

Ans^{r}. Yes.

Pros^{r}. Is there one amongst them against any punishment being inflicted without my immediate orders?

Ans^{r}. I don't know.

Mr. Slade order'd to withdraw, and Thomas Riddle, Quarter Master, sworn.

Prosecutor Were you upon deck when the circumstance stated in my charge against the prisoner took place?

Ans^{r}. Yes.

Pros^{r}. State all you know concerning it.

Ans^{r}. When the prisoner called the gunner, I was walking betwixt the after carronade and the taffrail, looking out for the captain on the starboard side. The prisoner called me to seize up Flynn to the fore brace. I did so and he desired the b^{ns}. mate to beat him. I then went aft to look out for the captain.

Pros^{r}. Do you know that the man was beat?

Answer Yes.

Pros^{r}. Do you know if the boatswain's mate was beaten?

Ans^{r}. No.

Thomas Riddle order'd to withdraw, and Moses Veale, Boats^{ns}. Mate, sworn.

Pros^{r}. Did you, on Saturday night last, receive orders from the prisoner to punish Flynn, one of the Gunner's Crew?

Ans^{r}. Yes.

Pros^{r}. After your receiving that order, state to the court what passed.

Ans^{r}. I was order'd to take the end of the fore brace; I did so and was order'd to start Flynn, the Gunner. After I had hit him three times, he fell down. I did not strike him when he was down; the prisoner did. The prisoner then called for the quar^{r}. master to seize him up to the starb^{d}. fore brace; he did so. I was then order'd to start him again, which I did until the prisoner said I was not doing my duty. He then took the end of the fore topsail brace and struck me over the head, which occasioned me to stagger to the starb^{d}. side of the ship. I then left off starting the man and the prisoner order'd me a second time to give him another dozen, when M^{r}. Blight came up and said he would not allow any such thing to be carried on while he was in the ship, it being the captain's orders not to allow it. Mr. Blight then order'd Flynn to be cast off.

Moses Veale order'd to withdraw.

The evidence in support of the charge being finish'd, the prisoner was called upon to make his defence, who put into the hands of the judge advocate a written paper signed by himself, which was read to the court as follows:

… I beg leave respectfully to state that I have been 30 years at sea; 17 of that period, I have had the honour to serve His Majesty as midshipman, master's mate, and for the last 11 years as master. I produce certificates, some of which the court will please to observe are strongly in my favour. I was taken prisoner in 1794 when I lost everything belonging to me, which accounts for my not having any of a date previous to that time. I beg leave to call on Captain Corbet, Lieutenant Tailour, and Lieutenant Blight; if during the time I have been in the *Nereide*, they ever saw or heard of my behaving in a tyrannical or oppressive manner to any of the men previous to the unfortunate business now before the court, in defence of which I am fully aware I have nothing further to offer than being hurried away by the heat of passion and I humbly hope the court will consider my long services and I trust be as lenient in their decision as possible.

Off Montevideo
26th August 1807

…

The prisoner then requested that Lieutenant Tailour of the said ship may be called in to speak to his general character, who said he never saw any act of tyranny or oppression used by the prisoner since they had been shipmates in the *Nereide*.

Lieutenant Tailour withdrew.

The prisoner having nothing further to offer in his defence, the court was cleared and proceeded to deliberate upon and form the sentence.

The court, having heard the evidence in support of the charge as well as what the prisoner had to offer in his defence and the evidence adduced in his behalf and very maturely and deliberately weighed and consider'd the same, was of opinion that the charge had been proved against the prisoner, M^r^. Corthine Parker, and did in consequence thereof adjudge the said M^r^. Corthine Parker to be dismissed from His Majesty's ship *Nereide*, and to be put back three years upon the list of masters of His Majesty's navy.

The court was open'd, the prisoner brought in, the evidence and audience admitted, and sentence passed accordingly. …

D. Contempt, Insolence and Disrespect

104. *Court Martial of Thomas Ratsey*

[ADM 1/5336]

Minutes of a court martial assembled and held on board His Majesty's ship *Dictator* at the Mole S^t^. Nicholas Island, S^t^. Domingo, the 13th day of June 1796.

Present

George Bowen, Esqr., Captain of the *Canada* and third officer in the command of His Majesty's ships at S^t^. Domingo and Jamaica, President.

Captains

Thomas Totty	Thomas Lewis
George Tripp	Thomas Parr
Thomas Bertie	Robert Parker

The court being assembled, the prisoner present and audience admitted, the order for assembling the court martial was read as follows:[1]

[1] This order is to Captain George Bowen, third officer in command on the Jamaica Station.

… Captain Thomas Totty of His Majesty's ship *Dictator* having transmitted to me a letter he had received from Lieutenant Richard Horsley of His Majesty's said ship, dated the 7th day of May last, requesting a court martial might be assembled to try M^r^. Thomas Ratsey, Master's Mate belonging to the *Dictator*, for treating the said Lieutenant with great contempt while in the execution of his duty. And whereas for the better keeping good order and discipline in the squadron, I think it proper that Lieutenant Horsley's request be complied with.

By virtue of the power & authority vested in me, I do hereby require and direct you to assemble a court martial on Saturday morning next (or as soon after as convenient) on board any one of His Majesty's ships, which court, you being president, is hereby required and directed to try the said M^r^. Thomas Ratsey for the offence above mentioned as set forth in the said Lieutenant Horsley's letter. For further particulars, the original letters are to be applied to, which are enclosed herewith.

Given on board the *Swiftsure* at the Mole St. Nicholas,
the 9th June 1796.

…

… Whereas a court martial is ordered to be assembled to try Mr. Thomas Ratsey, Master's Mate of His Majesty's ship *Dictator*, for behaving with contempt to Lieut. Horsley of the said ship while in the execution of his duty, I do, with the consent of the members who compose the court martial, hereby authorize & appoint you to officiate as judge advocate upon this occasion.

Given on board the *Dictator*
the 13th June 1796[1]

…

The court and judge advocate were then sworn, and Captain Totty's and Lieutenant Horsley's letters read as follows:[2]

Dictator, Cape Nicholas Mole
the 14th May 1796

… I have the honour to transmit to you the enclosed letter from L^t^. Horsley of His Majesty's ship *Dictator* under my command for your consideration …

[1]This warrant is from Captain Bowen to William Goddard.
[2]Captain Totty's letter is to Admiral Parker, Commander in Chief of the Jamaica Station at the time; Lieutenant Horsley's letter is to Captain Totty.

His Majesty's ship *Dictator*
May the 7th, 1796

… I beg leave to inform you that M[r]. Thomas Ratsey, Master's Mate on board His Majesty's ship *Dictator* under your command, has treated me with great contempt while in the execution of my duty. I think it a duty incumbent on me for the good of His Majesty's service to request you will be pleased to write to the commander in chief for a court martial on the said M[r]. Thomas Ratsey …

All the witnesses were then ordered to withdraw, except Lieutenant Richard Crocombe of the *Dictator*, who was sworn.

Lieut. Rich[d]. Crocombe sworn

Q. Prosecutor – Did I relieve you at 15 minutes past 4 o'clock in the morning watch of the 7th day of May last?
Ans[r]. – You did.
Q – Did you leave orders with me to dispatch the launch with all expedition for water?
Ans[r] – I did.
Q – Did I call for the gentleman of the watch & did M[r]. Ratsey answer; and did I tell him to call the launch's crew and what did he say?
A – He said, 'I have called them.'
Q – Did I order him to call them again?
A – You did.
Q – Did M[r]. Ratsey go to the gangway and call the launches in so low a voice as scarcely to be heard?
A – Yes he did and in my opinion not low enough to be heard on the lower gun deck, he being on the gangway.
Q – Did I order M[r]. Ratsey to see the boat manned instantly and did I say if he did not, damn my soul if I would not confine him?
A – You did.
Q – Did M[r]. Ratsey say I might confine him, but that he would not be damned by me?
A – Yes, he did.
Q – Did you go over to M[r]. Ratsey, and what did you say to him?
A – I went over to M[r]. Ratsey to convince him that Lieu[t]. Horsley had not damned his soul, but his own. M[r]. Ratsey's reply to me was that he did damn his soul,

and I then said, 'Sir, you may as well tell me I lie,' upon which I went below. That is all I know of the affair.

Q Court – Were you near enough to distinguish the words that passed and to be positive that Mr. Horsley damned his own soul and not Mr. Ratsey's?

A – Yes, I am certain I was near enough or I had not given such evidence.

Q. C. – Did you see the prisoner use any exertions to get the boat manned?

A. – Being relieved, I went below, and saw no further proceedings.

Q. C. – When you went to explain what Mr. Horsley said, in what manner did Mr. Ratsey reply?

A. – In a very contemptuous manner, such as I thought I did not merit from him.

Q. C. – The first time Lieut. Horsley spoke to Mr. Ratsey to man the launch, did he proceed upon that service as an officer ought to do or did he receive the orders in a slight or disrespectful manner?

A. – He did not proceed at all, only gave Mr. Horsley an answer that he had called them and walked aft.

Ordered to withdraw, and Joseph Atwell, Quarter Master belonging to the *Dictator*, was called in.

Joseph Atwell sworn.

Q. Pros. – Was you upon deck when I relieved Lieut. Crocombe on the morning of the 7th day of May last?

A. – On the 8th day of May, I was upon deck in the morning, and saw you relieve Lieut. Crocombe at a little after 4 o'clock, but I know of no such transaction on the morning of the 7th.

Ordered to withdraw, and here the evidence for the prosecution closed.

The prisoner was then put upon his defence, who declared he had not the watch at the time he is charged with treating the prosecutor, Lieutenant Horsley, with contempt; to prove which, he requested that Joseph Atwell might be recalled into the court.

Joseph Atwell recalled & examined by the prisoner.

Q. – Had you the morning watch on the 7th day of May last?

A. – No! I had not.

Q. – Had I the morning watch on the 7th day of May?
A. – No, but you had on the 8th when the launch was sent away by Lieut. Horsley for water.

Ordered to withdraw, and Mr. James Bowden, Midshipman, called in and sworn.

Mr. James Bowden sworn.

Q. Prisr. – Had I the morning watch on the 7th day of May last?
A. – No!
Q. Court – Do you know who had the morning watch on that day?
A. – I do not recollect, but I am positive Mr. Ratsey had not.

Ordered to withdraw, and Lieut. Trelawney of the *Dictator*, called in and sworn.

Lieut. Trelawney sworn.

Q. Pris. – Had you my watch on the 7th day of May last, and what watch was it?
A. – Yes! The morning watch.

Here the prisoner closed his defence and the court was cleared to sum up the evidence, which being done & audience admitted, the sentence was read as follows:

… and having examined evidence produced in support of the charge, and those called by the prisoner, and heard his defence, and maturely and deliberately considered the whole, the court is of opinion that the charge is not proved, it appearing by the evidence produced by the prisoner, that he had not the watch at the time stated. Mr. Thomas Ratsey is therefore acquitted, and he is hereby acquitted of having behaved with contempt to Lieutenant Richd. Horsley on the 7th day of May last as stated accordingly. …

105. *Court Martial of Joseph Ramsay*

[ADM 1/5349]

Minutes of the proceedings at a court martial held on board His Majesty's ship *Monarch*, off the Texel, on 25 June 1799.

Present

Archibald Dickson, Esqr, Vice Admiral of the Red and second in command, &c, &c.

Captains

Robert Dev^{x}. Fancourt	James Robt Mosse
Jno Step^{n} Hall	George Hart
Thomas Bertie	Rowley Bulteel
Jno Lawford	Arch^{d} Collingw^{d} Dickson

The prisoner was brought into court and audience admitted.

Read the order of the Right Honourable, The Lords Commissioners of the Admiralty, dated the 13th day of June 1799, directed to Archibald Dickson, Esqr., Vice Admiral of the Red and first officer in command of His Majesty's ship and vessels off the Texel, to try Mr Joseph Ramsay, Master of His Majesty's ship *Director*, for having replied to Captain Bligh of the said ship in a very improper manner and impertinently said, 'If I am not able to work the ship, it is better to have some other person else here.' Then the members of the court and judge advocate, in open court and before they proceeded to trial, respectively took the oaths directed by Act of Parliament.

The letter from Captain William Bligh of His Majesty's ship *Director* (containing the charges against the prisoner) was read and all the witnesses being ordered to withdraw and attend their examinations separately, they all withdrew accordingly, except the first to be sworn and the court proceeded to trial as follows:

Evidence in support of the charge, Mr Peter Blaeguire, Midshipman of His Majesty's ship *Director*, first sworn.

Prosecutor – Relate to the court what you know respecting the charge against the prisoner.

Ans^{r} – Captain Bligh said, 'Mr Ramsay, if you was to get the pendant clear, you would be able to see much better;' Mr Ramsay replied, 'Thank God, Sir, my eye sight is tolerably good.' Captain Bligh then said, 'Sir you have handled the ship very badly then;' Mr Ramsay replied, 'If I cannot do it, some one else had better be here,' or words to that effect.

Court – In what manner did the prisoner reply to Captain Bligh; was it coolly and dispassionately or was it contemptuously?

Ans^{r} – In my opinion, perfectly cool.

Court – Did the ship miss stays in consequence of inattention?

Ans^{r} – No.

Prisoner – Do you recollect whether the ship was about at the time Captain Bligh spoke to me?

Ans^{r} – Yes, she was.

Pris^{r} – Do you recollect in what part of the ship I was standing when Captain Bligh spoke to me?

Ans^{r} – To the best of my recollection, on the starboard side of the quarter deck.

Pris^{r} – Do you recollect where Captain Bligh was standing when I addressed him?

Ans^{r} – To the best of my recollection, he was standing on the gratings on the quarter deck.

Pris^{r} – Was the pendant clear or foul at that time?

Answ^{r} – I did not take notice.

Prisoner – Did I say to Captain Bligh, 'If, Sir, you think me not equal to working of the ship, had not some one else better do it.'

Ans^{r} – I do not recollect exactly the words.

Pris^{r} – Have you repeatedly heard Captain Bligh find fault with my working the ship in a very violent manner?

Ans^{r} – I cannot say I have.

This witness retired, when M^{r}. John Robinson, Midshipman of His Majesty's ship *Director*, next called in and sworn.

Prosecutor – On the 5th of May about 5 o'clock in the evening off the Texel, did you hear me say to the prisoner, M^{r}. Ramsay, 'If you would make them hoist the pendant clear, you would see better how to haul the ship,' or words to that effect?

Ans^{r} – Yes.

Pros^{r} – Did you hear M^{r}. Ramsay say to me in answer, 'If I am not able to work the ship, it is better to have some person else,' or words to that effect?

Ans^{r} – I heard him say, 'If I am not able to work the ship, some one else had better do it,' or words to that effect.

Prosecutor – Did you hear me tell him that was not a proper way to express himself?

Ans^{r} – I do not remember hearing that.

Prosecutor – Did you hear the prisoner say to me, 'I said so, and will say so before anyone and anywhere?'

Ans^{r} – I heard Mr Ramsay say so, or words to that effect just before the poop awning.

Pros^{r} – Did you hear the prisoner say, 'Thank God, my eye sight is very good?'

Ans^{r} – No.

Court – How did the prisoner express himself to Captain Bligh? Was it respectfully or was it in a quick, passionate manner?

Ansr – I do not conceive myself a sufficient judge to answer that question.

The prisoner had no question to ask this witness; he retired.

John Brown, Quarter Master of His Majesty's ship *Director*, next called and sworn.

Prosecutor – On the 5 of May about 5 o'clock in the evening off the Texel, did you hear me say to the prisoner, Mr Ramsay, 'If you would make them hoist the pendant clear, you would see better how to haul the ship,' or words to that effect?

Ansr – Yes.

Prosecutor – Did you hear Mr. Ramsay say to me, 'If I am not able to work the ship, it is better to have some person else?'

Ansr – Yes.

Prosr – Did you hear me tell him that it was not a proper way to express himself?

Ansr – Yes.

Prosr – Did you hear the prisoner say to me, 'I said so; and will say so before anyone and anywhere?'

Ansr – Yes.

Prosr – Did you hear the prisoner say that thank God his eye sight was very good?

Ansr – Yes, I did.

Court – Were the prisoner's answers to Captain Bligh and the words he made use of spoken in a respectful manner to his superior officer or were they expressed passionately and in anger?

Ansr – They seemed to be passionately spoken.

Court – In what manner did they appear to you passionately spoken?

Ansr – On account of the prisoner being forward and then coming aft in a hurry to where the Captain was standing.

Court – Did the prisoner's behaviour & manner of reply appear to you impertinent and improper?

Ansr – It appeared to me to be very improper.

Court – Where were you at the time you heard this pass?

Answr – At the conn.

Court – Describe the position of Captain Bligh and Mr Ramsay when the conversation passed between them.

Ansr – Captain Bligh was standing on the quarter deck gratings and Mr. Ramsay on the starboard side of the poop ladder.

Prisoner – Do you recollect, at the time Captain Bligh found fault with my hauling the ship, whether the main top bowline was let go before I hauled the ship?

Ansr – I do not recollect.

Prisoner – When the Captain found fault first with my hauling the ship, in what part of her was I standing?

Ansr – On the fore part of the quarter deck.

Prisoner – Where was Captain Bligh standing at that time?

Ansr – On the mid-ship grating of the quarter deck.

Prisoner – Were the head yards hauled at that time?

Ansr – I do not recollect.

Prisoner – Do you recollect at the time I addressed Captain Bligh, whether I tipped my hat to him when I spoke and was I close to him?

Ansr – I do not recollect; I did not see it.

This witness withdrew.

David Dickson, Seaman belonging to His Majesty's ship *Director*, next called in and sworn.

Prosecutor – Relate to the court what you know respecting the charge against the prisoner.

Answer – The first words I took notice of was Captain Bligh told Mr Ramsay that if he would see the pendant clear, he would see better how to put the ship about. Mr Ramsay answered that God be thanked his eye sight was tolerably good. Captain Bligh told him that was not the answer to give him; Mr. Ramsay said that if he could not put the ship about, that he had better get some other body. Captain Bligh said that was an improper answer to give him; Mr. Ramsay said that he was not afraid to say so in any place.

Court – Did those words you have mentioned to come from Mr. Ramsay appear to be in an angry tone of voice?

Ansr – No Sir, I cannot say; he generally speaks very low. I cannot say whether they were in anger or not.

Court – Did he speak in his usual manner?

Ans[r] – He did not, nor did the Captain; they spoke as if they did not like each other's words.

Court – Did the prisoner's behaviour during the conversation between him and Captain Bligh appear to you improper and impertinent?

Answer – Only the words that if he could not put the ship about, he had better get some other body.

Prisoner – Did I haul the head yards after the first conversation that you have stated to have taken place before I addressed Captain Bligh?

Ans[r] – I do not recollect, but while they were talking together, M[r]. Johnstone, First Lieutenant, trimmed the sails.

Prisoner – Where were you at the time?

Ans[r] – Standing at the foot of the poop ladder.

Lieutenant W[m] Tindall, of His Majesty's ship *Director*, next called in and sworn. Dismissed, knowing nothing relative to the charge; as were Lieutenants Samuel Roscow and W[m] Oxbrough of the said ship. Captain Tho[s] Davy and Lieutenant George Keith, of the marines of His Majesty's ship *Director*, next called in and sworn; but each declaring they knew nothing relative to the charge were dismissed.

M[r]. James Lewis, Pilot of the *Director*, called in and sworn.

Prosecutor – Relate to the court what you know respecting the charge against the prisoner.

Answer – I was doing my duty as pilot of the *Director*, and it is the captain's order for one of the pilots to see the land after the ship has stayed from the shore, and I was with the compass on the fore part of the poop, on the column chest until such time as the ship was in stays. While I stood there, I heard the captain say, 'M[r]. Ramsay, you either haul too soon or too late, Sir.' I then went aft to the after part of the poop, and set the land; I did not hear any reply given or do I know anything further about the charge.

Court – Did it appear to you that the ship was hauled too soon or too late?

Answer – I really did not observe.

Court – Did you hear Captain Bligh make any observations to the prisoner about the pendant?

Ans[r] – I did not.

The evidence for the Crown being closed, the prisoner was desired to relate what he had to say in his defence; he produced two letters from the

Captains Sir Wm Geo. Fairfax and Ja^{s} Alms to his good character, with sundry letters, numbered from no. 1 to no. 6 inclusive,[1] and addressed the court as follows, viz:

I beg to impress the court that on my first being appointed master and pilot of the *Director*, I found Captain Bligh very much against it and he has repeatedly declared he would suffer no such appointment in his ship, in consequence of which I wrote the letters from no.1 to no.6 inclusive, which with their respective answers, I have troubled the court with. Captain Bligh, in consequence of the Navy Board having persisted in my appointment, has done everything in his power to distress me by seeking every opportunity to hurt my feelings in the execution of my duty and by violent expressions to throw me off my guard.

That Captain Bligh, in the instance before the court, has in some measure succeeded appears upon the minutes; but I trust when the letters produced shall have been read, the court will duly consider my unpleasant situation. A captain predetermined to take every opportunity to find fault with me in the execution of my duty and, by constant harsh language, harassing my feelings (to a man, regularly bred to the sea and perfectly master of his duty, is truly distressing) I might, in an unguarded moment, have dropped an expression very foreign to my ideas and contrary to the discipline of the Navy; I trust the humanity of the court, will make an allowance for the frailty of human nature, thus taken by surprise. And I hope further to prove that the general tenor of Captain Bligh's conduct has been rather to get rid of the appointment than the man.

Lieutenant William Oxbrough of the *Director* examined on the part of the prisoner.

Prisoner	–	Have you ever known me neglect my duty as master or as pilot while onboard the *Director*?
Answer	–	No.
Question	–	While I was constantly at watch and watch, have I repeatedly been called out of my bed to work the ship when the watch only was upon deck?
Answer	–	Yes.
Question	–	Did you hear me murmur on account if it?
Answer	–	No.
Question	–	Did you ever know me flurried or appear confused in doing my duty as master or pilot?
Answer	–	No, I never did.
Prisoner	–	Have you heard Captain Bligh, often, on deck, call to me in a violent manner to know why such and such

[1]These letters are not bound with the transcript.

		things were not executed; in the same time, have I been doing my utmost to obey the orders given?
Answer	–	I have heard Captain Bligh speak loud often; when, to the best of my knowledge, M[r]. Ramsay (the prisoner) was doing his utmost to obey orders.
Question	–	Has it been the constant practice of Captain Bligh to use very harsh expressions to me while doing my duty?
Answer	–	No.
Court	–	Did you ever know the master behave in a contemptuous manner to Captain Bligh at any time?
Answer	–	No.
Question	–	Does the prisoner in general work the ship as becomes an officer and a seaman?
Answer	–	Yes.
Question	–	Did you hear Captain Bligh admonish the prisoner for incivility and inattention to him since he had been in the ship?
Answer	–	No.
Captain Bligh	–	Was it my written orders, before M[r]. Ramsay came into the ship, for the master to tack the ship always whether with watch or all hands?
Answer	–	The first lieutenant and master have always been called for the purpose.
Question	–	Do you think I might have seen things not attended to, which in some cases you might not?
Answer	–	Yes; I do.

Lieutenant William Tindall of His Majesty's ship *Director*.

Prisoner	–	Have you ever known me neglect my duty as master or as pilot while onboard the *Director*?
Answer	–	No.
Question	–	While I was constantly at watch and watch, have I not repeatedly been called out of my sleep to work the ship when she was worked by the watch only?
Answer	–	Yes.
Question	–	Did you ever hear me murmur on account of it?
Answer	–	No.
Question	–	Did you ever know me flurried or appear confused in doing my duty as the master or pilot?
Answer	–	No.
Prisoner	–	Have you heard Captain Bligh, often on deck, call to me in a violent manner to know why such and such

things were not executed, at the same time I was doing my utmost to obey the orders given?

Answer – I have heard Captain Bligh speak loud often when, to the best of my knowledge, the prisoner was doing his utmost to obey orders.

Question – Has it been the constant practice of Captain Bligh to make use of very harsh expressions to me while doing my duty?

Answer – I do not recollect. My station was in the waist and I did not hear them.

Question – Did I obey all orders cheerfully?

Answer – All that I ever heard him desire you to execute.

Court – You were lieutenant of the *Director* before M[r]. Ramsay was appointed in Captain Bligh's time. Was it the order and practice then for the master to be called at all times to put the ship about?

Answer – Yes, it was.

Court – Did you ever know the master behave in a contemptuous manner to the captain?

Answer – No.

Court – Was the former master, pilot; and did he keep watch and watch?

Answer – He was not pilot nor did he keep watch and watch.

Prosecutor – Why was the prisoner, as master of the ship, at watch and watch?

Answer – On account of his being appointed to do duty as pilot.

Question – Have you always known the pilots on board the *Director* at watch and watch, with my orders strictly to attend to the lead and my written orders that they were to consult with the officer of the watch upon the rate of the ship going, so as to have it marked correctly?

Answer – I have always known them at watch and watch, for the purpose you represent.

Question – Do you think that I might have seen things not attended to that in some cases you might not?

Answer – Probably you might.

Lieutenant Samuel Roscow, of His Majesty's ship *Director*, next called.

Prisoner – Have you ever known me neglect my duty as master or as pilot when on board the *Director*?

Answer – No.
Question – While I was constantly at watch and watch, have I repeatedly been called out of my bed to work the ship, when the watch only was upon deck?
Answer – Yes.
Question – Did you hear me murmur on account of it?
Answer – No.
Question – Did you ever know me flurried, or appear confused, in doing my duty as master or pilot?
Answer – No; I never did, by no means.
Question – Have you heard Captain Bligh, often on deck, call to me in a violent manner to know why such and such things were not executed; at the same time, have I been doing my utmost to obey the orders given?
Answer – I have heard Captain Bligh speak loud often when, to the best of my knowledge, the prisoner was doing his utmost to obey orders.
Question – Has it been the constant practice of Captain Bligh to use very harsh expressions to me, while doing my duty?
Answer – Very often, I have heard him.
Question – Did I appear to obey all orders of my captain or other superior officer with alacrity and cheerfulness?
Answer – At all times.
Question – Whether from that conduct, do you suppose the words made use of in the charge could be with an intention of offending my captain or injuring the discipline of the service?
Answer – No; I think not.
Court – Did you, at any time, know the master behave in a contemptuous manner to the captain, in the execution of his duty?
Answer – No, never.
Court – You have said in your evidence you have often heard the captain make use of harsh expression to the master, do you remember any & what were they?
Answer – I cannot immediately relate the words; but often, when working the ship, the captain has accused him of not forwarding the duty when he appeared to be doing his utmost and Captain Bligh kept calling in a loud manner, why he did not do it, repeatedly, why

is it not done, for shame, at the same time accusing him of neglect.

President – Do you term those harsh expressions?

Answer – Yes, from the manner they were spoken.

Prosecutor – Was it my written orders as well as verbal ones before Mr Ramsay (the prisoner) came into the ship for the master always to tack her with the watch or all hands?

Answer – Yes, it was.

Question – Do you think that I might have seen things not attended to, which, in some cases, you might not?

Answer – Certainly.

Question – Why was the prisoner at watch and watch?

Answer – In compliance with your order (as a pilot).

Question – Did ever a master, belonging to the *Director*, keep watch before the prisoner?

Answer – Yes; they have.

Question – Why did they keep watch?

Answer – Because some officer was absent or sick.

Question – Was, therefore, the reason of the master's keeping watch owing to my kindness in orienting him to do so, because you officers of the ship should not be at watch and watch?

Answer – I considered it as such.

Question – Have not the pilots always been at watch and watch behind the lead, & to consult with the officers of the watch of the rate of the ship's going?

Answer – Always.

Lieutenant George Keith, of the Marines belonging to His Majesty's ship *Director*, next called.

Prisoner – Have you heard Captain Bligh make use of violent & harsh expressions to me in the execution of my duty?

Answer – I have heard Captain Bligh make use of hardy expressions when the ship has been tacking, but I do not know whether to the prisoner or not.

President – Relate the words, if you recollect them.

Answer – I have heard him hastily enquire why things had not been done.

Captain Thomas Davy, of the Marines of His Majesty's ship *Director*, next called.

Prisoner – Have you heard Captain Bligh make use of harsh expressions to me in the execution of my duty?

Answer – I have heard that such things had happened, but I have not heard them myself.

Captain Davy acquainted the court that the prisoner had always conducted himself (as far as came within his knowledge) with decency & great respect. The defence rested here. The court was then cleared; and, the judge advocate, having read the minutes, and the court, having maturely and deliberately considered the whole, agreed that the charge was proved. The court, therefore, adjudged the prisoner to be dismissed from his situation as Master of His Majesty's ship *Director*.

The court was opened, and audience admitted, and sentence passed accordingly. …

NEGLECT OF DUTY

106. *Court Martial of William Little*

[ADM 1/5338]

Minutes of the proceedings or a court martial assembled and held on board His Majesty's ship *Cambridge* in Hamoaze, on Saturday the 7th of January 1797 for the trial of M^r^. William Little, Gunner of His Majesty's ship *Camilla*, 'for having carelessly and negligently left, and suffered to remain a quantity of gunpowder in the light room of the magazine, whereby an explosion took place on the night of the first of December last.'

Present
Augustus Montgomery, Esqr., Captain of His Majesty's ship *Theseus* and second officer in the command of His Majesty's ships and vessels at Plymouth,

President.

Theophilus Jones	Henry D. Darby
Thomas Louis	Jno. Mc Dougall
Alexander John Ball	Edwd. O'Brien
Davidge Gould	R^d^. Goodwin Keats
Charles Boyles	P^p^. Chas. Durham
John Loring	George Parker

H.M. Stokes, D. J. A.

The surgeons of the *Cambridge* and *Sampson* certified Captains Boger's and Trip's inability to attend thro' ill health.

The prosecution opened with reading the 5th Article of the Gunner's instructions.[1]

M^r^. John George Cock, First Lieutenant, sworn.

Prosecutor – Do you remember on my taking the command of the *Camilla*, after I read my orders to the ship's company, that I sent for all the warrant officers and enquired into the state of the stores they had under their respective charges?

[1]The Fifth Article of the Gunner's Instructions read: 'He is to give timely notice to the Captain upon all occasions of bringing powder on board and not to remove any out of the ship or from one part of her to another or fill cartridges or prepare fuzees, fireworks, &c. without the captain's directions, that he may give orders for extinguishing the fire and candles and posting sentinels at all proper places to prevent accidents and the decks are immediately after to be thoroughly swabbed and cleaned of the loose powder that may have fallen.'

A. – Yes, I do.

P. – Did the prisoner at that time or any other, to your knowledge, inform me of any gunpowder being in the light room or any other improper place?

A. – Not to my recollection.

P. – Did you ever before the accident of the explosion on the night of the first of December last acquaint me of any powder being improperly deposited?

A. – No.

P. – Did you know of any being so or did the prisoner ever mention it to you?

A. – No.

P. – Inform the court of the orders I gave you as officer of the first watch on the night of the first of December last?

A. – You ordered me to tell the sergeant to be particular in seeing all the lights out and that the gunner, nor any of his crew, went into the magazine with knives in their pockets or buckles in their shoes.

P. – Did you not know it was my intention to fill powder some time before that evening?

A. – Yes, but it was put off on account of bad weather.

P. – What were the directions you gave in consequence of my orders to you?

A. – At ten o'clock, I sent for the sergeant and told him to see all the lights out and report to me when they were out.

P. – After I had given you these orders and retired, were there not two boxes of musket and pistol cartridges handed from out of the light room with other things and did you not acquaint me therewith the next morning?

A. – Yes.

Prosecutor – Inform the court of all the circumstances you know respecting the explosion on the night of the 1st December last.

A. – On the night of the accident, I was officer of the first watch. To the best of my recollection, Captain Rotheram sent for me about ¼ past 10, respecting some further orders about tacking the ship. On my return from him, I saw a great explosion of smoke come up the after hatchway. I ask'd what was the occasion of it; someone in the dark, under the half deck, answered me, twas from the magazine, but I did not know his voice. I instantly ran down into the cockpit, where I found the prisoner, the sergeant of Marines, gunner's mate and ship's cook. I ask'd how the accident happened. The sergeant told me in putting the light into the light room, a spark fell from the candle on some loose powder in the light room. When I came down, they had got out a box of cartridges, and was getting a second one out of the light room. I ordered the cartridges to be carried on the quarter deck, there to remain till further order.

P. – Do you know the contents of those boxes that were handed up and examined next morning?

A. – They contain'd fill'd musket cartridges; the boxes were such as are generally used for that purpose.

P. – Was there not a quantity of loose powder also in the boxes?

A. – Yes, there was.

P. – Was there not an iron knife and a flint in the boxes with the loose powder?

A. – Yes, there was.

C. – When musket cartridges were required for the use of the ship, do you recollect whether the gunner was in the habit of applying to you for the keys of the magazine to get them?

A. – I do not recollect that any were wanting from the magazine from the time the prisoner became gunner of the ship to the time of the accident.

C. – Did you suppose all the powder was kept in the magazine?

A. – Yes, all except one or two gun cartridges for smoking the ship.[1]

C. – Had the gunner access to the magazine without previously asking the commanding officer and in what manner were the keys delivered to him?

A. – The gunner never had access to the magazine without coming to me first and the sergeant going with him there.

C. – How long had the prisoner been gunner of the ship at the time of the accident?

A. – Between two and three months.

[1]Filling the lower decks of a ship with smoke was thought to purify the air below. According to Falconer, 'the frequent fumigation of ships is highly necessary in order to prevent disease produced by confined or infected air' (Falconer, *A New Universal Dictionary*, s.v. Fumigate). Among the materials used to create the smoke were brimstone, sawdust, nitre with vitriolic acid, salt with vitriolic acid and wetted gunpowder.

Prisoner – Were the keys of the light room kept with the keys of the magazine?

A. – They were constantly in my cabin, but separate with a label to each.

P. – Did you not give me orders to complete the Marine cartouch boxes with ball cartridges?

A. – Not to my recollection.

M[r]. Thomas Penrose, Master, sworn.

Prosecutor – Do you remember on my taking command of the *Camilla* after I read my order to the ship's company that I sent for all the warrant officers and enquired into the state of the stores they had under their respective charges?

A. – Yes, I do.

P. – Did the prisoner at that time, or any other to your knowledge, inform one of any gunpowder being in the light room or any other improper place?

A. – Not to my knowledge.

P. – Inform the court of everything you know, relative to the explosion on the night of the first of December last and the steps taken by me the next morning.

A. – When you came on deck about half past seven o'clock, I told you there had been some powder blown up in the light room the night before. You then immediately sent for the first lieutenant and the gunner, whom you ordered to his cabin.

P. – Do you recollect the gunner's reply when I enquired why powder had been deposited in the light room?

A. – He said he had several times reported to the first lieutenant of the powder being in the light room.

P. – And did not Lieutenant Cock deny of his having any knowledge thereof or that the prisoner had ever given him any information of the kind?

A. – Yes.

P. – How long had you been master prior to the accident?

A. – About ten months.

P. – Did it ever come to your knowledge that any cartridges of powder were deposited in the light room prior to the accident?

A. – I never knew there were any there.

C. – To your knowledge was there no report made to the captain till the time in the morning you say you made it and who reported it to you?

A. – I do not know of any report being made to the captain before I made it and Mr. Desert, mate of the middle watch, reported it to me.

C. – Who was the officer of the middle watch that you relieved and did he not mention it to you?

A. – I relieved Mr. Andrews, Second Lieutenant, but he did not report to me the accident.

Prisoner – Do you know of any cartridges being issued to complete the Marine cartouch boxes since I have been gunner of the ship?

A. – No.

Thomas Harrogan, Ship's Cook, sworn.

Prosecutor – Are you stationed to attend the light room of the magazine on board the *Camilla*?

A. – Yes, I am.

P. – Do you remember being ordered there on the night of the first of December last?

A. – Yes, I do.

C. – Relate to the court, as circumstantially as you can, what happened from the time you went into the light room to the time of your coming out again.

A. – I went down into the light room as I was ordered and there being no snuffers, on my snuffing the candle with my fingers before I put it into the sconce, a part of the snuff fell from my fingers on the floor of the light room, upon which an explosion took place. I then came out into the cockpit and, in a few minutes after, went on deck.

P. – What injury did you receive from the explosion?

A. – I lost the sight of one eye four, and the other five, days.

P. – Have you usually attended the light room when the gunner has been employed in the magazine?

A. – Yes.

P. – Do you remember ever to have seen boxes handed out of the light room on these occasions?

A. – Yes.

P. – Were they supposed to contain powder?

A. – I cannot say with respect to their contents.

P. – What sort of boxes were they?

A. – Boxes for the purpose of containing powder.

P. – Were those boxes handed out of the light room at such times as you were ordered to the light room prior to the time of the prisoner becoming gunner of the *Camilla*?

A. – They were.
C. – Prisoner have you any questions to ask this evidence?
A. – No.

Thomas Breary, Quarter Gunner, sworn.

P. – Do you remember that on the morning of the second of December last, I ordered you to count the contents of two boxes of musket and pistol cartridges and loose powder then on the quarter deck?
A. – Yes.

Contents, viz.:

(Mark		No.	
M.	Box	1	Exercising cartridges 280, one iron knife, one flint, five formers, two funnels, and one tin measure.
	Box	2	Musket ball cartridges 80, pistol ball cartridges 23, one funnel, one tin measure, several balls, and about ½ pound of loose powder.

Two cases of musket balls, one keg of pistol balls)

P. – Do you know the account, which the judge advocate read to you, of their contents is right?
A. – Yes.
P. – Do you know how many musket cartridges were filled out of the loose powder found in the boxes?
A. – Thirty.
P. – Where were those boxes brought from the quarter deck?
A. – From the light room.
P. – Do you know how long they had been in the light room?
A. – No, I do not.
P. – Relate to the court all the circumstances you know respecting the explosion on the night of the first of December last.
A. – On the first of December when we went down to fill powder, the gunner called me down to take the boxes out of the light room, which I did, and took all out, except one box of musket balls. I told the cook to snuff the candle before he put it into the lantern, which he did with his fingers, and some of the snuff fell down where was some loose powder, which took fire, and flashed up in his face.
P. – Had it, to your knowledge, been the custom to keep those boxes with cartridges in the light room?
A. – I never was in the light room before; the last time I saw them there was in M^r^. Tricey's, the former Gunner, cabin and told

him it was not a fit place to keep them where there was always a light, but where he removed them, I don't know.

P. – When cartridges were wanting for sentinels or for exercising, did you ever assist in getting them up, or do you know from whence they were generally brought?

A. – No, nor do I know from whence they were brought.

Court – Prisoner have you any questions to ask this evidence?

A. – No.

Edward Fudge, Yeoman Powder Room, sworn.

Prosecutor – Do you know of any powder being kept in the light room of the *Camilla* before the explosion on the night of the first of December last?

A. – Yes, there were two boxes kept in it.

P. – When were they put there?

A. – I cannot say.

P. – Did you see them put there?

A. – No, they were there before I had anything to do with it.

P. – Were there ever any cartridges for the great guns kept there?

A. – No.

C. – Were the boxes there in the time of the former gunner?

A. – Yes, they were.

C. – Do you recollect any orders being given for filling the Marine cartouch boxes during the time of the present gunner?

A. – Yes, there were.

C. – Can you say by whom those orders were given?

A. – No.

C. – Do you know the reason why these boxes of cartridges were handed out of the light room just prior to the explosion?

A. – I cannot say.

C. – Was it customary to hand them out on going into the light room with lights?

A. – Yes, to put them on one side in the cockpit.

C. – Were there any hides round the boxes or any precaution taken to hinder the communication of fire to them?[1]

A. – No.

[1]The 1815 revision of Falconer's *A New Universal Dictionary* defined hides as 'the skins of animals, either raw or dressed; the first are allowed ships for service, the second for the gunner's department' (s.v. Hides). From this example it is clear that dressed hides were used to prevent the guns from igniting spare ammunition during firing.

Prisoner – Did you know of my ever having the key of the light room, or to be there with a light before the explosion?

A. – No.

Thomas Burley, Sergeant of Marines, sworn.

P. – Inform the court, as circumstantially as you can, of what happened after you sent Thomas Harrogan, the Ship's Cook, into the light room on the night of the first of December last till after the explosion took place.

A. – I was doing duty as master at arms (there being none on board), and on being ordered to put the lights out by the first lieutenant, I did so and then went down to the light room. And, as the cook was taking the light out of my lantern, Thomas Breary told him he'd better snuff it before he put it into the sconce again, which he did with his fingers, and some of the snuff falling down, an explosion took place.

P. – Do you know of any boxes with filled cartridges being kept in the light room and did you see any at the time of the explosion, either there or in the cockpit?

A. – Yes, we first took the boxes out, as we could not put the lights into the sconce without doing so.

P. – Do you know if it had been customary to keep boxes in the light room?

A. – Yes, it has ever since I've been in the ship, but I did not know their contents.

P. – When you had occasion to demand either ball or exercising cartridges, do you know from what part of the ship they were taken to supply you?

A, – We have had them taken out of the light room and out of the magazine ever since I have been in the ship and when any had been left after exercising, instead of opening the magazine, it has been customary to leave them in the light room.

P. – Did you see them deposited there yourself?

A. – Yes.

P. – Were the keys of the magazine and light room always deposited in the first lieutenant's cabin and were you the person employed to take them from thence when wanted?

A. – Yes.

P. – Have you any reason to think the prisoner took the keys from thence to go into the magazine or light room without being accompanied by you?

A. – No.

C. – Were the keys of the light room and magazine tied together?

A. – They were not.

C. – Did you ever take the keys of the light room away without the keys of the magazine and, if so, what was the light room opened for?

A. – Many times, to get blank cartridges.

C. – Was that done with the first lieutenant's knowledge?

A. – Yes.

C. – Was it ever particularly specified to the first lieutenant by you that the keys of the light room only were wanted for that purpose?

A. – Yes.

Prosecution closed.

C. – Prisoner, the prosecution being closed, have you any defence to make or evidence to call in your behalf?

A. – Yes, I have an evidence to prove I warned Lieut.[t] Cock of the impropriety of keeping the cartridges in the light room.

John Shadwell, Armourer, sworn.

Prisoner – When we completed the marines' and seamen's cartouch boxes, did you hear me say to Lieut.[t] Cock that the light room was an improper place for the boxes containing powder, or some words to that effect?

A. – Yes, and M[r]. Cock said they had been kept there before. You then asked me if they used to be kept there in the late gunner's time. I told you they had and that I had been assisting him in taking some out of the light room before.

Prosecutor – Was it before or after I took command of the ship?

A. – It was before.

Charges proved in part.

Sentence:

To be severely reprimanded.

…

107. *Court Martial of John Thomas*

[ADM 1/5366]

Minutes of proceedings at a court martial held on board His Majesty's ship *Salvador del Mundo* in Hamoaze on Thursday the fourteenth day of June 1804.

Present

John Sutton, Esquire, Rear Admiral of the Blue and second officer in the command of His Majesty's ships and vessels at Plymouth, President.

Captains

Davidge Gould	Edward Buller
William Henry Jervis	William Bligh
the Hble. Fra[s]. Farrington Gardner	Robert Waller Otway
Peter Puget	James Wallis
Tho[s]. Elphinstone	Patrick Campbell
Christopher Cole	George Reynolds

Robert Liddel
Deputy Judge Advocate

Being all the admiral [*sic*] and captains of post ships according to seniority, except Captain Vesey of His Majesty's ship *Brilliant*, who is rendered by illness incapable of attending the court, and Captain Dilkes of His Majesty's ship *Salvador del Mundo*, who is prosecutor on the occasion.

The prisoner was brought into court and the evidence & audience admitted.

The surgeon of His Majesty's ship *Brilliant* appeared before the court and reported that Francis Vesey, Esq[r]., Captain of the said ship, was afflicted with inflamed eye and that he could not attend the court without endangering his life and declared that he was ready, if required, to make oath to the truth of such report; whereupon, the court thought proper to dispense with the attendance of Captain Vesey.

Read the order of the Right Honourable the Lords Commissioners of the Admiralty, dated the sixth day of June 1804, directed to John Sutton, Esq[r]., Rear Admiral of the Blue and second officer in the command of His Majesty's ships and vessels at Plymouth, to try John Thomas, a Seaman belonging to His Majesty's ship *Salvador del Mundo*, for neglect of duty in quitting the boat of which he was one of the crew on, or about, the 23d. of May last.

Read the warrant appointing a judge advocate.

Then the members of the court and judge advocate, in open court and before they proceeded to trial, respectively took the oaths directed by Act of Parliament passed in the twenty-second year of the reign of King George the Second, entitled: *An Act for Amending, Explaining and Reducing into one Act of Parliament the Laws Relating to the Government of His Majesty's Ships, Vessels and Forces by Sea.*

A letter from John Dilkes, Esqr., Captain of His Majesty's ship *Salvador del Mundo*, to William Young, Esqr., Vice Admiral of the Red, &c^{a}., &c^{a}., &c^{a}., was then read as follows:

Salvador del Mundo in Hamoaze
4th June 1804

... I must beg leave to trouble you with requesting the Lords Commissioners of the Admiralty to order a court martial to try and adjudge John Thomas, Seaman belonging to His Majesty's ship under my command, for neglect of duty, in quitting the boat of which he was one of the crew, on, or about, the 23d. of May last, and being apprehended on shore upon suspicion of some crime against civil society, was delivered up as a deserter from His Majesty's service. ...

Captain Elphinstone produced to the court a letter from the commander in chief,[1] which was read as follows:

Plymouth Dock, 14th June 1804

... His Majesty's service requiring that the *Diamond* should go to sea as soon as possible, I am to request the court to dispense with the attendance of Captain Elphinstone, if it should not think his attendance absolutely necessary. ...

Whereupon the court thought proper to dispense with the further attendance of Captain Elphinstone and he withdrew accordingly.

All the evidence being then ordered to withdraw and to attend their examinations separately, they all withdrew accordingly, except the first to be sworn and the court proceeded to trial as follows:

Evidence in support of the charge

M^{r}. John Wheatly, Captain's Clerk of His Majesty's ship *Salvador del Mundo*, sworn and examined as follows:

Court — Produce to the court the muster books of this ship.

[1]This letter is from Vice Admiral William Young to Rear Admiral John Sutton.

The books produced, by which it appears that John Thomas, Ord., No. 235, was entered as p^r^. former book on the 1st October 1803, and that he was made Run on the 23d. May 1804, and returned a prisoner on the 31st of May, having been apprehended.

Court — Is the muster book produced to the court kept by you?

Answer — Yes.

Court — Are the records therein of the entry, Run, and return of John Thomas true records?

Answer — Yes.

Court — Is the prisoner the man whose name is so recorded?

Answer — Yes.

The Witness withdrew.

Lieutenant Joseph Priest of His Majesty's ship *Salvador del Mundo* sworn and examined as follows:

Prosecutor — Do you know the prisoner?

Answer — I do; I know him to be John Thomas, belonging to the *Salvador.*

Prosecutor — Relate what you know of his leaving the boat and returning on board again.

Answer — I sent him on shore in the jolly boat, as one of the boat's crew on the 22d. or 23d. of May last and the boat returned without him. I think about a week after he was brought on board by a constable from Plymouth as a deserter.

The witness withdrew.

M^{r}. John Tuckerman, a constable of Plymouth, sworn and examined as follows:

Prosecutor — Do you know the prisoner?

Answer — Yes, he is the man I apprehended.

Prosecutor — Relate to the court all the circumstances of your apprehending him, and what first induced you to take notice of the man.

Answer — On the 18th of May last I believe, but I am not quite certain, about 8 o'clock in the evening going down Saint Andrews Street in the Borough of Plymouth, I met the prisoner with a female child in his arms with about fifty boys following him. I asked what was the matter? I stopped the man. They told me he had been playing tricks with the child. I took the prisoner into the prison. I went to the magistrate with the father of the child and the following day, he was examined by the magistrate.

Prosecutor Did the prisoner acknowledge that he belonged to the *Salvador del Mundo*?

Answer He did and said he had come on shore on liberty.

Prosecutor Did he make any resistance?

Answer None.

Court How many days is it since you brought the prisoner on board?

Answer I cannot recollect.

Lieutenant Joseph Priest further examined as follows:

Court You have said you sent the prisoner on shore on the 22d. or 23d. of May last, might it not have been on the 18th?

Answer I am almost certain that it was the 22d. or 23d.

The witness withdrew.

The evidence in support of the charge being finished, the prisoner was called upon to make his defence, who said that he had been left behind by the boat, having been to the post office on the twenty third of May and was apprehended on the twenty fourth and was in prison a week.

The prisoner then called on Captain Buller at [*sic*] Captain Otway, members of the court with whom he had sailed in the late war, to speak to his character, who both said they never recollected anything against the man and believed he always did his duty very well.

The prisoner not having anything further to offer in his defence, the court was cleared, and proceeded to deliberate upon and form the sentence.

The court, having heard the evidence in support of the charge as well as what the prisoner had to offer in his defence and very maturely and deliberately weighed and considered the same, the court was of opinion that the charge had not been proved against the prisoner, John Thomas, and did in consequence thereof adjudge the said John Thomas to be acquitted.

The court was opened, the prisoner brought in, the evidence and audience admitted, and sentence passed accordingly. …

LOSS OF SHIP AND GROUNDING

108. *Court Martial of Captain Blake, the Officers and Crew of* L'Amaranthe

[ADM 1/5351]

An account of the proceedings of a court martial held on board His Majesty's ship *Hannibal* in Port Royal Harbour, Jamaica, on Monday the 30th December 1799, for the trial of Captain George Hans Blake, his officers and crew for the loss of His Majesty's sloop *L'Amaranthe*.

Present
Edward Tyrrel Smith, Esqr., President

Robert Rolles	Temple Hardy
Edward Fellowes	Man Dobson
W^{m}. Gordon Rutherford	Thomas Dundas
John Crawley	Christopher La Roche

Admiral Sir Hyde Parker's order for the trial read.
The court duly sworn.
The letter from Captain Blake to the admiral read:[1]

S^{t}. Augustine, 9th November 1799

… It is with concern, I inform you of the loss of His Majesty's sloop *L'Amaranthe* under my command on the night of the 25th of October last, at 9 (p.m.) on the coast of Florida, near Cape Canaveral. When the brig grounded the wind was at ENE, with a heavy sea and strong gale setting on the shore, so that in less than two hours, she parted. And, I have the misfortune to add that two warrant officers, as named in the margin [M^{r}. Stanby Cummings, M^{r}. John Curnside], and twenty men perished in endeavouring to gain the land.

I continued near the wreck until the 27th in hopes to procure some provisions, but, failing in my wish, I proceeded to the northward with the remaining officers and ship's company; and, after travelling thirteen days and nights bareheaded and barefooted along the uninhabited sands, and without any other sustenance than prickly pears and wild grapes, and a great part of the time without water, I arrived on the 8th of November at the Spanish fort of the Matanzas, where I was obliged through necessity to surrender prisoner of war and was the next day sent to this place, where

[1]This letter is to Sir Hyde Parker.

I was received with the greatest humanity by his excellency Governor Whyte and has given [*sic*] me leave to depart for Charleston in a schooner, which is to sail in a few days. I have accepted it in order to return to Jamaica as soon as possible and, in so doing, I hope to meet your approbation. …

Captain George Hans Blake sworn.

Court –	Inform the court of the situation of the brig before she got on shore, the course you was steering and everything else relative to the loss of her.
Capt. Blake –	At 12 noon of Thursday, the 24th of October last, the master observed in latitude 27° 56′ and, by our reckoning, longitude 78° 23′ W^{t}., Cape Canaveral bearing W b N°. 41 leag^{s}. At a little after 12, two sail were discovered to the eastward, to which I immediately gave chase, the wind at ENE till one p.m., when I tacked and stood north, until I came near enough to know the chase to be one I had spoke before [*sic*]. At half past 2, tacked and stood to the SE until 6 o'clock, when I consulted with the master whether he did not think the *Quebec* and *Arab* were further to the westward. He was of opinion with me that they were. I then said, 'If you think we can with safety run ten leagues further westward, we will do it.' His answer was, 'I am pretty confident of my latitude, and we may run twenty if you please.' I immediately ordered the helm to be put up and steer west. It was then blowing pretty fresh and were under double reefed topsails and foresail. At sunset, the master went, as was his usual custom, to the mast head to look round; there was no land in sight nor anything to indicate soundings. At 8, I went below; at 9, the gunner, whose watch it was on deck, came down in a great hurry, and said, 'Sir, the ship's aground.' The helm was *hard a port*, but before I could get on deck, she was among the breakers; and in less than five minutes, the carpenter reported to me she was bilged. The masts were cut away; the stern boat and boat on

the booms immediately cleared. I then sent the stern boat with the only sick man in her on shore and also endeavoured to get a rope on shore, but the surf was so very high that she stove. While this was doing, the people on board were launching spars and making rafts. At a little before 11, one heavy surf struck her and she went all to pieces. I then, with the master and a few people that were not before on the raft, swam to it and, after much difficulty, the raft, having been upset by the great force of surf, reached the land.

Court – Had you every reason to believe that the master's reckoning was good?

Answer – I had, having frequently compared it with the reckoning of the *Quebec* and *Arab*.

Court – Had you been in the habit of frequently sounding off Cape Canaveral?

Answer – I was never near enough to the land, but twice, to gain soundings.

Court – What appearance had the water when you got soundings?

Answer – Muddy green.

Court – Did you judge yourself at sunset of the night the sloop was lost to be much to the northward of the Marinilla Reef and if you did, how much to the northward?

Answer – I judged myself to be to the northward of the Marinilla Reef about 26 or 28 miles.

Court – What course did you steer from noon, when you was in the latitude of 27°. 56′ N°. by observation until sunset?

Answer – When I tacked after the chase, we lay up N°., which course I kept until I knew the chase to be one that we had spoke before. I then steered S°. E^{t}. till 6 o'clock.

Court – How many miles from the time you bore up, did you run until the sloop struck?

Answer – About 22 or 23 west till 8 o'clock; from 8 to 9, W^{t}. by S°.

Court – When did you see the land you took your departure from?

Answer –	The last land we took our departure from was Cape Canaveral about three weeks or more before the accident happened.
Court –	Where are the orders you were under?
Answer –	I did not save a single paper or a single thing.
Court –	Have you any blame to attach to the master or any of the ship's company for her loss.
Answer –	None whatever.
Court –	Was it customary to place men forward to lookout?
Answer –	It was always done.
Court –	Was the lead hove any time during that evening before the sloop got on shore?
Answer –	It was not.
Court –	Was the land seen or any alarm given before the sloop struck?
Answer –	The land was not seen; nor was there any alarm given until she was on shore.

(Captain Blake withdrew)

M[r]. Gillespie, Surgeon, sworn.

Court –	By the oath that you have taken, do you know of any blame to be attached to the master or any of the ship's company for the loss of the *L'Amaranthe*?
Answer –	None that I know.
Court –	Do you know of any observations that were made on the evening before the sloop struck, respecting her situation?
Answer –	I heard Captain Blake ask the master if he might stand on ten leagues further. I can't positively say the course, as he expected to find the commodore farther to the westward. The master's answer was he might stand on twenty if he pleased.
Court –	Was the master perfectly sober that evening?
Answer –	I had not seen him till he came upon deck, when he appeared perfectly sober.
Court –	Was he esteemed as a good navigator and his reckoning to be depended upon in general?
Answer –	I have always understood him to be a very clever fellow and a good navigator.

Court – Was everything done, to the best of your knowledge, for the preservation of the ship after she struck?

Answer – It was.

Court – Do you know any more of the circumstances of the loss of *L'Amaranthe* than those you have already related?

Answer – No more.

Court – When had you seen the land last and what was it?

Answer – I don't know.

(M^{r}. Gillespie withdrew)

Henry Clarkson, Seaman, sworn.

Court – Relate what you know of the loss of *L'Amaranthe*.

Answer – I do not recollect what latitude we were in or longitude; on that day the *Quebec* made our signal to chase S.E. I believe we continued the chase till about 6 o'clock in the evening. At 6, we lost sight of the chase, and bore up under the topsails, steering W^{t}. & by S^{o}.; at ½ past 7, set the foresail. At or about 9 o'clock, the ship struck; about two minutes before she struck, put the helm hard a port, but, before she came to the wind, she struck. The masts were cut away about five minutes after by Captain Blake's orders. We got the boat off the booms, but in getting her off, stove her bottom; cut away the booms to make rafts, and on them a good many of the people got on shore. In about two hours from her first striking, she went to pieces.

Court – When was the last time that you saw the land?

Answer – About three weeks before, we saw Cape Canaveral.

Court – Do you think that anybody was to blame for the loss of the sloop?

Answer – I think there was not.

Court – Did you ever sound off Cape Canaveral?

Answer – Yes.

Court – What distance did you think yourself from the land at six o'clock that evening?

Answer –	I heard M[r]. Baxler, the Master, say that he was about 41 leagues at 12 o'clock by his reckoning.
Court –	Were there people after sunset placed to lookout for the land, or to see the colour of the water changed [*sic*]?
Answer –	There was a man placed at the cathead to lookout.

(Withdrew)

Daniel Day, Seaman, sworn.

Court –	Relate all that you know of the loss of *L'Amaranthe*.
Answer –	I was below in my berth; between 7 and 8 o'clock, the captain rung the bell for me. I went into the cabin to him. M[r]. Baxler, the Master, was with him. They were conversing together and then one of the men came from the quarter deck to the master and told him to come upon deck or else he was afraid the ship would be lost. The captain, master & surgeon went immediately upon deck. In a very few minutes after she struck, she laid down on her broad side and filled directly, so that there was no getting below at all hardly. Her middle deck came up all at once, with part of the quarter deck.
Court –	Had you, from your knowledge, any reason to suppose the sloop was near to land?
Answer –	Not the least idea of it.
Court –	How long was it from the time the man came down to the master to the time the ship struck?
Answer –	As near as I can say, about five minutes.
Court –	Do you know whether there was any order given for altering the course immediately after the man came down?
Answer –	I did not hear any.
Court –	Was there any blame attached to any person for the loss of the sloop?
Answer –	I never heard of any. I have been with the captain ever since.
Captain Blake to Daniel Day –	Where was I at the time the person came down to me?

Answer –	In the cabin.
Captain B. –	Was the master with me then?
Answer –	Yes.
Captain Blake to M^{r}. Gillespie –	Where was I at the time the officer of the watch came down and said the ship was on shore?
Answer –	In the gun room at supper.
Captn. Blake to D^{o}. –	Was the master with me, or was he in his cabin at the time?
Answer –	He was not in the gun room; I understood him to be in his cabin.
Captn. Blake to D^{o}. –	Before I could get upon deck, was not the ship on shore?
Answer –	The ship was on shore.
Court to Day –	Do you know the person, who, you say, came into Captain Blake's cabin and told the master to come upon deck, as the vessel was likely to be lost?
Answer –	I think it was one of the quarter masters, but whose name I do not recollect.
Court to Day –	Had the bell struck eight before the quarter master came into the cabin?
Answer –	I think it had struck eight.
Court to Day –	What was the last bell you heard struck before the ship got on shore?
Answer –	Two bells, or seven o'clock.
Court to Day –	Did you hear the bell strike three, or did you hear it ring?
Answer –	No.
Court –	What was your reason for supposing it was past eight o'clock?
Answer –	The time of evening.
Court –	Was you drunk or sober that evening?
Answer –	Sober.
Court –	What did Captain Blake ring his bell for?
Answer –	To give some fishing hooks to M^{r}. Baxler.
Court –	How do you know?
Answer –	The captain told me to unlock the trunk and take them out.
Court –	How long was it from the time you came first into the cabin before the quarter master came down to the master?

Answer –	About two minutes.
Captain Blake to Mr. Hewson –	Did you heave the log at 8 o'clock?
Answer –	I did.
Captain Blake to Dº. –	When the officer of the watch came to report to me it was 8 o'clock, where was I?
Answer –	I do not recollect.
Captain Blake to Dº. –	Do you know whether I supped with the officers of the gun room that night?
Answer –	Yes.
Captain Blake to Dº. –	Was their usual hour of supper eight o'clock?
Answer –	It was.
Captain Blake to Dº. –	How long was it after that time that the ship grounded?
Answer –	Nearly an hour, almost two bells.
Court to Day –	Where did Captain Blake sup that night?
Answer –	In the gun room, I believe.
Court to Dº. –	Did Captain Blake go into the gun room before 8 o'clock?
Answer –	I can't say.
Court –	What time did the officers of the gun room sup that night?
Answer –	I do not know.
Court to Day –	Upon the solemn oath you have taken, do you positively declare that Captain Blake, between the hours of 7 & 8 o'clock or about 8 o'clock, rung the bell, and when you came into the cabin to answer it, told you to give some fish hooks to the master?
Answer –	Yes.
Court to Day –	Did Captain Blake go into the gun room after you gave the fish hooks to the master?
Answer –	Not that I know of. (The trial here closed.)

The court retired to deliberate.

And came to the resolution:

That Captain Blake, his officers and crew remaining be acquitted for the loss of the said sloop *L'Amaranthe*.

But are of opinion notwithstanding that blame is to be attached to Captain Blake for running at such a rate after dark on such a course, and in not keeping the lead going, and in putting too much dependence on the master's reckoning being in the stream of Gulf and not having seen the land for three weeks.

The court opened, Captain Blake, his remaining officers and crew all present.

The following sentence was read by the judge advocate:

… The court do acquit Captain Blake, the said remaining officers and crew for the loss of the said sloop, but are of opinion that Captain Blake is highly blameable in running at such a rate after dark upon such a course and in not keeping the lead going and in putting too much dependence on the master's reckoning being in the stream of the Gulf and not having seen the land for three weeks.

And it appearing to the court that Daniel Day, who was sworn and examined, did prevaricate in his evidence, do sentence him to suffer one month's imprisonment. …

The court dissolved. …

109. *Court Martial of Quamin*

[ADM 1/5363]

Minutes of proceedings at a court martial held on board His Majesty's ship *Theseus* in Port Royal Harbour, Jamaica on Thursday the 23d. day of June 1803.

Present

John Bligh, Esq[r]., Captain of His Majesty's ship *Theseus* and second officer in the command of His Majesty's ships and vessels in Port Royal Harbour, Jamaica, President.

Captains

Andrew Fitzherbert Evans	Wilson Rathborne
William Roberts	George LeGeyt

The prisoner was brought into court and the evidence and audience admitted.

Read the order of Sir John Thomas Duckworth, K.B., Rear Admiral of the Red, Commander in Chief, &[c]., &[c]., dated the 22d. day of June 1803 and directed to John Bligh, Esq[r]., Captain of His Majesty's ship *Theseus* and second officer in the command of His Majesty's ships and vessels in Port Royal Harbour, Jamaica, to try Quamin, a black pilot, for having taken charge of His Majesty's sloop *Hunter* on the morning of the 22d. instant to pilot her into Port Royal Harbour, did run the said sloop on one of the keys at the entrance of the said port and that the captain of the *Hunter* had every reason to suppose the said pilot must have run the *Hunter* on shore on purpose.

Then the members of the court and judge advocate, in open court and before they proceeded to trial, respectively took the oath enjoined them by Act of Parliament.

A letter from Captain S. H. Inglefield, commanding His Majesty's sloop *Hunter*, to the commander in chief was read as follows, *viz.*:

H.M. sloop *Hunter*, Port Royal Harbour
22d. June 1803

… I beg leave to acquaint you that Quamin, a black pilot, having taken charge of H.M. sloop under my command to pilot her into this harbour, did run her on shore on one of the keys at the entrance of the port. I have every reason to suppose (as he was repeatedly cautioned by me and the master to beware of the shoal we were approaching) that he must have run the sloop on shore on purpose. I have therefore to request you will please to order a court martial to try him for the same offence. …

All the witnesses were ordered out of court and Captain Inglefield, the prosecutor, was sworn and examined.

Court — Is the prisoner the pilot who had charge of the *Hunter* on the 22d. instant?

Ans[r]. — Yes, he is.

Quest. — Relate to the court the circumstances attending his running the sloop on shore and your reasons for believing he run her on shore intentionally?

Ans[r]. — I was looking out when we were approaching the keys and repeatedly cautioned the prisoner not to go too near them and to speak in time if it was necessary to take in sail. His answers were: 'There is no fear, we are going very well' or words to that effect. And, I had reasons from understanding him to be an old pilot, he could not be ignorant of the shoals; and, when the ship struck, he did not appear to be the least alarmed or give any advice how to get her off.

Quest. — At what time did he take charge of the *Hunter*?

Ans[r]. — About six P.M., the 21st instant.

Court — Did you, on his coming on board, give the charge of conducting the ship to the prisoner?

Ans[r]. — I followed his advice in heaving the ship to that night and making sail in the morning, not being acquainted with the coast myself. I should suppose he must have known he had the charge of the ship from his cunning of her the whole morning.

Quest. — Did you bear him on the ship's books as pilot?

Ans[r]. No.

Quest. Does he appear on the ship's books?

Ans[r]. No.

Quest. Was he drunk or sober when she struck?

Ans[r]. In my opinion, perfectly sober.

Quest. When she run aground, did he appear to know where he was or did he seem to be ignorant of the place?

Ans[r]. He did not seemed moved at all when she struck; just before she did strike, he ordered the helm to port and she immediately struck on her answering the helm.

Cross questioned by the prisoner.

Prisoner When the ship came near the shoals, did I desire the helm to be put to starboard, but for fear of running a canoe down, it was put to port?

Ans[r]. I do not recollect that the helm was put to port or starboard for the canoe, but I mentioned several times to you we should run the canoe down and I conceive if the helm had been put to port, she must inevitably been run down, as she was close on our starboard bow.

Prisoner When I desired the helm to be put to port before we came to the entrance of the keys, did you order it to be put to starboard?

Ans[r]. To the best of my recollection, I did not once interfere with the helm while you had charge of the ship.

No further questions were asked, and Captain Inglefield withdrew to his proper place to carry on the prosecution.

M[r]. Butcher, the Master, was then called and sworn.

Prosecutor Relate to the court what you know respecting the charge against the prisoner.

Ans[r]. In coming down near the keys, Captain Inglefield told the pilot to take care not to get the ship on shore, as we were coming near the shoal. The pilot told him to never mind, he was going very well. Captain Inglefield called him once or twice and showed him the keys and told him we were very near and desired him to look out that he did not get her on shore. He answered that he would look out and that she went very well. I told him myself several times that we were getting very near the keys and, when I got on to the booms, I told Captain Inglefield that the pilot would run the brig on shore if he did not keep farther off. Captain Inglefield called to the pilot and told him we were very near. The pilot ordered the helmsman to port and told the captain she went very well; soon after, about a minute or two, she struck.

Quest. Did you conceive during the time the pilot was on board that he had charge of the ship or not?

Ans[r]. I did conceive he had charge.

Court Was the pilot thwarted at any time before the ship struck?

Ans[r]. No, not to my knowledge.

Court Did you see the captain or any of the officers interfere with the pilot at any time before she struck?

Ans[r]. No, only the captain cautioning and showing him the shoals.

Quest. From your observation, did it appear that the pilot ever intended to pass between the keys or to the southward of them?

Ans[r]. I asked him if he was going to pass between the two keys and he said no, that he meant to go the outside of them.

Quest. How was the wind at the time?

Ans[r]. Free, abaft the beam, nearly aft.

Quest. Do you believe the pilot run the ship on shore on purpose?

Ans[r]. From hearing he had brought ships in before, I have every reason to suppose he did.

Cross questioned by the prisoner.

Prisoner Was the ship in the entrance of the two keys?

Ans[r]. She might have been in the entrance of two keys, but there were two between the shore and where we were aground.

Court At the time the ship was run aground was the pilot sober?

Ans[r]. He appeared to me perfectly sober.

This witness was asked nothing further and M[r]. Phillis, the Purser, called and sworn.

Prosecutor Relate to the court what you know respecting the charge against the prisoner.

Ans[r]. I was standing on the starboard gangway when we were approaching the shoal. I heard Captain Inglefield and M[r]. Butcher, the Master, repeatedly say to the prisoner, 'Pilot, you will run us on shore mind what you are about.' Immediately after, she struck.

Prosecutor Do you recollect what answer the pilot made?

Ans[r]. He said he was perfectly acquainted, and had taken ships in before.

Court Did you, during the time the prisoner was on board the *Hunter*, observe any interference on the part of the captain or any of the officers that could possibly cause the ship to have run on shore?

Ans^{r}. I did not.

Court Was the prisoner sober at the time she went on shore?

Ans^{r}. To all appearance, perfectly so.

Cross questioned by the prisoner.

Prisoner Do you suppose I run the ship on shore intentionally?

Ans^{r}. I cannot say.

Prisoner Did you hear me request to go between the two islands?

Ans^{r}. I did not.

This witness was asked no further questions, and M^{r}. Smart, the boatswain, called and sworn.

Prosecutor Relate to the court what you know respecting the charge against the prisoner.

Ans^{r}. I was standing on the hen coop on the larboard side close to the forecastle. The pilot stepped forward and looked over the bow. I said to him, ‘Pilot, I think we are too near the keys.’ He said, ‘Oh no, water enough.’ Then he went aft on the quarter deck again and I think, to the best of my recollection, about two minutes after, she struck.

Prosecutor Do you recollect hearing me caution the pilot of our being too near the keys?

Ans^{r}. Not to my knowledge.

Court Did you observe the captain or any other of the officers interfere with the pilot at any time before the ship struck?

Ans^{r}. Yes, M^{r}. Butcher, the Master, was standing on the stern of the six oar’d cutter before the booms, looking forward toward the starboard bow, and said. ‘Pilot, I think the water looks shoal ahead.’

No further questions asked this witness, he withdrew, and Owen Mc Carthy, Quarter Master, was sworn.

Prosecutor Was you steering the ship when coming into the harbour?

Ans^{r}. Yes.

Pros^{r}. Do you recollect, just before the ship struck, how the pilot ordered you to put the helm?

Ans^{r}. Yes, he told me to port the helm, which I did by his orders; and the captain told him, ‘Pilot, mind do not run me aground.’

Quest. Relate to the court any other circumstances of the charge against the prisoner.

Ans[r]. The pilot said, 'Ground, Sir! There is no fear of ground.'

Court How long was you at the helm before the ship struck?

Ans[r]. I cannot exactly recollect the time, but it was before she came near the keys.

Quest. Did you, during the time you were at the helm, consider the prisoner as cunning the ship?

Ans[r]. I did and took directions from him.

Quest. Before you took the helm at the time you were at the cun, from whom did you receive directions?

Ans[r]. From the pilot.

Quest. Did you see or hear any person interfere with the pilot?

Ans[r]. I did not; I went by his order only.

Cross questioned by the prisoner.

Prisoner Do you remember hearing the captain say he would run the canoe down?

Ans[r] [ ][1]

This witness was asked nothing further, and John Gallagher, Seaman, called and sworn.

Prosecutor Relate to the court all you know respecting the charge against the prisoner.

Ans[r]. When I was at the wheel from six to eight in the morning, I heard Captain Inglefield say to the pilot that he was going too nigh hand the breakers; the pilot said that there was no fear at all. The captain then said to the pilot, 'Speak in time if you want sail to be taken in; it shall be done so soon as ever you say the word.'

Court Did any officer interfere with the pilot?

Ans[r]. No, not that I heard.

Court From whom did you receive directions in cunning the ship?

Ans[r]. From the pilot.

Nothing further asked this witness and M[r]. Owens, the Master of the *Theseus*, called and sworn.

Prosecutor From the situation of the *Hunter*, do you think the pilot intended to bring her through the passage that is usual for ships of war to come into this harbour?

Ans[r]. From the situation of the *Hunter* the time she was aground, I did not think she was intended to come through the passage that I have seen ships come into this harbour.

[1]The space for the answer is left blank in the original transcript.

Court From the state of the wind, was there a necessity for her coming into the harbour through that passage?

Ans^r. None.

Quest. Is there a passage to the southward of the keys and was it possible for the *Hunter* to pass that way without getting on shore?

Ans^r. There is a good passage to the southward of the keys and the *Hunter* or any ship might go through with safety with a leading wind.

No further questions asked this witness and M^r. Cole, the Master Attendant, was called and sworn.

Court From the situation of the *Hunter* when aground, did she appear to have gone through the channel that ships usually go in coming into this harbour?

Ans^r. No, she went to the southward of the keys instead of between the two as ships generally do.

Court Is there a passage for ships to the southward of keys?

Ans^r. A ship of any size may go to the southward of the keys with a leading wind.

Quest. Is any common sea breeze a leading wind for that channel?

Ans^r. It is.

No further questions were asked, and the evidence on the part of the prosecution was then closed.

The prisoner was called upon for his defence, which was read as follows, *viz.*:

… I have been a pilot for upwards of five years, but have only been accustomed to pilot large ships for about two years of the time and, during all that time, I have not ever made a mistake in conducting ships in or out of the harbour until I unfortunately overshot the landmark, which was occasioned by a great cold and dimness over my eyes in consequence of sleeping on the beach, looking out for ships to pilot in, and, when I found I had run the ship so far, I was terrified so much as not to know what to do. This, Gentlemen, is a true statement of the business and trust entirely to the mercy of the court and also that you do not conceive I could be guilty of running the ship on shore on purpose. …

The prisoner having nothing further to offer in his defence, the court was cleared to deliberate upon and form the sentence.

…

... And having heard the evidence on the part of the prosecution and also what the prisoner had to offer in his defence and very maturely and deliberately weighed and considered the same, the court is of opinion that the charge of running His Majesty's sloop *Hunter* on shore intentionally is proved in part and do therefore adjudge him to be mulcted of his pilotage for the said sloop and rendered incapable of ever taking charge as a pilot of any of His Majesty's ships in future. And, the court does further adjudge that the prisoner be imprisoned for a term not exceeding the space of two years in such place as the commander in chief shall think proper to direct and he is hereby sentenced accordingly. ...

110. *Court Martial of Acting Lieutenant Westcott, the Officers and Crew of the* Fort Diamond

[ADM 1/5367]

Minutes of the proceedings at a court martial held on board His Majesty's ship *Galatea* at English Harbour, Antigua on the 4th of October 1804.

Present

Henry Heathcote, Esquire, Captain of His Majesty's ship *Galatea* and senior officer of His Majesty's ships & vessels at English Harbour, Antigua, President.

Captains

James O'Bryen	Kenneth M^c^Kenzie
Jno. C. Woolcombe	Edwd. Woolcombe

The prisoner was brought into court and the evidence and audience admitted. Read the order from Commodore Hood, Commander in Chief &^c^., &^c^., &^c^., dated 6th of September and directed to Henry Heathcote, Esqr., Captain of His Majesty's ship *Galatea* and senior officer at Antigua, for to try Acting Lieutenant Benjamin Westcott, commanding officer of His Majesty's sloop *Fort Diamond*, together with the petty officers and men under his command for the loss of that vessel by suffering her to be captured in Roseau Bay, S^t^. Lucia by two of the enemy's boats, as set forth in his letter.

Then the members of the court and the judge advocate, in open court and before they proceeded to trial, respectively took the oaths directed by Act of Parliament made and passed in the 22nd year of the reign of His late Majesty George the 2nd, entitled: *An Act for Amending, Explaining and Reducing into one Act of Parliament the Laws Relating to the Government of His Majesty's Ships, Vessels and Forces by Sea.*

A letter from Lieutenant Benjamin Westcott to Commodore Hood, Commander in Chief &^{c}., &^{c}., &^{c}., was then read as follows:

Blenheim, Carlisle Bay, Barbados
20th July 1804

… In pursuance of directions from Captain Maurice, I proceeded with His Majesty's sloop *Fort Diamond* to Roseau Bay in the Island of St. Lucia for wood and water for the Rock. Three days had elapsed on this service when we were boarded and taken possession of, at ½ past 7 o'clock P. M. 23d June by two French row boats; there was little resistance made, most part of the crew being asleep and the arms all below in consequence of having no chest on board to keep them in. …

All the evidences ordered to withdraw, except Thomas Batch, Seaman of the *Fort Diamond*, who was sworn.

By the Court – Relate to the court what you know respecting the loss of His Majesty's late sloop, the *Fort Diamond*.

Answer – Laying in Roseau Bay, most of the people had been on shore watering and cutting bamboo. They returned about 7 o'clock in the evening; some of them went below. L^{t}. Westcott was, at the time of the boat coming in sight, fishing on the taffrail. He was the first person that saw the boat; he hailed her without receiving an answer. He hailed a second time and they answered it was a boat from the shore. He then enquired who was in that boat; they gave no answer, but fired several muskets. M^{r}. Westcott then called for the cutlasses to be handed up. I went down and was clearing the muskets & cutlasses in the locker when Lieut^{t}. Westcott came down and got a cutlass out. He stood by the hatchway awhile and then turned about and said it was no use, it was too late. I heard him say no more, for a considerable time after. The people were by that time all below. The Frenchmen were on board and had sentries over all the hatches; they cut the cable. L^{t}. Westcott told us the quieter we kept ourselves then, it would be the better for us. He hailed the Frenchmen on deck after a while and asked permission to go on deck; they allowed him that, but no one else to go on deck till we got alongside the schooner. They called us up and ordered us into a boat and sent us on board the schooner.

Court –	How many men did the row boats carry?
Answer –	I saw but one boat and don't know how many men was in her.
Court –	At what distance was the boat from the vessel when discovered?
Answer –	About a ship's length off.
Court –	Was it very dark?
Answer –	Yes, but not *very* dark.
Court –	Did you hear Lieut[t]. Westcott call the crew on deck or make any preparation for defence before the boat fired at the *Fort Diamond*?
Answer –	No sir.
Court –	Did L[t]. Westcott afterwards use any exertions to get the men on deck?
Answer –	None.
Court –	Were the enemy absolutely in possession when he said it was too late?
Answer –	Yes, I believe they were all on board.
Court –	Where was L[t]. Westcott standing at that time?
Answer –	In the cabin, below.
Court –	Was any exertion used or proposed by the crew to L[t]. Westcott to regain the vessel from the enemy?
Answer –	None that I heard.
Court –	Was the schooner perceived before the vessel was given up?
Answer –	No.
Court –	Did any second boat come on board after the vessel was taken?
Answer –	I believe not till we got near the schooner.
Court –	What number of men were on board the *Fort Diamond*?
Answer –	Eighteen in all.
Court –	What distance was the *Fort Diamond* from the shore?
Answer –	She was then ab[t]. a mile & a half, owing to her having drifted that day.
Court –	When the boat was first discovered coming on board, did she appear as if coming from the shore or from the sea?
Answer –	Coming from the shore.
Court –	At sunset that evening, were there any suspicious small vessels in sight or near the bay?
Answer –	I don't know there was.
Court –	Was it customary to set a sentry at sunset?

Answer – No, not till eight o'clock.

Court – Was the men upon deck armed?

Answer – No.

Court – Were there any arms on deck?

Answer – Nothing but boarding pikes round the booms.

Court – When the boat first fired at the *Fort Diamond*, did her commander order her people to arm themselves and defend her?

Answer – I did not hear him, but he called for cutlasses.

Court – How many men do you suppose were on deck when the boat came alongside?

Answer – About seven.

Court – Where were the arms usually kept?

Answer – In a locker in the cabin.

Court – Do you know if there was any defence made or were any of the crew of the *Fort Diamond* wounded?

Answer – I believe not.

Court – After the crew went off the deck had they been properly cheered & headed, do you suppose they could have got up and regained the vessel?

Answer – I think they could.

Court – Was it possible for the commander to communicate to the people from the cabin?

Answer – Yes sir; there was a passage into the hold.

Court – You say L^{t}. Westcott went down to get arms; what effort did he make to get on deck again?

Answer – None that I perceived.

Court – How long did L^{t}. Westcott stand at the hatchway after he got the cutlasses before you heard him say it was too late?

Answer – Not above a minute.

Court – How long do you think it was from the time the boat fired till the people got on board of you?

Answer – Not a minute I believe; they were close to when they fired.

Court – You have said there was boarding pikes, was there any shot upon deck?

Answer – Yes sir.

Court – Do you think that if the officer commanding and crew had made what defence they could with the boarding pikes & shot that you might have repulsed the French boat?

Answer –	Yes sir.
Court –	Where did the people go off the deck?
Answer –	Into the cabin for arms.
Court –	Could those men that went to the passage for arms have had arms put into their hands time enough to repulse the men before they got on board?
Answer –	No.
Court –	How long were these men below before any arms could be got at?
Answer –	About 4 or 5 minutes.
Court –	How many places of communication had you with the deck below?
Answer –	Four.
Court –	Were the hatches put on?
Answer –	The main hatch and cabin slide.
Court –	Did you hear any of the crew say they were ready to assist in retaking the vessel?
Answer –	No.
L[t]. Westcott –	When the enemy's boat first fired, did you hear me call the people to arms?
Answer –	I heard L[t]. Westcott call to hand the cutlasses.
L[t]. Westcott –	When you saw me in the cabin for cutlasses, did I make any attempt to get on deck?
Answer –	None that I observed.

Evidence withdrew.

Tho[s]. Ferris, Seaman, called and sworn.

By the court –	Relate to the court what you know respecting the capture of the *Fort Diamond*?
Answer –	I was upon deck when the boat was hailed and they answered a boat from the shore. Then the Lieut[t]. asked who was in that boat; they made no answer. Then he asked a second time and they fired. Then the Lieut[t]. called out to us to jump down and get the arms; and while we were below, they boarded us. We could not get the arms clear when we were below, except 2 or three cutlasses. Then he said it was no use, for they had taken her; he told us all to sit down and be quiet and the quieter we were, the better they'd use us. That was all I heard him say. One man asked if we should go upon deck and retake her; and L[t]. Westcott said it was no use, for they had possession of her.

Court –	Did the Lieut[t], at any time, use any exertions to get the men on deck?
Answer –	No.
Court –	Did he try to hurry the men?
Answer –	No.
Court –	Was there any sentry looking out?
Answer –	No.
Court –	Was it customary to place a man to look out at sunset?
Answer –	Not till 8 o'clock.
Court –	Did you see any of the men board?
Answer –	Yes, one man.
Court –	Was any attempt made to drive him back?
Answer –	No.
Court –	Do you think if the men upon deck had thrown shot and used the handspikes, you could have driven them away?
Answer –	Yes.
Court –	Would the crew, do you think, if anyone had headed them, force their way on deck to retake the vessel?
Answer –	Yes sir.
Court –	When it was proposed by one of the men to go on deck and retake the vessel, did any of the other men give their opinion or make an answer as to the possibility of doing it?
Answer –	Yes sir; they said they were all willing to come upon deck.
L[t]. Westcott –	When I desired the people to be quiet in the hold, did I ask their opinions if anything could be done to regain the vessel?
Answer –	Not that I heard of.
Court –	Did you hear L[t]. Westcott at any one time propose retaking the vessel?
Answer –	No.
Court –	Did the boat appear to be a large boat or small?
Answer –	Small.
Court –	How many men do you suppose were in the boat?
Answer –	About 8 or ten.
L[t]. Westcott –	Was you in the cabin getting arms when first we were boarded?
Answer –	No, I was on deck when the first man boarded.
L[t]. Westcott –	Did you hear any person propose blowing the magazine up?

Answer – No.

Evidence withdrew.

The evidence on the part of the prosecution being closed, the prisoner requested time for his defence, which was allowed. The court was again opened, and called upon the prisoner for his defence, which he gave as follows:

… all I can say in my defence is that I have been unfortunate in the evidence which has been brought down, as neither of them had heard what was actually the case: that I proposed to the crew retaking the vessel and that I (after getting a cutlass) made every effort to get upon deck, but could not with the cutlass in my hand as the only way of getting up was by small steps to a bulkhead and on looking up saw two or three muskets with bayonets fixed pointed downwards. I then saw it was too late to make resistance, as they had complete possession of the vessel and had secured the main hatchway and cabin scuttle. The reason the men could not get armed sooner was owing to the arms being kept in a locker, when the door was so small that not more than one man could get in to hand them out. The reason I went down myself on the first alarm was to get the people armed as quick as possible, supposing most of them were asleep, they being much fatigued from hard labour that day and had not in the vessel an officer of any description to encourage the few men on deck to use what they could get in their defence. Out of the men belonging to the *Fort Diamond*, there were two sick, one boy, one Frenchman a Spaniard and two Dutchmen. Having nothing more to add in my defence, I must now throw myself on the mercy of this honourable court, hoping & relying on their known justice and lenity that they will see my conduct in a favourable light. …

Lieut[t]. Westcott examined by the court:

Did you apply for any evidence on this trial that was denied you?

Answer – No.

Court – Had you an opportunity given you of selecting such evidences from your crew as you supposed were best?

Answer – Yes.

Court – Have you anything to say against the crew of the *Fort Diamond*?

Answer – No.

The prisoner having nothing farther to offer in his defence, court was cleared and proceeded to deliberate upon and form the sentence.

The court, having carefully and deliberately weighed and considered the evidence produced on the part of the charge and what the prisoner had to offer in his defence, were of opinion that the charge of suffering the said vessel to be captured by the enemy in Roseau Bay, S[t]. Lucia is proved and that he falls under the first part of the 10th Article of War, in consequence of which the court do adjudge Lieut[t]. Benjamin Westcott to be dismissed His Majesty's service and rendered incapable of ever serving in the naval service of His Majesty, his heirs and successors; and he was therefore dismissed His Majesty's service. And nothing appearing against the crew of the said vessel, the court did adjudge that they should be acquitted.

The court was opened, audience admitted and sentence pronounced accordingly. …

111. *Court Martial of Edward Ellicott, the Officers and Crew of the* Explosion

[ADM 1/5383]

Minutes of the proceeding of a court martial assembled and held on board His Majesty's ship the *Quebec* in Yarmouth Roads, the 24th day of September 1807, for the trial of Edward Ellicott, Esq[re]., Commander of His Majesty's late bomb vessel the *Explosion*, together with his officer and men in consequence of the pilot having run her on a reef extending to the NW. of Sandy Island, adjoining to the island of Heligoland; and that notwithstanding every exertion used by the squadron under Vice Admiral Russell's orders, it was found necessary to run her on Sandy Island Beach on the 10th instant.

Present

George Hart, Esquire, Captain of His Majesty's ship the *Majestic* and third officer in the command of His Majesty's ships and vessels in Yarmouth Roads, President.

Captains

John Broughton	Rich[d]. Curry
The Right Hon[ble]. Lord Viscount Falkland	Lord Geo. Stuart

The prisoners being brought into court, and audience admitted, the order of the Right Honourable the Lords Commissioners of the Admiralty, dated the 21st of September 1807, and directed to George Hart, Esquire, Captain of His Majesty's ship the *Majestic* and third officer in the command of His Majesty's ships and vessels in Yarmouth Roads, for the trial of Edward Ellicott, Esq[r]., Commander of His Majesty's late bomb vessel *Explosion*, together with his officer and men in consequence of the pilot having run her on a reef extending to the NW. of Sandy Island, adjoining to the island of Heligoland and that notwithstanding every exertion used by the squadron under Vice Admiral Russell's orders, it was found necessary to run her on Sandy Island Beach on the 10th September 1807, was read. The members of the court and judge advocate then, in open court and before they proceeded to trial, respectively took the oath enjoined by Act of Parliament. The letter from Vice Admiral Russell, Commander in Chief of His Majesty's ships and vessels employed off Heligoland, containing the information, was then read, as also one from Captain Edward Ellicott; and the court proceeded to trial as follows:

Captain Edward Ellicott's narrative of the loss of His Majesty's late bomb vessel the *Explosion*, late under his command.

... On the 3rd day of September 1807, pursuant to directions from Vice Admiral Douglas, I sailed from Yarmouth Roads in His Majesty's late ship *Explosion* with the *Wanderer* and *Exertion*; under my orders agreeable to the orders marked No. 1 and, on opening the secret orders therein alluded to at the place directed, I proceeded with the above mentioned vessels to the Texel for the purpose of delivering to Vice Admiral Russell the dispatches I was charged with. I directed the pilot, John Parkinson, as the wind was to the southward and westward and blowing fresh, to make the land to the southward of the Texel, supposing the vice admiral might be to windward of that place. On making the land the 4th instant, I directed the pilot, about ½ past 9 a.m., to steer for Heligoland, who shaped his course accordingly and at 11 a.m. when steering agreeable to the pilot's directions the ship struck on the Haaks.

I had previously observed to the pilot that I thought we were very close in and recommended keeping a little more off. He replied there was no necessity for keeping further out, but said, 'We will have a cast of the lead,' which I immediately ordered to be hove and, in the act of which, the ship struck. We then set the main sail and got her head off and in about 10 minutes forced her clear of the shoal without having received any apparent injury and again steered for Heligoland, which we descried about 5 o'clock a.m. of the 6th instant and, about ½ past 8, saw the admiral and squadron at anchor under the island. I asked the pilot if he could go to the northward of the island. He replied certainly, but said there was a reef of rocks to the northward of the island. I told him to give them a wide berth and immediately made sail and steered according to his (the pilot's) directions, who cunned the ship himself and, about ½ past 9 o'clock, the ship struck on the reef of rocks to the northward of the island where she lay, striking very hard, until about 11, when, with the assistance of the pilots from the island, we got clear of the reef and anchored with near 4 feet of water in the hold. I trust that it will appear to this honourable court that from that period till the morning of the 10th, the time we were under the painful necessity of running her on the beach on Sandy Island, that every effort was used by the officers and crew of His Majesty's late ship *Explosion* to save her, the stores & provisions. …

Acting Lieutenant Christopher Wallis of His Majesty's late bomb *Explosion* sworn and examined as follows:

Presd[t]. State to the court what you know respecting the loss of His Majesty's late bomb, the *Explosion.*

Ans[r]. After we had bore up for Heligoland on the morning of the 4th instant, I heard Captain Ellicott say to the pilot he thought the ship was too close in and he thought we had better keep further off. The pilot answered he thought the ship was far enough off and that he wou'd have a cast of the lead if Captain Ellicott pleased. In the act of heaving the lead, the ship struck on the Haaks. The Helder Point then bore nearly east; I set the land myself. Captain Ellicott immediately ordered the main sail to be set and hauled off. After we got off some distance, we shaped our course for Heligoland according to the pilot's directions. We continued our course till the morning of the 6th; about 5 o'clock in the morning, we saw Heligoland from the mast head, then bearing about E.S.E. We stood in for the land and saw the admiral at anchor to the northward and westward of the island. Captain Ellicott then asked the pilot if we could go to the northward of the island. The pilot said yes, but there was a reef of rocks extending to the northward and westward about 4 miles. We then bore up and set top gallant sails and steered according to the pilot's directions till the ship struck.

Presd[t]. Did you sound frequently and was every precaution taken to conduct the ship to Heligoland?

Ans[r]. Yes.

Presd[t]. Was the pilot's conduct proper?

Ans[r]. Yes.

Presd[t]. Was he sober and attentive in directing the course?

Ans[r]. He was.

Presd[t]. Did he express any doubt of his ability of the coast?
Ans[r]. He did not.
Court Were all the wishes and requests of the pilot complied with?
Ans[r]. They were in every respect as far as came within my knowledge.
Presd[t]. When the ship did get on the reef, was every exertion used by Captain Ellicott, his officers & men?
Ans[r]. Yes.
Court Do you conceive the loss of the ship was occasioned by the ignorance of the pilot?
Ans[r]. Yes, I do.

M[r]. John King, Gunner of His Majesty's late bomb *Explosion*, sworn & examined as follows:

Court Had you charge of the watch when the *Explosion* was run on shore?
Ans[r]. Yes.
Court Relate the circumstances.
Ans[r]. On the 6th of September 1807, it was my watch from 8 till 12 in the forenoon. Between 8 & 9, I observed the admiral's flag flying in Heligoland Roads. I immediately acquainted my captain of it, who, then in my hearing, told the pilot to keep the ship clear of the rocks. I don't recollect the pilot making any answer. Between 9 & 10, the ship struck and, about 11, we got off and anchored. The Church of Heligoland then bore S. ½ W. 5 or 6 miles distance. There was every exertion made by Captain Ellicott, officers & men to keep the ship from sinking. The ship was cunned by the pilot from the time I saw the admiral's flag till she struck.
Presd[t]. Did you know there was a reef there before she struck?
Ans[r]. I did not.
Court Was every precaution used?
Ans[r]. Yes.
Court Do you conceive the loss of her was thro' the ignorance of the pilot?
Ans[r]. Yes.
Court Was it fine weather when the ship struck on the Haaks and Heligoland & was it such weather as to enable the pilot to see clearly?
Ans[r]. Both mornings were fine.

James Harris, Quarter Master of His Majesty's late bomb *Explosion*, sworn & examined as follows:

Court Were you at the helm at the time the *Explosion* struck?
Ans^r^. Yes.
Court Who cunned the ship?
Ans^r^. The pilot.
Court Was there any interference on the part of any other person?
Ans^r^. I heard Captain Ellicot tell him (the pilot) to be very particular and to keep clear of the rocks. I steered by the pilot's cunn until she struck.
Court Was it fine weather when she struck on the Haaks and Heligoland, so as to enable the pilot to see clearly?
Ans^r^. You could see very clearly, as it was fine weather both mornings.
Court Was every precaution used by Captain Ellicott, his officers & men to save the ship?
Ans^r^. Yes.

Captain Edward Ellicott, late Commander of His Majesty's bomb the *Explosion*, sworn & examined as follows:

Court Have you any complaint relative to the officers and ship's company in want of exertion from the time she struck until the time she was abandoned?
Ans^r^. None; they obeyed my orders in every respect and I always found them an excellent set of men.
Court To what circumstance do you impute the loss of the *Explosion*?
Ans^r^. Entirely to the ignorance of the pilot.
Court Have you ever been in that part of the world before?
Ans^r^. Never.

Captain, the Right Honourable Lord Viscount Falkland bearing testimony of the conduct of Captain Ellicott, his officers & ship's company:

I went on board the *Explosion* immediately after she was got off and frequently afterwards and had reason to be perfectly convinced that every exertion possible was made by Captain Ellicott, his officers & ship's company to keep the ship from sinking, save her stores and provisions and for every other purpose until it was necessary to beach her and abandon her.

M^{r}. John Parkinson, Pilot of His Majesty's late bomb the *Explosion*, sworn & examined as follows:

Court Are you pilot for the North Seas?
Ans^{r}. Yes.
Court How many years have you been a pilot?
Ans^{r}. Four years.
Court Have you a branch?
Ans^{r}. Yes.
Presd^{t}. Did you acknowledge yourself to Captain Ellicott to be a pilot generally for the N^{o}. Seas?
Ans^{r}. Yes.
Presd^{t}. Have you ever been at Heligoland before?
Ans^{r}. Yes.
Court Was every wish and direction of yours complied with by Captain Ellicott?
Ans^{r}. Yes.
Presd^{t}. What was the reason you got to the northward of the island?
Ans^{r}. By the wind and tide preventing my weathering it.
Presd^{t}. You knew of the reef?
Ans^{r}. Yes, but I did not think it extended so far; I thought about 3 miles by my chart.
Court How came you to be so much out in your reckoning on the Haaks?
Ans^{r}. By fatigue.
Presd^{t}. Had you any other pilot to assist you?
Ans^{r}. No.
Presd^{t}. What land did you make on first approaching the Texel?
Ans^{r}. Camperdown.
Presd^{t}. Were you told to shape a course for Heligoland?
Ans^{r}. Yes.
Presd^{t}. What distance do you think you were from the land when you struck & how did it bear?

Ans[r]. About 4 miles and it bore about E.S.E.
Court How old are you?
Ans[r]. Sixty years of age.
Court Can you see clearly?
Ans[r]. Pretty well.

The court, being cleared and the judge advocate having read the minutes and the court having maturely considered the whole, is of opinion that the loss of His Majesty's late bomb the *Explosion* was occasioned by the ignorance of the pilot, John Parkinson, and adjudged him to be imprisoned in the Marshalsea for six months, to be mulct of his pay and rendered incapable of ever taking charge of any of His Majesty's ships or vessels. And, it appearing to the court that every exertion was made on the part of the captain, officers and ship's company to save the ship, they are hereby acquitted, but it is recommended by the court to Captain Ellicott not to place such unlimited confidence in the abilities of his pilots in future. The court was then opened, audience admitted and sentence passed accordingly. …

112. *Court Martial of George Montague Higginson, the Officers and Crew of the* Pigmy

[ADM 1/5443]

Minutes of proceedings at a court martial held on board His Majesty's ship *Salvador del Mundo* in Hamoaze on Friday the 10th day of June 1814.

Present

Thomas Byam Martin, Esq[r]., Rear Admiral of the White and second officer in command of His Majesty's ships and vessels at Plymouth, President.

Captains

Robert Hall — Geo. Tobin
Henry Prescott — D'Arcy Preston

Geo. Eastlake, Jun[r].
officiating Judge Advocate

Being all the captains then and there present next in seniority to the president.

The prisoners, Lieut^{t}. George Montague Higginson and the officers and ship's company of His Majesty's late cutter *Pigmy*, were brought into court and the audience admitted.

Read – the order of the Right Honourable the Lords Commissioners of the Admiralty, dated the 6th day of June 1814 directed to the president 'to enquire into the cause and circumstances of the loss of His Majesty's late cutter *Pigmy* and to try the said L^{t}. George Montague Higginson, his officers and ship's company for their conduct on that occasion.'

Read – the warrant appointing a judge advocate.

The members of the court and judge advocate were then duly sworn.

Read – the annexed letter and narrative from the said Lieut^{t}. Higginson to J. W. Croker, Esqr., detailing the circumstances attending the loss of the said cutter.

The court then asked the officers and crew of the *Pigmy* cutter:

Q – Have any of you any complaint to make against any others of the officers and crew of the *Pigmy* cutter for improper conduct on the occasion of her loss?

A by all – None.

Lieut^{t}. W. McLeod of His Majesty's sloop *Snap* sworn and examined as follows:

Co^{t}. – Is the narrative you have just heard read a true account of the circumstances relating to the loss of the *Pigmy*?

A – It is. I was Mid^{n}. of the *Pigmy* at the time.

Co^{t}. – Relate all you know respecting the circumstances of her loss.

A – I was called to relieve the deck in the middle watch. I went on deck, found the pilot had charge of the watch and was directed by the commander on going down to him to see that everything that the pilot ordered was punctually executed and to obey him in everything. The *Pigmy* was at the time of my coming on deck in Antioche Passage on the starboard tack. At one we tacked; we continued standing to the E. at E. until ¾ past 1, when we hove to with the main topsail to the mast. We continued lying to for half an hour, when the pilot directed her to be kept away about SE, luffing to occasionally to sound; we were always in 9 fathoms. At this time, we wore on the other tack and, the cabin bell ringing, I went down to the commander, who enquired the bearing of the Chassiron Light; I told him NW. I told the commander likewise that the wind was freshening; he desired me to tell the pilot to take another reef in the topsails and to be careful that the ebb tide did not sweep us into the Breton Passage, which I did. The pilot remarked the weather was getting bad and told me to go down and tell the commander of it and that he thought it would be better to run out a little. I did so and the commander said the pilot had charge of the vessel and if he thought it prudent to run out, he would do so. About ¼ before 3, the pilot desired the helm to be put up and we steered NW. The vessel going pretty fast through the water as the wind was fresh, it became rather difficult to sound. About ¼ past 3, she shoaled from 9 fathoms to 4, I had previously sent the quarter master of the watch to the lead; I jumped down immediately to call the commander. When I was on the ladder going down, she struck; the commander came up immediately and I roused all hands on deck. She was down on her beam ends. Almost immediately we got the boat out and the commander went to sound astern of her. In the meantime, by his directions, I fired signal guns and hoisted an ensign union downwards. The boat was obliged to return; she was nearly swamped with the surf. Every exertion was that could possibly be made to save her and stuff was prepared to burn her; as the tide flowed, she filled entirely and, about 6, we hauled the ensign down and we got on shore.

Co^{t}. – How was the wind?

A – NE.

Co^{t}. – At what time did the *Pigmy* enter the passage?

A – I don't know at what hour; she was in the passage when I got on deck.

Co^{t}. – How did the Chassiron Light bear when you got on deck?

A – W & by S.

Co^{t}. – What induced the pilot to keep away SE?

A – He said the ebb tide was made and he wanted to stem against it.

Co^{t}. – Was the light distinctly seen throughout the night?

A – It was.

Co^{t}. – When you brought the light so much to the northward, did the pilot appear satisfied with the situation of the cutter?

A – Perfectly.

Co^{t}. – When and what land was seen before dark?

A – Both the islands of Rea and Oleron.

Co^{t}. – What was the object of going into the passage?

A – To watch the movement of the enemy.

Co^{t}. – Was the lead kept constantly going?

A – Constantly.

Co^{t}. – Was the lieut^{t}. informed when you brought to and bore up as you have described?

A – He was not informed when we brought to and bore up in consequence of his agreeing to its being done.

Co^{t}. – Did the lieut^{t}. go on deck when the light bore NW and the wind was blowing strong?

A – No.

Co^{t}. – What was the state of the health of Lieut^{t}. Higginson at the time?

A – He was much indisposed from constant fatigue.

Co^{t}. – Where was the master at the time?

A – In bed, having had the first watch.

Co^{t}. – Was it usual for the pilot to have charge of the watch?

A – No it was not.

Co^{t}. – Who ought to have had charge of the watch properly?

A – The master as near as I can remember, had the watches not been altered. The commander used to remain up generally the first watch and I ought to have the morning watch.

Co^{t}. – Were the cables ranged and the anchors clear?

A – The best bower was clear and a part of the range of cable up; it was not bitted. I had been desired in the fore part of the watch, 2 hours and a half before the vessel struck, to tell the pilot to get a range of cable; we begun to get it up and he said he wanted all the men on deck. I afterwards reminded him of it and again begun to get it up; the cable was not bitted, when he again wanted the men.

Co^{t}. – How did the light bear?

A – I don't know, but it was on the larboard bow after we had shaped our course.

Co^{t}. – Did the pilot appear confident of the situation and was he sober?

A – He was perfectly sober and did not appear otherwise than confident.

Co^{t}. – Would a cable have run out clear from the tier without being ranged?

A – It would.

Co[t]. – How far from the lighthouse did the vessel go on shore?
A – About a mile and half or a mile.
Co[t]. – When you informed the lieut[t]. that the light bore NW, did he make any observation upon it?
A – He told me to ask the pilot whether we had not better wear and we wore in consequence.
Co[t]. – Did the pilot express a wish at any time to anchor?
A – No.

The witness withdrew.

M[r]. John M[c]Dousal, Master on board His Majesty's late cutter *Pigmy*, sworn and examined as follows:

Co[t]. – Relate what you know of the circumstances respecting the loss of the *Pigmy*.
A – I had the first watch. We wore at 12 o'clock with her head off the island of Oleron towards the Island of Rea, got the anchors off the gunwale, saw the cable tiers clear, reported it to the commander who said that if any alteration in the weather took place to call him on all occasions. I then was relieved from the watch by the pilot and went down and told the commander so. The light then bore N and by S to the best of my recollection.
Co[t]. – Did you consider the vessel in such safety that you could with perfect propriety leave the deck and go to bed?
A – I did.
Co[t]. – Was there a leadsman in the chains?
A – Yes generally.
Co[t]. – How was the night?
A – A very dark, cloudy night.
Co[t]. – Did you from the appearance of the night consider it safe and prudent to steer into the passage?
A – We went in in consequence of a signal from the *Pomone* to the best of my recollection to reconnoitre.
Co[t]. – To what do you attribute the loss of the *Pigmy*?
A – To the ignorance of the pilot; I believe he lost sight of the light.
Co[t]. – Was everything done that could be done to save the vessel after she was on shore?
A – Everything was done.
Co[t]. – At what distance was the lighthouse when it bore W & by S?
A – From 7 to 8 miles.
Co[t]. – Did you vary the bearing of the light during the first watch?

A – Yes, I don't recollect what it was. When I went below, we wore with her head up towards the Isle of Rea.

Co^{t}. – Did you suppose there would have been any difficulty in keeping the light in nearly the same situation during the middle watch?

A – No.

Co^{t}. – Were you well acquainted with Basque Roads?

A – Not very well.

L^{t}. H – How many men had we capable of taking the lead?

A – About 2 or 3, we had the misfortune to lose some of our best men.

L^{t}. H – Was not the man at the helm sometimes obliged to quit it to take the lead in consequence of having no other in the watch to take it?

A – Very often.

The witness withdrew.

Lieutt. Higginson stated that he was 15 short of complement, that he and the master were both ill, that he had made a signal by telegraph to Captain Barrie of the *Pomone*, 'May I be allowed to anchor at dark,' and was answered in the negative.

The court was cleared and proceeded to deliberate upon and form the sentence.

The court, having very maturely and deliberately weighed and considered the before mentioned narrative from the said Lieut^{t}. Higginson and the evidence that had been given, was of opinion that the conduct of the said Lieut^{t}. George Montague Higginson was blameable in having placed such unlimited confidence in the pilot and in not having himself gone on deck when the bearings of the Chassiron Light indicated a dangerous position and the wind was reported to be freshening so fast, but in consideration of his having been indisposed (arising from previous fatigue) the court did only admonish the said Lieut^{t}. George Montague Higginson to be more circumspect in his future conduct and the court was further of opinion that no blame was imputable to any other of the officers or to the ship's company of the *Pigmy* for their conduct upon the occasion abovementioned and the court did in consequence adjudge them to be acquitted.

The court was opened, the prisoners brought in, the audience admitted and the sentence pronounced accordingly. …

112A. *Higginson to Croker*

[ADM 1/5443]

No. 11 Navy Row Stoke
Plymouth Dock
May 19. 1814

… I have to request you will be pleased to lay before the Right Honble. my Lords Commissioners of the Admiralty the enclosed statement of the loss of His Majesty's brig *Pigmy* on the 5th of March 1807 then under my command. At same time be pleased to state that I landed here only yesterday from France &, that this being the place of residence of my family, I trust their Lordships will have the indulgence to direct that my court martial may take place at this port. Lieut. McLeod of H.M. brig *Snap* was midshipman of the watch on board the *Pigmy* at the time of her loss. The residence of any of the other officers or crew I am not acquainted with. …

112B. *Lieutenant Higginson's Narrative*

[ADM 1/5443]

March 3rd. 1807. Having completed my provisions & water from one of the line of battle ships off Rochefort, got under way by orders from Commodore Keats to proceed into the Passage D'Antioche to observe the movements of the French squadron (they having shown a disposition to proceed to sea the two preceding days) & relieve the *Colpoys* brig then on that service. I did not succeed in getting into the passage till the 4th in the morng., the *Pomone* frigate being at anchor in the passage in consequence of HM brig *Pigmy* under my command being extremely bad manned, nearly one third short of complement.[1] The master & self in an ill state of health from constant bad weather & fatigue, I requested permission by telegraph to Captn. Barry of the *Pomone* to be allowed to anchor at night and was answer'd in the negative. After seeing the vessel under snug sail & giving the necessary directions for being call'd in the event of any change of circumstances, about 10 o'clock went to bed, informing the master the pilot was to be obeyed in altering the situation of the vessel as he thought fit & that the pilot would take charge of the middle watch & relieve him, myself taking charge of the morning watch.

[1]A brig had a full complement of 67 (*Regulations and Instructions*, 2nd edn, Table One: 'A Table Shewing the Number of Commission, Warrant and Petty Officers and the Ratings of every Description both Seamen and Marines allowed to each Class of His Majesty's Ships with their Present Rate of Pay').

I placed Mr. McLeod, Midshipman (the only one I had)[1] in the pilot's watch expressly to see the pilot's orders enforced & from time to time to make me acquainted with the soundings & weather, but immediately in case of any sudden change. I believe it was about ½ past 3 AM on the 5th when I was awoke by the striking of the vessel; I went instantly on deck. The wind blowing strong in heavy squalls and extremely dark, the vessel had run some time trailing on the sand and then struck fast, laying over to port with the sails shaking and the wind on our starboard beam, I believe about NE.

The pilot told me he believed us to be over on the island of Rea on a bank which lays about 2 miles off the shore. I immediately braced the yards round & fill'd, thinking by that means to force her over; after running constantly touching for the space of about 2 or 3 minutes, she again brought up, laying very much over to port. The sails were then clew'd up & before I had time to get the boat out, she was nearly on her beam ends & it was with difficulty the men could stand the deck to hoist her out; at dawn of day, I perceived the land on our lee beam very close to us & blowing a gale directly on shore. With about only 2 hours strong ebb, the vessel's bilge taking the ground, the[n] shortly after fill'd; with only one boat & that not capable of carrying out an anchor from the very heavy surf, I saw the impossibility of saving the vessel. I therefore hauled down the ensign (which I had hoisted at daylight as a signal of distress to the *Pomone*). As a signal I had struck to the fort that was then firing at us & after destroying all the signals, orders &c, went on shore with the crew on the island of Oleron. When I left her, the flood had made, her larboard gun whale was under water and her hold full up to the combings of the main hatchway. …

[1]A brig was allowed two midshipmen (*Regulations and Instructions*, 2nd edn, Table One).

UNOFFICERLIKE CONDUCT

113. *Court Martial of John Harford*

[ADM 1/5351]

Minutes at a court martial assembled on board His Majesty's ship *Gladiator* in Portsmouth Harbour on the 16th day of January 1800.

Present

Sir Richard Bickerton, Bar[t]., Rear Admiral of the Red and second officer in the command of His Majesty's ships and vessels at Portsmouth and Spithead, President.

Captain	Sir William George Fairfax	Captain	John Child Purvis
	William Domett		George Murray
	Richard Grindall		Thomas Foley
	Sir Charles Hamilton, Bar[t].		Sir Harry Neale, Bar[t].
	William Taylor		William Brown
	Charles William Paterson		Robert Barton

The prisoner was brought in and audience admitted.

The order from the Right Honble. Lords Commissioners of the Admiralty, dated the 11th of January Inst. and directed to the president, setting forth that Admiral Milbanke, Commander in Chief of His Majesty's ships and vessels at Portsmouth and Spithead, had transmitted to their Lordships a letter which he had received from Captain Thomas Wolley, Commander of His Majesty's ship *Arethusa*, inclosing one addressed to him by Lieut[t]. James Ayscough, dated the 9th of December 1799, stating that on the evening of the 7th of the said month, on his return from duty on board His Majesty's brig *Minorca*, he received the most intolerable treatment from M[r]. John Harford, then first Lieut[t]. the commanding officer on board, who struck him, threw a cup of tea in his face and took a horsewhip threatening and abusing him in the most unofficer and ungentlemanlike manner and for the trial of the said Lieutenant John Harford for the offences with which he is charged by Lieutenant James Ayscough in his aforesaid letter accordingly was read.

The president reported to the court that Captains the Honble. Alexander Cochrane, Charles Stirling, Francis Pickmore and Sir Thomas Williams were absent on Admiralty leave.

The members of the court and the judge advocate, then, in open court and before they proceeded to trial, respectively took the several oaths enjoined and directed in and by an Act of Parliament made and passed in the 22nd year of the reign of His late Majesty George the 2nd, entitled:

An Act for Amending, Explaining and Reducing into one Act of Parliament the Laws Relating to the Government of His Majesty's Ships, Vessels and Forces by Sea.

Then the letter from the said Lieut.[t] James Ayscough, dated the 9th of December Inst[t]., containing the charges was read and the witnesses were ordered to withdraw and attend their examinations separately, which they did as follows:

Lieut.[t] John Hindes Sparks, 2nd Lieut.[t] of the *Arethusa*, called in and sworn.

Lieut.[t] Ayscough asked:

Q. Relate to the court the conversation and transaction that passed between Lieut.[t] Harford and myself, on the evening of the 7th of December last, on my return from duty from His Majesty's brig *Minorca*.

A. I did not attend the conversation previous to his being struck; the first I saw was his being struck by M[r]. Harford and the next observation was he threatened to horsewhip him. M[r]. Harford then sat down; M[r]. Ayscough said, 'Do you think I will be treated in such a manner as this by such a fellow as you?' After that a cup of tea was thrown by M[r]. Harford at M[r]. Ayscough; whether it reached him or not, I cannot tell, but it went from M[r]. Harford.

Q. Was Lieutenant Harford commanding officer at the time?

A. He was.

Q. Did you observe anything in my deportment or language that could induce Lieutenant Harford to commit such acts of violence as you have related?

A. I did not.

Q. Did Lieutenant Harford, in addition to the violence he offered me, make use of the most aggravating satirical and insulting language to me as an officer?

A. I cannot speak positively to the conversation or language; I did not attend to it. I did not consider them in the first instance as quarrelling.

Q. Did you hear Lieutenant Harford say that if I fought him, he would afterwards kick me or words to that effect?

A. I do not.

Q. Did you hear me say, 'Gentlemen take notice of what has passed, for I mean to bring it forward. I am happy I did not allow my passion to get the better of me?'

A. I heard him say he would bring M[r]. Harford to a court martial, that he was glad that his passion did not get the better of him or words to that effect.

The Court asked:

Do you recollect the day on which this passed?

A. I do not remember the day; it was in the early part of December.

Q. How long had Mr. Ayscough been in the gun room when this passed?

Anr. About half an hour, we were at the distance of about the length of the table.

Q. Where was Mr. Harford sitting?

A. About midway of the table.

Q. Did you hear any provoking language from one of them to the other?

A. I did not attend to it. It appeared to me that they were quizzing each other; it was relative to the brig and the launch. I was reading at the time. It was about five and six o'clock; we were at tea at the time.

Lieutenant Harford asked:

You have said you did not hear any abusive language pass from the prosecutor to me; might such have passed?

A. It might.

Q. Did you conceive the prosecutor to be on service at the time this transaction happened?

A. I did not.

Q. What was my general character as an officer on board the *Arethusa*, quarrelsome or not?

A. I never observed Mr. Harford to be quarrelsome.

The Court asked:

When Lieutenant Harford threatened to horsewhip Lieutenant Ayscough, had he a horsewhip in his hand?

A. He had.

Q. Where did he get the horsewhip?

A. He went to his cabin for it.

Q. Do you know if the dispute arose about the jib or any sails of the launch?

A. I cannot tell whether it was the launch or the brig.

Mr. Henry Craddock, Master of the *Arethusa*, called in and sworn.

Lieutenant Ayscough asked:

Relate to the court the conversation and transactions that passed between Lieut. Harford and myself on the evening of the seventh of December last on my return from duty from His Majesty's brig *Minorca*.

Lieutenant Harford was asking Lieutenant Ayscough the state of the *Minorca*, the language I did not particularly take notice of, and the cutting of the launch's sails. M^{r}. Harford asked M^{r}. Ayscough how he liked them how they stood. He said he did not like them at all; he thought they were not well cut. Lieutenant Harford said, 'Are they cut in a seamanlike manner?' He said he did not know; he did like them, particularly the jib. Something passed between M^{r}. Harford and M^{r}. Ayscough which I did not notice, as I was talking to M^{r}. Curry. I think M^{r}. Harford said, 'Do not insult me Sir,' but what caused him to say so, I know not. I do not recollect the answer by and by; I heard something like a stroke (my back was towards them). I was sitting between them. M^{r}. Harford got up and went round me to strike him, and M^{r}. Ayscough rose and said, 'What shall I do, shall I resent it or not?' Nobody made answer that I heard. M^{r}. Harford sat down again and he said to M^{r}. Ayscough, 'Recollect Sir, do not provoke me,' but what was the language from M^{r}. Ayscough, I do not know; I did not hear him. I only heard M^{r}. Harford's voice. After M^{r}. Harford sat down again, I heard M^{r}. Ayscough say 'If you are strong, be merciful.' My head was laying on the table; I was between them. M^{r}. Harford threw a cup of tea in M^{r}. Ayscough's face across me and directly the cup of tea was thrown in his face.

Q. Why did you put your face on the table?

A. Because I was ashamed of the language used.

Q. Of whose language?

A. M^{r}. Harford's.

Q. What was there in M^{r}. Harford's language that you was ashamed of?

A. He said he would treat Lieutenant Ayscough like a boy; I believe that was for some expression used by Lieutenant Ayscough relative to the launch's sail, but I declare I did not hear what he said. He threatened to horsewhip him; he called for his horsewhip, and one of his servants brought it to him. He stood behind me and threatened to horsewhip him, but did not do it.

Q. Did you make any attempt to prevent it?

A. I did not.

Q. When you had your head down on the table, did you put your fingers in your ears?

A. No.

Q. Did you hear any provoking language from M^{r}. Ayscough at all?

A. He rose up and said, 'Can I take this from such a fellow as you?' I did not hear any provoking language from M^{r}. Ayscough before he was struck. I heard him say, 'I will try you, by God, Sir.' It was after he received the blow.

Q. Did Mr. Ayscough provoke him by any action or threat across the table?

A. He did not.

Lieutenant Ayscough asked:

Was he commanding officer at the time?

A. Yes, Mr. Harford was.

The Court asked:

Was Lieutenant Sparks at the table at the time?

A. Yes.

Q. Did he appear to attend to the concern, or hide his head as you did?

A. I did not see.

Q. Who were present in the gun room at the time this circumstance happened?

A. Mr. Sparks, Mr. Curry and Mr. Hayes, myself and Mr. Harford and the servants, Brown and Manning.

Lieutenant Harford asked:

Was my general character on board the *Arethusa* quarrelsome or otherwise?

A. No, not particularly quarrelsome. In his general character, he was not a quarrelsome man, rather passionate, I think, at times. I think it was merely in passion this happened.

Lieutenant Robert Hayes of the Marines belonging to the *Arethusa* called in and sworn.

Lieut.t Ayscough asked:

Relate to the court the conversation and transactions that passed between Lieutenant Harford and myself on the evening of the seventh of December last on my return from duty from His Majesty's brig *Minorca*.

Mr. Harford asked Lieutenant Ayscough a great many questions respecting the *Minorca*, seemingly in jest, which Mr. Ayscough did not like. Then Mr. Harford asked him concerning the launch whether the sails stood well; Mr. Ayscough said they did not. Mr. Harford then asked him if he thought they were cut sailor or seaman fashion. 'No,' said he, 'I do not; I do not like them at all. I do not think they hoist or stand well.' That appeared on both sides in a sneering manner, both the question and the answer. Then Mr. Harford asked him some more questions respecting the *Minorca*; they appeared to be satirical. Mr. Ayscough said he would not answer them, that if he wished to know about the *Minorca* particularly, he might go on board. Mr. Harford then said, 'Nay, Nay. James, or Jimmy, I asked you that I might be able to inform my captain when he came on board.' 'No,' said he, 'I do not think you did. You did not ask me in an officerlike manner; it was to quiz me.' M^{r}. Harford said, 'Nay, if you come to quizzing, there is no one tries to do it more than yourself and is less capable. M^{r}. Ayscough laughed and sneered at that. M^{r}. Harford appeared then to be in a passion and said, 'I have been at sea, man and boy, thirty years and I am not going to be treated with contempt by such a puppy of a boy as you and if you dare to do it, I'll cuff you.' And at the same time, he got up from his chair and went round to M^{r}. Ayscough, who said, 'Do it if you please, I do not care for you!! Do it, Sir.' Upon which, M^{r}. Harford gave him a slap on his cheek with his flat hand. M^{r}. Ayscough then put his right arm out against M^{r}. Harford's breast and said, 'This is too bad. I wish the captain was on board for your sake. By God, I'll try you by a court martial.' M^{r}. Harford said he was a dirty puppy and went towards his chair again and said he would horsewhip him as soon as look at him if he dared to treat him with contempt. M^{r}. Ayscough said he did not care for him. 'Don't insult me,' said M^{r}. Harford, 'By God, I'll horsewhip you if you do' and called out to Manning, his servant, to get him his whip. His servant went to get it and M^{r}. Harford went towards him and I believe received it from the servant's hand. He went then to M^{r}. Ayscough and said he would horsewhip him if he durst treat him with contempt. M^{r}. Ayscough replied, 'Do it sir;' but M^{r}. Harford did not and sat down in his chair. I believe there was silence for about a minute at that time. M^{r}. Harford then said that when he asked questions, he should not treat him with contempt or he would teach him not to treat him with contempt. M^{r}. Ayscough said, 'You did not ask me in an officerlike manner; do you think I am going to put up with this treatment from such a fellow as you?' M^{r}. Harford said, 'Don't dare to insult me; hold your tongue, or I'll dash the cup of tea in your face.' 'Do it sir if you please,' the other replied, 'I don't care for you. Do it sir.' M^{r}. Harford then threw the cup of tea in his face. M^{r}. Ayscough then partly got up from his chair, and said, 'By God, this is too bad,' and stretched his arm out towards the slop basin or sugar basin, I don't know which, and said, 'Shall I or shall I not,' but I got up from my chair and said, 'For shame gentlemen, don't make the gun room a Hell of Wapping,' upon which M^{r}. Ayscough sat down again and said he was glad his passion had not got the better of him very well sir, and I believe he said, 'You all see gentleman.'

Q. Was there anything in my deportment or language that could provoke him to insult me in this manner?

A. There was not anything in my opinion that would have tempted me to have struck a man.

The court asked:

Q. Were Lieut.^{t} Sparks and M^{r}. Craddock, the Master, at the table at the time?

A. They were.

Q. Is it possible they could not have heard what you have related?

A. They must have heard it, but it being a month ago, they might not recollect it.

Q. Was the conversation in a low or high tone of voice?

A. In a high tone of voice.

Q. Did either of these officers interfere to prevent the quarrel?

A. No, they did not.

Q. When Lieut.^{t} Ayscough declined to answer the questions of the first lieu^{t}., was it done to avoid a quarrel as to provoke the first lieu^{t}.?

A. It was to prevent his quizzing him, as he said.

Q. Did you imagine the manner in which M^{r}. Harford questioned M^{r}. Ayscough relative to the brig was done by way of ridiculing him or to get information to give his captain?

A. I do not think it was to get information to give his captain. I do not think M^{r}. Harford at first intended to insult M^{r}. Ayscough, but merely what they call 'quizzing,' which has happened in the mess before, but never brought on a quarrel before.

Lieut.^{t} Harford asked:

Q. Did the conversation used by the prosecutor relative to the boat's sails appear insulting and disrespectful to me?

A. It appeared in a sneering manner; he said he did not like them. They did not stand well, which appeared to hurt M^{r}. Harford's feelings.

Q. Do you know if the sails were made by my directions?

A. Yes, particularly the launch had been fresh rigged. I believe they had been trying the sails that very morning or the day before.

Q. Did you suppose M^{r}. Ayscough on service at the time?

A. Yes.

The prosecution was here closed, and the prisoner, being called on for his defence, produced the same, which was read by the judge advocate, which is hereto annexed.

William Brown, Gun Room Steward on board His Majesty's ship *Arethusa*, called in and sworn.

Lieutenant Harford asked:

Was you in the gun room on the evening of the 7th of Decr. last?

A. Yes.

Q. Relate to the court the conversation that passed between the pros^{r}. and me relative to the sails of the boat.

A. In the first place, M^{r}. Harford asked M^{r}. Ayscough what he had being [*sic*] doing in the brig. M^{r}. Ayscough did not make him any ans^{r}. Then M^{r}. Harford asked him how the launch sailed and how he liked the cut of the jib. M^{r}. Ayscough answered him that he did not like it at all; it had not hoist enough. M^{r}. Harford asked him how he liked the main sail; M^{r}. Ayscough answered that he did not like it at all. He asked him if he did not think the jib was cut seaman fashion. M^{r}. Ayscough said he did not think it was and they were lubbers who cut it and them that ordered it. M^{r}. Harford asked him again what he had been doing in the brig. M^{r}. Ayscough said it would be best for him to go in the launch and he would be a better judge. M^{r}. Harford asked him if he meant to affront him and that he did not think it was usage for a person of his years, that he had been in His Majesty's service twenty two years and never met with such an insult before. M^{r}. Harford told him he would not wish him to insult him too much and that he was bred above a seaman and did not see he had given him any offence, that he would not be insulted by a boy. He told him if he insulted him any more, he would have a cup of tea in his face. M^{r}. Ayscough dared him to do it three or four times; M^{r}. Harford told him if he dared him any more, he would lick him like a boy. M^{r}. Ayscough said, 'I dare you to do it' three or four times over. M^{r}. Harford got up out of his chair and just struck M^{r}. Ayscough with his back hand in his face very slightly. M^{r}. Ayscough jumped up out of the chair and said, 'Shall I resent it or not?' He immediately told M^{r}. Harford he would try him by a court martial, and break him. I was then called out of the room and did not see or hear anything more.

Q. Did the gestures and behaviour of the prosecutor upon that occasion appear to you to be contempt towards him?

A. I rather think it did.

Q. Were the sails you have spoken of made by my particular direction?

A. I believe they were.

The court asked:

Q. Are you positive you heard Lieut.^{t} Ayscough say whoever ordered those sails to be cut was a lubber?

A. Whoever cut them and them that ordered them.

The prisoner called on Captain Foley for his character:

Captain Foley said he served as lieutenant on board the *St. George* under my command for more than two years. At the beginning of this war, he conducted himself always very much to my satisfaction and I have every reason to speak well of him for the time I knew him. He was very much sought after by some very good officers to serve with them as first lieutenant. He left the *St. George* to join Lord Hood's ship on promotion. He was third lieutenant of the *Victory* when his Lordship struck his flag. He surely is a very good seaman and officer. The *St. George* had the flag of Admirals Sir Hyde Parker and Gill during the time; it appeared to me he was a favourite officer with both those gentlemen.

He called on Sir Charles Hamilton to speak to his character. He said:

Sometime back when I was in want of a first lieutenant, I sought for Lieutenant Harford, but found him already in the *Arethusa* (I was induced so to do for his public character and my own private knowledge of him).

M^{r}. Thomas Bell, Surveying Master, said:

I have known M^{r}. Harford upwards of ten years, during which time I sat at the table with him for about two years in the *St. George*, under the command of Captain Foley, and always considered him to be a gentleman and a good officer.

The court was cleared and agreed that the charge had been proved against the said Lieutenant John Harford, and did adjudge him to be dismissed from His Majesty's service.

The court was again opened, the prisoner brought in, audience admitted and sentence passed accordingly. …

113A. *Ayscough to Wolley*

[ADM 1/5351] His Majesty's ship *Arethusa*, River Tagus
December the 9th, 1799

… I have to acquaint you that on the evening of the 7th. of December, on my return from duty on board His Majesty's brig *Minorca*, I received the most intolerable treatment from M^{r}. John Harford, the first Lieu^{t}. the commanding officer on board, who struck me, threw a cup of tea in my face & took a horsewhip, threatening and abusing me in the most unofficer and ungentlemanlike manner.

I have therefore to request that you will take the earliest opportunity of transmitting this my letter to my Lords Commissioners of the Admiralty, requesting a court martial may be held on him for his conduct. …

113B. *Defence of Harford*

[ADM 1/5351]

… I have very little to offer in my defence, but must from the circumstances that have been related to the court in the course of the prosecution; the court may be induced to believe that the contemptuous and insolent language which transpired from the prosecutor was such as to irritate the passions of an officer and to palliate my conduct on the occasion.

I have been nearly twenty years in His Majesty's service and, during that time, have had the good fortune to give general satisfaction to all the officers under whom I have had the honour to serve; and I think, I may venture to say, I have always been on the best of terms with those officers on a footing with me and have not conducted myself unpleasantly to those under me. Under these impressions, I am in hopes the court will take the circumstances under consideration and believe that my conduct was actuated by my feelings at the moment from the aspersions cast by the prosecutor on the sails of the boat, which he knew had been planned by me and to the trimming of which I had paid particular attention.

In the course of my life, I have met with many unpleasant circumstances and disappointments, which may, in some measure, have soured my temper, and rendered it more irascible than men in general and that, added to the language made use of by the prosecutor, may have hurried me to the rash method of obtaining satisfaction, which I unfortunately adopted.

I certainly did not think it a matter of service, but perhaps the prosecutor, being more wise, takes the advantage of the laws under which we sail. The prosecutor wrote to withdraw his charge, but, I am sorry to say, it was not complied with.

I have no desire to detain the court or give them further trouble on the occasion, but beg to recommend myself to their consideration.

114. *Court Martial of John George Nops*

[ADM 1/5363]

Minutes taken at a court martial assembled on board His Majesty's ship *Diamond* in Portsmouth Harbour on the 8th day of March 1803.

Present

William O'Bryen Drury, Esqr., Captain of His Majesty's ship *Neptune* and third officer in the command of His Majesty's ships and vessels at Portsmouth and Spithead, President.

Captain	John Clarke Searle	Captain	Thomas Elphinstone
	Robert Williams		Thos. Masterman Hardy
	John W^{m}. Taylor Dixon		John Stiles
	Micajah Malbon		George Wolfe
	George Mundy		Frederick Lewis Maitland
	Richard Peacocke		William Parker

The prisoner was brought in and audience admitted.

The president reported to the court that Captain William Granville Lobb of His Majesty's ship *Isis* was absent on Admiralty leave.

The order from the Right Honourable Lords Commissioners of the Admiralty, dated the 6th March Instant and directed to the president, for the trial of Lieutenant John George Nops, belonging to His Majesty's ship *La Determinee*, for having on the evening of the 29th of December 'treated M^{r}. Richard Cull, a Midshipman, in a manner unbecoming the character of an officer and a gentleman by pulling his ears and felling him to the deck,' was read.

The members of the court and judge advocate, then, in open court and before they proceeded to trial, respectively took the several oaths enjoined and directed in and by an Act of Parliament made and passed in the 22nd year of the reign of His late Majesty George the Second, entitled: *An Act for Amending, Explaining and Reducing into one Act of Parliament the Laws Relating to the Government of His Majesty's Ships, Vessels and Forces by Sea*.

Then the letter from Captain Alexander Becher, Commander of His Majesty's ship *La Determinee*, dated the 31st of December 1802, and directed to Admiral Milbanke, Commander in Chief of His Majesty's ships and vessels at Portsmouth and Spithead, containing the charge was read, and the witnesses were ordered to attend their examinations separately, which they did as follows:

M^{r}. Richard Cull, a Midshipman belonging to His Majesty's ship *Determinee*, called in and sworn.

Captain Becher asked:

Q. Relate to the court the treatment M^{r}. Nops showed you on the evening of the 29th of December.

A. I had the from 4 to 6 watch. I was not relieved at the time; about quarter past 6, Lieutenant Nops came upon deck. I was on the larboard side of the deck. He came over to me and asked me my name; I answered him, 'M^{r}. Cull.' He then pulled me by the ears. I asked him what he did it for, as I had not given any provocation or disobeyed any command. He came over and shoved me with his hand on the breast insomuch that I came down in the quarter deck. After that, Mr. Nops went into the cabin, and on the morning afterwards I complained to the captain.

The court asked:

Q. When you were shoved, what did you stagger against that made you fall down?

A. I did not stagger against anything.

Q. Was it a push or blow?

A. It was with his open hand against my breast; it was a push.

Q. Did he say anything to you when he pulled your ears and shoved you?

A. He only asked me my name; that was all the conversation that passed.

Q. Did he appear very angry with you at the time?

A. Yes.

Q. In what way did he express that anger?

A. I thought by Mr. Nops' looks that he appeared to be more angry with me than I had ever seen him before.

Q. Was it dark at the time?

A. Yes, very near.

Q. Could you see his countenance?

A. Yes.

Q. Was Mr. Nops commanding officer at the time?

A. No.

Q. Had he at any time that day given you any orders or were any left with you by the midshipman you relieved?

A. None in particular, such as to keep a clear hawse.

Q. Did the ship tend while you were upon deck?

A. No.

Q. Do you know any reason for his pulling your ears and shoving you?

A. I do not.

Q. Were you the mate of the watch?

A. No.

Q. Was anybody in the watch beside you?

A. Yes.

Q. Was Mr. Nops lieutenant of the watch?

A. No.

Lieutenant Nops asked:

Q. Are you sure I asked you your name?

A. Yes.

Q. Are you not somewhat deaf?

A. A little.

Q. Did it blow at the time?
A. No, not so much, but I could hear Mr. Nops.
Q. Had we topmasts struck at the time?
A. I cannot say.
Q. Had you any reason to think I had any particular pique against you?
A. No.

John Monatt, Quarter Master belonging to the *Determinee*, called and sworn.

Captain Becher asked:

Q. Did you see Mr. Nops upon deck about 6 o'clock on the evening of the 29th of December?
A. I saw him after six.
Q. Did you see Mr. Cull on the deck at the same time?
A. No, not that I recollect. I saw nothing of the matter.

John Miller, a Quarter Master belonging to the *Determinee*, called in and sworn.

Q. Did you see Mr. Nops upon deck about 6 o'clock on the evening of the 29th of December?
A. Not at 6 o'clock, I went off the deck about 5 minutes after six. Mr. Nops had not then come on deck.
Q. Did you see Mr. Nops and Mr. Cull on deck at the same time?
A. No.
Q. Do you know anything of the charge?
A. No, I do not.

Benjamin Fowler, a Marine belonging to the *Determinee*, called in and sworn.

Q. Was you sentinel at the cabin door from 4 to 6 on the evening of the 29th of Decr.?
A. Yes.
Q. Had you a light?
A. No.
Q. Did you see Mr. Nops on the deck?
A. No.
Q. Did you see Mr. Cull there?
A. No.
Q. Who relieved you?
A. George Townsend at 6 o'clock.
Q. Did you see Mr. Cull on the deck?
A. No.
Q. Was there any midshipman on the deck between 4 and 6 o'clock?

A. I do not know.

John Monatt called in again.

The court asked:

Q. Was Mr. Cull on deck?

A. I saw him on deck a little after six.

Andrew Mc Cullock, a Seaman belonging to the *Determinee*, called in and sworn.

Captain Becher asked:

Q. Did you see Mr. Nops on the deck on the evening of the 29th of December?

A. I did.

Q. Did you see Mr. Cull there at the same time?

A. Yes.

Q. Did you observe anything pass between them?

A. No.

Q. Did you see Mr. Cull lying on the deck?

A. Yes, I did.

Q. How did he come there?

A. I do not know.

Q. Did you hear him say anything at the time?

A. No.

Q. At any time shortly before, did you hear him say anything?

A. No, I perceived him walk up to Mr. Nops, and afterwards I saw him lying on the deck.

Q. Did it appear to you that Mr. Cull had fallen to the deck by means of Mr. Nops pushing him?

A. I cannot say; his great coat was laying by him at the time.

Q. Was Mr. Nops near him?

A. He was about a yard from him. I was walking on the deck and, on turning round, I saw Mr. Cull on the deck.

Q. What weather was it?

A. Moderate weather.

Q. Do you know anything of the charge?

A. I saw him laying on the deck, but how he came there I do not know. I saw him get up and heard him speaking to Mr. Nops, but did not hear what Mr. Nops said. He immediately went into the captain's cabin and then Mr. Cull said he had pulled his ears and shoved or knocked him down.

Q. Do you believe that Mr. Nops could have treated Mr. Cull with any degree of violence on the quarter deck of the *Determinee* without your hearing or seeing it?

A. No, not with any degree of violence.

Lieutenant Nops asked:

Q. Did I appear angry with him?

A. I did not take any particular notice.

The prisoner, being called on for his defence, produced a paper writing, which was read by the judge advocate and is hereto annexed.

M^r^. W^m^. Parry, Master of the *Determinee*, called in and sworn.

Lieutenant Nops asked:

Q. Did you ever know me, during the time I have belonged to the ship, give occasion to suppose that I could treat M^r^. Cull in an ungentlemanlike manner?

A. No, I never did.

The court was cleared and agreed that the charge had not been proved against the said Lieutenant John George Nops, but appeared to be trifling, and did adjudge him to be acquitted.

The court was again opened, the prisoner brought in, audience admitted and sentence passed accordingly. …

114A. *Defence of Nops*

[ADM 1/5363]

Being called upon by this honble. court for my defence, I beg leave to state in the most concise manner what occurred and gave rise to this trifling tho' unpleasant affair from a clear conviction that I was actuated by no other motive whatever (jocularity excepted) to commit a crime, which I trust will appear as unintentional in the eyes of the court, as it did to me, when I unguardedly exposed myself to the power of a boy, whose wish of prosecuting me, I was a perfect stranger to and whose conduct on the occasion excited the greatest surprise.

On the evening of the 29th of Decr. 1802, I went on deck to speak to M^r^. Lockwood, then 1st. Lieutenant and, not finding him there, went to M^r^. Cull, who was then walking the deck, and said to him 'have you ever seen London,' or words to that effect, at the same time taking him by the ears in order to lift him up as a youngster, which at the time I did not consider any impropriety when he immediately said, 'Recollect, sir, you are on the quarter deck.' On which I replied, 'Oh sir are you for that,' and laid him gently on his back, far from felling him as represented. I then went into the cabin & found ---[1] the 1st Lieu^t^., but did not mention it to him or anyone belonging to the ship, considering it in that trivial light,

[1]Several words are obscured by the tattered condition of the paper.

that for some time after I was made acquainted of the accusation I could not recall it to my memory.

This, gen^{t}., is the whole of the affair and, if anything can tend to remove the embarrassment I now feel on this occasion, it is from a confidence that this honble. court will not allow a matter like the present to affect not only my present character, but my future prospects in the navy.

I shall not say anything of the witnesses I have brought forward on my behalf, as their evidence speak [*sic*] for itself, but beg leave to remind the court that a bare acquittal for want of evidence will not by any means take away the stigma the accusation has lain me under, and therefore trust to the mercy of the court & hope for an honble. acquittal of the charges preferred against me. …

BRUTALITY

115. *Court Martial of Richard Maundrell*

[ADM 1/5332]

Minutes taken at a court martial assembled on board His Majesty's ship *Royal William* at Spithead on the 30th day of March 1795.

Present

The Honble. William Cornwallis, Vice Admiral of the Blue and second officer in the command of His Majesty's ships and vessels at Portsmouth and Spithead, President.

Rear Admiral Sir George Keith Elphinstone K.B.	Captain
Captain	Alexander Graeme
Francis Parry	Andrew Mitchell
Charles Edmund Nugent	Charles Powel Hamilton
The Honble. Thomas Packenham	Sir Andrew Snape Douglas, Kn^{t}.
James Richard Dacres	James Douglas
William George Fairfax	The Right Honble. Lord Cranstoun

The president reported to the court that Captains Mason, Packenham, Lord Charles Fitzgerald, Duckworth, Hood and Knight were absent on Admiralty leave.

The prisoner was brought in and audience admitted.

The order from the Right Honble Lords Commissioners of the Admiralty, dated the 25th of March instant, directed to the president, setting forth that Captain Thomas Wooley, Commander of His Majesty's ship *Active* had acquainted their Lordships by his letter to their secretary of the preceding day's date that, upon a representation made to him by one of the petty officers belonging to the said ship of murmurings and discontent amongst her company owing to the cruel and severe treatment they had experienced from M^{r}. Richard Maundrell, the first Lieutenant, particularly during his absence from the ship, he had felt it his duty instantly to inquire into the cause of complaint, which he had found too well founded, especially in one instance where a man whom he had beat was many days confined from the blows he had received, although he was not returned to him upon the sick list when he rejoined the ship and for the trial of the said Richard Maundrell for the charge aforesaid, was read.

Then the members of the court and judge advocate, in open court and before they proceeded to trial, respectively took the several oaths enjoined and directed in and by an Act of Parliament made and passed in the 22nd year of the reign of His late Majesty George the Second, entitled: *An Act for Amending, Explaining and Reducing into one Act of Parliament the Laws Relating to the Government of His Majesty's Ships, Vessels and Forces by Sea.*

Then the said letter from Captain Thomas Wooley containing the charge was read, and the witnesses were ordered to withdraw and attend their examinations separately, which they did as follows:

M^{r}. Maundrell produced a paper writing to the court, which was read by the judge advocate and is hereto annexed.

The court was cleared and agreed to examine witnesses as to the facts.

John Bennett, Boatswain's Mate belonging to the *Active*, called in and sworn.

Captain Wooley asked:

Q. Relate to the court the circumstance and manner of your being beaten by Lieutenant Maundrell and the effect it had on you.

A. I was desired by M^{r}. Maundrell, it was the first Saturday after we went alongside the hulk in Portsmouth Harbour, to go with some hands on board the frigate and work with them. I accordingly went on board the *Active*; and M^{r}. Quail, the commanding officer, ordered me to take what hands I could, and go and clear the wings of what old rope and stuff there was to be found, which I accordingly did, but had none but soldiers to do it. I then, after I had got it up, put it all by his orders into the boat. He told me sometime after to get two spars and some men, and go and get ready for gambling [*sic*] the bowsprit: I told him there were no other hands but the soldiers that were with me, but what was employed upon other duty. He cursed me and told me I might find men if I would look for them and damned me for a son of a bitch of a boatswain's mate. I told him I was more like a labourer or a slave than a boatswain's mate and for all that could not give satisfaction. He then left me, and told me he would acquaint M^{r}. Maundrell of the words I had expressed. When he had gone away some men that were about other duty told me they would go and help me if I thought proper to let them leave off what they were about. I went out with them and had got the first spar just rigged out, when M^{r}. Maundrell came on board. I was then called down off the bowsprit to him on the quarter deck; he asked me did I make mention of such words to M^{r}. Quail of my not being boatswain's mate. I told him I had been faulty and said I had none but soldiers to do it. He then took a piece of rope; I believe it was 2½ inches and two foot and a half long. He had whipped the end of it before I came, least it should fag out. He told me did I remember that Captain Wooley had promised to flog me in the North Sea and now he would pay me for that and this together and he made me strip, which I accordingly did. He then began to beat me with all the power that he was able; I stood as long as possibly I could, and then I endeavoured to go away. He called me back; I went, when I knew it was in vain to refuse. He then began again and I stayed with him about much the same length of time. I went to go the second time, but he told me he had not done. I put my hat up to my left shoulder to save the blows, for I told him my arm was useless and, if he meant to beat me any longer, to strike me about the back more. He made me down with my hat from that shoulder and to the last of the beating seemed principally to aim at it. I stayed a few minutes afterwards and then he left off and told me to walk aft to the taffrail, and stay there, which I did, but had scarce reached it when I found myself very weak by the blows and the cold together that, I was obliged to support myself by the railing to save falling on deck. I there stayed till the boat came to fetch me on board of the hulk I then applied to the surgeon and got two or three men to help me down and strip me and show to him the manner I was in. He asked me how I came by such flesh; I told him M^r^. Maundrell had given it to me. He ordered me into the sick bay, amongst the rest of the sick; there I was off and on for three weeks. The ship's company, when they saw me strip, desired me to go on shore and acquaint the port admiral of it. I told them that I would not think of doing anything of the kind, as I could not get liberty, and, to do that, I should lay at his mercy again. They told me that since there was no likelihood of his leaving that ship, she being then most ready for sea that they would not stay any longer.

The court asked:

Q. Did you see Lieutenant Maundrell whip the rope?

A. No, but the man is here who saw it.

Q. When your captain returned, did you acquaint him of it?

A. No, not until the ship's company insisted I should come forward.

M[r]. Thomas Heron, Surgeon of the *Active*, called in and sworn.

Captain Wooley asked:

Q. Relate to the court the state you found Bennett in on his application to you and how long he was unable to do duty from the beating he received from Lieu[t]. Maundrell.

A. When Bennett applied to me, his arm and shoulder were considerably swelled in consequence of a beating which he said he had received from Lieu[t]. Maundrell, from which he was unable to do duty about four days I think.

The court asked:

Q. When was this?

A. I cannot recollect; we were in the harbour.

Q. How long was he under your care?

A. About four days in all.

Q. Did he come down or was he brought down?

A. He came down.

Q. Did he appear to you to be cruelly beaten?

A. It appeared to be severe.

Q. Were there any marks on his back?

A. It was swelled and discoloured, but not cut.

Captain Wooley asked:

Q. Did you not say that if he had been in a hot country, the beating would have been very dangerous?

A. I do not recollect it.

The court asked:

Q. Do you think he was cruelly beaten?

A. Yes. I think it was very severe; it appeared to have been by a repetition of blows.

Captain Wooley asked:

Q. Do you recollect William Jacobs being ill in consequence of blows given him by Lieutenant Maundrell?

A. I recollect Jacobs telling me that he felt himself very sore from blows; I attended him for some other complaint.

The court asked:

Q. Have you dressed any other persons' backs in consequence of being beaten?

A. No, I have not.

Q. Did Jacobs' illness proceed from beating?

A. I think not; I believe it was from drunkenness.

Q. Do you know that the prisoner was in the habit of striking the ship's company?

A. I have seen him strike some of the ship's company; I don't think more than once or twice.

Q. Did it appear to be in a cruel manner?

A. It appeared to be severe.

William Hayman, a Seaman belonging to the *Active*, called in and sworn.

Captain Wooley asked:

Q. Did you see Lieu[t]. Maundrell beat John Bennett?

A. Yes, I did. I was on the forecastle at the time. Mr. Maundrell called the man aft on the quarter deck and struck him.

The court asked:

Q. How many blows did he give him?
A. More than two dozen with a rope.
Q. Did you see any cause of complaint?
A. None that I know of.
Q. Did you see him go down to the surgeon?
A. I did not.
Q. How long was he before he did his duty again?
A. About three weeks
Q. Is Bennett, the Boatswain's Mate, diligent, sober and a well behaved man in his station?
A. As far as ever I see him.
Q. Did you ever see Mr. Maundrell beat or strike others of the ship's company?
A. Yes, I have seen him strike a great many of the ship's company.
Q. On such occasions did the beating appear to you to be excessive?
A. Yes.
Q. Relate how the beating happened.
A. They were beaten with the end of a rope.
Q. Was it done deliberately or merely in the hurry of duty?
A. There has been most cruel beatings by Lieut. Maundrell; many of the men, who are gone away from the ship, were cruelly beaten.

William Jacobs, a Seaman belonging to the *Active*, called in and sworn.

The court asked:

Q. Where do you do your duty?
A. In the cockpit along with the surgeon.

Captain Wooley asked:

Q. Relate to the court the manner of your being beat by Lieut. Maundrell on that day in which you told me you was confined to your hammock in consequence of it.
A. The surgeon desired me to serve out medicines to the sick, as he had no mate on board, every two hours in the day. Mr. Johnston, the Master's Mate, desired me to come on deck to pull at the fall. I was just got into the steward's room to cut out the butter and cheese as he was on shore and had nobody to help him and I told Mr. Johnston I would follow him on deck directly, which I did; as soon as I got upon deck, Mr. Maundrell sent for me and said he wanted me. He then cut a piece of rope that lay on the deck

and beat me with it while he could stand over me almost and he then knocked me down with his fist. I got up and ran away from him. He told me to come back and followed me and beat me more. He beat me with his fist very much afterwards and knocked me down three or four times. I fell down betwixt two casks, as he knocked me down with his fist, and was hardly able to get up again; he then took a rope that lay by his foot, a very big rope, and struck me with it, and I got up and ran away from him.

The court asked:

Q. Was the captain on board at the time?

A. No.

Q. Did you complain to the surgeon?

A. Lieu[t]. Maundrell made me pull at the fall that afternoon. In the evening, I went to the hammock, and in the morning, complained to the surgeon. He asked me if I was bruised about the back; I told him my head was worst. He did not examine me at all; he gave me some medicine that morning. I told him my head was so sore with blows that I could not get up.

Q. Was anybody by, when you was beaten?

A. Yes.

Captain Wooley asked:

Q. Was you in liquor at the time Lieu[t]. Maundrell began to beat you?

A. No, I had not tasted a drop of liquor.

William Billinge, a Marine belonging to the *Active*, called in and sworn.

Captain Wooley asked:

Q. Relate to the court the manner in which you saw Lieu[t]. Maundrell beat William Jacobs and the effect it appeared to have on him.

A. The first I saw was he sent for him up out of the cockpit and he came. Lieu[t]. Maundrell said, 'Come here Jacobs.' Jacobs would fain have told him what he was doing there, but he would not hear him. He cut the end of a rope off. He beat him as long as he could stand over him; he cried out for mercy a great while. The rope slipped out of his hand and he struck him several times with his fist. He broke loose from him and ran forward; and the Lieu[t]. followed and struck him several times there. And he ran from him again; he struck him with his fist and knocked him down between two casks. And I thought he was almost dead, for he could not move. The lieutenant took him a rope of 2 or 2½ inches and struck at him with both hands as hard as he could and said, 'I'll teach you to sham.' He then sent him to the spar deck and bid him to clap on the fall clearing lighter; he could scarce stand or walk on deck. He stayed while the lighter was clearing and then went down to his hammock and was in it for two days.

Q. Did Jacobs appear to be in liquor at the time?

A. No.

Captain Wooley said he was happy to have to say that 'when the ship was in the North Sea, in a dangerous sea, it was owing to the exertion of Lieutenant Maundrell that the mainmast was saved. He went into the top and exerted himself very much and set a very good example to both officers and ship's company and, until this unfortunate business came forward, I looked on him to be an active, sober, good officer.'

The court was cleared and agreed that the charge had been proved against the said Lieutenant Richard Maundrell and did therefore adjudge him to be dismissed from His Majesty's service.

The court was again opened, audience admitted and sentence passed accordingly. …

115A. *Defence of Maundrell*

[ADM 1/5332]

… To every feeling mind, but particularly to a professionary one, so awful an arraignment for a young officer to be brought before so honourable a tribunal must be impressive, affective, and distressing.

If erroneous zeal for the service has hurried me to inconsiderate measures, my private feelings has been sacrific'd to what I esteem'd the good of the service. I wish not to extenuate my errors, but, briefly from narration, endeavour to save the court every unnecessary trouble I feel particularly unhappy at having occasion'd.

In answer to the charge laid against me, I shall not intrude upon the court further than to acknowledge the truth of it and, in extenuation, to offer that nothing premeditated on my part was the cause of the offence, but a zeal as first lieutenant for the service, which I doubt not I could prove were I to trouble the court with instances of it from the testimony of (I may trust) every officer I have had the honour to serve under for 13 years past; and I also trust that tho' my conduct cannot be justified, my earnest wish and zeal in the service will plead in my behalf

For as I should be sorry to intrude too much on this honourable court and the candour of the prosecutor, whose conduct I confess with the greatest sense of gratitude and shall ever feel it my duty to acknowledge.

I shall waver adducing any evidence in support of what I allege for if in that zeal, I have done more than my duty lead me to do, I am at the mercy of the court for its consequences.

But, if my general character, which I am not conscious was before impeach'd, and my service in the present war, which gave me the commission which as yet I hold and which was not obtain'd in the general way, but as may be in the recollection of the court by duty in Holland where I was severely wounded, and which at the time not only gave me rank but also entitled me to a gold medal from the States General, which I beg leave to certify by a letter from Lord Auckland and which I trust may have weight.

I shall here with all respect and humility waver any other defence and throw myself on the mercy of the court, humbly hoping that whatever may be their decision, they may be pleas'd from the above circumstances to recommend me to the Lords of the Admiralty for further service to my country in which my time heretofore shall ever be devoted.

I cannot conclude without observing that the very handsome manner the prosecutor has from my knowledge and acquaintance with him ever behav'd claim'd my warmest thanks, and such is the confidence I place on his candour that I feel happy to have it in my power to ask him before this honourable court his opinions of my conduct (to which he has been an eye witness and particularly when with him in the North Seas).

A gold medal, the honourable testimony of the approbation of their High Mightiness, I have waived to wear till wth the sword that gained it and which as a prisoner I am at present depriv'd of may from the indulgence of the court enable me to add additional honours to both in the service of my king & country. …

115B. *Auckland to Maundrell*

[ADM 1/5332] Hague, 30th April 1793

… I am desired to transmit to you a gold chain & medal given by the States General of the United Provinces as a mark of their acknowledgement of your services to this Republic under our friend Captain Cornewall Berkeley. It is with much pleasure that I avail myself of so honourable an occasion to assure you that I am with sentiments of real & great esteem. …

116. *Court Martial of George William Blamey*

[ADM 1/5350]

Minutes of proceedings at a court martial held on board His Majesty's ship *Cleopatra* in Halifax Harbour on the 25 July 1799.

Present

Robert Murray, Esqre., Commander of H.M. ship *Asia* and senior captain of His Majesty's ships and vessels at Halifax, President.

Captains

Israel Pellew	John E. Douglas
And^{w}. F. Evans	John Seater

The prisoner was brought into court and the evidence and audience admitted.

Read the order from George Vandeput, Esqre., Admiral of the Blue and Commander in Chief of His Majesty's ships and vessels in the River St. Lawrence, the coast of Nova Scotia, &^{c}., &^{c}., &^{c}., dated the 20th & directed to Robert Murray, Esqre., Captain of His Majesty's ship *Asia* and senior captain of His Majesty's ships in Halifax Harbour, to try Lieu^{t}. Geo^{e}. W^{m}. Blamey for behaving in a cruel, oppressive manner unbecoming the character of an officer on the evening of the 15th ins^{t}. in violation of the thirty-third Article of War.

The judge advocate then, in open court and before they proceeded to trial, administer'd the oath enjoin'd by Act of Parliament to the several members, after which, the president administer'd the usual oath to the judge advocate.

Captain Skipsey's letter and the letter of complaint from M^{r}. Edwd. Egan, Clerk of the *Pheasant*, was then read by the judge advocate as follows,[1] vizt.:

Pheasant, Halifax, 20th July 1799

… The enclosed is a letter from the clerk of His Majesty's sloop under my command, who recriminates upon the 1st lieutenant upon what pass'd on the 15th ins^{t}. …

Pheasant, Halifax Harbour, 18th July 1799

… I have to request you will be pleased to apply to the Commander in Chief for a court martial on M^{r}. George W^{m}. Blamey, First Lieutenant of

[1]The first is from Skipsey to Vandeput; the second is from Egan to Skipsey.

His Majesty's sloop under your command, for behaving to me in a cruel, oppressive manner unbecoming the character of an officer on the evening of the 15th ins^{t}. in violation of the thirty third Article of War. …

All the evidences were order'd to withdraw out of court, except M^{r}. Nisbit, who was sworn.

M^{r}. Nisbit sworn

Pros$^{r's}$ Question — Relate, as far as you know, M^{r}. Blamey's conduct to me on the evening of the 15th ins^{t}.

Answer — I was at a small distance on larboard gangway from the quarter deck. I perceived M^{r}. Egan talking to Lieu^{t}. Blamey, the subject I do not know. I heard M^{r}. Blamey call somebody up by the words. 'Come up here sir,' which made me take notice. I saw M^{r}. Egan come up the ladder when M^{r}. Blamey said, 'Go aft sir.' When he was going aft, M^{r}. Blamey called him to him again and what pass'd I do not know. I went to my duty on the forecastle; I saw M^{r}. Blamey and M^{r}. Egan talking together, but did not hear what was said. M^{r}. Blamey held his hand towards M^{r}. Egan (The evidence describing the manner.); M^{r}. Egan went below after that.

Pro^{r}. Ques^{n}. — In the manner that Mr. Blamey held his fist to me did it not appear to you that he was going to strike me?

Answer — I thought he was very angry with you.

Ques^{n}. — Upon your oath did you not see him shake me by the shoulder?

Answer — No.

M^{r}. Geo^{e}. Fred^{k}. Davis sworn.

Pro^{r}. Ques^{n}. — Relate, as far as you know, M^{r}. Blamey's conduct to me on the evening of the 15th ins^{t}.

Answer — I was on the quarter deck when Lieu^{t}. Blamey refused M^{r}. Egan leave to go on shore, saying he appear'd to him to be drunk. M^{r}. Egan said he was not so; M^{r}. Blamey order'd silence, for if he said a word, he wou'd drive his fist down his throat, and order'd him down below. Before M^{r}. Egan was off the quarter deck ladder, Lieu^{t}. Blamey order'd him up to go aft; before he had got aft, he called him forward to him and sent M^{r}. W^{m}. Davis into the gunroom for M^{r}. Money, M^{r}. Whitney and M^{r}. Collins. When they came up, M^{r}. Egan was walking aft; Lieu^{t}. Blamey order'd them to take notice of M^{r}. Egan's conduct.

Pro[r]. Ques[n]. Did you see Lieu[t]. Blamey strike me on the shoulder and shake me violently?

Answer No, I did not; I saw him put his hand on your shoulder and turn you round.

Ques[n]. Did you hear the orders that Lieu[t]. Blamey gave the sergeant of Marines relative to my confinement?

Answer Yes, I did.

Ques[n]. What were they?

Answer I heard Lieu. Blamey order the sergeant to take M[r]. Egan down to his cabin.

Ques[n]. Did Lieu. Blamey say, 'Confine him and do not let him come out of his cabin, nor let anybody see him on any pretext whatever?'

Answer I did not. I heard Lieu. Blamey order the sergeant not to allow him to come out of his cabin without leave from the commanding officer.

Court Do you know of any cruel or oppressive conduct in M[r]. Blamey towards the prosecutor on the even[g]. of the 15th July? If you do relate what it was.

Answer I know of none farther than I have related.

M[r]. William Davis sworn.

Prosecu[r]. Relate, as far as you know, M[r]. Blamey's conduct to me on the evening 15th ins[t] [*sic*].

Answer M[r]. Egan came up and ask'd leave to go on shore. M[r]. Blamey denied him and told him to go down to his cabin; and M[r]. Egan went down the ladder and ask'd if he was a prisoner 3 or 4 times. M[r]. Blamey called him up again and told him not to say a word and go aft. He went aft and said he wou'd sooner see himself damn'd first. M[r]. Blamey said, 'Not a word sir.' M[r]. Blamey sent me down to acquaint the officers. They came on deck. M[r]. Blamey desired them to see what state he was in. M[r]. Blamey call'd the sergeant & Quarter Master Bailey off the larboard gangway. M[r]. Blamey desired them also to see what state the prisoner was in. M[r]. Blamey took hold of M[r]. Egan by the shoulder and held his fist in his face. I went to the other side of the deck and heard no more till M[r]. Blamey order'd the sergeant to take him below.

Court Do you know of any cruel or oppressive conduct in M[r]. Blamey towards the prosecutor on the evening of the 15th July? If you do, relate what it was.

Answer	I know of none further than I have already described.

Rich^{d}. Cavanaugh sworn.

Pros^{r}.	Relate as far as you know M^{r}. Blamey's conduct to me on the evening of the 15th ins^{t}.

Answer	M^{r}. Blamey desired M^{r}. Egan to go down below to his cabin. M^{r}. Egan was going down and said some words, but I do not know what they were. M^{r}. Blamey call'd him up & said, 'Not a word, or I will knock your soul out.'

Pros^{r}.	Did you see M^{r}. Blamey hold his fist in my face?

Answer	No.

Pros^{r}.	Did you hear him say, 'Damn your blood you rascal. If you say another word, I shall ram my fist down your throat?'

Answer	No.

Court	Do you know of any cruel or oppressive conduct in M^{r}. Blamey towards the prosecutor on the evening of the 15th July? If you do, relate what it was.

Answer	Nothing, but that he wou'd knock his soul out.

M^{r}. James Nisbit again call'd in.

Court	Do you know of any cruel or oppressive conduct in M^{r}. Blamey towards the prosecutor on the evening of the 15th July? If you do, relate what it was.

Answer	No, not any.

The court, being clear'd to consider of a paper of remarks presented by the prosecutor, are of opinion that they ought not to be read.

Sergeant Escher sworn.

Court	Relate to the court as distinctly as you can the orders you rec^{d}. from Lieu. Blamey respecting putting M^{r}. Egan in confinement on the 15th July.

Answer	The first order I rec^{d}. on the even^{g}. of the 15th was on the quarter deck when Lieu. Blamey told me to take charge of M^{r}. Egan and confine him to his cabin and put a sentinel over him. After I had executed this order, I was called by M^{r}. Blamey, who order'd me not to let M^{r}. Egan have any communication with anybody, not that he shou'd be allow'd to go out of his cabin on any pretext whatsoever. To my recollection, about ½ an hour afterwards, M^{r}. Blamey call'd me again & order'd me to allow the prisoner to go to the round house with a sentinel over him, but he was to go to no other place.

This is all the orders I rec^{d}. on the evening of the 15 July.

Pros^{r}. After you had inform'd me of the orders you had rec^{d}. from Lieu^{t}. Blamey, did I not ask you if I was allowed to go to the round house and you say you did not know, but you wou'd go and ask?

Answer Yes.

Pros^{r}. Q. Was not a bucket sent down and did you not say that I was not to go out any more for the night, but must use that?

Answer Yes, I did.

Court Do you know of any cruel or oppressive conduct in M^{r}. Blamey towards the prosecutor on the evening of the 15th July? If you do, relate what it was.

Answer I thought the orders I rec^{d}. were proper as from a commanding officer and I do not think they were cruel or oppressive.

Lieu. Morrey sworn.

Court Do you know of any cruel or offensive conduct in M^{r}. Blamey towards the prosecutor on the evening of the 15 July? If you do, relate what it was.

Answer I do not know of any while I was on deck.

M^{r}. Whitney sworn.

Lieu^{t}. Blamey Did I on the evening of the 15th July behave towards M^{r}. Egan in a cruel, oppressive manner unbecoming the character of an officer?

Answer Not by any means.

M^{r}. Collins sworn.

L^{t}. Blamey Did I on the evening of the 15th July behave towards M^{r}. Egan in a cruel, oppressive manner unbecoming the character of an officer?

Answer Not by any means.

John Bailey sworn

Lieu^{t}. Blamey Did I on the evening of the 15th July behave towards M^{r}. Egan in a cruel, oppressive manner unbecoming the character of an officer?

Answer No, I did not see you behave any ways but as an officer.

The evidence in support of the charge being finished, the prisoner was called upon to make his defence; but, not having anything to offer, the court was clear & proceeded to deliberate upon and form the sentence.

The court, having carefully & deliberately weighed and considered the evidence produced (the prisoner not offering anything in his defence), were of opinion that the charges are not proved, but are malicious and ill-founded and the court do therefore honourably acquit the said Lieutenant George William Blamey of the charges against him; and he is hereby fully acquitted accordingly.

The court, being again open'd & audience admitted, the sentence was read accordingly. …

116A. *Warrant Appointing Henry Long Deputy Judge Advocate*

[ADM 1/5350]

By Robert Murray, Esquire, Captain of His Majesty's ship *Asia* and second in command of His Majesty's ships in Halifax Harbour.

Whereas Admiral Vandeput has directed me by an order dated the 20th July to assemble a court martial to try Lieu^{t}. George W^{m}. Blamey for behaving in a cruel, oppressive manner unbecoming the character of an officer on the evening of the 15th inst. in violation of the thirty third Article of War, 'And whereas by an Act passed in the 22nd year of the reign of King George the Second, entitled: *An Act for Amending, Explaining and Reducing into one Act of Parliament the Laws Relating to the Government of His Majesty's Ships, Vessels and Forces by Sea*, it is order'd that 'in the absence of the judge advocate and his deputy, the court martial shall have full power and authority to appoint any person to execute the office of judge advocate,'

I do, with the consent & approbation of the members of this court martial, hereby authorize & appoint you to execute the office of judge advocate on the above occasion, for which this shall be your warrant.

Given on board His Majesty's ship *Cleopatra*, where the court is assembled at Halifax, the 25th July 1799.

4

MULTIPLE OFFENCES

The courts martial presented in this, the fourth and final, chapter involve cases in which defendants were charged with more than one offence. These trials were fairly common. Indeed, almost 37 per cent of the men in the sample, 490 of a total of 1,149, stood accused of committing more than one crime. A few such trials arose from extremely serious episodes [119]. Some were the result of feuds, real or supposed slights and the like [122, 134]. Others were the consequence of attempts to throw the book at the defendant, such as charging a man with drunkenness and neglect of duty, since to be found guilty of drunkenness meant that the accused was deemed guilty of being so intoxicated as to be incapable of performing his duty [136, 141]. Still others were the outcome of a single act of indiscretion [120, 121, 123, 125, 128, 129, 136, 138, 139, 141, 144]. However, most adjudication of multiple offences simply occurred because the miscreant had been presumed by his accuser to have committed more than one crime, such as using a ship's boat to desert [117, 118, 124, 126, 127, 130, 131, 132, 133, 137, 140, 143, 145, 146, 147, 148].

117. *Court Martial of John Kent*

[ADM 1/5330]

Minutes of proceedings at a court martial held on board His Majesty's ship the *Defence* at Blackstakes on the 9th day of September 1793.

Present

James Cumming, Esqr., Captain of His Majesty's Ship *Resolution* and second officer in the command of His Majesty's ships and vessels in the river Medway and the buoy of the Nore, President.

Captains

John Henry	James Gambier
John Brown	Francis John Hartwell
George Wilson	Thomas West
William Clark	James Robert Mosse

Being all the captains of the post ships in the river Medway and at the buoy of the Nore, except Captain, the Honble Alexander Fr. Cochrane of His Majesty's Ship *Hind*, Captain John Maude of His Majesty's ship the *Leopard*, and Captain V. C. Berkley of His Majesty's Ship *Assurance*, who are absent with leave from the Lords Commissioners of the Admiralty.

The prisoner was brought into court and the evidence and audience admitted.

Read the order of the Right Honourable, the Lords Commissioners of the Admiralty, dated the 4th instant, directed to James Cumming, Esqr., Captain of His Majesty's Ship *Resolution* and second officer in the command of His Majesty's ships and vessels in the river Medway and at the buoy of the Nore, to try John Kent, Carpenter of His Majesty's Sloop *Scorpion*, for behaving with contempt and disobedience of orders to M^{r}. Emanuel Hungerford, the Second Lieut^{t} [of?] the said sloop, being then at sea.

Then the members of the court and judge advocate, in open court and before they proceeded to trial, respectively took the oaths directed by Act of Parliament made and passed in the 22nd year of the reign of His late Majesty King George the Second, entitled *An Act for Amending, Explain^{g} and Reducing into one Act of Parliament the Laws relating to the Government of His Majesty's Ships, Vessels and Forces by Sea*.

Copies of letters, referred to in and sent with the Admiralty order above mentioned, upon the subject of the said order, from the said Lieut^{t} Hungersford, Captn Ferris and Rear Admiral Gardner were read as follows:

> 'A copy of a letter received from Lieutenant Hungerford.'
> Sir, Whereas Mr. John Kent, Carpenter of His Majesty's Sloop *Scorpion* under your command, this day behaved to me with contempt and disobedience of orders,
>
> I have therefore to request you will be pleased to cause a court martial to try him for the above charges. …

All the evidences were then ordered to withdraw out of the court, except Thomas Moore, Gunner of His Majesty's Sloop *Scorpion*, who, being sworn, was desired by the court to relate what he knew.
Witness – Lieut^{t} Hungerford desired me to fix the boarding pikes round the driver boom; as the pikes were not of equal length, I asked Lieut^{t} Hungerford whether I should cut them so as to make them even. I was answer'd, 'You are to go about it immediately.' I immediately went to the prisoner, who was then caulking of the pinnace, for a saw; he told me there was a man sawing in the waist; he said he would be much obliged to me if I would get the saw from the man and do it myself, as he wanted to get done with that job. I got the saw from the man and began sawing the pike staves, when Allen, the Carpenter's Mate, came to me and desired I would let him have the saw and that he would give me another. I told him I would, provided he would give me a better; he then went and brought me a turning saw. I told him I was afraid I should break it. Lieut^{t} Hungerford heard what I said and said, 'Saw away. Damn the saw, break it and let it go to Hell.' I had scarce sawed one stave through, before I broke the saw; I immediately said to the prisoner, who was still caulking the pinnace, 'Mr. Kent, I have broke the saw. I am sorry for it, for it was Allen's fault more than mine by giving me such a ticklish tool.' The prisoner immediately answered, 'Damn my blood, you had better break everything I have; you are continually playing pranks with my tools.' Lieut^{t} Hungerford said, 'Let me have no words about the saw; it's broke. I'll either buy you another, or pay for it; do your work and be damn'd to ye, if you know how.' The prisoner made answer, 'It is not the value of the saw. Sir, it is the utility of it, for I have not got a saw in the ship that I can cut a log out with, for no man can saw with this tool now it is broke.' Lieut^{t} Hungerford said, 'Damn you Sir, come aft; you are damned impertinent. By God Sir, I'll send you to your cabin.' The prisoner answered, 'I don't think I am impertinent, Sir, I never was impertinent to any officer and I hope I never shall.' Lieut^{t} Hungerford s^{d}., 'By God, you shall not to me; by God, I'll send you to your cabin in half a shake. Go along Sir, and do your work; and let me not hear a syllable out of your lips.' The prisoner went to the pinnace and going by me, when I was standing by the barricade on the quarter

deck, said, 'Damn me this all your fault; you see how I have been served.' I was going to make a reply, but Lieut^{t} Hungerford said, 'Silence, don't let me hear another word; do your work and be damn'd to you, if you know how, for you have never done your work like a man, since you have been in the ship; nor, damn you, do I think you know how to do it.' The prisoner answered, 'It's well known by several officers in the ship that I both know my duty and have done it; and I have certificates from former captains to show, Sir, as good as any man, from captains of this ship.' Lieut^{t} Hungerford then said to me, 'M^{r}. Moore, take notice;' and then he said to the prisoner, 'I'll confine ye, by God Sir, come aft Sir. M^{r}. Port, go call the sergeant of the marines;' but, recollecting himself, said, 'Never mind, go aft Sir; I am damn'd, but I'll fix your business and consider yourself as a prisoner till I acquaint Captn Ferris of your behaviour.' The prisoner went aft. Lieut^{t} Hungerford said to me, 'M^{r}. Moore, take full notice of every word that has passed and mind and recollect it.' I answered, 'I have taken notice of every word that has passed, and shall take care to recollect it.' I heard no more.

Questions by Captn Ferris, 1st – Do you recollect Lieut^{t} Hungerford putting the prisoner in mind during this business of who he was talking to?

Answer – I don't recollect that Lieut^{t} Hungerford said any of them words.

Query 2nd – Do you recollect the prisoner's pulling off his hat whilst he was talking to the lieut^{t}?

Answer – I saw him move his hat.

Query 3rd – Do you recollect anything the prisoner [did?] at the time of moving his hat?

Answer – The prisoner answered 'Sir,' and made the replies I have mentioned before.

Court – On what day did the business happen?

Answer – On the 30th of April.

Court – At what time of the day did this happen?

Answer – Between 3 and 4 o'clock in the afternoon.

Court – Where was the ship?

Answer – At sea.

Court – Did you keep any minutes of this conversation to refresh your memory?

Answer – Yes; at the desire of Captain Ferris and Lieut^{t} Hungerford.

Court – Did you and the prisoner mess together?

Answer – We generally eat together, but do not mess together.

Court – Did the prisoner's manner during this conversation appear contemptuous or disobedient to Lieut.^{t} Hungerford?

Answer – I don't think it was.
Court to the prisoner – Have you any questions to ask the witness?
Answer – No.
Witness was then ordered to withdraw.
M^{r}. George Roe Port, a midshipman, was called into court and sworn.
The court desired him to relate what he knew of the business.
Witness – On the 29th of April 1793, between 3 & 4 in the afternoon, I was on the quarter deck; I heard Lieut.^{t} Hungerford speak louder than usual. As I was coming forward, he ordered me to attend to what the prisoner said, who I heard say that M^{r}. Moore had broke his saw and that he had no other to make logs with; Lieut.^{t} Hungerford said, he had before told him that he would pay him for it and desired him to hold his tongue and go and attend to his duty. He stood still and repeated that he had no other saw in the ship to make logs with. Lieut.^{t} Hungerford again told him to hold his tongue and attend his duty, that if he did not, he would confine him. The prisoner went on the gangway and Lieutenant Hungerford told him that if he did not pay every attention to his duty, he would confine him; the prisoner said he always had paid every attention to his duty, always should do so and could show certificates of his having done so. Lieut.^{t} Hungerford then called him on the quarter deck, desired him to go aft and to consider himself as doing no more duty. The prisoner went aft on the larboard side, abaft the mizzen mast. Lieut.^{t} Hungerford ordered him over on the starboard side; he came over and immediately sat down on the hen coop. Lieut.^{t} Hungerford ordered him to stand up, which he did with his body bent, owing to the poop awning being spread. The prisoner asked Lieut.^{t} Hungerford if he would have him come forward. Lieut. Hungerford told him, 'No.' He then got up on the top of the hen coop and stood strait up. Lieut.^{t} Hungerford ordered him to come down, which he did and went forward as far as the after part of the quarter deck awning and leant with his arm over the quarter deck railing and so continued till the captain came up. Lieut.^{t} Hungerford went off the quarter deck prior to the captain's coming on deck and (as I supposed) to complain of the prisoner.
Court – Did the prisoner's manner appear contemptuous or disobedient to Lieut.^{t} Hungerford?
Answer – When the prisoner spoke from the gangway, he spoke louder than usual.
Court – Were they not at a greater distance from each other when he spoke louder than in the previous part of the conversation?
Answer – They were.
Court – Did you or did you not hear the Lieut.^{t} or the prisoner make use of any oaths?

Answer – To the best of my recollection, I did not hear them.
Court – Was you present at the whole time of the conversation between the lieut[t]. and prisoner or only part.
Answer – Only part of it.
Court – What part of the time was you present?
Answer – The latter.
Court – Do you mean to say, the only instance of disobedience in the prisoner was not holding his tongue when ordered?
Answer – Was not holding his tongue and not immediately going to his duty?
Court – How long do you suppose it to have been between the lieut.[t] ordering him to hold his tongue and go to his duty and his passing across the gangway the first time?
Answer – Immediately.
Court – Did the prisoner continue speaking after being ordered by the lieut.[t] to be silent and do his duty of himself or was it in reply to the lieut.[t] only?
Answer – In reply.
Court – Did the prisoner, either upon the first or second time when the lieut.[t] told him to go off the deck and if he did not he wo[d] confine him, comply with the lieut[t].'s order?
Answer – He did the last time, but not the first.
Court to the prisoner – Have you any questions to ask this witness?
Answer – No.
The witness was then ordered to withdraw.

M[r]. William Marsh, a Midshipman, was then called into court and sworn.
Court – Did you hear the prisoner make use of any disrespectful language to Lieut.[t] Hungerford in the afternoon of the 29th of April last?
Answer – No.
Court – Did you observe the prisoner disobey any order given by Lieut.[t] Hungerford?
Answer – No.
Court – Did you observe, at any part of the time, the prisoner behave with contempt to Lieut.[t] Hungerford?
Answer – I am no judge.
Court to the prisoner – Would you wish to ask this witness any questions?
Answer – No.
Court – Have you anything to say or would you wish to call any witnesses?
Answer – No.

Court – Would you wish to ask the first witness, M[r]. Moore, any questions?
Answer – No.

The court was then cleared and proceeded to deliberate upon and form the sentence.
The court, having carefully and deliberately weighed and considered the evidences produced and the prisoner's answers, were of opinion that the charges had not been proved and that the prisoner was acquitted.
The court was again opened. The prisoner was again brought into the court and the audience admitted.
The above sentence and opinion of the court was then read to the prisoner and he was acquitted accordingly. …

117A. *S. Ferris to Edmund Dod*

[ADM 1/5330]
Scorpion at Sea (A copy) E. Hungerford
April the 29th 1793

A copy of a letter sent the Commodore Dod of H.M. Ship *Charon*

Scorpion in Carlisle Bay, Barbados

Lieutenant Hungerford, 2nd Lieut. of His Maj. sloop *Scorpion* under my command, having represented to me by letter of the 29th April last that M[r]. John Kent, Carpenter of the said sloop, had that day behaved to him with contempt and disobedience of orders,

I am therefore to request you will please [*sic*] to apply for a court martial on the said Mr. John Kent for the above charges. …

117B. *Gardner to Ferris*

[ADM 1/5330]

A copy of a letter received from Rear Admiral Gardner

Queen, Carlisle Bay, Barbados
24th May 1793

Captain Dod of His Majesty's Ship the *Charon*, having transmitted to me your letter of the 8 instant requesting he would apply for a court martial to try John Kent, Carpenter of the sloop under your command, on the charges exhibited against him by Lieut.[t] Hungerford, the second Lieut.[t] of the said sloop, I am to acquaint you that the court martial cannot take place at present, as His Maj. Service requires that your sloop should proceed from hence immediately, without waiting the return of the *Experiment*, on board which ship Lieutenant Hungerford (the prosecutor) now is, in consequence of the exchange allow'd of by Capt.[n] Dod. …

117C. *Ferris to Philip Stephens*

[ADM 1/5330]

A letter from Captain Ferris likewise referred to in, and sent with the Admiralty order above mentioned, was then read as follows, *viz[t]*.

Scorpion, at the Nore
August the 11th 1793

The enclosed are letters respecting M[r]. John Kent, Carpenter of His Majesty's sloop *Scorpion* under my command, who was confined on the 29th of April 1793 for behaving with contempt and disobedience of orders to Lieut.[t] Hungerford of the said sloop, then officer of the watch at sea.

I am therefore to request you will please to lay them before their Lordships in order that a court martial may take place, as I am acquainted with the charges, although Lieutenant Hungerford is not present. …

118. *Court Martial of John Bell, John Rodney, Stephen Murphy, John Long and David Connolly*

[ADM 1/5331]

Minutes of the proceedings at a court martial assembled on board His Majesty's ship *Vengeance* in Fort Royal Bay, Martinique for the trial of John Bell, John Rodney, Stephen Murphy, John Long and David Connolly, Seaman belonging to His Majesty's ship *Vengeance*, commencing the 11th of March 1794 and continued by adjournment to the 12th of the same month.

Present
Commodore Charles Thompson, President.

Captains

John Henry	John Brown
Chas. Edm^{d}. Nugent	George Grey
Henry Powlett	

The prisoners being brought into court and the evidence and audience admitted, an order was read from Sir John Jervis, Knight of the Bath, Vice Admiral of the Blue and Commander in Chief of His Majesty's ships and vessels employed and to be employed at Barbados and the Leeward Islands and the seas adjacent, and dated the 10th day of March 1794, directed to Charles Thompson, Esquire, Commodore and second in command &c., &c., &c., to assemble a court martial and try John Bell, John Rodney, Stephen Murphy, John Long and David Connolly, Seaman belonging to His Majesty's ship *Vengeance*, for having committed a most atrocious offence on the person of a Negro belonging to the estate of Monsieur Chapelle, named John, and for having beaten and robbed a mulatto by the name of Felix.

Then the members and judge advocate respectively took the oaths enjoined them by Act of Parliament.

Read the following letter from Captain Eliab Harvey of His Majesty's ship *Santa Margarita*:[1]

Station Monsieur River
March 10th, 1794.

… The five men named in the margin [John Bell, John Rodney, Stephen Murphy, John Long, David Connolly], having committed an atrocious offence on the person of a Negro belonging to the estate of Monsieur Chapelle, named John [*sic*],

They are also accused of having beaten and robbed a mulatto of the name of Felix, one of the evidence [*sic*] respecting the offence mentioned above.

…

Read also a letter from Captain Henry Powlett, Commander of His Majesty's ship *Vengeance*, contents as follows, viz.:[2]

[1]This letter is addressed to Captain Powlett.

[2]This letter is to Commodore Thompson, the second in command on the Leeward Islands Station at the time.

Vengeance, March 10, 1794
Fort Royal, Martinique

… Having received the enclosed from Captain Harvey, I am to request you will be pleased to apply to the commander in chief for a court martial on John Bell, John Rodney, Stephen Murphy, John Long and David Connolly, Seaman belonging to His Majesty's ship under my command for the crimes therein mentioned. …

	Then all the evidences were ordered to withdraw out of court, except Felix, a mulatto man, who was sworn.
Court	Do you know the prisoners?
Answer	Yes.
Court	Relate what you know concerning the charge against the prisoners.
Answer	The prisoners came in a party to my hut on Thursday night last about ten o'clock and the prisoner John Bell, who called himself commander of the party, threatened to kill me with a cutlass; he took his handkerchief and tied my hands and directed the prisoners David Connolly and John Rodney to murder me with their pikes. After binding me, John Long and Stephen Murphy, the prisoners, broke open my box and took there out four Dollars and four handkerchiefs; those two then beat the Negro women who were in the hut. Then I followed the party some distance and saw John Bell and David Connolly cut a Negro named John, belonging to Monsieur Chapelle, with their cutlasses because he would not give them rum; the other three pierced him with their pikes in many places. Then I followed the prisoners to the tent, where they went in; and I found them there next morning when I went to complain of them.

The evidence then withdrew.

Annie, a Negro woman, sworn.

Court	Do you know the prisoners?
Answer	I know this man (pointing out David Connolly). He came into my hut several nights ago, when I was in bed and caught hold of me. I pushed him away and some others who were with him gave me several blows with their fists in the head and back.

The evidence was ordered to withdraw.

Olive, Negro woman, sworn.

Court	Do you know the prisoners?
Answer	No; but some men came last Thursday night into my hut, which was adjoining to that of Felix, twas about midnight. They offered me some violence and I escaped from them. I heard Felix cry out and a noise like the breaking of bottles.

The evidence withdrew.

Lieutenant Duncan Forbes Mitchell of the *Vengeance* sworn.

Court	Do you know where the prisoners were on Thursday night last?
Answer	About half past nine that night they were in their huts. I saw them again in their huts at day break. Some time in the forenoon, a mulatto named Felix came and complained to Captain Harvey and said that some men belonging to a tent, which he pointed out, had robbed him and wounded another man about ten o'clock the night before. He was desired to return in the evening, when the people came from work, which he did. Myself and Captain Carpenter had the men drawn up, when the mulatto picked out John Long, Stephen Murphy and John Rodney, & at the same time described David Connolly by a scar in his cheek, whom he knew immediately as soon as he was shown him (as he happened then to be in confinement for drunkenness), as the persons who had committed the robbery and wounded the man. They were then put in confinement. Then I went up to see the black man, whom I found wounded, his right arm broke [*sic*] and the little finger of it cut nearly off; his head and body wounded in many places. He said he received those wounds from some seamen about ten o'clock the night before. The day following, the mulatto, Felix, returned with a handkerchief, which he said they had bound him with. On seeing 'J. B.' marked in the corner of the handkerchief, we called John Bell and the mulatto, Felix, then pointed him out as the commander of the party (The evidence then produced the handkerchief he alluded to, which is marked 'J. B.' in the corner.). Captain Harvey, on this, ordered him in close

	confinement, as he had been confined for drunkenness the day before.
Court	Did you examine the prisoners' clothes the next day?
Answer	I examined them the next evening and found no marks of blood upon them.
Prisoner Stephen Murphy	Do you recollect my answering you on your speaking to me on Thursday night, while you were in the tent, and what time was it?
Answer	I do remember your answering me about one or two in the morning, as near as I can guess.
Prisoner John Bell	What time did you ask for Isaac Hickman's blanket?
Answer	About nine o'clock in the evening.

The evidence then withdrew.

Here the prosecution closed and the prisoners were put on their defence, which they made in the following words:

Stephen Murphy	As soon as we came from work on Thursday evening last, we had our grog. I went into the tent and opened my blanket and spread it, when Daniel Eagan came in and got his blanket and we both lay down together till morning, when we were called up by M^r^. Mitchell. I lay next to M^r^. Mitchell but one and Daniel Eagan the other side of me.
John Bell	The mulatto says I was in a blue jacket. I have no such thing on shore. There is another man in the same tent, whose name is James Brune and the handkerchief might belong to him, as he has the same initials as me.
David Connolly	Thursday night last, I slept in the tent the whole night and I have evidence to prove it.
John Long	I have evidence to prove that I was in the tent all that night.

Daniel Eagan, Seaman belonging to the *Vengeance*, sworn.

Stephen Murphy	Did I not lie under the same blanket with you in the tent on Thursday night last?
Answer	Yes.
Court	Are you clear that the prisoner, Stephen Murphy, lay under the same blanket with you the whole night?
Answer	I firmly believe he did, as I never heard him get up and found him there in the morning. I awoke twice

	in the night to get a drink of water and found him there each time.
Court	What time did you awake?
Answer	As nearly as I can guess, the first time about midnight and the second near day break.
John Rodney	At the times you awoke, did you miss any of the men out of the tent?
Answer	No. In particular, the first time I had occasion to pass over them to get at the water.

This evidence then withdrew.

Isaac Hickman, Seaman of the *Vengeance*, sworn.

David Connolly	Do you know whether I was in the tent the whole night on Thursday last?
Answer	It was late when we left off work; about eight o'clock we came down and got our grog and supper all together. We all sat together at the tent door. We all went in and spread our blankets. I lay down and fell asleep; the prisoners were in the tent at that time and I awoke about an hour and a half afterwards, to the best of my judgement, and found the tent full and the tent holds no more than eight. I lay awake about half an hour.

This evidence withdrew.

James Brune, Seaman of the *Vengeance*, sworn.

John Rodney	Did I spread my blanket over you and me in the tent on Thursday night last?
Answer	Yes.
John Rodney	Did you miss me till the morning?
Answer	No.
John Rodney	Did you miss any of the prisoners out of the tent till the morning?
Answer	No. To the best of my knowledge, about twelve o'clock, M[r]. Mitchell awoke and called out to Murphy, who was outside the tent and answered him at that time; to the best of my belief, all the rest of the prisoners were in the tent.

John Mulholland, Marine of the *Santa Margarita*, sworn.

John Bell	Were you present in the guard house when the mulatto, Felix, came to point out some men he complained of?
Answer	I was. Bell, the prisoner, and two other men were in the guard house and, as far as I could understand, he

declared neither of those three men were of the party he complained of. Next day, John Bell, the prisoner was pointed out by the mulatto as one of the party.

This evidence withdrew and the court adjourned till eight o'clock tomorrow morning.

Wednesday 12 March

The court assembled again and proceeded on the trial.

Felix the Mulatto called in again and interrogated.

Court	Had you any light in your house to enable you to know the prisoners on seeing them again at the camp?
Answer	Yes, there was a light in my house when they came in.
Court	Did the prisoners put out the light on entering?
Answer	They struck me on the hand as I held the candle and put it out.

The prisoners having nothing more to offer in their defence, the court was cleared and the members proceeded to deliberate and pass sentence.

The court, having maturely and deliberately considered the evidence produced in the support of the charge, as well as what the prisoners had to offer in their defence, are of opinion that the charge is in part proved and therefore adjudged the said John Bell to receive three hundred lashes and the said John Rodney, Stephen Murphy, John Long and David Connolly to receive two hundred lashes each, on their bare backs with a cat of nine tails, alongside, or on board, of such ships, at such times and places, and in such proportions, as the commander in chief shall direct.

The court was then opened, audience admitted and sentence passed accordingly.

119. *Court Martial of Anthony Mark, alias Antonio Marco, John Elliot, Joseph Mansell and Peter Delany, alias Pierre D'Orlanie*

[ADM 1/5343]

Proceedings of a court martial held on board His Majesty's ship *York* at Mole S[t]. Nicholas on the 17th of March 1798 in pursuance of an order from Sir Hyde Parker, Kn[t]., Vice Admiral of the Red & Commander in Chief of His Majesty's ships & vessels employed and to be employed at & about Jamaica &[ca]., & addressed to George Bowen, Esq[re]., Captain of His Majesty's Ship *Carnatic* & third in Command.

The court being assembled, the order for the court martial & deputy judge advocate's warrant read, the court sworn; & evidences for the prosecution present, the following exact copies of letters and deposition were audibly & solemnly read.[1]

Diligence, Dona Maria Bay, S^{t}. Doming 27th October 1798.

... It is with inexpressible pain I inform you of the fate of His Majesty's ship *Hermione*, the uncertainty of which to me had long been a source of the most mortifying reflections, now ascertained beyond all doubt to have been such as mocks our warmest passions and remained for these times to produce [*sic*].

By the master of a Spanish schooner which I captured on the twentieth of October to windward of Altavella from La Guira bound to S^{t}. Domingo, I am informed that the *Hermoine* arrived at this latter place on the twenty-sixth of last month at three p.m., having been ran away with by her crew, who, not content with such atrocity, added to it the last, the most horrible of all human actions, a general indiscriminate slaughter of their captain & officers, excepting the surgeon and one of the master's mates; who concealed themselves; most of the Marines, six women, and in all about forty souls: it appears that Captain Pigot about the time of going to bed was murdered by his coxswain, who was nominated commander afterwards and in that character delivered her with all papers, signals & instructions to the Spanish governor on conditions of arrears of wages being paid, to be considered as Spanish subjects and not given up to the English when the war is over. The ship was carried round to Porta Cavallo unrigged and her guns and stores landed.

The last time that I saw her was at eleven o'clock at night on the twenty-second of September; we were both in chase of a privateer off Mona, the weather extremely dark & gloomy; and I apprehend it was at this time the abominable purpose was effected. It seems from the declaration which they gave in at La Guira, that there had been a correspondence held with the *Diligence*'s crew to this end; and that at all events had we not separated, they would have taken us along with them. The master of the schooner charged me to take care of myself when he related this. Having weighed this part of the information against the truly gallant, good tempered disposition of my people, I called them together and fairly related the case in all its circumstances. Never could any body of men be more shocked at hearing of such unexampled barbarism, nor ever was

[1]The first letter is from R. Mends to Vice Admiral Hyde Parker, who was Commander in Chief of the Jamaica Station at the time; the second is from John Crawley to Vice Admiral Parker.

indignation marked stronger than when they were told of the intention of breeding a mutiny in or of seizing the *Diligence* by force[;] to a man I was assured that had we been in company when this fatal catastrophe took place, that they would have retaken the *Hermione* or perished alongside of her.

The master of the Spanish schooner informs me that the mutineers are held in the utmost detestation at La Guira, the scorn and contempt of everyone; nor had, or were likely to meet with, any employment; their offer of going to sea on the ship under Spanish colours being rejected by the Governor. …

Valiant, Cape Nichola Mole, S^{t}. Domingo
8th March 1798

… In obedience to your signal on the 1st inst, after a five hours chase I came up with & captured *La Magicienne*, French corsair of sixteen guns and eighty-eight men, and it being hinted to me that James Mason, late Carpenter's Mate of His Majesty's ship *Hermione,* was one of the corsair's crew and was desirous of relating what he knew concerning the mutiny, murder, and piracy committed onboard His Majesty's ship *Hermione*, I thought proper to avail myself of the opportunity of bringing to light such an atrocious act and accordingly took the enclosed deposition (upon oath) in presence of Lieutenants Philpot and Hancock: also on mustering the prisoners, I discovered three of them to be deserters from His Majesty's ship *Aquilon*. …

Valiant at sea, 2nd March 1798.

The deposition of John[1] Mason, late Carpenter's Mate of His Majesty's ship *Hermione*, taken before the under mentioned officers, sayeth:

First

That he was onboard His Majesty's ship *Hermione* then cruising off the Mona, at the time the mutiny, murder & piracy were committed onboard the said ship.

Secondly

He further sayeth that Anthony Mark, John Elliot, Joseph Montell, and Peter Delany, now prisoners onboard His Majesty's ship *Valiant*, were actually onboard His Majesty's ship *Hermione* at the time of the above murder, mutiny & piracy.

[1]John Parker is referred to as James Mason earlier in the transcript.

Thirdly

That he knows the officers who were murdered, namely Captain Pigot; M$^{r.}$ Reid, 1st Lieut^{t}.; M^{r}. Douglass, 2nd Lieut^{t}.; Mr Faucher, 3rd Lieut^{t}.; Lieutenant of Marines; M^{r}. Martin, Boatswain; M^{r}. Smith, Mid^{n}; Captain's Clerke; M^{r}. Pacey, Purser; and M^{r}. Sampson, Surgeon; and these to the best of his knowledge, are the only persons who were murdered.

Fourthly

That the following persons are still prisoners at La Guira vizt. M^{r}. Southgate, Master; M^{r}. Price, Carpenter; M^{r}. Sall, Gunner; M^{r}. Casey Mid^{n} & William Moncrieff, the ship's cook.

Fifthly

That M^{r}. Turner, Master's Mate, took charge of His Majesty's ship *Hermione* shortly after the crew had got possession of her and conducted her into La Guira, where he transacted the terms for the crew, and was absolutely present when the Spanish commandant paid the seamen of His Majesty's ship *Hermione* twenty-five dollars each and is now at Porto Cavallo, never having been confined.

Sixthly

That M^{r}. ——— (name not recollected), Mid^{n}., is now onboard His Majesty's ship *Hermione* at Porto Cavallo and that John Crigh, Seaman; David Forrester, D^{o}.[;] Simon Holmes, Cook's Mate, and another seaman (whose name he does not recollect), late of the *Hermione,* are now onboard a French schooner privateer called *L'Espoir*, lying at S^{t}. Domingo. …

All the evidences were ordered to withdraw except:

Lieutenant Harris, of the *Queen*, & formerly of the *Hermione*, who being duly sworn:

Court Did you know any of the prisoners, as belonging to the *Hermione*?

Ans^{r}. Yes, since the 17th of June last, when I left her, they all belonged to her.

Court Specify their names.

Ans^{r}. John Mason, Carpenter's Mate, Joseph Montell, alias Mansell, a Main Topman; Antonio Marco, one of the afterguard; Pierre D'Orlanie one of the afterguard also; and John Elliot one of the Main Topmen.

Withdrew.

M^{r}. William Seal, Gunner of the *Valiant*, sworn.

Court Do you know any of the five men said to belong to the *Hermione*?

Ans^r^. Yes. John Mason and John Elliot, who belonged to the *Success* and were turned over into the *Hermione*, when Captain Pigot removed into and took the command of that ship. Withdrew.

John Kelly, a Seaman belonging to the *Hannibal* and formerly one of the *Hermione*'s, sworn upon the Cross as a Roman Catholic.

Court Look at the prisoners. Did you belong to the *Hermione*, and when?

Ans^r^. Yes and about five months ago.

Court Were you put onboard a prize when the *Hermione* was cruising in the Mona Passage, the last cruise?

Ans^r^. Yes to the best of my knowledge.

Court At the time you was put onboard the prize, was it the same time that the *Hermione* went a cruise with the *Diligence*.

Ans^r^. Yes.

Court Inform the court if you know the four prisoners and the other man, John Mason.

Ans^r^. Yes I know them as belonging to the *Hermione* when I was put onboard the prize. Withdrew.

Daniel Parry of the *Adventure* and late of the *Hermione*, sworn.

Court Inform the court at what time you went onboard the *Hermione*.

Ans^r^. I entered from a Guineaman, Captain John Wills, onboard the *Hermione,* the 30th July 1793 and left her the 4th of September 1797, when I was put onboard a prize schooner, the *Diligence* & *Hermione* in company.

Court Look at the prisoners and John Mason. Do you know those men?

Ans^r^. Yes I know that they belonged to the *Hermione,* when I was put onboard the prize, the 4th of September last.

This evidence ordered to withdraw.

The deposition (as already inserted in these minutes) of John Mason, late carpenter's mate of the *Hermione,* was now sworn to and signed by him, the said John Mason; and he was further sworn to give evidence against the prisoners.

Court Look at the prisoners. Do you know them personally?

Ans^r^. Yes.

Court Tell their names.

Ans^r^. Peter Delany, Antonio Marco, John Elliot, Joseph Montell.

Court On the night of the mutiny, murder and piracy committed onboard the *Hermione,* were these men actually onboard? And at what time did it take place to the best of your knowledge?

Ans^r^. They were actually onboard. I do not recollect the day, but the ship was cruising off the Mona Passage.

Court Were there any men of war cruising in company with the *Hermione*?

Ans^r^. Yes, the *Diligence* brig.

Court Inform the court what you know of the transactions relating to the mutiny, murders & piracy which took place onboard the *Hermione*?

Ans^r^. It was about ten o'clock at night. I was in my hammock and I heard the ship's company cheering and saying that 'the ship was their own'. I went up the main hatchway ladder and just as I got up in crossing the hatchway, the sentinel from the cabin door came running forward, ran right against me and set me backwards. There were no lights in the ship at that time that I could see. I went down between decks and saw the gunner sitting in his cabin, stripped and crying, & the carpenter likewise. The whole cry of the ship's company was 'hand them up', meaning the officers.

Court Was it down the skylight that is over the gun room where the officers messed?

Ans^r^. Yes. After this the carpenter and gunner went into the gun room to the master. At this time I went upon deck and heard Thomas Nash, a Forecastleman, call out, 'every man in his station about ship.' M^r^.Turner, a Master's Mate, conducted the ship to La Guira. He went on shore with a boat's crew, was two days absent and then brought a letter from the Spanish Governor, which contained a promise not to deliver up the ship's company to the English. Two or three days after this we went on shore and were all put into one house or barrack. The five officers, M^r^. Southgate, the Master, M^r^. Sall, the Gunner, M^r^. Price, the Carpenter, M^r^. Casey, who had been a Midshipman; and William Moncrieff, the Ship's Cook, were put into prison. James Bell, John Farrel, Thomas Nash and Robert M^c^Cready lent a hand to conduct the ship to La Guira.

Court Was Turner, the Master's Mate, considered as their captain or commander after the captain and lieutenants were murdered?

Ans^r^. Yes, he was.

Court Could you, from your situation, know who took the lead, and were the most active persons in murdering their captain & officers?

Ans^r^. I do not.

Court When you saw the gunner & carpenter go into the gun room to the master, did you see any of the other officers either dead or alive or anything else that particularly struck you attention?

Ans^r^. I did not.

Court You have stated in the former part of your evidence, that you heard the ship's company cry out, down the skylight over the gun room, 'Hand them up'. Did you observe any persons active in the gun room at that time in offering violence to any of the officers?

Ans^{r}. No, I did not.

Court Was there a light in the gun room at that time?

Ans^{r}. No.

Court How then could you see the master?

Ans^{r}. I did not see him, but heard the gunner say he would go in and see the master, having been hurt by a boy falling on him from the mizen top sail yard the day before.

Court Have you anything to relate to the court, respecting the transactions of the crew and what was done to the *Hermione* after she went to La Guira?

Ans^{r}. The ship was about a fortnight at La Guira and then she went to Porto Cavallo. Twenty-four of the ship's company went in her and I was one of the number. When we got to Porto Cavallo, there were six men kept in the ship to keep her clean and a short time after the Spaniards prest men to fit her out. At the time they heard of the English cruisers being off, they hauled her in under the fort and stripped her.

Court At the time the Spaniards were equipping the *Hermione* at Port Cavallo, who commanded her?

Ans^{r}. A Spaniard.

Court Were any Englishmen at that time onboard her as officers or part of her complement when considered as a man of war in the Spanish service?

Ans^{r}. Yes.

Court Relate who they were.

Ans^{r}. M^{r}. Turner was the former master's mate, but I don't know what rank he held.

Court Were there any others?

Ans^{r}. Yes. M^{r}. Wiltshire, who had been a Midshipman; the Boatswain's Mate, Th^{d}. Jay; Hans Christopher, a Seaman; Robert Stewart, a Seaman also; there were several more, but I do not remember their names.

Court Relate to the court, how you escaped and were [*sic*] you went to from Porto Cavallo?

Ans$^{r.}$ I went in a schooner to Curacao, and there I entered onboard *La Magicienne*, a French privateer.

Court Where and when did the prisoners at the bar enter onboard of this French privateer?

Ans[r]. John Elliot entered at Curacao, at the same time that I did.
Court Do you know when the other prisoners entered onboard *La Magicienne*?
Ans[r]. After we came in her to the harbour of S[t]. Domingo, they arrived there in a French privateer, *L'Espoir.* After they came in, they left *L'Espoir* and entered onboard *La Magicienne* and remained onboard until captured by the *Valiant*.
Court Upon what terms did you enter onboard *La Magicienne*?
Ans[r]. At twenty-four dollars advance and went upon shares.
Court Did the prisoners enter upon the same terms as you and receive the advance?
Ans[r]. Yes, they did.
Court Was there any money given to you and the rest of the *Hermiones* on your arrival at La Guira by the Spanish Governor?
Ans[r]. Yes, twenty-five dollars each man.
Court Were there any reasons given for advancing you this money?
Ans[r]. Yes.
Court What were the reasons?
Ans[r]. A man by the name of William Carter, one of the *Hermiones*, enquired of the Governor, for what purpose it was given him? He told him it was a present to subsist on.
Court How many days was the *Hermione* in possession of the crew, before they delivered her up to the Spanish Governor at La Guira?
Ans[r]. Five days to the best of my recollection.
Court Did M[r]. Turner or those people who acted as officers after the mutiny receive more money than you?
Ans[r]. I cannot tell. Withdrew

Lieutenant Harris of the *Queen* & late of the *Hermione* called to the general character of John Mason.

Court What was the character of John Mason, who has given in his deposition, while he was onboard the *Hermione* with you?
Ans[r]. He was a man of great credibility, sober, honest and attentive. Withdrew.

The evidence for the Crown here closed.

The prisoners separately and severally asked if they had any evidence to produce, or any defence to offer in their behalf. None.

Court cleared and retired.

Came to the following resolutions:

That the charges of mutiny, murder and piracy, running away with and delivering His Majesty's ship *Hermione* into the hands of the enemy and being found in arms against His Majesty are fully proved.

That the prisoners Anthony Mark, alias Antonio Marco, John Elliot, Joseph Mansell and Peter Delany, or Pierre D'Orlanie, do suffer death, by being hung by their necks, onboard such of His Majesty's ships as the commander in chief shall direct, until they are dead.

And as a further example and to deter others from committing or being accessory to such heinous crimes, that when dead, the bodies of the said prisoners be hung in chains upon gibbets, on such conspicuous points or headlands as the commander in chief shall think proper. And

That the said prisoners be sentenced to be so hung & gibbeted accordingly.

The Court opened.

Prisoners brought in and evidences present.

The Deputy Judge Advocate read the

Sentence

… And having heard the evidence produced to identify the persons of the prisoners, and very maturely & deliberately weighed and considered the several circumstances in the letters and paper above mentioned, and the prisoners having no evidence to produce, or anything to offer in their own defence, the court is of opinion that the charges of mutiny, murder and running away with His Majesty's said ship *Hermione* and delivering her up to the enemy and being found actually in arms against His Majesty and his subjects onboard *La Magicienne*, a French Privateer, are fully proved.

The court do therefore adjudge the said Anthony Mark, alias Antonio Marco, John Elliot, Joseph Mansell and Peter Delany, Alias Pierre D'Orlanie, to be hung by their necks until they are dead at the yard arms of such of His Majesty's ships and at such times as shall be directed by the commander in chief.

And as a further example to deter others from committing or being accessory to such shocking and atrocious crimes that when dead, their bodies be hung in chains upon gibbets on such conspicuous points or headlands as the commander in chief shall direct. And they are hereby sentenced to be so hung until they are dead and their bodies gibbeted accordingly. …

120. *Court Martial of Sampson Jefferies*

[ADM 1/5352]

Proceedings of a court martial held onboard His Majesty's ship *Hannibal* in Port Royal Harbour, Jamaica on Monday the 3rd February 1800 for the trial of Sampson Jefferies, Seaman of His Majesty's ship *Carnatic*.

Present
Edward Tyrrel Smith, Esq[r]. President

Captains	Robert Waller Otway	Samuel Peter Forster
	John Crawley	Francis Vesey
	Christopher Laroche	

M[r]. George Newell, Surgeon of the *Thunderer*, attended to inform the court that Captain Hardy was incapable from illness to attend his duty.

Prosecutor		*Prisoner*
Captain Loring	*evidences present*	*Sampson Jefferies*

The order for trial read:[1]

By Sir Hyde Parker, Kn[t]., Admiral of the Blue and Commander in Chief of His Majesty's ships and vessels employed and to be employed at and about Jamaica and the Bahama Islands &[ca]., &[ca]., &[ca].

Captain Loring of His Majesty's ship *Carnatic* having in his letter of yesterday's date represented to me that Sampson Jefferies, a Seaman belonging to the said ship, had been accused of making use of mutinous and seditious words to M[r]. Shoubel Kelly, Master's Mate of the said ship when onboard the prize brig *Minerva*, where he was sent to assist in navigating her and that he refused to do his duty when ordered by the said M[r]. Shoubel Kelly and requested I would be pleased to order a court martial to be held to try the said Sampson Jefferies for making use of mutinous and seditious words onboard the prize brig *Minerva* to M[r]. Shoubel Kelly on the third day of December last and for refusing to do his duty when ordered.

You are hereby authorized and required to assemble a court martial, and try the said Sampson Jefferies for making use of mutinous and seditious words, and refusing to do his duty, agreeable to the charges exhibited against him in M[r]. Shoubel Kelly's letter, which with Captain Loring's letter is herewith enclosed for your guidance and information.

Given under my hand on board His Majesty's ship *Queen* in Port Royal Harbour, Jamaica, this thirtieth day

[1]This order is to Captain Edward Tyrrel Smith.

of January one thousand eight hundred.

...

The Court duly sworn

M^r^. George Newell, Surgeon, *Thunderer*, sworn to Captain Hardy's inability to attend the court.

The charge read:[1]

Carnatic Port Royal Harbour
Jamaica 29th January 1800

... M^r^. Shoubel Kelly, Master's Mate of His Majesty's ship under my command having represented to me by letter of the 27th instant, which I herewith enclose for your information, that onboard the prize brig *Minerva*, which he had the charge of, on the third day of December last, Sampson Jefferies, a Seaman belonging to the *Carnatic*, who was put onboard to assist in navigating her, made use of mutinous and seditious words and refused to do his duty when ordered.

I am therefore to request you will be pleased to order a court martial to try the said Sampson Jefferies for the above offences. ...

Mr Shoubel Kelly's letter of complaint read:

Carnatic Port Royal Harbour
27th January 1800

... Sampson Jefferies, Seaman belonging to His Majesty's ship under your command, having on the third day of December last whilst onboard the Spanish prize brig *Minerva* entrusted by you to my charge behaved in a mutinous and seditious manner and to the best of my belief with an intention to take the vessel from me, in consequence of which behaviour stating at my arrival in Port Royal Harbour the circumstances to Captain Hardy who advised me to send him onboard the *Abergavenny* to be confined in irons. I am to request you will be pleased to apply to the commander in chief for a court martial to try the said seaman, for the said mutinous and seditious behaviour accordingly. ...

M^r^. Shoubel Kelly, Master's Mate, *Carnatic*, sworn

Prosecutor Relate to the Court, the expressions the prisoner made use of on the 3rd of December last onboard the prize brig *Minerva*, which you had the command of, and his behaviour

[1]The letter containing the charge is from Captain John Loring to Admiral Parker; the second is from Shoubel Kelly to Captain Loring.

	from the time of his leaving the *Carnatic* to your taking him onboard the *Abergavenny*.
Answer	The brig *Minerva*, which I had the charge of, was captured by His Majesty's ship *Carnatic* on the 3rd day of December last. At half past one (p.m.) I desired the people to set up the rigging. Sampson Jefferies, the prisoner, told me he had not smoked his pipe. I desired him to go to his duty immediately; he told me he was neither onboard the *Carnatic* nor yet at Port Royal. I asked if he meant to take the vessel from me? He told me he was at sea and this was the only time to take the advantage for, he said, he did not care what he said or did on board a brig. In the course of the passage he used to light his pipe and sit over the hatchway under which was 15 or 1600 w^{t}. of powder, which I desired him several times not to do.
Court	What time of the day was it this discourse happened?
Answer	At half past one as near as I can guess.
Court	Was the prisoner perfectly sober at the time?
Answer	Yes, I believe he was.
Court	Was there any persons near you that heard the conversation and who were they?
Answer	Yes, John Anderson, the Quarter Master, John Runthwaite and Samuel Dobitoe.
Court	Relate any further conversation that passed at the time or any altercation that took place.
Answer	I ordered the prisoner the second time to go to his duty when he went and at this time he made use of the expressions before stated.
Prosecutor	Did you ask Anderson, the Quarter Master, if he was concerned with the prisoner in making an attempt to take the vessel from you and what was his reply?
Answer	Yes, and he said he was not concerned in it.
Prosecutor	Did he say anything more?
Answer	He said he was not concerned in it & should be very sorry to be so.
Court	How did you know that the prisoner meant to take the vessel from you?
Answer	I don't know that he meant to take the vessel from me, but it was the best of my belief.
Court	What reason had you to believe so?
Answer	From the words that he made use of to me, which I have mentioned before.

Court Did your suspicion arise from those words only?

Answer Only from those words.

Court Did he make use of any other seditious or mutinous words but what you have before mentioned?

Answer Not on that day. (M^{r}. Kelly withdrew)

John Anderson, Quarter Master, *Carnatic*, sworn

Prosecutor Relate to the Court the expressions the prisoner made use of on the 3rd December last onboard the prize brig *Minerva*.

Answer On the 3rd of December last, at 12 o'clock I was sitting at dinner on deck when M^{r}. Kelly told me to get a pull of the lee main rigging after dinner. He inquired of me if I thought the people had had their time. I went over to the starboard side of the main deck and asked them if they had had their dinners; they said yes. I desired them to come over and get a pull of the lee main rigging. Samuel Dobitoe got up and came over with me and got the tackle to set the rigging up; the rest did not start. M^{r}. Kelly went over and spoke rash to them. They came over to the main rigging. Sampson Jefferies said he had not time to smoke his pipe; he would rather be onboard his own ship and that now was the time to speak; 'we are at sea and not in harbour. When we was in harbour in the last prize you gave me liberty to go on shore; I got drunk and you put me onboard the *Abergavenny*.'

Court Did you at any time on the 3rd December last hear any seditious or mutinous words come from the prisoner?

Answer No.

Court Did you suppose from the prisoner's conversation & conduct on the 3rd Decem^{r} that he had any intention of taking the prize from M^{r}. Kelly?

Answer I do not think he could have any intention at all to do so.

Court Was you asked any question by the prisoner upon the subject of taking the vessel or any discontent?

Answer Not any.

Court Were you not asked by M^{r}. Kelly if you had any intention of joining the prisoner in taking the prize?

Answer No.

Court Did he never speak to you upon the subject?

Answer Yes. He spoke to me about Jefferies, that he thought he could depend upon me and two or three more that were in the brig; he said he might depend on me to stand by him and added that I should be very sorry if any such thing as a mutiny should happen and that I would stand by him to the last drop of my blood. Mr. Kelly replied he was very glad.

(John Anderson) withdrew.

Samuel Dobitoe, Seaman, sworn

Prosecutor — Relate to the Court the expressions the prisoner made use of on the 3rd December last onboard the prize brig *Minerva.*

Answer — On the 3rd or 4th of December last, I don't know which exactly, we had all been at dinner about half past one. Mr. Kelly ordered us to set the lee main rigging up. Jefferies, the prisoner, replied it was not his watch upon deck, that he thought the watch on deck were enough to set it up and added that he and Mr. Kelly had words when in harbour last time, but as they were now at sea, now is our time.

Court — Did you at any time on the 3rd of December hear any seditious or mutinous words come from the prisoner?

Answer — No more than what I have related.

Court — Was the prisoner in liquor?

Answer — He was perfectly sober. (Dobitoe withdrew)

John Runthwaite, Seaman, sworn

Prosecutor — Relate to the Court the expressions the prisoner made use of on the 3rd of December last onboard the prize brig *Minerva.*

Answer — About one o'clock that day, the prisoner Jefferies rose up after eating his dinner and went to the caboose to light his pipe. Mr. Kelly said, 'Jefferies, it is no time for smoking now.' Jefferies replied, 'For why Mr. Kelly?' Mr. Kelly told him to get the main boom tackle up and down to set the larboard main rigging up. Jefferies said there are four in the other watch and that he thought three would be enough without keeping all hands. Mr. Kelly asked him what he meant by that. 'Do you mean to take the brig from me? If you do, I'll go below.' Jefferies made answer and said 'No Sir, God forbid.' And this is all that I can recollect that happened between them then.

Court — Was the prisoner ordered to set the main rigging up before he arose to light his pipe?

Answer — Not that I heard. Runthwaite withdrew

The evidence for the Prosecution closed.

The prisoner was called on for his defence.

Defence read by the Judge Advocate:

… It is with the utmost concern that I stand before you accused of using mutinous and seditious words to M[r]. Kelly, my officer, and refusing to do my duty when ordered. But with respect to a design of taking the command of the brig from him, I declare most solemnly I never had any such intention. I acknowledge some words escaped me for which I am very sorry and hope the gentlemen of the court will consider my inexperience and ignorance and extend their clemency to me. I have been five years in the service and never had a complaint made against me by any officer. …

Daniel George, Seaman, sworn

Prisoner Did you on the 3rd December last hear me make use of any mutinous or seditious words to M[r]. Kelly.

Answer No.

Court Was you upon deck at the time the men were ordered to set the lee main rigging up?

Answer No.

The prisoner, having no other evidence, requests Captain Loring to speak to his character.

Captain Loring: The prisoner has a very fair character in the ship in so much that he has been three times in a prize and I never had a complaint before against him.

Lieutenant Hunt: During the time that I have belonged to the *Carnatic*, the prisoner Jefferies has been a very quiet, sober and attentive man and obedient to command.

M[r]. Stevenson the Gunner: I have ever known the prisoner to be a sober and peaceable man and ever attentive to his duty. He has been in the *Carnatic* and *Colossus* with me between four and five years.

The trial closed.

The court retired to deliberate and came to the following resolutions:

That the charge of using seditious words is proved, but do acquit him of any mutinous intentions. That in consideration of the very good character given him by his officers, he be adjudged to receive only fifty lashes on his bare back with a cat of nine tails, onboard the *Carnatic* at such time as the commander in chief shall direct.

The court opened, prisoner brought up, evidences present.

The following sentence was pronounced by the Judge Advocate:

… The court is of opinion that the charge of using seditious words is proved, but do acquit him of any mutinous intention. In consequence of which and the very good character given him by his officers, the court do adjudge him to receive only fifty lashes on his bare back with a cat of nine tails, onboard His Majesty's ship *Carnatic* at such time as the commander in chief shall think proper to direct.

And he is hereby sentenced to be so punished accordingly. …

121. *Court Martial of Lieutenant John Spinney*

[ADM 1/5354]

Minutes of the proceedings of a court martial held onboard His Majesty's ship the *Royal Sovereign*, in Torbay the 27th of October 1800 in pursuance of an order from the Right Honourable the Lords Commissioners of the Admiralty, dated the 20th October 1800, to try Lieutenant John Spinney of the Marines, belonging to His Majesty's ship the *Captain*, for having behaved on the 1st of August 1800 in an unofficer-like manner, made a disturbance in the gun room, quarrelled with one of the master's mates and struck the gunner and one of the midshipmen and for having behaved in a disrespectful manner to Captain Sir Richard John Strachan, Bart, Commander of the said ship, by not paying attention when he spoke to him and when going to confinement, acted in such an outrageous manner, as to make it necessary to take his pistols and offensive weapons from him.

Present

Sir Henry Harvey K.B., Vice Admiral of the White, and second officer in the command of His Majesty's ships and vessels in Torbay, President.

Sir Andrew Mitchell, K.B. Vice Admiral of the Blue	Sir Charles Cotton, Bar^{t}., Rear Admiral of the Red
Cuthb^{t}. Collingwood, Esqr., Rear Admiral of the White	Sir Robt. Calder, Bar^{t}, Rear Admiral of the Blue
Captain Thos. M. Russel	Capt. Edwd. Thornborough
Capt. Sampson Edwards	Capt. Sir W^{m}. G. Fairfax
Capt. Thomas Totty	Capt. Earl Northesk
Capt. James Vashon	Capt. Thos. Wells

The prisoner being brought into court, attended by the provost martial and all the witnesses and every other person that thought proper being admitted, the court was sworn, agreeable to the Act of Parliament, and the order for assembling the court was first read, together with a warrant from the president appointing M^{r}. John Smith Tracey to officiate as judge advocate on the occasion; the following letter was then read, containing the charges against the prisoner.[1]

Captain, off Brest, 29th Augt. 1800

… Lieutenant Hennah, the senior officer of His Majesty's ship under my command, having represented to me in the afternoon of the 1st instant that Lieu^{t}. John Spinney of the Marines had behaved in an unofficer-like manner, making a disturbance in the gun room, quarrelling with one of the master's mates and striking the gunner and one of the midshipmen, I directed he should be confined: I have to add that he behaved disrespectfully to me, in not paying attention while I spoke to him and, when going to confinement, acted in such an outrageous manner, as to make it necessary to take his pistols and offensive weapons from him and on the following night was so troublesome, as to cause the gunner to complain to the officer of the watch of his conduct.

I request, my Lord, that Lieutenant Spinney may be brought to a court martial for the before mentioned offences. …

All the witnesses were now ordered to withdraw, except Lieutenant Willm. Hennah, who was sworn and examined as follows:

Prosecutor Relate to the court what you informed me of in the cabin respecting the prisoner and also what passed in consequence of the order I then gave you upon the quarter deck.

Answer On Friday the 1st of August, M^{r}. Foreman, the Master's Mate, complained to me on the quarter deck, that Lieu^{t}. Spinney was very quarrelsome and troublesome in the gun room, that there was no staying below; I desired him to wait a few minutes, till the captain had dined, when I would make him acquainted with the circumstance. In about two minutes more M^{r}. Collet, the Gunner, made a similar complaint against Lieu^{t}. Spinney and that he had struck him with a German flute. I gave him the same answer, desiring him to wait a few minutes. M^{r}. Collet and M^{r}. Young, Midshipmen, likewise made a complaint of the prisoner and that he had struck M^{r}. Young. Soon after this Captain Mortimer of the Marines came on the quarter deck and told me there was a great noise in the gun room and pistols going to work and that he was afraid some mischief would ensue unless some

[1]This letter is from Captain Sir Richard Strachan to Admiral the Earl of St Vincent.

person went down to stop it. I immediately went down to the gun room, where I found M^r^. Spinney and M^r^. Foreman, the Master's Mate, quarrelling and very high words passing. I ordered them to desist, or I would acquaint the captain; Lieu^t^. Spinney then went the other side of the gun room and said something to M^r^. Collet, the Gunner, which I did not distinctly hear, and soon after struck him; I then returned to the quarter deck, and immediately made it known to the captain in his cabin and he gave me directions to put Lieu^t^. Spinney under confinement. I acquainted Lieu^t^. Spinney with the captain's orders and he was going down the quarter deck ladder when Sir Richard came out, who desired Lieu^t^. Spinney to come on the quarter deck again, that he had something to say, but Lieu^t^. Spinney still persisted in going down, saying he was ordered into confinement. M^r^. Martin, one of the Midshipmen, was then directed by the captain to acquaint Lieutenant Spinney that he wanted to speak to him and he returned to the quarter deck and said he threatened to blow his brains out; the captain then ordered me and Lieutenant Courtenay to go down and take Lieu^t^. Spinney's arms from him and place a sentinel over him, which, as soon as I had done, I reported to the captain.

Prosecutor Did it appear to you that it was necessary to take the arms from Lieutenant Spinney for fear he should do some mischief to himself or some other person?

Answer Yes, it did. Lieutenant Spinney appeared to me to be in a state of delirium at the time and to be worked up into a fit of rage and frenzy, that he seemed not to know what he was about at the time.

Court What did the general conduct and behaviour of the prisoner appear to you to be previous to the 1st of August?

Answer I have seen him frequently in those kind of passions and rage and it appeared to me to be the effect of mental derangement.

Lieutenant Hennah was now desired to withdraw and M^r^. William Collet, the Gunner, called and sworn and examined as follows.

Prosecutor Relate to the court the circumstance of Lieutenant Spinney's having struck you, as well as what you know respecting the other part of the charges.

Answer On the 31st of July Lieutenant Spinney was walking the starboard side of the gunroom at different times during the day, making use of provoking speeches, which I conceived to stir up a quarrel with me. I, that day, took no notice of it. On the following day he also came into the gunroom, passed my cabin door and behaved in like manner. He called me a blackguard old gunner, then pointed at me; he had in his left hand a flute. I was sitting at the gunroom table when he came and spit in my face; he up with the flute and made a blow at me in the face which I fended off with my left hand, which broke the flute to pieces and very much bruised my finger. I went on the quarter deck and reported his conduct to M^{r}. Hennah, the First Lieutenant, who told me that Sir Richard was at dinner and, as soon as he had dined, he would acquaint him of it. I afterwards came down into the gunroom and sat in the same place. Then the Master's Mate, M^{r}. Foreman, came down to get his tea and Lieutenant Spinney began to quarrel with him and strip'd his waistcoat and tore open his shirt to fight him in a great passion. After that, Lieut^{t}. Spinney went to his cabin and wanted to fight with M^{r}. Foreman there with pistols and pointed one of the pistols out of the cabin at M^{r}. Foreman. I went on deck to the first lieutenant and related the circumstance and he came down into the gunroom and talking to M^{r}. Foreman and I was sitting in the same place. Lieut^{t}. Spinney was walking the same side, he had his left fist clenched and struck me under the right eye. I beg'd M^{r}. Hennah to take notice of it and the rest of the gentlemen. I put my hand to my face and felt it was swelled and got my hand full of blood where he had cut me (at the same time showing a bloody handkerchief).

Prosecutor Relate the circumstance of your complaining to the officer of the watch the night after.

Answer Lieutenant Spinney was walking in the gunroom before my cabin door, making use of threatening speeches, that when he went on shore he would buy a horsewhip to whip his friends or something to that purpose.

Prosecutor Relate to the court what you have observed of the prisoner's general conduct and behaviour during the time you have been in the ship with him.

Answer I never saw anything amiss of him before this affair happened with me, except when he quarrelled with me because I turned him out of my mess.

Court Did it appear to you at the time he struck you that the prisoner laboured under any mental derangement?

Answer	I used to think at times that the prisoner was a little deranged and particularly so on that evening that he struck me.
Court	How did the dispute between M[r]. Foreman and the prisoner begin, when the latter came down into the gunroom?
Answer	It appeared to me from some provoking speeches the prisoner made use of to the gentlemen of the mess and M[r]. Foreman took it up.
Court	Did you ever observe in the prisoner any of this outrageous conduct before dinner?
Answer	No, chiefly in the afternoon and evening.
Court	Did he take his glass freely at dinner?
Answer	He took his allowance and sometimes more.
Court	Did you ever see the prisoner drunk?
Answer	No.
Court	Was the prisoner accustomed to drink to an excess?
Answer	No.

Prisoner's Defence

… It is not my intention to trespass upon your patience by entering into any exculpation of my conduct or to attempt to refute the charges that have been preferred against me; on the contrary, I acknowledge myself to be greatly in fault, for which I am most sincerely and heartily concerned and truly sorry. Unhappily for me, I possess a warmth of temperament and irascibility of disposition, which I cannot control when my passion is roused or provoked. I am then no longer master of my actions or conduct; such unfortunately was the case on the 1st of August last. I have therefore to entreat you gentlemen to have compassion on my infirmity; and that you will take into your consideration my long confinement and ill health, the distress and anxiety of mind that I feel at being brought to a public trial after having been flattered with an idea that it would have been dispensed with and that you will, in your goodness, represent my case to the right Honourable the Lords Commissioners of the Admiralty that I may be allowed to retire upon half-pay, as I have no other means of support. And I have served His Majesty seventeen years. …

Cap[t]. Sir Richard John Strachan, speaking of the prisoner's character:

I think, in general, that he has been a very attentive officer, except in the circumstance now before the court, and he has been long in confinement, ever since the first of August, and I think he is subject to violent passions when he has no command of himself and I certainly think, when he is aggravated, that he labours under mental derangement. And I think Lieu[t]. Spinney has reason to expect that he would have been allowed to retire on his half-pay, having by my consent and approbation applied to the commander and chief to solicit that favour from the Admiralty; but in consequence of the order having been given out, their Lordships said that the court would be able to judge how far he was entitled to that indulgence.

Captain Mortimer of the Marines, speaking of the prisoner's character:

During the time that Lieutenant Spinney has been onboard the *Captain* I have always observed that he has discharged his duty with diligence and punctuality and I feel myself much indebted to him for his attention to the discipline of the party. I think at times he is subject to a degree of mental infirmity.

The prisoner, having no other person to call or anything more to say in his defence, all persons were ordered to withdraw and the court, having very maturely and deliberately considered the same, was of opinion that the charges was proved, the said Lieu^t^. John Spinney was therefore sentenced to be dismissed from full pay in His Majesty's service and rendered incapable of ever serving His Majesty, his heirs or successors in any military capacity, but in consideration of circumstances to retain his half pay.

The sentence being drawn up in the usual form and signed by the court, all persons were again admitted and the prisoner brought in, the judge advocate, by the direction of the president, pronounced the same and the court broke up. …

122. *Court Martial of William Cuming*

[ADM 1/5356]

Minutes of the proceedings of a court martial assembled on board His Majesty's ship *Russell*, at anchor, off the Island of Bornholm, the 22 day of June 1801 for the trial of William Cuming Esqr., Captain of His Majesty's said ship, for a breach of the second and thirty-third Articles of War.

Present

Thomas Totty Esqr., Rear Admiral of the Blue, &c^a^., &c^a^., &c^a^., President

Captains

John Dilkes
Sir Thos. Williams, K^t^.
Sir Fra^s^. Laforey, B^t^.
Robert Lambert
James Brisbane
Charles Tyler
George Duff
Saml. H. Linzee
Arch^d^. C^d^. Dickson

The prisoner being brought in Court and the evidence and audience admitted, the order of the Right Honourable Lord Viscount Nelson, KB, Vice Admiral of the Blue and Commander in Chief of a squadron of His Majesty's ships and vessels employed and to be employed on a particular service, bearing date the 15th day of June 1801 and directed to Thomas Totty, Esqr., Rear Admiral of the Blue, &c^{a}., &c^{a}., &c^{a}., to try William Cuming Esqr., Captain of His Majesty's ship *Russell*, on charges exhibited against him by Lieutenant Nesbit Josiah Willoughby of the said ship, for a breach of the second and thirty-third Articles of War and the president's warrant, appointing M^{r}. Thomas Crispe to officiate as judge advocate at the said trial, were read.

Then, the judge advocate, in open court, administered the oath to the members and, before the president, took the oath of secrecy himself, in due form of law.

The charge, contained in a letter from Lieutenant Nesbit Josiah Willoughby of His Majesty's ship *Russell*, addressed to Thomas Totty Esqr., Rear Admiral of the Blue, &c^{a}., &c^{a}., &c^{a}., was then read and was as follows, *vis^{t}*:

His Majesty's ship *Russell*,
Off Bornholm, June 9th, 1801

… I have to request you will be pleased to order a court martial on the conduct of W^{m}. Cuming, Esqr., Captain of His Majesty's ship *Russell*, for a breach of the second Article of War, in being guilty of uncleanness, and of the thirty-third, having conducted himself toward his officers in an unofficerlike and oppressive manner, in having struck or *forcibly shoved* them while in the execution of their duty, particularly Lieutenant Samuel Bateman upon the twelfth of March 1801 and for having made use of infamous & ungentlemanlike language, damning, blasting and threatening to cut them down publicly before the ship's company and at periods when they were using every exertion to forward His Majesty's service and particularly for charging me with falsehood upon the seventh of June 1801; in support of which charges, I shall produce the most substantial evidence. …

All the evidence were then ordered to withdraw, except John Sharpless, Seaman, who was sworn.

Prosecutor	Relate to the Court an order which Captain Cuming gave you upon the 20th of last May or thereabouts.
Witness	I was sent down off the poop in a hurry to hoist the jib. I happened to spit out upon the poop and Captain Cuming made me go back and lick it up.

Court Was the order for not spitting about the decks publicly made to the ship's company prior to this?

Answer I never heard it.

Prisoner You have said it was on the poop, are you clear in what you have sworn to?

A. Yes.

P^{r}. Was it on the poop ladder or at the bottom of it?

A. No, on the brink of the poop on the larboard side.

The Prosecutor, having no further question to put to the witness, he was ordered to withdraw.

W^{m}. Ja^{s}. Niven, Mids^{n}., called in and sworn.

Prosec^{r}. Relate to the Court the substance of an order which Captain Cuming gave to John Sharpless, upon the 20th of May last.

Witness He gave him an order to lick up the spittle which was on the poop.

P. Did you see him lick it up?

A. Yes.

Court How long have you been a midshipman in the *Russell*?

A. About twenty months.

C. Do you know whether any order was ever given for the men not to spit about the decks?

A. Yes, I have heard it given.

C. In what way was that order given?

A. Publicly to the ship's company.

C. Did you ever hear the captain declare, after having given the order, that no one should spit upon the deck, that the next person he found committing so nasty an act, that he (the captain) would make that man lick it up?

A. No.

The prosecutor, having no further question to ask the witness, nor the prisoner any, ordered to withdraw.

Lieu^{t}. Geo. Crespin, of Marines, called in and sworn.

Prosecutor Relate to the court the conversation that took place between you & Captain Cuming upon the poop, on or about the 2nd of last April.

Witness Captain Cuming had issued an order for the great guns to be exercised. I was on the poop instructing the Marines in the use of the great guns. Captain Cuming came up and said, unless the guns were better pointed, it would be of no more use than to fart at them, meaning the enemy.

P. Did you see the people laugh?
A. All that were within hearing smiled.
P. Was you hurt by the remark?
A. I certainly was. It hurt my feelings.
Court What was it hurt your feelings in that remark?
A. It being an ungentlemanlike expression, particularly before the men.
C. Were there any ladies present at the time?
A. None.
C. As you felt yourself so much hurt, did you conceive the remark was particularly made to you?
A. No.

The prosecutor had no further question to ask the witness, nor the prisoner any, withdrew.

Sergeant Rob[t]. Johnson, Marines, called in, and sworn.

Prosecutor Did you ever hear Captain Cuming treat Lieutenant Crespin in an unofficerlike manner?
A. No.
P. Did you hear Captain Cuming say to Lieutenant Crespin he might as well fart as point his guns as they were?
A. He said so on the poop, but I did not conceive it was meant to Lieutenant Crespin particularly.
Prisoner Do you remember the cannonades on the poop ever to be exercised but on a general exercising day?
A. No.

Witness withdrew.

W[m]. Peter Burn, Master, called in and sworn.

Prosecutor Has Captain Cuming very forcibly shoved you whilst in the execution of your duty?
A. Yes, he has shoved me.
P. Did he hurt your feelings by such an unofficerlike conduct?
A. Yes, very much.
P. Relate to the Court the circumstances of his thrusting his speaking trumpet against your side and shoving you with it while in the execution of your duty.
Witness I do not recollect exactly the time, but one night when I was going to execute an order of Captain Cuming and going down the midship ladder, Captain Cuming thrust his speaking trumpet against my right side. I did not stop, but

went immediately forward and put the order into execution.

Court — What was the order?

A. — I do not recollect.

C. — How do you know you did execute the order when you cannot recollect what it was?

A. — I think it was something respecting the cable.

P. — Have you ever seen Captain Cuming shove Lieutenant Samuel Bateman in an unofficerlike manner?

A. — I have seen Captain Cuming shove Lieutenant Bateman and will relate one circumstance. One day near the larboard gangway, I saw Captain Cuming run forward and appeared to shove Lieutenant Bateman, who jumped into the waist and afterwards said that he was obliged to do so to prevent him from falling.

Court — Did Lieutenant Bateman say so in presence of the prisoner?

A. — No.

Prosecr. — Did you consider Captain Cuming's oppressive and unofficerlike conduct to Lieutenant Bateman and yourself degraded and lessened your consequence in the eyes of the petty officers and ship's company?

A. — Yes, certainly it must, as it was observed by some of the young gentlemen who were on the poop and afterwards spoke of it as Mr. Willoughby told me and they told me also themselves.

P. — Have you ever heard Captain Cuming, in carrying on duty, express himself in an unofficerlike manner by swearing, clinching his fist and stamping his foot to his officers?

A. — I have heard him swear in a manner which I thought unbecoming his rank, but cannot say to whom he addressed himself.

Court — Did you ever complain to Captain Cuming of his having shoved you with his speaking trumpet in a forcible manner?

A. — No, but I hope I will be able to give satisfactory reasons for not taking notice of it when it happened.

C. — What was the situation of the ship when Captain Cuming ordered you upon that point of duty which you cannot recollect?

A. — All hands on deck and I think at an anchor, about nine o'clock at night and quite dark. But I do not perfectly recollect.

C. You say it was quite dark. Are you certain that Captain Cuming knew your person at the time you say he shoved you with the trumpet?

A. He spoke to me just before and, hearing him give an order, I was going forward to execute it.

C. What do you call just before?

A. Not more than one minute.

C. Did he call you by your name at the time he pushed you with the trumpet?

A. I do not recollect.

C. Did you conceive, when Captain Cuming shoved you with the trumpet, he meant it as a blow to insult or hurt you or in order to expedite the service he wished to have executed and he was sending you upon?

A. I cannot say what his intentions were.

C. I should like to know, as you say your feelings were much hurt at the time, whether on that night or next morning, you mentioned this transaction to any of your messmates, that you had been degraded or insulted by Captain Cuming in the execution of your duty.

A. Yes, that night or next morning, I mentioned in the ward room, having been shoved with the trumpet and that I thought it strange conduct, having never been accustomed to anything of the kind before.

C. At the time you mentioned this, who were present and about what time was it?

A. I do not exactly recollect. I should not have thought any more of it, had not Lieutenant Willoughby brought it to my remembrance.

Prisoner You have said that I shoved you. Had I any animosity against you previous to this time or had any misunderstanding taken place between us?

A. Not that I know of.

P. You have said you saw me shove Lieutenant Bateman, for what purpose or on what duty was he ordered that he went in the waist?

A. As near as I can recollect, we were taking a ship in tow and I suppose he was employed on that duty.

P. Do you recollect the situation of the *Duckington Hall* and the weather at the time?

A. She was in distress and the weather squally, at times blowing very strong.

P. If Lieutenant Bateman was ordered in the waist, do you conceive it was for the purpose of taking the ship in tow?

A. Yes.

P. Was every officer and man busily employed for the purpose of taking in sail to take the ship in tow again?

A. Yes.

Witness withdrew.

Lieutenant Jam[s]. Bateman called in and sworn.

Prosecutor. Did you ever jump from the larboard gangway into the waist to avoid being shoved into it by Captain Cuming?

A. I did jump into the waist. Captain Cuming had ordered a hawser to be paid out from the larboard port, which I believe was not clear. Captain Cuming came near me and I jumped into the waist immediately, for fear of his pushing me down.

P. Did Captain Cuming forcibly shove you on the twelfth of last March? And relate to the court the circumstances.

A. The ship was short and we were heaving through all. I was then standing on the brink of the tank and Captain Cuming put his hand on my shoulder, told me to go down and see the reason of their heaving through all. I caught hold of the ladder and slipped down on the main deck, the ship being in a ticklish situation, with other ships on each quarter.

P. Was you near falling into the hold or on the orlop deck in consequence of a forcible shove Captain Cuming gave you and the gratings being unlaid?

A. Yes.

P. Did you mention this circumstance to any officer soon afterwards as a grievance?

A. Yes.

P. Did Captain Cuming ever damn or blast you publicly while in the execution of your duty?

A. Yes. Once something went wrong and I believe he said 'Damn you, go to leeward and see the staying sheets hauled aft.'

P. Did Captain Cuming make use of the expression 'Damn and blast you and your rheumatism' publicly on the quarter deck, when you mentioned to him you had it?

A. We were letting the reefs out of the topsails and, while they were hoisting, Captain Cuming ordered me to go up on the poop to see when the maintop sail was taut by the lee leech. I said, 'Sir, I have got the rheumatism so bad I can hardly walk.' Whether he said 'Damn and blast your rheumatism,' or 'Damn & blast you and your rheumatism' I don't know, but I think the first.

P. Do you think Captain Cuming's conduct on the twelfth of March last and afterward in damning & blasting you and your rheumatism, lessened and degraded you in the eyes of the inferior officers and ship's company?

A. No, I do not, as I never had an order disobeyed by officer or man.

P. Did Captain Cuming, on the fifth & seventh instant, treat me in an unofficerlike manner by repeatedly thrusting his clenched fist, but with one finger extended within six or seven inches of my face?

A. I saw Captain Cuming talking to you in that manner, but I cannot say at what distance exactly.

P. Was his address unofficerlike? And state in what it consisted.

A. Not in my opinion.

P. Did Captain Cuming, upon the seventh instant, declare with asperity that I was guilty of a falsehood?

A. He said what you had stated was false.

Court Do you know what the subject was that Captain Cuming was in conversation about when you state that he had thrust his clenched fist in the face of Lieutenant Willoughby on the fifth and seventh instant? Did it relate to His Majesty's service, or private matters?

A. His Majesty's service; the Court must have mistaken me respecting Captain Cuming's thrusting his hand into Lieutenant Willoughby's face, it was his usual custom to extend his arm in that way when in conversation.

C. Did you ever complain to Captain Cuming of the various damnings he had given you?

A. Never.

C. When Captain Cuming went forward upon the gangway to expedite the service by getting a hawser to take the ship in tow, was there room on the break of the quarter deck for Captain Cuming to pass by you without you going into the waist?

A. I believe there was, but the ship had a good deal of motion.

C. Did Captain Cuming speak to you or order you to go down

in the waist on that point of duty or did you go in consequence of a wish to expedite the service?

A. By Captain Cuming's order.

C. Was it given in public orders that any man found spitting on the deck that he (Captain Cuming) should direct the person guilty of such nasty actions to lick it up?

A. Yes. Captain Cuming had given those orders. I have frequently told the men and all must have known such orders.

C. When Captain Cuming ordered you to go down and enquire the reason that they were heaving through all and that he put his hand upon your shoulder by way of enforcing the orders, do you consider it as done in his zeal for the service or to affront you?

A. His zeal for the service.

C. When you mentioned in the ward room Captain Cuming having pushed you, was it complaining that you had been degraded or insulted in the execution of your duty by having been so pushed?

A. I said that Captain Cuming had shoved me and that I was near falling down the hatchway. I did think it degrading at that time, but not since.

C. As first lieutenant of this ship and an experienced officer, I beg to ask you if Captain Cuming, since he has commanded the *Russell*, has been guilty of any scandalous actions in derogation of God's honour and corruption of good manners in breach of the second Article of War?

A. Not to my knowledge.

C. Has Captain Cuming during this period ever behaved himself in an infamous, cruel, oppressive, or fraudulent manner, unbecoming the character of an officer in breach of the thirty-third Article of War?

A. No, never.

Witness withdrew.

M^r^. John Palfreman, Master's Mate, called in and sworn.

Prosecutor. Relate to the Court if you have ever seen Lieutenant Bateman shoved in a forcible manner by Captain Cuming.

Witness. The morning we left Yarmouth, I was standing on the main deck, close to the main hatchway, and saw Captain Cuming shove Lieutenant Bateman and he was near falling down the main hatchway.

Prisoner	Did you see me shove Lieutenant Bateman down the hatchway with an intent to do him an injury or was it for the purpose of expediting the service I had sent him on?
A.	I cannot say; I only saw Captain Cuming put his hand on Lieutenant Bateman's shoulder and shove him.
P.	Do you know for what purpose he was going below?
A.	I do not.
P.	Where are you stationed at mooring and unmooring ship?
A.	At the third and fourth bars of the capstern.
P.	Were we heaving through all at the time?
A.	I don't recollect.

Witness withdrew.

Lieu[t]. Geo. Taylor called in & sworn.

Prosecutor	Relate to the court the conduct of Captain Cuming to you on the morning he ordered you to go on board the *Duckington Hall*.
Witness	I was desired to go on board the *Duckington Hall* to bring a towline belonging to the *Russell*, to take the particulars how she was dismasted, her name, and that of the owners and to return immediately to the *Russell*, which I gave on my return to Captain Cuming. He, being in a passion at the time, tore the paper and threw it overboard.
Court	Have you anything to relate respecting the charges you have heard read?
A.	No.
Prosec[r].	Did he snatch the paper in an abrupt manner, damn it and throw it overboard?
A.	Yes.
P.	Did Captain Cuming, upon the fifth & seventh instant, thrust his clinch'd hand, but with one finger extended, within a few inches of my face?
A.	Yes.
P.	Did he, on the seventh instant, say that what I had stated was false, 'by God'?
A.	Yes.
Court	Do you know what it was that Lieutenant Willoughby had stated?
A.	That Captain Cuming had shoved him over some of the guns.
C.	Did you believe it to be true or false?
A.	I had never heard of it before.

C. What lieutenant are you in the ship and how long in the Naval Service?

A. Third Lieutenant and been nine years in the service.

C. As an officer of such standing in the service, I beg to ask you if Captain Cuming, since he has commanded the *Russell*, has been guilty of any scandalous actions in derogation of God's honour and corruption of good manners in breach of the second Article of War?

A. Not to my knowledge.

C. Has Captain Cuming, during this period, ever behaved himself in an infamous, cruel, oppressive, or fraudulent manner, unbecoming the character of an officer in breach of the thirty-third Article of War?

A. I cannot say he has.

Witness withdrew.

Lieu^t^. John Roberts called in and sworn.

Prosecutor Did Captain Cuming, on the fifth and seventh instant, address me with his fist clinched, but with one finger extended, within a few inches of my face?

A. The fifth I know nothing of. On the seventh I was in the cabin with Captain Cuming, when M^r^. Willoughby accused Captain Cuming of shoving him over a gun. Captain Cuming, at the time, seemed very much agitated at being accused of it and told M^r^. Willoughby, shaking his finger in his usual manner, that it was false. How near it was to his face I cannot exactly say.

Court What lieutenant are you in the ship and how long have you been in the navy?

A. Fourth Lieutenant, eight years in the service.

C. As an officer of such standing, I beg to ask you if Captain Cuming, since he has commanded the *Russell*, has been guilty of any scandalous actions in derogation of God's honour and corruption of good manners in breach of the second Article of War.

A. I do not think he has.

C. Has Captain Cuming, during this period, ever behaved himself in an infamous, cruel, oppressive, or fraudulent manner, unbecoming the character of an officer in breach of the thirty-third Article of War.

A. I do not think he has.

Witness withdrew.

Lieu^t^. Hole, of Marines, called in and sworn.

Prosecutor. Has Captain Cuming ever treated you in an unofficerlike manner publicly on the quarter deck?

A. In my opinion, he has.

P. Relate to the court the circumstance.

Witness Soon after we passed the grounds, Captain Cuming sent for me on the quarter deck and asked me the reason why his orders respecting the sentinels on the gangway were not carried into execution. I answered that the fault was not mine, as I had given his orders to the sergeant; upon this, Captain Cuming appeared very much infuriated, clinched his fingers, with the exception of the fore one, and shook it at me several times.

Court Do you ever see Captain Cuming make use of that action on other occasions?

A. Once in the cabin.

C. Did you conceive at the time that he meant it as a threat or to strike you?

A. No. I was at too great a distance for that.

Prisoner When I desired you to put the sentries on the gangways and at my cabin door, did you conceive it your duty to see those orders into execution?

A. I conceived it to be the duty of the officer of the guard.

P. Was you commanding officer of the Marines at the time?

A. Yes.

Witness withdrew.

Lieut. Heny Trevor, of Marines, called in and sworn.

Prosecutor Relate to the court a conversation that passed between you and Captain Cuming on the second of April, relative to his threatening to cut you down when in the execution of your duty?

Witness I was then quarter'd on the forecastle and after the *Russell* had commenced firing, the sergeant reported to me that, from a want of ammunition, we were prevented from annoying the enemy, when a favourable opportunity presented itself; and upon my acquainting Captain Cuming with it, he replied that, if I spoke to him then about ammunition, while the ship was aground, that he would cut me down.

Court Did he lift his hand in a threatening way and had he a sword or any weapon in it?

A. He extended his arm & had a trumpet in his hand, but I was at too great a distance from him to receive any injury from him, if he had any such intention.

C. At the time this happened, did it then enter your mind that it would ever be brought before a court martial or did you mention it the next day to Captain Cuming?

A. No. I was advised by the chaplain not to mention it.

C. Was you quartered on the forecastle?

A. Yes.

Witness withdrew.

The Prosecutor not wishing to call in any further witness and the prisoner saying he had no defence to offer, the court was cleared. And, after having maturely and deliberately weighed and considered the evidence in support of the prosecution, the Court was of opinion that the charges were frivolous, scandalous, malicious, and totally unfounded, tending to lessen the dignity and to subvert the good order and discipline of His Majesty's Naval Service and did therefore adjudge the said Captain William Cuming to be acquitted.

The court was then opened, audience admitted; and, the judge advocate having read the sentence, the court broke up. …

123. *Court Martial of Charles Coleman*

[ADM 1/5362]

Minutes of the proceedings of a court martial assembled and held onboard His Majesty's ship *Venus* in Fort Royal Bay, Martinique, 6 July 1802.

Present

Thomas Graves, Esqr., Captain of His Majesty's ship the *Venus*, and second officer in the command of His Majesty's ships and vessels in Fort Royal Bay, Martinique, President.

Captains

James O'Bryen	George Barker
Robert Fanshawe	Christopher Cole

The prisoner was brought into court and the evidence and audience admitted.

Read the order from the Honble Robert Stopford, Commodore and Commander in Chief for the time being of His Majesty's ships and vessels employed at Barbados and the Leeward Islands &c., &c., &c., dated the 5th July 1802 and directed to Thomas Graves, Esqr., Captain of His Majesty's ship the *Venus* and second officer in the command of His

Majesty's ships and vessels in Fort Royal Bay, Martinique, to try Charles Coleman (Seaman), belonging to His Majesty's ship the *Excellent*, for quarrelling and fighting onboard the said ship on the night of the 2d of July 1802.

Then the members of the court and judge advocate, in open court and before they proceeded to trial, respectively took the oaths as directed by an Act of Parliament made and passed in the 22d year of the reign of His late Majesty King George the Second, entitled *An Act for Amending, Explaining and Reducing into One Act of Parliament the Laws relating to the Government of His Majesty's Ship's, Vessels of War and Forces by Sea*.

A letter from John Nash, Esq[r]., Captain of His Majesty's ship the *Excellent* to the Hon[ble]. Robert Stopford, Commodore and Commander in Chief of His Majesty's ships and vessels employed at Barbados and the Leeward Islands &c., &c., &c. was read as follows:

His Majesty's ship *Excellent*
Fort Royal Bay, Martinique
5th July 1802

… Charles Coleman, a Seaman belonging to His Majesty's ship under my command, being guilty of quarrelling and fighting on the night of the 2nd instant, I have to request you will be pleased to order a court martial to try him for the said offence. …

All the evidence were then ordered to withdraw out of court, except Hugh Campbell, Corporal of Marines belonging to His Majesty's ship the *Excellent*, who was sworn.

Prosecutor:

Q. – Was you present at the quarrel between the prisoner and Thomas Burrows, the Marine, on the night of the 2nd instant?

A. – Yes.

Q. – Did you hear them quarrel and see them fight?

A. – Yes.

Court:

Q. – What began the wrangle?

A. – I can't tell.

Q. – Was you certain blows passed on both sides?

A. – No; I only saw the prisoner strike blows.

Prisoner:

Q. – Was you present when Thomas Burrows dragged me out of the berth?

A. – No.

Evidence was ordered to withdraw; and Hugh Tye, seaman, was called into court and sworn.

Prosecutor:

Q. – Was you near the prisoner and Burrows, the Marine, when they were quarrelling on the night of the 2nd instant?

A. – Yes.

Q. – Did you see them fight?

A. – Yes.

Q. – Did you see the prisoner strike Burrows?

A. – I saw him strike at him, but could not tell whether he hit him or not.

Court:

Q. – What began the quarrel?

A. – The first beginning of the quarrel was Burrow's hammock was quite low from any of the rest in the berth; the prisoner said then if he hung in the berth as he had done before, he should make him hang higher or otherwise lower him down. Burrows, going over to the other side of the table, he fell upon the prisoner, who shoved him up. Burrows was in liquor. The prisoner asked him if he wanted anything and Burrows said he did not care whether or not; the prisoner gave him a shove and told him to stay off him. Burrows catched [*sic*] him by the collar and dragged him out of the berth and said he would take him to Sergeant Monday. The prisoner said he would stand it no longer; the prisoner let go his right hand and struck at him several times. The man fell and, when I looked, the prisoner's shirt was torn.

Evidence was ordered to withdraw and Joseph Carr (Marine) was called into court and sworn.

Prosecutor:

Q. – Was you present at the quarrel between the prisoner and Burrows, the Marine, on the night of the 2d instant?

A. – Not at the first beginning.

Q. – Did you see the prisoner strike him?

A. – Yes.

The evidence in support of the charge being finished, the prisoner was called upon to make his defence, which he did in writing as follows and which was read by the judge advocate:

> … I shall not take up much of your time in attempting to do away what has come out upon evidence, but confine myself to a few remarks and submit my case to the mercy of this honourable court.

I have been in the King's service 13 years and upwards and, until the unfortunate evening of the 2nd July, never was accused of doing amiss; on the contrary, I have always been so fortunate as to gain the approbation of the officers with whom I have served, some of whom are now in court. The court then will judge how I feel at the present moment better than I can possibly express. Old age, as can easily be perceived, has greatly overtaken me and, although I may be so fortunate as to meet the indulgence of this hon^{ble} court, still I shall always feel unhappy at what happened on the evening alluded to. My captain, for whom I have the greatest respect, I trust has only brought the present charges against me to prove the impropriety of men taking the law into their own hands, when redress can be so easily obtained by applying through the proper channel. All I can now say then is that I am truly sorry for what has happened and pray this hon^{ble} court to show me all the indulgence in their power. …

The prisoner then requested Lieutenants Henderson Bain and Sir Norborne Thompson, Bart., and Mr John Keiler, Master of the *Excellent*, to speak to his character, who all said that they never heard any complaint against him from any officer, except that for which he stands charged, that they never saw him drunk and always considered him as a willing and hard working man.

The prisoner having nothing further to offer in his defence, the court was cleared and proceeded to deliberate upon and form the sentence.

The court, having carefully and deliberately weighed and considered the evidence produced and what the prisoner alleged in his defence, were of opinion that the charge had been proved; but in consideration of his very good character, the court only adjudge the prisoner, Charles Coleman, to receive thirty-six lashes upon his bare back with a cat o'nine tails onboard His Majesty's ship to which he belongs at such time as the commander in chief shall think proper to direct.

The court was then opened, audience and evidence admitted and sentence passed accordingly. …

124. *Court Martial of John Scriven and George Blanchard*

[ADM 1/5362]

Minutes taken at a court martial, assembled on board his Majesty's ship *Hercule* in Portsmouth Harbour, the twenty-fifth day of September, One Thousand Eight Hundred and Two.

Present

Solomon Ferris Esqr., Captain of His Majesty's ship *Hercule* and second officer in the command of His Majesty's ships and vessels at Portsmouth and Spithead, President.

Captain	William Robert Broughton	Captain	James Athol Wood
	Thomas Elphinstone		Robert Williams
	William Cumberland		John Stiles
	Sir Thomas Livingstone Bar^{r}.		John Wood
	Frederick Lewis Maitland		Charles Fielding
	Edward Henry Columbine		Alexander Skene

The prisoners were brought in and audience admitted.

Then the order from the Right Honourable Lords Commissioners of the Admiralty, dated the 10th instant and directed to the president, for the trial of John Scriven and George Blanchard, two Marines belonging to His Majesty's gun vessel *Locust* 'for having, when on sentry on the 5th instant at midnight, taken away the cutter from the stern and deserted to the shore and also for having robbed Andrew Hanlin, a Seaman belonging to the said gun vessel, of a watch and a bag of clothes,' was read.

The president reported to the Court that Captains Sir Rich^{d}. I Strachan Bar^{t}., Francis William Austen and Peter Turner Bover were absent on Admiralty leave.

M^{r}. W^{m}. Mustard, Surgeon of His Majesty's Ship *Leda*, being sworn, stated to the court that Captain James Hardy, her Commander, was ill and could not with safety to his health attend his duty as a member of the court.

The members of the court and the judge advocate then, in open court and before they proceeded to trial, respectively took the several oaths enjoined and directed in and by an Act of Parliament made and passed in the 22nd year of the reign of His Late Majesty King George the Second, entitled *An Act for Amending, Explaining and Reducing into One Act of Parliament the Laws Relating to the Government of his Majesty's Ships, Vessels and Forces by Sea.*

M^{r}. William Allen, Gunner of His Majesty's gun brig *Locust* called in & sworn

Lieut^{t}. Lake asked:

Q. State to the court what you know of the prisoners on the night of the 5th of September.

A. At 4 o'clock in the morning I was going down to call the watch and the sentry told me to give them a good rouse up. I asked him who I should call of his side; he told me George Wilmot. Soon after that the corporal of Marines got up and went upon the deck and then came and stood on the fore ladder and sung out, where was the sentry three or four times. I told him he was standing before him as he was there three or four minutes before. I went on deck and sung out for the sentry myself, who was John Scriven, the prisoner, and who was the person who had desired me to give them a good rouse up. I looked about the hammer cloths and saw nothing there but his musket, which I happened to knock down. I went to the head to look if he was there and I heard a noise aft; I ran aft and saw one boat and two people making away in her from the ship. I could not distinguish their features as it was foggy. I hailed the boat and told them if they did not come back I would fire at them. I ran for the musket, but she did not go off the first time. The second time she did, but they went on. I sung out for more ammunition. By this time the captain and officers came up and most part of the ship's company and the captain ordered the jolly boat to be lowered down immediately. I went into her & the boatswain and George Wilmot, a Marine, and pursued, but could see nothing of the boat.

Q. Was it the *Locust*'s boat that was going from the vessel?

A. In my opinion, it was.

Q. Was there an enquiry who the deserters were?

A. Yes and it was reported Blanchard and Scriven.

Q. Did you see the prisoners brought on board afterwards by a party of the Bow Street officers?

A. Yes, I did.

The court asked:

Q. Are you positive that the prisoners are the two men?

A. Yes, I am.

Q. Was Blanchard on board on the night the two men went away?

A. I do not know, but I saw Scriven on his post as before stated.

Q. Who was in the watch with you?

A. John Scriven.

Q. Were Scriven and Blanchard both sentries?

A. Scriven was the only sentry. He desired me to call Wilmot, but I believe it was Blanchard's turn, but I am not sure of it.

Q. Who was in the practice of planting the sentries?

A. The Corporal of Marines, Richard Dawson.

Q. Where was the vessel at this time?

A. In the stream off Deptford.

Q. Are you certain the boat was fast astern or alongside at the time you called Wilmot?

A. I saw her in the course of my watch fastened astern.
Q. Had the boat been ordered away on any duty in the course of your watch?
A. No, she had not.
Q. When you discovered the men going from the vessel, did you examine if the boat was gone?
A. Yes and she was gone.
Q. Was there any boat on board during your watch?
A. No.
Q. Were there any oars in the boat?
A. Not that I know of.
Q. Was it customary to have them out at sunset?
A. Yes.

Richard Dawson, Corporal of Marines belonging to the *Locust*, called in & sworn

Lieut[t]. Lake asked:
Q. Relate to the court the Marines that were placed as sentinel on Sunday, the 5th instant.
A. The first watch was Richard Lowe, the next watch was John Scriven, the next watch should have been George Blanchard, but George Wilmot was placed in his stead.
Q. Do you know that at the setting the watch at 8 o'clock that the two prisoners were on board the *Locust*?
A. Yes they were; I saw them both.
Q. Do you know that at 4 o'clock on the alarm being given on mustering the ship's company that the two prisoners were absent?
A. Yes, they were.
Q. Do you know that the boat was gone?
A. Yes.
Q. Have I at all times given you orders to direct the sentries to take particular care that the boat was not taken away by any of the supernumeraries in the night?
A. Yes and I always delivered such orders to them when I planted them. I told them not to let any boat come alongside nor any person to take away any boat. I delivered this order to Lowe at 8 o'clock.
Q. After the jolly boat was sent for the cutter, did you see the cutter return on board again?
A. I did not see her at first; I was below.
Q. Were the persons missing the next day?
A. Yes.

Andrew Hanlin, a Seaman belonging to the *Locust*, called in and sworn

Lieut[t]. Lake asked:

Q. Do you recollect the cutter being taken from the stern of the *Locust* on Sunday the 5th instant?

A. I heard them talking about it; I was sick in my hammock.

Q. Did you on that night lose your watch & clothes?

A. Yes.

Q. Where were they placed?

A. Very close to where I hung in my hammock and, about a quarter after 4 o'clock, I missed the bag. There was a pay list, a pension ticket and two certificates in the bag; one for the *Isis* and one for the *Victory*. The watch was in a bag rolled up, to the best of my opinion, in a pair of stockings.

Q. Can you tell who took them away?

A. No.

Q. Have you seen any of the clothes since?

A. The jacket and waistcoat now on Scriven are mine. I have had the waistcoat two years. I lost two pair of trousers, one pair blue. I think those Scriven has were the blue trousers I lost. If so, they had a round patch on the back of them.

On the prisoner Scriven being directed to turn round, a round patch appeared upon his trousers. The witness further said, 'I am clear they are my trousers.'

Q. Did you ever lend or give the prisoners any clothes?

A. Never.

M[r]. Sinclair Collin M[c]Kenzie, Surgeon of His Majesty's gun vessel *Locust,* called in and sworn.

Lieut[t]. Lake asked:

Q. Relate to the court what passed on the night the cutter was taken away.

A. I was in bed and was alarmed by the report of a musket. I immediately went upon deck with my clothes. I heard them call that some men had run off with the boat. I ran to the stern of the vessel to look out if I could see the boat, but could see nothing of her. I assisted to lower down the jolly boat when two or three hands leaped into her and went in search of the cutter, but did not find her.

Q. At what time was the cutter brought back again?

A. In the morning before I was up.

George Wilmot, a Marine belonging to the *Locust,* called in and sworn.

Q. Were you sent for the cutter on the night of the 5th instant?
A. Yes.
Q. Where did you find her?
A. In a creek between Deptford and Greenwich on the Deptford side of the water and the painter made fast to a pile and she was taken on board again. There were two oars in her.
Q. Was there any clothing in the boat?
A. None.
Q. Do you know that the two prisoners were on board on that night?
A. Yes. I saw them at 8 o'clock & they were afterwards missing.

M^r^. William Allen, a Midshipman belonging to the *Locust,* called in & sworn

Lieut^t^. Lake asked:
Q. Have I, at all times, given you directions to see the boat properly moored and everything taken out of her for the night?
A. Yes.
Q. Had the oars been taken out of her on the evening of the 5th?
A. Yes, I saw them taken out about 8 o'clock.
Q. Did you muster the ship's company soon after the boat was taken away?
A. Yes, past 4 o'clock and the prisoners were missing. I had seen Scriven in the course of the afternoon on board.

Richard Rogers, a peace officer belonging to the police office at Bow Street, called in and sworn.

The Court asked:
Q. State to the court what you know against the prisoner.
A. Upon an information I received I went to the Star and Garter public house at Bromley and there took the two prisoners. On searching Scriven, I found this watch in his waistcoat pocket. He had a bad seven shilling piece and a half crown tied up in the flap of his shirt and five shillings and six pence and some halfpence for which they had sold some shoes to persons in the house, which I gave to them and received back the shoes. By the information of Blanchard, who went with me and Brassington to M^r^. Charles Long's wood at Bromley, I found two bags containing wearing apparel and I have had several articles in my possession ever since. Scriven confessed at Bow Street to M^r^. Bond that they belonged to the *Locust*.

Andrew Hanlin said he was certain it was his watch and the stocking in which it was was his stocking. A piece of written paper was in a handkerchief with the watch, which Hanlin said was of his handwriting, and was signed by him and was in the bag when he lost it.

On the bag being opened, a waistcoat, a pair of canvas trousers and a shirt were found, which Hanlin said were his property.

Richard Rogers further said: 'Blanchard told us everything with the greatest civility and said they had shipped themselves in the old buildings, meaning Sir Gregory Page's, and the marine jacket (which he produced) was found there.

John Brassington, a peace officer belonging to the police office at Bow Street, being called in & sworn

Q. State to the court what you know against the prisoners.

A. We were in search of two foot pads. The prisoners answered the description of them very much, we were shooting and going by the bye lanes; we heard of the different people who had been robbed. On the road to Lewesham we heard at a public house that two men had been there inquiring the nighest way to town – without going the public road. We went then to Sydenham and stopped at a public house. A man came and gave us information that two men had gone to Bromley. We immediately followed and at the first public house, I believe the Star and Garter, we found the two prisoners. We stayed some while before we spoke to them. When they were going away we stopped and searched them. I found on Blanchard a pocket book, a knife, a six pence and a handkerchief, which were all he had about him. We said they had two bags with them. They denied it at first and we took them before the justices and, while Scriven was examined before a magistrate, I took Blanchard down in a parlour and he acknowledged that he was a Marine and a deserter from the *Locust,* but denied having committed any robbery. He then told where the bags were, and we went and found them in the place he said. He said the clothes on him were not his own. He was a Marine and had changed his clothes. Scriven afterwards acknowledged he was a deserter.

Hanlin said that neither the book, the knife or the handkerchief were his property.

The prosecution being closed, the prisoners were called on for their defence.

George Blanchard said his father was dead and his mother left with nine children and his motive for going away was to endeavour to assist her, that he did not take the clothes.

Lieuten^{t}. Lake, being desired to speak to his character, said: 'Since Blanchard has been under my command, I never saw a better disposed or quieter young man.'

John Scriven said: 'On the morning when I left the ship, the sentry called me. I got up and came on deck. When I came on deck, as I came to the top of the steps, the other sentry went down. I walked backwards and forwards the deck some time, talking with the Quarter Master. He went aft and I went down below and took down a bag (I laid with my bed on the deck that night, close by where the bags hung). After I took down the bag, I took down my knapsack and put some things into it. I thought the bag had been my own; it was very dark. I brought the bag on deck & walked about deck awhile and went down to call Blanchard as he showed me over night where he laid and told me to call him. Blanchard brought his bag upon deck and when he came up with his bag, I walked about deck awhile and put my bag in the boat. I got into the boat; it was on the larboard side. Blanchard, after a bit, came and got into the boat and told me to go aft and he then coiled the rope in the boat and said shove off. There were two oars in the boat. We shoved off. I never was in a boat before and made a bad hand of rowing. At last we came to the shore. Blanchard jumped out of the boat and took his bag and I got out of the boat myself and said I would make the boat fast and got my own bag out and handed it up to him. We went towards Blackheath when it got a little light and I there found I had got the wrong bag. The reason I put the things on was I was all over mud with hauling the things up.'

Corporal Richard Dawson called in again.

The court asked:

Q. Did the prisoner, John Scriven, leave any bag on board?

A. No. He left his knapsack, but I could not find any bag of his on board. I never saw him with a bag.

Q. Did he mess on the same side with Hanlin?

A. Yes.

Q. Did he leave any clothes on board?

A. He left his new uniform jacket waistcoat and breeches on board.

Q. How long have you been in the brig?

A. About eighteen months.

Q. Was any search made for Scriven's clothes on the next morning?

A. Yes, I searched everywhere for all their things but could find no bag.

Q. What was the character of John Scriven on board?

A. He always behaved in a good soldier-like manner on board. He was attentive to his duty.

Lieutenant Lake, being asked to speak to Scriven's character, said his character stood very high on board & he behaved so well that he thought himself happy in having such a man and made him a lance corporal.

The Court was cleared and agreed that the charges had been proved against the said John Scriven and proved in part against the said George Blanchard and did adjudge the said John Scriven to receive five hundred lashes and the said George Blanchard to receive two hundred lashes on their bare backs with a cat o'nine tails on board of or alongside such ship or ships of His Majesty at Spithead or in Portsmouth Harbour at such time or times & in such manner and proportions as the commander in chief of His Majesty's ships and vessels for the time being at Portsmouth aforesaid should direct.

The court was again opened, the prisoners brought in, audience admitted and sentence passed accordingly. …

124A. *Lake to Nepean*

[ADM 1/5362] His Majesty's Gun Vessel *Locust* at Deptford
September 9th, 1802

… I have to request you will be pleased to represent to their Lordships that the two Marines named in the margin [John Scriven, George Blanchard] did, when on sentry, Sunday the 5th ins^t^. at midnight, take away the cutter from the stern and desert to the shore, robbing Andrew Hanlin, a Seaman belonging to the *Locust,* of a watch and a bag of clothes; about on Wednesday the 8th ins^t^., a party of the Bow Street officers took these two men on the highway habited in seaman dress and brought them on board the *Locust* at Deptford where they now lay.

I beg leave to move their Lordships that a court marshal may be ordered to try them for the same. …

125. *Court Martial of John Murray.*

[ADM 1/5363]

Minutes of the proceedings of a court martial assembled and held on board His Majesty's ship the *Gibraltar* in the harbour of Valletta on Friday the 14th January 1803 for the trial of M^r^. John Murray, Master of His Majesty's ship *Charon.*

Present

William Hancock Kelly, Esqre., Captain of His Majesty's ship the *Gibraltar* and second officer in the command of His Majesty's ships and vessels at Malta, President.

Captains

Richard Goodwin Keats — Sir Robert Barlow, Kn^t^.
George Fred^k^. Ryves — William Skipsey
Edward O'Bryen

The court was opened, the prisoner brought in, and evidence and audience admitted. The judge advocate read the order from Rear Admiral Sir Richard Bickerton, Bar^{t}., Commander in Chief of His Majesty's ships and vessels in the Mediterranean, dated the 10th instant and addressed to the president, for the trial of M^{r}. John Murray, Master of His Majesty's ship the *Charon*, for having on the evening of the 25 of December last made use of unofficerlike speeches and behaved with contempt and disrespect to his superior officer on board the said ship. Then the members of the court and officiating judge advocate, in open court and before they proceeded to trial, respectively took the oath enjoined by Act of Parliament; after which, the letter from Captain Schomberg, Commander of His Majesty's ship *Charon*, containing the charges was read.[1] And all the witnesses being ordered to withdraw, they withdrew accordingly, except the first to be sworn; and the court proceeded to trial as follows: Captain Charles Marsh Schomberg being the Prosecutor.

	Lieutenant Henry Tom Marsdin of His Majesty's ship *Charon* sworn.
Prosecutor	Was you commanding officer on board the *Charon* the evening of the 25 December last?
Answer	I was.
Prosecutor	State to the court the conduct of the prisoner that night.
Answer	Coming upon deck between the hours of nine and ten, I found a boat had been sent from the ship by the orders of the prisoner, which boat I had ordered to be manned and to wait alongside; on my calling the boat back to the ship, the prisoner disputed my authority as commanding officer and treated me with the utmost contempt. He said I had nothing to do with the boat: it was the captain's boat. He was officer of the watch and I had nothing to do with her. I desired him to recollect I was commanding officer of the ship; he said, 'You, commanding officer of the ship! I am officer of the watch and you have no command of the deck.' I told him again, I was commanding officer and, in the absence of my captain, considered myself, to all intents and purposes, captain of the ship. The prisoner replied, 'You, captain of the ship! If I was captain of a ship, I would not trust you with my long boat.' I told him he should not throw me off my guard, as I intended to lay the business before the captain, and I immediately quitted the deck.

[1]This letter is not bound in ADM 1/5363 with the transcript.

Court Did you send the prisoner to order the boat to be manned?

Answer No, I sent the coxswain to get the boat manned and ordered him to wait alongside. I was told that he informed the prisoner.

Court How long had the boat put off when you came on deck?

Answer She had just cleared the ship.

Court How do you know it was by the prisoner's order the boat quitted the ship?

Answer I was told so by Lieutenant Pridham of the Marines upon my coming upon deck.

Court Were the words you state the prisoner to have made use of expressed with any particular marks of contempt and disrespect?

Answer Yes, he expressed them with a raised voice and dwelt much on the word 'you!'

Court Were any other persons present at the time?

Answer Yes, the witnesses who came forward: M[r]. Bundock, Lieutenant Pridham, M[r]. Humphries, Midshipman, and the sentry at the gangway.

Court Had the prisoner charge of the watch on deck by your order?

Answer Yes, I ordered him to be called upon setting the watch at eight o'clock.

Court Is it customary in the ship for the officer of the watch to give permission for boats to leave the ship without the knowledge of the commanding officer?

Answer No.

Court Where was the boat going?

Answer On shore for the captain.

Court And to whom did the prisoner give orders for the boat to put off?

Answer To the captain's coxswain, I suppose.

Prisoner Were you on deck at eight o'clock that evening?

Answer No, I sent the midshipman of the watch to desire M[r]. Murray to take charge of the first watch.

Prisoner Is it customary in the ship to send a midshipman with such orders?

Answer On all messages to officers of the ship.

This witness withdrew by order of the court, the prisoner having no further questions to ask.

M[r]. William Bundock, Naval Storekeeper, called and sworn.

Prosecutor Was you on the *Charon*'s quarter deck on the night of the

25 December last when a conversation took place between Lieutenant Marsdin and the prisoner?

Answer — Yes, I was.

Prosecutor — Did the prisoner behave with contempt and disrespect to Lieutenant Marsdin as commanding officer?

Answer — I will relate the conversation. I came on the quarter deck about nine o'clock and the prisoner was looking over the gangway, calling to the coxswain of a boat, and asked if that was the boat which was going for the captain. The coxswain replied, 'Yes' and he desired him immediately to put off. At this time, Lieutenant Marsdin came on deck and said, 'Mr. Murray, I ordered the boat to wait.' The prisoner replied, 'I am officer of the watch and will send her if I please.' Mr. Marsdin then said to him, 'Give me none of your airs Mr. Murray.' The prisoner replied, 'You! You poor little creature! You, commanding officer; I would not trust you with the command of a long boat. You may take my warrant if you please; I don't care a damn for it.' The boat was alongside at this time; I went into it and heard no more of the conversation.

Prosecutor — Was the conduct of the prisoner, during the whole of the conversation which you heard, contemptuous and disrespectful to Lieutenant Marsdin?

Answer — Yes, it was.

Court — Was there anything in the manner or conduct of Lieut. Marsdin that might have irritated the prisoner and thrown him off his guard?

Answer — Not in the least.

Court — Was the prisoner sober?

Answer — I really cannot answer.

The prisoner having no question to ask, the witness withdrew.

Mr. George Humphries, Midshipman of the *Charon*, called and sworn.

Prosecutor — Did you come upon the quarter deck on the night of the 25 December last at the time a conversation took place between Lieutenant Marsdin and the prisoner?

Answer — I did.

Prosecutor — Did you observe the prisoner to behave with contempt and disrespect to Lieutenant Marsdin, then commanding officer?

Answer — I did.

Prosecutor — State to the court what passed and the manner it was delivered.

Answer I heard Lieutenant Marsdin tell the prisoner that he, in the captain's absence, was considered to all intents and purposes captain of the ship. The prisoner replied, 'You, captain! You are no seaman.' Lieutenant Marsdin said he should hold no conversation with him upon that subject; the prisoner replied, if he was captain of a ship, 'I would not trust you with a long boat.' That is all I heard.

Court Was you upon deck when Lieutenant Marsdin came up and did you remain there during the whole conversation?

Answer No, I found Lieutenant Marsdin on deck when I came up. I remained on deck afterwards till the conversation was ended.

Court Was the language the prisoner made use of spoke in a common way or in a high contemptuous manner?

Answer In a high contemptuous manner.

The prisoner, having no question to ask, this witness, withdrew.

Lieutenant William Pridham of Marines called and sworn.

Prosecutor Was you on the quarter deck the night of the 25 of December last?

Answer Yes.

Prosecutor Relate to the court the conversation which took place between Lieutenant Marsdin and the prisoner.

Answer On going to the gangway to enquire if the boat was ready, which was to take M[r]. Bundock out of the ship, I saw the prisoner there, who ordered the boat to put off. I told him it was Lieutenant Marsdin's orders she should wait; the prisoner then said that it was his orders the boat should put off immediately. I returned on the quarter deck and met Lieutenant Marsdin, who had just come from below, and told him the prisoner had ordered the boat to put off, on which Lieutenant Marsdin went to the gangway and called the boat back. Lieutenant Marsdin returned to the quarter deck and spoke to the prisoner, who told him that he was commanding officer of the ship while officer of the watch and that he, Lieutenant Marsdin, had nothing to do with it. Lieutenant Marsdin then told the prisoner to recollect that he was commanding officer, on which I went below. On my going down the ladder, I heard some words pass, which I cannot immediately recollect.

Prosecutor Did you observe the prisoner's conduct to be highly contemptuous and disrespectful to Lieutenant Marsdin?

Answer In my opinion, in the highest degree.

Court — Did you hear the prisoner tell Lieutenant Marsdin that if he was captain of a ship, he would not trust him with a long boat?

Answer — No, I do not recollect that.

This witness withdrew without being questioned by the prisoner.

William Page, a Marine of the *Charon*, called and sworn.

Prosecutor — Was you sentinel at the cabin door the night of the 25 December last between the hours of eight and ten o'clock?

Answer — Yes.

Prosecutor — Relate to the court the language the prisoner made use of to Lieutenant Marsdin and his manner of speaking.

Answer — The prisoner said he was officer of the watch and Lieu[t]. Marsdin had no command of the deck; and, afterwards, the prisoner said he would not trust him with a long boat.

Prosecutor — Did the prisoner speak to Lieutenant Marsdin in the manner that officers usually speak to their superiors?

Answer — They were at high words and did not appear to speak as officers should speak together.

Court — What distance were they from you at the time of the conversation?

Answer — Part of the time at the mizzen mast and part at the gangway.

Court — Did the prisoner speak in so loud a tone of voice at the gangway that you could distinctly hear him at your post at the cabin door?

Answer — Yes.

This witness withdrew by order of the court.

Henry Glover, Marine, called and sworn.

Prosecutor — Was you sentinel on the starboard gangway between the hours of 8 and 10 o'clock the evening of the 25 December last?

Answer — Yes.

Prosecutor — Relate to the court the expressions you heard pass between Lieutenant Marsdin and the prisoner.

Answer — When I was on the starboard gangway, the prisoner was officer of the watch, ordered a boat to be manned and asked the coxswain if she was ready. He replied she was and the prisoner asked if it was time to go for the captain. The coxswain said it was half an hour past the time and the prisoner told him to shove off. After the boat was gone, the first Lieutenant, M[r]. Marsdin, came on deck and enquired the reason the boat went away without his orders. The prisoner said it was half an hour past the time the boat should go for the captain and he had sent her away. The first lieutenant said he should call her back. The prisoner said it was not proper to call her back as she was going for the captain and it was half an hour past the time. The first lieutenant said he should do as he pleased; he was commanding officer. The prisoner made answer, saying, 'If you command the ship, I command the deck as officer of the watch; it is not your place to insult me.' The first Lieutenant and the prisoner went aft on the quarter deck and I heard Lieutenant Marsdin tell the prisoner he was drunk. The prisoner replied, 'If I am drunk, I would not trust you with the command of a long boat.' I heard no more of the conversation.

Prosecutor Was the prisoner's manner of speaking to Lieutenant Marsdin contemptuous and disrespectful?

Answer Yes, the prisoner spoke rather disrespectful.

This witness withdrew.

John Davis, Coxswain of the boat, called and sworn.

Prosecutor Did you inform the prisoner that it was Lieutenant Marsdin's orders the boat should not shove off the evening of the 25 December last between the hours of eight and ten o'clock?

Answer Yes, I did.

Prosecutor Did you shove off by the orders of the prisoner?

Answer Yes, I did.

Prosecutor Were you called back and did you come back by the orders of Lieutenant Marsdin?

Answer Yes.

Court Did the prisoner say anything to you when he sent the boat away, more than giving you orders to put off?

Answer He told me the captain's boat should not be detained.

Court Did the prisoner ask you any question, while you were alongside, relative to the time of night?

Answer He asked if it was time to go for the captain; I told him yes.

Prisoner When you came on deck, did you not tell me it was past the time the captain had ordered the boat to go for him?

Answer No.

The witness withdrew, the prisoner having no further questions to ask.

The prosecution here closed.

The prisoner was called upon for his defence, but having nothing to offer or any evidence to call to disprove the charges, the court was cleared and proceeded to deliberate upon and form the sentence.

The court, having maturely and deliberately weighed and considered the whole of the evidence, was of opinion that the charges had been proved, and did therefore adjudge the said M^r^. John Murray to be dismissed from His Majesty's service, and rendered incapable of again serving in the naval service of His Majesty, His heirs or successors.

The court being opened & the prisoner brought in, the sentence was read. …

126. *Court Martial of Peter Casey*

[ADM 1/5366]

Minutes of proceedings at a court martial held on board His Majesty's ship *Salvador del Mundo* in Hamoaze on Wednesday, the second day of May 1804.

Present

Herbert Sawyer, Esquire, Captain of His Majesty's ship *Princess Royal* and second officer in the command of His Majesty's ships and vessels at Plymouth, President.

Captains

John Dilkes
Israel Pellew
the Hble. Charles Paget
Wilson Rathborne
Charles Boyles
William Bedford
Micajah Malbon

Robert Liddel
Deputy Judge Advocate

Being all the captains of post ships according to seniority, except Joseph Sydney Yorke, Esqr., Captain of His Majesty's ship *Prince George*, who is absent with leave from the Lords Commissioners of the Admiralty.

The prisoner was brought into court and the evidence & audience admitted.

Read the order of the Right Honourable the Lords Commissioners of the Admiralty, dated the twenty seventh day of April 1804, directed to Herbert Sawyer, Esqr., Captain of His Majesty's ship *Princess Royal* and second officer in the command of His Majesty's ships and vessels at Plymouth, to try Peter Casey, a Private Marine belonging to His Majesty's ship *Foudroyant*, for getting drunk on his post on the fourteenth of April last between the hours of four and six in the afternoon, and for stealing some wine from a cask belonging to the officers of the *Foudroyant*, which was slung in the ward room of the ship, of which he had particular charge as sentinel at the wardroom door.

Read the warrant appointing a judge advocate.

Then the members of the court and the judge advocate, in open court and before they proceeded to trial, respectively took the oaths directed by an Act of Parliament passed in the twenty second year of the reign of King George the Second, entitled *An Act for Amending, Explaining and Reducing into One Act of Parliament the Law Relating to the Government of His Majesty's Ships, Vessels and Forces by Sea.*

A letter from Captain Puget of the *Foudroyant* to Sir John Colpoys, K.B., &c[a], &c[a], &c[a]., was then read as follows:

His Majesty's ship *Foudroyant*, Hamoaze
April 24th, 1804

… Peter Casey, a Private Marine serving on board His Majesty's ship *Foudroyant* under my command, having on the afternoon of the 14th of April last been found drunk on his post whilst sentinel at the wardroom door of that ship and having stolen some wine from a cask slung in the *Foudroyant*'s wardroom belonging to that ship's officers, which cask was under his charge as sentinel, I have to request you will be pleased to apply to the Lords Commissioners of the Admiralty that the said Peter Casey may be tried at a court martial for the above offences. …

All the evidences being then ordered to withdraw, and to attend their examinations separately, they all withdrew accordingly, except the first to be sworn, and the court proceeded to trial as follows:

Evidence in support of the charge.

James Thomas, Corporal of Marines of His Majesty's ship *Foudroyant*, was sworn and examined as follows:

Prosecutor	Did you plant the prisoner sentinel at the wardroom door of the *Foudroyant* on the afternoon of the fourteenth of April last?
Answer	Yes.
Prosecutor	Was he sober when you planted him there?
Answer	He appeared to me as such.
Prosecutor	What was his condition when relieved?
Answer	He was then very drunk.
Prosecutor	Do you know anything of a bottle of wine found in his possession while sentinel on that post?

Answer No. It was found by the sergeant.

Prosecutor Had the prisoner, at the time he was sentinel as before mentioned, charge of the cask of wine belonging to the officers of the *Foudroyant*?

Answer Yes, I gave him charge of it at four o'clock.

Court State the orders you gave the prisoner at the time you planted him as before mentioned.

Answer I took him into the wardroom and showed him the cask of wine, the lock of which was secured with white marline. I told him to let nobody draw any wine from thence, but the wardroom steward.

Court At what time did you plant the prisoner, and how long was he to remain on the post?

Answer I planted him at four o'clock; he was to remain till six.

Court Was any other person in the wardroom when you took the prisoner and showed him the cask?

Answer None, but the other sentinel.

Court What was the other sentinel?

Answer He was sentinel over the wine and took me in to see the state of it.

Court Did you relieve the prisoner at six o'clock?

Answer Yes.

Court When you relieved the prisoner was the lock of the wine cask under his charge in the state as when you planted him?

Answer The marline was there and tied round the lock.

Court Did you visit the post between the hours of four and six and, did you then find the prisoner in the same state as when you planted him?

Answer I visited the post and thought the man was something in liquor and reported it immediately to the sergeant.

Court Was wine served to the ship's company at this time?

Answer No, beer was served.

Prisoner Was the sentinel that I relieved drunk at the time that you planted me?

Answer He was not drunk.

The witness withdrew.

William King, Sergeant of Marines of His Majesty's ship *Foudroyant*, sworn and examined as follows:

Prosecutor Was the prisoner sentinel at the wardroom door of the *Foudroyant* between the hours of 4 and 6 of the afternoon of the fourteenth of April last?

Answer He was.
Prosecutor Did you see him on or about four o'clock?
Answer I did, a little before he was placed sentinel.
Prosecutor Did he appear at that time to be sober?
Answer He appeared at that time to be sober.
Prosecutor What was the condition of the prisoner when relieved and taken to the officer of the guard?
Answer He was drunk.
Prosecutor Relate what you know respecting a bottle of wine found on the prisoner, while sentinel at the wardroom door.
Answer When he was relieved, he had a bottle of wine in his hand, which I took from him and gave to the officer of the guard. He was very much in liquor and ordered to be confined on the poop by the commanding officer.
Prosecutor Did you visit the cask in the wardroom during the time the prisoner was sentinel at the wardroom door?
Answer I did. I found the wine was spilt about in the wardroom. I sent for the wardroom steward and asked him if the cask was as he had left it; he said no, the string was cast off from the lock, and that the lock had been turned and wine drawn.
Court Where was the cask of wine?
Answer It was hung up in the wardroom of the *Foudroyant*. The officers were living in an hulk.
Court When you took the bottle of wine from the prisoner, did he give you any account how he came by it?
Answer No.

The witness withdrew.

William Hallahan, Wardroom Steward on board His Majesty's ship *Foudroyant*, sworn and examined as follows:

Prosecutor Did you draw some wine from a cask slung in the *Foudroyant*'s wardroom on the fourteenth of April last?
Answer Yes, five bottles, about a quarter before four in the afternoon.
Prosecutor Did you, after you had so done, make the lock fast and was any wine spilt on the deck, to your knowledge, at that time?
Answer Yes, I seized it fast that it could not be turned. There was not any wine spilt on the deck at that time, except a small drop or so.
Prosecutor State at what time you visited that cask again and in what state you found it.

Answer — It was between five and six o'clock of the same afternoon. I found the seizing of the lock was cast loose and there was wine spilt under it on the deck, perhaps about half a tumbler full.

Prosecutor — What wine was in the cask?

Answer — Port wine.

Court — What did you do with the five bottles of wine which you drew from that cask before four o'clock?

Answer — I carried them into the hulk and they were expended at the wardroom table.

The witness withdrew.

Lieutenant David Ross of the Royal Marines serving on board His Majesty's ship *Foudroyant* sworn and examined as follows:

Prosecutor — Was you officer of the guard on the afternoon of the fourteenth of April last on board the *Foudroyant*'s hulk?

Answer — Yes.

Prosecutor — What was the condition of the prisoner when brought to you on that afternoon and what report did the sergeant make of him?

Answer — When he was brought aft, I cannot recollect the time, but I believe it was between four and six o'clock, he was drunk. The sergeant reported that he had found the prisoner drunk upon his post and found a bottle of wine in his possession, which bottle of wine I took from the sergeant and delivered to the commanding officer.

Court — Did the sergeant bring the prisoner to you with any complaint and what was the complaint?

Answer — He did not bring the prisoner with him when he came the first, but complained of the prisoner being drunk and that he had found a bottle of wine on him and said he had relieved him. I ordered the sergeant to confine him.

The witness withdrew.

Lieutenant Henry Potter Malpass of His Majesty's ship *Foudroyant* sworn and examined as follows:

Prosecutor — What report did Lieutenant Ross of the Marines make to you of the prisoner on the afternoon of the fourteenth of April last, you being then commanding officer of the *Foudroyant*?

Answer — I was in the wardroom at nearly six o'clock when Lieutenant Ross brought a bottle of wine in his hand, which he told me was taken from a man of the name of Casey, who he said was at that time sentinel at the wardroom door of the

Foudroyant. I went on deck and ordered the prisoner to be relieved and brought over. I found him perfectly drunk. I ordered him to be confined.

Prosecutor Did you compare the wine taken from the prisoner with the wine in use of the wardroom at that time?

Answer I did and it appeared to me to be the same.

The witness withdrew.

Corporal James Thomas further examined as follows:

Court Was the prisoner relieved before six o'clock in consequence of his being drunk or was he relieved at the regular time?

Answer He was relieved at the regular time; I reported him drunk about ten or fifteen minutes before that.

The witness withdrew.

The evidence in support of the charges being finished, the prisoner was called upon to make his defence, who said he had not anything to offer, but lay himself at the mercy of the court.

The prisoner not having anything further to offer, the court was cleared and proceeded to deliberate upon and form the sentence.

The court, having heard the evidence in support of the charges, the prisoner not having anything to offer in his defence, and very maturely and deliberately weighed and considered the same, was of opinion that the charges had been proved against the prisoner, Peter Casey, and did in consequence thereof adjudge the said Peter Casey to receive two hundred lashes with a cat of nine tails on his bare back alongside such of His Majesty's ships at such times and in such proportions as the commander in chief of His Majesty's ships and vessels at this port shall direct.

The court was opened, the prisoner brought in, the evidence and audience admitted and sentence passed accordingly. …

127. *Court Martial of John Dow*

[ADM 1/5368]

Minutes taken at a court martial assembled on board His Majesty's ship *Gladiator* in Portsmouth Harbour on the first day of January 1805.

Present

Sir Isaac Coffin, Bar^{t}., Rear Admiral of the White and second officer in the command of His Majesty's ships and vessels at Portsmouth and Spithead, President.

Captains	George Martin	Captains	John Irwin
	William Cuming		Loftus Otway Bland
	James Dunbar		John Wainwright
	George Nicholas Hardinge		

The Prisoner was brought in and audience admitted.

The President reported to the court that Captains John Gore, Henry Hill, Edward Stirling Dickson, John Acworth Ommaney and Micajah Malbon were absent on Admiralty leave.

The order from the Right Honourable Lords Commissioners of the Admiralty, dated the twenty-ninth day of December last and directed to the President to assemble a court martial for the trial of M^r^. John Dow, Carpenter of His Majesty's Ship *Calcutta*, for having been repeatedly guilty of drunkenness and disobedience by absenting himself for several days together from his duty was read.

The members of the court and the judge advocate then, in open court and before they proceeded to trial, respectively took the several oaths enjoined and directed in and by an Act of Parliament made and passed in the twenty second year of the reign of His late Majesty King George the Second, entitled *An Act for Amending, Explaining and Reducing into One Act of Parliament the Law Relating to the Government of His Majesty's Ships, Vessels and Forces by Sea.*

Then the letter from Captain Daniel Woodriff, Commander of His Majesty's ship *Calcutta*, dated the twenty-eighth day of December last and directed to Admiral Montague, Commander in Chief of His Majesty's ships and vessels at Portsmouth and Spithead, containing the charge, was read and is hereto annexed and the witnesses were ordered to withdraw and attend their examinations separately, which they did as follows:

Lieutenant Richard Donovan of His Majesty's ship *Calcutta* called in and sworn.

Captain Woodriff asked:

Q. Do you know the prisoner?

A. I do.

Q. Do you remember upon the passage from New South Wales to have seen the prisoner repeatedly drunk when he came on the quarter deck at eight o'clock in the evening to report the state of the well and the security of the store rooms?

A. I have.

Q. Do you remember my causing his cabin to be searched for liquor shortly after our leaving New South Wales or rather between New Zealand and making Cape Horn?

A. I was not present myself.

Q. Do you recollect my directing the allowance of spirits of M^r^. Dow and his boy to be stopped in consequence of M^r^. Dow's frequent intoxication?

A. Yes.

Q. Do you recollect M^r^. Dow's repeatedly absenting himself from his duty for several days together, since the ship came into this harbour?

A. Twice.

Q. Was you ever sent on shore after Mr Dow to endeavour to find him and bring him on board?

A. I was once, the evening after last Christmas Day, but I did not find him.

Q. Do you remember that a few days subsequent to the docking of the ship Mr Dow was brought on board after several days absence and that he wanted to escape from the hulk the same evening?

A. Yes, I do.

Q. Do you remember the apparent contrition of M^r^. Dow the next morning, his supplicating forgiveness and promising nothing of the kind should ever happen again?

A. I do.

Q. When did Mr Dow get leave to go on shore last and for how long?

A. Saturday evening the twenty-third of December last until Monday morning.

Q. When did he return and in what state?

A. On Friday following, very much intoxicated.

The court asked:

Q. When you have seen him in this state, was he incapable of doing his duty?

A. I have frequently seen him very much intoxicated and not capable of doing his duty properly.

Q. What has been his general conduct?

A. He was a very good man when sober, which he would be for a month or six weeks together; I never saw a more hardworking man and more attentive to his duty when sober.

Q. Did you ever know him guilty of disobedience of orders?

A. Never, but in the instances I have mentioned.

M^r^. Dickson, a Midshipman belonging to the *Calcutta*, called in and sworn.

Captain Woodriff asked:

Q. Do you know the prisoner?

A. Yes.

Q. Do you recollect M^r^. Dow's having repeatedly absented himself from the ship several days together since the ship has been in the harbour?

A. Yes.

Q. Do you remember being sent on shore accompanied by the sergeant of Marines both to Portsmouth and Gosport in search of Mr. Dow in the month of November?

A. It was on or about that time.

Q. Do you remember seeing Mr. Dow on board between Saturday the twenty-second of December and Friday the twenty-eighth?

A. No.

Q. Do you remember his being brought on board the twenty-eighth and in what state?

A. I did not see him brought on board, but saw him soon afterwards; he appeared to be rather intoxicated.

The court asked:

Q. Was you in the ship when she left Chatham?

A. Yes.

Q. Have you frequently seen the prisoner drunk and incapable of doing his duty?

A. Yes.

Mr. Wm. Lennard, Gunner of the *Calcutta*, called in and sworn.

Captain Woodriff asked:

Q. Do you know the prisoner?

A. Yes.

Q. Do you recollect at any time during the passage home to have seen Mr. Dow intoxicated?

A. Once, that is a long time back.

Q. Do you recollect that his allowance of spirits was stopped at sea?

A. Yes.

Q. Do you know for what reason?

A. I believe about the middle of last April; one evening he was deficient of coming up to make his report and he was sent for and he was intoxicated. I believe it was for that.

Q. Do you know that he has been repeatedly absent from the ship without leave for several days together since she has been in the harbour?

A. I have known him to be absent, but do not know what leave he had.

Q. Have you been sent after him on those occasions?

A. Yes.

The court asked:

Q. Did you go out from England in the ship?

A. Yes.

Q. Have you often seen the prisoner drunk and incapable of doing his duty in the passage from New South Wales?

A. Only once when he was actually wanted on duty, he might have been, and I [did?] not see him.

Q. Have you ever seen him drunk on board?

A. Yes but only once at sea. I have seen him intoxicated in harbour at Port Jackson; I have seen him drunk on shore in Portsmouth and when he came on board.

Q. Do you consider the prisoner to be a drunken or a sober man?

A. I cannot say he is a sober man.

The prosecution being closed, the prisoner was called on for his defence; he requested Captain Woodriff to speak to his character.

He said M[r]. Dow is in my opinion a very fit person to be carpenter of one of His Majesty's ships and appears to me very well qualified, is active and diligent and is everything I would desire in a carpenter, except his addiction to liquor.

The court was cleared and agreed that the charge had been proved against the said John Dow, and did adjudge him to be dismissed from his office of Carpenter of His Majesty's ship *Calcutta* and to serve in such other situation and on board such ship of His Majesty's as the Commander in Chief of His Majesty's ships and vessels at Portsmouth aforesaid should direct.

The court was again opened, the prisoner brought in, audience admitted and sentence passed accordingly. …

127A. *Woodriff to Montagu*

[ADM 1/5368] *Calcutta*, Portsmouth Harbour
28th December 1804

… M[r]. John Dow, Carpenter of His Majesty's ship under my command, having been repeatedly guilty of drunkenness and disobedience by absenting himself for several days together from his duty, I have, in consequence thereof, ordered him under arrest and have to request you will be pleased to move their Lordships to grant an order to try M[r]. John Dow, Carpenter of the *Calcutta*, by a court martial for the aforesaid offences. …

128. *Court Martial of David Henderson and John Baikie*

[ADM 1/5374]

Minutes of proceedings at a court martial held on board His Majesty's ship *L'Aimable* at Yarmouth Roads on the eleventh day of July 1806.

Present

Joseph Hanwell, Esqr., Captain of His Maj^s^. ship *Majestic* and third officer in command of His Majesty's ships and vessels at Yarmouth Roads, President.

Captains

George Burlton	George Parker
John Draper	James Macnamara
Robt. Campbell	Henry Hill
Richard Curry	

being all the post captains of His Majesty's ships at this place, except Captain Clotsworthy Upton, the prosecutor.

The prisoners were brought into court and the evidence and audience admitted.

Read the order of the Right Honourable the Lords Commissioners of the Admiralty, dated the eighth day of July 1806, directed to Joseph Hanwell, Esquire, Captain of His Majesty's ship *Majestic* and third officer in command of His Maj^s^. ships & vessels at Yarmouth Roads, to try M^r^. David Henderson & M^r^. John Baikie, Master's Mates belonging to His Majesty's ship *L'Aimable*, for drunkenness, quarrelling & fighting as stated in a letter from Captain Upton of that ship, dated the 5th day of July 1806.

The members of the court and judge advocate, before they proceeded to trial, respectively took their oaths agreeable to Act of Parliament.

Read a letter from Captain Upton[1] as follows, *Viz.*:

His Majesty's ship *L'Aimable*
Yarmouth, 5th July 1806

… I beg leave to state to you that the conduct of Messrs. John Baikie and David Henderson, Master's Mates of His Maj^s^. ship under my command, has been so disgraceful to the characters of officers and of gentlemen (while getting under weigh on the morning of the 4th) that I am under the necessity of requesting you will be pleased to cause their removal from His Maj^s^. ship *Aimable*.

[1]This letter is addressed to Vice Admiral Thomas Macnamara Russell.

M^{r}. Henderson, at the early hour of three in the morning, appeared at his station intoxicated, when he entered into a quarrel and altercation with M^{r}. Baikie, striking and otherwise maltreating him. M^{r}. Baikie, with the ferocity of a savage, availed himself of superior strength and sobriety, has beaten him in the most brutal, shameful manner. It is unnecessary for me to say anything on the bad example there shown in the most public manner; it is but too evident. But it may be necessary for me to add that, as we weighed with the watch, only the main deck necessarily became under the immediate direction of these officers and where they then sacrificed the discipline and good order of the ship.

…

The evidences ordered to withdraw out of court, except M^{r}. *Geo^{e}. Bateman*, who was sworn.

Captain Upton, Prosecutor	Did you see the quarrel and drunkenness exhibited in the charges against the prisoner?
Answer	Part of it.
Capt. Upton	Was M^{r}. Henderson drunk?
Ans^{r}.	He appeared to me to be much intoxicated indeed.
Capt. Upton	Did you see M^{r}. Henderson strike M^{r}. Baikie.
Answer	I saw M^{r}. Henderson run out of the galley and strike M^{r}. Baikie at same time [*sic*] saying, 'you damned rascal.'
Capt. Upton	Did you see M^{r}. Baikie beat M^{r}. Henderson?
Answer	I saw them scuffling together, but cannot say whether M^{r}. Baikie struck him or not.
Court	Do you mess with M^{r}. Baikie and M^{r}. Henderson?
Answer	I do.
Capt. Upton	Do you recollect in what state M^{r}. Henderson's face was the morning after the quarrel happened?
Ans^{r}.	It was contused & very much swelled; he could hardly see out of his eyes.
Capt. Upton	Do you know of your own knowledge whether that proceeded from the beating he got from M^{r}. Baikie?
Answer	I cannot say I saw M^{r}. Baikie beat his face.

Captain Upton observed he had no further question to put to that gentleman.

Court	Can you give any further relation?
Ansr.	No.
Court	You don't know then the cause of their quarrel?
Ansr.	I cannot say, but believe it was an old grudge.
Prisoner, Mr. Baikie	Did you hear me tell Jno. Lynch to hold Mr. Henderson and to prevent him from striking me?
Ansr.	I heard Mr. Baikie say, 'Haul him away. Haul him away.'

William Teague, Boatsn. Mate, sworn.

Captain Upton	State to the court what you know respecting the charges against the prisoners.
Answer	At 3 o'clock, I was ordered to turn the hands up to make sail. And I went then down and called Mr. Baikie and Mr. Moody and came on deck again and was getting the topsail sheets manned when Mr. Henderson ordered him to go on the starboard side of the main deck; & Mr. Baikie replied he would go on which side the main deck he thought proper. And then, Mr. Henderson told Mr. Baikie a 2d. time to go on the starboard side of the main deck & gave Mr. Baikie a shove with his hand. Then Mr. Baikie gave Mr. Henderson a shove and then Mr. Henderson gave Mr. Baikie a kick in the bowels and then Mr. Baikie took hold of the cat fall. Then they both began a kicking each other.
Capt. Upton	Was Mr. Henderson drunk?
Ansr.	Yes.
Capt. Upton	Did you see in what state Mr. Henderson's face was after the quarrel?
Answer	Yes, he was all cut over the eye and bleeding very much both at nose & eye.
Capt. Upton	Do you know if that was done by Mr. Baikie?
Answer	Yes.
Court	Do you know of any other circumstance?

Answer	Only that his face was not in that state when he came on deck.
Court	In what manner did M^{r}. Henderson get that swelled face; do you know if it proceeded from a blow of the fist, kick or cat fall or if otherwise?
Answer	I cannot say.
Prisoner, M^{r}. Baikie	Did you hear me tell anyone to hold him in order to prevent M^{r}. Henderson striking me?
Answer	Yes, I did.
Court	Was it after his face was bruised, or before, that the prisoner (M^{r}. Baikie) requested someone to hold him?
Answer	It was after and he ordered his servant to fetch another coat and shirt that M^{r}. Henderson had torn of [*sic*] M^{r}. Baikie's back.
James Flaxman sworn.	
Capt. Upton	Did you see M^{r}. Henderson drunk on Friday morning the 4th instant.?
Answer	Yes.
Capt. Upton	Did you see him strike M^{r}. Baikie or ill use him in any other way?
	M^{r}. Henderson ord^{d}. M^{r}. Baikie over on the starboard side the waist. M^{r}. Baikie asked who he was ordering; M^{r}. Henderson shoved him by the shoulder, ordered him over on the starboard side the main deck. M^{r}. Baikie told him he would stop on either side he pleased; with that, M^{r}. Henderson kicked him in the bowels.
Capt. Upton	Did you see M^{r}. Baikie strike and beat M^{r}. Henderson?
Answer	They parted and, after we hauled the main topsail sheet home, we turned the people on the fore topsail sheet. I saw M^{r}. Henderson and M^{r}. Baikie then fighting.
	Did you see M^{r}. Henderson's face after they had done fighting & what state was it in?
Ans^{r}.	All of a gore of blood.
Capt. Upton	Do you know if it was caused by M^{r}. Baikie beating him?

Answer	Whether it was by a fall on the cable or blow, I cannot say.
Prisoner, M^{r}. Baikie	Did I request anyone to hold him for the purpose of avoiding quarrelling with M^{r}. Henderson?
Answer	Yes, he called Jno. Lynch, but the quarrel was all over then.
Prisoner, M^{r}. Baikie	Do you think I was very grossly insulted?
Answ^{r}.	Yes.

The prisoners had no further questions to put, but M^{r}. Henderson called on Captain Upton for a character.

Captain Upton declared that, during the time M^{r}. Henderson had been under his command, his conduct had merited his approbation until this circumstance arose, & which he (Captain Upton) could not pass over without sacrificing the discipline of the ship, and was also persuaded that every officer in the ship had the same good opinion of M^{r}. Henderson, the prisoner.

Lieutenant Oliphant also declared that, ever since he had been in the *Aimable*, he had observed M^{r}. Henderson do his duty as a steady, sober man & attentive, good officer, & never knew him before in a fault.

Lieutenant Hewitt had known the prisoner, M^{r}. Henderson, about twelve months and always found him do his duty with alacrity, sobriety & steadiness and never knew him in a fault.

The other prisoner, M^{r}. Baikie, was extremely sorry for what had happened and submitted to the court his having been struck and provoked, and trusts his general good character as an officer will be taken into consideration and hopes he will be found still fit to serve His Maj^{s}. in the situation he now fills.

The prisoner, M^{r}. Baikie, then called on Captain Upton for a character.

Captain Upton replied, 'The strongest proof that I can give of M^{r}. Baikie's conduct having met my approbation is his having served with me in three ships and that, during the time I was on half pay, he was by my recommendation under the patronage and protection of Admiral George Martin, that I deeply regret the necessity of bringing him before a court martial, as I had the most anxious wish to forward his views in the service, but that I could not sacrifice the discipline of the ship or suffer a bad example to be held out on any consideration whatsoever. And Rear Admiral George Martin has given certificates of M^{r}. Baikie's general good character and I am fully persuaded that every officer in each of the three ships had the same good opinion of M^{r}. Baikie as myself.'

The prisoners having nothing further to offer in their defence, the court was cleared and proceeded to deliberate upon and form the sentence.

The court, having carefully and deliberately weighed and considered the evidence produced and what the prisoners had to allege in their defence, was of opinion that the charges against Mr. David Henderson were proved and in consideration of Mr. Henderson's good character as related to the court by Captain Upton and officers of the *Aimable*, the court only adjudge Mr. Henderson to be reprimanded, disrated and removed to such other ship as Vice Admiral Russell shall please to direct. The court were also of further opinion that the charge of beating Mr. David Henderson was proved, but that it did not amount to ferocious, savage, brutal, or shameful manner, but appears to have arisen from the impulse of the moment, from having received a blow and other provocation, and from the great and many testimonials of his (Mr. John Baikie's) good conduct both from his captain and by certificates, the court only adjudged Mr. Jno. Baikie to be reprimanded. And Messrs. David Henderson and Jno. Baikie were reprimanded and sentenced accordingly.

The court was opened, audience admitted and sentence passed accordingly. …

129. *Court Martial of Francis Broadfoot*

[ADM 1/5381]

Minutes of proceedings at a court martial held on board His Majesty's ship *Salvador del Mundo* in Hamoaze on Saturday the second day of May 1807.

Present

The honourable Alan Hyde Gardner, Captain of His Majesty's ship *Hero* and second officer in the command of His Majesty's ships and vessels at Plymouth, President.

Captains

Israel Pellew	John Loring
Thomas Rogers	George Eyre
John Halliday	John Bligh
Edward Rotheram	Richard Peacocke
Charles Fielding	Richard Hawkins
John Conn	Murray Maxwell

George Eastlake, Jr.
officiating Judge Advocate

Being all captains of post ships according to seniority then & there present.

The prisoner was brought into court and the evidence and audience admitted.

Read – The order of the Right Hon. The Lords Commissioners of the Admiralty, dated the 28th day of April 1807, directed to the Honourable Alan Hyde Gardner, Capt. of His Majesty's ship *Hero* and second officer in the command of His Majesty's ships and vessels at Plymouth, to try M^{r}. Francis Broadfoot, Second Master and Pilot of His Majesty's cutter *Entreprenante*, for having, since her arrival in Hamoaze, conducted himself unbecoming the character of an officer by neglecting his duty, taking on the 14th of the said month part of the crew on shore, associating with them and returning on board in a state of intoxication.

Read – The warrant appointing a judge advocate.

Then the members of the court and judge advocate, in open court and before they proceeded to trial, respectively took the oaths directed by Act of Parliament passed in the 22d year of the reign of George the Second.

The annexed letter from Lieutenant Robert Benjn. Young, commanding His Majesty's cutter *Entreprenante*, to William Young, Esqr., Admiral of the Blue, &c., &c. was then read.

All the witnesses, except the first to be sworn, being then ordered to withdraw and to attend their examinations separately, they all withdrew accordingly and the court proceeded to trial as follows:

Evidence in support of the charge.

M^{r}. Henry Heatherly, Midshipman belonging to His Majesty's cutter *Entreprenante*, sworn and examined as follows:

Pros^{r}. Did the prisoner absent himself without leave from the *Entreprenante* on the morning of 14th April last?

Ans^{r}. He did.

Pros^{r}. Did he take the boatswain's mate and boat's crew with him?

Ans^{r}. He did.

Pros^{r}. What did the prisoner say to the boatswain before he went over the side?

Ans^{r}. He sent for the boatswain's mate upon deck and asked him to go on shore with him to take his morning. Boatswain's mate went with him reluctantly with 2 men as the boat's crew.

Pros^{r}. Were you sent on shore by me that morning to find the boatswain?

Ans^{r}. I was.

Pros^{r}. Relate to the court where you found the boatswain and in what state the prisoner was seen with him and the names of the crew who were smoking and drinking with him.

Ans^{r}. I found the boatswain at an alehouse in Richmond Walk and the prisoner drinking and smoking with Abraham Burt, William Benjamin and Henry Parker; the prisoner was something the worse for liquor, not intoxicated. He had been drinking; he was not incapable of doing his duty at that time. I also informed him the survey was holding on board and Mr. Young expected to see him there; he [did?] not come.

Pros^{r}. What time did the prisoner return? Relate his conduct to you and his state.

Ans^{r}. The prisoner returned at 5 o'clock the same day; on his coming on board, he stripped to fight me and, finding him intoxicated, incapable of duty, I took no notice of it, till M^{r}. Young returned in the morning. He appeared to have been much beaten with fighting, having a black eye and swelled face.

Co^{t}. Did the boat's crew return at the same time?

Ans^{r}. They returned before with the boatswain about 12 o'clock.

Co^{t}. What time did the prisoner leave the ship?

Ans^{r}. About half past 8 in the morning.

Co^{t}. Are you acquainted with the conduct of the prisoner on the 18th of January?

Ans^{r}. Yes.

Co^{t}. Relate it to the court.

Ans^{r}. On the 18th of January, being under sailing orders, Lieut. Young went on shore on duty, on coming on board about half past three in the afternoon and enquiring for the prisoner, he was found lying on the arm chest in the galley dead drunk. [He?] did not come upon deck till the next morning.

The witness withdrew.

George Chapman, Boatswain's Mate belonging to His Majesty's cutter *Entreprenante*, sworn and examined as follows:

Pros^{r}. Did the prisoner, on the morning of the 14 April last, invite you on shore with him?

Ans^{r}. Yes.

Pros^{r}. What were the words he said to you before he went over the side?

Ans^{r}. He asked me to go on shore to get my morning. I told him I had a [great deal?] of duty to do and I could not go; he persisted and I went with him. I drank one glass of grog with him. I asked him if he was going on board; he told me he was going to his tailor for some clothes. I returned on board.

Co^{t}. Were Abraham Burt, William Benjamin and Henry Payne associating and drinking in an alehouse in company with yourself and the prisoner on the 14th of April last?

Ans^{r}. Yes.

The witness withdrew.

William Evans, Quarter Master belonging to His Majesty's cutter *Entreprenante*, sworn and examined as follows:

Pros^{r}. Were you quarter master of the watch on the 14 April last?

Ans^{r}. Yes.

Co^{t}. Did you see the prisoner come on board on that day? State his conduct to the midshipman and whether he was in a state of intoxication.

Ans^{r}. I saw the prisoner come on board; he seemed to be disguised in liquor. M^{r}. Heatherly informed him he was left commanding officer of the vessel; the prisoner said he should not acknowledge his command till he heard it from M^{r}. Young. Several words ensued in a wrangling manner; the prisoner clinched his hand against M^{r}. Heatherly. I did not see him strike him.

Co^{t}. Did he strip?

Ans^{r}. He stripped off his jacket in a menacing manner.

Co^{t}. Did you see the prisoner on the 18 January last, when getting under way, drunk and incapable of doing his duty?

Ans^{r}. I saw the prisoner at that time lying down on a chest in the galley, but I don't know that he was drunk.

Co^{t}. Did you see him on deck at any time then doing his duty?

Ansr. I did not.

The evidence in support of the charge being finished, the prisoner was called upon to make his defence, who addressed the court.[1]

The prisoner having no written defence or anything further to offer, the court was cleared and proceeded to deliberate upon and form the sentence.

The court, having heard the evidence in support of the charge as well as what the prisoner had offered in his defence and very maturely and deliberately weighed and considered the same, was of opinion that the charge had been proved against the prisoner, Francis Broadfoot, and did in consequence adjudge said Francis Broadfoot to be dismissed from his present situation of second master, to serve before the mast in such ship of His Majesty as the commander in chief at this port should direct and be rendered incapable of ever serving again as an officer in the navy of His Majesty, His heirs and successors.

[1]This letter is not bound with the transcript in ADM 1/5381.

The court was opened, the prisoner brought in, the evidence and audience admitted and sentence passed accordingly. …

129A. *Robert Benjamin Young to William Young*

[ADM 1/5381] His Majesty's cutter *Entreprenante*
26 April 1807

… M^{r}. Francis Broadfoot, Second Master and Pilot of His Majesty's cutter under my command, having, since the arrival of the vessel in Hamoaze, conducted himself unbecoming the character of an officer by neglecting his duty, taking, on the 14 ins^{t}., part of the crew on shore, associating with them and returning on board in a state of intoxication and from his former conduct in the vessel when getting under weigh on the 18th January last, laying down in the galley unable to perform his duty, urges me to request you will be pleased to order a court martial to be held on him. …

130. *Court Martial of George Lonis*

[ADM 1/5383]

Minutes of the proceedings of a court martial held on board the *Magnanime* in Sheerness Harbour on Friday the 2nd day of October 1807.

Present
George Parker, Esqre., Captain of His Majesty's ship *Stately* and second officer in the command of His Majesty's ships and vessels in the River Medway and at the buoy of the Nore, President.

Captains

John Broughton	Richard Jones
Edwards D. Graham	John Richards

There being no other post captains at this port, except Captain E.D. Graham, on leave from the Lords Commissioners of the Admiralty.

The prisoner was brought into court and the evidence and audience admitted. Witnesses called over by the judge advocate.

Read the order of the Right Honble. the Lords Commissioners of the Admiralty, dated the 29th ult^{o}. and directed to George Parker, Esqre., Captain of His Majesty's ship *Stately* and second officer in the command of His Majesty's ships and vessels employed in the River Medway and at the buoy of the Nore, and that appointing M^r^. John Gunnell to execute the office of judge advocate, which were as follows, *vizt*.:[1]

… Whereas Rear Admiral Wells hath transmitted to us a letter, dated the 19th September 1807, which he had received from Lieutenant Chas. Champion, commanding His Majesty's gun brig *Snipe*, representing that in the night of the 17th of the same month George Lonis, Quarter Master of the said gun brig, was drunk, behaved in a very outrageous and mutinous manner, threatening to strike the master and making use of mutinous expressions against the officers of the *Snipe* and requesting that he (the said George Lonis) may be tried by a court martial for the same. We send you herewith Lieutenant Champion's above mentioned letter and do hereby require and direct you to assemble a court martial so soon as conveniently may be, which court (you being president thereof) is hereby required and directed to try the said George Lonis, Quarter Master of the *Snipe* for the offences with which he stands charged by Lieut. Champion and particularly set forth in his above mentioned letter accordingly.

Given under our hands this 29th Septem^r^. 1807

…

… Whereas the Right Honble the Lords Commissioners of the Admiralty have directed me by an order, dated the 29th ultimo, to assemble a court martial and try George Lonis, Quarter Master of His Majesty's gun brig *Snipe*, for behaving, on the night of the 17th of the same month, in a very outrageous and mutinous manner, threatening to strike the master and making use of mutinous expressions against the officers of the *Snipe*; and whereas by an Act passed in the 22nd year of the reign of King George the Second, entitled *An Act for Amending, Explaining and Reducing into One Act of Parliament the Law Relating to the Government of His Majesty's Ships and Vessels and Forces by Sea*, it is ordered that in the absence of judge advocate [*sic*] and his deputy, the court martial shall have full power and authority to appoint any person to execute the office of judge advocate,

I do with the consent and approbation of the members who constitute this court hereby authorize and appoint you to execute the office of judge advocate on the above occasion, for which this shall be your warrant.

Given on board the *Magnanime* (where the court is assembled) in Sheerness Harbour this 2d. October 1807.

…

[1]This warrant was issued by Captain Parker to John Gunnell.

Then the members of the court and the judge advocate took the oaths prescribed by Act of Parliament.

A letter from Lieutenant Champion exhibiting the complaint was read, and is as follows, *vizt*.:[1]

Snipe, Sheerness
19th September 1807

… I beg leave to state that on the night of the 17th instant George Lonis, Quarter Master of His Majesty's gun brig under my command, was drunk and behaved in a very outrageous manner, threaten'd to strike the master, besides making use of mutinous expressions against the officers of the said brig.

I therefore am to request that you will be pleased to transmit my letter to the Lords Commissioners of the Admiralty in order that the said George Lonis may be tried for the same. …

All the evidences withdrew, except M^r^. James John Blenkins, Sub Lieutenant, who was sworn.

Did you see the prisoner on the night of the 17 ultimo?

Yes.

Was he drunk?

Yes.

Relate to the court what [you] saw of the prisoner's conduct on that night.

Between 7 and 8 o'clock, I was walking the quarter deck, and heard a noise forward crying out 'murder.' I went forward and, on seeing the master, I went down the fore ladder. I ordered him to bring, with the corporal Marines, the people that were making a noise and they brought aft James Gaunt, naked all but his trousers, and George Lonis. Gaunt immediately told me that Geo. Lonis endeavour'd to kill him by pulling out his eyes. I then ordered Geo. Lonis to be put in irons and, after being below in irons, I heard him damning all the officers of the ship and called the midshipman 'a bloody villain' before he was put in irons on the quarter deck. I observed him to go to the master and lift both his fists to him, and threatened to knock him down. I went over to the larboard side of the quarter deck and ask'd him if he knew the consequence of lifting his hand to an officer.

[1]This letter is addressed to Rear Admiral Thomas Wells.

On my ordering the prisoner to be brought aft the following morning do you think his behaviour respectful or that he appeared sorry for his conduct?

No, on the contrary, he lean'd against the bulwark of the quarter deck, never pulled off his hat and seemed to care nothing about the officers on the quarter deck.

Court

Did you see the prisoner attempt to strike the master?

I saw him lift his hand against the master and threaten to strike him. I don't know whether he meant it; he held out his hand and said, 'If you offer to strike me, I will knock you down.'

Did the master attempt to strike the prisoner?

I saw the master push him against the skylight. I did not see him strike him.

Withdrew.

M^{r}. James Ross, Master, called in and sworn.

Did you see the prisoner on the night of the 17th September last?

Yes.

Was he drunk?

Yes.

Relate to the court what you saw of the prisoner's conduct on that night.

Between 7 and 8 o'clock I was below writing the log in my cabin. I heard 'murder' cried out forward and directly went forward with my light, saw George Lonis sitting alongside of the coppers on the starboard side, making use of very improper expressions to the ship's company. I requested him to hold his tongue, and not make so much noise to disturb the ship's company; he still persisted in his conduct and instantly my light was blown out, whether by the prisoner I cannot tell. I judged by the position of the prisoner, it could be no other person and struck him directly. I called for the assistance of the corporal Marines. I took him by the collar and took him up the hatchway. I carried him aft to Lieutenant Blenkins. He sat down upon the gratings and he made use of some very improper expressions to me and I struck him 3 or 4 times. He lifted his hand, but whether to strike me, I am not certain. Every time he lifted his hand, I knocked him down. He called me a 'bugger,' which was the cause of my striking him.

Did the prisoner make any resistance when you carried him aft?

No, he was so drunk he could not. I carried him aft.

What expressions did he make use of to the ship's company?

'You buggers, I'll murder you all.'

Did you hear the prisoner making use of any mutinous expressions against the officers of the brig?

No further than that he had all their duties and he called the midshipman a 'bloody buggerer villain.'

To your knowledge, was the prisoner allowed any liberty liquor that day?

Not that I know of, I was on shore in the dock yard.

You say you struck the prisoner repeatedly, is it therefore not probable when he held his hands against you on the quarter deck, it was more with a view to save himself than with an intention to strike you?

I did not offer to strike him until he held his hand up.

Did he make use of any threatening language at the time he lifted his hand up?

Nothing but the expression of a 'bugger,' which caused me to strike him.

Did you at any time hear the prisoner threaten to knock you down?

No.

Withdrew.

James Gaunt called in, and sworn.

Was the prisoner drunk on the night of the 17 September?

Yes.

Relate to the court what you saw of the prisoner's conduct and his treatment to you on that night.

The prisoner came forward and knocked at my store room and told me to open the door. I opened the door and asked him what he wanted; he told me to let him see. I shut the door and he knocked again. I open'd it and he rush'd at me and a scuffle ensued betwixt us. We were at blows and we fell down over a chest by the galley. There was no light and I found two hands upon me, but cannot swear to the prisoner.

Who tore your shirt off your back?

It was tore by the prisoner in the scuffle before the lights were out.

Had you a light in your store room when the prisoner knocked at the door?

I had.

How was that light put out? Was it before or after the scuffle?

It was put out in the scuffle.

Withdrew.

M^{r}. John Gibbs, Midshipman, called in, and sworn.

Did you see the prisoner on the night of the 17th ulto?

I did.

Was he drunk?

He was.

Did you hear him make use of any abusive language to yourself or any other officer on board that night?

I did; he made use of several abusive expressions, such as damning and blasting the whole of us.

On the prisoner's being brought aft the following morning, was his behaviour respectful or did he appear sorry for his conduct?

He seemed to express his sorrow for his improper conduct on the night before. He came aft with his hat in his hand and appeared sorry, to the best of my recollection.

Did I order him to lean off the gunnell and take his hat off?

I don't recollect that.

Did you hear him call you a 'bloody villain' or words to that effect on the night of the 17th Septem^{r}.?[1]

[ ]

Withdrew.

Richard Hayward, Corporal of Marines, called in and sworn.

Was the prisoner drunk on the night of the 17th September last?

Yes, he was.

Relate what you saw of his conduct on that night.

I went forward and saw the prisoner and another man fighting and I endeavoured to part them and took them aft on the quarter deck. What passed on the quarter deck, I cannot say.

Did you hear him abuse any of the officers?

No, I did not.

Withdrew.

The evidence in support of the charge being finished, the prisoner was called upon to make his defence.

Duncan Forbett called in and sworn.

Pris^{r}.

Did you see me offer to lift my hand up against M^{r}. Ross to strike him?

I did not.

Court

Where was you at the time the prisoner was taken aft on the quarter deck?

I was in my hammock.

Withdrew.

John Jeune called in and sworn.

[1]The answer to this question is left blank in the transcript.

Did you see M^{r}. Ross beat me betwixt decks before I was a prisoner?

Yes.

Did M^{r}. Ross beat me after I was a prisoner?

Yes.

Where?

On the quarter deck.

What did M^{r}. Blenkins say to M^{r}. Ross when he struck me and [M^{r}. Blenkins] took him away from me?

M^{r}. Blenkins said, 'M^{r}. Ross don't strike him while he is a prisoner.'

Pro^{r}.

Was there a sentinel over the prisoner at the time?

No, there was not.

Withdrew.

Walter Arnott called in, and sworn.

Pris^{r}.

Did you see M^{r}. Ross beat me after I was brought on the quarter deck?

Yes, I did.

Did I lift my hand up and offer to strike M^{r}. Ross?

You held up your hand and said, 'Don't strike me while I am a prisoner;' and the master said, 'You Rascal, hold down your hand.' M^{r}. Blenkins was at the main hatchway, calling for the corporal and, when he heard those words, he went aft and push'd the master away from you.

Did I call the master a 'bugger?'

Not in my hearing

Withdrew.

Alexander Donald, Quarter Master, called in, and sworn.

Pris^{r}.

Did you see M^{r}. Ross beat me after I was on the quarter deck?

Yes.

Did I offer to strike him?

No.

Did I call M^{r}. Ross a 'bugger?'

Not in my hcaring.

Court

Was you present on the quarter deck the whole of the time?

Yes.

Did you hear anything that passed forward between M^{r}. Ross and the prisoner previous to his being brought aft?

No.

Withdrew.

The prisoner requested Lieutenant Blenkins to speak to his character and to his general conduct. Lieutenant Blenkins said that since he has belonged to the ship, he has always considered the prisoner as a very good, trusty man and believes him to be a very good sailor.

He also requested M^r^. Ross (Master) to speak to his general conduct.

M^r^. Ross said, 'Since he belonged to the brig about four months, I have always found him a very steady, good man' and this is the first time he had ever known him drunk. 'M^r^. Champion recommended him to me as a very steady, good man, which I have always found until the present instance.'

[Pris^r^] Did you ever know me make use of abusive language before this time?

I never did.

[Pro^r^] When I recommended Lonis to you as a steady man, did I observe at the same time you must be cautious?

Yes, you did.

M^r^. Blenkins was again called in.

Court

Did you give the prisoner permission to take up any extra allowance of spirits on the 17th September?

I allowed him a gill extra in addition to his allowance. I told him I had no objection if the steward would allow it, as a gunner and some other officer had come on board to see him.

Withdrew.

The prisoner having nothing further to offer in his defence, the court was cleared and proceeded to deliberate upon, and form sentence.

The court, having carefully and deliberately weighed and considered the evidence produced and what the prisoner had to offer in his defence, are of opinion that the charge of drunkenness is proved, that the charges of behaving in an outrageous and mutinous manner is proved in part and that the charge of threatening to strike the master, besides making use of mutinous expressions against the officers of the brig, is not proved. The court doth therefore, in consideration of his having been allowed an extra allowance of spirits and his having been severely beaten by the master as appears in his own evidence, only adjudge him to be severely reprimanded and admonished to be particularly circumspect in his conduct in future; and he is hereby so sentenced accordingly. …

131. *Court Martial of Thomas Allen Barnard and Terence Clark*

[ADM 1/5387]

Minutes taken at a court martial assembled on board His Majesty's ship *Gladiator* in Portsmouth Harbour on the twenty-eighth day of May 1808.

Present

Charles Tyler, Esq[r]., Rear Admiral of the Blue and second officer in the command of His Majesty's ships and vessels at Portsmouth and Spithead, President.

Captain	John Laugharne	Captain	John Irwin
	William Robert Broughton		The Honble. Courtnay Boyle
	Adam Drummond		James Brisbane
	James Carthew		John Wainwright
	Thomas Charles Brodie		William Pryce Cumby
	The Honble George Cadogan		Samuel Jackson

The prisoners were brought in and audience admitted.

The president reported to the court that Captains Sir Joseph Yorke, Kn[t]., E. L. Graham, and George Le Geyt were absent on Admiralty leave.

The order from the Right Honble. Lords Commissioners of the Admiralty, dated the 26th day of May instant, and directed to the president to assemble a court martial for the trial of Thomas Allen Barnard, Sub-Lieutenant, and M[r]. Terence Clark, Assistant Surgeon, both belonging to His Majesty's gun brig *Resolute*, for having gone on shore from the *Resolute* on the evening of the fifth on May instant without Lieutenant Edward Harris's special leave and in defiance of his standing orders, and for having slept on shore on the night of the said day contrary to the Articles of War, the General Printed Instructions and his standing orders, was read.

The members of the court and judge advocate then, in open court and before they proceeded to trial, respectively took the several oaths enjoined and directed in and by an Act of Parliament made and passed in the twenty second year of the reign of His late Majesty King George the Second, entitled: *An Act for Amending, Explaining and Reducing into one Act of Parliament the Laws Relating to the Government of His Majesty's Ships, Vessels and Forces by Sea.*

Then the letter from the said Lieutenant Edward Harris, commander of the said gun brig, dated the seventh day of May instant and directed to Vice Admiral Whitshed, containing the charges was read and is hereto annexed and the witnesses were ordered to withdraw and attend their examinations separately, which they did as follows:

Lieutenant Edward Harris, commanding the gun brig *Resolute*, called in and sworn.

The court asked:

Q. Produce the written standing orders of the brig relative to the granting leave of absence.

It was produced and is as follows, 'no leave of absence can be granted without my permission.'

Q. Were the prisoners acquainted with this order?
A. Yes, they were.
Q. Where were you when you state they disobeyed this order?
A. I was on shore at Spike Island at dinner with Colonel Fenwick.
Q. How long had these officers been under your command?
A. The sub-lieutenant, about three months; the assistant surgeon, more than a twelve month.
Q. Did either of those officers ever go on shore without your permission before?
A. Yes.
Q. Had you given them leave of absence on the fifth of May or for the succeeding night?
A. No.
Q. At what time did they return the next day?
A. About half past eight o'clock in the morning, they came off in a shore boat.
Q. Was any officer left on board on the fifth?
A. The second master.
Q. Were your standing orders made public?
A. Yes and they were read to the prisoners.
Q. Were they copied for them?
A. They were not.

Lieutenant Barnard asked:

Q. When were those orders read to me?
A. I really cannot say, but it was soon after that officer came on board in consequence of some impropriety he had committed.
Q. Was it between nine and ten o'clock in the evening?
A. I think it was about eight o'clock.

M^r^. Daniel Mc Arthur, Second Master of the *Resolute*, called in and sworn.

The court asked:

Q. At what time on the fifth of May did the prisoners go on shore from the *Resolute*?
A. Betwixt four and five o'clock in the afternoon.
Q. Where was she then?

A. At the Cove of Cork.
Q. Was Lieutenant Harris then on board?
A. He was not.
Q. Do you know if they had any leave of absence from the commander?
A. I do not know whether they had or not.
Q. When did they return on board?
A. At seven or eight o'clock.
Q. Was Lieutenant Harris then on board?
A. He was.
Q. When Lieutenant Barnard quitted the ship, did he leave any orders or directions with you?
A. None.
Q. Was the order respecting leave of absence ever read in the presence of the prisoners?
A. I never heard it until after they were in confinement.
Q. Was you acquainted with that order before?
A. I joined her the eleventh of last March.
Q. Is a copy of those orders hung up in any conspicuous part of the ship?
A. No
Q. Were those orders understood to be known in the ship?
A. I had heard of them; I understood it to be the standing order.
Q. During Lieutenant Harris' absence, has it been customary for the commanding officer left on board to take leave to go on shore himself or to give other persons leave?
A. Never that I know of. His orders to me were that no person was to quit the ship without his leave.
Q. Do you know this book to be the public orders of the *Resolute*?
A. This is the only one I saw on board.

Lieutenant Barnard asked:
Q. Was it four o'clock that you accompanied the commander to Spike Island?
A. Yes, about that time, a little earlier; I was back again before five.
Q. Was it seven o'clock when I went on shore?
A. It was nearly about five; he quitted the ship quickly after I came on board.

M[r]. Clarke asked:
Q. On my arrival at Cove, did I ask you leave to go on shore on duty?
A. Yes, he did.
Q. On the fifth of May, did I go on shore on duty?

A. Mr. Clarke, as he went over the side, held up a paper and said, 'I am going on shore to get this signed.'

The court asked:

Q. What was the paper?

A. I do not know.

Mr. Clarke asked:

Q. Was it a printed paper?

A. Yes, like the one Mr. Clarke now shows to me.

Q. On the first evening I went on shore, did you represent it to the commander?

A. I did.

Q. What did he say?

A. He made no answer; he neither approved or disapproved of it.

Henry Smith, Quarter Master of the *Resolute*, called in & sworn.

Q. At what time on the fifth of May, did the prisoners go on shore?

A. About seven o'clock in the evening.

Q. Did they remain on shore all night?

A. Yes.

Q. At what time did they return the next day?

A. At half past eight o'clock.

Q. At what time did the commander come on board?

A. At a quarter past nine o'clock in the evening and was on board all night.

Q. Had the prisoners any leave of absence to your knowledge?

A. No.

The prosecution being closed, the prisoners were called on for their defence.

Sub-Lieutenant Barnard said that he had always asked leave before; and, when the commander left the ship, he did not know that he was going to Spike Island and he expected him to return, but not doing so, he left word with the acting master that he was gone on shore.

Mr. Clarke said he had gone twice before on shore in the same way and it was mentioned to the commander, who made no objection, that on the present occasion, he showed the second master, who was commander, a paper that he was going on shore to get signed and he said very well and he could not get back.

Mr. Barnard produced a letter he had received from the prosecution, annexed hereto, to show that he did not always expect that he should not quit the ship without his special leave.[1]

[1]This letter is not bound with the transcript in ADM 1/5387.

Lieutenant Harris called in, and the letter shown to him.
The court asked:

Q. Is that letter of your handwriting?

A. Yes.

Q. Was it written before the fifth of May?

A. Yes, it was written when I was ill on shore; the admiral knew I was on shore in a very ill state.

The court was cleared and agreed that the charges had been in part proved against the said M^{r}. Thomas Allen Barnard and did adjudge him to be severely reprimanded and that the charges had not been proved against the said M^{r}. Terence Clarke and did adjudge him to be acquitted.

The court was again opened, the prisoners brought in, audience admitted and sentence passed accordingly. …

131A. *Harris to Whitshed*

[ADM 1/5387]

His Majesty's gun brig *Resolute*
Cove of Cork, 7th May 1808

… I have to request you will be pleased to move the Right Honble. the Lords Commissioners of the Admiralty that a court martial may be held on Sub Lieut^{t}. Thos. Allen Barnard & M^{r}. Terence Clark, Assistant Surgeon, of His Majesty's gun brig *Resolute* (under my command) for having gone on shore from the said brig on the evening of the 5th inst^{t}. without my special leave & in defiance of my standing orders & for having slept on shore on the night of the 5th inst^{t}. contrary to the Articles of War, the general printed instructions & my standing orders. …

132. *Court Martial of John Ensor*

[ADM 1/5388]

Minutes of the proceedings of a court martial assembled on board His Majesty's ship *Magnanime* in Sheerness Harbour on Tuesday the 5th of July 1808.

Present

By George Parker, Esqre., Captain of His Majesty's ship *Aboukir* and second officer in the command of His Majesty's ships and vessels in the River Medway and at the buoy of the Nore, President.

Captains

Charles Ekins	William Cuming
Richard Curry	James Giles Vashon
Henry Lambert	Honble. Edwd. Rodney

Being all the captains of post ships at this port, except Captains the Honble T. B. Capel of the *Endymion*, Richard Jones of the *Namur*, Robert Henderson of the *Agincourt*, and the Honble. G. Poulett of the *Quebec*, who are on leave from the Lords Commissioners of the Admiralty.

The prisoner was brought in by the Provost Martial.[1]

Witnesses called over by the judge advocate.

Read the order of the Right Honble. the Lords Commissioners of the Admiralty, dated the 28th ultimo., directed to the president, and that appointing M^{r}. John Gunnell to officiate as judge advocate, which were as follows, *vizt*.:[2]

… Whereas Vice Admiral Vashon hath transmitted to us a letter, dated the 13th day of June 1808, which he had received from John Ellis, Esqre., Commander of His Majesty's sloop *Spitfire*, requesting that Lieutenant John Ensor of the said sloop may be tried by a court martial 'for unofficerlike conduct and for inflicting punishment at different times and on different people in his watch on deck at night, particularly on or about the 27th and 28th of May last in contempt of orders to the contrary in having one tied up by the thumbs to the main stay, ordering the boys rub his posterior with sand stones and to swab and beat with swabs, in ordering another a severe beating from the cable tier to the spar deck and from the main hatchway forward and back again and also for contempt'. We send you enclosed Captain Ellis' above mentioned letter and do hereby require and direct you to assemble a court martial so soon as conveniently may be after the arrival of the *Spitfire* at the Nore, which court (you being president thereof) is hereby required and directed to try the said Lieutenant John Ensor for the offences with which he is charged by Captain Ellis in his above mentioned letter accordingly.

Given under our hands the 28 day of June 1808.

…

… Whereas the Right Honourable the Lords Commissioners of the Admiralty have directed me by an order dated the 28th ult^{o}. to assemble a court martial to try Lieutenant John Ensor of His Majesty's sloop *Spitfire*

[1]The provost martial had charge of prisoners at courts martial until their sentences were executed (Falconer, *A New Universal Dictionary*, s.v. Provost Martial).

[2]The order appointing Gunnell was signed by Captain George Parker.

'for unofficerlike conduct, and afflicting [*sic*] punishment at different times and on different people in his watch on deck at night, particularly on or about the 27th and 28th of May last in contempt of orders to the contrary.'

And whereas by an Act passed in the 22nd year of the reign of George the Second, entitled *An Act for Amending, Explaining and Reducing into One Act of Parliament the Law Relating to the Government of His Majesty's Ships, Vessels and Forces by Sea*, it is ordered 'that in the absence of the judge advocate and his deputy, the court martial shall have full power and authority to appoint any person to execute the office of judge advocate.'

I do with the consent and approbation of the members who constitute this court hereby authorize and appoint you to execute the office of judge advocate on the above occasion, for which this shall be your warrant.

Given on board the *Magnanime* this 5th day of July 1808.

...

Then the members of the court and the judge advocate took the oaths prescribed by Act of Parliament.

The letter of complaint from Captain Ellis of the *Spitfire* was read and is as follows, *vizt*.:[1]

His Majesty's ship *Spitfire*
Leith Roads, the 13th June 1808

... I have to request you would be pleased to move my Lords Commissioners of the Admiralty for an order to assemble a court martial, the first convenient opportunity, to try Lieutenant John Ensor of His Majesty's sloop *Spitfire* under my command,

for unofficerlike conduct and having inflicted punishment at different times and on different people in his watch on deck at night, particularly on or about the 27th and 28th of May last in contempt of orders to the contrary in having one tied up by the thumbs to the main stay, ordering the boys rub his posterior with sand stones and to swab and beat him with swabs,

In ordering another severe beating from the cable tier to the spar deck and from the main hatchway forward and back again,

And for contempt. ...

All the witnesses withdrew, except George Story, who was sworn.

[1]This letter is addressed to Vice Admiral James Vashon.

Prosecutor

Was you punished by the prisoner about the 28th May in a middle watch, and in what manner?

Yes, in the first instance the lance corporal tied me up by the thumbs to the main stay, and flogged me over the backside with a swab, then the boys were ordered up and rubb'd me with the holy stones;[1] and, after swab'd me dry, they then put a swab and a purser's bread bag before my mouth and, after he cast me off, they took a rope and put about my neck and drove me fore and aft.

Court

What had you been guilty of to incur such punishment?

They said I had been taking something out of a man's pocket.

Did the prisoner beat you severely and with what?

Yes, with swabs and holy stones. The boys followed me with my trousers down with ropes and beat me fore and aft the deck from 7 bells till after 4 o'clock.

Where was the captain at the time?

In bed on board the ship.

How were you tied up and how were the sand stones applied?

I was tied up by my thumbs with my breeches down and the boys rub'd my backside and took it by spells for nearly half an hour. And I was so sore, I could not sit down.

Prisoner

Did ever you make any complaint of this to Captain Ellis?

No.

Withdrew.

William Smith called in and sworn.

Pros[r].

Was you punished by the prisoner's orders in a first watch on or about the 28th of May last?

Yes.

Relate to the court in what manner.

I had orders by the captain to keep no watch and to turn out at 7 bells to sound the well and work all day. The quarter master's or boatswain's mate was to call me. I was not called, but the boatswain's mate came and beat me from my hammock up the after ladder, fore and aft the deck.

Did you make any complaint to me on the quarter deck on the next afternoon of that circumstance?

[1]According to Falconer's *A New Universal Dictionary*, a holy stone was 'a soft porous stone used in most ships for the purpose of rubbing and scouring the decks with sand every morning' (s.v. Holy Stone).

Yes, to ask to keep my watch again.

When I sent for the prisoner to enquire into it, did he accuse me of letting a mutineer out of irons without punishment?

Yes.

When I told him I should bring him to a court martial, did he likewise say he thank'd me, he was obliged to me and after he got to the bottom of the ladder on the after hatchway, repeat it?

Yes.

Court

At the time he made use of the words, 'I thank you, & am obliged to you,' what was his manner? Was it in a threatening tone? Was his manner respectful?

To the best of my knowledge, it was in a disrespectful manner.

What impression did the circumstance of punishing George Story make on the minds of the ship's company?

They said it was very barbarous usage.

Prisoner

Was you urged by any person to make the complaint to Captain Ellis or did you make it from your own choice?

From my own choice.

Had you ever been punished by any other person since you belonged to the ship?

Never, by any person.

How long have you been in the ship?

A 12 month next September.

Withdrew.

M^r^. Edwd. Mc Douall called in and sworn.

Was you midshipman of the prisoner's watch on or about the 27 or 28 of May last?

Yes.

Relate what you know of the punishment of Story and Smith.

Story was punished about ½ past 3 in the morning. When one of the seamen accused him of theft, he was by order of M^r^. Ensor tied up to the main stay by his thumbs with a rope round his body; his feet rested on the starboard cable. He was then flogg'd with a wet swab on his posterior. I went below at 4 o'clock and did not come on deck after.

When and how was Smith, the Carpenter's Mate, punished?

On the 27th of May, Lieutenant Ensor ordered the boatswain's mate to go down below and start him upon deck, first giving him time to put on his clothes. He sent me down to see the boatswain's mate did his duty. I, thinking the man had had sufficient time to put on his clothes, ordered the boatswain's mate to start him up and do his duty. Lieutenant Ensor sent the quarter master down to me and I went upon deck. He asked me if the man was coming up; I told him he was. He then came upon deck. Lieutenant Ensor asked him why he was not up to sound the well, before he went down with an end of rope from the main hatchway to the fore hatchway and back again. He then went down and sounded the well and came up and reported 8 inches.

Was there any specified time allowed him to dress in?

Three minutes.

Did you hear the prisoner, when I accused him of having beat Smith and threaten to try him by a court martial, say he thank'd me and was very much obliged to me?

No. I was not there.

Withdrew.

John M[c]Grath called in and sworn.

Pros[r].

Relate to the court what you know of the punishment of Story.

He was brought up and seiz'd to the main stay by the 2 thumbs and was there a few minutes with one foot touching the cable and afterwards made a rope fast round his body and made it fast to the stay to bear the weight off his thumbs. Corporal Wallis beat him over the backside with a wet swab; and afterwards the boys were turned up to holy stone his backside and the swab was used after the holy stones again. He was then cast off and a rope made fast round his arms and neck and the boys hauled him about the decks.

Relate what you know about Smith's punishment.

I had orders from M[r]. Ensor a little before 7 bells to go down in the tier and beat him up in 2 minutes out of the tier and not to let him know before 7 bells; and, if I did not have him on deck in 2 minutes, he would start me. I beat him after I came on deck by Lieutenant Ensor's orders.

Did you hear the prisoner, when I threatened to try him by a court martial for having beaten Smith, say he thank'd me and was very much obliged to me?

No.

Did you hear him say I had released a mutineer from irons without punishing him?

No.

Did you hear him say anything as he went down the after ladder?

No; I did not go with him.

Court

Do you know what crime Story was guilty of?

It was reported he had been picking a man's jacket pocket, which lay on the booms.

Did you consider the punishment on him as severe or cruel?

It was pretty severe; it was a hard punishment.

Did you ever tell Smith that the lieutenant ordered you to beat him?

No, not that I recollect.

Should you have called the man at 7 bells, if you had been desired not to do it before that time?

I never had any orders, except on that night.

Did the prisoner make it a practice of beating the men when they were not on deck in their watch or at any other time?

No, I never saw him beat them at any other time.

How long have you been in the ship?

About 4 or 5 months.

Did you ever hear the men complain of the prisoner's beating them?

No, not that I recollect.

Did you consider him as severe on the people?

Sometimes he was severe.

How long had the prisoner been doing duty in the ship from the time you joined the ship till he beat him?

About a month or better, to the best of my recollection.

Withdrew.

Joshua Wallas, Marine, called in and sworn.

Pros[r].

Relate to the court what you know of Story's punishment?

As I was going round the decks to report how things were below, I saw two men talking to Story. I asked them what was the matter; they told me directly that Story had been guilty of taking a man's jacket and they had taken notice of everything he had done with his hand in the pocket and they supposed he wanted to plunder out of the pocket. I made the same known to the commanding officer of the deck, taking the prisoner on deck. He was ordered to be tied up to the main stay by his thumbs. After he was tied up by his thumbs to punish him to disgrace the watch, after a few minutes, I was called to punish the same person, upon which I took a wet swab by order of the commanding officer of the deck to punish him upon the bottom, receiving orders to get one of the bread bags to wet overboard to put over his head. While going thro' the punishment, after 2 or 3 minutes being confined by his thumbs, one got loose, bearing with one leg upon the cables. After a time, he was then ordered to be seiz'd up below the wrist, to the wrist to the stay. The boys were then called forth to make use of the holy stone to holy stone his bottom, but no sand used, the boys rubbing his fundament, which made it look very red and angry. After his being released from that punishment, he was drove below by the boys to punish him. After being below, he seemed to make a jeer of what had happen'd, being hardened to everything that was bad.

Court

Was the captain on board at that time?

Yes, he was.

Did you think he was punished severely?

I should have thought so, but I don't think he feels anything.

Prisoner

Did he say to you he would go thro' the punishment again for a chew of tobacco?

Yes.

Withdrew.

The evidence in support of the charge being finished, the prisoner was called upon to make his defence, which he did in the following words:

… Captain Ellis having thought proper to bring me before you to answer charges of the most serious nature, I trust this Honble. Court will, from the evidence before it, acquit me of unofficerlike conduct, having at all times endeavoured to support that character, which would best enable me to forward my views in His Majesty's service as an officer and a gentleman.

Geo. Story was a most notorious, dirty thief, swarming with vermin and a disgrace to the ship in which he served, for which crimes he has been repeatedly punished without making the smallest alteration in his person or conduct, which was represented to Captain Ellis, mentioning particularly that this man was in the habit of stealing the boys daily allowance of provisions, thereby putting them in a state of starvation, which representation I am sorry to say was not taken notice of by the captain.

With respect to my having ordered a man to be severely beaten from the cable tier to the spar deck, &c., I beg the indulgence of the court to state that this man would not come up to perform his duty after allowing him proper and sufficient time so to do and that the punishment he received in consequence was by no means severe; nor was it inflicted thro' wantonness, but, on the contrary, to preserve the discipline and good order which I had been accustomed to observe on board every one of His Majesty's ships in which I have had the honour to serve, more particularly upon considering the state the ship was in at the time, there being mutinous sentences written in different parts of the ship and Captain Ellis, so far from bringing the person or persons to punishment, told them that he would not punish them further than sending them into one of His Majesty's gun brigs or schooners, taking into consideration the evil consequences which has at various times occurred in the navy for the want of due subordination.

As to Captain Ellis's written order forbidding any punishment to be inflicted, I knew nothing of until I was sent for to answer the charge of having broken or acted against it.

With regard to my having behaved in a contemptuous manner to Captain Ellis, I humbly beg leave to state that I am not aware of having acted contrary to the character of an officer inferior to him, but, at all times and in all places, have endeavoured to treat him with the respect due to his rank as my captain.

I have also to beg the honble. court will take into their consideration that I have served nearly twelve years in His Majesty's navy with honour and credit to myself until this unfortunate circumstance took place, in which, if I have acted wrong, I submit to the consideration of this honourable court the long and close confinement which I have suffered, being forbid even to appear on the quarter deck, notwithstanding the weak state of my health required that I should take the air. I hope the court will do me the justice to believe that the punishment inflicted on these men was not done with a cruel or oppressive design on my part. I have therefore to rely on the clemency of this honourable court. …

Lieutenant John Donaldson called in and sworn.

Prisoner

Have you been in the habit, both before and since my being in confinement, of punishing the men for the neglect of their duty and to the knowledge of Captain Ellis?

Some trifling punishments I have given, but I can't exactly say to the knowledge of Captain Ellis.

Did you ever know of my behaving in a cruel or oppressive manner to the men, which I was charged with or with contempt to Captain Ellis or in an unofficerlike manner?

No.

Relate to the court the character of Geo. Story when in the *Inflexible* with you and since he has been in the *Spitfire*.

When he was on board of the *Inflexible*, he kept himself in such a filthy, lousy state, I was obliged, as 1st Lieutenant, to order him to be cleaned by the master at arms; he has been much in the same state since he has belonged to the *Spitfire*.

Will you relate to the court the message you brought me from Captain Ellis on the 29th of May last and on the 14 June last, the latter being by desire of Vice Adm^{l}. Vashon, [and] whether the answers which I returned to Captn. Ellis were, in your opinion, contemptuous?

Captain Ellis told me about that time that it was impossible for him and Mr. Ensor to sail together and that he must quit the ship by remaining sick till we got into harbour and go to sick quarters, also of his requesting an apology to be made to Captain Ellis. His answer was that the crimes of which Captain Ellis had accused him before the ship's company were such that he could not possibly quit the ship without being tried by a court martial. On the 14 of June, Captain Ellis told me that Admiral Vashon wished M^{r}. Ensor to drop the business and to go to sick quarters and requesting that a public apology might be made to Captain Ellis and he returned the same answer as before.

Court

Did you ever know the prisoner behave with contempt to Captain Ellis?

No.

Was the prisoner's general conduct cruel and oppressive to the ship's company in general?

No; he was an attentive, good officer and attentive to the ship's company's comfort.

Withdrew.

M^{r}. James Matthews, Master, called in and sworn.

Prisoner

Relate to the court what passed on the 28th May last and whether I behaved in a contemptuous manner to Captain Ellis on the quarter deck when ordered under arrest.

I did not see you behave in a contemptuous manner.

Did you ever know of my behaving in a cruel, oppressive manner to the men or with contempt to Captain Ellis or in an unofficerlike manner?

Never, to my knowledge.

Court

What reply did M^{r}. Ensor make to his captain when he put him under arrest?

I heard M^{r}. Ensor say, when he was about half way down the ladder of the after hatchway, 'it was time.' The rest of the words, I could not make out.

Did there seem to be any conversation or any heat at the time?

No, none.

Withdrew.

Mr. Thos. Davies, Purser, called in and sworn.

Prisoner

Did you ever know of my behaving in a cruel, oppressive manner to the men or with contempt to Captain Ellis or in an unofficerlike manner?

Never.

Withdrew.

Mr. John Owen Martin called in and sworn.

Prisoner

Did you ever know of my behaving in a cruel, oppressive manner to the men or with contempt to Captain Ellis or in an unofficerlike manner?

Never.

Withdrew.

Mr. McDouall, Midshipman, called in and sworn.

Did you ever know of my behaving in a cruel, oppressive manner to the men in my watch on deck?

No.

Withdrew.

William Emblin called in and sworn.

Did you ever know of my behaving in a cruel or oppressive manner to any of the men in the *Spitfire*?

Only to one, Geo. Story

Withdrew

The prisoner having nothing further to offer in his defence, the court was cleared and proceeded to deliberate upon and form sentence.

The court, having carefully and deliberately weighed and considered the evidence produced and what the prisoner had to offer in his defence, are of opinion the charges are proved. The court do therefore adjudge the prisoner, Lieutenant John Ensor, to be dismissed His Majesty's service and he is hereby so sentenced accordingly. …

133. *Court Martial of Thomas Purnell*

[ADM 1/5388]

Minutes of the proceedings of a court martial assembled and held on board His Majesty's ship the *Trident* in the harbour of Valletta, Malta the 17th day of August 1808 for the trial of Mr. Thomas Purnell, Master of His Majesty's ship the *Volage*, for unofficerlike conduct and neglect of duty.

Present

Sir Alexander John Ball, Baronet, Rear Admiral of the White and senior officer in the command of His Majesty's ships and vessels in the harbour of Valletta, President.

Captain

Richard Hussey Moutray	John Stewart
William Durban	Ja^s^. Alex^r^. Gordon

being all the captains of the post ships at Malta, except Captain Robert Bell Campbell of His Majesty's ship the *Trident*, the surgeon of which ship certified the president his inability to attend through ill health.

The prisoner being brought into court and the audience admitted, the order of the Right Honourable Cuthbert Lord Collingwood, Vice Admiral of the Red, Commander in Chief, &c., &c., &c., dated the 8th February last, directed to Sir Alexander John Ball, Baronet, Rear Admiral of the Blue and senior officer in the command of His Majesty's ships and vessels in the harbour of Valletta, Malta to try M^r^. Thomas Purnell, Master of His Majesty's ship the *Volage*, for unofficerlike conduct and neglect of duty, was read.

Then the members of the court and judge advocate, in open court and before they proceeded to trial, respectively took the oaths enjoined by Act of Parliament made and passed in the 22d. year of the reign of His late Majesty King George the Second, entitled *An Act for Amending, Explaining and Reducing into One Act of Parliament the Laws Relating to the Government of His Majesty's Ships, Vessels and Forces by Sea.*

A letter from Philip Rosenhagen, Esquire, Captain of His Majesty's ship the *Volage*, to Rear Admiral Sir Alexander John Ball, Bart., &c., &c., was read as follows, *viz.*:

His Majesty's ship *Volage*
in Valletta, the 1st February 1808

… M^r^. Thomas Purnell, Master of His Majesty's ship under my command, having returned to her from the hospital, it is my duty to represent to you that the day before the ship sailed from Plymouth with dispatches, M^r^. Purnell was ordered on shore by me to procure charts for this country, that he returned on board in such a state of intoxication as to be totally unfit to do his duty the next day, in consequence of which I was under the necessity of taking a pilot to work the ship out of Plymouth Sound, not being acquainted with it myself. I have further to add that M^r^. Purnell, even on his first joining the ship, was so far intoxicated as to be unfit to do his duty and have therefore to request you will apply to the commander in chief for a court martial to try the said Mr. Thomas Purnell for such unofficerlike conduct and neglect of duty. …

All the evidences were then ordered to withdraw out of court, except:

Lieut. William Woolridge of the *Volage*, who was sworn and examined as follows, *viz.*:

Q. by Prosecutor. Do you remember Mr. Purnell joining the ship as master in Plymouth Sound?
I do.
Was he drunk or sober?
He was not sober.
Do you remember Mr. Purnell being ordered on shore by me the day before we sailed from Plymouth to purchase charts for this country?
I do.
In what state did he return on board?
In a state of intoxication.
Was I, in consequence of his inability to do his duty the next day, obliged to take a pilot to work the ship out of Plymouth Sound?
Yes.
Do you think I should at any time have been justified in placing any confidence in Mr. Purnell in conducting or navigating the ship?
I think not.

The prisoner had no questions to ask this witness and he was desired to withdraw.

Mr. Joseph Henry Fitch, Purser of the *Volage*, called in and sworn.

Q. by prosr. Do you remember Mr. Purnell joining the ship as master in Plymouth Sound?
Yes.
Was he drunk or sober?
In my opinion, he was drunk.
Do you know that Mr. Purnell was on shore the day before we sailed from Plymouth to purchase charts for this country?
I know that Mr. Purnell was on shore.
In what state did he return on board?
I saw him in a short time after he returned on board; he appeared to me to be then intoxicated.

Was I, in consequence of his inability to do his duty the next day, obliged to take a pilot to work the ship out of Plymouth Sound?
A pilot was taken on board.

The prisoner asked this witness no question.

The evidence being closed on the part of the prosecution and the prisoner, being put upon his defence, had no witnesses to call nor anything to offer in mitigation of his offences, or to speak to his general character while in that ship, requested to throw himself on the mercy of the court.

The court was then cleared, and, having very maturely considered the evidence produced and what the prisoner had offered when called upon for his defence, were of opinion that the charge was proved and did therefore adjudge him to be dismissed from His Majesty's service.

The court was opened, audience admitted, and sentence passed accordingly. …

134. *Court Martial of John Callan*

[ADM 1/5395]

Minutes of proceedings at a court martial held on board His Majesty's ship *Salvador del Mundo* in Hamoaze on Tuesday the 4th day of April 1809.

Present

John Sutton, Esq[r]., Rear Admiral of the Red and second officer in the command of His Majesty's ships & vessels at Plymouth, President.

Captains

Thomas Wolley	Henry Hotham
Sir Tho[s]. Masterman Hardy, Bart.	Zachary Mudge
John Serrell	The Hon. George Poulett

George Eastlake, J[r].
officiating Judge Advocate

Being all the admirals & captains of post ships then & there present next in seniority to the president, except Capt. Cha[s]. Worsley Boys of His Majesty's ship *Statira*, who was absent on admiralty leave.

The prisoner, M[r]. John Callan, acting Surgeon on board His Majesty's sloop *Orestes*, was brought into court and the witnesses and audience admitted.

Read – The order of the Right Honble. the Lords Commissioners of the Admiralty, dated the 27 day of March 1809, directed to the president to try the said Mr. John Callan for repeated quarrelling & fighting in the gun room, for endeavouring to make a mutinous assembly, making use seditious words & for breeding a nuisance in the ship by making use of the pot in his cabin instead of going to the round house.

Read – The warrant appointing a judge advocate.

Then the members of the court & judge advocate, in open court and before they proceeded to trial, respectively took the oaths directed by Act of Parliament passed in the 22d. year of the reign of King George the 2nd.

Read – The annexed letter of charge from Capt. J. R. Lapenotiere of His Majesty's sloop *Orestes* to Admiral Young, Commander in Chief at Plymouth.

All the witnesses, except the first to be sworn, being then ordered to withdraw, and to attend to their examinations separately, they all withdrew accordingly and the court proceeded to trial as follows:

Evidence in support of the charge.

Mr. Joseph Mills Briggs, Gunner of His Majesty's sloop *Orestes*, sworn & examined as follows:

Pro. Has the prisoner frequently come to your cabin and there asked in a private manner what was your opinion of your captain?

A. Yes, he has several times and said very disrespectful words of his captain. At one time he went so far as to call the captain a 'scoundrel' (This was a few months ago.). To the best of my recollection, the ship was at sea.

Pro. Did the prisoner, at other times, tell you that the captain had a bad opinion of you and thought you a scamp?

A. He did once.

Pro. Did you soon afterwards make the circumstance known of the prisoner's calling me a 'scoundrel' and of his repeatedly asking you your opinion of your captain to a superior officer?

A. I did report it to Mr. Southcott, the Master, & Mr. Doyle. The reason of the prisoner's frequenting my cabin was that he complained to me he had no regular place to make up his medicines. I told him he was at liberty at any time when I was in my cabin to come there and do it. He never came there since he called the captain 'scoundrel.'

Pro. Did you think at the time the prisoner came to your cabin to ask you your opinion of your captain that it was done for the purpose of drawing your sentiments and to prejudice you against your captain?

A. I did, as I believed at the time that no other officer of the ship associated with the prisoner but the purser.

Pro. Has the prisoner been in the habit of coming to your cabin on those intimate terms independent of mixing medicines?

A. No.

Pro. Has he been in your cabin at any time without mixing medicines?

A. He has been there and gone out without mixing medicines.

Pro. Have you seen the prisoner's servant empty his master's pot and do you know what it contained?

A. I went forward with Capt. Lapenotiere's spy glass. Putting my hand over the wash board, I put it in some human nuisance that came out of the chamber pot. I went aft immediately and caught the prisoner's boy going down the main hatchway with an empty chamber pot in his hand. I asked the boy what he had emptied out of the pot; he told me dirty water. I took him forward by the collar, showed him what I had put my hand into and asked him if that was dirty water. The boy then owned that he had thrown it out of the pot. I asked him whose it was; he said his master's.

Co^{t}. What occasioned the prisoner to come to your cabin when he called the captain 'scoundrel?'

A. I don't know. He came and sat himself down by me. After asking me how I was in the morning, he began to discourse on several things that I don't remember, about what he was accused of, but I remember very plain that he said the captain had spoke very disrespectful of him and called the captain 'scoundrel' and said he had used him unlike a gentleman and that the captain had no great opinion of me. The prisoner asked my opinion of the captain several times. I thought it was best to keep myself on my guard, as I thought it was the prisoner's intention to bias my mind against the captain.

Co^{t}. Was there any person present or within hearing when the prisoner called the captain 'scoundrel?'

A. Not to my knowledge; the prisoner shut the door himself on his entering the cabin.

Pris. Have you complained of me to the commanding officer before M^{r}. Southcott became master?

A. Not to my knowledge.

Pris. Did you tell the captain I called him a 'scoundrel?'

A. Not until I was called forward by M^{r}. Southcott and the captain likewise to prove it.

The witness withdrew.

Lieut. William Hewitt of His Majesty's sloop *Orestes* sworn & examined as follows:

Pro. Have you ever refused the prisoner leave to see his friends since the 24th of March last?

A. I never did when they asked me.

Pro. Have you received instructions from me to let anyone see the prisoner whom he thought proper, except the purser and 2d. lieutenant who were under arrest?

A. I informed the prisoner that he was to see his friends.

Pro. Have there been repeated quarrels between the prisoner and the purser since they have been in the ship?

A. There have.

Pro. Have you been obliged to send for the sergeant of marines to confine the prisoner for fighting with the purser?

A. I have seen the prisoner and purser collar each other and I did send for the sergeant of marines.

Pro. Were their clothes torn?

A. I saw one of their shirts torn.

Pro. Was you near me on the 22d. of March last when the surgeon's papers were taken?

A. Yes.

Pro. Did I ask what he wished to have done with these papers?

A. Yes, he said he wished to have them sent to the admiral.

Pro. Were those papers sealed up in your presence?

A. Yes.

Pro. Was you present next morning when I sent for the prisoner to have them opened for the purpose of numbering?

A. Yes.

Pro. Did the prisoner say after they were numbered that those papers were his property, I had no authority to take them and that it was the greatest robbery that could be committed upon man?

A. Yes.

Pro. Have I frequently sent for you to know what occasioned the unpleasant smell which came out of the gun room?

A. Yes.

Pro. Did you sometime after come to me and say that you had at last found out what occasioned that smell I had so frequently complained of, that it was the surgeon had made use of his pot and that you had that morning discovered it and that that was not the first time by many and that his first servant left him on that account?

A. I told the captain so.

Pro. Did I immediately send for the prisoner on the quarter deck and ask him what could induce him to be guilty of so dirty a trick?

A. Yes, his answer was that he did not know there was any orders to the contrary.

Cot. Have you known the prisoner repeatedly quarrel with the purser?

A. Yes.

Cot. Was the circumstance you have related respecting the surgeon's making use of his pot in his cabin considered as a nuisance in the ship?

A. Yes.

Cot. Has the prisoner been allowed to see his friends since his confinement without the presence of a third person?

A. The sergeant has mostly been present; I told him always to attend to hear what passed.

Cot. Why did you prevent the prisoner's seeing his friends without the sergeant being present?

A. I thought I was doing my duty.

Pris. Would you allow the physician of the fleet to speak to me privately respecting my own health about a week ago while I was under arrest?

A. I attended by the physician's desire, as he said he came on board on service, and it was proper the commanding officer should attend.

The witness withdrew.

Mr. John Southcott, acting Master of H. Majesty's sloop *Orestes*, sworn & examined as follows:

Pro. Was you present on the 22d. of March when the prisoner's papers were taken?

A. I was; the prisoner agreed with the purser that they might be enclosed to Adml. Young and thought it was an honourable transaction in so doing.

Pro. Were they sealed up in your presence unexamined?

A. They were.

Pro. Were you and the prisoner present when they were opened the next morning to be numbered?

A. We were.

Pro. Relate the prisoner's conduct upon the occasion.

A. He said he did not think the captain authorized to take them and conceived it high robbery by so doing.

Pro. Has the prisoner had free communication with his friends since his arrival at Plymouth or do you know that he has been prevented in any way from seeing them?

A. I know it was your orders that he should see his friends and, when commanding officer myself, I allowed it.

The witness withdrew.

M^r^. Lawrence Doyle, Carpenter of His Majesty's sloop *Orestes*, sworn & examined as follows:

Pro. Did the prisoner come to your cabin in March last and enter into conversation with you respecting a show?

A. Yes, the prisoner came and said they were taking him off in a show on board, alluding to a puppet show which was exhibiting by the gunner.

Pro. Did he say that he had seen by the log that there was a hawser expended at Vigo and ask you if you knew anything of it?

A. Yes I told him it did not relate to me.

Pro. What was your reasons for making that kind of answer?

A. I did not like to have anything to say about it, as I heard from the gunner, the prisoner had been speaking disrespectful of his captain and I did not wish him to come near my cabin.

The witness withdrew.

John Quinn, Seaman of His Majesty's sloop *Orestes*, sworn & examined as follows:

Pro. How long was you the prisoner's servant?

A. About 3 weeks.

Pro. How often have you emptied your master's pot after his easing himself in it during that period?

A. Twice.

The witness withdrew.

The evidence in support of the charge being here closed, the prisoner was acquainted therewith and asked if he had anything to offer in his behalf, upon which the prisoner requested to be allowed an hour to prepare his defence; whereupon the court was cleared and, at the expiration of an hour, was reopened , when the prisoner put into the hands of the judge advocate the annexed written paper signed by himself, which was read to the court.

The prisoner then called the following witnesses:

Evidence in behalf of the prisoner.

M^r^. Thomas Harris, late 2d. Lieut. of His Majesty's sloop *Orestes*, sworn & examined as follows:

Pris. Have you frequently observed a harness cask under the table in the gun room and did it occasion a disagreeable smell?

A. Yes, it proceeded from the pickle that was in the cask. I had it started and cleaned out and sent upon deck.

Pris. Did you see me exhibited in a show by the gunner, giving the purser a glyster[1] and imitating my brogue?

[1] A glyster is an antiquated term for an enema (*Oxford English Dictionary*, s.v. Clyster).

A. Yes, frequently and representing the prisoner's giving a pill.
Pro. Were the figures alluded to cut out at the gun room table?
A. Some, by the Spanish passenger.
Pro. Did you and the prisoner see those figures before they were exhibited?
A. I did; I don't know that the prisoner did.
Pro. Were you & the prisoner present at the show?
A. I believe once, but cannot exactly say.
Pro. Have you heard the prisoner say after, he was highly entertained?
A. No, but he had a great mind to rise up & break them.
Pro. Why do you think it was the prisoner that was represented?
A. Because of the prisoner's brogue being imitated & calling for his boy Jones by name.
Co[t]. What part of the ship was the show?
A. Before the mainmast between decks.

The witness withdrew.

M[r]. Stephen Godfrey Goddard, Purser of His Majesty's sloop *Orestes*, sworn & examined as follows:

Pris. Do you recollect that there was a complaint lodged against me that my cabin had a bad smell and was there then stinking tripe under the gun room table?
A. There was.
Pris. Did I tell you at that time that I had a disorder in my bowels?
A. You did.
Pris. Did you see me represented in a show and hear my boy's name mentioned in the representation?
A. Yes.
Pris. Did you ever hear me speak disrespectful of Capt. Lapenotiere?
A. Never.
Pris. How long ago was it that a little dispute took place between you and me?
A. About 7 months.
Pris. Have we been friends ever since?
A. Ever since.
Co[t]. Has the prisoner at any period frequently quarrelled with you?
A. Never, but in the instance before mentioned, which was merely jocular.

The witness withdrew.

And the prisoner called on the following persons to speak to his general character:

Capt. Tho[s]. Wolley of His Majesty's ship *Salvador del Mundo* said: 'The prisoner has always been spoken of by the surgeon as very indefatigable in his duty and as a person in whose abilities he had a confidence and his general conduct in the ship was always inoffensive and rather gave me a good opinion of him.'

Lieut. Joseph Priest of His Majesty's ship *Salvador del Mundo* said: 'The prisoner was assistant surgeon in this ship near 12 months and, during that time, he behaved remarkably attentive, obedient and sober and I have heard the surgeon frequently represent him very able in his profession.'

M^r^. Alexander Whyte, Surgeon of His Majesty's ship *Salvador del Mundo* said: 'M^r^. Callan was under me about 12 months &, during that period, his conduct was uniformly correct. In a professional view, it was marked by a knowledge of his profession and by a most faithful application of that knowledge to the relief of the sick & his conduct upon every occasion was such as to induce me strongly to recommend him to Capt. Wolley, D^r^. Baird, the Inspector, and to the Transport Board, as a sober, diligent & attentive, good surgeon, well worthy of promotion; and I believe it was attended to by Capt. Wolley & D^r^. Baird.'

The prisoner having nothing further to offer, the court was cleared and proceeded to deliberate upon and form the sentence.

The court, having very maturely and deliberately weighed and considered the evidence in support of the charge as well as what the prisoner had offered in his behalf, was of opinion that the charges had been in part proved against the prisoner, M^r^. John Callan, and did in consequence adjudge the said M^r^. John Callan to be dismissed his situation of acting surgeon in His Majesty's sloop *Orestes* to which he belongs.

The court was opened, the prisoner brought in, the witnesses and audience readmitted and sentence pronounced accordingly. …

134A. *Defence of John Callan*

[ADM 1/ 5395]

… At the very serious nature of the charges which were exhibited on paper against me by my captain, I must confess I was considerably alarmed and agitated, not from a consciousness of my having been ever guilty of mutiny or sedition, but from a very natural supposition that such charges serious & very serious as they are, the most serious that could be alleged would not have been made unless my captain had it in his power to give the court some proof upon such a charge for their judgement and decision. For what reasons he made such a charge or upon what grounds I am after this day's examination left to consider, but certain it is that nothing like mutiny and sedition has been ever attempted to be proved against me; &

I must for the present set down the circumstance of their being made to motives not the most prudent or honourable. If they were introduced solely for the purpose of swelling the prosecutor's case with an unnecessary appearance of magnitude, it is not such conduct as a well disposed prosecutor standing only for a distribution of justice between him and his prisoner would have pursued.

Gentlemen, two years have now elapsed since I have had the honour to be in H.M. service; during that period until the cry that has called for this inquiry, I have the satisfaction to say my conduct has been considered as praiseworthy & exemplary, ever regardful to the duties of my situation & the respect due my superiors. When this be as it will be proved, I think gent. you will be left in some degree of wonder to account for reasons to actuate me to the sudden breach of that conduct as is attempted to be fixed on me this day, gentlemen. I am accused of having called my captain a scoundrel, but that is substantiated by the evidence of the gunner alone, a person who at this moment is at my instance under order for a court martial for having made me the ridicule and contempt of all the ship's company & for great immorality.

Such an evidence as this cannot surely be considered as the most unbiased or well disposed as all evidences should be upon which a man is either to be condemned or acquitted. But gents, it is true I am in his hands as to this particular & it is said by him that I made use of this expression at a time when no one was present. How is it possible I can refute it? My own testimony I am aware is not admissible, but I would, in the latest moment of my existence, sacramentally depose to my having never made use of the expression. Such a deposition to those who know me would be sufficient to weigh down the scale of evidence in my favour, but shut out as I necessarily am, prevented as I am from the possibility of refutation. It is by circumstances alone, as I humbly submit that the credit due to the gunner must be tried.

If gent. I am right in this position, it is an addition to the observations just before made on his evidence that he has sworn before you this day that he made the alleged expression known to the master immedy. as it is said it escaped me. But gent. did my prosecutor venture to ask Mr. Southcott if such was or not the case? And it is another addition that he, the gunner, deposed that he never complained of me before Southcott was the master & immedy. afterwards stood contradicted by the evidence of Mr. Hewitt, who stated that a complaint had been made & of such a nature, namely my being troublesome to his cabin as must have prevented & did actually prevent my going to his cabin afterwards on any familiar terms, such as it must be presumed I was on with him at the time of the alleged expression. With these observations gent., I leave this part of the case.

Gent., as to the alleged nuisance, it is only proved that my servant emptied the pot twice. It is true that it was so emptied, but necessity compelled me to use it. I was at that time labouring under a serious complaint of diarrhoea, & of my being so I told the purser, who will prove it to you. It could be no very agreeable companion to my cabin & certainly, but from necessity, would I a moment have allowed it to remain. As to my having said that I did not know it was contrary to orders, I certainly did not know that an officer labouring under such a complaint was obliged to go to the roundhouse. The stench arising from the gun room was occasioned as I shall prove by a keg of stinking tripe & the harness cask in a very foul state being in the gun room.

As to quarrelling with the purser, it is but once only that it happened. No blows passed & this took place many months since. It was then overlooked & since that the captain has passed it over in silence. Is not this also referable to evidence of the disposition of my prosce^{r}., who has charged me with repeated quarrels & broils, &.

Then gent., as it is regards my saying of the seizure of the papers that it was like to robbery, I certainly felt warm, and perhaps too much so, but gent. the arbitrary and perhaps unusual power which was exercised in the seizure of my private papers is some little excuse for expressions used in the moment of impulse.

I now humbly beg leave to lay (hereto annexed) before the court a *letter written* by the prosecutor to the Transport Board in July last, which will speak for itself why I have been since, as I have been under the captain's permission exhibited in pictures showing the practice used by surgeons in their patients I must also learn.

And, with the remainder of my proofs as to character, I commit myself to the disposition of this hon. co^{t}., well knowing that they will temper their pronunciation on my case with mercy & justice. …

134B. *'Letters Referred to in the Prisoner's Defence.'*[1]

[ADM 1/5395] *Orestes*, Plymouth Sound
19th July 1808

… I have to request that M^{r}. John Callan (who was appointed acting surgeon of the sloop I command by Admiral Young) may not be superseded, as his conduct since with me has been such as to merit my warmest approbation. …

[1]The first of these letters is from Captain Lapenotiere to the Commissioners for Transports; the second is from Alex McLeary of the Transport Office to Callan.

Transport Office
31st March 1809

… Having laid before the Commissioners for Transports, &c. your letter of the 28 instant (which was not received until this day), I am directed to send you herewith agreeably to your request an attached copy of Captain Lapenotiere's letter[1] to this board in July last, requesting that you might not be superseded in the *Orestes*. …

134C. *Lapenotiere to Young*

[ADM 1/5395]

Charge

His Majesty's sloop *Orestes*
Plymouth Sound, March 24th, 1809

… I am to beg you will be pleased to apply to my Lords Commissioners of the Admiralty to order a court martial to be held on Mr. John Callan, Acting Surgeon of His Majesty's sloop under my command for repeated quarrelling and fighting in the gun room, also for endeavouring to make a mutinous assembly, making use of seditious words and for breeding a nuisance in the ship by making use of the pot in his cabin, instead of going to the round house to the great annoyance of myself and officers. …

135. *Court Martial of William Edward Fiott*

[ADM 1/5404]

Minutes of proceedings of a court martial assembled and held on board His Majesty's ship *Bucephalus* in Madras Roads, the 27th day of April 1810 for the trial of Lieutenant William Edward Fiott, belonging to His Majesty's ship *Bucephalus*, for uttering words of sedition & traitorous words to prejudice of His Majesty's [*sic*] and government.

Viz.:

Present

George Byng, Esquire, Commodore &c., &c., &c. of His Majesty's ship *Belliqueux* and second officer in the command of His Majesty's ships and vessels employed in the East Indies, President.

[1]This letter is not included among the supporting evidence bound with the transcript in ADM 1/5395.

Captains

Thomas Gordon Caulfield
Honble. George Elliot
Hugh Cook
Charles Gordon
Christopher Cole
William Jones Lye
Charles Foot

William Bailey, Deputy Judge Advocate.

The prisoner being brought into court and audience admitted, the order from William O'Bryen Drury, Esquire, Rear Admiral of the Red and Commander in Chief for the time being of His Majesty's ships and vessels employed in the East Indies, directed to Commodore George Byng, &c., &c., &c. His Majesty's ship *Belliqueux*, dated the 26th day of April 1810, for the trial of William Edwd. Fiott, Lieutenant belonging to His Majesty's ship *Bucephalus*, for uttering words of sedition and traitorous words to the prejudice of His Majesty's [*sic*] and government was read. The members of the court and judge advocate then, in open court and before they proceeded to trial, respectively took the oaths enjoined by Act of Parliament.

The letter from Captain Charles Pelly[1] of His Majesty's ship *Bucephalus* (containing the charges against the prisoner) was then read as follows, *viz*.:

His Majesty's ship *Bucephalus*
Madras Roads, 25 Ap^{l}.1810

… I beg leave to inform you that Lieutenant William Edward Fiott, belonging to His Majesty's ship *Bucephalus* under my command did, on the afternoon of the 18th March last at sea on board the said ship at the gun room mess table, utter words of sedition & traitorous words to the prejudice of His Majesty and government, by saying the king (alluding to the King of England) was only an old fool and would only select fools to be his ministers and rejected every man of sense and further that Bonaparte was the greatest man in the world or words nearly to that effect with other expressions to the same meaning all in my opinion highly seditious & traitorous. A fuller account of what occurred, I herewith beg to enclose for your further information I think likewise my duty to lay before you a letter of apology he sent me after he was in confinement, but, which from a consideration of circumstances, I did not feel myself justified in so doing until I had laid the case before you.

[1]This letter is addressed to Rear Admiral Drury.

I have therefore to beg you will direct a court martial to try him for the said offences. …

All the witnesses being ordered to withdraw and attend their examination separately, they all withdrew accordingly, except Captain Charles Pelly of H.M. ship *Bucephalus*, who was sworn, and gave his evidence in support of the charges.

Court	Relate to the court all you know respecting the charges against the prisoner.
Answer	On the 18th day of March last (Sunday), as stated in the charge, I was dining in the gun room. Shortly after the cloth was removed, when the prisoner was in conversation generally, he was talking upon politics. I sometimes was conversing with him on the subject &, at other times, with the rest of the gentlemen present upon other subjects, when my attention was particularly taken by hearing the prisoner speaking louder than anyone else present, saying Bonaparte, or the Emperor Napoleon, was the greatest man in the world, that he had conquered the whole world, even England, and that the King was only an old fool. If he would but select men of sense to be his ministers, the country might be saved; but as we now stood, it was only money that saved us or words nearly to that effect, which he uttered so hastily and violently, I could not stop the conversation till he had finished his sentence. When I spoke rather louder than is usual for me to speak, calling him by name to command attention and remonstrated with him upon using such language, by saying it's impossible any person entertaining such ideas can hold a situation of an officer and further that such expressions must not be made use of, even if he meant it as a joke or quiz upon anyone or for the sake of making conversation. I do not believe he could have heard the whole of my remonstrance before he answered, '*Yes*, but I do mean it *and dare say it*.' Doctor Milne then took up the conversation about a minute, when I again called him by name and said, at the same time rising from my chair, 'I cannot set at any table to hear such conversation, therefore I shall immediately retire;

under any other circumstances, I should immediately have ordered you under an arrest, but as it is a conversation that occurred over wine, I shall retire to consider of what measures to pursue.' He only answered, he was sorry if he had 'offended me,' to which I answered it was no personal insult to me, farther than what my duty required of me.

Court — It so often happens that subjects are started merely for the sake of argument or *to quiz*, might not the prisoner be actuated by the above motives?

Answer — He might, but whether *he* was or was not, I cannot say.

Court — When he said the King was an old fool, did he express himself the King of England or what reason had you to suppose he meant the King of England?

Answer — I believe he did not express the King of England, but the conversation was upon the government of England and therefore it was alluding to the King of England.

Court — Did some oppose or others defend any part of the prisoner's argument when at table?

Answer — The conversation was gentlemanly, rational and orderly and no appearance of agreement between the prisoner or anyone present, but several were delivering their sentiments quite different, expressive of England's greatness.

Question by Prisoner — You stated I was talking generally on politics on the 18th March 1810 and other subjects and you were also conversing with me and at other times with the other gentlemen at table; when you were in conversation with me, was my conversation seditious, traitorous, or prejudicial to His Majesty's government previous to those words you state to have been made use of by me?

Answer — I heard nothing traitorous or seditious previous to what I have already related or should have taken notice of it.

Prisoner — Do you imagine those words were premeditated or spoken in hurry of argument, I that entertained any traitorous or seditious principles [*sic*] toward the King or government?

Answer — It is impossible for me to say whether they were premeditated, but I can state that they were spoken in a great hurry. It is equally impossible to state whether he entertains any seditious or traitorous principles. I was prompt'd to take the measures I did from the duty incumbent on me to notice words spoken to the prejudice of His Majesty or government.

Captain Pelly withdrew and proceeded in the prosecution when Lieut.[t] Haverfield was called into court & sworn.

Court — Relate to the court what you know respecting the charges against the prisoner on the 18th day of March last.

Answer — In the afternoon, on Sunday the 18th March 1810, Captain Pelly was dining with the officers in the gun room. In the course of an argument which arose I don't know between whom except that the prisoner, Lieut.[t] Fiott, took a part. I heard him say that the King was an old fool & that Bonaparte was one of the greatest men in the world. I recollect that Captain Pelly called him to an account, saying it was all very well for a joke and that M[r]. Fiott certainly could not mean what he was saying. M[r]. Fiott in answer said he did mean *it*. Captain Pelly very shortly after got up from table, saying as it was a private conversation, he should not take immediately notice of it or words to that effect, that he could not sit at table and hear the name of our Sovereign so insulted. Captain Pelly then left the table &, very shortly after, the conversation closed.

Court — Did the prisoner say the King was an old fool and that he only selected fools to advise him?

Answer — I recollect his saying that the King was an old fool, and that he had only selected fools for his ministers or words to that effect.

Court — Did you hear the prisoner say that the King rejected men of sense?

Answer — I did not, to my recollection.

Evidence withdrew, & M[r]. Alex[r]. Milne, Passenger in the *Bucephalus* & Surgeon in the Royal Navy, who was sworn.

Court — Relate to the court what you know respecting the charges against the prisoner on the 18th day of March last.

Answer	I was present in the gun room on the 18th day of March last when the conversation related to Bonaparte, when the prisoner observed that Bonaparte was the greatest man in the world, and that he had conquered all the world. Upon myself observing to him that England was not yet conquered, he replied it was not from the abilities of the King (meaning the King of England) that the nation had not been conquered and that he was an old fool and that he either had, or deserved, only fools for his ministers. Upon the representation of Captain Pelly that the prisoner's conversation was highly improper and hoped that he did not mean what he said, the prisoner's reply was '*I certainly do*,' upon which Captain Pelly left the table and then there was a considerable pause on the former conversation. About half an hour after Captain Pelly left the table, the conversation was renewed and he seemed then to feel considerable contrition for what he had previously said.
Court	Did you hear the prisoner say that the King rejected every man of sense?
Answer	I do not recollect any word like that.
Court	Did the prisoner appear to be heated in argument during the time he made use of these expressions?
Answer	I thought there appeared in the prisoner a considerable degree of warmth when he made use of those expressions.

Evidence withdrew and closed on the part of the prosecution, when the prisoner was called on to make his defence, which he did in the following words:

Mr. President and gentlemen of this honble. court, for the indulgence you have granted me in allowing me time to prepare my defence, I have to make my most sincere acknowledgements to you. It is now I am called upon to answer to charges at which my very soul revolts, those of sedition and traitorous acting to prejudice of His Majesty's government. It is, however, in my unfortunate situation no small consolation to be brought before a court so honourably constituted. Twelve years have I served my King, and I [have?] ever been proud of my profession. I regret there are not more officers present with whom I have chiefly served, as I should, I feel confident, be able then to do away with any idea of my entertaining seditious and traitorous principles; I hope I shall yet be able to show the honble. court whatever words I may have made use of in an incusetious [*sic*] moment that I hold the person of my Sovereign in the highest veneration and, should I be fortunate enough to obtain a favourable sentence, I still hope I may have an opportunity to convince the world that His Majesty's [*sic*] has not a more loyal subject than myself. Could I, as I have already said, produce the officers with whom I have chiefly served, it would, I am confident, appear that no one felt more zeal or would more readily have sacrificed his life for the service of my Sovereign and country.

I beg leave to declare that I never for one moment had an idea of my words being seditious, traitorous or prejudicial to His Majesty's government or I never should have been induced to make use of them.

Gentlemen, such are my sentiments, and my every wish, every thought is centred in the service of my King and country, my whole soul is elevated when I see myself associated with its defenders and with extreme ardour I long for an opportunity of rendering myself worthy the appellation of a British officer.

Here the defence closed and the prisoner requested to call a few witnesses in support of his defence.

Lieutenant Haverfield of His Majesty's ship *Bucephalus*, who was sworn

Prisoner	Didn't I feel extremely sorry, after Captn. Pelly left the table, for having spoken so disrespectfully of the King and did I not, when His Majesty's health was proposed to be drunk, drink to it most readily?
Answer	The prisoner appeared extremely sorry at the conduct he had been guilty of before Captain Pelly and he drank the King's health most readily.
Prisoner	Did you conceive I ever entertained disloyal sentiments or have I ever shown any prejudice against His Majesty's service?
Answer	I never thought so, quite the contrary, and have always observed the prisoner to possess the greatest zeal for His Majesty's service.
Prisoner	Did you hear me say, I hoped to be the man to humble Bonaparte?
Answer	I did not.
Prisoner	Have you often heard me drink the King & God bless him and confusion to Bonaparte?
Answer	Frequently.
Question Prisoner	Do you think my expressions proceeded from any want of respect or attachment to His Majesty or

government or from the heat of argument which made me forget myself?

Answer I think they were spoken inadvertently and the impression on my mind at the moment was that the prisoner was not aware of what he was saying, altho' he said he meant it. I think it was rather from bravado, for he appeared very much heated in argument.

Evidence withdrew, & Lieutenant Orr of the Royal Marines was next called in & sworn.

Prisoner Didn't I feel extremely sorry, after Captn. Pelly left the table, for having spoken so disrespectfully of the King and did I not, when His Majesty's health was proposed to be drunk, drink to it most readily?

Answer The prisoner appeared extremely sorry at the conduct he had been guilty of before Captain Pelly and he drank the King's health most cheerfully, and that he was very ready to make any apology which Captn. Pelly or the officers might think sufficient and that he had also to apologize to the officers for having been the cause of Captain Pelly's leaving the table.

Prisoner What was the impression made on your mind by my expressions on the 18th March last; did you conceive they were my sentiments or unmeaning words of an unguarded moment?

Answer I think the prisoner frequently has been very unguarded and, at that time, I think he then was.

Prisoner Did you *conceive* I ever entertained disloyal sentiments or have I ever shown any prejudice against His Majesty's service?

Answer Never to my knowledge, except on the 18th day of March last.

Evidence withdrew, and Lieut^{t}. Abraham Pike of the *Bucephalus* was next called in and sworn.

Prisoner Do you suppose or entertain any idea from my general conduct, of my entertaining any principles of sedition or prejudice to His Majesty's service?

Answer No.

Evidence withdrew, and M^{r}. George Palmer Cranch, Purser of the *Bucephalus* was next called in and sworn.

Prisoner Do you suppose or entertain any idea from my general conduct, of my entertaining any principles of sedition or prejudice to His Majesty's service?

Answer — No, I do not.

Evidence withdrew and the prisoner then called on Captain Pelly to relate to the court his general conduct during the time he had sailed with him.

Answer by Captain Pelly — He was always active, and ready to exert himself, but constantly put me under the necessity of giving him severe reprehensions [*sic*] for his injudicious and inconsiderate conduct.

The prisoner having nothing else to offer in defence, the court was cleared and proceeded to deliberate upon and form the sentence.

The court, having carefully, minutely & deliberately considered the evidence produced and what the prisoner alleged in his defence, is of opinion that the charge is fully proved, but in consequence of the prisoner's youth and of circumstances brought forward in his defence, they do only adjudge him to be dismissed from His Majesty's ship *Bucephalus* and to be placed at the bottom of the list of lieutenants in His Majesty's Royal Navy, this twenty-seventh day of April 1810.

And the said Lieutenant William Edward Fiott is hereby dismissed from His Majesty's ship *Bucephalus*, and put at the bottom of the list of lieutenants, this 27th day of April 1810. …

136. *Court Martial of James Davison*

[ADM 1/5412]

Minutes of proceedings at a court martial held on board His Majesty's ship *Abercrombie* in the Tagus on the 2nd day of January 1811.

Present

Sir Thomas Williams, Knight, Rear Admiral of the White, and second officer in the command of His Majesty's ships and vessels in the Tagus, President.

Captains

John Lawford	Samuel Hood Linzee
Sir John Gore, Kn^t^.	John Poo Beresford
Donald Campbell	William Charles Fahie
Thomas Boys	Sir Thomas Masterman Hardy, B^t^.
William Granger	Right Honble. Lord William Fitzroy
Charles Richardson	William Kent

Thomas Williams
Deputy Judge Advocate

Being all the Admirals and Captains of post ships according to seniority, except Captain John Surman Carden of His Majesty's ship *Mars*, who was from bodily indisposition rendered incapable of attending the court.

The prisoner was brought into court and the prosecutor, the witnesses and audience admitted.

The surgeon of His Majesty's ship *Mars* appeared before the court and reported that John Surman Carden, Esq[r]., Captain of the said ship, was from bodily indisposition unable to attend the court without endangering his health and declared he was ready, if required, to make oath to the truth of such report; in consequence whereof the court thought proper to dispense with Captain Carden's attendance.

Read the order of the Honourable George Cranfield Berkeley, Admiral of the Blue and Commander in Chief of His Majesty's ships and vessels employed on the Coast of Spain and Portugal, &c[a]. and in the Tagus, dated the 26th day of December 1810 and directed to the president, to try Sergeant James Davison of the Royal Marines, belonging to His Majesty's ship *Abercrombie*, for having, when on guard at the British minister's house on the 23rd of December 1810 lost his hat and sash, been guilty of great impropriety in getting drunk and absenting himself from the said guard for the most part of the night of the 23rd of December.

Read the warrant appointing a judge advocate.

Then the members of the court and judge advocate, in open court and before they proceeded to trial, respectively took the oaths directed by Act of Parliament passed in the twenty second year of the reign of King George the Second.

A letter from Captain H. Waring of the Royal Marines, belonging to His Majesty's ship *Abercrombie*, addressed to William Charles Fahie, Esq[r], Captain of the said ship, and by him transmitted to Admiral the Honble. G. C. Berkeley, Commander in Chief, &c[a]., was then read as follows:

H.M. ship *Abercrombie*, Tagus
24th December 1810

… A report having been made to me that Sergeant James Davison, who had the guard yesterday at the envoys house, had lost his hat and sash. On inquiry, I found he had been guilty of great impropriety in getting drunk and absenting himself from the said guard for the most part of the night of the 23rd ins[t].

I have therefore to request you will be pleased to apply to the commander in chief for a court martial on the said Ja[s]. Davison for a breach of the Articles of War. …

All the witnesses, except the first to be sworn, being then ordered to withdraw and to attend their examination separately, they all withdrew accordingly, and the court proceeded to trial as follows:

Evidence in support of the charge.

Lieutenant William White of the Royal Marines, belonging to His Majesty's ship *Abercrombie*, sworn and examined as follows:

Questioned by the prosecutor.

Q. Did you take (Sergeant James Davison) the prisoner on shore and give him charge of the guard at the envoys house on the 23rd of December 1810?

A. Yes.

Questioned by the court.

Q At what time did you give the prisoner the guard?

A. At half past 9 in the morning.

Q. Was he then perfectly sober?

A. Yes.

Q. What orders did you give him?

A. To be particularly alert during the night doing duty and to report any particular occurrence in the morning.

The witness withdrew.

Sergeant Esau Sheldrake of the Royal Marines, belonging to His Majesty's ship *Abercrombie*, sworn and examined as follows:

Questioned by the prosecutor.

Q. Relate to the court what you know respecting the charge against the prisoner.

A. I was present when the prisoner came on board the *Abercrombie* on the 24th between 8 and 12 in the morning. I saw him without a hat and he went down on the lower deck and I went down also and asked him where his hat was; he said he had lost it and likewise his sash, and I came and reported this to Captain Waring of the Royal Marines.

Q. Did he inform you how he lost it?

A. Afterwards, he did.

Q. Do you know that the prisoner accompanied a party of Marines from the *Abercrombie* for the purpose of mounting guard on shore on the morning of the 23rd of December?

A. Yes, I do.

The witness withdrew.

John Watson, Private Marine acting Corporal belonging to His Majesty's ship *Abercrombie*, sworn and examined as follows:

Questioned by the prosecutor.

Q. Relate to the court what you know respecting the charge against the prisoner.

A. About half past seven at night a week ago last Sunday, the prisoner told me to take charge of the guard at the envoy's house, that he was going out, but he would not stop any time; he did not return to me until about half past seven the next morning, without his hat or sash.

Q. Was the prisoner drunk before he left the guard that night?

A. He appeared capable of doing his duty when he left me.

Q. Did he threaten to put you in confinement before he went away that night?

A. Yes.

Q. Did you ever see the prisoner behave in the same manner as he did that night, without being drunk?

A. No.

Q. Did he not appear as if he had been drinking a great deal more than usual?

A. He had been drinking, but he was not drunk.

Q. Did not you tell him that he would do better to remain with his guard than to go out that night?

A. Yes, he said he would stop no time.

Questioned by the court.

Q. When the prisoner left you when you were on shore on guard, was he then as sober as you are at this moment?

A. No.

Q. When he returned in the morning, was he as sober as you are now?

A. He appeared to me, when he returned, as sober as a man could be.

Q. What offence had you committed that the prisoner should have threatened to confine you at the time you have stated?

A. He gave me liberty to go out for 2 or 3 minutes and he said I had stopped too long.

Q. Did you conceive your offence to be such that, if the prisoner had been perfectly sober, he would have so threatened you?

A. No.

Q. Then you considered that threat to proceed from the prisoner in consequence of his being drunk?

A. If he had not been drinking, he would not have threatened me, but he was capable of doing his duty.

Q. Were you with the guard yourself the whole of that night?

A. Yes.

Q. If the prisoner had returned to his duty, should you have seen him?
A. Yes.
Q. In the absence of the prisoner, were you the commanding officer of the guard?
A. Yes.
Q. Did he account to you in the morning for his absence during the night?
A. He said he was badly used by some of the Portuguese soldiers and was not able to return.
Q. Did he account for the loss of his hat and sash?
A. He said the Portuguese soldiers had taken them from him.
Q. Was the prisoner drunk any part of the day or evening in which you were on guard with him, previous to ½ past 7 when he left you?
A. No, not in my presence.

Questioned by prisoner.

Q. Did I not acquaint you, on my return, with having lost my money in the same manner in which I had lost my hat and sash?
A. Yes.

The witness withdrew.

Corporal James Smith of the Royal Marines, belonging to His Majesty's ship *Abercrombie*, sworn and examined as follows:

Questioned by the prosecutor.

Q. Had you the guard at the admiral's house on the 23rd of Dec[r]. last?
A. Yes.
Q. Did the prisoner visit you on that night?
A. No, he did not.

Questioned by the court.

Q. Did you consider yourself at the time you was doing duty at the admiral's house under the command of the prisoner?
A. Yes.
Q. Do you know that the prisoner during the day or night of the 23d. of December last got drunk or absented himself from his duty?
A. No, I do not.
Q. Did you see the prisoner any part of the day or night of the 23d. of December?
A. I did not see him after the time we parted till we returned together on board the next morning.

The witness withdrew.

Samuel Woodrough, Private Marine belonging to His Majesty's ship *Abercrombie*, sworn and examined as follows:

Questioned by the prosecutor.

Q. Relate to the court what you know respecting the charge against the prisoner.

A. He went away from the guard at the envoy's on Sunday week at 7 o'clock in the evening and did not return until the next morning at 7. He had no sword, hat or sash when he came back.

Q. Did you hear anything pass between the prisoner and the corporal, Watson, before he left the guard on that night?

A. I only heard the prisoner give him charge of the guard, saying he should be back in a few minutes.

Q. Was the prisoner drunk when he went away?

A. I know he had been drinking, but I cannot say he was drunk.

Q. Was he sober when he returned the next morning?

A. Yes.

Questioned by the court.

Q. How do you know the prisoner had been drinking?

A. I saw him coming out of a grog shop.

Q. Had you any other reason to suppose he had been drinking?

A. He looked very red in the face.

Q. Was there anything in his conduct or conversation to lead you to suppose he had been drinking?

A. No.

Q. How long after you saw him come out of the grog shop was it before he left the guard in charge of the corporal, Watson?

A. About an hour.

Q. At the time you heard the prisoner give the corporal charge of the guard, was he then as sober as you are at this moment?

A. No, I cannot say he was.

Q. Were you at the place where the guard was mounted the whole of the night?

A. Yes.

Q. If the prisoner had returned to it after you heard him leave the guard in charge of the corporal, should you have seen him?

A. Yes, I should.

Q. Did you hear the prisoner threaten to confine Corporal Watson during that afternoon?

A. No.

Q. Was Corporal Watson sober that night when he was left in charge of the guard?

A. Yes.

Q. Did you hear the prisoner give any reasons for having lost his hat, sword and sash?

A. No.

Q. When the prisoner returned, did he come alone?

A. Yes.

Q. Were you supplied with your day's provisions from your ship on that day?

A. Yes, at ½ past one.

The witness withdrew.

The evidence in support of the charge being finished, the prisoner was called upon to make his defence, who put into the hands of the judge advocate a written paper signed by himself, which was read to the court as follows:

… The underneath is the substance of the defence or declaration I have to offer in reply to the charges I now stand arraigned for, and which I could have wished to have personally delivered to the court were I not I fearful lest the iudes[1] position I labour under, both of body and mind, might perhaps render that deliverance not altogether so clear or comprehensive as I could wish; I therefore commit the following to paper, which I pledge myself to contain nothing but the plain and unvarnished truth and which I most respectfully submit to the consideration of the court. On Sunday the 23rd ultimo, I was ordered to remain at the envoy's house to do duty with a small party of Marines. About the hour of ½ past 7 in the evening, I had occasion to go to the necessary house, but being wholly unacquainted with the place, I went up different lanes in order to find out one, when at last I was overtaken by four Portuguese dragoons, who knocked me down, beat me severely, dragged me thro' the gutter a considerable distance, when at last they left me almost suffocated with dirt and mire, first picking my pockets of a two Pound note, three one Pound notes, two seven Shilling pieces and three Shillings; they also robbed me of my uniform hat, sword, sash and shoes. After I had remained some while in this wretchedly deplorable condition, I recovered my senses and strength sufficiently to enable me to crawl to the first house that presented itself to me, which happened to be one where they were employed baking bread and where they permitted me to remain the entire night until the following morning, when I returned to the guard and remained there until a fresh guard relieved it from another ship, when I marched my party to the packet stairs, where we waited for a boat to receive and put us on board this ship. Thus gentlemen have I stated to you the particulars of my case as briefly as I could and have now only to

[1]Iudes is a Latin term derived from iudicium, a judicial investigation (Roger Morriss to John Byrn, 13 June 2005).

hope that if I have said anything wrong or mistaken the manner of stating the business that you will pardon me, as I never before had the misfortune of being placed in the predicament I now stand in. …

The prisoner then requested that witnesses might be examined in his behalf, whereupon:

John Rowland, Private Marine of His Majesty's ship *Abercrombie*, was sworn and examined as follows:

Questioned by the prisoner.

Q. In what state was I when I returned to the guard on the morning of the 24th?

A. He was very dirty; he had neither hat, sash nor sword on. He appeared as if he had been dragged in the dirt.

Questioned by the court.

Q. Had he any wound or bruise about him, as if he had been beaten?

A. No.

Q. Might not the dirt which you saw on him have been caused by his falling in the dirt?

A. I cannot tell; he was very dirty.

Q. Were his clothes or pantaloons torn?

A. No.

Q. Did you know if the prisoner had any money when he came on shore?

A. No.

Q. Did he inform you on his return that he had been robbed or beaten?

A. Yes.

The witness withdrew

Captain William Charles Fahie of HM ship *Abercrombie* (in his place) stated that the prisoner was recommended to him by Captain Waring as a sergeant; he has been in the ship ever since last August twelvemonth and his conduct during that time has been always correct until the present instance.

Captain Waring of the Royal Marines, stated that he found the prisoner in December twelvemonth acting sergeant in the *Abercrombie* and, from his good and regular behaviour, he recommended him to Captain Fahie as a sergeant; he also had recommended him to headquarters to be confirmed.

Lieutenant Durnsford, Royal Navy, said he had observed him to be in general a sober man and, when on shore at different times, he had behaved very much to his satisfaction.

The prisoner not having anything farther to offer in his defence, the court was cleared and proceeded to deliberate upon and form the sentence.

The court, having heard the evidence in support of the charge as well as what the prisoner had to offer in his defence and the evidence adduced on his behalf and very maturely and deliberately weighed and considered the same, was of opinion that the charges had been in part proved against the prisoner, James Davison, and did in consequence thereof and in consideration of his very good character and circumstances, only adjudge the said James Davison to be broke as a sergeant and reduced to the ranks.

The court was opened, the prisoner brought in, the prosecutor, the witnesses and the audience admitted and sentence passed accordingly. …

137. *Court Martial of Terrence Macmanoes*

[ADM 1/5420]

Minutes of the proceedings of a court martial held on board His Majesty's ship *Monmouth* in the Downes on the 28 day of Novr. 1811.

Present

Thomas Foley, Esq., Rear Admiral of the Red & third officer in the command of His Majesty's ships and vessels in the Downes, President.

Edward Griffith, Esqre., Captain of the Fleet.

Captains

Matthew Henry Scott	J. P. Beresford
Robert Rolles	Henry Raper
Robert D. Oliver	J. S. Rainier
E. W. C. R. Owen	Adam Mackenzie
Hyde Parker	George C. Mackenzie
Charles Gill	

The prisoner was brought into court and the evidence & audience admitted. Read the order of the Right Honble. the Lords Commissioners of the Admiralty, dated 27 ins^t^. & address'd to Thomas Foley, Esqre., Rear Admiral of the Red and third officer in the command of His Majesty's ships & vessels in the Downes, to try Terrence Macmanoes, a Marine belonging to His Majesty's ship *Courageux*, for obstructing Serg^t^. Sheppard in the execution of his duty on the afternoon of the 21st ins^t^. & shortly after for quarrelling with & beating three private Marines without any provocation on their part.

Then the members of the court & judge advocate, in open court and before they proceeded to trial, respectively took the oaths prescribed by Act of Parliament.

A letter from Capt[n]. Phillip Wilkinson, Commander of His Majesty's ship *Courageux*, was read containing the above charge. All the evidences were ordered to withdraw out of court, except Serg[t]. Samuel Sheppard of His Majesty's ship *Courageux*, who was sworn.

Q. State to the court when you were going to stop two boys who were fighting what the prisoner did to prevent you & the language he made use of on that occasion.

Ans. Thursday last, the 21st, in the afternoon about 3 o'clock, there were two Marine boys fighting on the larboard side & the people around them making a great noise; I went to part them & as I was going along, the prisoner laid hold of my left arm & held me for a considerable time before I could get clear & when I got clear, I parted the two boys & dispersed the people &, as I was returning, the prisoner was endeavouring to pick a quarrel with one of the private Marines, James Sparks. Afterwards, I went & sat down in my berth. The prisoner came to the end of the table of the berth & I told him I should report him for hindering me in the execution of my duty &, no doubt, he would be punished for it. Next he held up his right arm & struck his fist in the table & said that neither I nor any other serg[t]. should threaten to report him; it was in a very contemptuous manner.

Q. C. At the time you state to have been detained by the prisoner, did he address any language &, if he did, what was it & were his actions violent?

Ans. He said never mind, they are only skylarking; he held me fast. I had a hard matter to get out of his arms.

Q. C. Did you desire him to let you go and not obstruct you?

Answ. Yes, I desired him more than once and I was forced at last to wrench myself out of his arms.

The prisoner having no questions to ask this witness, the latter withdrew & Thomas Saxon, Corporal of Marines, was call'd & sworn.

Q. Did you see the prisoner take hold of Serg[t]. Sheppard's arm to prevent him from separating the boys on the afternoon of the 21st Ins[t].?

Ans. Yes.

Q. State what you saw & what you heard the prisoner say at that time?

Ans. On the 21st in the afternoon about 3 o'clock, two boys were fighting. Serg[t]. Sheppard stepping forward to part the boys, the prisoner, Macmanoes, seized hold of Serg[t]. Sheppard & after that he told Serg[t]. S. he knew his duty better than him & that he would take the Serg[t]. on the quarter deck if he threatened him with anything. Afterwards, he struck the table in a very vicious way, said he did not care if he could but get him a flogging.

The prisoner having no questions to ask this evidence, the latter withdrew & Richard Goodwilly was sworn.

Q. State to the court the behaviour of the prisoner to you on the afternoon of the 21st ins[t].

Ans. I was sitting in my berth peeling potatoes. The prisoner came down & shoved himself up against me. I thought he was in fun at first; I said, 'Macmanoes, keep your fun to yourself.' 'Damn your eyes,' says he, 'Are you going to give us any of your cheek?' And he immediately up with his fist & gave me a blow in the eye.

Q. Did you see the prisoner beat John Hicks & Thomas Bates?

Answ. No.

Q. C. Did he give you more than one blow?

Answ. No.

The prisoner having no questions to ask this evidence, the latter withdrew & Thomas [*sic*] Hicks was call'd & sworn.

Q. Did you see the prisoner strike Richard Goodwilly on the afternoon of the 21st ins[t].?

Ans. Yes.

Q. State his behaviour to you on that afternoon.

Ans. About 6 in the evening, he came into the berth & shoved up against Richard Goodwilly, who begg'd him to be quiet. He did not want any skylarking from him. He struck him directly; &, as Thomas Bates & I were taken upon the quarter deck to speak to the prisoner's conduct, when we return'd below, he struck us both, me twice & the other once on the face and head with his fist.

Q. Prisoner Did I strike you below before I went on the q[r]. deck?

Ans. No, you struck Goodwilly.

The prisoner having no further questions to ask this evidence, he withdrew & Thomas Bates was call'd & sworn.

Q. State the prisoner's conduct to you on the afternoon of the 21st ins[t].?

Ans. Last Thursday evening, he came into the berth & shoved up against Richard Goodwilly & he desired him to be quiet & he up with his fist, & struck him. He immediately went & complained of him, call'd John Hicks & me on the q^{r}. deck as witnesses & we came down in the berth again & he immediately came down with the ship's [company] &, in passing the berth, he came into it & struck John Hicks & me, John Hicks once & me twice.

Then the evidence on the part of the prosecution closed & the prisoner was called upon for his defence, which he made by throwing himself on the mercy of the court.

The prisoner having nothing further to offer in his defence, the court was cleared & proceeded to deliberate upon & form the sentence.

The court, having carefully and deliberately weigh'd & consider'd the evidence produced as well as the prisoner's defence, were of opinion that the charge had been fully proved; in consequence thereof, the court adjudged the prisoner, Terrence Macmanoes, to receive seventy two lashes on his bare back with a cat of nine tails on board His Majesty's ship *Courageux* at such time or times as the captain of that ship should direct.

The court was then open'd, audience admitted & sentence pass'd accordingly. …

138. *Court Martial of John Moon*

[ADM 1/5422]

Minutes of proceedings of a court martial held on board His Majesty's ship *Elephant* in the Downs on the 16th day of Jan^{ry}. 1812.

Present

John Ferrier, Esq., Rear Admiral of the White and third officer in the command of His Majesty's ships and vessels in the Downs, President

Captains

George Byng	Joseph Bingham
James Walker	E. W. C. R. Owen
Richard Raggett	Philip Carteret
Hyde Parker	John Hatsted

The prisoner was brought into court and the evidence and audience admitted.

Read the order of the Right Honble. Lords Commissioners of the Admiralty, dated the 15 inst. and addressed to the president; proceeded to try John Moon, Private Marine of 3d class belonging to His Majesty's ship *Elephant*, for having on the evening of the 10th inst. struck Serg[t]. John Rider of the Royal Marines, also of the same ship, whilst in the execution of his duty and for having otherwise conducted himself in a most riotous manner.

Then the members of the court and off[g]. judge advocate, in open court and before they proceeded to trial, respectively took the oaths enjoined by Act of Parliament.

A letter from Captain Francis William Austen, Comm[r] of the *Elephant*, was then read as follows, addressed to Vice Adm[l] Sir R J Strachan, &c., &c., &c.:

(Copy) His Majesty's Ship *Elephant*
in the Downs Jan[ry] 11, 1812

… John Moon, Private Marine of the 3d Class belonging to His Majesty's ship under my command, having on the evening of yesterday the 10th inst. struck Serg[t]. John Rider of the Royal Marines also belonging to the same ship whilst in the execution of his duty and otherwise conducted himself in a most riotous manner, I have to request you will be pleased to make application to my Lords Commissioners of the Admiralty for a court martial to try him for the same. …

All the evidences were order'd to withdraw except Serg[t]. John Rider who was sworn.

Prosecutor. State to the court what you know of the charge against the prisoner.

Ans. Last Friday evening, the 10th inst., between the hours of six and seven John Gregson, Seaman, came to me in my birth and said that the prisoner, John Moon, was in his birth challenging to fight one of his messmates and he would thank me if I would order him away as he did not wish to quarrel with him. I instantly went with John Gregson to his birth and found the prisoner standing up by the table where John Gregson messes. I order'd him to his birth; he said he would not go for me & put his fist in my face. I instantly collar'd him & told him he should go with me on the quarter deck. He then knock'd me down. I got up & forced myself from under him &, before I could recover myself, he knock'd me down the second time and fell upon me. I threw him off me & threw him on his back. I there held him and call'd for the sergeant of the guard; the sergeant instantly came to my assistance & with his assistance and two men more (Marines), we forced him aft on the quarter deck. When he came there, he attempted to make his escape & was prevented by corporal of the guard. I reported his behaviour to the 1st lieut^{t}. who sent for the master at arms and order'd the prisoner in irons.

Q. C. What do you mean by saying he attempted to escape?

Ans. To escape from our custody.

The prisoner having no questions to ask this evidence, he withdrew & Sergeant Charles Cubett, also of the Royal Marines & belonging to the same ship, was call'd & sworn.

Prosecutor. State to the court what you know of the charge against the prisoner.

Ans. On the 10th inst. in the evening I heard Serg^{t}. Rider call for the sergeant of the guard; upon which, I went over on the starboard side of the ship. I saw Serg^{t}. Rider had hold of the prisoner and before I could get nigh enough him for to lay hold of him, he struck Serg^{t}. Rider twice. I caught hold of him and broke the hold between prisoner & the Serg^{t}. I then call'd for the corporal of guard to my assistance to take him on deck. He came and the prisoner behaved in such an obstreperous manner that we were obliged to force him on deck; when we got there, the 1st lieut. not being present on deck, the prisoner swore he would not stay there longer in the cold, made an attempt to get off, which corporal & I prevented.

Q. Court. Did you see the prisoner knock Sergeant Rider down on the deck?

Ans. No, I can't say I saw him knock him down; he (the Serg^{t}.) never fell from the blows I saw him give the Sergeant.

Court. Was prisoner drunk or sober at that time?

Ans. I can't call him sober.

Court. Were Sergeant & prisoner lying upon deck when you saw them first?

Ans. They were rising from the deck; the Sergeant was on his legs fast hold of him. They were scuffling.

The prisoner having no questions to ask this evidence, he withdrew and John Gregson, alias John Greegson, was call'd and sworn.

Prosecutor. Did you on the evening of the 10th inst. go to Sergeant Rider for any purpose relative to the prisoner and if so, state for what?

Answer. He was making a noise in my berth and I went to Serg^{t}. Rider to ask him to take him away. Sergt. Rider took him away & after that Moon (prisoner) struck him on the breast once. That was all I saw.

Court. Did you see the Sergeant fall from any blow you saw him receive?

Answer. No.

The prisoner ask'd this witness no questions but denied having any knowledge of the charges. This evidence then withdrew and Samuel Letts, Private Marine also of the same ship, was call'd and sworn.

Pros[r]. Did you see Sergeant Rider and the prisoner, John Moon, at or near the berth of John Gregson on the evening of the 10th inst.?
Ans. Yes.
Pros[r]. Relate what you saw pass between them at that time.
Ans. I saw John Moon strike Sergeant Rider on the breast once. The Serg[t]. did not fall in consequence of that blow. They were scuffling together, the Serg[t]. was taking him aft & I followed assisting the Serg[t]. There were three others – Rich'd Stead, John Gregson and Serg[t]. Cubett.

The prisoner had no questions to ask this evidence and he withdrew.

The evidence on the part of the prosecution being closed, the prisoner was call'd upon to make his defence. He said he did not know what he was doing, he was so tipsy; he said he did not know whether he committed the crime or no, said he had been six months aboard this ship. The prisoner further said he had no evidence nor written defence nor witness to character.

Sergeant Rider was call'd again & being interrogated said he hardly thought it possible the prisoner could not have known him the sergeant.

The prisoner having nothing further to offer in his defence, the court was clear'd and proceeded to deliberate upon and form the sentence.

The court, having maturely and deliberately weigh'd and consider'd the evidence produced in support of the charge as well as what the prisoner had to offer in his defence, were of opinion that the charge was proved; in consequence thereof the court adjudged the said prisoner, John Moon, to be hang'd by the neck until he be dead at the yardarm of His Majesty's said ship, the *Elephant*, or such other of His Majesty's ships and at such time as should be directed by the Lords Commissioners of the Admiralty.

The court open'd, audience admitted & sentence pass'd accordingly.
…

139. *Court Martial of Jacob Simpson*

[ADM 1/5426]

Minutes of the proceedings of a court martial assembled and held on board His Majesty's ship *Monmouth* in the Downs the 28th day of May 1812.

Present

Graham Moore, Esq., Captain of His Majesty's ship *Chatham* and second officer in the command of His Majesty's ships and vessels in the Downs, President.

Captains

William Nowell
Robert Dudley Oliver
Richard Raggett
Henry Lidgbird Ball
William Prowse

Being all the post captains of His Majesty's ships and vessels in the Downs, except Captain Hancock of His Majesty's ship *Nymphen*, who certified to the court by the surgeon his inability to attend through ill health.

The prisoner being brought into court and the audience admitted, the order of the Right Honble the Lords Commissioners of the Admiralty, dated the 27th instant, directed to Graham Moore, Esq., Captain of His Majesty's ship *Chatham*, proceeded to try Mr. Jacob Simpson, Carpenter of His Majesty's sloop *Griffon*, for drunkenness, disobedience of orders and unofficerlike conduct on the evening of the 30th of April last was read. The order appointing Mr. John Symmons to officiate as judge advocate and the letter from Captain Trollope containing the charges preferred against the prisoner were then also read.[1]

The members of the court and judge advocate then, in open court and before they proceeded to trial, took the oaths as enjoined by Act of Parliament and all the witnesses being ordered to withdraw and attend their examinations separately, they all withdrew accordingly, except the first to be sworn and the court proceeded to trial as follows:

Lieutenant Sheppard of the *Griffon* called & sworn.

Prosecutor – Do you remember a complaint being made to you as officer of the watch on the evening of the 30th of April respecting Mr Simpson?

Answer – Yes.

Prosecutor – Relate to the court what you know respecting the circumstances.

Answer – It was my watch on deck from six till eight o'clock. About seven, the carpenter's servant, Aaron Munn, came aft and told me his master had been beating of him. I stripped the boy and, on examining his back, observed he had been very inhumanely beaten and very much bruised. I acquainted Captain Trollope; he sent for the carpenter, who came on deck. When the carpenter came, I saw he was much intoxicated. When Captain Trollope asked him what he had been beating his boy for, he said he had not dressed his dinner. Captain Trollope asked him if he knew it was contrary to his orders that any one should be struck in the ship; the carpenter said he did. Captain Trollope ordered him to his cabin

[1]This letter is not bound with the transcript in ADM 1/5426.

and sent for the sergeant to put him under an arrest; shortly after, the sergeant reported to me he was very riotous in his cabin.
Prosecutor – Did you hear any improper language from Mr Simpson after I had ordered him to be put under an arrest?
Answer – Yes, he said he would go down and bring his warrant up; he would not do his duty as carpenter of the ship any longer; he would do it as carpenter's mate.
Prosecutor – Do you recollect the order being publicly read that no person should be started or beat in the ship?
Answer – Yes.
Court – Did this happen in the evening between seven and eight?
Answer – Yes.
Court – Was the sloop at sea at this time?
Answer – Yes.
Court – What marks of intoxication did he show except what you have mentioned?
Answer – He could scarcely walk; he treated Captain Trollope in a contemptuous manner with his hands in his pockets.
Samuel Gardner, Seaman, called & sworn.
Prosecutor – Do you recollect on the evening of the 30th April seeing the carpenter, Mr Simpson, beating his boy, Aaron Munn?
Answer – Yes. I saw him beating him with about an inch and a half rope; he was holding him with one hand and beating him with the other. I went to him and took the boy from him.
Prosecutor – Did you hear the prisoner offer to fight John Carthness?
Answer – Yes.
Prosecutor – What state did Mr Simpson appear to be in?
Answer – Groggy.
Court – Was this about the same time?
Answer – Yes, about five minutes after he had done beating the boy.
Court – Do you know it was contrary to my orders that no person should be started or beat in the ship?
Answer – Yes.
Court – Do you know whether there was any altercation between the prisoner and John Carthness?
Answer – John Carthness interfered with him when he was beating the boy and he offered to fight him.
John Carthness, Seaman, was sworn.
Prosecutor – Do you recollect on the evening of the 30 of April seeing Mr Simpson, the Carpenter, beat his boy, Aaron Munn?
Answer – No, I did not see him.
Prosecutor – Was you there at the time the boy was heard singing out?

Answer – Yes.
Prosecutor – Relate what passed between you and the carpenter.
Answer – Mr Simpson came out of his cabin and said, 'Who is that going to take me on the quarter deck?' No one spoke for some time. He said, 'That is you Mr Carthness.' I said, 'No sir, I never spoke a word.' He said, 'Come out here and I'll fight you.' I refused and then after that Mr Simpson was ordered on the quarter deck.
Prosecutor – What state did Mr Simpson appear to you to be in?
Answer – In liquor.
Court – Did you see any more of it and is that all you know of the matter? Did he say anything more to you after you refused to fight him?
Answer – No.
Court – When you came to the carpenter's cabin, was boy in the cabin?
Answer – Yes.
Court – Was the boy singing out for some time?
Answer – Not long, about a minute.
Court – Was it dark?
Answer – The hammocks were down and it was dark. My berth is close to the carpenter's cabin. I heard all this as I was sitting in my berth; the prisoner passed by my berth.
Court – Were there any people crowding about the cabin?
Answer – No, Samuel Gardner was in my berth. I heard someone say the boy ought to go on the quarter deck to complain.

Samuel Gardner was recalled.

Court – State to the court what you know further relative to Mr Simpson beating his boy.
Answer – Upon hearing the boy cry in the carpenter's cabin, I went and interfered and took the boy; I was sitting at that time in Carthness's berth. He appeared to me to be beating the boy very severely. Carthness said the boy ought to take him to the quarter deck.

John Cullen called & sworn.

Prosecutor – Do you recollect on the evening of the 30 April seeing Mr Simpson, the Carpenter, beat his boy, Aaron Munn?
Answer – Yes, I was sitting down in the berth and Carthness said the boy should be taken out and Gardner open'd the door. Someone said the carpenter should be taken aft and he took off his waistcoat and offered to fight him.
Court – Was the prisoner drunk or sober?
Answer – He appeared to me to be drunk.
Court – Was the ship at sea?
Answer – Yes.
Court – Did the prisoner appear to be beating the boy in a severe manner?

Answer – Yes, he was holding him with one hand and beating him with the other with an inch and an half rope.

The prisoner here was called upon for his defence, who said he had none but left himself to the mercy of the court, had been 16 years in the service, four years in the *Griffon* and called upon Captain Trollope for his character, who said it was the first complaint he had had of him since he had been in the *Griffon* four months. The carpenter also produced certificates giving him a good character and some recommending him to a larger ship.

Prisoner – Since you commanded the *Griffon* has my character been that of a sober man?

Answer – Yes.

Prisoner – Have I ever been known to be cruel?

Answer – Not to my knowledge.

Prisoner – Has my conduct in general been respectful to my superior officers?

Answer – Yes.

The prisoner having nothing further to urge in his defence, the court was clear'd and proceeded to deliberate upon and form the sentence.

The court, having heard the evidence in support of the charge as well as what the prisoner had to offer in his defence and having very maturely and deliberately weighed and considered the whole and every part thereof, were of opinion the charge was proved. The court did therefore adjudge the said prisoner, Mr Jacob Simpson, to be very severely reprimanded and rendered incapable of promotion for two years; and he was thereby so reprimanded and sentenced accordingly.

The court was opened, audience admitted and sentence passed accordingly.

140. *Court Martial of James Emery*

[ADM 1/5434]

Minutes of proceedings at a court martial held on board His Majesty's ship *Raisonnable* in Sheerness Harbour on Monday the 11th day of January 1813.

Present

Edward Sneyd Clay, Esqre., Captain of His Majesty's ship *Raisonnable* and second officer in the command of His Majesty's ships and vessels in the River Medway below Oakham Ness and at the buoy of the Nore, President.

Captains
Edmund Heywood
Charles John Austen

Commanders
Thomas Richard Toker
Thomas Renwick

Thomas Williams, officiating as Judge Advocate

Being all the captains of post ships at this port, except Thomas Boys, Esqre., Captain of His Majesty's ship *Zealous*, absent on Admiralty leave.

The prisoner was brought into court and the prosecutor, the witnesses and audience admitted.

Read the order of the Lords Commissioners of the Admiralty, dated the 9th day of January 1813, directed to Edward Sneyd Clay, Esqre., Captain of His Majesty's ship *Raisonnable* and second officer in the command of His Majesty's ships and vessels in the River Medway below Oakham Ness and at the buoy of the Nore, to assemble a court martial and try M^{r}. James Emery, Boatswain of HM sloop *Mosquito*, for disobedience of orders and contempt.

Read the warrant appointing a judge advocate.

Then the members of the court and judge advocate, in open court and before they proceeded to trial, respectively took the oaths directed by an Act of Parliament passed in the twenty second year of the reign of King George the Second.

A letter from Lieutenant James Long, First of His Majesty's sloop *Mosquito* to Captain James Tomkinson of that sloop was then read as follows:

His Majesty's sloop *Mosquito*
In the Downes 21st Decr. 1812

… I beg leave to acquaint you that M^{r}. James Emery, Boatswain of this sloop, behaved in a contemptuous manner to me last evening and refused to obey the orders I gave him,

I have therefore to request you will be pleased to make application to the commander in chief for a court martial to be held on him for the same. …

Read a letter from Captain James Tomkinson of His Majesty's sloop *Mosquito* to William Young, Esquire, Admiral of the White, Commander in Chief, &^{ca}. as follows:

His Majesty's sloop *Mosquito*
In the Downes 23rd Dec[r] 1812

… I have the honour to enclose a letter from Lieut. James Long, 1st Lieut. of His Majesty's sloop under my command, requesting a court martial may be held on M[r]. James Emery, the Boatswain of the *Mosquito*, as therein stated. Having enquired into the circumstance, it appears that Lieutenant Long had ordered the boatswain, M[r]. James Emery, to attend the side to clear a lighter of water (one boatswain's mate being sick and the other employ'd about the hold) which he repeatedly and positively refused to do in a contemptuous manner. I have therefore to request you will be pleased to make application that a court martial may be held on M[r]. James Emery accordingly for 'disobedience of orders & contempt' as expressed in the enclosed letter. …

All the witnesses, except the first to be sworn, being then ordered to withdraw and to attend their examinations separately, they all withdrew accordingly and the court proceeded to trial as follows:

Evidence in support of the charge

Lieutenant James Long of HM Sloop *Mosquito* sworn and examined as follows:

Prosecutor – Relate to the court all the particulars you know relative to the charge you have heard read against the prisoner.

Answer – On Sunday the 20th December last, the hands had been turned up after dinner to clear a lighter of water. They had been employed some time in clearing the lighter and did not do it so smartly as I wished. I sent Pryce Pugh to tell the prisoner I wanted him; he came and asked me if I wanted him. I told him to attend the quarter fall in the waist; he paid no attention to my order, turned round from me, looked over the larboard gangway. From there, he went to the quarter masters abaft the mainmast (who were then pointing the ends of the small bower cable); he gave them some order. I observed his motions and went over on the starboard side of the quarter deck, called out myself to the prisoner, 'Emery, you will attend at the gangway in hoisting in the casks and send the boatswain's mate to attend the quarter tackle fall in the waist, as one of your mates is sick.' His answer to me was that he would not do it; he did not conceive it his duty and he would not do it, with his hands in his pantaloon pockets. I called to Daniel

Johnston and Wm. Irvin, Quarter Masters, who were then close by, and asked them if they heard the order I gave Mr. Emery & his answer to me and the contemptuous way in which he stood. They both answered yes; I sent immediately for the sergeant of Marines and desired him to confine Mr. Emery, the prisoner, to his cabin for disobedience of orders and contempt.

Prosecutor – Had you any doubt when you first ordered the prisoner to attend to that duty whether he heard you or not?

Answer – No.

Prosecutor – Do you conceive the manner and attitude of the prisoner (when you gave him the order) contemptuous or not?

Answer – Contemptuous.

Court – On which side was the craft containing the water?

Answer – On the starboard side.

Prisoner – Did I splice a piece of rope on to the quarter tackle and did I go down for rope for tails of the cable?

Answer – Yes.

Court – Was this before or after you first gave the prisoner orders to attend to the quarter tackle in the waist?

Answer – Before.

Court – Where was the prisoner at the time you sent for him, as the hands had been previously turned up?

Answer – In his cabin.

The witness withdrew

Pryce Pugh, Private Marine belonging to HM Sloop *Mosquito*, sworn and examined as follows:

Prosecutor – Was you sent by Lieut. Long on the 20th December last in the afternoon to the prisoner to desire him to go to him?

Answer – Yes.

Prosecutor – Where was the prisoner when you delivered the message to him?

Answer – In his cabin.

Prosecutor – Had the hands been turned up to clear [the?] lighter previously to this?

Answer – Yes.

The witness withdrew.

William Johnstone, a Quarter Master belonging to HM Sloop *Mosquito*, sworn & examined as follows:

Prosecutor – Relate to the court the order you heard Lieut. Long give the prisoner on the 20th December last in the afternoon relative to the clearing the lighter of water.

Answer – Lieut. Long sent for the prisoner and when he came up, Lieut. Long told him to attend at the side clearing a lighter; the prisoner said, 'No.' 'No,' says M^{r}. Long; 'no sir,' says he, 'I will not. It is not my duty and I will not do it.' Then Lieut. Long told me and the other quarter master, Irvin, to take notice of what he said.

Prosecutor – Do you recollect in what posture the prisoner stood at the time he was addressing Lieut. Long?

Answer – Yes, he stood with his hands in his pockets.

Prosecutor – Did you conceive the prisoner stood in a proper or in an improper manner at the time?

Answer – In an improper manner.

Court – Did you in a clear and distinct manner hear the prisoner refuse to obey the orders of Lieut. Long?

Answer – Yes.

The witness withdrew.

William Irvin, Quarter Master belonging to HM Sloop *Mosquito*, sworn and examined as follows:

Prosecutor – Relate to the court the order you heard Lieutenant Long give the prisoner on the 20th December last in the afternoon relative to the clearing the lighter of water.

Answer – Lieutenant Long told the prisoner to attend the side to clear the lighter; the prisoner said he would not. M^{r}. Long said, 'You won't sir'; 'no sir,' the prisoner said, 'It is not my duty and I will not do it.'

Prosecutor – Do you recollect in what posture the prisoner stood at the time he was addressing Lieut. Long?

Answer – Yes, he stood with his hands in his pockets.

Prosecutor – Did you conceive the prisoner stood in a proper or in an improper manner at the time?

Answer – He did not stand in a respectful manner.

The witness withdrew.

The evidence in support of the charge being finished, the prisoner was called upon to make his defence, who put into the hands of the judge advocate a written paper signed by himself, which was read to the court as follows:

… As a prisoner before you, it is with regret that after my long services of 28 years I should, as you might expect, feel the remorse, stings of ungratitude on being forced to call the honourable gentleman in question, who got me made after sailing with him only 6 months in the quality of a petty officer, which I have been fifteen years in His Majesty's service. And in the whole course of my trial, if I have in any other way behaved unbecoming the character of an officer and a seaman, I likewise hope that your clemency will still farther accede to me as I have an aged mother to support whom all dependence is on me; and for the future, I shall make it my utmost diligence to serve in any station with pleasure and rectitude and with gratitude remain in duty bound. …

The prisoner not having anything farther to offer in his defence, the court was cleared and proceeded to deliberate upon and form the sentence, of which the following is an extract:

And, having heard the evidence produced in support of the charge as well as what the prisoner had to offer in his defence, the court is of opinion that the charges are proved against the prisoner, M^r^. James Emery, and doth in consequence thereof adjudge the said James Emery to be dismissed from his employment as boatswain in His Majesty's navy and to serve before the mast on board such of His Majesty's ships as the commander in chief of His Majesty's ships and vessels at this port shall direct.

And the prisoner, M^r^. James Emery, is hereby so sentenced accordingly.

The court was then reopened, the prisoner brought in, and the prosecutor, the witnesses and the audience admitted and sentence passed accordingly. …

141. *Court Martial of Andrew Graham*

[ADM 1/5434]

Minutes of proceedings at a court martial held on board His Majesty's ship *Raisonnable* in Sheerness Harbour on Monday the 11th day of January 1813.

Present

Edward Sneyd Clay, Esqre., Captain of His Majesty's ship *Raisonnable* and second officer in the command of His Majesty's ships and vessels in the River Medway below Oakham Ness and at the buoy of the Nore, President.

Captains
Edmund Heywood
Charles John Austen

Commanders
Thomas Richard Toker
Thomas Renwick

Thomas Williams, officiating as Judge Advocate

Being all the captains of post ships at this port, except Thomas Boys, Esqre., Captain of His Majesty's ship *Zealous*, absent on Admiralty leave.

The prisoner was brought into court and the prosecutor, the witnesses and audience admitted.

Read the order of the Lords Commissioners of the Admiralty, dated the 9th day of January 1813 and directed to Edward Sneyd Clay, Esqre., Captain of His Majesty's ship *Raisonnable* and second officer in the command of His Majesty's ships and vessels in the River Medway below Oakham Ness and at the buoy of the Nore, to assemble a court martial to try Mr. Andrew Graham, Boatswain of His Majesty's sloop *Nightingale* for drunkenness and contempt.

Read the warrant appointing a judge advocate.

Then the members of the court and judge advocate, in open court and before they proceeded to trial, respectively took the oaths directed by an Act of Parliament passed in the twenty second year of the reign of King George the Second.

A letter from Captain Nixon of His Majesty's sloop *Nightingale* to Vice Admiral Otway, Commander in Chief &^c^, Leith, was read as follows:

His Majesty's sloop *Nightingale*
Leith Roads, 30th Novr 1812

… I have to request you will be pleased to apply to their Lordships for a court martial to be held on M^r^. Andrew Graham, Boatswain of His Majesty's sloop *Nightingale* under my command, for drunkenness and contempt to his superior officer on or about the 21st day of October last. …

All the witnesses, except the first to be sworn, being then ordered to withdraw and attend their examinations separately, they all withdrew accordingly and the court proceeded to trial as follows:

Evidence in support of the charge

Lieutenant Lacey Dickenson of His Majesty's sloop *Nightingale* sworn and examined as follows:

Prosecutor – Relate to the court what you know of the charges against the prisoner.

Answer – On the 21st of October last between two and four in the afternoon, John Evett, one of the seamen, came to me with his face bloody and complained that the prisoner had struck him whilst in his berth between decks. I sent for the prisoner, who came aft perfectly drunk. I desired him to go below to his cabin and said that I should request the captain to apply for a court martial on him; he said, 'Do it. Do it. That's right, that's what I want; break me and send me to hell.' I then told him that if he did not go immediately below to his cabin, I would put him in irons; he then went forward but would not go below. I sent for the corporal of Marines and desired another Marine, who was standing forward, to assist in dragging him below to his cabin, where I placed a sentry on him.

The witness withdrew

M[r]. John Kennedy, Master of His Majesty's sloop *Nightingale*, sworn and examined as follows:

Prosecutor – Relate to the court what you know of the charges against the prisoner.

Answer – On the 21st of October last between the hours of 12 and one in the forenoon, the prisoner came on board very much intoxicated and reported himself to the first lieutenant, who then told him to go below, that he was a disgrace to the ship and not think of doing any duty till he was perfectly sober. He went below then and in the afternoon between three and four, I came on deck and saw John Evett with his face covered with blood; and immediately afterwards, the prisoner came on deck. M[r]. Dickenson asked him how he dared make any disturbance below after he had told him to go below and not do any duty; the prisoner said he had struck the man for insolence. M[r]. Dickenson then told him to go below again and that he would acquaint the captain with his conduct and that if he did not take care he would be tried by a court martial; the prisoner then said that was what he wanted, to break him and send him to hell. M^r^. Dickenson then ordered him below again; the prisoner not appearing to obey the order, M^r^. Dickenson then ordered a corporal of Marines to take his men and put him below by force, which was done and a sentry put over him. He then made a great disturbance below, calling out to the sentry why he did not run him through with a cutlass.

Court – When the prisoner made use of the expressions you have asserted, did he do so in a contemptuous manner?

Answer – Yes.

Court – When the prisoner came on board, was he returning from leave or duty?

Answer – I believe from leave, I am not sure.

The witness withdrew

John Evett, Seaman belonging to HM sloop *Nightingale*, sworn and examined as follows:

Prosecutor – Upon what occasion did you complain to Lieut. Dickenson of the prisoner on or about the 21st of October last?

Answer – I had just come on board and was sitting in my berth eating my victuals; the prisoner was sitting alongside of me and he slewed round and struck me. I never said anything to him.

Prosecutor – Was the prisoner drunk or sober at the time?

Answer – He was drunk.

Prosecutor – Were you present when the prisoner was ordered below by Lieut. Dickenson?

Answer – Yes.

Prosecutor – What reply did the prisoner make?

Answer – He told him he would not go.

Prosecutor – Do you think he expressed himself in a contemptuous manner to M^r^. Dickenson?

Answer – Yes.

Court – Did the prisoner refuse going below when ordered to do so by Lieut. Dickenson?

Answer – Yes.

The witness withdrew

M^r^. James Reid, Surgeon of HM sloop *Nightingale*, sworn and examined as follows:

Prosecutor – Was you present when the prisoner was ordered below by Lieut. Dickenson on or about the 21st October last?

Answer – I was.

Prosecutor – What reply did the prisoner make to Lieut. Dickenson and in what manner did he make that reply?

Answer – When Lieut. Dickenson desired the prisoner to go below, observing he was in a state of intoxication and saying that if he did his duty he ought to try him by a court martial, the prisoner said he wished that he would, as that was what he wanted which he repeated several times in an impertinent manner. As he did not seem to obey the order immediately, Lieut. Dickenson ordered the corporal of Marines to take him below and the prisoner then complied and went down.

The witness withdrew

The evidence in support of the charge being finished, the prisoner was called upon to make his defence, who said he had not anything to offer but requested Captain Tomkinson to speak to his character, who said:

'The prisoner was boatswain's mate with me when I had command of the *Ceylon* after her recapture and behaved particularly smart & active in fitting her out when she was a perfect wreck and I think through his activity, she was ready for sea in about 15 days. He remained in her about three months, during which time he behaved much to my satisfaction.'

The prisoner not having anything farther to offer in his defence, the court was cleared and proceeded to deliberate upon and form the sentence, of which the following is an extract:

And, having heard the evidence produced in support of the charge as well as what the prisoner had to offer in his defence, the court is of opinion that the charges are proved against the prisoner, M^r^. Andrew Graham, and doth in consequence thereof adjudge the said Andrew Graham to be dismissed from his employment of boatswain in His Majesty's navy and to serve before the mast in such one of His Majesty's ships as the commander in chief of His Majesty's ships and vessels at this port shall direct.

The court was then reopened, the prisoner brought in and the prosecutor, the witnesses and audience admitted and sentence passed accordingly. …

142. *Court Martial of Alexander Meldrum*

[ADM 1/5439]

Minutes of proceedings at a court martial held onboard His Majesty's ship *La Hogue* at Halifax the 23rd November 1813.

Present

Edward Griffith, Esquire, Rear Admiral of the Blue and second officer in the command of His Majesty's ships and vessels at Halifax, President
The Honourable Henry Hotham, Captain of the Fleet

Captains

John Talbot
William Skipsey
Hyde Parker
Alexander Gordon
The Honble Thomas Bladen Capel
Farmery Predam Epworth
Samuel John Pechell

The prisoner was brought into court, and the evidence and audience admitted.

Read the order of the Right Honble Sir John Borlase Warren, Bt., KB, Admiral of the Blue and Commander in Chief &^{ca}, &^{ca}, &^{ca}., dated the 20th instant, directed to Edward Griffith, Esquire, Rear Admiral of the Blue and second officer in the command of His Majesty's ships and vessels at Halifax, to try M^{r}. Alexander Meldrum, Master of His Majesty's ship *Maidstone*, for neglect of duty in not returning onboard his ship until after she had been twenty two hours on shore and for unofficerlike conduct and want of zeal for His Majesty's service.

Then the members of the court and judge advocate, in open court and before they proceeded to trial, respectively took the oaths directed by Act of Parliament made and passed in the 22nd year of the reign of His late Majesty King George the Second entitled *An Act for Amending, Explaining and Reducing into One Act of Parliament the Laws relating to the Government of His Majesty's Ships, Vessels and Forces by Sea.*

A letter from Captain George Burdett of His Majesty's ship *Maidstone* was read as follows,[1] vizt.:

[1]This letter is addressed to Sir J. B. Warren, Commander in Chief of the Halifax Station.

His Majesty's ship *Maidstone*
Halifax Harbour, 15 Novr 1813

… M^{r}. Alexander Meldrum, Master of His Maj. ship under my command, having been onshore on the night of the 12th ins^{t}. during a violent gale of wind, in which the ship broke from her anchor and drifted onshore, and the conduct of M^{r}. Alexander Meldrum being so negligent and unofficerlike in not using every exertion to repair onboard in the state the ship was then lying – on her beam ends – more particularly as the signal was flying for every officer to repair onboard from daylight of the morning of the 13th ins^{t}. and repeated with a gun. I have therefore to request you will please to order a court martial to try the said M^{r}. Alexander Meldrum for neglect of duty in not returning onb^{d}. his ship till nearly dark on the evening of the 13th, twenty two hours after the ship had been onshore, and for unofficerlike conduct and want of zeal for His Maj. Service. …

	All the evidences were ordered to withdraw out of court except Lieutenant John Taylor, 1st L^{t}, who was sworn.
Question by Prosecutor	Did HMS *Maidstone* under my command drive onshore on or about the night of the 12th ins^{t}.?
Answer	She did.
Question by Pros^{r}.	Was the prisoner onboard?
Ans^{r}.	No.
Question by Pros^{r}.	How long had she been in that situation before the prisoner came onb^{d}.?
Ans^{r}.	From about 7 in the evening of the 12th till between 4 and 5 on the following afternoon.
Question by Pros^{r}.	Was he put under an arrest by my order immediately on making his appearance onb^{d}.?
Ans^{r}.	Yes.
Question by Pros^{r}.	Was the signal made with a gun on the morning of the 13th for everyone to repair onboard?
Ans^{r}.	The signal was made for everyone to repair onb^{d}. and 2 or 3 guns were fired, but whether they were fired to cnforcc thc signal or as distress guns I can't say.
Quest^{n} by Pros^{r}.	Was any signal flying at the time for distress?
Ans^{r}.	I believe not.
Quest^{n} by Pros^{r}.	At the time those guns were fired, what did you suppose they were fired for?

Ans^{r}.	I was on the main deck when the guns were fired and I did not know what they were fired for.
Quest^{n} by Pros^{r}.	Had the prisoner your leave to go off the spot?
Ans^{r}.	He had my leave to go onshore and to return onb^{d}. the next day. I did not know that he was going off the spot.
Quest^{n} by Pros^{r}.	Did I inform you that he had my leave to go off the spot?
Ans^{r}.	No.
	The prosecution had no other question to ask of this witness.
	The court asked the following:
Question by Court	When the prisoner came onboard on the afternoon of the 13th, did he account to you for not having come before?
	No.
Quest^{n}. By Court	Were you authorized to give leave of absence to the off^{rs}. of the *Maidstone* and what leave were you authorized to grant?
Ansr.	I was authorized to give leave by Capt. Burdett and I have taken upon myself to grant 24 hours leave, but I should not venture to give more without the captain's particular permission.
Quest^{n}. By Court	Were there any written orders of Capt. Burdett's onb^{d}. and if there were what were they with respect to leave?
Ans^{r}.	There were; no officer was to leave the ship when he was onb^{d}. without his permission or to sleep out of the ship without his leave, but, since we have been in harbour, the captain has ordered me to regulate the leave.
	The court had nothing further to ask.
	The prisoner asked this witness the following questions:
Question	Had I your permission to go onshore on Friday the 12th ins^{t}.?
Ans^{r}.	You had.
Question	Was that permission granted till the evening of the 13th.?

Ans^{r}.	Permission was granted from the afternoon of the 12th till the afternoon of the 13th.
Question	Did I return onboard the ship within the time limited by you for returning onb^{d}.?
Ans^{r}.	There was no hour particularly mentioned and I conceived that you returned to your leave.
Question	Have you ever since you have been 1st Lieutt. of the *Maidstone* witnessed any want of zeal in me for the benefit of HM Service?
Ans^{r}.	No, except in this instance.
Question	Did I tell you immediately after my being put under arrest why I did not return onb^{d}. earlier on the 13th?
Ans^{r}.	You told me you were off the spot and that you did not consider your leave out.
Question	Do you mean to say that you consider this an instance of my want of zeal for His Maj. Service?
Ans^{r}.	If there had been a possibility of your getting onb^{d}. and you did not avail yourself of it, I should conceive it a want of zeal.
	The p^{r}. having nothing further to ask of this witness, he withdrew.
	M^{r}. Robert Higgins, Master at Arms of the *Maidstone*, was next called into court and sworn.
Quest^{n}. by Prosecutor	Did you put the prisoner under an arrest by my orders?
Ans^{r}.	I did.
Quest^{n}. by Pros^{r}.	State to the court when and at what time of the day?
Ans^{r}.	At about 5 o'clock on the evening of the 13th.
Quest^{n}. by Pros^{r}.	How long had the *Maidstone* then been onshore?
Ans^{r}.	From about 8 o'clock of the preceding night.
	The prosecutor had nothing further to ask of this witness.
	The court asked the following questions:
Question by Court	When you rec'ed orders to put the prisoner under an arrest, had you any conversation with him?

Ans^{r}. Nothing more than my desiring him to consider himself a prisoner to his cabin.

Question by Court Was the p^{r}. onb^{d}. all the day previous to his being put under an arrest?

Ans^{r}. I don't know.

The evidence in support of the charges being finished, the prisoner was asked whether he had any defence and he offered the following, which was read by the judge advocate:

… I beg to state to you that I received leave from the first lieutenant on the noon of the 12th Ins^{t}. to be absent from HMS *Maidstone* till the following day and, from no particular hour having been specified for my return, I naturally supposed, as had frequently been the case before, that if I returned at any hour on the following day I should not have exceeded my leave. And this I was the further induced to suppose as the first lieutenant said to me on leaving the ship, 'Be onboard on Saturday as I wished to go onshore on Sunday.' After having settled all my business in town, I walked out in the country to a house beyond the Rockingham Inn, where, in consequence of its coming on to rain, I spent the night of the 12th; and I beg most solemnly to assure this court that altho' it appeared to blow hard, I had not the most distant idea of any of HM ships having driven onshore. I did not rise till about 9 o'clock on the morning of the 13th and, having breakfasted, I returned to town on foot, where I arrived about 3 o'clock and immediately on discovering the situation of the *Maidstone*, I made every possible exertion to obtain a shore boat to put me onboard, which (from the difficulty of obtaining, they having been all hired by the merchants looking after their vessels) I did not succeed in doing till about 4 o'clock. On my arriving onb^{d}., I was immediately put under arrest without being asked a question or any explanation taking place. I regret that I cannot, from the very nature of the thing, prove by evidence what I have asserted, having gone into the country alone, but I can most positively assure this court that what I have stated is an exact history of my case. I have been upwards of six years in the service, the whole of which time I have served as master and I feel it will not be presumption in me to say that I have hitherto supported an unblemished character, both as an officer and a gentleman …

The prisoner then requested to call Lieutenant Kelly Nazer, 2nd Lieutenant of the *Maidstone*, who was called into court and sworn

Quest^{n}. by Prisoner During the time you have been lieutenant of the *Maidstone*, have you witnessed any want of

	zeal or neglect of duty on my part as master of that ship?
Ans^{r}.	I have never observed any want of zeal on your part or neglect of duty; on the contrary, I have found you very attentive and you always appeared to have the safety of the ship much at heart.
	The prisoner had nothing further to ask of the witness, who withdrew.
	Lieutenant Matthew Lidden, 3rd L^{t}. of the *Maidstone*, was next called in and sworn.
Question by Prisoner	Have you been Lieu^{t}. of the *Maidstone* ever since I have belonged to her?
Ans^{r}.	Yes.
Question by Pris^{r}.	What is your opinion of my conduct as master of that ship and have you ever noticed any want of zeal in me for HM service?
Answer	I have a good opinion of you as master of the ship and I never saw an order given which you did not obey with all the promptness and decision in your power. And I never have noticed any want of zeal in you for His Maj. service.

The prisoner having nothing further to offer in his defence, the court was cleared and proceeded to deliberate upon and form the sentence.

The court, having maturely and deliberately weighed and considered the evidence produced in support of the charges and what the prisoner had to offer in his defence, were of opinion that the charges were not proved against the prisoner, M^{r}. Alexander Meldrum, Master of His Majesty's ship *Maidstone*, and did therefore adjudge him to be acquitted.

143. *Court Martial of Alexander McLaren*

[ADM 1/5443]

Minutes of proceedings of a court martial held onboard His Majesty's ship *Salvador del Mundo* in Hamoaze on Wednesday the 29th of June 1814.

Present

Tho[s] Boys, Esq[r]. Captain of His Majesty's ship *Zealous* and second officer in command of His Majesty's ships and vessels at Plymouth, President

Captains

Thomas Elphinstone — Robert Hall
Frederick Warren

Commander
John Parish

Geo Eastlake Jr
officiating Judge Advocate

Being all the captains then and there present next in seniority to the president.

The prisoner, Alexander M[c]Laren, Seaman of His Majesty's sloop *Avon*, was brought into court and the witnesses and audience admitted.

Read the order of the Right Honourable the Lords Commissioners of the Admiralty, dated the 15th day of June 1814, directed to the president, to try the said Alexander M[c]Laren for having acted in a very mutinous manner to M[r]. Jordan, the Master, and for attempting to desert.

Read – the warrant appointing a judge advocate.

The members of the court and judge advocate were then duly sworn.

Read – the annexed letter from Captain G. R. Sartorius, late of His Majesty's sloop *Avon* to Vice Admiral Sawyer

All the witnesses, except the first to be sworn, being then ordered to withdraw and to attend their examinations separately, they all withdrew accordingly and the court proceeded to trial as follows:

Evidence in support of the charges

M[r]. John Jordan, Master of His Majesty's sloop *Avon*, sworn and examined as follows:

Co[t]. Relate to the court all you know respecting the charges against the prisoner.

A. On the evening of the 11th of May last being ordered by the commanding officer of the *Avon* to proceed on board of a merchant ship in the Cove of Cork to get the wages due to Alexander Campbell, who was pressed out of the said ship. After departing from the ship, the boat's crew, of whom the prisoner was one, directed their course to the shore by backing and pulling occasionally in spite of the helm; I repeatedly ordered them to pull onboard. Finding that would not do, I took up the boat hook and directed it at the said Campbell in order to deter him from pulling the boat towards the shore. Finding that threats would not do, I made a thrust at him with the boat hook, which he evaded. The prisoner was on the bow of the boat rowing the bow oar and also endeavoured to pull the boat towards the shore. The wind blowing towards the shore and finding it impossible to regain the ship, I directed the boat as near as possible towards the garrison, in which I succeeded in getting the boat on shore close to the east end of the garrison in order to get the necessary assistance from the soldiers; on the boats landing, the prisoner and Campbell jumped out of the boat and run for the country. I immediately hastened to the garrison for the guard and with the assistance of the guard pursued them, came up the prisoner and took him in custody and conveyed him to the guard house and afterwards on board the *Avon*.

Co[t]. Did the prisoner attempt to draw his knife or use any threat?

A. A knife was threatened to be drawn at the time I was in the struggle with Campbell, but I can't say by whom.

Co[t]. How many men had you in the boat?

A. Four, the other two were Frenchmen, the prisoner being in the bow pulled harder than the other.

Co[t]. Did the prisoner make any resistance when he was taken?

A. No.

Co[t]. You say you were struggling with Alexander Campbell, are you sure that the prisoner was endeavouring to pull the boat on shore?

A. He was.

The witness withdrew.

Antonio Massey (a German), Seaman on board His Majesty's sloop *Avon*, sworn and examined as follows:

Co[t]. Relate all that you know respecting the charge against the prisoner.

A. About 5 or 6 weeks ago, we were going on board the brig at Cork with the master of the *Avon*, the prisoner, me, Campbell and another man. I and the Frenchman stopped in the boat alongside the brig and the prisoner came down in the boat and afterwards Campbell came with the master; then we shoved off and Campbell asked the prisoner to pull on shore and the prisoner made no answer. They pulled two or three times round and Campbell and the prisoner wanted to pull on shore; Campbell took hold of my oar to prevent me from pulling and the master told him to let me alone. Then Campbell struck the master, then the master sung out to the ship as we passed by, but no one heard. The master said to me, as no one heard, we must go on shore; on landing on shore, Campbell was the first to jump out of the boat and the prisoner after him and the master called to the sentry to catch the men who were running away. The master told me and the Frenchmen to stay in the boat, which we did, and after some time we went off to the *Avon* and at night the master came off by himself and the next day the prisoner was brought on board.

Co[t]. Did the prisoner or Campbell threaten to draw his knife?

A. I did not see it.

The witness withdrew.

Joseph Goude (a Frenchman), Seaman on board His Majesty's sloop *Avon*, sworn and examined as follows:

Co[t]. Relate what you know respecting the charge against the prisoner.

A. We first went alongside the merchant vessel with Campbell. On board of the first, we remained about ½ an hour; we then went to the next. The prisoner, Campbell and the master went on board the second; I and Antonio Massey remained in the boat. They remained an hour or hour and half on board talking, but I could not tell what they said; after that a boy came to us with a bottle of rum. Then Campbell said, 'I want you to pull me ashore;' I said I would go where I am ordered. The master desired us to go into the boat; after we had the rum, the prisoner immediately went in, but Campbell remained ½ an hour before he would go into the boat. As soon as he got into the boat, the master went in also and then shoved off. Campbell and the prisoner were both drunk, the prisoner was most drunk; when he was asked by Campbell to pull on shore, he said, 'Go to Hell.' After that, Campbell took hold of Antonio Massey's oar and prevented him from pulling because he would not pull to the shore; the master then took hold of the boat hook and threatened Campbell to prevent him from pulling on shore. Campbell then took the master by the arm, but whether he struck him or not, I can't say. After that, the master said pull on shore; during this time, the prisoner did nothing. He was in such a state of drunkenness that he did not know how he was pulling. I said to the master I would pull on shore as I was not in the plot with Campbell. The master was steering the boat to go on shore near the guard house and when Campbell perceived that he called to the prisoner to pull to a brig for the master would have them stopped by the guard if they went on shore; the prisoner replied, 'Pull yourself.' When we had landed, Campbell jumped out; the master followed him and so did the prisoner. And I and the German remained to take care of the boat; we stayed half an hour. On pulling round to the usual landing place, we met the gig coming on shore with the sergeant of marines, who went in pursuit of the prisoner and Campbell; on coming on shore I turned to the prisoner frequently to see if he was pulling, but never saw him draw or attempt to draw his knife.

The witness withdrew.

Antonio Massey again called in and examined as follows:

Co^{t}. Did the prisoner appear to be drunk when going on shore with the master?

A. Yes, I don't think he knew which way he was going.

Co^{t}. Had you any rum given you when alongside the brig?

A. Yes, one glass each.

The witness withdrew.

The evidence in support of the charges being here closed, the prisoner was asked if he had anything to offer in his defence, when he desired the annexed certificate of his character might be read to the court and the same was read accordingly.

The prisoner also laid before the court his 'protection from being impressed' and stated that it was not regarded at the time he was impressed although he showed it to Captain Sartorius.[1]

The prisoner having nothing farther to offer, the court was cleared and proceeded to deliberate upon and form the sentence.

The court, having very maturely and deliberately weighed and considered the evidence in support of the charges as well as what the prisoner has offered in his behalf, was of opinion that the charges had been in part proved against the prisoner, Alexander McLaren, but in consideration of the very good character that had been given him by his captain and other favourable circumstances, the court did only adjudge the said Alexander McLaren to receive two dozen lashes with a cat of nine tails on his bare back on board His Majesty's sloop *Avon* to which he belongs.

The court was opened, the prisoner brought in, the witnesses and audience re-admitted and the sentence pronounced accordingly. …

[1]This protection is not bound with the transcript in ADM 1/5443.

143A. *Sartorius to Sawyer*

[ADM 1/5443] His Majesty's sloop *Avon*
Cove of Cork, 14th May 1814

... Alexander McLaren, a Seaman belonging to His Majesty's sloop under my command, having on the evening of the 11th instant acted in a very mutinous manner to M^{r}. Jordan, the Master, by endeavouring with Alexander Campbell to pull the boat on shore contrary to his orders and wishes, and even threatening to make use of their knives if anyone prevented them from executing their intentions, and ultimately attempting to desert, in which attempt Alexander Campbell succeeded, but Alexander McLaren was apprehended,

I therefore beg you will be pleased to move their Lordships to grant a court martial on Alexander McLaren to try him for the same. ...

143B. *Sartorius's Certificate of Alexander McLaren's Character*

[ADM 1/5443] June 28, 1814

In extenuation of Alex^{r}. McLaren's conduct, I beg to say that except in the present instance his conduct has invariably been such as to afford me the highest satisfaction.

I always conceived him to be an intelligent, attentive, good man & firmly believe that the breach of discipline he has been guilty of originated partly from ignorance of the degree of guilt attached to it (he having been lately pressed) as well as from the persuasions & example of the man who escaped. ...

144. *Court Martial of John Davies*

[ADM 1/5444]

Minutes of proceedings at a court martial held on board His Majesty's ship *Namur* in Sheerness Harbour on Tuesday the 19th day of July 1814.

Present

John Maitland, Esquire, Captain of His Majesty's ship *Barfleur* and third officer in the command of His Majesty's ships and vessels in the River Medway and at the buoy of the Nore, President

Captains
Arthur Farquhar
John Hancock
Thomas Garth
Charles John Austin

Thomas Williams officiating as
Judge Advocate

Being all the captains of post ships at this port.

The prisoner was brought into court and the prosecutor, the witnesses and audience admitted.

Read the order of the Lords Commissioners of the Admiralty, dated the 16th of July 1814 and directed to John Maitland, Esquire, Captain of His Majesty's ship *Barfleur* and third officer in the command of His Majesty's ships and vessels in the River Medway and at the buoy of the Nore, to try Mr John Davies, Boatswain of His Majesty's sloop *Portia*, for having behaved himself on the evening of the 2nd of May in a most mutinous and contemptuous manner to Lieut. Charles Pitt on the quarter deck, being also at that time in a state of intoxication.

Read the warrant appointing a judge advocate. Then the members of the court and judge advocate, in open court and before they proceeded to trial, respectively took the oaths directed by an Act of Parliament passed in the twenty second year of the reign of King George the Second.

A letter from Lieut. Charles Pitt to Captain Thomson was then read as follows:

HMS *Portia*, Yarmouth Roads
3 May 1814

… M^r^. John Davies, Boatswain of the above sloop, having last evening behaved himself in a most mutinous and contemptuous manner to me publicly on the quarter deck and being likewise in a state of intoxication,

I have to request you will be pleased to apply to the commander in chief to order a court martial to be held on him for a breach of the second and 19th Articles of War. …

All the witnesses, except the first to be sworn, being then ordered to withdraw and to attend their examinations separately, they all withdrew accordingly and the court proceeded to trial as follows:

Evidence in support of the charge

Mr. Robert Smith, Gunner of H M Sloop *Portia* sworn and examined as follows:

Prosecutor – Were you aware of the prisoner's conduct to me on the quarter deck on the 2nd of May last between the hours of 6 and eight on the evening?

Answer – Yes, Lieut. Pitt ordered the prisoner to go down below to bed and he would not go down. Lieut. Pitt called for the sergeant or corporal, I am not sure which, to take him down to his cabin, which he refused to do at first but about five or six minutes after, he went down. The prisoner was very much in liquor at this time.

Prosecutor – Do you recollect my warning the prisoner of his conduct after repeated disobedience of my orders and his making use of the expressions 'That the ship was a buggering privateer and that he did not care damn for any of us?'

Answer – I recollect Lieut. Pitt's speaking to him concerning the expressions he had made use of before and what they were, I do not know.

Prosecutor – Do you recollect the prisoner's heaving his warrant at me while on the starboard side of the quarter deck?

Answer – I don't.

Court – In what part of the ship were you when this circumstance took place?

Answer – By the main hatchway, the prisoner was standing on the larboard side of the ladder.

Court – Could these expressions have been made use of without your hearing them?

Answer – They might.

The witness withdrew

William Ogleby, Quartermaster, H M Sloop *Portia*, sworn and examined as follows:

Prosecutor – Were you aware of the prisoner's conduct to me on the quarter deck on the 2nd of May last between the hours of six and eight on that evening?

Answer – In the beginning of hoisting the boats in, the prisoner stamped his foot upon the main deck and swore that he was once on board a man of war, 'but now I am aboard of a buggering privateer;' after that, Lieut. Pitt called him and desired him to go to his cabin. This he refused to do; Lieut. Pitt then ordered the corporal of Marines to call the party to take him to his cabin when he refused to go. He went down a little while after.

Prosecutor – Do you recollect the prisoner's heaving his warrant at me while on the starboard side of the quarter deck?
Answer – I did not see it.
Prosecutor – Was the prisoner drunk?
Answer – Yes.

The witness withdrew

William Caribane, Corporal of Marines belonging to HMS *Portia*, sworn and examined as follows:

Prosecutor – When I ordered the prisoner below in the evening of the 2nd of May last under your charge, did he make resistance?
Answer – Yes, he stood with his fist ready to knock me down in case I took hold of him.
Prosecutor – Did he repeatedly disobey my orders to go below?
Answer – He stood a considerable time before he would go down.
Prosecutor – Was the prisoner drunk?
Answer – Yes.

The witness withdrew

Thomas Chetham, Private Marine of HMS *Portia*, sworn and examined as follows:

Prosecutor – When I ordered the prisoner below on the evening of the 2nd of May last under your charge, did he make resistance?
Answer – Yes, he would not go when he was ordered to his cabin.
Prosecutor – Did he repeatedly disobey my orders to go below?
Answer – Yes.
Prosecutor – Are you aware of his standing on the ladder when in your charge in a menacing attitude?
Answer – Yes.
Prosecutor – Was the prisoner drunk?
Answer – Yes.
Prosecutor – Do you recollect his making use of the expressions that he was once on board a man of war but now on board a buggering privateer?
Answer – Yes.
Court – Did you see the prisoner throw his warrant at the first lieutenant?
Answer – No.

The witness withdrew

The evidence in support of the charge being finished, the prisoner was called upon to make his defence, who said he had not anything to offer but requested Captain Thomson to speak to his character, who said the prisoner had always conducted himself well until this circumstance and since. When the sloop carried away her bowsprit, he made himself very useful and that he has been two years in the *Portia*. The prisoner then requested Lieut. Pitt to speak to his character, who said that his former conduct had been very good and that he had never before seen any disposition to this kind of behaviour.

The prisoner also produced certificates of good conduct.

The prisoner not having anything farther to offer in his defence, the court was cleared and proceeded to deliberate upon and form the sentence of which the following is an extract:

> And having heard the evidence produced in support of the charge as well as what the prisoner had to offer in his defence and maturely weighed the same, the court is of opinion that the charge is proved against the prisoner, M^{r}. John Davies, but in consideration of his good character does only adjudge him to be dismissed his situation of boatswain in His Majesty's navy and to be disposed of as the commander in chief of His Majesty's ships and vessels at this port shall direct.

. . .

145. *Court Martial of John Wheeler*

[ADM 1/5446]

Minutes of proceedings at a court martial held on board His Majesty's ship *Salvador del Mundo* in Hamoaze at Plymouth on Saturday the first day of October 1814.

Present

Thomas Byam Martin, Esqre., Rear Admiral of the Red and second officer in the command of His Majesty's ships and vessels at Plymouth, President.

Captains

Sir Josias Rowley, B^{t} (R^{r}. Adm^{l}., but serving as Capt. of the *America*)
John Chambers White
Alexander Wilmot Schomberg
Archibald Duff
Thomas Forrest
James Slade
The R^{t}. Honble Lord James O'Bryen
Robert Hall (1)
Tristram Roberts Ricketts
Francis Newcombe
John Davie
Charles Montague Fabian

George Eastlake, officiating Judge Advocate

Being all captains of post ships next in seniority to the president, except Captain George Burdett, who was absent attending a court martial at Portsmouth.

The prisoner, John Wheeler, Private Marine serving on board His Majesty's ship *Ulysses*, was brought into court and the witnesses and audience admitted.

Capt. Thomas Browne of the *Ulysses* appeared as prosecutor.

Read – The order of the Right Honble the Lords Commissioners of the Admiralty, dated the 28th day of September 1814, directed to the president, to try the said John Wheeler for disobedience of orders and striking his superior officer. The members of the court and judge advocate were then duly sworn.

Read – The annexed letter from the said Capt. Browne to Vice Admiral Domett, being the charges against the prisoner (No 1).

All the witnesses, except the first to be sworn, being then ordered to withdraw and to attend their examinations separately, they all withdrew accordingly and the court proceeded to trial as follows:

Charles Allen, Corporal of Royal Marines serving on board His Majesty's ship *Ulysses*, sworn and examined as follows:

Pros[r]. Were you on the lower deck of the *Ulysses* on the evening of Saturday the 24th of September last when the hands were turned up to range the sheet cable?

A, I was.

Pros[r]. Did you order the prisoner to go to the cable and assist?

A. Yes.

Pros[r]. Where was he at that time?

A. Standing in his berth just opposite the after hatchway, I ordered him forward to assist ranging the sheet cable. He turned round, collared me and asked what I wanted of him; I said I wanted him to do his duty. As he collared me, I was going to take him aft on the quarter deck and Sergeant Brown came to my assistance. When we got him as far as the main hatchway, Serg[t]. Horridge was standing there and ordered him to be taken aft immediately and he was taken aft by me and Serg[t]. Brown. M[r]. Jackson, the Master's Mate, was standing ranging the sheet cable at the time it happened.

Court Did he immediately collar you on being desired to range the cable without any conversation?

A. Yes, he appeared to be intoxicated with liquor rather. When I spoke to him, I said, 'Wheeler go forward and range the sheet cable; don't you hear the hands ordered forward?' I could not take him aft myself; he was very stubborn.

Court Was anything said or done to take the prisoner that could irritate him so as to put him so much off his guard as to strike the sergeant?

A. I spoke to him civilly; he was quarrelling with a woman at the time.

Court Did the quarrel with the woman appear to have provoked him and put him in a passion, so that you found him in a passion?

A. Yes, I think it did and he appeared a little in liquor. He was in an angry state; if it had not been for his quarrelling with the woman, perhaps it would not have happened.

Court Did you see him strike Sergeant Brown?

A. Yes.

Court Was the blow aimed at the sergeant?

A. Yes, it was fairly aimed at him.

The witness withdrew.

Serg^{t}. Thomas Horridge of the Royal Marines serving on board His Majesty's ship *Ulysses* sworn and examined as follows:

Pros^{r}. Were you on the lower deck of the *Ulysses* on Saturday the 24th of September last when Serg^{t} Brown and Corporal Allen were taking the prisoner up the main hatchway?

A. Yes.

Pros^{r}. Did you see the prisoner strike the sergeant?

A. I saw the prisoner entangled with Corporal Allen and Sergeant Brown. I requested them to take the prisoner aft on the quarter deck. I saw the prisoner strike Serg^{t}. Brown, on which Serg^{t}. Brown fell on the chest. I took the prisoner up on the quarter deck and reported him to the officer of the watch.

Court Did the prisoner strike at the sergeant or could it, by possibility, have been accidental?

A. He struck the sergeant after he had broke loose from him and not in any struggle at the time.

Court Did you hear Serg^{t}. Brown or Corporal Allen say anything that could have provoked him?

A. Nothing but desiring him to go forward to the sheet cable. I did not see or hear anything beside.

Court Was the prisoner sufficiently sober to do this duty?

A. I don't think he was.

Court Are you of opinion that the prisoner was sufficiently sober to be aware of the enormity of the offence he is charged with having committed?

A. I don't think that he was.

The witness withdrew.

Serg[t]. James Brown of the Royal Marines serving on board His Majesty's ship *Ulysses* sworn and examined as follows:

Pros[r]. Were you assisting Corporal Allen in taking the prisoner aft on the quarter deck on Saturday evening the 24th of September last?

A. Yes. In the evening of that day, between 5 and 6 o'clock, the hands were turned up to range the sheet cable; the prisoner was quarrelling in his berth with a woman. Corporal Allen ordered him to go forward to assist ranging the sheet cable; he said he would not go for him. I ordered Corporal [Allen] to take him on the quarter deck; as we were taking him along by the main hatchway, he struck me on the left side of my head with his fist, which caused me to fall on a chest. I got up again and assisted in taking the prisoner on the quarter deck.

Court When you found him quarrelling with this woman, did he appear in an angry and provoked state of mind?

A. He was very much in liquor and appeared very angry indeed.

Co[t]. Do you mean very violently angry?

A. Yes.

Co[t]. Was the blow you received accidental or was it purposely and evidently levelled at you?

A. It was purposely levelled at me.

Co[t]. Was it after the prisoner broke loose from you?

A. Yes.

Co[t]. Was the prisoner sufficiently sober to know you?

A. Yes, he knew me and called me by name.

The witness withdrew.

M[r]. George Jackson, Master's Mate of His Majesty's ship *Ulysses*, sworn and examined as follows:

Pros[r]. Were you on the lower deck of the *Ulysses* on Saturday the 24th of September last when Serg[t]. Brown and Corporal Allen were taking the prisoner up the main hatchway?

A. Yes.

Pros[r]. Did you see the prisoner strike the sergeant?

A. Yes. Corporal Allen and Serg[t]. Brown were taking him up the main hatchway; the prisoner struck the sergeant on the side of his head and knocked him over a chest. The blow was not accidental; he disengaged himself and struck it. The prisoner appeared in an angry state of mind; I don't know from what cause. He was half drunk.

The witness withdrew.

The evidence in support of the charge being here closed, the prisoner was asked if he had anything to offer in his behalf, when the prisoner delivered in the annexed written paper (No. 2), which was read to the court.

The prosecutor (Capt. Browne) admitted that the transaction took place on pay day as stated by the prisoner.

The prisoner having nothing further to offer, the court was cleared and proceeded to deliberate upon and form the sentence.

The court, having very maturely and deliberately weighed and considered the evidence in support of the charges as well as what the prisoner had offered in his behalf, was of opinion that the charges had been proved against the prisoner, John Wheeler, and the court did, in consequence, adjudge the said John Wheeler 'to be hanged by the neck until he is dead at the yardarm of such one of His Majesty's ships and at such time as the commissioners for executing the office of Lord High Admiral of the United Kingdom of Great Britain and Ireland shall direct.'

The court was then opened, the prisoner brought in, the witnesses and audience re-admitted and the sentence pronounced accordingly. …

145A. *Browne to Domett*

[ADM 1/5446]

His Majesty's ship *Ulysses*
Plymouth Sound, 26th September 1814

(No. 1)

… On Saturday evening the 24th instant at half past five o'clock, the hands having been turned up on board His Majesty's ship under my command to range the sheet cables and other immediate duties, Charles Allen, Corporal of Marines, finding that John Wheeler, Private, was in his berth, ordered him to go and assist at the cable, which he refused to do. The corporal then attempted to take him aft on the quarter deck when he collared the corporal, and Sergeant James Brown coming to his assistance, John Wheeler struck the sergeant with his fist and knocked him over a chest.

I have to request you will be pleased to apply to the Lords Commissioners of the Admiralty to order a court martial on the said John Wheeler, Private Marine, for disobedience of orders and striking his superior officer.

I enclose a list of evidences.[1] …

[1]The list is not bound with the transcript in ADM 1/5446.

145B. *John Wheeler's Defence*

[ADM 1/5446] HMS *Ulysses*, Plymouth
October 1st, 1814

(No. 2)

… I here stand indicted before you for a crime of the greatest breach of discipline in His Majesty's navy – a navy which has so universally merited honour and esteem from every nation. Allow me to say I sensibly feel the disgrace I have brought upon myself, a crime that I am perfectly ignorant of, being in a state of intoxication. It was on pay day and I was not aware of my irregular conduct and I now throw myself on the mercy of this honble court. …

145C. *Lord Melville's Petition to the King*

[ADM 1/5446] Admiralty Office
13th October 1814

Minutes of court martial and sentence of death on John Wheeler, Private Marine of His Majesty's ship *Ulysses*, for disobedience of orders and striking his sergeant

Lord Melville, finding on a perusal of the minutes some circumstances which appear in extenuation of the prisoner's offence, begs leave most humbly to recommend him as a fit object of your Royal clemency, but that, for the sake of public example, your Royal Highness's merciful intentions should not be made known until the prisoner is brought to the cathead as if for execution.

Approved
…
4th Novr. 14

146. *Court Martial of Alexander Johnston*

[ADM 1/5447]

> Minutes of the proceedings of a court martial assembled and held onboard His Majesty's ship *Bellerophon* in Saint John's, Newfoundland on Monday the fourteenth day of November 1814.

Present
Edward Hawker, Esqre, Captain of His Majesty's ship *Bellerophon* and second officer in the command of His Majesty's ships and vessels in S^{t}. John's Harbour, President

Captains
William Henry Dillon
Henry Bourchier
William Kempthorne
John Skekel

The prisoner was brought into court and the evidence and audience admitted.

Read The order of Sir Richard Goodwin Keats, Knight of the Bath, Vice Admiral of the White and Commander in Chief of a squadron of His Majesty's ships and vessels employed and to be employed at and about the island of Newfoundland and the coast of Labrador from Mount Joli to the entrance of Hudson's Streights, dated the 12th of Novem^{r} 1814 and directed to Edward Hawker, Esqre, Captain of His Majesty's ship *Bellerophon*, to try M^{r}. Alexander Johnston, Master of His Majesty's ship *Crocodile*, on the charges therein stated against him by Captn. Elliott of His Majesty's said ship *Crocodile*.

Then the members of the court and judge advocate, in open court and before they proceeded to trial, respectively took the oaths prescribed by Act of Parliament.

Read A letter from Captain William Elliott of His Majesty's ship *Crocodile* to Vice Admiral Sir Richard Goodwin Keats, K.B., containing the charges against the prisoner, as follows, *viz:*

His Majesty's ship *Crocodile*
S^{t}. John's, November 12, 1814

… Mr Alexander Johnston, Master of His Majesty's ship *Crocodile* under my command, having been so drunk on the evening of the 7th instant as to be incapable of doing his duty and last night, being officer of the first watch, quitted the deck and sat drinking in the gunner's cabin, at the same time gave permission to the midshipmen to keep their lights in after 10 o'clock in direct disobedience to the written orders of the ship,

I have to request you will be pleased to order a court martial to try the said Mr Alex^r^ Johnston for the above mentioned offences. …

All the witnesses were then ordered to withdraw out of court except the first to be examined, Lieutenant William John Cole of the *Crocodile*, who was sworn and examined by the prosecutor.

Question Did you see the prisoner on the evening of the 7th instant?
Answer Yes.
Question Where was he?
Answer On the quarter deck.
Question Was he so drunk as to be incapable of doing his duty?
Answer Yes. I thought he was incapable of doing his duty.
Question Was it necessary that another officer should keep his watch and did you order the gunner to do so?
Answer Yes.
Question Where was the ship at this time?
Answer Close off the mouth of S[t]. John's harbour.

There being no further question put to the witness, he was ordered to withdraw and Lieutenant Henry Bowman Wodehouse called and sworn.

Examined by the prosecutor

Question Did you see the prisoner on the evening of the 7th instant?
Answer I saw him about ½ past 6 or 7 o'clock on that evening.
Question Was he sober at that time or was he drunk?
Answer He did not appear to me to be drunk. I only saw him for a few moments and did not take particular notice.
President It being your middle watch, did you relieve the prisoner on deck?
Answer No. I went on deck about ten minutes after one bell and did not see any officer on deck.
Court Do you know that the prisoner had the first watch?
Answer Yes.

The prisoner having no question to ask the witness, he was ordered to withdraw and M[r]. John Seagrove, Gunner of the *Crocodile*, called and sworn.

Examined by the prosecutor

Question Did the prisoner come into your cabin on the evening of the 11th instant between the hours of 8 and 12?
Answer Yes.
Question How long did he remain there?
Answer Better than half an hour.

Question What did he do while he was there?
Answer He drank one glass of grog.
Question Did you see the prisoner on the evening of the 7th instant?
Answer The first lieutenant sent for me on the evening of the 7th instant about ½ past 8. I stood on the top of the ladder when he ordered me to keep the first watch. I saw M[r]. Johnston standing behind M[r]. Cole at that time, but going below again directly, I did not take further notice. When I came up again, the prisoner was gone below. I relieved the first lieutenant from the deck, who told me the reason of ordering me to keep the first watch was that the prisoner was incapable of his duty.
President You say the prisoner drank one glass of grog in your cabin; did he drink more?
Answer No.
Question What were considered the general orders of the ship respecting the lights being put out at night?
Answer Ten o'clock.
Question Do you know the lights were kept in after that time on the night of the 11th instant and by whose authority?
Answer They were kept in after that time, but I do not know by whose authority.
Question Have you ever known any discretionary power allowed to the officer of the watch or any other officer to grant leave for the lights to be kept in after that time?
Answer No.
Court Had you a light in your cabin on the night of the 11th instant after the usual time, when the master was in the cabin?
Answer Yes.
Court By whose permission was it granted?
Answer The sergeant did not come at the usual time to put the lights out.

The prisoner having no question to ask the witness, he was ordered to withdraw and M[r]. William Leaper, Carpenter of the *Crocodile*, was called and sworn.

Examined by the prosecutor

Question Did you see the prisoner on the evening of the 11th instant between the hours of 8 and 12 in the gunner's cabin?
Answer Yes.
Question How long did he remain there?
Answer It was about seven bells when he came in and some time after 12 when he went away?

Question What did he do while he was there?

Answer When he came in, I told M[r]. Johnston that M[r]. Seagrove and me was spending the evening together and there was either grog or wine for him to drink if he would drink it and away as we did not wish to be disturbed. He still interrupted us till I shoved him out of the cabin. While he was in, he drank some grog.

The prisoner having no question to put to the witness, he was ordered to withdraw and Sergeant Nathaniel Moore of the Marines called and sworn.

Examined by the prosecutor

Question You have heard the charges read; relate to the court all you know respecting them.

Answer On the evening of the 11th instant, I went on deck at 10 o'clock to report the lights. The prisoner was on deck. I said the lights were not out in the gentlemen's cabin. He told me they might have a light provided they kept quiet below. At 7 bells, I saw the prisoner come down into the steerage and go into the gunner's cabin.

The written orders of the ship were given in, in which appeared the following article:

> Art. 18 – 'The warrant and petty officers' lights are to be put out at 9 o'clock at sea and 10 in harbour and reported to me or the commanding officer and it is my positive order that neither the officer of the watch or commanding officer (if I am out of the ship) will ever give them leave for lights after that hour.'

The prisoner having no question to ask the witness, he was ordered to withdraw and M[r]. Robert Frederick Fitzwilliam, Volunteer 1st Class, called and sworn.

Examined by the prosecutor

Question Was you sent by the master's mates or by any of your messmates on deck to the officer of the watch on the evening of the 11th instant and did you ask permission for the lights to be allowed to be kept in after 10 o'clock?

Answer Yes.

Question Who desired you to ask?

Answer Several of the gentlemen.

Question Who was the officer of the watch?

Answer The prisoner.

Question Did you get permission and for how long?

Answer I got permission from the prisoner, but not for any stated time. He desired that we would not make noise.

The prisoner having no question to ask the witness, he was ordered to withdraw and John Reynolds, Quarter Master of the *Crocodile*, called and sworn.

Examined by the prosecutor

Question Was you quarter master of the first watch on the evening of the 7th instant?

Answer Yes.

Question Did you see the prisoner in that watch?

Answer Yes, I saw him come on deck to relieve the first lieutenant.

Question Was he so drunk as to be incapable of doing his duty?

Answer I can't say if he was incapable of doing his duty, but he was intoxicated. The prisoner relieved the first lieutenant who went below, but came on deck shortly after and desired me to call the gunner, which I did. When the gunner came on deck, the first lieutenant gave him charge of the deck and the prisoner went below.

The prisoner having no questions to ask the witness, he was ordered to withdraw and Conrad Forster, Marine of the *Crocodile*, called and sworn.

Examined by the prosecutor

Question Did you see the prisoner on the evening of the 7th instant when the ship was off the harbour's mouth?

Answer Yes.

Question Was he drunk or sober?

Answer I can't say that he was drunk. He came out of the gunroom and went on deck directly.

Question Did you see him when he came down again and was he sober?

Answer I did. I cannot say that he was sober or that he was drunk.

The prisoner having no question to ask of the witness, he was ordered to withdraw and the evidence on the part of the prosecution being closed, the prisoner was informed that the court was ready to hear anything he had to offer in his defence, when he requested leave to retire for a short time.

On the court being opened again, the prisoner requested the judge advocate to read the paper which he delivered to him signed.

The judge advocate then read the following, *viz.*:

> … Sensible of the degrading situation to which I have heedlessly brought myself and under severe repentance, I am desirous not to occupy the time of the court unnecessarily but to leave my case entirely to it's mercy; relying that in it's justice and lenity, it will make some distinction between the

effects of a casual indiscretion and that of an habitual course of inebriety.

During ten years that I have served in His Majesty's navy, I have hitherto received the approbation of the officers under whom I have served, certificates of which I could have produced but they were lodged at the Navy Office when I passed for master. I beg however to submit one that I have from the captain of the last ship in which I served and, with extreme concern for my misconduct, to leave my case to the lenient consideration of the court. …

A certificate from Captain Hopkins of the *Helicon* was also read of the prisoner's service as acting master and master from January 1813 to April 1814 during which time he behaved with sobriety, attention to his duty and much to his entire satisfaction.

The prisoner requested Captain Elliott to speak to his character as a navigator.

Captain Elliott said:

'M^r^. Johnston has been between 7 and 8 months in the ship. I have found him a very good navigator and as good a seaman as I could wish to have in a ship.'

The prisoner having nothing further to offer in his defence, the court was cleared and proceeded to deliberate upon and form the sentence.

The court, having maturely and deliberately weighed and considered the evidence produced on the part of the prosecution and what the prisoner had to allege in his defence, was of opinion that the charges against the prisoner had been proved and did thereupon adjudge him to be dismissed from His Majesty's service.

The court was then opened, evidence and audience admitted, and sentence passed accordingly. …

147. *Court Martial of Hugh M^c^Crenon*

[ADM 1/5448]

Minutes of proceedings at a court martial held on board His Majesty's ship *York* in Hamoaze at Plymouth on Wednesday the 19th day of April 1815.

Present

Alexander Wilmot Schomberg, Esqre., Captain of His Majesty's ship *York* and second officer in the command of His Majesty's ships and vessels at Plymouth, President.

Captains

Tristram Robert Ricketts	Henry Edward Reginald Baker
James Nash	William Henry Webly
James Richard Dacres	The Honble Henry Duncan
Archibald Duff	Thomas Brown
Sir Thomas John Cochrane, Kn^{t}.	Gilbert Heathcote
Matthew Smith	Edward Pelham Brenton

George Eastlake Junr., officiating Judge Advocate

Being all captains of post ships then and there present and next in seniority to the president, except Captain Somerville of the *Rota* who was sick.

The prisoner, Hugh McCrenon, Seaman of His Majesty's ship *Lee*, was brought into court and the witnesses and audience admitted.

Capt. J. J. G. Bremer of the *Lee* appeared as prosecutor.

The surgeon of the *Rota* certified on oath the illness of Capt Somerville & his consequent inability to attend the court whereupon the members thought fit to dispense with the attendance of the said Captain Somerville.

Read – The order of the Right Honble. the Lords Commissioners of the Admiralty, dated the 14th day of April 1815 directed to the president, to try the said Hugh McCrenon for having absented himself without leave on the evening of the 9th or early on the morning of the 10th of the same month and having behaved in a most outrageous and contemptuous manner to M^{r}. Leeworth, Midshipman, who was sent to apprehend him on the evening of the 11th at Plymouth.

The members of the court and judge advocate were then duly sworn.

Read – The annexed letter of charge from the said Capt. Bremer to Adm^{l}. Sir J. T. Duckworth, Commander in Chief at Plymouth.

The witnesses, except the first to be sworn, then withdrew.

Lieut. John Thomas Shortland of His Majesty's ship *Lee* sworn & examined as follows:

Pros^{r}. Did you as first lieutenant of the *Lee* order the ship's company to be mustered on the morning of the 10th ins^{t}.?

A. I did.

Pro. Was the prisoner missing?

A. He was.

Pro. Had he your leave to be absent from the ship?

A. He had not.

Pro. When had you last seen the prisoner?

A. On Sunday forenoon, the 9th; he belonged to the *Lee* and did his duty on the forecastle.

Co^{t}. Where was the ship at the time of the prisoner's absenting himself?

A. In Hamoze; on Monday morning, when I was going to send one of the carpenters over the quarter, I found the carpenter was missing and that one of the cutters was gone. In consequence of this, I turned the hands up to muster and found the prisoner and 5 or 6 others missing.

Co[t]. Who was commanding officer of the ship on the night of the 9th ins[t].?

A. M[r]. Lurchin, the Master, till 9 o'clock, when I took the command in coming on board.

Co[t]. Do you know who had charge of the watches during the night?

A. M[r]. Lurchin had the first, Lieut. Rothery the 2d. and M[r]. Warner, the Gunner, the 3d.

Co[t]. Was it reported to you by either of those officers that a boat had been taken away during the night?

A. It was not.

Co[t]. Do you know by what means this man made his escape from the ship?

A. I do not.

Co[t]. When was the cutter reported missing?

A, About 5 o'clock on Monday morning by M[r]. Ellison, Midshipman.

The witness withdrew.

M[r]. Henry Leeworthy, Midshipman of His Majesty's ship *Lee*, sworn and examined as follows:

Pro. Do you know the prisoner?

A. Yes.

Pro. Relate the circumstances attending your finding him on shore.

A. After we got on shore at Plymouth, we got a peace officer and proceeded to Castle Street; on entering the street, we perceived two seamen conversing together. On perceiving us, they immediately ran different ways; the master followed one and I the other. Having pursued the prisoner as far as the quay, there happened to be a heap of rubbish, over which he fell; and I immediately took him by the collar and put my knee on his breast, drawing my sword at the same time, declaring if he moved I would run him through. He answered he would be damned if he cared, for he would not be taken on board; he would rather die first. After a great struggle, he was nearly effecting his escape when two marines came to my assistance. He still persisted in struggling and struck me repeatedly. With great difficulty, we dragged him to the house where the master was in search of others. The prisoner at the same time declared he would take one of our lives before we took him on board. He still persisted in struggling and the master placed me and a marine over him, ordering us to draw our arms and to run him through if he moved. After the search was over, we seized his arms and took him to the guildhall and there lodged him for the night. The next day, he was taken on board.

Co^{t}. Did he make use of any other expression?

A. Yes, he said he knew the marines to be a damned set of rascals disguised. He also said he knew where the other deserters were, but would not tell.

Co^{t}. Was he drunk or sober?

A. From the manner in which he ran, I should think he had been drinking, but he knew what he was about and knew me to be his officer.

The witness withdrew.

M^{r}. Thomas Lurchin, Master of the *Lee*, sworn & examined as follows:

Pro. Were you sent on shore on the evening of the 11th to search for the prisoner?

A. Yes.

Pro. Relate the circumstances of his being taken.

A. Pursuant to Capt. Bremer's order, I went and got a peace officer and then repaired to Castle Street where I saw the prisoner by himself and gave orders to M^{r}. Leeworthy, the midshipman who accompanied me, to lay hold of him, but, before that could be done, he ran away and M^{r}. Leeworthy and two marines after him. I did not follow them; in about half an hour, the midshipman and marines returned with the prisoner in custody. I heard the prisoner frequently make use of threatening language to the person who had taken him. I rather think it was meant to the marine until M^{r}. Leeworthy laid hold of him. He then persisted in struggling and shoved M^{r}. Leeworthy frequently from him. I asked him if he knew who he was shoving; he said yes. I then drew my sword and threatened if he did not behave more respectfully and quiet, I would run him through and gave the marine, who I placed sentinel over him, orders to do so if he attempted to make his escape.

Co^{t}. Was he drunk or sober?

A. He was sober.

Co^{t}. What is the general conduct of the prisoner on board?

A. Very sober and attentive to his duty.

Co^{t}. Were you commanding officer of the ship in the evening when he absented himself?

A. Yes.
Co^{t}. Had you given leave of absence to any of the ship's company?
A. No.
Co^{t}. Were the usual sentinels placed on the gangway?
A. Yes.

The witness withdrew.

William McCulloch, Private Marine serving on board the *Lee*, sworn & examined as follows:

Pro. Were you sent on shore at Plymouth to search for the prisoner on the night of the 11th ins^{t}.?
A. Yes, we met him in a street at Plymouth and he ran away and the midshipman (M^{r}. Leeworthy) after him, and I and another man followed. When I came up, he was lying on his back in the street and M^{r}. Leeworthy had his sword drawn over him. I drew my bayonet and took the prisoner by the breast, lifted him up off the ground and, with the other Marine, dragged him along the street to the house where the master was. I cannot tell what passed at the house, as I took post outside the door.
Co^{t}. Were any expressions made use of by the prisoner in your hearing?
A. Yes, he said once he would not go. I said, 'If you don't go, I'll die before I part with you.' After that, he went quietly.
Co^{t}. Was the prisoner sober enough to know his officer?
A. Yes.

The witness withdrew.

The evidence in support of the charges being here closed, the prisoner was asked if he had anything to offer in his behalf, when he stated

That he knew nothing of having ill used the midshipman and that he had no intention but to return to the ship.

The prisoner then called on the prosecutor to speak to his character, when

Capt. Bremer said, 'He is a hard working, good, steady man; he has behaved very well. I have been very well satisfied with him.'

The prisoner having nothing farther to offer, the court was cleared and proceeded to deliberate upon and form the sentence.

The court, having very maturely and deliberately weighed and considered the evidence in support of the charge as well as what the prisoner had offered in his behalf, was of opinion that the charges had been proved against the prisoner, Hugh McCrenon, and the court did in consequence adjudge the said Hugh McCrenon to receive one hundred and fifty lashes with a cat o' nine tails on his bare back alongside such of His Majesty's ships at such times and in such proportions as the commander in chief of His Majesty's ships and vessels at Plymouth should direct.

The court was opened, the prisoner brought in, the witnesses and audience re-admitted and the sentence pronounced accordingly.

The court observed that the sentence would not have been so lenient but for the good character that had been given to the prisoner. …

147A. *Bremer to Duckworth*

[ADM 1/5448]

HMS *Lee*, Hamoaze
12 April 1815

… Hugh McCrenon, Seaman of His Majesty's ship *Lee* under my command, having absented himself without leave on the evening of the ninth or early on the morning of the tenth inst. and having behaved in a most outrageous and contemptuous manner to M^{r}. Leeworthy, Midshipman, who was sent to apprehend him on the evening of the 11th inst. at Plymouth,

I have to request you will be pleased to move the Right Honble the Lords Commissioners of the Admiralty to order a court martial to be held on him to try him for the said offences. …

148. *Court Martial of Alexander Lyal*

[ADM 1/5449]

Minutes of proceedings at a court martial held on board His Majesty's ship *Saint George* in Hamoaze at Plymouth on Friday the 16th day of June 1815.

Present

Sir Richard John Strachan, Bar^{t}., G.C.B., Vice Admiral of the Red and third officer in the command of His Majesty's ships & vessels at Plymouth, President
Sir Benjamin Hallowell, K.C.B., Rear Admiral of the Red
Sir Thomas Byam Martin, K.C.B., Rear Admiral of the Red
Sir Graham Moore, K.C.B., Rear Admiral of the Red

Captains

	Charles Ogle
Sir Archibald Collingwood Dickson, Bar^{t}.	William Robert Broughton
David Lloyd	Richard Raggett
James Nash	Jeffery Raigersfeld

John Hayes James Hillyar

George Eastlake, Jun[r]., officiating Judge Advocate

Being all the admirals and captains of post ships then and there present, next in seniority to the president, except Capt. Robert Jackson, who was sick, and Capt. Robert Barrie, who was absent on Admiralty leave.

The prisoner, M[r]. Alexander Lyal, Master of His Majesty's ship *Wanderer*, was brought into court and the witnesses and audience admitted.

Capt. William Dowers of the *Wanderer* appeared as prosecutor.

The surgeon of the *Ville de Paris* appeared and certified the illness of Capt. Robert Jackson and his consequent inability to attend the court and declared that he was ready if required to make oath to the truth of such report, whereupon the members thought fit to dispense with the attendance of the said Captain Jackson.

Read – The order of the Right Honble the Lords Commissioners of the Admiralty, dated the 12th day of June 1815 directed to the president, to try the said M[r]. Alexander Lyal for neglect of duty, disobedience of orders and apparent drunkenness.

The members of the court and judge advocate were then duly sworn.

Read – The annexed letter of charge from the said Capt. Dowers to Adm[l]. Sir J. T. Duckworth, Commander in Chief at Plymouth.

The witnesses, except the first to be sworn, then withdrew.

The prosecutor stated that he alone could give evidence upon part of the charges, whereupon:

William Dowers, Esq[r]., Captain of His Majesty's ship *Wanderer*, was sworn and examined as follows:

Co[t]. Relate what you know respecting the charges against the Prisoner.

A. After delivering the night order, a copy of which has been just read to the court, to the officer of the watch on the night of the 5th ins[t]., I told the prisoner only to make a short tack off in order to get in shore for the tide, which would make down about midnight; the ship was then a few miles to the southward & eastward of Dungeness. At 3 o'clock in the morning of the 6th or thereabouts, I awoke and, on sending for the officer of the watch, found the ship still standing off shore. The master was directed to be sent to me and, on his coming into the cabin, I repeatedly asked him why the night orders had not been complied with and why the ship was still standing to the southward. And, on receiving no answer, I asked the prisoner why he did not reply to my questions. After repeating the same question to him, I heard him endeavouring to articulate and, as he could not do so, I was induced to lift the screen of my cot and then saw the prisoner apparently as drunk as I ever saw a man in my life. I remarked, 'I believe you are intoxicated M^r^. Lyal. Go out of my cabin.' As he neither made answer or went out of my cabin, I called the sentry to take him out. The first lieutenant was sent for, the ship tacked and the circumstance mentioned to him and my orders given to put the prisoner under arrest for drunkenness and disobedience of orders.

Co^{t}. Was the sentry present?

A. I believe the sentinel was standing near the door at the foot of my cot.

The witness resumed the place of prosecutor.

Lieut. Henry Whittle of His Majesty's ship *Wanderer* sworn & examined as follows:

Pros^{r}. Did you at 8 o'clock on the night of the 5th of June ins^{t}. receive my orders to direct M^{r}. Batt to keep the first watch and the prisoner to attend the pilotage of the ship and did you signify those orders to those officers?

A. I did.

Pro. After tacking to the eastward of the ships at anchor in Dungeness, did you hear me tell the master only to make a short tack off in order to keep in shore for the tide?

A. I did.

Pro. When I sent to you at 3 o'clock in the morning of the 6th & mentioned the circumstance of my believing M^{r}. Lyal to be drunk, did you see the prisoner and did he appear to be drunk?

A. I saw the prisoner at that time; he appeared to have drank more than he usually did and was rather stupid, but I could not say that he was drunk. He had been sitting up all the night and had been much up the night before. And I did not know whether to attribute it to fatigue or to drinking, as I had no conversation with him.

Pro. Do you know of any necessity for the prisoner's sitting up the night before?

A. None in particular, unless it was to keep the ship clear of her anchor.

Pro. Is the prisoner in the habit of keeping regular watch on board the *Wanderer*?

A. Yes.

Pro. Was there any order given to the prisoner not to keep his regular watch on the night before?

A. There was no order given to that effect.

Pro. Was there any effort made to get the ship down channel by tacking between the night of the 5th and the morning of the 6th ins^{t}. until I sent for you at 3 o'clock in the morning?

A. No.

Co^{t}. When you were desired by Capt. Dowers to put the prisoner under arrest for drunkenness, did he appear to you to be drunk?

A. I don't think he was drunk.

Co^{t}. Were the circumstances of the ship such as to have induced a diligent master to have been up on the night of the 4th?

A. Yes, being at single anchor in the tide's way.

Co^{t}. Had you any conversation with the prisoner after Capt. Dowers had ordered him under an arrest for drunkenness?

A. No.

Co^{t}. Did the prisoner speak at all afterwards?

A. Yes, he asked the surgeon if he thought he was drunk. I did not hear the surgeon give an answer.

Co^{t}. Was the prisoner's manner of speaking like a drunken man or a man that had been drinking?

A. His manner appeared as if he had been drinking but not drunk.

Co^{t}. Was he in that state that he could have put the ship about?

A. I think he could have put the ship about.

Co^{t}. Do you think when the ship is at single anchor in the tide's way and in moderate weather, there is any call for any extraordinary exertion so as to fatigue a man on the part of the master?

A. I do not.

Co^{t}. What kind of weather was it on the night preceding the 5th & where was the ship?

A. The ship was at single anchor in The Downs; it was a fresh breeze.

Co^{t}. Was it such a night as to require unusual exertion on the part of the master to keep the ship clear of her anchor?

A. No.

Co^{t}. Do you know of any neglect of duty or disobedience of orders on the part of the prisoner relative to the charge?

A. I think it was neglectful not going about before 3 o'clock according to the captain's orders. He was desired by the captain to make a short tack off in my presence.

Co^{t}. If you had been captain of the *Wanderer* on the night of the 5th, would you have trusted the master in any difficult or intricate situation from his appearance?

A. At the time Capt. Dowers sent for me in the morning of the 6th, I should not.

Co^{t}. Why would you not?

A. He appeared to me rather stupid or fatigued.

Co^{t}. Was the prisoner sober?

A. He appeared to me to be half drunk; he was capable of a certain part of his duty and not of all. I think he could have put a ship about, but I should not have trusted him with the pilotage in a narrow channel.

The witness withdrew.

M^{r}. John Bee, Midshipman of the *Wanderer*, sworn and examined as follows:

Pro^{r}. Did you, as officer of the middle watch, receive the night order book from M^{r}. Batt, the officer of the first watch, on the night of the 5th ins^{t}.?

A. I did.

Pro. Was any exertion made to get the ship down channel by tacking until I ordered it to be done after 3 o'clock on the morning of the 6th?

A. There was not.

Pro. As the ship lay off south and the variation was against her, would she have gone faster down channel on the other tack?

A. I think she would.

Pro. How often was the master on deck in the middle watch before I sent for him?

A. Once.

Pro. Did you go down to the master during the middle watch?

A. Not until I was ordered by the captain.

Pro. Where was the master at the time?

A. In the gun room, sitting at the table with the surgeon in conversation.

Co^{t}. Did the prisoner at that time appear to be sober?

A. He did.

Co^{t}. Were there bottles & glasses and cards on the table?

A. I did not observe; I merely called the master.

Co^{t}. When the master came upon deck at night as you have stated, did he appear to be sober?

A. Quite so.

Co^{t}. Had you any conversation together?

A. Yes, I spoke to him relative to the South Foreland and Dungeness lights. The master, when he came on deck, looked into the binnacle and observed how the ship lay which was south and also the bearings of Dungeness Light which was about N.W. by W. This was at three quarters past twelve. And the conversation

A. afterwards I don't remember exactly; it related to the fineness of the night. Previous to the prisoner's going below, I asked him whether he wished me to call him at any particular hour; his answer was no, as he intended again coming on deck. Between 6 and 7 bells, the sentinel told me the captain wished to see me; I went down and he asked me whether we had been standing on the starboard tack all night. I told him we had. He then ordered me to call the master, which I did. He was sitting at table in the gun room with the surgeon in conversation. The master rose up directly & said he would go and see him, which he did, first coming on deck and looking into the binnacle. After the master had been to the captain, the captain again sent for me and enquired if he was sober when he came on deck. I told him I thought he was.

Co^t^. At the time you have described, did the master appear to have been drinking?

A. I did not pay particular attention, as I was engaged about the ship.

Co^t^. As the captain had left directions at 11 o'clock to make only a short tack off in order to keep in shore for the tide, did the master, when he came on deck at ¾'s past 12, give any reason for not complying with that order?

A. He did not.

Co^t^. How far were you from Dungeness when the master came on deck at ¾ past 12?

A. About 8 miles to leeward of it.

Co^t^. From ¾ past 12 when Dungeness bore N.W. & by W. until half past 3 o'clock when it bore N.W. & by N., what distance had the ship ran off shore?

A. I think we could not have been more than 8 miles.

The witness withdrew

George Atkins, Private Marine serving on board the *Wanderer*, sworn and examined as follows:

Pro. Were you the sentinel at the cabin door of the *Wanderer* on the morning of the 6th ins^t^.?

A. Yes.

Pro. Did you observe the prisoner and the surgeon sitting at the gun room table while you were sentinel?

A. Yes.

Pro. What were they doing?

A. They were having a game at cards when I first went on sentry; I did not observe how long they played.

Pro. What was the latest time you observed them?

A. I went on sentry at 12 and saw them so late as about half past 12.

Pro. When I sent for the master at 3 o'clock, did you give me a light and hold the door open?

A. Yes, I gave a light and held the door open some part of the time.

Pro. Did you repeatedly hear me ask the prisoner some questions and why he did not answer me?

A. Yes, the captain said to him he thought he had been doing a very wrong thing to let the ship stand so long on one tack; this he repeated more than once. The master made no reply and Capt. Dowers asked why he did not answer his question; still he made no reply.

Pro. Did I tell you to take the master out of the cabin?

A. Yes, and I opened the door and the master walked out on the quarter deck.

Pro. Did the prisoner appear drunk or sober?

A. I don't know; I did not take particular notice.

Co[t]. Did you observe the prisoner to go on deck during your watch?

A. I did not till he left the captain's cabin; he might have gone and I not seen him.

Co[t]. As you were sentry at the cabin door, how could you see the prisoner and surgeon sitting together at the gun room table?

A. I saw them through the skylight.

The witness withdrew.

The evidence in support of the charges being here closed, the prisoner was asked if he had anything to offer in his behalf, when he desired leave to retire out of court for a few minutes, which was granted him. And, at the expiration of a short time, the prisoner again appeared and delivered in the annexed written paper signed by himself which was read to the court.

The prisoner then called on the following officers to speak to his general character:

Lieut. Henry Whittle (being already sworn) said, 'I have known the prisoner about 3 years; his general conduct has been very correct before this circumstance.'

Lieut. Tho[s]. Holbrook of the *Wanderer* (being first sworn) said, 'Since I have been with the prisoner, which is about ten months, he has behaved himself with sobriety and he is a temperate and correct character and attentive to his duty.'

The prisoner stated that his certificates to character were all at the Navy Office. And, having nothing further to offer, the court was cleared and proceeded to deliberate upon and form the sentence.

The court, having very maturely and deliberately weighed and considered the evidence in support of the charges as well as what the prisoner had offered in his behalf, was of opinion that the charges had not been proved against the prisoner, Mr. Alexander Lyal, and did in consequence adjudge him to be acquitted.

The court was opened, the prisoner brought in, the witnesses and audience re-admitted and the sentence pronounced accordingly. …

148A. *Defence of Alexander Lyal*

[ADM 1/5449]

… I have been ten years in His Majesty's service and, if I have not had the good fortune to have arrived at any particular degree of credit, I have at least had the satisfaction not to have incurred disgrace. I have ever been anxious to execute my duty with correctness and particularly desirous of becoming a proficient in the navigation of the Channel, to which I hope I may be permitted to lay some claim. I am fully aware of the dangerous consequence of not paying implicit obedience to the orders of a superior, but this is a case in which my own judgement was to guide me as fully appears by the night order.

It has already appeared that the ship was tacked off shore at 10:45 and was laying up south with a light breeze from W.S.W. I went on deck some time after eleven o'clock and again about one. When I took the bearings of the land and found that though the wind might continue the same, we should still weather the Ridge, but there was every appearance of its coming round to the southward which would have enabled us to lay quite clear of Dungeness. It was therefore my intention not to have tacked until four o'clock. I was quite certain of the bearings of the land and the dangers. If any blame can attach itself to me, it must be that of not acquainting Captain Dowers that I wished to stand on. He only wished to be acquainted when it was proper to go about; besides no advantage could have arisen from tacking sooner, for we should then have had the lee tide on the beam which did not make to the westward until 2:45. I do not recollect any verbal order about making short tacks. At all events, I should have considered the written night order as the one to govern my conduct.

I had kept the watch from twelve o'clock until four on Monday morning and part of the morning watch looking out for the swinging of the ship and was up the whole of the following night until Captain Dowers sent for me, which I hope will be considered sufficient cause for the appearance of fatigue. When on deck, I was talking with Mr. Bee, the officer of the watch, and pointing out to him the bearings of the land and of the Ridge, so that he must have observed if I had been in a state of intoxication. My only motive in playing cards (a custom very prevalent of late in the *Wanderer*) was to divert myself from sleep, though I am now fully aware of the impropriety and beg to express my deepest sorrow and concern for having thus violated the rules of the service, but neither on this nor any other occasion was there any gambling, the usual inducement to play at unseasonable hours.

I humbly beg to call the attention of the court to the testimony borne to my general character and conduct by the officers of the *Wanderer*, one of whom, Lieutenant Whittle, has known me upward of three years, and I throw myself on their indulgence which it will be my future study to deserve.

148B. *Dowers to Duckworth*

[ADM 1/5449]

His Majesty's ship *Wanderer*
Off Beachy Head, June 6th, 1815

… In obedience to your orders of the 2nd ins[t]. to return to Plymouth without loss of time after seeing the convoy in safely to The Downs,

Last night, His Majesty's ship was working down channel and, when I went to bed (after eleven o'clock), a copy of the enclosed night order was given to the officer of the watch and, at the same time, I told the master (M[r]. Alexander Lyal) 'we should only make a short tack off in order to keep in shore for the tide.'

I did not awake till near 3 o'clock AM and found, to my great surprise, the ship still standing off shore. And on sending for the master, he came to me so stupefied as not to be able to answer any question put to him.

On enquiry I learnt that the master had been sitting up till the moment I sent for him, playing cards and drinking at the gun room table with the surgeon.

Had we been in the narrow part of the Channel or had I not awoke at the time I did, His Majesty's ship and all on board might have fallen a sacrifice to the master's neglect and disobedience.

I request you will be pleased to apply for a court martial to try M[r]. Alexander Lyal, the Master, for the same and for apparent drunkenness, feeling it due to the King's service to make this application. …

148C. *Captain Dowers' Night Order*

[ADM 1/5449]

HM ship *Wanderer*, 11 PM
June 5th, 1815, off Dungeness

Copy of the Night Order, June 5th, 1815

Night Order

The master will attend to the pilotage of the ship and let me know when it is advisable to tack so as to get with all possible dispatch to Plymouth.

In standing inshore, the lead is to be kept going and the officers of the watch are to be responsible the ship does not go into danger.

All safe sail is to be carried and a most particular look out that we do not run foul of anything. Be also on the alert to prevent surprise. Other orders as usual.

Officers watch!!!

...

DOCUMENTS AND SOURCES

All the volumes used in the sample are to be found in The National Archives.

ADM 1/5330	1792 – January 1794
ADM 1/5331	February – December 1794
ADM 1/5333	July – December 1795
ADM 1/5334	January 1796
ADM 1/5349	April – June 1799
ADM 1/5355	December 1800 – March 1801
ADM 1/5362	July – December 1802
ADM 1/5363	January – September 1803
ADM 1/5368	January – February 1805
ADM 1/5383	August – October 1807
ADM 1/5388	July – August 1808
ADM 1/5389	September – October 1808
ADM 1/5404	April 1810
ADM 1/5416	May – June 1811
ADM 1/5426	May 1812
ADM 1/5434	January – February 1813
ADM 1/5436	May – June 1813
ADM 1/5442	April – May 1814
ADM 1/5444	July – August 1814
ADM 1/5447	November 1814 – January 1815
ADM 1/5448	February – April 1815

Numbered Document Sources

Chapter 1: Procedure

1	An Act for Amending, Explaining and Reducing into One Act of Parliament the Laws relating to the Government of His Majesty's Ships, Vessels and Forces by Sea.	22 Geo. II c. 33
2	An Act to Explain and Amend an Act made in the Twenty Second Year of the Reign of His Late Majesty King George the Second, Entitled An Act for Amending, Explaining and Reducing into One Act of Parliament the Laws Relating to the Government of His Majesty's Ships, Vessels and Forces by Sea.	19 Geo. III c. 17

3	Chapter on courts martial in *Regulations and Instructions Relating to His Majesty's Service at Sea*		1st edn (1731), pp. 3–6
4	Chapter on courts martial in *Regulations and Instructions*		2nd edn (1806), pp. 404–10
5	CM of Joseph Piper	11 Jan 1793	ADM 1/5330
5A	Report of CM of Joseph Piper	11 Jan 1793	ADM 1/5330
6	Report of CM of William Clark and John Rolfe	26 Mar 1793	ADM 1/5330
7	Orrok to Parker	4 July 1794	ADM 1/5331
8	CM of William Walker	13 Sept 1794	ADM 1/5331
8A	Report of CM of William Walker	13 Sept 1794	ADM 1/5331
9	Foote to Nepean	19 May 1795	ADM 1/1795
10	CM of Patrick Tarney, William Perkins, Henry Perkins, Patrick Morgan and John McLaughlin	26 Aug 1795	ADM 1/5333
10A	Report of CM of Patrick Tarney, William Perkins, Henry Perkins, Patrick Morgan and John McLaughlin	26 Aug 1795	ADM 1/5333
10B	Hand to Sotheron	24 Aug 1795	ADM 1/5333
11	Court to Nepean	11 Feb 1796	ADM 1/5334
12	Court to Nepean	12 Feb 1796	ADM 1/5334
12A	Enclosure in Court to Nepean	9 Mar 1796	ADM 1/5334
12B	Nepean's notes to Admiralty	9 Mar 1796	ADM 1/5334
13	CM of John Styles	23 Feb 1796	ADM 1/5335
14	CM of Henry Hone Haviland	20 Oct 1796	ADM 1/5337
15	CM of Peter Egan alias Peter Hugan	19 Nov 1796	ADM 1/5337
16	Mitford to Harvey	19 Dec 1797	ADM 1/5342
17	CM of Daniel Brennan	22 Feb 1798	ADM 1/5343
18	CM of Angus McMillan, Thomas Mack and William Logan	26 June 1798	ADM 1/5345
19	CM of John Kerr	10 Oct 1798	ADM 1/5347
19A	Kerr to Robins	22 Sept 1798	ADM 1/5347
19B	Defence of John Kerr	10 Oct 1798	ADM 1/5347
20	Tripp to Goddard	29 May 1799	ADM 1/5349
21	CM of William Johnson	11 June 1799	ADM 1/5349
22	Dawson to Nepean	30 Sept 1799	ADM 1/1721
23	Oake to Lords Commissioners of the Admiralty	20 Nov 1799	ADM 1/3093
24	Roberts to Nepean	22 Nov 1799	ADM 1/3093
25	Brasington to Lords Commissioners of the Admiralty	19 Dec 1799	ADM 1/5349
26	Gomm to Nepean	22 April 1800	ADM 1/2895
26A	Midgley to Gomm	25 April 1799	ADM 1/2895
27	Report of the CM of William Connor	30 Jan 1801	ADM 1/5355
28	CM of Charles Burne	8 April 1802	ADM 1/5361

29	CM of Edward Nicholas Conner, Green Berry, Henry Keal and Thomas Hemmett	6 July 1804	ADM 1/5366
30	Byam to Heathcote	2 Oct 1804	ADM 1/5367
31	CM of Woodford Simms	5 Feb 1805	ADM 1/5368
32	CM of Captain Patrick Campbell, the officers and crew of the *Doris*	6 Feb 1805	ADM 1/5368
33	CM of George Marshall	27 May 1805	ADM 1/5369
34	CM of Michael Raven	9 June 1810	ADM 1/5406
35	CM of John Bathie	1 Oct 1811	ADM 1/5419
35A	Buller, Richardson and Scobell to Calder	18 Feb 1811	ADM 1/5419
36	CM of William Craig	1 Nov 1811	ADM 1/5420
37	Orders for executions of John Smith and Jean Tourney	15 Jan 1812	ADM 1/5422
38	CM of Charles Clark Dobson	20 Jan 1812	ADM 1/5423
39	CM of William Kinder	12 May 1812	ADM 1/5426
39A	Seymour to Cotton	18 Jan 1812	ADM 1/5426
40	CM of James Scaby	22 May 1812	ADM 1/5426
41	Sawyer to Evans	25 May 1812	ADM 1/5426
42	CM of Simon Thomas	12 June 1812	ADM 1/5427
43	CM of Thomas Harris	9 Jan 1813	ADM 1/5434
44	Bicknell to Croker	1 Mar 1813	ADM 1/3704
45	CM of Edwin Henry Chamberlayne	3 Jan 1814	ADM 1/5440
45A	Crozier to Pellew	26 Dec 1813	ADM 1/5440
45B	Crozier's charges	[No date]	ADM 1/5440
45C	Crozier's charges	[No date]	ADM 1/5440
45D	Report of CM of Acheson Crozier	29 Dec 1813	ADM 1/5440
46	Martin to Principal Officers and Commissioners of the Navy	14 Oct 1814	ADM 1/835
46A	Eastlake to Martin	[No date]	ADM 1/835
47	Jefferson to Croker	7 Jan 1815	ADM 1/4782
48	Martyn to Croker	23 April 1815	ADM 1/4910
49	Bicknell to Croker	8 June 1815	ADM 1/3707
50	Bicknell to Croker	17 Aug 1815	ADM 1/3707

Chapter 2: Social Crimes

51	CM of James Flanagan	9 Mar 1801	ADM 1/5355
52	CM of David Lawson	27 June 1803	ADM 1/5363
52A	Somerville to Nepean	15 May 1803	ADM 1/5363
53	CM of John Farrel and John Barry	7 Mar 1806	ADM 1/5372
54	CM of Joseph Fountain	23 Sept 1809	ADM 1/5399
55	CM of Samuel Pike	24 June 1813	ADM 1/5436
56	CM of William Robson	18 April 1814	ADM 1/5442
56A	Robson's defence	18 April 1814	ADM 1/5442
56B	Saurin to Bickerton	13 April 1814	ADM 1/5442

57	CM of Thomas Beecher and George Delany	10–11 June 1799	ADM 1/5349
57A	Defence of Beecher and Delany	11 June 1799	ADM 1/5349
58	CM of John Hazlehurst, William Wilson and Richmond Norton	4 Feb 1800	ADM 1/5352
59	CM of Solomon Barnett and Robert Dent	8 July 1805	ADM 1/5370
59A	Hope to Montagu	4 July 1805	ADM 1/5370
60	CM of John Goodridge	6 Oct 1808	ADM 1/5389
61	CM of Mark Moore	10 Mar 1796	ADM 1/5335
61A	Shipman to Lords Commissioners of the Admiralty	18 Feb 1796	ADM 1/5335
62	CM of Jonathan Sturdy	27 April 1798	ADM 1/5344
62A	Rogers to Parker	23 April 1798	ADM 1/5344
63	CM of William Henry Brown Tremlett	9 Sept 1800	ADM 1/5354
63A	McIntosh to Milbank	20 July 1800	ADM 1/5354
64	CM of David Richards	17 Jan 1814	ADM 1/5440
64A	Shaw to Pellew	14 Jan 1814	ADM 1/5440
64B	Richards's Paper	14 Jan 1814	ADM 1/5440
65	CM of Edward Smith	29 Dec 1794	ADM 1/5331
66	CM of Richard Probert	4 Jan 1796	ADM 1/5334
67	CM of James Smith	19 Dec 1808	ADM 1/5390
67A	Steventon to Young	13 Dec 1808	ADM 1/5390
68	CM of William Mason, Stephen Rolls and John M^c^Carthy	24 Sept 1812	ADM 1/5430
68A	Fahie to Keith	3 Sept 1812	ADM 1/5430
68B	Mason to Court	[No date]	ADM 1/5430
68C	Mason's defence	24 Sept 1812	ADM 1/5430
69	CM of Edward Patton	15 April 1793	ADM 1/5330
69A	Report of CM of Edward Patton	15 April 1793	ADM 1/5330
70	CM of Thomas Brown	23 Aug 1799	ADM 1/5350
71	CM of Richard Gaff	26 Dec 1800	ADM 1/5355
71A	Harvey to the Earl of St Vincent	26 Dec 1800	ADM 1/5355
72	CM of Robert Pring	3 Sept 1801	ADM 1/5358
73	CM of John Wheeler	8 Nov 1811	ADM 1/5420
73A	Gore to Cotton	5 Sept 1811	ADM 1/5420
73B	Wheeler's Defence	8 Nov 1811	ADM 1/5420
74	CM of Thomas Nelson	30 July 1800	ADM 1/5353
74A	Pickmore to Milbanke	17 July 1800	ADM 1/5353
75	CM of William Downes	28 April 1809	ADM 1/5395
76	CM of William M^c^Master and John Callaughan	29 July 1799	ADM 1/5350
77	CM of John Harrison, William Harris, John Ware and John Douglas	14–16 June 1800	ADM 1/5355
78	CM of Thomas Hubbard and George Hynes	10 Dec 1800	ADM 1/5355
78A	Greetham to Nepean	12 Dec 1800	ADM 1/5355
78B	Edwards to St Vincent	14 Nov 1800	ADM 1/5355

78C	Greetham to Nepean	14 Dec 1800	ADM 1/5355
78D	Hubbard to Hubbard	4 Sept [1800?]	ADM 1/5355
79	CM of Isaac Wilson	1 April 1809	ADM 1/5395
80	CM of John Sherwood	15 May 1812	ADM 1/5426

Chapter 3: Naval Crimes

81	CM of Michael Jenking	27 Jan 1794	ADM 1/5330
82	CM of Robert Tillford	25 Jan 1796	ADM 1/5334
83	CM of John Maloney	30 Dec 1796	ADM 1/5337
83A	Elphinstone to Nelson	26 Dec 1796	ADM 1/5337
84	CM of John Jacobs	27 Mar 1797	ADM 1/5338
84A	Extract of report of CM of John Jacobs	27 Mar 1797	ADM 1/5338
85	CM of John McKinley and Robert Smith	24 April 1799	ADM 1/5349
86	CM of Henry Carey	18 Oct 1802	ADM 1/5362
86A	Barclay to Nepean	16 Aug 1802	ADM 1/5362
86B	Duncan, Winslow and Palmer to Nepean	2 Sept 1802	ADM 1/5362
87	CM of John Biggs	23 Jan 1805	ADM 1/5368
88	CM of Thomas Lee and Robert Jackson	10 Aug 1807	ADM 1/5383
88A	Murray to Pole	26 July 1807	ADM 1/5383
88B	Spence to Lee	29 July 1807	ADM 1/5383
89	CM of William Downes	12 Jan 1809	ADM 1/5391
90	CM of John Hyde	16 Aug 1813	ADM 1/5437
91	CM of John Harland, Joseph Nicholes and Charles Robinson alias Dougherty	22 July 1814	ADM 1/5444
92	CM of John Brown	16 Nov 1814	ADM 1/5447
92A	Caulfield to Martin	9 Nov 1814	ADM 1/5447
92B	Brown's defence	9 Nov 1814	ADM 1/5447
93	CM of Robert Eccles and George Chapman	7 Dec 1814	ADM 1/5447
93A	Carroll to Martin	1 Dec 1814	ADM 1/5447
94	CM of Major Reynolds	13 April 1815	ADM 1/5448
95	CM of Michael Goley, Robert Powell, Peter Wair and Robert Field	29 April 1796	ADM 1/5335
95A	Members of the court to Nepean	29 April 1796	ADM 1/5335
95B	Stokes to Nepean	3 May 1796	ADM 1/5335
96	CM of James Dollard and Garrett Caine	9 April 1799	ADM 1/5349
96A	Meares to Faulknor	11 Sept 1798	ADM 1/5349
96B	Defence of Dollard and Caine	9 April 1799	ADM 1/5349
97	CM of David Roach, Nicholas Harrison and Naiad Suare	3 Nov 1806	ADM 1/5376
97A	Member of the court to Cochrane	3 Nov 1806	ADM 1/5376
98	CM of John Mose	11 Dec 1806	ADM 1/5376

98A	Bertie to Coffin	8 Dec 1806	ADM 1/5376
99	CM of William Morison and John Moral	9 July 1794	ADM 1/5331
100	CM of James Seymonds alias Simmons	27 June 1808	ADM 1/5387
101	CM of Thomas Taylor	10 Mar 1810	ADM 1/5403
102	CM of George Lumsdaine	1 Nov 1793	ADM 1/5330
102A	Report of CM of George Lumsdaine	1 Nov 1793	ADM 1/5330
103	CM of Corthine Parker	26 Aug 1807	ADM 1/5383
104	CM of Thomas Ratsey	13 June 1796	ADM 1/5336
105	CM of Joseph Ramsay	25 June 1799	ADM 1/5349
106	CM of William Little	7 Jan 1797	ADM 1/5338
107	CM of John Thomas	14 June 1804	ADM 1/5366
108	CM of Captain Blake, the officers and crew of *L'Amaranthe*	30 Dec 1799	ADM 1/5351
109	CM of Quamin	23 June 1803	ADM 1/5363
110	CM of Acting Lieutenant Westcott, the officers and crew of the *Fort Diamond*	4 Oct 1804	ADM 1/5367
111	CM of Edward Ellicott, the officers and crew of the *Explosion*	24 Sept 1807	ADM 1/5383
112	CM of George Montague Higginson, the officers and crew of the *Pigmy*	10 June 1814	ADM 1/5443
112A	Higginson to Croker	19 May 1814	ADM 1/5443
112B	Higginson's narrative	3 Mar 1807	ADM 1/5443
113	CM of John Harford	16 Jan 1800	ADM 1/5351
113A	Ayscough to Wolley	9 Dec 1799	ADM 1/5351
113B	Harford's defence	16 Jan 1800	ADM 1/5351
114	CM of John George Nops	8 Mar 1803	ADM 1/5363
114A	Nops's defence	8 Mar 1803	ADM 1/5363
115	CM of Richard Maundrell	30 Mar 1795	ADM 1/5332
115A	Maundrell's defence	30 Mar 1795	ADM 1/5332
115B	Auckland to Maundrell	30 April 1793	ADM 1/5332
116	CM of George William Blamey	25 July 1799	ADM 1/5350
116A	Warrant appointing Henry Long Deputy Judge Advocate	25 July 1799	ADM 1/5350

Chapter 4: Multiple Offences

117	CM of John Kent	9 Sept 1793	ADM 1/5330
117A	Ferris to Dod	29 April 1793	ADM 1/5330
117B	Gardner to Ferris	24 May 1793	ADM 1/5330
117C	Ferris to Stephens	11 Aug 1793	ADM 1/5330
118	CM of John Bell, John Rodney, Stephen Murphy, John Long and David Connolly	11 Mar 1794	ADM 1/5331

119	CM of Anthony Mark, alias Antonio Marco, John Elliot, Joseph Mansell and Peter Delany, alias Pierre D'Orlanie	17 Mar 1798	ADM 1/5343
120	CM of Sampson Jefferies	3 Feb 1800	ADM 1/5352
121	CM of John Spinney	27 Oct 1800	ADM 1/5354
122	CM of William Cuming	22 June 1801	ADM 1/5356
123	CM of Charles Coleman	6 July 1802	ADM 1/5362
124	CM of John Scriven and George Blanchard	25 Sept 1802	ADM 1/5362
124A	Lake to Nepean	9 Sept 1802	ADM 1/5362
125	CM of John Murray	14 Jan 1803	ADM 1/5363
126	CM of Peter Casey	2 May 1804	ADM 1/5366
127	CM of John Dow	1 Jan 1805	ADM 1/5368
127A	Woodriff to Montagu	28 Dec 1804	ADM 1/5368
128	CM of David Henderson and John Baikie	11 July 1806	ADM 1/5374
129	CM of Francis Broadfoot	2 May 1807	ADM 1/5381
129A	Young to Young	26 April 1807	ADM 1/5381
130	CM of George Lonis	2 Oct 1807	ADM 1/5383
131	CM of Thomas Allen Barnard and Terence Clark	28 May 1808	ADM 1/5387
131A	Harris to Whitshed	7 May 1808	ADM 1/5387
132	CM of John Ensor	5 July 1808	ADM 1/5388
133	CM of Thomas Purnell	17 Aug 1808	ADM 1/5388
134	CM of John Callan	4 April 1809	ADM 1/5395
134A	Callan's Defence	4 April 1809	ADM 1/5395
134B	Letters referred to in Callan's defence	19 July 1808 and 31 Mar 1809	ADM 1/5395
134C	Lapenotiere to Young	24 Mar 1809	ADM 1/5395
135	CM of William Edward Fiott	27 April 1810	ADM 1/5404
136	CM of James Davison	2 Jan 1811	ADM 1/5412
137	CM of Terrence Macmanoes	28 Nov 1811	ADM 1/5420
138	CM of John Moon	16 Jan 1812	ADM 1/5422
139	CM of Jacob Simpson	28 May 1812	ADM 1/5426
140	CM of James Emery	11 Jan 1813	ADM 1/5434
141	CM of Andrew Graham	11 Jan 1813	ADM 1/5434
142	CM of Alexander Meldrum	23 Nov 1813	ADM 1/5439
143	CM of Alexander McLaren	29 June 1814	ADM 1/5443
143A	Sartorius to Sawyer	14 May 1814	ADM 1/5443
143B	Sartorius's certificate of McLaren's character	28 June 1814	ADM 1/5443
144	CM of John Davies	19 July 1814	ADM 1/5444
145	CM of John Wheeler	1 Oct 1814	ADM 1/5446
145A	Browne to Domett	26 Sept 1814	ADM 1/5446
145B	Wheeler's Defence	1 Oct 1814	ADM 1/5446
145C	Lord Melville's petition to the King	13 Oct 1814	ADM 1/5446
146	CM of Alexander Johnston	14 Nov 1814	ADM 1/5447
147	CM of Hugh McCrenon	19 April 1815	ADM 1/5448

147A	Bremer to Duckworth	12 April 1815	ADM 1/5448
148	CM of Alexander Lyal	16 June 1815	ADM 1/5449
148A	Lyal's Defence	16 June 1815	ADM 1/5449
148B	Dowers to Duckworth	6 June 1815	ADM 1/5449
148C	Dowers' Night Order	5 June 1815	ADM 1/5449

INDEX

Abercrombie 249, 250, 251, 252, 253, 254, 255, 684, 685, 686, 688, 691
Abergavenny 149, 371, 372, 582, 583
Aboukir 653
absence without leave 391–403, 407–11
Actaeon 418
Active 544
Adam, Charles 193, 314
Adamant 40
Adamson, James 445
Adventure 576
Africa 131, 459
Agamemnon 70
Agincourt 385, 654
Alexander 412
Alexander, Thomas 116, 125, 314, 387, 388
Alfred 29
Alkmaar 283, 286
Allen, Alexander 412
Allen, Charles 727
Allen, William 608, 612
Alms, James 473
Ambuscade 179, 187
Amethyst 126
Amity 208, 209
Amphitrite
An Act for Amending, Explaining and Reducing into One Act of Parliament the Laws relating to the Government of His Majesty's Ships, Vessels and Forces by Sea 4–20, 155, 167, 171, 189, 193, 205, 211, 215, 229–30, 269, 294, 309, 313–14, 327, 349, 353, 374, 380, 384, 392, 421, 436, 489, 507, 529, 538, 544, 557, 560, 605, 608, 628, 623, 642, 649, 664, 712
An Act to Explain and Amend an Act made in the Twenty Second Year of the Reign of His Late Majesty King George the Second entitled An Act for Amending, Explaining and Reducing into One Act of Parliament the Laws relating to the Government of His Majesty's Ships, Vessels and Forces by Sea 20–22
Anderson, John 583, 584
Anna Theresa 179, 180, 181, 182, 183, 184, 188
Anson 215
Aquilon 574
Arab 493
Arethusa 528, 529, 530, 534, 536
Argo 340
Armstrong, John 392
Arnott, Walter 647
Arrow 178
Arthur, William 252
Articles of War 437, 438
Asia 70, 552, 557
Assistance 34, 205
Assurance 560
Astle, George 436
Astrea 120
Atkins, David 427
Atkins, George 747
Atkinson, Christopher 69
Atlas 269, 270, 271, 272, 273, 274, 275, 276
Atwell, Joseph 466
Audacious 30
Austen, Charles John 723
Austen, Francis William 122, 171
Austin, Charles John 703, 708
Austin, Francis William 608
Austrea 356, 357, 358, 359
Avon 305, 397, 718, 719, 720, 721, 722
Aylmer, Frederick William 391
Ayscough, James 37, 528, 529

Back Bay, Trincomale 313
Baikie, John 449
Bailey, John 632
Bailey, William 677
Bain, Henderson 607
Baker, Henry Edward Reginald 167, 408, 738
Baker, Thomas 99, 155
Balcombe, William 35, 39
Balhetchet, William 452
Ball, Alexander John 479

Ball, Henry Lidgbird 699
Ball, John 664
Ballard, Volant Vashon 452
Barclay, John 376
Barfleur 50, 722, 723
Barker, George 604
Barlow, Sir Robert 615
Barnard, Thomas Allen 649
Barnett, Solomon 193
Barrie, Robert 743
Barry, John 157, 158
Barry, William 131, 132
Barton, Robert 125, 528
Barton, William 424
Basseterre Roads, Guadeloupe 114
Bastard, John 404
Batch, Thomas 508
Batcher, Samuel 146
Bateman, James 598
Bates, Thomas 694
Bathie, John 116, 120
Batt, William 301
Baylis, Robert 214
Bayntun, Henry William 420, 459
Bazeley, John 412
Bazely, John 30, 231, 283
Beauclerk, Amelius 157, 238
Beaufort, Francis 459
Beauman, Francis 384
Beaver, Philip 120
Becher, Alexander 538
Bedford, William 93, 99, 167 420, 622
Bedworth, John 405, 406
Bee, John 746
Beecher, Thomas 179
Belam, George 298
Bell, Edward 236
Bell, John 566
Bell, Thomas 536
Belle Isle 103, 104, 105
Bellerophon 30, 300, 301, 302, 731, 732
Belliqueux 676, 677
Bellona 361
Belona 178, 210
Belvidera 395
Benequet 100, 103, 104, 105
Bennett, John 545
Benning, James 444
Beresford, John Poo 309, 684, 692
Berkeley, Velters Cornewall 231
Berkely, George Cranfield 685
Berkley, V.C. 560
Bermuda 392
Berry, Edward 134, 137, 141, 223, 327
Berry, George 131
Berry, Green 86
Bertie, Albemarle 155, 420, 463
Bertie, Thomas 468
Berwick 135
bestiality 335–45
Bevins, John 445
Bickerton, Richard 171, 210
Bicknell, Charles 136
Biggs, John 377
Billinge, William 549
Bingham, Joseph 52, 122, 373, 695
Binks, William 131, 132
Bissete, James 452
Bissett, James 114, 115, 231
Black, Christopher 397
Blackstakes 560
Blackwood, The Honble Henry 155, 178, 384, 448
Blaeguire, Peter 468
Blake, George Hans 493
Blake, Randal 316, 317, 318
Blake, Robert 179, 185
Blamey, George William 552
Blanchard, George 607
Bland, Loftus Otway 628
Blenheim 508
Blenkins, James John 643
Blewitt, John 395
Bligh, John 106, 335, 500, 637
Bligh, Richard Rodney 52, 204
Bligh, William 468, 488
Blight, William 460
Blinkhorn, Thomas 336
Bloom, James 211
Bloye, Robert 400
Bodley, William 194, 273
Bogar, Richard 412
Boger, Richard 29, 57
Bonny, John 30
Bookless, Thomas 283
Bornholm Island 592
Botherwicke, David 169
Bourchier, Henry 732
Bourne, Richard 130
Bouverie, Duncombe Pleydell 125
Bover, Peter Turner 373, 608
Bowden, James 467
Bowen, George 52, 463, 572
Bowen, James 52, 155, 327
Bowen, John 126
Boyce, William 173
Boyle, Courtenay 380
Boyle, Courtnay 436, 649
Boyle, The Honble Courtney 63, 155, 178
Boyle, John 93, 99
Boyles, Charles 479, 622
Boyne 352

Boys, Charles Worsley 335, 436, 666, 684
Boys, R.P. 131
Boys, Thomas 294, 703, 708, 718
Brace, Edward 135, 138, 141, 223
Brackenbridge, William 69
Brassington, Ann 75–6
Brassington, John 613
Brassington, Thomas 75–6
Breary, Thomas 484
Bremer, James John Gordon 408, 738
Brennan, Daniel 55
Brenton, Edward Pelham 738
Brest 588
Brevdragerer 122, 123, 124
Briggs, Thomas 238, 400, 667
Bright, Thomas 156
Brilliant 488
Brisbane, James 116, 288, 592, 649
Bristol 123, 124
Britannia 31, 353
Brixham 79, 80, 85
Broadfoot, Francis 637
Brocanture 116, 117, 118, 120
Brodie, Thomas Charles 649
Broke, Philip Bowes Vere 238
Bromley, Robert Howe 380
Brooks, Thomas 410
Broughton, John 514, 641
Broughton, William Robert 373, 384, 608, 649, 742
Brown, James 317, 398, 729
Brown, John 381, 400, 470, 560, 567
Brown, Thomas 219, 269, 408, 738
Brown, William 205, 528, 534
Browne, Richard 55
Browne, Thomas 400, 404, 727
Browning, Francis 332
Brune, James 571
Brunswick 53
brutality 544–57
Bucephalus 676, 677, 678, 680, 682, 683, 684
Buchan, John 424
Bucke, John 437
buggery 309–35
Bulldog 457
Bullen, Charles 157
Buller, Sir Edward 29, 116, 249, 257, 288, 436, 488
Bulteel, Rowley 468
Bundock, William 617
Burdett, George 354, 712, 727
Burdon, George 420
Burgess, Richard Rundle 412
Burlton, George 137, 141, 223, 632
Burn, William Peter 595
Burne, Charles 79–86
Burnett, John 369
Burns, Patrick 163, 164
Burosse, John 316
Burrow, Alexander 55
Burrows, Thomas 605
Button, Daniel 87, 91
Butts, M. 89
Byng, George 676, 677, 695
Byron, Richard 391

Cadogan, George 649
Cain, James 30
Caine, Garrett 420–27
Cains, James 30
Calcutta 628 630, 631
Calder, Robert 50, 587
Caledonia 141
Caley, William 361
Callan, John 339
Callaughan, John 309
Cambridge 42, 49, 179, 182, 257, 355, 412, 420, 479
Camilla 479, 483, 485
Campbell, Colin 114
Campbell, Collin 433
Campbell, Donald 249, 684
Campbell, George 269
Campbell, Hugh 605
Campbell, John 342
Campbell, Patrick 94, 99–106, 134, 488
Campbell, Robert 137, 448, 632
Campbell, Robert Bell 664
Canada 463
Canfield, Paul 53, 191
Cape of Good Hope 121, 189
Cape Nichola Mole, St Domingo 654, 712
Captain 229, 268, 354, 587, 588, 592
Carden, John Surman 125, 685
Carey, Henry 373
Caribane, William 725
Carlisle Bay, Barbados 349, 427, 435, 565
Carnatic 149, 572, 580, 581, 582, 583, 584, 586, 587
Carpenter, Charles 268
Carroll, William Fairbrother 404, 408
Carter, Richard 442
Carteret, Philip 122, 695
Carthew, James 649
Carthew, Robert 294
Carthew, William 231
Carthness, John 700
Casey, Peter 622
Castang, John P. 356
Castor 42, 46, 115, 412, 420, 452, 453
Caulder, Robert 353

Caulfield, Edward 437
Caulfield, Thomas Gordon 155, 401, 404, 677
Cayley, William 69, 204, 309
Censor 123, 124
Centaur 92, 401, 402, 403
Chamberlayne, Edward Henry 138, 139, 141
Champion, Charles 642, 643
Chapman, George 404, 639
Chapple, John 223, 225
Charon 27, 29, 565, 615, 616, 617, 618, 620
Chatham 29, 375, 698, 699
Cheater, John 118
Chetham, Thomas 725
Chichester 381
Child, John 149
Christian 383, 384
Church, Stephen George 446
Circe 427
Civita Vechia, Italy 358
Clark, George 215
Clark, Henry 61
Clark, Terence 649
Clark, William 29–30, 314, 560
Clarke, George 294
Clarke, John 355
Clarkson, Henry 496
Clay, Edward Sneyd 702, 708
Cleave, Thomas 278, 280
Clements, William 226
Cleopatra 70, 552, 557
Clist, Richard 385
Clyde 375, 376
Cochrane, Alexander 115, 392, 452, 560
Cochrane, Sir Thomas 249
Cochrane, Sir Thomas John 738
Cock, John George 479
Cockbourne, George 210
Cockburn, George 356
Cockburne, George 63, 210
Codrington, Edward 193, 384, 391, 436
Coffin, Francis Holmes 116
Coffin, Isaac 193, 288, 436, 627
Colby, David 106
Cole, Christopher 488, 604, 677
Cole, Francis 412
Cole, William John 733
Coleman, Charles 604
Collett, William 589
Collingwood, Cuthbert 157, 268, 353, 587, 664
Colossus 116, 586
Colpoys, John 229
Columbine, Edward Henry 608
Combe, William M. 131, 132
confinement 73, 90, 91
Conn, John 157, 637
Conner, Edward Nicholas 86
Conner, Philip 397
Connolly, David 566
Connor, Terrence 70
Connor, William 78
contempt 78, 463–7, 723
convoys 31–3
Conway, Hugh S. 30
Cook, Edward 31
Cook, Hugh 677
Cooke (1), John 93, 99
Coombes, William 241
Corbet, Robert 178, 459
Cornwallis, William 229, 544
Cotton, Charles 30 126, 269, 277, 289, 587
Courageux 692, 693
courts of enquiry 120
Crabb, William 138
Cracraft, William Edward 283
Craddock, Henry 530
Cragie, Jason 135
Craig, William 120, 121
Cranch, George Palmer 683
Crawley, Edmund 204, 275
Crawley, John 492, 581
Creighton, David 230
Crespin, George 594
Crispe, Thomas 593
Crispin, Benjamin 340
Crocker, J.W. 136
Crocodile 732, 733, 734, 736
Crocombe, Richard 465
Crofton, Ambrose 34
Crozier, Acheson 138, 141
Crump, Thomas 276
Cubett, Charles 697
Cull, Richard 538
Cullis, William 53
Culloden 29
Cumberland 74
Cumberland, William 373, 448, 608
Cumby, William Price 161, 162, 649
Cuming, William 384, 592, 628, 654
Cumming, James 560
Cunningham, Charles 57
Curran, Matthew 388
Curry, Richard 448, 514, 632, 654
Curtis, Roger 189, 204
Cuttle 131
Cyrus 404, 405, 406, 407

Dacres, Barrington 106

Dacres, James Richard 50, 86, 107, 353, 377, 408, 410, 738
Dannemark 114, 451, 452
Darby, Henry D'Esterre 34, 204, 294, 479
Dartmouth Harbour 172
Dashwood, Charles 161, 162, 171, 377
Davers, Charles Sidney 361
Davidson, James 684–92
Davie, John 171, 726
Davie, Thomas 402
Davies, John 663, 722–6
Davis, George Frederick 553
Davis, John 93, 94, 97, 621
Davy, Thomas 472, 477
Dawson, John 74
Dawson, Richard 610, 614
Day, Daniel 497
Day, George 360
de Courey, Michael 57, 93, 99, 106, 107
de Frane, Frederick 124
Dean, William 427
Defence 193, 194, 195, 196, 197, 198, 199, 560
Delany, George 179
Delany, Peter 572
Delgarno, Maurice 42
Denbigshire 132
Denman, Edmund 162, 163
Dent, Robert 193
Deptford 615
Deputy Judge Advocate 557
Derby Militia 132, 133
desertion 27–9, 34–9, 86, 130, 132, 349–89, 404, 407
Devastation 387, 388
Diadem 74
Diamond 99, 441, 489, 537
Diana 420, 421, 422, 425
Dickenson, Lacey 709
Dickson, Archibald 454, 467, 468
Dickson, Archibald Collingwood 468, 742
Dickson, David 471
Dickson, Edward Stirling 134, 223, 628
Dictator 229, 230, 463, 464, 465, 466
Diligence 573, 574, 576, 577
Diligent 107
Dilkes, John 55, 231, 361, 592, 622
Dillon, William Henry 134, 732
Director 468, 469, 470, 471, 472, 473, 474, 477
disobedience of orders 454–63, 727, 743
disturbances of the peace 294–308
Dixon, John William Taylor 538
Dixon, William 58
Dobitoe, Samuel 583, 584, 585
Dobson, Charles Clark 122
Dobson, Man 52, 367, 492
Dod, Edmund 229, 230
Dollard, James 420–27
Domett, William 528
Dominica 427, 428, 432, 433, 434, 435
Dona Maria Bay, St Domingo 573
Donald, Alexander 647
Donald, William 135
Donelly, Ross 210
Donnelly, Ross 368, 384
Donovan, Richard 628
Doris 93, 94, 96, 97, 99, 103, 104, 105
D'Orlanie, Pierre 572
Dormett, William 327
Douglas, Sir Andrew Snape 205, 229, 544
Douglas, James 544
Douglas, John 313, 318
Douglas, John Erskine 134, 137, 178, 552
Dow, John 627
Dowers, William 743, 745
Down, Edward Augustus 340
Downes, the 692, 695, 698, 703
Downes, William 383
Doyle, Lawrence 671
Drake 167, 168
Drake, John 385
Draper, John 632
Dreadnought 157
Drew, John 412
Driskill, John 249
Drougherty, Hugh 258, 263, 266
Drummond, Adam 193, 649
Drummond, John 301
drunkenness 79, 81, 83, 85, 149–78, 743
Drury, Thomas 30
Drury, William O'Bryen 373, 537, 677
Duckington Hall 601
Duckworth, John Thomas 52, 86, 377, 408, 500, 738
Duell, James 135
Duff, Archibald 726, 738
Duff, George 592
Duff, W.A. 60
Dunbar, James 59, 200, 628
Duncan, The Honble Henry 408, 738
Dundas, George Heneage Lawrence 340
Dundas, Thomas 492
Dunn, Richard Dalling 377
Durban, William 664
Durham, Philip Charles 125, 155, 215, 327, 479
Dwarf 137
Dymock, Thomas 83

Eagle, Meleken 416

Eastlake, George 116, 126, 143, 238, 249, 288, 335, 400, 404, 408, 520, 637, 666, 718, 726, 738, 743
Eccles, Robert 404
Edwards, Sampson 269, 327, 587
Edwards, William 333
Egan, Edward 552
Egan, Peter a.k.a Peter Hugan 52
Egmont 353
Ekins, Charles 384, 654
Elback, Edward 176
Elder, Robert 450
Elephant 695
Elizabeth 135
Ellicott, Edward 518
Elliot, George 677
Elliot, Robert 200
Elliot, William 171, 732
Ellis, John 654
Ellison, Joseph 29, 42
Elphinstone, George Keith 30, 229, 544
Elphinstone, Thomas 93, 99, 356, 373, 488, 538, 608, 718
embezzlement 204–28
Emblin, William 663
Emery, James 702–7
Endymion 654
English Harbour, Antigua 92, 93
Englishman's Head, Guadeloupe 451
Ensor, John 653
Entreprenante 639, 640, 641
Epworth, Farmery Predam 712
Erskine, John 223
Eurus 361, 362, 364, 366
Evans, Andrew Fitzherbert 70, 131, 391, 500, 552
Evans, Ellis 202
Evans, William 640
Evett, John 710
Excellent 605
Exertion 515
Explosion 515–20
Eyre, George 367, 637

Fabian, Charles Montagu 726
Fahie, William Charles 452, 684, 685, 691
Fairfax, William George 231, 269, 278, 473, 528, 544, 587
Fancourt, Robert Devereux 468
Fane, Francis William 125
Fanshawe, Robert 604
Farquhar, Arthur 723
Farrel, John 157, 158
Farrier, John 261
Faulkner, Jonathan 57, 440
Fayerman, Francis 63, 210
Fellowes, Edward 492
Ferara, Antony 366
Ferrier, John 122, 283, 695
Ferrieres, Isaac 427
Ferris, Able 179
Ferris, Solomon 373, 608
Ferris, Thomas 511
Ferris, William 116, 288
Fice, Thomas 402
Field, Robert 412
Fielding, Charles 608, 637
Fielding, Richard 375
Fighting 667
Finn, Richard 181
Fiott, William Edward 676–84
Fisher, Richard 440
Fitch, Joseph Henry 665
Fitzgerald, Charles 229
Fitzroy, Augustus 204
Fitzroy, William 684
Fitzwilliam, Robert Frederick 735
Flanigan, James 149
Flaxman, James 635
Fly 384
Foley, Andrew 317
Foley, Thomas 50, 119, 353, 528, 692
Folville, Samuel 354
Foot, Charles 677
Foote, Edward James 33, 171, 373
Forbes, Robert 249
Forbett, Duncan 646
Forrest, Thomas 726
Forster, Conrad 736
Forster, Samuel Peter 581
Fort Diamond 507–14
Fort Royal Bay, Martinique 309, 361, 566, 568, 605
Foss, Joseph 399
Foster, Joseph 330
Foudroyant 622, 623, 624, 625, 626, 627
Fountain, Joseph 161, 162
Fowke, George 171, 179, 215
Fowler, Benjamin 540
Fowler, William 223
Franchise 161
Franson, Derk 190
Fraser, Alexander 420
Fraser, Perry 57
Frederick, Thomas Lenox 31, 50, 353
Fremantle, Thomas Francis 158, 161, 215, 340, 341
Fudge, Edward 485
Furious 374, 376, 377
Fury 74–5

Gaff, Richard 277

Gage, William Hall 167, 223
Gaite 78
Galatea 92, 93, 427, 507
Galbraith, George 245
Gallagher, John 505
Galway, Edward 288
Gambier, James 560
Gardner, Alan 269
Gardner, Alan Hyde 93, 99, 327, 448, 637
Gardner, The Honble Francis Farrington 106, 488
Gardner, Samuel 700
Garth, Thomas 723
Gaunt, James 645
George, Daniel 586
Gibbs, John 645
Gibraltar 615
Gifford, John 157
Gilbert, Joseph 284, 285
Gill, Charles 692
Gill, James 276
Gill, Patrick 179, 183, 184, 186, 187
Gillespie, Robert 168, 170
Gilmore, Alexander 174
Gilmore, Andrew 257, 258, 268
Gladiator 155, 171, 193, 198, 215, 294, 295, 327, 379, 381, 382, 420, 436, 627, 649
Glascock, William 409
Glatton 231, 232
Glover, Henry 620
Glynn, Henry Richard 288
Goddard, Stephen Godfrey 672
Goddard, William 69
Goley, Michael 412
Gomm, James 76–7
Goodall, Samuel Granston 454
Goodridge, John 200
Goodwilly, Richard 694
Goodwin, George 376
Gordon, Alexander 712
Gordon, Charles 677
Gordon, James Alexander 664
Gore, Sir John 31, 288, 289, 628, 684
Goselin, Thomas Leeth 309
Gosselin, Thomas Le Marchand 436
Goude, Joseph 720
Gould, Davidge 479, 488
Gower, Erasmus 229
Grace, James 172
Graeme, Alexander 544
Graham, Andrew 707–12
Graham, Edwards D. 641
Graham, Edwards L. 649
Graham, James 69
Graham, Thomas 399
Granger, William 684
Grant, Charles 134, 138, 141, 223
Grant, George 269
Grant, Gregory 167
Grant, Thomas 205
Graves, Thomas 93, 99, 105, 278, 604
Gray, Francis 399
Green, Thomas 162, 163, 165
Grey, Sir George 50 349, 567
Grey, York George 294
Gridall, Richard 42, 412
Griffith, Edward 692, 712
Griffiths, Anselm John 116, 288
Griffon 699
Grindall, Richard 327, 528
Groundwater, Magnus 179 186
Gunnell, John 642, 654

Hagarly, William 132
Hailey, John 176
Halifax Harbour, Nova Scotia 552, 557, 712
Hall, George 30
Hall, Henry John 449
Hall, John 34
Hall, John Stephen 468
Hall, Joseph 386
Hall, Justice 163, 165
Hall, Miles 181
Hall, Robert 193, 400, 404, 520, 718, 726
Hallahan, William 625
Halliday, John 125, 171, 637
Hallowell, Sir Benjamin 31, 50, 448, 454, 742
Halsted, John 122
Hamilton, Sir Charles 179, 215, 294, 380, 528, 536
Hamilton, Charles Powel 205, 229, 544
Hammick, John Love 163
Hammick, Stephen Love 241
Hamoaze, Plymouth 93, 99, 116, 120, 125, 142, 179, 237, 249, 257, 288, 335, 400, 404, 406, 407, 412, 419, 420, 479, 488, 520, 623, 637, 641, 666, 717, 726, 737, 742
Hampden 455
Hamphatrite 178
Hanchet, John Martin 171
Hancock, John 723
Hancock, William 268
Hanlin, Andrew 611
Hannay, Peter 225
Hannibal 221, 367, 492, 576, 580
Hanwell, Joseph 632
Harding, William 296
Hardinge, George Nicholas 628

Hardy, James 294, 373, 608
Hardy, John 270, 271, 272
Hardy, John Oakes 42, 70, 193
Hardy, Temple 492
Hardy, The Honble Thomas Masterman 283, 335, 373, 448, 538, 666, 684
Harford, John 528–37
Hargood, William 210, 436, 441
Harland, John 391
Harper, Robert 61
Harris, Edward 650
Harris, George 249
Harris, James 518
Harris, John 352
Harris, Thomas 134, 135, 136, 671
Harris, William 313
Harrison, John 313
Harrison, Nicholas 427
Harrogan, Thomas 483
Hart, George 468, 514
Hartwell, Francis John 560
Harvey, Eliab 52, 215, 294, 567
Harvey, Henry 30, 54, 277, 361, 587
Harvey, John 63, 384
Harvey, Thomas 157, 309, 361
Hatsted, John 695
Haviland, Henry Hone 50–52
Hawker, Edward 171, 732
Hawker, Thomas 179
Hawkins, Richard 637
Hayerman, Francis 420
Hayes, John 452, 743
Hayman, William 547
Hayward, Richard 646
Hazlehurst, John 189
Hearn, Thomas 179, 182
Heathcote, Gilbert 400, 408, 738
Heathcote, Henry 120, 121, 155, 193, 408, 507
Hebrus 391
Helicon 737
Heligoland 123, 514, 515
Heligoland Roads 517
Hellard, Samuel 452
Hemmett, Thomas 86, 89
Henderson, David 632
Henderson, Robert 654
Henry, John 349, 560, 567
Herbert, Charles 179
Hercule 79–86, 89, 377, 607, 608
Hermione 152, 153, 170, 294, 295, 302, 573, 574, 576, 577, 578, 579
Hero 637
Heron, Thomas 546
Hewitt, William 337, 668
Heynwood, Peter 459
Heywood, Edmund 703, 708
Hibbs, Robert John 265
Hibernia 134, 137, 139, 141, 222
Hickman, Isaac 571
Hicks, John 694
Higgins, Robert 715
Higginson, George Montague 520, 521, 526
Hill, Henry 193, 628
Hill, William 80, 387
Hillyar, James 157, 400, 404, 743
Hind 560
Hodgson, Brian 384
Holbrook, Thomas 748
Holland, James 323
Holloway, John 31, 63, 155, 215, 294, 327, 454
Holson, Aaron 251
homicide 229–56
Hood, Samuel 50
Hooper, George 159
Hope 171, 172, 173, 175, 176, 177, 178
Hope, George 193
Hope, Henry 200
Horridge, Thomas 728
Horsley, Richard 464
Hosie, William 196
Hoste, William 380
Hotham, Henry 666, 712
Hotham, William 454
Howel, Michael 53
Howell, George 66
Hoy, Robert 274
Hubbard, Thomas 327, 334
Hughes, Alford 278
Humphries, George 618
Hungerford, Emmanuel 560
Hunt, Anthony 412
Hunt, Edward 363
Hunt, James 63
Hunt, Paul 131, 132
Hunter 500, 501, 504, 505, 506, 507
Hunter, John 300
Hurrill, Richard 158
Huson, John 310, 311
Hyde, John 387
Hydra 78
Hynes, George 327, 334

Impregnable 400, 404
Indefatigable 412
infamous behaviour 107
Inflexible 661
Inglefield, John Nicholas 30
Inglefield, Samuel Hood 161, 500
insanity 130

Insolent 93
Invincible 69, 309, 310
Iris 457
Irvin, William 706
Irwin, John 193, 380, 436, 628, 649
Isis 231, 232, 235, 538, 611
Isle Dieu 105
Isle of France 120, 121

Jackson, George 729
Jackson, Robert 379, 743
Jackson, Samuel 391, 649
Jacob, James Gledstances 127, 129, 130
Jacobs, John 361
Jacobs, William 548
James, Bartholomew 352
Jefferies, Sampson 580, 582, 583
Jefferson, John 143
Jenking, Michael 349
Jenkins, Henry 52
Jerratt, John 223
Jervis, John 194, 349, 567
Jervis, William Henry 155
Jessip, Thomas Freeman 427
Jeune, John 646
Johns, William 43, 414
Johnson, Robert 595
Johnson, William 70, 706
Johnston, Alexander 731–7
Johnston, James 120
Johnstone, Arthur 137
Johnstone, Rob 394
Johnstone, William 165
Jones, David 71–2
Jones, Henry 98
Jones, Jacob 385
Jones, John 294
Jones, Nathaniel Charles 78
Jones, Richard 641, 654
Jones, Theophilus 63, 204, 269, 479
Jones, Thomas 30
Jones, William 71
Jordan, John 718
Judge Advocate 23, 25, 26, 27, 70

Keal, Henry 86
Keats, Richard Goodwin 57, 479, 615, 732
Keiler, John 607
Keith, George 472, 477
Kell, John 232
Kelly, John 576
Kelly, Shoubel 581, 582
Kelly, William Hancock 29, 615
Kempthorne, William 732
Kennedy, John 709
Kent, John 560
Kent, William 684
Kerr, John 62, 69
Kinder, William 125, 126, 130
King, Andrew 116, 384
King, John 517
King, Sir Richard 222, 288
King, Richard 137, 141
King, William 624
Kinner, George 207
Kite 121, 122
Knight, John 31, 278, 454
Knight, Joseph 107
Knight, William 238
Knight, William Bolton 391
Knowles, Charles Henry 50

La Conception 200, 202
La Determinee 538
La Fleche 31
La Hogue 712
La Magicienne 579
La Minerve 356
La Nouville Entreprize 200
La Roche, Christopher 492, 581
Laforey, Francis 210, 380, 529
L'Aimable 123, 632
Lake, Willoughby Thomas 93, 99, 125
L'Amaranthe 492–500
Lamb, William 236
Lambert, Henry 654
Lambert, Robert 592
Lambeth 76
Lancaster 189
Lance, James 374
Lapenotiere, J.R. 336
Larcoin, Joseph 294
Larcom, Joseph 70
Larcom, Thomas 189
Larkan, Robert 63
Laugharne, John 436, 649
Lawford, John 93, 99, 468, 684
Lawson, David 155–7
Layton, Frederick 131, 132
Le Conquerante 75
Le Geyt, George 500, 649
Le Nerve, Peter Anselm 448
Le Tonnant 100
Leaper, William 734
Learson, William 35, 37
Leary, Cornelius 438
Lechmere, Charles 405
Lechmere, William 42, 63
Leda 608
Lee 738, 739, 740, 741, 742
Lee, John 189
Lee, Thomas 379

Lee, William 136
Leeworthy, Henry 739
Legal, Jean 104, 106
Legge, Arthur Kaye 42
Leghorn 31, 353, 358, 359
Lennard, William 630
Leopard 560
L'Espoir 579
Lewis, Drury Thomas 579
Lewis, James 472
Lewis, Robert 304
Lewis, Thomas 463
Liddel, Robert 93, 99, 488, 622
Lidden, Matthew 717
Lilley, Joseph 338
Lily 162, 163
Lincoln's Inn Fields 143
Linzee, Robert 31, 353
Linzee, Samuel Hood 125, 189, 592, 684
Little Hampton Harbour 381
Little, William 479–87
Livingstone, Sir Thomas 608
Lloyd, David 742
Lobb, William Granville 538
Locust 608, 610, 611, 612, 615
Logan, William 57
Loney, Peter 269, 270
Long, Henry 557
Long, James 704
Long, John 566
Lonis, George 641
Loring, John 215, 479, 582, 586, 637
Loring, John Wentworth 193
Losack, George 436
loss of ship 99–106, 492–527
Louis, Thomas 479
Lovington, John 132
Lowbridge, Thomas 133
Lowe, Richard 610
Lowenstoffe 27
Luke, Robert 365
Lukin, William 63, 215, 294
Lumsdaine, George 441, 454–9
Lurchin, Thomas 740
Lutin 36–7
Lutwidge, Henry Thomas 408
Lutwidge, Skeffington 454
Lyal, Alexander 742–51
Lye, William Jones 677
Lymington 74
Lynn, John 365
Lyons, Alexander 305

Maccraken, William 399
Macdaniel, Jeremiah 393
Mack, Thomas 57
Mackenzie, Adam 692
Mackenzie, George C 692
Macmanoes, Terrence 692–5
Macnamara, James 215
Madden, Daniel 284
Madras 55
Madras Roads 676
Magnanime 183, 186, 641, 642, 653
Maidstone 367, 368, 369, 370, 375, 712, 713, 714, 715, 716, 717
Mainwaring, Jemmett 215
Mainwaring, Thomas Francis Charles 141
Maitland, Charles 94
Maitland, Frederick Lewis 538, 608
Maitland, John 722, 723
Majestic 447, 448, 449, 514, 632
Malbon, Micajah 538, 622, 628
Malcolm, Charles 116, 404
Malcolm, Pultney 125
Maling, Thomas James 436
Maloney, John 356
Malpass, Henry Potter 626
Malta 138
Man, Robert 31
Manby, Thomas 155, 380
Manley, John 42, 440
Mansell, Joseph 572
Mansfield, Charles John Moore 420
Marco, Antonio 572
Mark, Anthony 572
Mars 685
Marsdin, Henry Tom 616
Marsh, William 564
Marshall, George 107, 628
Marshall, Robert 305
Martin, George 42, 412
Martin, John Owen 663
Martin, T.W. 142
Martin, Thomas 368
Martin, Sir Thomas Byam 179, 520, 726, 742
Martinique 604
Martyn, Charles 144
Mason, Christopher 440, 441
Mason, Francis 459
Mason, John 576, 579
Mason, William 249–56
Massey, Antonio 719, 721
Matson, Richard 309
Matthews, James 662
Matthews, John 454
Maude, John 560
Maugham, John 132
Maundrell, Richard 544
Maurrin, John 418
Mawdesly, Othuel 345

Maxwell, Murray 637
Maya, James 102
McArthur, Daniel 650
McCarthy, John 249–56
McCrenon, Hugh 737–42
McCulloch, William 741
McCullock, Andrew 541
McCullock, James 53
McCullum, William 406
McDonald, Alexander 332
McDouall, Edward 657
McDouall, John 281
McDougall, John 479
McDousal, John 524
McGrath, John 658
McIntosh, James 215
McKenzie, George Charles 167
McKenzie, Kenneth 507
McKenzie, Sinclair Collin 611
McKinley, George 116, 288
McKinley, John 367
McLaren, Alexander
McLaughlin, John 34, 38
McLear, Daniel 432
McMaster, William 309
McMillan, Angus 57
McSharry, Patrick 418
Meares, James 421
Medley, William 397
Megson, Francis 257
Meldrum, Alexander 712–17
Melville 427
Melville, Peter 329
Mends, Robert 52
Mercury 211, 212, 214
Meredith, James 131, 132
Mermaid 455
Merope 116, 117, 120
Merrifield, John 290
Middleman, Robert Gambier 31
Midgley, William 77
Milford 341, 345
Miller, John 540
Mills, Robert 307
Milne, Alexander 680
Milne, Robert 83
Milner, James 362
Minds, Robert 149
Minerva 528, 529, 530, 531, 532, 536, 581, 582, 583, 584, 585
Mitchell, Andrew 277, 544, 587
Mitchell, Duncan Forbes 569
Mitchell, James 250
Mitford, Henry 54
Mole St Nicholas Island, St Domingo 463
Monarch 467
Monkton, John 327
Monmouth 122, 692, 698
Montagu, Charles 400
Montagu, Robert 204, 210, 268
Montague, William Augustus 249
Montevideo 459
Montgomery, Augustus 479
Moon, John 695–8
Moore, Sir Graham 93, 99, 387, 742, 698
Moore, Mark 204, 205
Moore, Nathaniel 735
Moore, Thomas 561
Moral, John 440
Morgan, John 206, 423
Morgan, Patrick 34, 37
Moriority, James R. 131, 132
Morison, William 440
Morris, George 378
Morsley, George 53
Mortimer, George 80
Mose, John 436
Mose, Samuel 30
Mosquito 703, 704, 705, 706
Mosse, James Robert 441, 468, 560
Moubray, Richard Hussey 134, 664
Mowat, Henry 34, 205
Mudge, Zachary 335, 666
Mulholland, John 571
Mulock, Joshua 57
Mundy, George 538
Munn, Aaron 699
Murphy, Stephen 566
Murray, George 459, 528
Murray, John 233, 236, 380, 615
Murray, Robert 70, 552
Murray, William 68, 310
Mustard, William 608
mutinous expressions 86, 440–44
mutiny 412–40, 667, 723
Myrtle 143

Nagle, Edmund 441
Namur 654, 722
Nancy 205, 206, 207, 208, 210
Naples, Italy 356
Nash, James 116, 125, 288, 408, 738, 742
Nash, John 605
Nazer, Kelly 716
Neale, Sir Harry 528
Negapalnam Roads 314
negligence 93, 479–91, 663, 712, 743
Nelson, Horatio 30–31, 356
Nelson, Thomas 294
Nemesis 156, 157
Nepean, Evan 33, 40–41, 74, 77, 155

Neptune 79, 158, 157, 161, 223, 224, 225, 226, 227, 373, 537
Nereide 459, 462
Netherwood, William 117
Newcombe, Francis 400, 404, 726
Newell, George 581, 582
Newman, James Newman 106, 179, 384
Newman, William 300
Nicholes, Joseph 391
Nicholls, James 431
Nicholls, Kelly Henry 268
Nicolls, Edward 132
Nieman 126, 127, 128, 129, 130
Niger 33
Nightingale 708, 709, 710
Niven, William James 594
Nops, John George 537–43
Nore 440
Northesk, Rt Honble William Earl of 155, 157, 278, 587
Northumberland 427
Norton, Richmond 189
Nowell, William 699
Nugent, Charles Edmond 205, 544, 567
Nugent, Charles Edward 229
Nymphen 699

Oake, John 74–5
O'Brien, Edward 479
O'Brien, William 268
O'Bryen, Edward 507, 615
O'Bryen, Rt Honble James 604, 726
Ogle, Charles 63, 157, 792
Ogleby, William 724
Older, Edward 33
Oliver, Robert Dudley 171, 193, 692, 699
Ommanney, John Acworth 628
Orde, John 229, 440
Orestes 335, 336, 337, 338, 339, 666, 667, 668, 670, 671, 672, 676
Orpheus 193
Orr, John 371
Orrok, Thomas Archibald 30
Osborn, John 189, 412
Osborn, Richard 427
Otway, Robert Waller 278, 488, 581
Owen, Edward William Campbell Rich 122, 692, 895
Owen, Lloyd 253
Owen, William 306
Oxbrough, William 472,

Packenham, Thomas 544
Page, William 620
Paget, Charles 374, 622
Paige, Benjamin William 171
Paignton Hospital 85
Palermo Bay 340
Palfreman, John 600
Parish, John 50, 718
Parkenham, Thomas 229
Parker, Christopher 229
Parker, Corthine 459–63
Parker, George 171, 327, 479, 641, 653
Parker, Sir Hyde 53, 122, 353, 454, 572, 581, 692, 695, 712
Parker, Peter 30, 211, 229, 367
Parker, Robert 463
Parker, William 30, 538
Parkinson, John 519
Parr, Thomas 463
Parry, Daniel 576
Parry, Francis 229, 544
Parthian 238, 241, 243, 245, 246, 247, 248
Pasley, Thomas 30
Pater, Dudley 178
Paterson, Charles William 528
Paterson, William 408
Patterson, John 443
Patton, Edward 257
Paul, Thomas 42
Paulet, Lord Henry 327
Payne, John 370
Payne, John Willett 211
Peacocke, Richard 538, 637
Peard, Shuldam 50
Pechell, Samuel John 712
Pegasus 204
Pelican 87, 89
Pellew, Edward 135, 138, 141, 341, 412
Pellew, Israel 70, 134, 137, 141, 222, 412, 441, 552, 622, 637
Pelly, Charles 677, 678, 684
Penguin 377, 378, 379
Pennelope, James Padgett 178
Penrose, Charles Vinicombe 149
Perkins, William 34
Peter, Samuel 367
Peterel 446
Petit Mont 104
Peyton, Thomas 204
Pheasant 552
Phillip, Arthur 412
Philomel 223, 225, 226, 227
Philpot, Samuel 180
Pickmore, Francis 63, 134, 141, 204, 210, 215, 222, 294, 327
Pickmore, James 137
Pierce, Robert 36
Pierpoint, William 57
Pigley, Charles 197
Pigmy 520–27

Pigot, Hugh 427
Pigot, James 30
Pike, Abraham 683
Pike, Samuel 167
Pimins, Hro[t] 132
Pimmins, Samuel 133
Pinnegar, David 289
Pitt, Charles 723
Plampin, Robert 134, 137, 223
Plunder 179–88
Plymouth 116, 126, 248, 268, 731
Plymouth Dock 489
Plymouth Sound 157, 336, 407
Point le Marie 104
Pole, C.M. 269
Pole, Charles Morice 268, 454
Pole, W.W. 380
Pollard, Charles 172
Polsom, William 133
Polyphemus 161, 162, 163, 166
Pomona 207
Ponsonby, Anthony 350
Porcupine 200, 202, 257, 258, 261, 268
Port, George Roe 563
Port Louis, Isle of France 121
Port Mahon 134, 137, 140, 141, 222
Port Royal Harbour, Jamaica 86, 106, 149, 161, 367, 368, 377, 492, 500, 580
Portia 723, 724, 725
Portsmouth 210, 365, 366
Portsmouth Harbour 155, 171, 193, 199, 204, 210, 215, 229, 294, 327, 373, 379 420, 436, 537, 607, 631, 649
Poulden, Richard 282
Poulett, George 335, 654, 666
Powdrill, Samuel 30
Powell, James 48
Powell, Robert 412, 415, 417
Powlett, Henry 349, 567
Prescott, Henry 520
Preston, D'Arcy 356, 520
Preston, Robert 452
Prideaux, Robert 165
Pridham, William 619
Priest, Joseph 490, 491, 673
Prince of Wales 141
Prince, Richard 212
Princess Charlotte 107
Princess of Orange 383
Princess Royal 622
Pring, Robert 283
Probert, Richard 231
Prouse, William 215
Prowse, William 93, 99, 167, 693
Pryce, Henry 401
Puddicembre, Peter 132
Puget, Peter 488
Pugh, Pryce 705
Puissant 294, 380
Purnell, Thomas 663–6
Purvis, John Child 278, 353, 454, 528
Pym, Samuel 106, 125

Quamin 500–507
quarrelling 667
Quebec 493, 514, 654
Queen 368, 565, 575, 579, 581
Queen of Sicily 141
Quiberon Bay 100, 101, 103
Quilliam, John 238
Quinn, John 671

Raggett, Richard 122, 387, 695, 699, 742
Raigersfeld, Jeffery 742
Rainer, J.S. 692
Rainer, John Sprat 167
Rainer, Peter 30, 314
Raisonnable 702, 703, 707, 708
Ramsay, Joseph 467–78
Raper, Henry 692
Rathborne, Wilson 500, 622
Ratsey, Thomas 463–7
Raven, Michael 115
Read, George 67–9
Read, W.H. 27
Reding, Edward 168
Redmill, Robert 294
Reed, Joseph 368, 371
Reeve, John 425
Reeve, Samuel 31, 268, 454
Reid, James 710
Reigs, Clements 191
Renelagh, Viscount 179
Renou, Adrian 309
Renwick, Thomas 703, 708
reproachful speeches 107
Repulse 223
Resolute 650, 652, 653
Resolution 560
Retalick, Richard 356
Reunion 221
Reynolds, John 488
Reynolds, Major 407, 736
Reynolds, Robert Carthew 57, 179, 412
Rhin 116, 117, 119, 120
Rich, Edward 384
Richard, James 544
Richards, David 222–8
Richards, James 96, 104
Richards, John 641
Richardson, Charles 684
Ricketts, Tristram Roberts 726, 738

Riddle, Thomas 461
Rinker, Charles 131
Riou, Reynolds Edward 294
Roach, David 427
Roach, John 87, 88
Robbins, Thomas 285
Roberts, David 251
Roberts, John 602
Roberts, William 500
Robins, Thomas Lawton 64–6
Robinson, Charles 391
Robinson, John 59, 469
Robinson, William 195
Robinson, William Henry 131
Robley, Lewis 131
Robson, William 171, 177
Rochford 101
Rodney, Edward 654
Rodney, John 566
Roebottom, Richard 283, 285
Roebuck 447
Rogers, Richard 612, 613
Rogers, Thomas 211, 637
Rolfe, John 29–30
Rolles, Douglas Robert 223
Rolles, Robert 134, 137, 141, 492, 692
Rolls, Stephen 249–56
Romney 35, 37, 38, 39
Roscow, Samuel 472, 475
Rose 31, 33
Rose, James 302
Roseau Bay, St Lucia 507
Rosenhagan, Philip 664
Ross, Daniel 85
Ross, David 626
Ross, George 149
Ross, James 55, 362, 644
Rostock 387
Rota 738
Rotheram, Edward 637
Rotherford, Thomas 35
Row, Robert 118
Rowe, Joshua Latimer 123
Rowland, John 691
Rowley, Bartholomew Samuel 161, 162
Rowley, Charles 157
Rowley, Josias 134, 137, 141, 726
Rowley, Samuel Campbell 408
Roy, Daniel 33
Royal George 277, 278
Royal Sovereign 269, 277, 282, 587
Royal William 294, 300, 302, 364, 365, 544
Rozier, James 235
Ruby 392, 393, 395, 397
Runthwaite, John 582, 585
Runy, James 418
Russel, Thomas M. 278, 361, 587
Russell 592, 593, 594, 600, 602
Russell, Thomas Macnamara 55, 278
Rutherford, William Gordon 52, 155, 157, 492
Ryan, John 207
Ryan, Patrick 229
Ryan, William 263
Ryves, George Frederick 615

Saint George 106, 107, 327, 330, 332, 334, 335, 437, 438, 440, 742
Saint Johns, Newfoundland 731, 732
Saint Sodora 76
Salter, Robert 254
Salvador del Mundo 93, 99, 116, 120, 125, 142, 237, 238, 249, 288, 335, 488, 489, 490, 491, 520, 622, 637, 666, 672, 717, 726
Sanderson, Forster William 367
Sandwich 440
Santa Margarita 567
Sartorius, George Rose 408, 718
Saturn 179, 238, 269
Saumarez, James 204, 269
Saurin, Edward 171
Sawyer, Herbert 131, 231, 622
Saxmundham 124
Saxon, Thomas 693
Sayer, George 427
Scaby, James 130
Scamander 408
scandalous behaviour 107
Scantling, James 339
Scarth, William 345
Schomberg, Alexander Wilmot 400, 404, 408, 726, 737
Schomberg, Charles Marsh 120, 616
Schultz, George Augustus 246
Scobell, Edward 114
Scorpion 352, 560, 561, 565, 566
Scott, George 380
Scott, Matthew Henry 238, 692
Scott, Robert 380
Scourge 441, 442, 443, 444, 445
Scriven, John 607
Seagrove, John 733
Seal, William 575
Searle, Charles Clark 327
Searle, John Clarke 538
Seater, John 70, 552
sedition 86, 447–53
seditious expressions 667
Seine 427, 435
Selby, William 193

Serrell, John 161, 335, 666
Seymonds, James 447–51
Seymour, Hugh 149, 229
Seymour, Michael 116, 126, 171, 436
Seymour, Rodd Michael 238
Shark 166, 304, 305, 306, 307
Sharpless, John 593
Sharps, Reuben 306
Shaw, John 160, 393
Sheerness Harbour 78, 641, 642, 643, 653, 702, 707, 722
Sheldrake, Esau 686
Sheppard, Edward 230
Sheppard, Samuel 693
Sheraton, Thomas 358
Sherman, Henry 132
Sherwood, John 340
Shield, William 32
Shirreff, William Henry 161, 162
Shortland, John Thomas 738
Sickmore, Francis 420
Sidney, Joseph 294
Simmonds, John 283, 284, 285
Simpson, Jacob 698–702
Sims, Charles 49
Sims, Woodford 93–9, 106
Sincere 32
Sittingbourne 375
Skedel, John 732
Skene, Alexander 608
Skipsey, William 615, 712
Slade, George 460
Slade, James 726
Slaney 408
Smellie, Alexander 378
Smith, Charles Thurlow 141
Smith, Edward 229
Smith, Edward Tyrrel 52, 149, 367, 492, 581
Smith, Henry 652
Smith, James 237–48, 688
Smith, John 121
Smith, Matthew 408, 738
Smith, Robert 367, 724
Smith, Samuel 337, 353
Smith, Thomas 321
Smith, William 207, 311, 409, 656
Smith, Sir William Sidney 63, 134, 135, 137, 138, 141, 222, 441
Smyth, Thomas 238
Snap 521
Snape, John 243
Snipe 642, 643
Somerville, Philip 155, 288
Sonnerat, Thomas 389
Sophie 74
Sorlings 380, 381, 382
Sotheby, Thomas 353
Sothoron, Frank 34, 42
South Foreland 746
Southby, Thomas 50
Southcott, John 670
Sparkes, John Hindes 529
Sparks, James 693
Speed, John Henry 381
Speedy 356, 357, 359, 360, 361
Spence, David 457
Spencer 302
Spinney, John 587
Spitfire 654, 663
Spithead 170, 171, 178, 349, 376, 377, 440, 544
Sproule, Andrew 380
Spurry, John 443
Squirrel 445
St Albans 70, 376
St Domingo 573
St Fiorenzo Bay 353
St George 27, 29, 536
St Helens 33
St John's Harbour, Newfoundland 34
Stap, William 441
Stately 229, 641
Statira 335, 666
Stenhouse, William 290
Stephens, Matthew 74
Stevens, John 177
Stevens, Thomas 355
Stevenson, James 63
Steventon, Thomas 238
Stewart, Edward H. 131, 132
Stewart, John 664
Stiles, John 193, 538, 608
Stirling, Charles 204
Stoddart, Thomas 194
Stokes, H.M. 57, 179, 412, 479
Stone, Charles 279
Stopford, Robert 42, 120, 237, 605
Strachan, Richard 608
Strachan, Sir Richard John 211, 373, 420, 604, 742
Strees, Samuel 133
striking a superior officer 86, 87, 126, 257–83, 727
Stuart, Lord George 123, 514
Stuart, James 283, 284, 285
Sturdy, Jonathan 210–15
Styles, John 42
Suare, Naiad 427–36
Success 170, 576
Surprize 150
Sutherland, Andrew 268

Sutton, John 99, 237, 327, 335, 420, 488, 666
Sutton, Robert Manners 454
Sutton, Samuel 283
Swatfield, William 231
swearing 85, 86
Swiftsure 464
Swithers, Jeremiah 230
Sykes, Edmond 286
Symes, Elias 156
Symmons, John 699

Table Bay 189
Tagus River 536, 684, 685
Tailour, John 404
Tait, Thomas 157
Talbot, John 294, 712
Tarney, Patrick 34
Tatham, Sanford 349
Taylor, Benjamin 162
Taylor, George 601
Taylor, John 713
Taylor, Thomas 451–3
Taylor, William 179, 442, 447, 528
Teague, William 634
Tealsted, Lawrence William 420
Teaser 63, 67
The Downes 122, 231, 283, 383, 384
The Texel 467
Theft 189–204
Theseus 86, 87, 167, 479, 500, 505
Thomas, James 623, 627
Thomas, John 204, 488–91
Thomas, Richard 157
Thomas, Simon 132
Thombrough, Edward 269
Thompson, Charles 349, 566
Thompson, John 175,
Thompson, Norborn 138, 141
Thompson, Norborne 114, 607
Thompson, William 85
Thornborough, Edward 587
Thornbrough, Edward 200, 278
Three Brothers 190, 192
Thunderer 581, 582
Tiber 408, 409, 410
Tickler 76, 77
Tigress 215, 216, 217, 218, 219, 220
Tillford, Robert 353
Tindall, William 472, 474
Tisiphone 454, 455
Tobin, George 288, 520
Todd, William 30
Tode, Edward James 215
Toker, Thomas Richard 703, 708
Tomkinson, James 703
Tonnant 94, 288, 289, 290, 292, 391, 392
Torbay 79, 277, 278, 282, 361, 587, 592, 593
Totty, Thomas 179, 269, 327, 361, 463, 587, 592, 593
Toulon 454
Tourey, George Henry 210
Tourney, Jean 121, 122
Touzeau, Charles 84
Tracey, John Smith 278, 587
Trelore, John 422
Tremayne, John 238
Tremendous 42, 135, 189, 191
Tremlett, William Henry Brown 215
Trevor, Henry 603
Trident 200, 313, 314, 663, 664
Tripp, George 69, 463
Trollope, Henry 210, 231, 232, 269, 278
Troth, William 374
Troubridge, Thomas 50
Tuckerman, John 490
Turnbull, Cornelius 445
Twysden, Thomas 57
Tye, Hugh 606
Tyler, Charles 210, 294, 592, 649

Ulysses 727, 728, 729, 730, 731
Unite 138, 139, 140, 141, 309
ungentlemanly conduct 79
unofficerlike conduct 142, 528–43, 663, 712
Upton Clotsworthy 116, 238, 288 632

Valiant 574, 575, 579
Valletta, Malta 200, 615, 663, 664
Vandeput, George 70, 552
Vansitart, Henry 149
Vansittart, Henry 377
Varlo, George 131, 132
Vashon, James 278, 654
Veale, Moses 461
Vengeance 349, 566, 567, 568, 569
Venus 604
Vesey, Francis 581
Victorious 314
Victory 536, 611
Vidal, Emeric [?] Essex 387
Vigo 137, 387
Ville de Paris 79, 743
Vincent, Richard Btrd 178, 200
Volage 553, 664, 665
Voltiguer 179, 182, 183, 182, 185, 186, 187, 188
Vosper, William 356

Waaksamheid 69

Wade, James 128
Wainwright, John 392, 398, 628, 649
Wair, Peter 412
Waldgrave, The Honble William 50, 353
Walker, Henry 131
Walker, James 122, 380, 695
Walker, Thomas 401, 402
Walker, William 31, 33
Wallace, James 34, 35
Wallas, Joshua 659
Walling, Peter 445
Wallis, Christopher 516
Wallis, James 294, 488
Wanderer 515, 743, 744, 745, 746, 747, 748, 750, 751
Ware, John 313, 318
Warren, Frederick 340, 718
Warren, John 85
Warren, John Borlase 269, 712
Warren, Samuel 120, 448
Waterford 257
Watkins, Frederick 179
Watson, Francis 257
Watson, John 686
Watson, Joshua Rowley 114, 452
Watson, Robert 232, 441, 447
Webber, Thomas 444
Webley, William Henry 738
Webster, Andrew 362
Weeks, William 220
Weir, Henry 400
Wells, Thomas 587
Wemyss, Francis 364
West, John 63
West, Thomas 560
Westcott, Benjamin 507
Western, Thomas 52, 309
Wharton, James 169
Wheatly, John 489
Wheeler, John 292, 726–31
Whitby, Henry 106, 377
White, John 167
White, John Chambers 726
White, Thomas 387
White, William 686
Whitehead, William Henry 449
Whitshed, Charles Hawkins 210
Whitshed, James Hawkins 269, 278
Whittle, Henry 744, 748
Whyte, Alexander 673
Wiley, Robert 128
Wilkinson, Phillip 693
Williams, Robert 373, 387, 608, 538
Williams, Sir Thomas 143, 420, 592, 684
Williams, Thomas 327, 684, 703, 708, 723
Willoughby, Nesbit Josiah 593
Wilmot, George 610, 611
Wilson, George 210, 361, 560
Wilson, Isaac 335
Wilson, John 216, 271
Wilson, William 189
Wodehouse, Henry Bowman 733
Wodehouse, Philip 356
Wolfe, George 538
Wolley, Thomas 528, 666, 672
Wood, James Athol 373, 452, 608
Wood, John 608
Woodriff, Daniel 628
Woodrough, Samuel 688
Woolcombe, Edwaed 507
Woolcombe, John C. 507
Wooldridge, William 171
Wooley, Thomas 544
Woolridge, William 665
Woolwich 130, 132
Wrexham 133
Wright, John 131
Wybourne 131
Wylie, Walter 46

Yarmouth Roads 170, 447, 514, 632
York 283, 407, 572, 737
Yorke, Joseph 649
Yorke, Joseph Sidney 42, 124, 215, 383, 384, 436
Young, Robert Benjamin 641
Young, William 197, 268, 641, 703

Zante 141
Zealous 440, 703, 708

NAVY RECORDS SOCIETY
(FOUNDED 1893)

The Navy Records Society was established for the purpose of printing unpublished manuscripts and rare works of naval interest. Membership of the Society is open to all who are interested in naval history, and any person wishing to become a member should apply to the Hon. Secretary, Robin Brodhurst, Pangbourne College, Pangbourne, Berks, RG8 8LA, United Kingdom. The annual subscription is £30, which entitles the member to receive one free copy of each work issued by the Society in that year, and to buy earlier issues at reduced prices.

A list of works, available to members only, is shown below; very few copies are left of those marked with an asterisk. Volumes out of print are indicated by **OP**. Prices for works in print are available on application to Mrs Annette Gould, 1 Avon Close, Petersfield, Hampshire, GU31 4LG, United Kingdom, to whom all enquiries concerning works in print should be sent. Those marked 'TS', 'SP' and 'A' are published for the Society by Temple Smith, Scolar Press and Ashgate, and are available to non-members from Ashgate Publishing Limited, Wey Court East, Union Road, Farnham, Surrey, GU9 7PT, United Kingdom. Those marked 'A & U' are published by George Allen & Unwin, and are available to non-members only through bookshops.

Vol. 1. *State papers relating to the Defeat of the Spanish Armada, Anno 1588*, Vol. I, ed. Professor J. K. Laughton. TS.

Vol. 2. *State papers relating to the Defeat of the Spanish Armada, Anno 1588*, Vol. II, ed. Professor J. K. Laughton. TS.

Vol. 3. *Letters of Lord Hood, 1781–1783*, ed. D. Hannay. **OP**.

Vol. 4. *Index to James's Naval History*, by C. G. Toogood, ed. by the Hon. T. A. Brassey. **OP**.

Vol. 5. *Life of Captain Stephen Martin, 1666–1740*, ed. Sir Clements R. Markham. **OP**.

Vol. 6. *Journal of Rear Admiral Bartholomew James, 1752–1828*, ed. Professor J. K. Laughton & Cdr. J. Y. F. Sullivan. **OP**.

Vol. 7. *Hollond's Discourses of the Navy, 1638 and 1659*, ed. J. R. Tanner. **OP**.

Vol. 8. *Naval Accounts and Inventories in the Reign of Henry VII*, ed. M. Oppenheim. **OP**.

Vol. 9. *Journal of Sir George Rooke*, ed. O. Browning. **OP**.

Vol. 10. *Letters and Papers relating to the War with France 1512–1513*, ed. M. Alfred Spont. **OP**.

Vol. 11. *Papers relating to the Spanish War 1585–1587*, ed. Julian S. Corbett. TS.

Vol. 12. *Journals and Letters of Admiral of the Fleet Sir Thomas Byam Martin, 1773–1854*, Vol. II (see No. 24), ed. Admiral Sir R. Vesey Hamilton. **OP**.

Vol. 13. *Papers relating to the First Dutch War, 1652–1654*, Vol. I, ed. Dr S. R. Gardiner. **OP**.

Vol. 14. *Papers relating to the Blockade of Brest, 1803–1805*, Vol. I, ed. J. Leyland. **OP**.

Vol. 15. *History of the Russian Fleet during the Reign of Peter the Great, by a Contemporary Englishman*, ed. Admiral Sir Cyprian Bridge. **OP**.

Vol. 16. *Logs of the Great Sea Fights, 1794–1805*, Vol. I, ed. Vice Admiral Sir T. Sturges Jackson. **OP**.

Vol. 17. *Papers relating to the First Dutch War, 1652–1654*, ed. Dr S. R. Gardiner. **OP**.

Vol. 18. *Logs of the Great Sea Fights*, Vol. II, ed. Vice Admiral Sir T. Sturges Jackson.

Vol. 19. *Journals and Letters of Admiral of the Fleet Sir Thomas Byam Martin*, Vol. II (see No. 24), ed. Admiral Sir R. Vesey Hamilton. **OP**.

Vol. 20. *The Naval Miscellany*, Vol. I, ed. Professor J. K. Laughton.

Vol. 21. *Papers relating to the Blockade of Brest, 1803–1805*, Vol. II, ed. J. Leyland. **OP**.

Vol. 22. *The Naval Tracts of Sir William Monson*, Vol. I, ed. M. Oppenheim. **OP**.

Vol. 23. *The Naval Tracts of Sir William Monson*, Vol. II, ed. M. Oppenheim. **OP**.

Vol. 24. *The Journals and Letters of Admiral of the Fleet Sir Thomas Byam Martin*, Vol. I, ed. Admiral Sir R. Vesey Hamilton.

Vol. 25. *Nelson and the Neapolitan Jacobins*, ed. H. C. Gutteridge. **OP**.

Vol. 26. *A Descriptive Catalogue of the Naval MSS in the Pepysian Library*, Vol. I, ed. J. R. Tanner. **OP**.

Vol. 27. *A Descriptive Catalogue of the Naval MSS in the Pepysian Library*, Vol. II, ed. J. R. Tanner. **OP**.

Vol. 28. *The Correspondence of Admiral John Markham, 1801–1807*, ed. Sir Clements R. Markham. **OP**.

Vol. 29. *Fighting Instructions, 1530–1816*, ed. Julian S. Corbett. **OP**.

Vol. 30. *Papers relating to the First Dutch War, 1652–1654*, Vol. III, ed. Dr S. R. Gardiner & C. T. Atkinson. **OP**.

Vol. 31. *The Recollections of Commander James Anthony Gardner, 1775–1814*, ed. Admiral Sir R. Vesey Hamilton & Professor J. K. Laughton.

Vol. 32. *Letters and Papers of Charles, Lord Barham, 1758–1813*, ed. Professor Sir John Laughton.

Vol. 33. *Naval Songs and Ballads*, ed. Professor C. H. Firth. **OP**.

Vol. 34. *Views of the Battles of the Third Dutch War*, ed. by Julian S. Corbett. **OP**.

Vol. 35. *Signals and Instructions, 1776–1794*, ed. Julian S. Corbett. **OP**.

Vol. 36. *A Descriptive Catalogue of the Naval MSS in the Pepysian Library*, Vol. III, ed. J. R. Tanner. **OP**.

Vol. 37. *Papers relating to the First Dutch War, 1652–1654*, Vol. IV, ed. C. T. Atkinson. **OP**.

Vol. 38. *Letters and Papers of Charles, Lord Barham, 1758–1813*, Vol. II, ed. Professor Sir John Laughton. **OP**.

Vol. 39. *Letters and Papers of Charles, Lord Barham, 1758–1813*, Vol. III, ed. Professor Sir John Laughton. **OP**.

Vol. 40. *The Naval Miscellany*, Vol. II, ed. Professor Sir John Laughton.

*Vol. 41. *Papers relating to the First Dutch War, 1652–1654*, Vol. V, ed. C. T. Atkinson.

Vol. 42. *Papers relating to the Loss of Minorca in 1756*, ed. Captain H. W. Richmond, R.N. **OP**.

*Vol. 43. *The Naval Tracts of Sir William Monson*, Vol. III, ed. M. Oppenheim.

Vol. 44. *The Old Scots Navy 1689–1710*, ed. James Grant. **OP**.

Vol. 45. *The Naval Tracts of Sir William Monson*, Vol. IV, ed. M. Oppenheim.

Vol. 46. *The Private Papers of George, 2nd Earl Spencer*, Vol. I, ed. Julian S. Corbett. **OP**.

Vol. 47. *The Naval Tracts of Sir William Monson*, Vol. V, ed. M. Oppenheim.

Vol. 48. *The Private Papers of George, 2nd Earl Spencer*, Vol. II, ed. Julian S. Corbett. **OP**.

Vol. 49. *Documents relating to Law and Custom of the Sea*, Vol. I, ed. R. G. Marsden. **OP**.

*Vol. 50. *Documents relating to Law and Custom of the Sea*, Vol. II, ed. R. G. Marsden. **OP**.

Vol. 51. *Autobiography of Phineas Pett*, ed. W. G. Perrin. **OP**.

Vol. 52. *The Life of Admiral Sir John Leake*, Vol. I, ed. Geoffrey Callender.

Vol. 53. *The Life of Admiral Sir John Leake*, Vol. II, ed. Geoffrey Callender.

Vol. 54. *The Life and Works of Sir Henry Mainwaring*, Vol. I, ed. G. E. Manwaring.

Vol. 55. *The Letters of Lord St Vincent, 1801–1804*, Vol. I, ed. D. B. Smith. **OP**.

Vol. 56. *The Life and Works of Sir Henry Mainwaring*, Vol. II, ed. G. E. Manwaring & W. G. Perrin. **OP**.

Vol. 57. *A Descriptive Catalogue of the Naval MSS in the Pepysian Library*, Vol. IV, ed. Dr J. R. Tanner. **OP**.

Vol. 58. *The Private Papers of George, 2nd Earl Spencer*, Vol. III, ed. Rear Admiral H. W. Richmond. **OP**.

Vol. 59. *The Private Papers of George, 2nd Earl Spencer*, Vol. IV, ed. Rear Admiral H. W. Richmond. **OP**.

Vol. 60. *Samuel Pepys's Naval Minutes*, ed. Dr J. R. Tanner.

Vol. 61. *The Letters of Lord St Vincent, 1801–1804*, Vol. II, ed. D. B. Smith. **OP**.

Vol. 62. *Letters and Papers of Admiral Viscount Keith*, Vol. I, ed. W. G. Perrin. **OP**.

Vol. 63. *The Naval Miscellany*, Vol. III, ed. W. G. Perrin. **OP**.

Vol. 64. *The Journal of the 1st Earl of Sandwich*, ed. R. C. Anderson. **OP**.

*Vol. 65. *Boteler's Dialogues*, ed. W. G. Perrin.

Vol. 66. *Papers relating to the First Dutch War, 1652–1654*, Vol. VI (with index), ed. C. T. Atkinson.

*Vol. 67. *The Byng Papers*, Vol. I, ed. W. C. B. Tunstall.

*Vol. 68. *The Byng Papers*, Vol. II, ed. W. C. B. Tunstall.

Vol. 69. *The Private Papers of John, Earl of Sandwich*, Vol. I, ed. G. R. Barnes & Lt. Cdr. J. H. Owen, R.N. Corrigenda to *Papers relating to the First Dutch War, 1652–1654, Vols I–VI*, ed. Captain A. C. Dewar, R.N. **OP**.

Vol. 70. *The Byng Papers*, Vol. III, ed. W. C. B. Tunstall.

Vol. 71. *The Private Papers of John, Earl of Sandwich*, Vol. II, ed. G. R. Barnes & Lt. Cdr. J. H. Owen, R.N. **OP**.

Vol. 72. *Piracy in the Levant, 1827–1828*, ed. Lt. Cdr. C. G. Pitcairn Jones, R.N. **OP**.

Vol. 73. *The Tangier Papers of Samuel Pepys*, ed. Edwin Chappell.

Vol. 74. *The Tomlinson Papers*, ed. J. G. Bullocke.

Vol. 75. *The Private Papers of John, Earl of Sandwich*, Vol. III, ed. G. R. Barnes & Cdr. J. H. Owen, R.N. **OP**.

Vol. 76. *The Letters of Robert Blake*, ed. the Rev. J. R. Powell. **OP**.
*Vol. 77. *Letters and Papers of Admiral the Hon. Samuel Barrington*, Vol. I, ed. D. Bonner-Smith.
Vol. 78. *The Private Papers of John, Earl of Sandwich*, Vol. IV, ed. G. R. Barnes & Cdr. J. H. Owen, R.N. **OP**.
*Vol. 79. *The Journals of Sir Thomas Allin, 1660–1678*, Vol. I *1660–1666*, ed. R. C. Anderson.
Vol. 80. *The Journals of Sir Thomas Allin, 1660–1678*, Vol. II *1667–1678*, ed. R. C. Anderson.
Vol. 81. *Letters and Papers of Admiral the Hon. Samuel Barrington*, Vol. II, ed. D. Bonner-Smith. **OP**.
Vol. 82. *Captain Boteler's Recollections, 1808–1830*, ed. D. Bonner-Smith. **OP**.
Vol. 83. *Russian War, 1854. Baltic and Black Sea: Official Correspondence*, ed. D. Bonner-Smith & Captain A. C. Dewar, R.N. **OP**.
Vol. 84. *Russian War, 1855. Baltic: Official Correspondence*, ed. D. Bonner-Smith. **OP**.
Vol. 85. *Russian War, 1855. Black Sea: Official Correspondence*, ed. Captain A.C. Dewar, R.N. **OP**.
Vol. 86. *Journals and Narratives of the Third Dutch War*, ed. R. C. Anderson. **OP**.
Vol. 87. *The Naval Brigades in the Indian Mutiny, 1857–1858*, ed. Cdr. W. B. Rowbotham, R.N. **OP**.
Vol. 88. *Patee Byng's Journal*, ed. J. L. Cranmer-Byng. **OP**.
*Vol. 89. *The Sergison Papers, 1688–1702*, ed. Cdr. R. D. Merriman, R.I.N.
Vol. 90. *The Keith Papers*, Vol. II, ed. Christopher Lloyd. **OP**.
Vol. 91. *Five Naval Journals, 1789–1817*, ed. Rear Admiral H. G. Thursfield. **OP**.
Vol. 92. *The Naval Miscellany*, Vol. IV, ed. Christopher Lloyd. **OP**.
Vol. 93. *Sir William Dillon's Narrative of Professional Adventures, 1790–1839*, Vol. I *1790–1802*, ed. Professor Michael Lewis. **OP**.
Vol. 94. *The Walker Expedition to Quebec, 1711*, ed. Professor Gerald S. Graham. **OP**.
Vol. 95. *The Second China War, 1856–1860*, ed. D. Bonner-Smith & E. W. R. Lumby. **OP**.
Vol. 96. *The Keith Papers, 1803–1815*, Vol. III, ed. Professor Christopher Lloyd.
Vol. 97. *Sir William Dillon's Narrative of Professional Adventures, 1790–1839*, Vol. II *1802–1839*, ed. Professor Michael Lewis. **OP**.
Vol. 98. *The Private Correspondence of Admiral Lord Collingwood*, ed. Professor Edward Hughes. **OP**.

Vol. 99. *The Vernon Papers, 1739–1745*, ed. B. McL. Ranft. **OP**.

Vol. 100. *Nelson's Letters to his Wife and Other Documents*, ed. Lt. Cdr. G. P. B. Naish, R.N.V.R.

Vol. 101. *A Memoir of James Trevenen, 1760–1790*, ed. Professor Christopher Lloyd & R. C. Anderson. **OP**.

Vol. 102. *The Papers of Admiral Sir John Fisher*, Vol. I, ed. Lt. Cdr. P. K. Kemp, R.N. **OP**.

Vol. 103. *Queen Anne's Navy*, ed. Cdr. R. D. Merriman, R.I.N. **OP**.

Vol. 104. *The Navy and South America, 1807–1823*, ed. Professor Gerald S. Graham & Professor R. A. Humphreys.

Vol. 105. *Documents relating to the Civil War, 1642–1648*, ed. The Rev. J. R. Powell & E. K. Timings. **OP**.

Vol. 106. *The Papers of Admiral Sir John Fisher*, Vol. II, ed. Lt. Cdr. P. K. Kemp, R.N. **OP**.

Vol. 107. *The Health of Seamen*, ed. Professor Christopher Lloyd.

Vol. 108. *The Jellicoe Papers*, Vol. I *1893–1916*, ed. A. Temple Patterson.

Vol. 109. *Documents relating to Anson's Voyage round the World, 1740–1744*, ed. Dr Glyndwr Williams. **OP**.

Vol. 110. *The Saumarez Papers: The Baltic, 1808–1812*, ed. A. N. Ryan. **OP**.

Vol. 111. *The Jellicoe Papers*, Vol. II *1916–1925*, ed. Professor A. Temple Patterson.

Vol. 112. *The Rupert and Monck Letterbook, 1666*, ed. The Rev. J. R. Powell & E. K. Timings. **OP** (damaged stock available).

Vol. 113. *Documents relating to the Royal Naval Air Service*, Vol. I (1908–1918), ed. Captain S. W. Roskill, R.N. **OP** (damaged stock available).

*Vol. 114. *The Siege and Capture of Havana, 1762*, ed. Professor David Syrett. **OP** (damaged stock available).

Vol. 115. *Policy and Operations in the Mediterranean, 1912–1914*, ed. E. W. R. Lumby. **OP**.

Vol. 116. *The Jacobean Commissions of Enquiry, 1608 and 1618*, ed. Dr A. P. McGowan.

Vol. 117. *The Keyes Papers*, Vol. I *1914–1918*, ed. Professor Paul Halpern.

Vol. 118. *The Royal Navy and North America: The Warren Papers, 1736–1752*, ed. Dr Julian Gwyn. **OP**.

Vol. 119. *The Manning of the Royal Navy: Selected Public Pamphlets, 1693–1873*, ed. Professor John Bromley.

Vol. 120. *Naval Administration, 1715–1750*, ed. Professor D. A. Baugh.

Vol. 121. *The Keyes Papers*, Vol. II *1919–1938*, ed. Professor Paul Halpern.

Vol. 122. *The Keyes Papers*, Vol. III *1939–1945*, ed. Professor Paul Halpern.

Vol. 123. *The Navy of the Lancastrian Kings: Accounts and Inventories of William Soper, Keeper of the King's Ships, 1422–1427*, ed. Dr Susan Rose.

Vol. 124. *The Pollen Papers: the Privately Circulated Printed Works of Arthur Hungerford Pollen, 1901–1916*, ed. Professor Jon T. Sumida. A. & U.

Vol. 125. *The Naval Miscellany*, Vol. V, ed. Dr N. A. M. Rodger. A & U.

Vol. 126. *The Royal Navy in the Mediterranean, 1915–1918*, ed. Professor Paul Halpern. TS.

Vol. 127. *The Expedition of Sir John Norris and Sir Francis Drake to Spain and Portugal, 1589*, ed. Professor R. B. Wernham. TS.

Vol. 128. *The Beatty Papers*, Vol. I *1902–1918*, ed. Professor B. McL. Ranft. SP.

Vol. 129. *The Hawke Papers: A Selection, 1743–1771*, ed. Dr R. F. Mackay. SP.

Vol. 130. *Anglo-American Naval Relations, 1917–1919*, ed. Michael Simpson. SP.

Vol. 131. *British Naval Documents, 1204–1960*, ed. Professor John B. Hattendorf, Dr Roger Knight, Alan Pearsall, Dr Nicholas Rodger & Professor Geoffrey Till. SP.

Vol. 132. *The Beatty Papers*, Vol. II *1916–1927*, ed. Professor B. McL. Ranft. SP

Vol. 133. *Samuel Pepys and the Second Dutch War*, transcribed by Professor William Matthews & Dr Charles Knighton; ed. Robert Latham. SP.

Vol. 134. *The Somerville Papers*, ed. Michael Simpson, with the assistance of John Somerville. SP.

Vol. 135. *The Royal Navy in the River Plate, 1806–1807*, ed. John D. Grainger. SP.

Vol. 136. *The Collective Naval Defence of the Empire, 1900–1940*, ed. Nicholas Tracy. A.

Vol. 137. *The Defeat of the Enemy Attack on Shipping, 1939–1945*, ed. Eric Grove. A.

Vol. 138. *Shipboard Life and Organisation, 1731–1815*, ed. Brian Lavery. A.

Vol. 139. *The Battle of the Atlantic and Signals Intelligence: U-boat Situations and Trends, 1941–1945*, ed. Professor David Syrett. A.

Vol. 140. *The Cunningham Papers*, Vol. I: *The Mediterranean Fleet, 1939–1942*, ed. Michael Simpson. A.
Vol. 141. *The Channel Fleet and the Blockade of Brest, 1793–1801*, ed. Roger Morriss. A.
Vol. 142. *The Submarine Service, 1900–1918*, ed. Nicholas Lambert. A.
Vol. 143. *Letters and Papers of Professor Sir John Knox Laughton (1830–1915)*, ed. Professor Andrew Lambert. A.
Vol. 144. *The Battle of the Atlantic and Signals Intelligence: U-Boat Tracking Papers 1941–1947*, ed. Professor David Syrett. A.
Vol. 145. *The Maritime Blockade of Germany in the Great War: The Northern Patrol, 1914–1918*, ed. John D. Grainger. A.
Vol. 146. *The Naval Miscellany*, Vol. VI, ed. Michael Duffy. A.
Vol. 147. *The Milne Papers*, Vol. I *1820–1859*, ed. Professor John Beeler. A.
Vol. 148. *The Rodney Papers*, Vol. I *1742–1763*, ed. Professor David Syrett. A.
Vol. 149. *Sea Power and the Control of Trade. Belligerent Rights from the Russian War to the Beira Patrol, 1854–1970*, ed. Nicholas Tracy. A.
Vol. 150. *The Cunningham Papers*, Vol. II: *The Triumph of Allied Sea Power 1942–1946*, ed. Michael Simpson. A.
Vol. 151. *The Rodney Papers*, Vol. II *1763–1780*, ed. Professor David Syrett. A.
Vol. 152. *Naval Intelligence from Germany: The Reports of the British Naval Attachés in Berlin, 1906–1914*, ed. Matthew S. Seligmann. A.
Vol. 153. *The Naval Miscellany*, Vol. VII, ed. Susan Rose. A.
Vol. 154. *The Chatham Dockyard, 1815–1865*, ed. Philip MacDougall. A.

Occasional Publications:

Vol. 1. *The Commissioned Sea Officers of the Royal Navy, 1660–1815*, ed. Professor David Syrett & Professor R. L. DiNardo. SP.
Vol. 2. *The Anthony Roll of Henry VIII's Navy*, ed. C. S. Knighton and D. M. Loades. A.